P. 386, 394

SOUTHERN NATION

Princeton Studies in American Politics: Historical, International, and Comparative Perspectives
Ira Katznelson, Eric Schickler, Martin Shefter, and Theda Skocpol, series editors

A list of titles in this series appears at the back of the book.

Southern Nation

Congress and White Supremacy after Reconstruction

David A. Bateman

Ira Katznelson

John S. Lapinski

RUSSELL SAGE FOUNDATION
NEW YORK

PRINCETON UNIVERSITY PRESS
PRINCETON AND OXFORD

Requests for permission to reproduce material from this work should be sent to Permissions, Princeton University Press

Published by Princeton University Press
41 William Street, Princeton, New Jersey 08540
6 Oxford Street, Woodstock, Oxfordshire OX20 1TR
and the Russell Sage Foundation
112 East 64th Street, New York, NY 10021

press.princeton.edu
russellsage.org

Jacket art courtesy of Shutterstock

LCCN 2017959010

ISBN 978-0-691-12649-4

British Library Cataloging-in-Publication Data is available

This book has been composed in Adobe Text Pro and Gotham

Printed on acid-free paper. ∞

Printed in the United States of America

10 9 8 7 6 5 4 3 2 1

CONTENTS

ACKNOWLEDGMENTS

There is a sense in which this project was born in a classroom on American Political Development at Columbia University. During a discussion of state-building in the late nineteenth and early twentieth centuries, John asked Ira about the absence of Congress, not only in that seminar but in APD more broadly. Much collaboration ensued, including the formation of the American Institutions Project at Columbia that, among other matters, housed a multi-year effort to substantively code congressional roll calls and statutes that was generously supported by the National Science Foundation (award #0318280).

After graduating at Columbia, John moved to Yale, then to the University of Pennsylvania. At Penn, John worked closely with his student, David, who since has gone on to teach at Cornell. This book's history thus spans three scholarly generations. Each author has been concerned to build analytical history with Congress at the center, and to illuminate patterns of political representation within a wider ambit, including the place of the South as a region for which congressional power, from the Founding, has been vital.

Southern Nation first was conceptualized as a set of questions about post-Reconstruction America in intellectual partnership with Rose Razaghian as she, too, was concluding her graduate studies at Columbia and soon began to teach at Yale before moving back to Columbia in an administrative role. In early days, Ira, John, and Rose shared a year as visiting scholars at the Russell Sage Foundation, an invaluable institution that has proved more than patient in its wait for this book. The three authors remain indebted to Rose for her formative contributions.

More broadly, the sheer quantity as well as depth of our debt to an incredible community of scholars who work on Congress are reminders that scholarship is a collective enterprise. We are especially grateful to Frances Lee, David Mayhew, Charles Stewart, and Richard Valelly who selflessly joined us for an uncommonly productive day-long book workshop where they were confronted with a not-fully-baked penultimate draft. That intensive colloquy truly was pivotal in shaping our extensive final revisions. We suspect that we have not been able to satisfy all of their critiques, but hope they will see in the book a genuine appreciation for their insights and perspectives, and our deep gratitude for their comradely efforts and keen intellectual support.

David Mayhew, to whom we dedicate this book, deserves particular thanks. As John's colleague at Yale for six years, he was instrumental from the beginning. As our collective colleague, he deserves credit for helping with various components of the book, and for providing no-holds-barred commentary throughout its construction. David's first book, *Party Loyalty among Congressmen*, moreover, was instrumental in pushing us to think about the importance of policy issue substance. Also especially noteworthy are Josh Clinton, who shaped the book more than he probably realizes; Wendy Schiller, whose combination of precise knowledge and sense for intellectual architecture proved especially valuable; and the peerless Matthew Holden, who not only informed the book's treatment of black disenfranchisement but demonstrated a special gift for working with younger scholars.

As *Southern Nation* took shape, it also benefited from the critical counsel of other scholars in addition to those already named or those at our home universities: Scott Adler, David Brady, John DiIulio, Gerald Gamm, Jeffrey Jenkins, Bryan Jones, Sunita Parikh, Justin Peck, Keith Poole, Eric Schickler, the late Barbara Sinclair, Tom Schwartz, and Stephen Skowronek. Two of the most significant were our anonymous reviewers, whose sharp insights and close reading of the text gave us much to think about and work with, and whose suggestions led to innumerable improvements, big and small.

The Center for the Study of Democratic Politics at Princeton University was where David's participation on this project began. His experience there early in his faculty career was formative in shaping his contributions to the book, which benefited especially from the feedback and support of Jean-François Godbout, Kyle Dropp, and Miguel R. Rueda, as well as Michele Epstein, Charles Cameron, Nolan McCarty, and Keith Whittington.

We also are indebted to Barbara Gilbert and Daniel Meyer at the University of Chicago for their assistance in reproducing a photo of James O'Hara, and for granting us permission to reprint it here, as well as Molly and Mary Bell Kirkpatrick for graciously allowing us to use an extended quote from their grandfather, Donald Davidson.

Colleagues and graduate students at our home universities have offered especially supportive intellectual milieus within which our work has proceeded. At Columbia, the project has gained much from presentations at the American Politics Seminar and from comments by Robert Erikson, Andrew Gelman, Fred Harris, Jeffrey Lax, Robert Shapiro, Greg Wawro, and Justin Phillips, whose office at the Russell Sage Foundation was adjacent to Ira's during an additional semester there as a visiting scholar. And we are grateful as well to those who, when graduate students. devoted many efforts to deepening the research and stimulated ideas that underpin the volume, including Alexander de la Paz, Sean Farhang, Christina Greer, Quinn Mulroy, Thomas

Ogorzalek, David Park, Eldon Porter, Charlie Riemann, Amy Semet, and Melanie Springer.

At Cornell, the book was considerably improved through a workshop and discussions with Bryce Corrigan, Peter Enns, Sergio Garcia-Rios, Claire Leavitt, Adam Levine, Alexander Livingston, Jamila Mitchener, Erica Salinas, Delphia Shanks-Booth, AshLee Smith Garrett, Mallory SoRelle, and others. Particularly helpful were the numerous conversations with Richard Bensel, Suzanne Mettler, and Elizabeth Sanders, who offered vital guidance about how to think through some of the difficult questions raised by southern history and policymaking, and whose individual contributions to the study of American political development informed *Southern Nation* at each stage of its development. A special debt is owed to Elizabeth for her determined insistence that southern political history not be flattened, and that its diversity, including ideological diversity, be integrated into our story.

At Penn, David would like to thank Brendan O'Leary and Rogers Smith for their unerring guidance and tireless mentorship, as well as Stephan Stohler, Tim Weaver, Meredith Wooten, Chelsea Schafer, and Emily Thorson, who have each provided generously of their time as intellectual interlocutors and as wonderful friends. There, a wonderful crew participated in the research venture, including two employees of the university, Hannah Hartig and Andrew Arenge, and a small army of graduate and undergraduate students, including Will Marble (now a PhD student at Stanford), Chris Brown, Zac Endter, Sarah Wilson, Sarah Engell, Max Levy, Chris Wogan, Hugh Hamilton, Isabella Gillstrom, and Annie Caccimelio.

We also wish to thank Daniel Galvin and Matt Glassman, who assisted this project at Yale.

The ideas in this book were tested at multiple venues: meetings of the Congress and History annual conference, and workshops at Cal-Tech, MIT, Yale, NYU, and Brown and at our present home institutions. We also gained from the institutional milieus at Yale's Institution for Social and Policy Studies, the Fox Leadership Program and the Program on Opinion Research and Election Studies (PORES) at Penn, and the Institute for Social Research and Policy at Columbia.

We have been incredibly fortunate to collaborate with the exceptional professionals at Princeton University Press and the Russell Sage Foundation. Eric Crahan has been a wonderful editor, who has believed in this book and waited for it ever since he inherited the portfolio from Chuck Myers, together with the estimable Suzanne Nichols at Russell Sage, who leads a vigorous publishing program at the foundation. We also have a special word of thanks for Cynthia Buck, whose copyediting of the manuscript was superb. Her work substantively improved the book in many ways. We also benefited from Natalie

Baan and Pamela Weidman at Princeton University Press. Mary Makarushka also deserves thanks for copyediting an early version of the book.

We close with special gratitude to four persons vital to our personal lives: For David, Begüm Adalet. For John, his dearly missed brother Jason, who passed away in the last stages of finishing the book, and Anjali Shaw. For Ira, Deborah Socolow Katznelson. We thank them for their loving support, critical engagement, inspiration, and degrees of forbearance that none of this book's authors quite possess.

PART I

Introduction

1

Southern Politics

The Southern political leader is yet somehow "Southern." He has a nationality inside of a nationality.[1]

We are a peculiar people. We have peculiar environments. Our conduct of our political affairs should be a bit peculiar.[2]

Maryland was represented at the First Federal Congress by Michael Jenifer Stone, one of six members sent by that state's voters to the House of Representatives. Stone owned a plantation called Equality. Filled with slaves, it embodied the new nation's haunting mutual constitution of race and democracy. From the start, as the historian Edmund Morgan put the point, "republican freedom" in the United States "came to be supported, at least in large part, by its opposite, slavery."[3]

Opening a century after the Founding, *Southern Nation* inquires about the long legacy of this relationship during the decades following secession, war, and military occupation—that is, between 1877 as Reconstruction concluded and the start of the New Deal in 1933. Focusing on what white southern Democrats did after they regained control of their congressional delegations by the close of Reconstruction, we investigate when and how the states that had practiced chattel slavery on the eve of the Civil War conducted themselves inside the national polity. How did the return to Congress by representatives committed to white supremacy further a particular view of southern nationhood? To what extent did they advance the South as a nation within the nation? And to what extent were they able to project the terms of this nationality beyond their region, making the United States a southern nation?

After abolition and the constitutional negation of the doctrine announced two decades earlier in *Dred Scott*, that no black person could be eligible for American citizenship, the Union again was made whole. With the South still suffering the devastation that had been wrought by the war, undergoing wrenching transformations to its economic and social order, experiencing a new racial pluralism in its state and local politics, and suffering a pervasive climate of uncertainty scored by violence, the region's representation in Washington became a focal and sometimes decisive instrument for adjudicating among white preferences. At stake were policies that would determine the degree to which the South could govern what most whites in the region believed to be its own racial affairs, as well as lawmaking that would shape the section's political economy. This combination proved vexed and difficult, posing knotty problems and forcing thorny choices.

Once again, as during the antebellum years, Congress became the chief arena within which southern delegations could seek to shape their region's— and the country's—character. Given its significance, the legislature's procedural rules, as before, also came into play, as southern members understood how shifts in procedures could affect influence and transform probabilities.

These substantive and institutional dimensions of post-Reconstruction America were fraught. The South was hardly a single territorial bloc with simple or uniform qualities. Not all of its states had seceded. Demographic realities varied. Not just the extent but the types of agriculture diverged. Political arrangements were multiple. In this context, it is important to inquire about the frequency and content of the emergence of a congressional "Solid South" and the conditions that facilitated southern success in extruding black citizens from public life, sometimes in tension with other valued goals, and to identify the issues and means by which southern ideas, practices, and priorities were projected beyond the region to shape the contours of the American state and the country's national policies. We thus want to know when the preferences, interests, and actions of southern representatives were mere tangents to the main story of American lawmaking and when, by contrast, their congressional presence became vital, even pivotal, thus making the whole of the United States into a southern nation.

Parallels and Complexity

We are not the first to attend to these fundamental themes about the effects of southern behavior and influence on the substance of lawmaking and the rules within which Congress operated.

Writing in 1949, the historian Richard Hofstadter reflected on "the present tension between the Solid South and American liberal democracy" and recalled that more than a century earlier the South Carolina statesman John C.

Calhoun had characterized the South as a force for stability and compromise in American political life. Calhoun argued that slavery provided a "central point of interest" around which the entire white South would unite, and that the South in turn provided a "central point of union" that protected the North from conflict "growing out of the division of wealth and poverty, and their concomitants, capital and labor." This role as a "balance wheel against labor agitation," he argued, could only be played if the South militantly maintained regional solidarity and abjured party divisions in national politics. For the young Republic to be a successful political entity, Calhoun counseled, the South had to act as a separate, coherent, and unified nation within a nation.[4]

Calhoun would fail to attain the constitutional guarantees he hoped would protect southern autonomy in matters of bondage and race. Ten years after his death, eleven of the fifteen states composing the slave South seceded and constituted themselves as an independent confederacy of sovereign states. The Union, a country that in 1860 was home to just under 27 million free whites, 476,000 free blacks, 400,000 slaveholders, and 4 million slaves, was forcibly splintered in two. The South's subsequent defeat, the termination of slavery, and the postwar military occupation ended any hope of formal institutional parity for the South within the Union. But it raised afresh the fate of Calhoun's fiercely expressed wish that in national political life the region should compose a southern nation determined to protect self-government as it worked to secure white supremacy and safeguard its leading role in national political institutions.

Comparing the post–World War II era to antebellum America, Hofstadter took note of the South having restored what in effect was *home rule*: local control over state government by elements of the white population free from federal interference. The region had reversed many of the consequences of Radical Reconstruction, defended local autonomy against federal intervention, and been restored in recent decades to its pivotal position in the national polity. Despite the emergence of anti–Jim Crow activism, Hofstadter could record that "the South has stood firm under a combination of the master-race theory and the one-party state," that "southern delegations in Congress . . . hold the balance of power," that southerners had learned to achieve Calhoun's dream of concurrent powers within the national legislature, and that the Democratic Party thus "finds itself in the anomalous position of being a party of 'liberalism,' whose achievements are subject to veto by a reactionary faction."[5]

Hofstadter's powerful parallelism invites the question of how the situation in the mid-twentieth century came to resemble that of the antebellum years. Was this simply a matter of continuity across a wide expanse of time? Attention to the post-Reconstruction era in fact reveals a complex and contingent patterning of southern behavior and influence. What was consistent, however, was the rock-solid commitment of southern members to safeguard the ability of their state and local governments to shape and police the region's racial order after slavery. Notwithstanding this passionate quest, three closely connected facets of political development varied a good deal during the half-century after Reconstruction: the degree of security for southern racial autonomy; how comfortable southerners felt to pursue diverse interests and build cross-regional and, at times, cross-party coalitions; and the scope of their legislative influence.

Southern political behavior, in short, was not all of one piece. It varied over time within changing situations of partisanship and across issue areas. If the outcome, ultimately, was the one identified by Hofstadter at midcentury, the path traveled beforehand had been uneven and circuitous. Further, the ways in which southern representatives journeyed in the national legislative arena, we will see, significantly shaped the political economy of the region itself, dooming it to a degree of deprivation that was far from inevitable.

As we understood our own voyage on this historical road, we were guided principally by V. O. Key's magnificent *Southern Politics in State and Nation,* a book based on a massive research program that appeared just as Hofstadter was underscoring the behavior of the South in Congress as a distinct nation in the spirit of Calhoun. Written by the country's leading political scientist, a Texan who had been induced to take on the subject by no less than President Harry S. Truman, Key's volume burst on the scene as a sharply etched portrait of the region and its politics, at the heart of which lay the status of the South's large black minority. "Whatever phase of the southern political process one seeks to understand," Key contended, "sooner or later the trail of inquiry leads to the Negro." A year later, Hofstadter opened a review of *Southern Politics* by observing that "the South has never lost its nationalism." Ever since the 1850s, when the United States ceased to be a secure setting for chattel slavery based on race, the region's "relations with the rest of the nation have been much like the conduct of foreign affairs, or as Professor Key calls it, 'a sort of sublimated foreign war.'" With the South believing itself to be under "a continuous state of siege," it deployed the Democratic Party as the primary instrument to manage this relationship. As the dominant political force in the South, the party served as both an "army of resistance and the diplomatic corps: through it the South has manifested its solidarity against the rest of the nation, and through it she has contracted valuable alliances with other elements in the country."[6]

As much as Hofstadter admired Key's book, he took note of a certain imbalance. Its focus on national politics, Hofstadter observed, "occup[ied] only a minor portion of the book," and its contribution was limited by Key's inability to systematically evaluate the importance of the issues and votes on which the South seemed to possess a distinctive set of policy concerns. The crucial question of southern politics, Hofstadter argued, was not simply whether the South voted more or less with the Democratic Party in Congress, but whether the region had succeeded in shaping national lawmaking through the variety of mechanisms at its representatives' disposal—by influencing the legislative agenda, by controlling congressional committees, or by directing debate and outcomes on the floor. The answer to this question, Hofstadter concluded, required "another book," one focused specifically "on the South's role in national politics."[7]

Southern Nation pursues this task by advancing an analysis of the role and influence of southern members of Congress from Reconstruction to the New Deal. This approach underscores the persistent possibilities of division among southern Democrats as they struggled to find cohesion in circumstances of very considerable sectional diversity. Southern achievements, which were considerable, were secured unevenly and haltingly. Rather than assume that the cohesion of southern representatives always came easily and was persistently high, or that southern members were always wily and masterful in deploying influence in Congress, we show how southern security and capacity were produced over time under conditions of anxiety and uncertainty.

So doing, the book also offers elements, we believe, that are vital pathways to our contemporary circumstances. Thus, from one vantage, we are deepening historical knowledge about a pivotal era. As signified by Hofstadter's temporal comparison and Key's empirical study, work on the South in American political life has been particularly robust for the early Republic through Reconstruction, and again from the New Deal to the present day. By contrast, work on the region from the moment of southern reintegration to the close of the Hoover administration has primarily concentrated on how the South managed to impose and regulate a holistic system of racial segregation within the region, rather than on the region's role in national politics. Because Jim Crow's triumph was made possible by the acquiescence of the Supreme Court and the bipartisan withdrawal of national attention to the South's racial order, questions about the South in national politics during the five and a half decades from 1877 to 1933, with some important exceptions, do not often focus on Congress, the key institutional site in which southern legislators conducted their region's "foreign affairs."[8]

As an analytical history, *Southern Nation* probes the role of the South in political development before the New Deal, with implications for understanding America during and since. The book also helps us understand how and why the subjugation of African Americans has been so deep and so entrenched even during periods of progressive achievement. Within the period under consideration, it aims to discern how the South shaped the parameters of the American state and influenced the content of its public policy and, just as importantly, the rules and practices that define Congress, the country's central lawmaking institution. In short, we are interested in how southern politics remade the United States above and below the Mason-Dixon Line.

An ancillary objective is to chip away at the wall that often separates the study of Congress from the study of public policy and American political development. As a contribution to historical political studies, *Southern Nation* demonstrates how attention to the substance of congressional representation can illuminate vexing historical questions. As a contribution to the study of Congress, the book shows how attention to historical context, to collective identities beyond parties, and to policy content can help us better understand the institution's workings. In all, we seek to connect understanding the South with its influence in relation to national party politics, economic development, and changes to Congress itself.

Southern Nation illuminates how white southern Democrats came to wield their influence once they regained control of their party during the "redemption." As a contribution to the history of Congress and to the place of the South in Congress, the book draws on both quantitative measures, in the spirit of V. O. Key, and the more qualitative approach suggested by Richard Hofstadter. Like Key, we rely on a range of quantitative measures of congressional behavior and theories of lawmaking to assess the potential influence and role of southern members of Congress. But we also follow Hofstadter's suggestion to more closely analyze, through in-depth qualitative case studies, the varying role of southern lawmakers in shaping policy in a larger number of important issue areas. In doing so, we believe that we present a more systematic account of the role of southern legislators in Congress than has previously been offered, as we disclose how white southern politicians obstructed their own region's economic and educational development by blocking policies that would have helped it advance in these areas, for fear of upsetting the region's increasingly rigid racial hierarchy. With the ideology of white supremacy pervading their deliberations and actions, they took decisions that had a lasting impact on southern and national politics, then and now, including the divided partisan nature of the North and the South, the degree of ideological polarization in American politics, and gaps in economic and educational standing—themes to which we return in the conclusion.

A Southern Nation

No question has loomed larger in America's experience than the role of the South. At the founding of the Republic, nearly two of five residents in the South were African slaves. The infamous three-fifths clause of the Constitution provided the states in which chattel slavery was continued or established with what amounted to a representational bonus of 25 percent in the U.S. House of Representatives. Westward expansion and the "first emancipation" in northern states resulted in fifteen states practicing slavery before the Civil War, each of which qualified for two Senate seats. From the admission of Louisiana to statehood in 1812 to 1849, southern states returned exactly half of the Senate, providing the institutional basis for an effective concurrent veto over national policy. As a result of these features of political representation, the slaveholding South received an additional boost in the Electoral College.

The combination of regional distinctiveness, an extreme system of human domination, and sectional political power produced what the historian Don Fehrenbacher calls "a slaveholding republic," referring not just to the South but to the United States as a whole. From the start, southern members used their outsized position in Congress to protect and fortify their social order. The majority of antebellum presidents were slaveholders. Most Supreme Court justices were southern. Federal authority enforced the right to buy, own, sell, inherit, and recover slaves, even in the nation's capital. The country's foreign policy routinely was mobilized to protect slavery by a variety of means, including remonstrations against any foreign recognition that slaves could escape across national boundaries. Enforcement of restrictions against participation in the slave trade, which continued to bring slaves to the American continents after it was proscribed in the United States, was meager. The judiciary routinely reinforced property rights in slaves, culminating in the 1857 case of *Dred Scott v. Sandford*, which also declared that even "a free negro of the African race . . . is not a 'citizen' within the meaning of the Constitution of the United States." Congress likewise recognized that fugitive slave laws were a condition of comity between the sections, and from 1836 to 1844 Congress even circumscribed its own ability to discuss slavery by imposing on itself the institutional mechanism of "gag rules." Overall, "the proslavery cause benefited from the structure of American politics, which required that any northerner serving in, or aspiring to, high federal office make some kind of peace with the nation's peculiar institution."[9]

The early Republic was a southern nation. Embedded inside a liberal polity—one organized around principles of individual rights, popular sovereignty, representation, limited government, and toleration—was the world's largest slave system, safeguarded through the procedures, institutions, laws, public administration, and jurisprudence of the national regime. Slavery could not have persisted without the sufferance, accommodation, and military security proffered by the rest of the country, while slavery's crops integrated the nation's domestic and overseas economic relationships. Moreover, the region's disproportionate political powers strongly shaped and directed policy decisions, not only about slavery but about territorial expansion, warfare, Indian policy, the contours of democratic reforms, internal improvements, the tariff, and other prominent policy issues of the period. Despite great variation across the South, the section acted politically in common when it believed it faced threats to its essential interests. Over time this commitment grew more intense as the northern states abolished slavery within their borders, the international environment grew more threatening, and the white South's defense of slavery as a positive institution faced increasing opposition from activists in the North and overseas. Slaves manifestly had allies, and the stakes of debates about the scope of slavery in the western territories grew more substantial.

It was a southern nation to which Alexis de Tocqueville and Gustave de Beaumont arrived three decades before the Civil War, during Andrew Jackson's second term. These French observers, who even met with the president who exemplified both the egalitarian and racially illiberal features of the still young republic, took stark measure of the country's racial order. Beaumont published the powerful *Marie; or, Slavery in the United States: A Novel of Jacksonian America* in 1835, and Tocqueville, in volume 1 of *Democracy in America*, also published that year, devoted one-quarter of the text to a concluding chapter, "Some Considerations Concerning the Present State and Probable Future of the Three Races That Inhabit the Territory of the United States."

"The Europeans," he wrote, "having scattered the Indian tribes far into the wilderness, condemned them to a wandering vagabond life full of inexpressible afflictions." And writing about the South, he took note of how "in one blow oppression has deprived the descendants of the Africans almost all the privileges of humanity." These "two unlucky races," Tocqueville observed, "have neither birth, physique, language, nor mores in common; only their misfortunes are alike. Both occupy an equally inferior position in the land where they dwell; both suffer the effects of tyranny, and though their afflictions are different, they have the same people to blame for them.... [The white man] makes them serve his convenience, and when he cannot bend them to his will he destroys them." In America, "slavery brutalizes" and produces a circumstance marked by "servile fear." White America, Tocqueville observed, presented blacks with no opportunity of integration, placing them in the impossible position of being unable either to separate from white America or to unite with it. But while Tocqueville reminded his readers that "there are other things in America besides an immense and complete democracy," he ultimately did not explicitly and thoroughly connect his passionate and systematic account of slavery and its consequences for the future of the country to his primary subject, the character of American democracy. Questions about the South, race, and slavery, he wrote, "are like tangents to my subject, being American, but not democratic, and my main business has been to describe democracy."[10]

In this respect, Tocqueville underplayed a key feature of his analysis that helped shape how we have proceeded here. Going beyond a multifaceted empirical description and ethical condemnation of American racism, he identified a crucial mechanism for the reproduction of racial hierarchy and subordination within the crucial liberal tenet of the rule of law. Lawfulness and legislation, he stressed, were put in play in America not to negate racial exclusion and brutality but as their instruments. In that way, he invited the reader to consider how liberal values—based, as he wrote, on "natural right and reason"—could have been consistent with their decisive negation. Read this way, Tocqueville's text is an anxiety-charged consideration of the borderland where egalitarian democracy and racial oppression overlap. It is thus an invitation to think hard about the mechanisms underlying this connection between democracy and oppression in the American context, and in particular to examine the role of the country's lawmaking institutions in buttressing, as well as challenging, racial exclusion and domination.

Emancipation and Redemption

If before the Civil War the United States was "a slaveholding republic," what was the standing of the South in the polity after the victory of the Union and the return of the South to the national political arena? Over the course of the long period from the close of Reconstruction to the start of the New Deal— and well beyond, at least to the enactment of the Voting Rights Act of 1965— the region remained a distinctive, albeit internally diverse, unit within the larger political, social, and economic order of the United States.

The South's rebellion, against its very intention, "inspired the most sweeping revolution of the nineteenth century, and shifted the social and political course of the Atlantic world." The Civil War became a revolution not just because President Lincoln issued the Emancipation Proclamation at the start of 1863, but also because hundreds of thousands of slaves rebelled against their masters, entering Union lines, while more than 140,000 blacks, the great majority former slaves, became Union soldiers, constituting about 10 percent of the U.S. military during the last year of the war. "The black military role in support of the Union," Steven Hahn notes, "made possible a revolution in American civil and political society that was barely on the horizon of official imagination as late as the middle of 1864"—a revolution that potentially extended to the redistribution of confiscated white property and the guarantee of political and civil rights for free and freed blacks.[11]

In the years immediately following the close of the Civil War, it appeared as if the degree of social transformation would be contained, as President Andrew Johnson sought to decide the terms of reconstructing the Union. It was Congress that acted to ensure that some of the more thoroughgoing transformative possibilities were realized. As secured by the Thirteenth Amendment of 1865, emancipation comprised a combination of human liberation and one of the most radical redistributions of property in history. Uniquely, American emancipation was both abrupt and uncompensated. Slavery, abolished with the Thirteenth Amendment, was forever extinguished by the extension of citizenship and voting rights to the formerly enslaved, who, aligning with the Republican Party, burst into American public life. An immense amount of "capital" was lost to the southern economic elite, as was their hegemonic political position in the face of military occupation and the radical democratization of political participation and officeholding across racial lines. Southern blacks, now wage laborers, had become citizens, voters, and officeholders, their rights protected by the federal government.

Even as most southern blacks had no choice but to sign labor contracts to work the land once more, the transformation in their standing under the aegis of the Military Reconstruction Acts was sweeping. With the extension of the franchise to adult men without regard to race, southern blacks quickly registered to vote en masse. By late 1867, every former Confederate state had enrolled at least 90 percent of eligible blacks in the electorate; even in laggard Mississippi a remarkable 83 percent were on the rolls. Soon black representatives were helping to write new, more egalitarian state constitutions; notwithstanding persistent antagonism and complaints about black usurpation, these efforts were crosscut by some interracial collaboration.[12]

The result was a profound transformation of southern life. When journalist Edward King and artist J. Wells Chamney traveled some 25,000 miles at the behest of *Scribner's Monthly* to produce their 1875 book *The Great South*, what they wrote in the opening chapter on Louisiana might well have been said about the region as a whole. They observed, in "Paradise Lost," that "a gigantic struggle is in progress. It is the battle of race with race, of the picturesque and unjust civilization of the past with the prosaic and leveling civilization of the present." This leveling primarily took political form. When they visited the legislature in South Carolina, once the cockpit of secession, Edwards and Chamney noted with surprise the outcome of the era's political transformation. The offices of the governor, treasurer, secretary of state, and superintendent of schools in the Columbia statehouse—a building "furnished with a richness and elegance," they noted—were "usually filled with colored people, discussing the issues of the hour." The speaker of the House and the president of the Senate were both black, and in total the South Carolina electorate was represented by forty-one white and eighty-three black members, the latter all Republican; the Senate contained fifteen black and ten white Republicans as well as eight white Democrats.[13]

Black representation rested on the remarkable political engagement of black citizens. In a comparative consideration of passages from slavery, Jürgen Osterhammel's magisterial global history of the nineteenth century observes that "in no other country did the abolition of slavery expand the scope of action as dramatically as it did in the United States." The uprising and participation of blacks during the Civil War was followed by a burst of citizen independence and participation based on free association. "In the transition to freedom," Osterhammel notes, African Americans were emplaced, if only for a time, within the fabric of free associational democratic citizenship that Tocqueville had so robustly described.

> Former slaves gave themselves new names, moved into new homes, brought their scattered families together again, and looked for ways of becoming economically independent. Those whom a master had previously denied free speech could now openly express themselves in public; black community institutions that had been operating underground—from churches and schools to burial societies—found their way to the surface. As slaves, black women and men had been their master's property and therefore not legal subjects in their own right. Now they could step out into the world, give testimony in court, conclude mutually binding contracts, sit on juries, cast their vote at elections, and stand for office.[14]

African Americans quickly used their new political power to bargain with other actors, impose restrictions on antiblack violence, and transform southern state governments and their policies, notably in education. Especially in the Deep South, where they often composed local or even statewide majorities, African Americans managed to radically invert older patterns of power. Congress protected these developments with laws to enforce voting rights and secure the new constitutional guarantees, and President Ulysses S. Grant and the new Department of Justice worked to implement these regulations in the courts.

But this was a world marked by fundamental, irreconcilable ambitions. Most land continued to be owned by white planters, who desperately sought to maintain black labor. Where they could, planters sought to secure control over this labor force "by intimidation; by vagrancy laws making idle Blacks susceptible to arrest and forced labor; by yearlong contracts restricting workers to the plantation under customary rules in return for a meager wage." In turn, this effort to secure "labor from a controlled, subordinate caste" was resisted by freed blacks, who "wanted land, literacy, a secure family life, and basic social equity."[15]

Quite soon, organized white supremacy made a comeback. Large numbers of southern whites fought back against the new conditions of freedom, often by extrapolitical means of intimidation and through the violence of the Ku Klux Klan, the Red Shirts, and the White Brotherhoods. By the early 1870s, the tide had begun to turn. By that decade's close, most black gains were on the path to negation—even as former slaves continued to pursue electoral alliances with whites despite stunning and remarkably violent assaults, often led by the Klan and other private organized vigilante forces, on their new status as rights-bearing citizens.

Both as symbol and as cause, the massacre of 81 black militia members in April 1873, on Easter Sunday, at Colfax, Louisiana, by a white militia numbering some 300 proved a critical juncture. Most of those arrested were either released or acquitted, and in 1875 the Supreme Court in *United States v. Cruikshank* declared unconstitutional the federal Enforcement Act of 1870, under which the indictments had been brought. Ruling that the postwar constitutional amendments "only empowered the federal government to prohibit violations of black rights by *states*," the Court concluded that "the responsibility for punishing crimes by individuals rested where it always had—with local and state authorities."[16]

The Democratic Party gained control of the House of Representatives in the midterm elections of 1874 as a sustained economic depression cut deeply into Republican support across the country, signaling the likely end of Reconstruction. The new Democratic majority, the first since the start of the Civil War, and 50 percent of whom were from the South, soon acted to prevent enforcement of the Civil Rights Acts of 1875 and signaled that it would act to curtail the federal government's military presence in the South. The stage was set for the formal ending of Reconstruction with the Compromise of 1877, which settled the contested presidential election. As the federal government withdrew from the enforcement of black rights, white southern lawmakers were increasingly free to shape the racial contours of citizenship, while white southern Democrats were reestablished in Washington as a key source of votes and lawmaking capability.

The Solid South and American History

From the end of Reconstruction until the New Deal, the South was repeatedly cast as a problem by northern elites and intellectuals—as an economic backwater in need of northern capital and expertise, ravaged by racism, by diseases such as hookworm and pellagra, and by seemingly unyielding poverty. Many southerners saw things from a different perspective and forcefully argued that the region's poverty was the product of a national political economy that was rigged against the South, subsidizing northern industry on the back of southern agriculture and draining money from the rest of the country to the financial Northeast. Until the New Deal, argued one former southern member of Congress, "most government activity in economic affairs had worked against the economic interests of the South," while the region's foremost historians have characterized the relation between the South and the rest of the country in the decades after 1877 as "colonial." Southerners would often complain that they were excluded from the halls of power, that "no man of discretion, North or South, would think of proposing a Southern man for President," and they frequently suggested that this exclusion was the cause of the region's economic underdevelopment.[17]

Southerners, it is true, had been out of power for a long time, their party a minority in Congress and the region denied what many saw as its fair share of offices in the executive and judicial branches. And yet the region's legislators were able to secure the borders of its "authoritarian enclave" even as they built episodic national majorities around progressive economic and political policy proposals. Southerners had taken a leading role in the Populist movement, and while the Populists were defeated for decades after the region was viewed as a hotbed of economic radicalism. It was the part of the country where the "Socialistic tendencies" of the period had gained widest favor. During the first presidential term of Woodrow Wilson, southern legislators helped frame much of the period's most important and far-reaching progressive legislation, and they did so while simultaneously ensuring that white supremacy was left not only undisturbed but strengthened. Nor was the region's influence exclusively domestic. In a reversal from the pattern of antebellum history, southern politicians helped curtail American imperialism (a sharp reversal of southern orientations during the antebellum period, when the South had spearheaded imperial expansion), strongly supported Wilsonian internationalism, and profoundly shaped the rise of the United States to a global power.[18]

Neither historians nor political scientists have sufficiently integrated the South and the complex relationship between white supremacy and liberal democracy into the larger American experience. The region, rather, has been absorbed into the significant literature on the impact of sectionalism on the national polity, too often as if the South were just one section among the others. This analytical placement diminishes the South's special qualities and its deeply uncommon role within the national polity. Neither racism nor a racial ordering of citizenship was ever confined to the South. But the region was exceptional in the pervasiveness, centrality, and elaborateness of its racial regime, which left its imprint on nearly every feature of southern life, including its low-wage and underdeveloped political economy and its unusual political system. Rendering the South as peripheral to the history of the United States minimizes the extent to which the South was a "co-creator of the nation's history" and obscures the ways in which the ideas and practices underpinning this racial order were projected across the United States.[19]

Notwithstanding Key's *Southern Politics*, scholarship on the politics of race in the region, and the recent recrudescence of interest in sectionalism by historians and political scientists, the place of the South in national state-making and the region's connections to the American liberal tradition have proved elusive. Following Key's insight that the hub of the relationship between southern and national politics lies in Congress, the point where constituency representation and national participation join, we aim to bring the South from the periphery to the center by emphasizing the region's lawmaking role in the House and Senate and its impact on American politics and policy, the organization of Congress, and the character of the region itself.[20]

Throughout the long period we consider, anxiety about potential federal action to curb the region's freedom of action often led the white South to rely on its congressional representatives to secure the long-term viability of what euphemistically was called "the southern way of life." White supremacy, they came to understand, was fraught and fragile, a view that was manifested in fact in the great fight over, and near-passage of, a federal elections bill in 1890. Only after this legislation had been thoroughly defeated, as evidenced by a declining interest among northern politicians about southern racial practices, did southern members become less anxious that they would be outmaneuvered on matters of race. In this changed situation, the South in Congress was able to move from confronting hard choices to being better able to control the character and terms of those choices.

With full-blown white supremacy encountering no resistance by other national political forces, the South could unleash efforts to advance black disfranchisement, secure control of black labor, and promote progressive policies to curb the excesses of the country's political-economic order. In turn, progressives from other regions proved quite willing to accommodate southern demands that progressive legislation be designed to accommodate white southern control over racial hierarchy. Southern priorities thus could triumph both within the region and in the framing of national policy.

Patterns of apportionment enhanced the ranks of southerners in the nation's legislature, insofar as the passage of the Fourteenth Amendment ensured that the region's entire population would count toward its share of seats despite the mass disfranchisement of southern blacks. Coming almost exclusively from one-party constituencies, southern representatives were in turn more likely to get reelected and accumulate seniority. But southern legislative influence fluctuated with institutional rules, with the size of the Democratic Party, and with the degree to which southerners' votes were needed for legislative action.

Flanked by regional apartheid and national liberalism, southern members nervously justified their racial society in terms that ranged from naked racism to a language of regret about the constraints imposed by black "backwardness." Their anxieties crested and ebbed as they interpreted national and international trends and as they pored over events and policies as diverse as Booker T. Washington's 1901 invitation to the White House by Theodore Roosevelt, the northern reaction to the 1906 Brownsville Affair, and even the official embrace of white supremacy by the British government in South Africa in 1909 for evidence of any "change of view" that might either secure or threaten the South.[21]

Some southern observers sought to convince their compatriots that "in its main purpose the South has been and is triumphant," that "nothing that will endanger [the South's] control of the situation . . . is any longer likely to be done by the North, or by the nation, against the will of the southern people." At the time, this was hardly an unreasonable position. Black citizens—especially in the South but in the North as well—lived in "the shadow of a vast despair" all through the era we consider. The southern system of organized humiliation was not considered to be a national problem, except perhaps when expressed in lynching, and few northern politicians desired any agitation on this issue.[22]

Still, most white southern Democrats did not believe that the question was permanently settled. Many believed that the nation could not be trusted for anything more than a "tacit acquiescence in what [southern] state governments may do." But "acquiescence does not evoke enthusiasm," and most of the political leadership of the white South believed that foreign interference in the region's racial hierarchy could again become a possibility.[23]

Despite a national indifference that set black rights aside, southern fears that potentially effective external pressure might be brought to bear were not easily allayed. The result was an unrelenting southern exaggeration of threat, one that ultimately made it difficult for Jim Crow and massive southern influence over most spheres of national public policy to persist. For most of the era we consider, these incongruities were masked and national politics proceeded as if nothing were more normal for a liberal regime than to have one very large and uncommonly powerful section constituted by an illiberal order based on the racial regulation of civil society, economic exploitation, and political repression; the South was different to be sure, but seemingly only one region among many in the national political order.

Notwithstanding the long-term play of this double-edged reality, the decades we are exploring were not all of one piece. Even before the New Deal and the civil rights eras, there was a good deal of variation in the preferences, behavior, and effects of the southern presence in Congress. This was a region of both factions and overarching consensus, depending on the moment, the issue, and the stakes. The core of *Southern Nation* traces these developments in two periods: after Reconstruction, when the three branches of the federal government wrestled with and ultimately failed to restrain a return to authorized racism; and the high moment of Jim Crow when the white South came to be the dominant force in the Democratic Party and the Republican Party conceded southern autonomy.

Throughout the period, southern anxieties played a key constitutive role. Shifts in the character and intensity of southern congressional members' apprehension for the security and persistence of the racial order powerfully affected their assessments of public policy options. It is impossible to understand how and by what means southern decision-making in Congress proceeded in each of these moments in diverse areas of public policy without taking these qualms about a potential federal role into account.

Our analysis begins with the great paradox at the core of V. O. Key's *Southern Politics*. Like Key, we are concerned to understand southern political behavior, especially how southern members of Congress fashioned a two-way relationship between that region and the country as a whole. We thus begin by identifying the propositions he placed at the heart of his study, then explain how we have sought to extend his reach geographically, temporally, and substantively.

Key advanced two principal analytical claims. With a stunted franchise and no party competition at home, the South entered the national scene with a constellation of Democrats who, however different, shared in the wish to preserve the region's capacity to decide its racial future on its own. Through the instrument of the Democratic Party, southerners were able to transform their diversity within Congress into a "Solid South," to act as a large and cohesive force within the national party and thereby bring to the region a long period of racial security.

Key's report on the status of the South detailed a region united by the race question and precious little else. "We ought to be both specific and candid about the regional interest that the Democratic party of the South has represented in national affairs," he wrote. "It must be conceded that there is one, and only one, real basis for southern unity: the Negro." Famously observing that "the politics of the South revolves around the position of the Negro," he argued that this matter alone—as a determinant of preferences, as a disciplining feature of imprisoned political discourse, as the controlling influence on institutional design, as the molder of public policies, and as the producer of public opinion and electoral participation—united an otherwise heterogeneous region.[24]

Focusing on the states that had composed the Confederacy, Key defined the South not in terms of secession as such but in terms of electoral behavior. The "critical" feature of southern politics was its solidarity, and there were "eleven states and only eleven [that] did not go Republican more than twice in the presidential elections from 1876 to 1944." He added, "not without importance," that "the eleven states that meet the test of partisan consistency also are the eleven states that seceded to form the Confederacy." Not without importance, one surmises, because these states, more than the six others that were practicing legally mandated racial segregation at the time he wrote, were caught up in collective memories of secession, war, occupation, and reintegration into the Union. But also because located within these states were the "Black Belt" counties, dominated by plantation agriculture and characterized by high proportions of African American residents, whose culture, economics, and politics set the tone and terms for southern political life as a whole. For it was the white elite in these areas of the South that had the strongest, least mediated, and least conflicted interest in upholding white supremacy.[25]

Nevertheless, as Key reminds us, these Black Belt counties were not characteristic of the region. As a southern liberal who hoped that social change could come from within the South, Key was deeply committed to informing the rest of the country about what every southerner knew: the region was complex. Southern economic, geographic, demographic, social, and political variety was quite remarkable—as Key showed in pointillist state-by-state descriptions. The region's politics were fragmented, local, face-to-face, often demagogic. Personalities frequently trumped issues, while the near total control of the Democratic Party effectively erased party as a force in state and local politics. The result, from a party vantage, was a politics of chaotic disorganization, with patterns that were quite dissimilar from state to state, or within various states over time.[26]

But this diversity not only was contained within but assumed as its background condition a broadly common racial order marked by official segregation, legal imposition, restricted voting, police repression, tolerated private violence, and national permissiveness—in all, a system of racial totalitarianism embedded inside a wider democracy. With race kept to the side of political conflict, and with race also serving as the implicit instrument defining the boundaries of political debate, southern politics could often appear overtly issue-less. Issues that defined political competition in other places were downplayed, and highly distinctive political cultures that other Americans often viewed as alien and odd, even primitive, dominated southern localities and states.[27]

Once Reconstruction ended and the potentialities of biracial class politics had been tamed, and once southern legality was altered to secure Jim Crow in terms that the nation's courts tolerated as somehow consistent with the Reconstruction Amendments, the race question was settled at the state level. In these circumstances, Key noted, "on the fundamental issue, only the Federal Government was to be feared" as a potential source of intervention. Thus, "unity on the national scene was essential" for the white South "in order that the largest possible bloc could be mobilized to resist any national move toward interference with southern authority to deal with the race question as was desired locally."[28]

Focusing on the 1930s and 1940s, Key argued that in Washington the South's great diversity and remoteness ceased to matter much. There, he stressed, southern fractionalization converted into southern solidarity. Within the South itself, race constituted the conditions in which factionalism prospered. The very same factor, he explained, especially as filtered through the preferences of its leading political voices on the national scene, advanced southern cohesion. "The maintenance of southern Democratic solidarity," he wrote, "has depended fundamentally on a willingness to subordinate to the race question all great social and economic issues that tend to divide people into opposing parties." The full range of the region's disparate interests and preferences was tamed, limited, and ordered by the paramount preference of southerners—as individual members, as constituency representatives, and as members of the Democratic Party—to defend the contours of the section's racial rules. Because the South lacked meaningful party competition, the region's representatives in the House and Senate were free to join together despite all their differences to preserve white supremacy whenever it was threatened. The responsibility of southerners to guard the region's autonomous capacity to regulate its internal affairs demanded cohesion despite divisions of style, political practice, and ideology. It was on those issues evaluated by southern members to be impinging on their section's core priorities that the South acted as a self-conscious and cohesive actor in national politics. The South, in short, converted multiplicity to singularity when its representatives converged on Washington. The section, as Key showed, acted in Congress as a "southern nation."[29]

To probe the frequency and conditions of southern cohesion in the House and Senate and to identify when and how southern legislative power shaped the character of the United States as a whole, *Southern Nation* extends and elaborates Key's brilliant account. By contrast to his historical snapshot of the 1930s and 1940s, we present a moving picture. While featuring issues and mechanisms that Key placed front and center, we undertake a systematic analysis of congressional behavior over an earlier and longer time span, focusing primarily on the five and a half decades spanning from the end of Reconstruction to the election of Franklin Roosevelt to the presidency. We thus begin in 1877, at a moment of economic depression and electoral crisis, and as some Republicans wagered that in giving up on more racially egalitarian aims they could protect the rules "regarding money, banks, tariffs, land, railroad, [and] subsidies" that favored the new type of capitalism that had been "placed on the lawbooks while the South was out of the Union." With Rutherford B. Hayes taking the presidency only with the contested votes of Florida, South Carolina, and Louisiana, the president, in turn, promoted a program of internal improvements in the region and presided over a policy of noninterference in the affairs of the South.[30]

The two core sections of the book grapple with the South in Congress during the region's return to the Union and during the Progressive era. We close with the 1932 election of Franklin Roosevelt, which inaugurated a reorganization of economic and political life that would both reflect southern priorities and foster new threats to the region's racial hierarchy. In all, we aim to apprehend the frequency and ways in which the South became a united nation in Washington and the consequences of this solidarity for the country. We trace the shifts in these patterns over time and identify the contextual and party-specific mechanisms that put stress on prevailing models of congressional behavior. We wish to better understand both how large-scale developments, including economic crises and wartime emergencies, pressured existing arrangements and how shifts in congressional practices and party rule affected southern unity and effectiveness by moving the South from majority status in a minority party to minority status in a majority party. These matters require a historical span a good deal longer than the one Key considered.

While we extend the time period under consideration, we also use a more expansive definition of the South than that used by Key, who focused on the eleven states that had most persistently voted for the Democratic presidential candidate and that, not incidentally, had also been the states that seceded to join the Confederacy. Our legal and institutional approach defines the region not in terms of the history of secession or patterns of electoral behavior but rather in terms of the distinctiveness of its racial order. We include all seventeen states in which racial segregation in schools was mandated by law before *Brown v. Board of Education* was adjudicated by the Supreme Court in 1954. Only these same seventeen still outlawed interracial marriage thirteen years after *Brown*, at the start of 1967, just as the Supreme Court was getting ready to rule in *Loving v. Virginia* that such laws were not constitutional.

Though our definition is institutional, it is not without broader historical, cultural, and political significance. For much of the period with which we are concerned, the South was not solely "the territory east of the Mississippi and south of the Ohio and Potomac Rivers, but a vast and varied empire reaching from the upper waters of the Chesapeake Bay or the desert land where New Mexico joins Texas, comprising one-third of all the States of the Union." For many, if not most, southern and northern writers in the late nineteenth and early twentieth centuries, the South included those fifteen states that still practiced slavery when the Civil War began, plus West Virginia, which broke away during the war, and later Oklahoma, which in 1860 was Indian Territory.[31] As late as 1964, "southern" meant "more than the former states of the Confederacy" to Frank Smith, congressman from Mississippi. "It includes border states like Maryland, West Virginia, Kentucky, and Oklahoma, and parts of states like Missouri and New Mexico."[32]

To be sure, these boundaries encompass great variation and invite debate about commonalities and differences. Thus, Albert Bushnell Hart, writing in 1910, argued that Maryland had become more "a middle state than a Southern," that West Virginia "has been cut off from the South, and is now essentially Western," and that the same was true for Missouri, but that Oklahoma was "a community imbued with a distinct Southern spirit." Even Virginia, North Carolina, Kentucky, and Tennessee were, in Bushnell's telling, outside the "true Southland."[33]

As David Carlton has noted, "much sterile debate about the region's character has arisen out of differences over which places qualify as 'southern' and which do not." We do not propose to resolve such debates. No definition of "the South" can satisfy all metrics and considerations across all periods. Rather, the approach we utilize permits us to take variation in time and space into account. As we hunt for southern cohesion, we have opted for the most expansive definition of the region, erring on the side of diversity and thus biasing against a finding of southern unity. Moreover, we do not presuppose fixed or singular answers to questions concerning the scope and content of the issues that motivated the region's representatives. The larger the region, the more diverse the economy, civil society, demography, built environment, and political interests. Our enlarged definition of the South thus introduces a bias against excessively swift or sure findings of southern unity and collective power. And with a wider South, we can better identify when the South's different kinds of heterogeneity actually shaped diversity in roll call behavior, and when they did not. In short, the way the South is defined, here and in other scholarship about the politics of the region, is not innocent with respect to models, mechanisms, and findings.[34]

We probe the role of the South in American lawmaking by developing a more systematic account of the role of southern legislators in Congress than previously has been possible, drawing on a range of new measures and data in tandem with an immersion in congressional debates and newspaper coverage and various primary sources, while also relying on a plethora of secondary scholarship. Rather than focus on a narrow set of policies over time or take a cross-sectional approach at key moments, we examine patterns of behavior regarding classes of public policies over a long swath of time. We hypothesize a lexical ordering to southern preferences that placed the region's distinct and racialized "way of life" first, so that this concern for preserving the social and racial hierarchies of the South would trump party cues and pressures when a given policy was thought to conflict with this primary consideration. Within this frame, southern representatives possessed a second key preference: to gain both relief and advantages from the new finance- and corporation-oriented political economy that the Republican Party was advancing for the country as a whole, but only if such economic goals could be secured without forfeiting local control over race. This consideration was deeply connected to a range of tasks that southern members had to carry out as they defended home rule and pursued national policy goals. These tasks included dealing with northern Democrats, cultivating occasional support among some Republicans, defeating third parties, and controlling black labor as they managed the stresses and realities of black politics.

By identifying the substance of roll calls and matching these to voting patterns in Congress, the set of policies that southern legislators perceived to most threaten the status quo can be more precisely identified. Readers will discern how southern Democrats were constantly seeking allies not only among other Democrats but among Republicans, especially progressive Republicans from the West and Midwest, on issues such as revenue policy, tobacco taxation, tariff rates, railroad regulation, currency matters, labor policy, war pensions, and educational investments to combat illiteracy, provided such policy activism could be shaped to be consonant with the region's racial order.

Pursuing this analysis, we not only confirm the arguments that have been made by historians and political scientists about the special importance of specific policies, including civil rights, but also identify other policies that southern members of Congress thought fundamental to their region's social, economic, and political arrangements, as well as policies that they believed would upset racial arrangements. We observe a very active federal government in matters of economic and educational policy, more so than most considerations to date. What southerners sought to do was bend this activism toward their needs and protect regional red lines, including respect for the emerging system of segregation.

Additionally, we apply a southern lens to the story of congressional development by identifying the elaboration of southern mastery over congressional procedures and examining how the institutional changes its representatives crucially crafted affected the way Congress legislated. We examine how these developments within the legislature increasingly made Congress into a southern institution as the region's representatives not only helped lead rules changes but took advantage of congressional reorganization.

Our analysis also raises some significant analytical questions about southern regional influence. Overall, the South had much success in advancing or blocking legislation, even at moments when its representatives lacked what congressional scholars identify as pivotal status—that is, when majorities could have been assembled without their consent—at least in part because many members from the rest of the country were situationally happy to go along with the South or were quite content for the United States to become a southern nation.

Overview

We begin with "Southern Lawmaking," a chapter that conceptualizes the potential for southern influence. Outlining measures that allow us to map regional preferences about specific policies onto legislative behavior and performance, we consider how the quasi-party status fashioned by southerners inside the Democratic Party intersects with prominent concepts and models in the political science of congressional lawmaking. We detail southern influence as rooted in these theories, which we reconstitute to accommodate southern distinctiveness. We also underscore the importance of the content of public policy as a causal factor, showing how shifts in the character and intensity of southern preferences for the security of racial arrangements at distinctive historical periods affected decision-making differently in diverse areas of public policy.

With these analytical tools in hand, we turn to the heart of the matter in the two core sections of *Southern Nation*. Part II, "Union Restored," presents an account of congressional behavior in the decades following the reintegration of the South into the Union. In 1877, the terms of the South's return remained to be negotiated, but were ultimately settled with the repeal of the Federal Elections Laws in 1894, the 1896 holding in *Plessy v. Ferguson*, and the refusal of President McKinley to intervene to halt the violent white supremacist campaigns at the end of the century.

Chapter 3 visits the internal tensions within the various southern Democratic parties, which successfully united competing factions around the cause of white supremacy but whose unity was always tense and insecure. Here we outline how southern legislators evaluated and voted across distinctive policy areas and offer close analysis of this crucial issue.

Chapter 4 explores this period's central southern lawmaking dilemma: the perennial necessity to weigh hopes for federal investment, regulation, and a reconfiguration of the national economy against the priority of preserving white supremacy. The white South's fears about the prospect of national intervention, we show, were key to the behavior of its representatives, who often made choices that strengthened regional autonomy at the expense of the standing and prosperity of the South. This combination proved fateful to the subsequent course of American political development.

Chapter 5 turns to home rule, in particular southern evaluations of prospects for a new national labor policy and attention to voting rights protections. Southern success in defeating a renewed consideration of the franchise established the terms of the broad national accommodation that came to characterize American policy and politics for the first half of the twentieth century. The South would be left alone to determine the contours of black citizenship, while the economic program of the Republican Party would be placed on a stable political foundation.

Part III, "Egalitarian Whiteness," charts the dramatic transformation of southern politics that accompanied black disfranchisement and the ascendancy of the Republican Party in national politics during the early twentieth century.

Chapter 6 identifies the issues and policy debates that underlay distinctive southern preferences and choices as national progressivism increasingly came to be shaped by the region's representatives. We underscore the transformations to southern politics in the first three decades of the century as southern legislators increasingly drove an economic program, much of it progressive, that ultimately would define the era's legislative accomplishments. The economic agenda of southern agrarians and populists had buffeted the region since the Civil War, but was now both tamed and channeled into the mainstream of southern political life, enabled by the successful suppression of black electoral politics and the rise of systematic racial segregation grounded in law.

Chapter 7 focuses on the period from 1900 to 1915, when an increasingly cohesive congressional bloc from the South remade the American state in its image. At first, these representatives participated in carefully crafted legislative coalitions as the weaker but often more engaged partner, a prolegomenon to the rush of Wilson presidency activism. In the process, the white South fashioned the type of regulatory regime it long had sought to achieve: relatively little bureaucracy in Washington combined with much implementation delegated either to the states or to public-private entities like farm credit boards. Utilizing a congressional capacity based on numbers, longevity, committee control, and support from the speaker, southern legislators imposed new restraints on northern capital while not allowing the South's racial order to be called into question.

Chapter 8 attends to the long moment when southern Democrats came to dominate their party in Congress, just as Republicans were gaining governing capacity after the war years. Here we are particularly concerned with highlighting how the South ever more successfully remade congressional institutions and practices to accommodate the peculiar fact that the region's heterogeneity and range of preferences were contained within a single political party. This achievement complemented the earlier era's policy outcomes, for it reshaped Congress for the long haul. Southern legislators designed and implemented the radical diffusion of authority in the House of Representatives, enabling the diversity of southern policy priorities to be worked out and advanced in the critical legislative committees. Through compromise, they also ensured that the creation in the Senate of a cloture mechanism that could end a filibuster would only further institutionalize their ability to obstruct legislation that called their region's racial hierarchy into question. What emerged overall, thanks to southern influence, was a pattern of national lawmaking that endured for decades, marked by arrangements in which coalitions were forged less by party than by lines of constituency interest and issue-specific policy preferences, with committees coming to serve as key sites of negotiation and brokerage.

These chapters invite a reconsideration of how scholars treat divisions in time during the pre–New Deal twentieth century. A key decision in that regard is our choice to divide the Wilson years, joining his administration's wartime period to the 1920s. Of course, any periodization is a simplification. We know, of course, that many of President Wilson's progressive initiatives were framed as preparedness measures, and that the Republican Party sought, in the 1920s, to restrain and reverse federal activism.

Notwithstanding, these familiar story lines, we argue, are not so much wrong as incomplete. The guiding logic behind the chronological breakpoint we have adopted is the history of movement within the Democratic Party. We show, in chapter 7, that in the early Wilson years Democrats across regions were able to maintain cohesion on core priorities and work out compromises as necessary, but generally achieved reforms that had been long-standing demands of the South with the backing of the entire party.

Lawmaking during Woodrow Wilson's first term was the culmination of southern ambitions during the century's first decade. The later Wilson years, however, witnessed moments during which party lines totally collapsed as progressive and conservative southern Democrats were in much less agreement about what should be done. The party caucus ceased to function as an effective coordinating mechanism, and western Republicans and progressive southerners often allied against northeastern Republicans and conservative southerners. This is a story of fragmentation within the Democratic Party once its priorities had been achieved and once the war had upended expectations about what Washington could, and ought, do.

With the end of the war and the Paris Peace, party lines were reestablished, especially after nearly all northern Democrats were defeated. But this emergent renewal was attenuated, with legislative coalitions forming that were more like those of the unstable war years than the prewar period early in the century. There was no return to political "normalcy." Rather, something significant and new developed as features of lawmaking that first were exhibited during World War I took a more settled form. During Wilson's second term, and more fully in the 1920s, the South as a cohesive actor started to give way to something more heterogeneous and situational as its legislators took advantage of the institutional reforms that created conditions for more policy-oriented political coalitions that crossed regional and party lines.

Southern Nation's historical account ends at a moment marked by the catastrophic collapse of global capitalism, the rise of totalitarianism, and the acceleration of fear, each a characteristic at the start of the New Deal and its governing capacity that was based on the astonishing Democratic Party landslides of 1932, 1934, and 1936.

Part IV locates this extraordinary moment of party hegemony as well as subsequent trends by showing how the period *Southern Nation* considers provided significant bases for future developments. We thus conclude the book with two sets of claims. First is a discussion of the Roosevelt and Truman years, during which the shift of southern Democrats from a majority of the minority party to a minority of the majority party temporarily overrode the lawmaking features that were fashioned after 1915. However, by the late 1930s, when Jim Crow Democrats came again to constitute more than half of the members of the House and Senate, and on into the conflict-charged civil rights era, southern influence over national policymaking reached its apex in ways that extended the pattern that had emerged in previous decades including support for a particular kind of hands-off progressivism, protection for southern racial autonomy, and cross-party coalitions on such key issues as labor policy and national security. These features of congressional behavior—in which political parties were, for a time, diminished as vehicles for collective government—were made possible both by southern members' substantive choices as they perceived their system of race relations to be increasingly fragile and by their ability to operate the institutional rules, practices, and expectations that had been molded in part to respond to the particular conditions of southern politics before the New Deal.[35]

The second question we address is whether, notwithstanding a remarkable array of changes in the postwar years, not least the civil rights revolution, the United States again has become defined by the preferences and priorities of the South. The era of post-1938 southern effectiveness in the last years of regional segregation went hand in hand with historically low rates of congressional polarization. With the passage of the Civil Rights and Voting Rights Acts in the mid-1960s, a once durably and overwhelmingly Democratic region became durably and overwhelmingly Republican. The result was a renewal of party polarization characterized by the effective growth of a conservatism that combined a preference for strong federalism with foreign policy assertiveness and traditional cultural priorities. Once again, the South dominated a significant ideological trend lodged within the region's dominant political party. As a result, Congress came to be characterized by cohesive political parties that are organized and mobilized to advance competing, indeed sharply diverging, legislative agendas. Now in the majority, one of these parties has advanced the cause of making the United States, yet again, a southern nation.

2

Southern Lawmaking

The South's way of dominating political situations without actually counting a numerical control has always been one of the most striking features of American political history.[1]

Writing in the late seventeenth century, John Locke declared "the first and fundamental positive law of all Commonwealths" to be the "establishing of the Legislative Power," the institutional authority that would "direct how the force of the commonwealth shall be employed for preserving the community and the members of it." Locke's emphasis on the importance of the legislative branch was often invoked in the first seven decades of the nineteenth century as the difficulties of reconciling democracy and slavery in an extended Republic came to be felt. When antislavery activism intensified in the antebellum United States, the House of Representatives—the "people's chamber," the "grand repository of the democratic principle of the government," and the branch that was expected to "know and sympathize with every part of the community"—passed the first in a series of "gag rules" that prevented antislavery petitions from being read or discussed, while the Senate bound itself by passing a rule making it impossible for the body to vote to receive but not accept a petition. At the time, the gag rule was widely understood to be a reasonable compromise, a way to ensure that Congress would continue to preserve the peculiar American community. After the rule's eventual rescission, recurring sectional crises erupted when the House and Senate were called on to act for or against slavery. Congress quickly became the center of the contradiction between freedom and slavery.[2]

Congress emerged again as a site of pitched battles when the Civil War and Reconstruction ended and the secessionist southern states were readmitted to full standing in the Union. As before the war, large majorities of southern legislators considered Congress to be a potential threat, since the institution could nullify home rule and the ongoing process of restoring the racial and economic hierarchies that Emancipation and Reconstruction had unsettled. Concurrently, the institution also held out the promise of a renewed role for the South in national life and of a reconfiguration of national policy to respond to the diverse material needs and principled commitments of the region.

Vital questions emerged in the years following the region's readmission to Congress. These included whether southern members could somehow regain the capacity to impose a gag rule on issues of race and home rule, whether the white South would persist in its solidarity with the Democratic Party, and whether the conflicting currents of radicalism and conservatism rushing through the region might lead to a renewal of two-party competition.

The five and a half decades at the core of this book present three analytical opportunities. The first is that of historical understanding. When, how, and to what effect did the South act politically as if it were a distinct nation within the larger polity? Second is the opportunity to deploy this history to better understand American political development, and in particular to examine how the range of southern priorities defined the content of national policy during formative periods of American state-building. Political development is, after all, largely defined by the public policies enacted or blocked at the national level. The role of the South in advancing and blocking development, especially in the period between the end of Reconstruction and the New Deal, has to date been probed only insufficiently. Third is the chance to draw on an analytical history of southern lawmaking to evaluate and reconceptualize the leading theories that currently guide the study of Congress, and especially to understand the ways in which the South shaped the country's central governing institutions. Leading preference-based theories of lawmaking do not often incorporate how the intensity of preferences, the substance of lawmaking, and the political environment matter for outcomes.

Southern Nation works at two points of connection—the intersection between history and political science, and between studies of public policy and Congress. Over the last several decades, Congress scholars have made enormous strides in understanding the institution's performance, operations, and internal organization. The bulk of this work is centered on understanding what motivates the behavior of individual members of Congress, with a focus primarily on the post–World War II period. Various methodological advances have allowed us to better assess the structure of political conflict and to trace change in the organization of conflict over time, while theoretical advances have provided a framework for better understanding the lawmaking process. Putting this literature to work, we use the tools assembled by Congress scholars to examine the role of the South as a "co-creator of the nation's history." An emphasis on the role of the South in Congress also offers valuable corrections. After a period in which much scholarship on Congress remained doggedly ahistorical, there has been a welcome turn to historically oriented questions, themes, and evidence, a trend that has dramatically widened understanding of the institution. The extensive documentation of the American Congress over time, combined with the efforts of scholars to compile and systematically analyze these data, has enabled the field to project its attention backwards without abandoning its methodological rigor. History thus has begun to achieve a welcome analytical substructure.[3]

This turn, however, has not come without limitations. Much of the (re)turn to history treats the past as a depository of cases to be employed to test theories that are assumed, at least implicitly, to operate equivalently across different historical contexts. By contrast, we believe that historically grounded understandings of congressional lawmaking require attention to how the institutional arrangements central to contemporary congressional theories came to be established, the identification of alternative development paths, and a focus on how the policy preferences and legislative actions of representatives were conditioned by the historical and political contexts within which they operated.[4]

The manner in which the South appears in much congressional scholarship also raises significant questions. Most theoretical work focuses on individual members, who are conceived of as independent, goal-oriented actors and, in some accounts, as members of a partisan organization that acts as their agent. To be sure, these emphases have been highly productive, but at the potential cost of obscuring the impact of other coalitions, whether these are rooted in a particular identity, cross party lines, or are firmly embedded within a particular party.

At the heart of this book lies a different idea. Most congressional scholarship has paid insufficient attention to the distinctive traits of southern congressional behavior, including the intensity of preferences on policy issues related to the region's racial order, how southern members in particular interpreted and sought to shape the content of public affairs, and the consequences of this behavior for American political development. Understanding the role of the South in shaping the American state and the content of its public policies requires that we situate the analysis in Congress, the institutional site where the broad and at times uneasy national accommodation that characterized American politics for the first half of the twentieth century was hammered out and secured. In turn, this approach necessitates a theory of southern congressional politics to illuminate how the region's legislators individually or collectively acted to influence the legislative process, and how a diverse region could come together in defense of its paramount priorities. In many ways, we are attempting to understand how southern legislators behaved as a group, not just a sum of aggregated preferences, and we offer a research design to evaluate our theoretical expectations, empirically assess the importance of southern lawmaking, and identify its mechanisms.

This chapter begins by detailing standard accounts of congressional lawmaking and influence, then turns to a discussion of southern exceptionalism. We outline a theory of southern representation that focuses on how lawmakers from a heterogeneous region balanced their diverse constituent and individual demands with the distinctive imperatives and constraints unique to the South. We suggest that standard accounts of congressional lawmaking need to be modified to accommodate the distinctive identity and goals of southern lawmakers across different historical and institutional contexts. We close by outlining a research strategy, inspired by the analytical approaches of V. O. Key and Richard Hofstadter, that allows us to evaluate our theoretical expectations, identify the mechanisms by which southerners were able to influence the national political agenda, and assess the importance of their influence for American political development.

Theories of Congressional Influence

Was the post-Reconstruction South, in the words of W. J. Cash, "a nation within a nation," or at least "the next thing to it"? We conceive of the South as a potentially cohesive political actor within the national polity, as unique among American regional identities in its self-conscious organization toward coordinated political action. Despite its considerable diversity during the period under study, we argue, the South constituted a *political* community rooted in a distinctive economic and social life, located within a well-defined territory, and organized to defend characteristic policy priorities. Preserving the political conditions for the "southern way of life" was the paramount concern of white southern politics, even though this was never the sole goal of all of its elected officials or necessarily even the primary preference for each individual representative.[5]

Congress was the key site for the South's defense against national interference. Sitting at the center of the American national state, Congress long has had additional importance when viewed from the perspective of the South. Members from the region repeatedly stressed, in the words of an Alabama congressman, that Congress was "the last refuge of the people of my beloved Southland," the branch of government that recurrently enabled the South to fight back, in the telling of white southerners, "when political passion and persecution sought to nullify their self-government." The region's representatives and senators were highly conscious of a collective responsibility to ensure that no legislation threatening white supremacy could be passed, a consciousness that the historian Ulrich B. Phillips called "the cardinal test of a Southerner."[6]

This assessment of Congress as the last great bastion of the South's once immense national political influence was on target empirically. The four panels of figure 2.1 show the relative proportion of offices occupied by southerners, of either party, across four different institutions: the top executive offices (the president and his cabinet), the Supreme Court, the House of Representatives, and the Senate. Southern representation in the cabinet (top-left panel) tended to be slightly greater than the southern share of the population before the Civil War; after the war, the region was at a consistent disadvantage, reaching proportionality only during Democratic administrations. Membership on the Supreme Court (top-right panel) followed the same basic pattern of overrepresentation before the Civil War, with a collapse afterwards during which proportionality was reached only occasionally.[7]

Congress was different. There, representation was set down in the Constitution rather than being dependent on the process of presidential selection. Though the South never regained the disproportionate representation it had enjoyed in the Senate before the Civil War (bottom-right panel), its proportion of seats hovered slightly above its share of the population until the 1980s. Further, the conclusion of the Civil War actually brought about an increase in southern representation in the House, as for the first time the region's entire population, white and black, came to be counted toward the apportionment of seats, notwithstanding the degree of black disfranchisement.

Congress became the focus of the white South's hopes because it had little reason to look for succor elsewhere. A central question concerned the conditions that could enable white southerners to exercise influence in Congress, either to protect their shared commitment to home rule and white supremacy by using the multiple veto checks embedded within the institution or to advance preferred policies in other areas. To answer these questions requires an approach to lawmaking and legislative influence that allows us to identify and detail the different ways in which the South could bend the legislative process toward regional ends. Current empirical and theoretical work on lawmaking inadequately captures this process.

Advances to the theoretical study of congressional lawmaking provide a set of theories that serve as our point of departure. We begin with an observation made by an anonymous member of the House of Representative to the political scientist Richard Fenno: "The process here is one where consent must be obtained before anything gets done. If you are one of those from whom consent must be obtained, then you are a more important person."[8]

The most influential accounts of lawmaking in recent decades have stressed the importance of *pivotal members*, legislators whose votes are ultimately

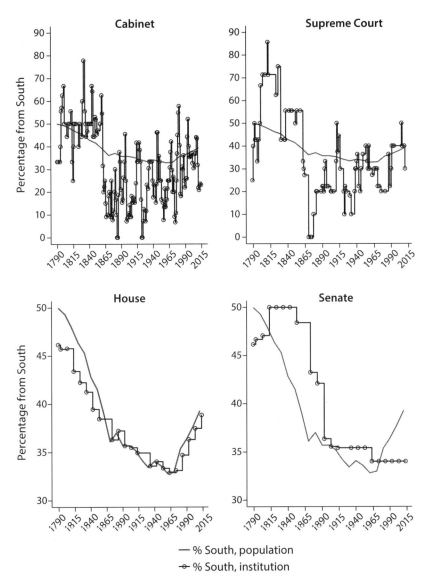

FIGURE 2.1. Southern Representation in Four Political Branches

needed for bills to pass. For example, according to nonpartisan models of lawmaking, if all members of the House were arrayed on a line from most liberal to most conservative, under majoritarian rules of the chamber the pivotal member would be the median member. Without the approval of the median members in both the House and Senate, legislation will be defeated; because consent must be obtained from these individuals, whoever they might be on any given issue, they can exercise substantial influence over the content of legislation. Since the inauguration of a cloture rule requiring a two-thirds majority to end debate, the Senate has the additional *filibuster pivot* of the sixty-seventh (or sixtieth since 1975) senator, again arrayed on a line from most liberal to most conservative on any particular policy issue.[9]

Pivotal politics models underscore that the rules of the chambers and legislators' preferences relative to their peers make some members much more influential than others; the rules, as well as the constitutional requirements of bicameralism, create several such veto actors, including the median members of each chamber, the filibuster pivot, the president, and the legislators in each chamber whose vote is needed to override a presidential veto; and that the configuration of preferences over a legislative proposal compared to existing policy determines the likelihood that the proposal will be enacted, as well as which members' preferences will be most accommodated in the process.

The theory's identification of members who are in a position to veto legislation and thus influence the content of public policy allows us to evaluate the likelihood of southern influence across time. Using a technique developed by Joshua Clinton, Simon Jackman, and Douglas Rivers, we can estimate the probability that the pivotal median member in each chamber was a southerner from either party in a particular year. This estimate in turn gives us a useful first approximation of the potential for southern influence over public policy.[10] Figure 2.2 shows this probability for the House of Representatives (top-left panel) and the Senate (top-right panel), with Congress-level probabilities represented by the thin gray line and the thick black line showing a smoothed trend. For the Senate, we also include the probability that the filibuster pivot was southern, beginning with the establishment of a cloture rule in 1917. The bottom-right panel shows the joint probability that at least one of these three pivotal positions was occupied by a southerner, highlighting the period from 1877 to the present.[11]

For nearly the entire period on which we concentrate, from 1877 to the New Deal, the South had a significantly lower probability of being pivotal than its share of seats would suggest. As we explain later, the measure of pivotality that we estimate is based on roll call voting data in Congress, which is only one of several ways in which we explore the importance of the South in the lawmaking process. As with southern representation in the other branches, the likelihood that the South would be pivotal in Congress collapsed with the Civil War and did not recover until the New Deal. By this measure, southern influence was at its zenith in the 1830s and 1840s, a period when the region divided almost equally between Whigs and Democrats. From 1877 to 1932, the region's legislators were largely contained within the Democratic Party and tended to be more extreme relative to the chamber; the implication of a pivotal politics approach is that during this period the region would have exercised relatively little influence over public policy. During and after the New Deal, however, southern legislators began moving to the center of the ideo-

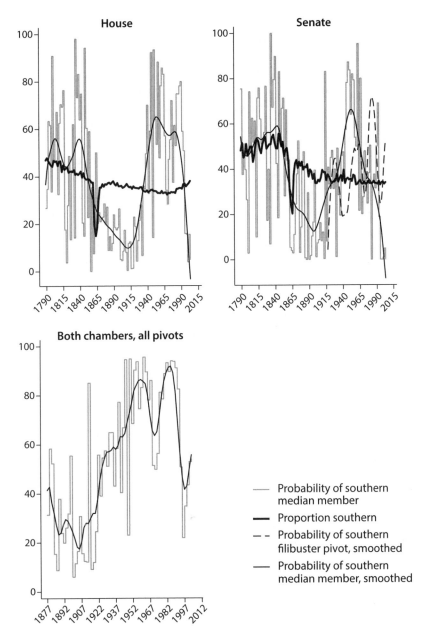

FIGURE 2.2. Probability That the Pivotal Members in Congress Were Southern

logical divide in Congress, forming issue-specific coalitions with Republicans and, as a result, frequently holding the policy balance.[12]

Within pivotal politics accounts, legislative influence is not a function of personal expertise, policy entrepreneurship, delegated authority, or legislative skill. Rather, the distribution of influence is entirely a product of the overall configuration of preferences on a particular issue and on the rules of the chamber. This sparse account contrasts with the emphasis that other scholars have placed on the role of parties and committees in structuring the legislative agenda and deciding which issues will be considered on the floor or even allowed to come to a vote. By deciding whether to hold back or bring up legislation, this literature argues, key party and committee actors are able to bias the subset of issues debated by the chamber; as a result, outcomes are not simply determined by the floor median. "Pivotal" members are not always pivotal, precisely because some issues are never considered by the full chamber. We take this insight fully into consideration in identifying who actually is pivotal in lawmaking in particular instances, while insisting that invaluable roll call voting measures may mask the importance of key veto players in the American policy process. We recognize that this may be critical in understanding why the South, though it often does not show up as being pivotal in quantitative indices, nonetheless achieved its desires more than its pivotality measures would predict.

Consider the influential *party cartel* model of Gary Cox and Mathew McCubbins. In their telling, the majority party in the House of Representatives operates as a procedural cartel that successfully monopolizes control over the legislative agenda. The speaker, the Rules Committee, and the chairs of the important House committees are empowered to effectively block legislation at different stages in the process, and together they can ensure that the majority party is squarely in control of the issues brought to the House floor. The members of the majority party cede this *negative agenda* power, they argue, to ensure that the reputation of the party—an important component of individual electoral fortunes—is adequately cared for, and especially that the party is seen to be up to the task of governing. It is the responsibility of the party leadership, then, to keep issues that will split the party, and thus tarnish the collective brand, off the legislative agenda. If the party is internally united on its policy priorities, the leadership might also be empowered to use its control over the agenda to advance issues that have broad support within the party, but this is a distinctively secondary grant of authority.[13]

The party cartel theory has been used less in the Senate, where individual senators have considerably more control over the agenda and the capacity for influence is much more widely diffused. Still, the Senate has seen shifts over time in the degree to which parties, committees, or individual members have been empowered. "In the Senate of the 1870s," write David Brady, Richard Brody, and David Epstein, "members behaved independently of party." But from roughly 1894 to 1910, the Senate was organized by the Big Five—Republican senators Eugene Hale of Maine, Orville Platt of Connecticut, John C. Spooner of Wisconsin, William B. Allison of Iowa, and Nelson Aldrich of Rhode Island—who collectively provided leadership to a relatively homogeneous Republican majority. They determined committee assignments, closely attended to the legislative agenda, and ultimately required members to "seek their favor or remain without influence in the chamber." After the Democratic takeover of the Senate in 1912, power was decentralized to committees, whose members gained "privileged access to decision making in the committee's area of jurisdiction." While party continued to be important in shaping the legislative agenda, influence would largely be concentrated in committees for the remainder of the period on which we focus.[14]

Like pivotal politics, *party cartel*– and *committee*-based theories of lawmaking allow us to sketch a preliminary assessment of the potential for southern influence over time. The left panel of figure 2.3 traces the percentage of the House majority party leadership offices occupied by southerners, as well as the proportion of seats they occupied on important committees. The right panel shows the proportion of important committees chaired by southern senators, as well as their overall membership on these committees. Unsurprisingly, in both chambers southern influence was closely bound up with the electoral success of the Democratic Party. But the South was also especially well placed within that party. The rules of the Democratic caucus, like the party's rules for selecting a presidential nominee, required a two-thirds vote before members could be bound, and Democrats could only be bound by the party on issues that did not involve a question of constitutional interpretation. The southern delegation regularly constituted more than two-thirds of the caucus. Just as important, with the disfranchisement of black voters and the advent of one-party politics in the region, southern lawmakers began accumulating seniority over their Democratic colleagues and thus were soon disproportionately represented in party leadership positions. This fact would contribute immensely to their heightened influence during the Wilson years and again during and after the New Deal.[15]

The *pivotal politics*, *party cartel*, and *committee* theories of legislative influence stress the importance of being able to effectively veto legislative proposals, whether by withholding needed votes for passage or by keeping an issue off the legislative agenda. They are not entirely equivalent in their implications for the type of influence that can be exercised, and they disagree on which legislators are the key veto players. Committee theories, whether implicitly or explicitly, understand committee action to be associated with influence early in the legislative process, when the basic structure, goals, and features of policy are established, and then again when the House and Senate go into conference to decide on the final terms of legislation. Individual expertise and policy entrepreneurship are likely to be most important at these moments.

The pivotal politics model argues that the House of Representatives is dominated by the median voter, and that this influence is perhaps more likely to be exercised relatively late in the process, after legislation has been drafted,

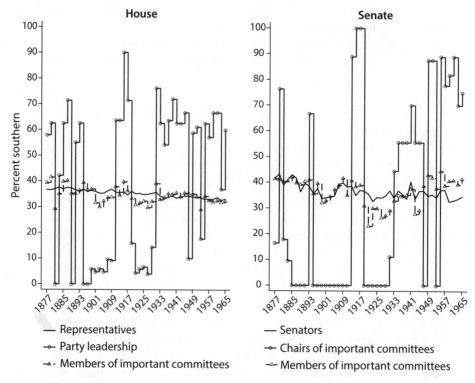

FIGURE 2.3. Percentage of Agenda-Setting Offices and Important Committee Seats Held by Southerners. Party leadership includes speaker, majority leader, and the chairmen of the Finance, Appropriations, Rules, and other important committees.

debated, and reworked in committee. Although norms and rules might limit the extent to which a committee-drafted bill is amended on the floor, leaving the pivotal members with what is effectively an up-or-down choice, on many issues we expect that the floor will be allowed to pass some amendments. Absent restrictive rules, either advanced by the party leadership or reflecting the general rules of the chamber, there is little limit to the ability of the floor to rewrite a bill altogether. Knowing this, legislators operating at earlier stages in the process are likely to take the median members' preferences into account, calibrating the bill to what they think is necessary for passage and devising rules that will protect the bills worked out in committees or in the party caucus from being modified on the floor.

All of these accounts are useful in sketching the broad strokes of southern potential, but they are not perfectly adequate to our task, precisely because they do not sufficiently take into account the distinctive commitments and features of southern politics. In particular, they do not adequately deal with policy content and preference intensity. Central to the party cartel account, for instance, is an assumption of a roughly equivalent ordering of priorities across members. While they might care about the substance of legislation, members of Congress are especially concerned with their own reelection and are thus willing to place considerable weight on the maintenance of their party's national reputation so that it does not become a drag on their own electoral prospects. Yet for much of the period we consider, there is little reason to assume that most southern legislators, even senior members of the party cartel, were concerned more with the national party brand than with achieving substantive policy ends.

. For southern Democrats, in fact, the cartel logic often was reversed. By the beginning of the twentieth century, a restricted franchise and the region's one-party system had ensured that party disunity was unlikely to cost southern Democrats their reelection. Moreover, after 1910, when legislative influence became increasingly concentrated in committees rather than in the majority party, southern Democrats might not even have been at a stark disadvantage in policy influence by being in the minority, though they certainly preferred to hold the committee chair position and to have majority status within a committee. The result was that southern Democratic lawmakers were perhaps uniquely free from the constraint of needing to worry about the success of the national party to win congressional elections. Even in minority status, they still held considerable power.

As the political scientist Paul Hasbrouck warned in 1927, the weakening of party authority and the high likelihood of reelection created an opportunity for senior members "to abuse their power"; entrenched committee chairs could become "blind to the general welfare—to the detriment of party, it is true, but with a dangerous leeway of personal immunity—and pursue a policy of class or sectional benefit." Indeed, it is the behavior of southern representatives occupying key committee positions during the 1930s and 1940s that provides the most important deviation to the pattern predicted by party cartel theory. The problem, we suggest, is in part that party cartel theory fails to appreciate how the distinctive preferences and commitments of southern members could shape the party loyalty even of the most senior members.[16]

Another limitation of party, committee, and pivotal politics accounts is their neglect of the intensity and cohesiveness of preferences and their impact on legislative influence. A huge weakness of preference-based theories of lawmaking is that they treat all preferences equally, with the distribution and rules determining which individuals will be best situated to enact their preferences into law. Preference intensity has no real place in these theories. Consider how pivotal politics treats the filibuster. Because invoking cloture and shutting down a filibuster in the Senate requires sixty votes, whichever senator is best situated to provide the sixtieth vote is empowered to close debate. A member who opposes the proposed legislation or wants accommodations on this or another issue may vote against cloture until these demands are met.

As political scientists have demonstrated, however, for much of congressional history the filibuster has been less a mechanical function of the distribution of preferences than an instrument in a war of attrition, with the advantage going to those who are most committed and to those who can muster groups sufficiently large to sustain the obstruction campaign. The amount of time remaining in the session is likewise a critical variable in a filibuster's success: with less time remaining, the threat of a sustained filibuster that would defeat a range of legislation becomes more credible. That is, a successful filibuster requires a collective willingness to sacrifice other desired legislation that will not be considered so long as the filibuster is under way, a consideration that poses a threat to the unity of the obstructionists. So long as filibustering demands a collective effort, its success is conditional in part on the cohesion and numbers brought to bear on a particular legislative fight, the willingness of its supporters to prioritize the issue under debate over others, and the parliamentary expertise to skillfully exploit the rules to maximum dilatory advantage.

The decision to sustain a filibuster has always been conditioned by the knowledge that a determined majority could ultimately change the rules and close off avenues for obstruction. Obstruction campaigns, then, have had to be waged with an eye to not pushing the majority too far and not blocking progress on issues of sufficient importance to provoke a reaction.[17] But where a minority is believed to be more intensely invested in the outcome than the majority, then even the threat of a filibuster has proved to be sufficient to lead the majority party to abandon its efforts. This logic applies to all members, depending on the rules of the chamber, but it particularly advantaged southern Democrats: by the 1890s, it undoubtedly was the case that white southerners were much more intensely invested in the defeat of policy proposals that directly impinged on white supremacy than were the white northerners whose votes and sustained commitments would be needed for passage.

The example of the filibuster suggests other ways in which the intensity of a legislative bloc's commitment and sense of common purpose conditions the level of influence it can exercise. Consider a case in which a bill with the support of a majority of the chamber is sent to any one of several committees; each committee is controlled by southerners, by virtue of chairmanships or committee majorities, but the pivotal median member of the chamber is a non-southerner. If one committee refuses to report the legislation, the chamber might vote to send the bill to another committee. But if across the different committees the southern legislators act as a cohesive unit in opposition to the bill, then most avenues for bringing the bill to the floor will be closed, requiring the bill's supporters to abandon the fight, make accommodations to southern preferences, or create new institutional avenues for legislative change.[18]

Southern Exceptionalism

This discussion suggests the need to modify theories of congressional law-making to account for the exceptional features of southern representation in national politics. During the period we consider, the region's members, we argue, were not quite like other legislators, most notably because their views about the wide array of issues before Congress were influenced by intense preferences regarding the region's racial hierarchy. This strong pre-dilection is important not only to understand their choices across policy areas but also, more broadly, to grasp central features of congressional be-havior and national policymaking in ways that familiar accounts risk ignoring or discounting.

THE SOURCES OF SOUTHERN DIVERSITY AND UNITY

The defining characteristic of southern politics in the national arena was a willingness to subordinate the considerable diversity of policy priorities in the region to the paramount need to maintain local control of the South's racial order. Understanding how this source of preferences played out in a larger seventeen-state South is critical for determining how its members of Congress behaved in lawmaking. It was "the South's practice," wrote Alabama's William Garrott Brown in 1910, to set "the supremacy of the white race" above all other issues, "to consider all other public questions whatsoever not primarily on their merits but primarily in relation to this question." The source of southern "unity despite its diversity," wrote the historian Ulrich B. Phillips in 1928, was a common resolve that the South "shall be and remain a white man's country." Or, as Josephus Daniels, an ardent white supremacist and progressive Demo-crat, had put the point in 1912, "the subjection of the negro, politically, and the separation of the negro, socially, are paramount to all other considerations in the South short of the preservation of the Republic itself."[19]

The "Solid South," the unity of most or all of the seventeen-state region within the Democratic Party, was in many ways a puzzling phenomenon in national politics. The region was cut through with important cleavages that could produce distinctive political priorities and patterns of politics. The most important line of cleavage mapped onto the region's racial geography and was defined by the uneven location of the South's large African American popula-tion. This varied network connected rural and urban communities, from the fiercely independent Mound Bayou, Mississippi, to the Gullah communities along the coast of South Carolina; to the region's reconstituted and reconfig-ured plantations and medium-sized farms; to the all-black towns of Oklahoma, settled by former slaves of the Indian nations and by migrants from the east; to the emerging black communities of the region's small towns and growing

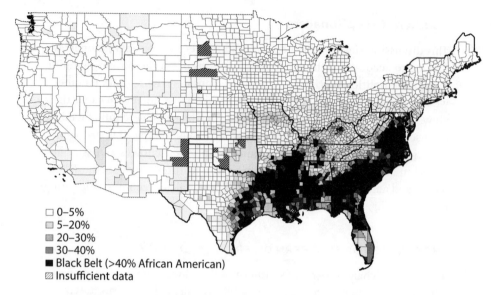

□ 0–5%
▨ 5–20%
▧ 20–30%
▩ 30–40%
■ Black Belt (>40% African American)
▨ Insufficient data

FIGURE 2.4. Black Belt Counties, 1900

cities. Figure 2.4 shows the distribution of African Americans across the country in 1900; the shaded counties had a greater number of black residents as a proportion of the total population. The southern states with comparatively small black populations—Missouri, Oklahoma, and West Virginia each had a black population around 5 percent of the state total—had proportionately larger black communities than any non-southern state.[20]

The spatial concentration of African Americans produced some of the region's most important political divisions. Foremost among these was the division between the so-called Black Belt districts, where the African American population constituted around 40 percent of the total, and non–Black Belt areas. The Black Belt counties as they stood in 1900 have been marked in bold in figure 2.4. During Reconstruction, and for decades afterwards, the size of the black population in these districts allowed black voters to either determine or at least substantially influence their district's representation in Congress, state legislatures, and local offices. After the disfranchisement of black voters, the maintenance of white political, social, and economic supremacy was an especially important priority for the representatives of these districts; the recognition of this concern, of course, was the basis for V. O. Key's claim that this subregion formed the "hard core" of southern sectionalism.[21]

By contrast, it was often outside the Black Belt that southern radical agrarianism was most persistent and marked. Populism fared best in non–Black Belt districts, where the movement made significant and, to the white elite of the Black Belt districts especially, threatening inroads. In 1908, and even more so in 1912, the Socialists were able to make more modest inroads in these regions, largely in the Southwest, winning 16 percent of the vote in Oklahoma, 9 percent in Florida, 8 percent in Texas, and 6 percent in Louisiana and Arkansas.

Another central break distinguished between states that had seceded in 1860–1861 and those that stayed loyal to the Union. Many border states had been internally divided, riven by conflict over whether to join the Confederacy or stay in the Union. Missouri and Kentucky both had separately organized Confederate and Union state governments and sent delegations to sit in the Confederate Congress. Each experienced sustained guerrilla warfare by pro-secession groups and Union forces, and ultimately both were placed under military authority. Maryland, whose state anthem continues to beseech its residents to respond to Virginia's call for aid, saw much of its legislature arrested for supporting secession. West Virginia fought to remain in the Union, but there were secessionist revolts across the state, and former Confederates dominated the state's post–Civil War politics. Even Delaware required federal troops to secure voters against intimidation by secessionist sympathizers. Whether or not a state seceded was influenced by the degree to which it depended on trade with nonslave states and the proportion of the population held in slavery, but in almost no southern state—neither those that would constitute the Confederacy nor those that remained in the Union—was the decision unanimous.

Secession, however, would have enduring consequences. The border states, for instance, were not subject to congressional Reconstruction, and though the Freedmen's Bureau operated there briefly, the inversion of political and economic authority was not nearly as dramatic as in the former Confederacy. Nor was the "lost cause" political culture that developed in the decades that followed as firmly rooted, although memorials to Confederate veterans and military leaders were erected in Kentucky and elsewhere. The fact that the border states had not left the Union, despite the best efforts of some of their most elite citizens, produced a different experience with emancipation and with American nationality. Combined with the smaller number of African Americans in the potential electorate, these features produced a version of the South's political culture that was at once recognizably southern yet distinctive as compared to how the more severely felt anxieties of the white population elsewhere in the region were expressed.

There were other features of the region, related to but distinct from the intensity of commitments to racial hierarchy and the legacy of the Civil War, that could both draw the South together and form potential fault lines upon which it might fracture. For one, the region was deeply invested—to a greater degree than anywhere outside the prairie states of Kansas, Iowa, Minnesota, Nebraska, and the Dakotas—in agriculture. This is implicit in the center and right panels of figure 2.5, which shows the proportion living in urban areas and engaged in manufacturing labor in the median congressional district of the border states, the former Confederacy, the Northeast and Great Lakes, and the West and Midwest. For all the repeated celebrations of the New South as an industrializing region, there were few southern constituencies outside of Baltimore, St. Louis, and the rapidly developing Birmingham that had sizable manufacturing districts. Only with the turn-of-the-century growth of cotton mills along the Eastern Seaboard and the petroleum industry in the Southwest would industrialization extend beyond these cities, allowing the region to match the level of manufacturing activity in the West and prairie Midwest. When combined with the extreme poverty in the region, the lack of economic diversification left the South poorly integrated into national labor or capital markets: not until World War I would southerners in large numbers begin leaving the region for employment, while the post-Civil War breakup of the large plantations removed one of the key financial intermediaries in the region that had previously allowed the region to attract and manage capital. The lack of capital and low levels of education in turn limited the extent to which industry could take advantage of the particular conditions in the region, whether in terms of iron manufacturing or cotton harvesting. "The South," notes Gavin Wright, "remained separate enough, as a labor market and as a people . . . to feel like citizens of a separate country. Yet it was a 'country' that was not large enough or strong enough or cohesively organized enough to have its own technology, its own industrial standards, specifications, techniques."[22]

As various observers recognized, the agricultural character of southern life was an important source of regional unity. Commenting on the "staunchness of the southern democracy" in 1884, the *Dallas Weekly Herald* noted that the "the people of the south are an agricultural and pastoral people. Their political views were not modified by the price of stocks, nor did they have the temptation presented for departure from their fixed ideas of republican government by such theories as affected their northern brethren in the nature of protection and legislation of that class. There was no surfeit of wealth, and having but few large cities among them the disease of monopoly did not become contagious." A republican tradition in America had long maintained that political independence and virtue were associated with productive ownership of land, while commercial trading and finance encouraged the vices of speculation, double-dealing, and a seeming perversion of government activity toward private ends. It was a frequent suggestion of the post–Civil War South that this region alone had stayed true to this tradition, as a consequence of its agricultural character and its supposedly Anglo-Saxon homogeneity. While the median northeastern constituency had a population that was between 15 and 20 percent foreign-born, as well as a growing and larger population of second-generation immigrants, the median southern constituency had almost no foreign-born residents, and the proportion of foreign-born popula-

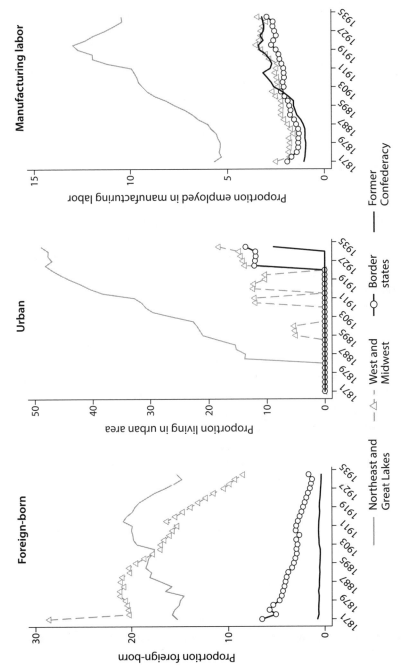

FIGURE 2.5. Proportion Foreign-Born, Urban, and Manufacturing Labor in the Median Congressional District of Different Regions

tion in the border states (left panel of figure 2.5) was declining. The average rather than median constituency was slightly higher in proportion foreign-born, but showed the same basic trend. The lack of immigration sustained a high degree of ethnic homogeneity among the South's white population (as did the assignment of any person recognized as having any African ancestry as "black"). But the dearth of immigrants also cut off a potential source of economic dynamism for the region, which failed to develop robust migration networks with the rest of the country until the 1920s. "Until the character of Southern occupation and mode of thought be changed by Northern and for-eign emigration," the *Weekly Herald* concluded, "here will be the abiding place of true republicanism among a race who believe in the equality of man and the rights of the states in the Union." Such "lost cause" narratives were nothing if not inconsistent.[23]

Although the region as a whole was agricultural, there was important varia-tion in the types and character of its agriculture. The Deep South was inten-sively invested in cotton, which was sold through New York intermediaries on a global market whose price largely reflected the size and quality of the south-ern harvest. For decades, cotton was the country's single largest export, and after the Civil War the amount of cotton grown increased enormously, displac-ing feed crops and livestock. This expansion of the cotton economy worked in many ways to the disadvantage of the South: fluctuations in global demand could throw the southern economy into crisis, with reverberations felt well beyond the immediate cotton-growing regions.[24]

Elsewhere in the South, other crops dominated. Figure 2.6 shows the county-level per capita concentration of three crops: tobacco, cotton, and cane sugar. Southern agriculture included wheat growing, especially in some of the border states, and wool harvesting in the southwest of Texas, but it was these three cash crops that most defined the regional and subregional econo-mies. In the Upper South and the border states, tobacco was much more important than cotton. Although tobacco prices were not entirely stable, and the crop was a major source of internal revenue taxation, they were relatively high and, by the end of the nineteenth century, rising, spurred on by the development of rolling technology that enabled the mass production of ciga-rettes. Sugar cane was grown in a few districts in the South—as well as the territories of Hawaii and Puerto Rico—and was a central part of the Louisiana economy in particular. To an even greater extent than cotton, sugar was re-quired large numbers of workers, who labored under grueling conditions. Cotton was grown primarily for export, buttressing the commitment to free trade of many southern planters, whereas sugar was sold on a domestic mar-ket in which the primary competition came from the West Indies. Sugar rep-resentatives and senators, then, were much more likely to support Republi-can tariff protections.

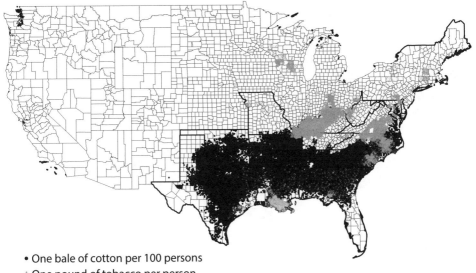

• One bale of cotton per 100 persons
△ One pound of tobacco per person
× One ton of sugar cane per 10 persons

FIGURE 2.6. Southern Cash Crop Production: Cotton, Tobacco, and Sugar

The South's unity and its internal heterogeneity were reflected in its patterns of partisanship. Figure 2.7 shows the average county-level vote share cast for a Republican House of Representatives, Senate, presidential, or gubernatorial candidate from 1877 to 1932. Admittedly, this is a lot of information to be compressed into a single image, but it nonetheless captures the basic distribution of partisanship across the country, at least in terms of relatively stable, long-term voting configurations.[25] The darker the county, the more its average share of the vote went to Democratic candidates; the lighter the county, the more the average share went to Republicans. There are two important sets of contrasts. Clearly, the white South's partisanship differed from that of other sections in its overwhelming support for the Democratic Party, which after the disfranchisements of the 1890s was often the only option for political advancement and engagement. But there also were notable intrasouthern variations, and some subregions could support competitive Republican parties, initially among black Americans but gradually superseded by white southerners. In Missouri, Oklahoma, Kentucky, Maryland, West Virginia, and Delaware, there were counties where politics was consistently Democratic, but in others it was consistently Republican; Tennessee, North Carolina, and Virginia likewise saw sustained pockets of Republicanism, albeit rarely strong enough to achieve statewide majorities. The Republican counties of east Tennessee, southeast Kentucky, and the Missouri Ozarks were among the most Republican in the Union, while the Democratic counties along the Missouri

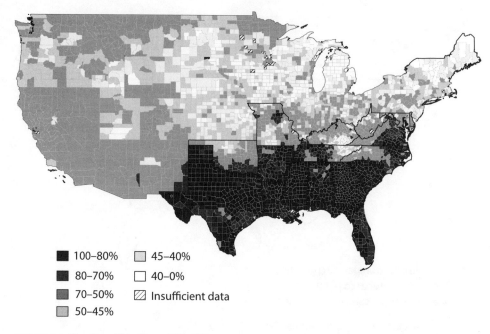

■ 100–80%   ▨ 45–40%
■ 80–70%   □ 40–0%
■ 70–50%   ▨ Insufficient data
▨ 50–45%

FIGURE 2.7. Two-Party Vote Share, 1877–1932

River or in southeastern Oklahoma were among the most Democratic outside the one-party Deep South. Even the Deep South witnessed rare exceptions to Democratic dominance. Winston County, Alabama, for instance, occasionally voted for the Republican presidential candidate.[26]

In short, there were multiple "Souths," with diverse policy interests and political cultures. In state and national politics, these divisions could result in political conflicts that sometimes manifested in competing partisan organizations, especially in the border states. In those states that substantially restricted the electorate in response to black political activism, a more common pattern was to see such divisions manifest in shifting factional support within the Democratic Party. In these circumstances, southern members of Congress, like their colleagues from other regions, were compelled by the electoral connection to represent their diverse constituencies in ways that often varied and were at odds with each other.

But crucially, and to a degree unequaled by other regions, white southerners shared a broader commitment to a vision of their region that, under certain circumstances, could suppress such differences as the different "Souths" amalgamated into a solid sectional bloc. In this respect, southern Democrats served both as representatives of their individual constituencies and as regional delegates. Although sectionalism undoubtedly also shaped the preferences of other members of Congress, the South was unique in the degree to which its members saw themselves as protectors and advocates for the whole *white* South, not simply as advocates for their district or state.

Central to the narrative of southern identity crafted in the half-century after the Civil War was the tale of the white South suppressing its political divisions in order to end Reconstruction and sustaining southern institutions by remaining united. It became a touchstone of southern political rhetoric that after the Civil War "the Southern people could and did attempt to resume their places in the Union with far greater unanimity than prevailed among them when attempting to go out," and that they had accepted the Thirteenth Amendment and submitted to the legality, if never the legitimacy or wisdom, of the Fourteenth and Fifteenth. But whenever the possibility of federal intervention to protect African American civil rights was raised, southern Democrats were quick to note that the precondition for reconciliation and loyalty had been the home rule they had secured in the late nineteenth century. "I am attached to my State and proud of our beloved Southland," declared one southern representative, using a term common through much of the late nineteenth and early twentieth centuries. "Above all and beyond all I love the Union of all the States, and desire to see no legislation . . . calculated to revive the bitter memories of the war or restore in the South the methods of reconstruction." Accordingly, when the foundations of white supremacy were perceived to be under threat, southern representatives weighed their diverse individual and constituent preferences about a given policy proposal against the risks the policy might pose to racial hierarchy. Even those whose foremost individual priority was not the maintenance of white supremacy found, on such occasions, that they were constrained by a broad regional consensus that could be enforced through race-baiting primary campaigns.[27]

This calculus could lead from time to time to the abandonment of desired legislation in order to better defeat a civil rights bill. More regularly, however, this reckoning took the form of evaluating significant legislation along two dimensions: the direct consequences of the policy under consideration, such as the regulation of food safety or funding for education, and the implications, direct or indirect, for the racial order. "The Government ownership of railroads," noted one southerner in 1907, "will be opposed by Southern statesmen because of the dangerous possibility of having negro conductors, even though without this danger such ownership might be expedient." In this way, southern political leaders considered "national questions not solely in their national character but always with the restraining thought of their bearing on the peculiar situation." One irony of southern representation, then, is that while large numbers of southern representatives championed a program of positive national assistance or regulation, support for these programs often was tempered by concern about "outside" intervention. The imperative to defend the region could contradict the drive to secure national programs for the region's impoverished constituents, unless mediated by a corresponding ability of the region's legislators to design policy in a way that would leave the foundations of white supremacy intact.[28]

To be clear, we do not expect these distinctively southern concerns to operate equally across all members or consistently across time. Indeed, given the region's considerable diversity and the central importance of racial variation in defining this variety, it would be astounding if such concerns were evenly diffused. Further, while all southern representatives were attuned to the broad consensus on racial hierarchy among their constituents, popular commitment to white supremacy was never equally strong across the region. Just as important, threats to white supremacy could be protean and uncertain, with southerners themselves heatedly debating whether or not a given policy might have more far-reaching effects than they were prepared to allow. The likely impact of civil rights proposals was more or less obvious. More subtle and difficult to assess was the effect, for example, of women's suffrage, or the regulation of monopolies. As a result, southerners could differ about whether policy benefits warranted any potential risk. These evaluations could vary across the region at any one moment, but also across moments according to the depth of southern racial anxieties and the degree to which members believed that northern Republicans and Democrats could be trusted to keep a hands-off position on matters of regional race relations.

When an issue was understood as implicating white supremacy, however, southern lawmakers could act with unparalleled cohesion and determination. Southern members well understood the rules of the game in Congress and shaped them to enhance the prospects of getting their way in terms of policy outcomes when it mattered most. When the South was in the majority, the seniority of the region's lawmakers—the product of the successful consolidation of black disfranchisement and one-party politics—conferred disproportionate influence over congressional committees. A high degree of collective determination across southern committee chairs, southern committee members, and southern party leaders greatly biased the policies that were brought to the floor. When the South was in the minority, this collective determination could greatly empower the region's ability to obstruct the progress of lawmaking by use of the filibuster. In these cases, southern lawmakers were often willing, however reluctantly, to temporarily abandon other legislative priorities to defend white supremacy.

This willingness to subordinate policy desires was not only manifested in legislative fights but evident earlier in the process as well—in the decision of the vast majority of white southern politicians to work through the Democratic Party even when they disagreed with the party on core issues. This allegiance carried a cost. Not only were white southerners often forced to choose between white supremacy and other policy priorities, but the region as a whole was made less likely to be pivotal in national elections and, when concentrated in the minority, more likely to be excluded from agenda-setting legislative offices. As white southerners recognized, and occasionally bemoaned, the region achieved "political solidarity at the price of provincial status."[29]

THE PROSPECTS FOR SOUTHERN INFLUENCE

We now have the building blocks for a theory of southern influence attuned to both southern diversity and sectional solidarity. The South's influence in Congress, like that of other regional or issue-specific blocs, was a product of its ability to occupy the different offices responsible for setting the agenda; the distribution of preferences in the chamber, such that southern support would be required to reach a majority or supermajority; and, vitally, the level of intensity southern members brought to specific issues. The more important congressional offices the South held, or the more its votes were needed for legislative action, the greater the probability that its representatives could exercise a formative or veto role in the legislative process; and the more cohesive the region's lawmakers, the higher their potential ability to individually or collectively block legislation, and thus their ability to extract concessions. What made the South unique, however, was the willingness of southern representatives to subordinate policy differences to the defense of white supremacy, to act as a large and coherent bloc when legislation threatening white supremacy appeared on the agenda.

Given the intensity of most southern members' preferences concerning race, the odds of a bill's defeat whenever white supremacy might be implicated in the policy proposal were considerably heightened unless the threat was limited, the accommodations to the South were generous, or the policy benefits were uncommonly great. As a result, we predict that when the region was empowered by occupying agenda-setting offices or the pivotal median spot, its representatives would secure policy concessions. Out of power, they could credibly commit to a sustained and costly filibuster. This ability to use veto authority in the Senate became even more powerful as the Senate reformed itself between 1913 and 1920. During this period, senators became directly elected; the Senate made institutional changes to the unanimous consent rules; and the chamber formalized rule XXII, which established a formal cloture procedure to cut off debate. These Senate reforms allowed the South to act even more effectively and cohesively in the lawmaking process, provided its representatives could mobilize to act as a unitary actor—a possibility strengthened by their concentration in a single political party.[30]

Crucially, the effective use of this potential to achieve collectively held goals was dependent on the empowered representatives' willingness to prioritize the "southern" position over other preferences that they or their constituents might hold, a willingness that never could be guaranteed, even on issues that, in our view, could have impinged on white supremacy. In general, we expect that southern preferences over a policy would be attuned to the broader political context as southern lawmakers made a series of evaluations of the likelihood that northern racial liberals would move beyond rhetorical defense of equal civil and political rights for black southerners and commit to more meaningful legislative action. When these evaluations heightened southerners' anxiety about the national political context, it became more likely that their role as regional delegates would dominate their desire to secure the policy priorities desired by their different constituencies.

Our account of southern lawmaking allows us to generate expectations about the behavior of southern members and prospects for their influence. As we anticipate that southern members regularly evaluated policy according to its potential impact on white supremacy, we should find both statistical and qualitative evidence of a powerful dimension structuring southern evaluations, one to which they were willing to subordinate other policy preferences if deemed sufficiently important. Qualitative evidence is particularly important, for the implication of our approach is that the South would have been able to prevent certain votes from happening; if that is the case, it would be difficult to discover quantitative evidence of the racial dimension distinctive to the region with roll call data.

Given the centrality of Congress to the circumstances of the region, we also expect southern members to have been especially attuned to the organization of the institution and the rules that allocate influence within the chambers. Thomas Brackett Reed, soon to be House speaker, made just this point in 1889. Since the appearance of slavery on the national agenda, he observed, "the rules of the House [had] been framed with the view of rendering legislation difficult," precisely because "the South was anxious that there should be ample means at its disposal to stop any measure detrimental to its cherished institution."[31]

Legislative rules that maximized opportunities for obstruction amounted to an effective veto for the South before the Civil War, a feature we expect southern lawmakers to have sought to restore. More specifically, we envisage southern lawmakers as generally supporting rules that advantaged political minorities by diffusing influence, as more likely to oppose changes that allowed decisive action by bare majorities, and as acting strategically to retain the ability of minorities to obstruct. Such rule changes might include imposing supermajority requirements for legislative action as well as decentralizing agenda control to committees where southerners might be more likely to be pivotal. Finally, we expect southern influence and the extent to which southern priorities were accommodated in national policy to wax and wane according to the strength of the Democratic Party, the rules of each chamber, and the likelihood that the region's representatives would be pivotal for a given policy area.

These expectations are historically contingent. During periods when the white South was especially anxious to preserve its racial order, southern Democratic representatives would have been more likely to act as regional delegates, subordinating their preferences over other issues to the one overarching imperative to defend white supremacy. When they believed that the threat was real and pressing, southern cohesion would be most intense, to the possible exclusion of other priorities. In these circumstances, the pressure to adopt a common position and to subordinate other policy priorities could put considerable strains on the southern coalition as those more marginally attached to the region's racial ordering weighed the cost of forgoing policy they might desire for security on an issue that was less important to them than to the Black Belt legislators who helped set the tone and priorities of southern politics. At the extreme, regional and partisan loyalty could break down altogether, pushing some constituencies and politicians out of the Democratic Party, as occurred with the Populist revolt in the 1890s. When members believed that the threat to home rule and white supremacy was distant, however, the impulse toward unity would lessen and the space for pursuing positive policy change would expand.

All else equal, we hypothesize that periods of heightened anxiety undermined the ability of southern lawmakers to advance a positive legislative agenda. At such times, they were more cautious about legislation and more likely to subordinate other priorities to white supremacy. As Key suggested in 1949 (one such period when racial anxieties were heightened), "the question may well be raised—but not necessarily answered—whether the compulsion toward unanimity on the race question does not carry over into other fields and produce a higher degree of solidarity than would exist under two party condition. The chances are that progressive[s] . . . lacking a real party system to back them up at home, may be under special pressure to trim their sails."[32]

This does not mean that even during such periods southern lawmakers abandoned all other policy objectives. Yet, as many representatives from the region complained, during periods of heightened racial anxiety it often was difficult to focus the attention of their constituents and fellow representatives from the South on other issues.[33] Heightened anxiety, we suggest, made southern lawmakers more exacting in their demands and increased the likelihood that they would require more substantial policy accommodations on a wider range of issues. Periods of dampened anxiety, by contrast, allowed southern members the freedom to advance a legislative program tailored to the needs and preferences of their constituents. Conservative southerners, more often than not, would still warn about the dangers of centralization and federal intervention and continue to be supported by more conservative constituencies, but crucially, progressive, populist, and liberal southerners would be free to support more far-reaching federal involvement in the region's economic and social affairs, and the racial appeals of conservatives would resonate with fewer members and fewer constituents.

The prospects for southern influence, and the ways in which it might be manifested in policy and politics, can be categorized by considering the interaction between southern anxieties and the region's ability to structure the legislative agenda or exercise a pivotal influence. Table 2.1 lists a series of expectations based on whether the region occupied the key offices and pivots (legislative influence) and whether the moment in question was a period of high or low southern anxiety about federal intervention in matters of race. The points in the table are derived from our reading of congressional theories of lawmaking, combined with our own expectation of how southerners' paramount priority would intersect with their other concerns.

On the basis of this schematic orientation, we can provide a rough overview of our expectations for the different periods into which we have subdivided the period we consider, summarized in table 2.2. Different temporal moments, defined by the level of southern Democrats' influence in national politics and our own reading of the intensity of conflict over race, have been placed into the schema of table 2.1, with a "moderate" level of influence and anxiety included to capture periods of divided government and moments that fall short of the full-fledged insurgency of the civil rights era or the persistence of black voting after Reconstruction and the "nadir" of black political opportunity in the early twentieth century. Our expectation is that the moments identified in table 2.2 will generally conform to the patterns of political influence discussed in table 2.1, and that those moments falling into the "moderate" categories will show a mix in the levels and mechanisms of influence.

The period from 1877 to 1900 witnessed a succession of divided governments in a climate of high anxiety over the prospect of federal intervention in southern racial practices. The South generally was not pivotal on most issues, though recurring Democratic control of the House of Representatives enabled southern legislators to count on occupying a significant portion of committee chairs and leadership roles. Legislation drafted or supported by southern members was, however, likely to be reworked by the pivotal members or by the other chamber, and we expect that the need for almost all white southern members to subordinate other policy priorities to the cause of white supremacy would result in the loss of policies that otherwise were considered important for the region.

TABLE 2.1. Predicted Patterns of Southern Lawmaking

Legislative Influence	Intensity of Anxieties	
	High	Low
High	• Committee leadership enables South to set legislative agenda and design policy • Influence on terms of final passage when pivotal • Southern filibuster effective but not needed • Broad range of legislation is suspected of threatening white supremacy • Southern "conservatives"—those opposed to federal activism—more likely to be empowered	• Committee leadership enables South to set legislative agenda and design policy • Influence on terms of final passage when pivotal • Filibuster not usually needed and relatively ineffective when used on non-core priorities • Southern lawmakers less likely to be unified across policy issue areas • Southern "progressives"—those more supportive of federal activism on nonrace issues—more likely to be empowered
Low	• South has little influence on policy design or passage • Reliant on obstruction to block action • Highly attentive to danger of provoking rule changes • Need and readiness to subordinate legislative priorities to defend white supremacy	• Lowest level of southern influence • Reliant on obstruction, but usually ineffective on nonrace issues (which are not usually on the agenda) • Ability to enact positive legislation contingent on cultivating Republican allies and willingness of South to forgo partisan gains

By contrast, the period from 1900 to 1932 was marked by sharp discontinuities in the level of southern influence. The first decade of the twentieth century saw the Republican Party entrenched in the presidency, the Senate, the House of Representatives, and the Supreme Court. During that period of tight opposition party control, the South was unable to set the agenda and rarely was pivotal on the chamber floor. If the white South could find a silver lining in this state of affairs, it was in the fact that the threat of federal intervention had largely dissipated. With the advent of Democratic control of the House in 1911, followed by the presidency and the Senate two years later, individual southern Democrats were extremely well positioned on committees to advance their legislative agendas. They were constrained, however, by their need to win the support of pivotal members from other regions, and thus we expect to see their legislative proposals frequently reworked.

TABLE 2.2. Periods of Southern Lawmaking

Legislative Influence	Intensity of Anxieties		
	High	Moderate	Low
High	*1893–1895*	*1941–1947*	*1913–1919*
	1935–1941	1951–1960*	*1933–1935*
	1949–1951		
	1961–1967		
Moderate	1875–1877*	1877–1889*	1911–1913*
	1891–1893*	1947–1949*	1921–1931
Low	1867–1875	1895–1901	1901–1911
	1889–1891		1919–1921

Notes: Periods of Democratic control are in italics, periods of divided government are marked with an asterisk, and periods of Republican control are in regular font. The years 1951–1960 are classified as "high legislative influence" because of the conservative coalition, while the years 1921–1931 are classified as "moderate legislative influence" because a series of bipartisan blocs comprising southern Democrats and midwestern Republicans played important roles in shaping legislation during this period.

The return of Republican ascendancy after World War I did not lead to a renewed exclusion of southerners from policy influence. Instead, the region's lawmakers benefited from institutional changes that had decentralized congressional authority to committees, creating a context in which bipartisan compromises could be more easily worked out. The region could thus exercise a level of influence somewhere between the highs of the Wilson years and the lows of the years between McKinley and Taft.

In sum, we have suggested a set of propositions about southern behavior and influence, each contingent upon the historical and political context but rooted in a more general approach to southern lawmaking. We have also named a set of expectations concerning the levels and types of southern influence over national policy at different moments that vary with the party's strength in Congress, the location of the region in an ideological space, and the intensity of southern racial anxiety.

Research Strategy

V. O. Key approached the study of the South's role in Congress in *Southern Politics* primarily by analyzing voting patterns on 873 roll call votes cast in seven sessions of the Senate and four sessions of the House from 1933 to 1945. From these, Key calculated quantitative measures of legislative behavior that enabled him to evaluate the extent of regional solidarity and the stability of party coalitions. His analyses led him to conclude that "on the race question, and on that question alone, does a genuine southern solidarity exist. On other questions southern Democrats split and southern solidarity becomes a matter of degree."[34]

In a review of *Southern Politics*, Richard Hofstadter commented that Key's text was limited by both its short time period and its exclusive reliance on roll calls without any measure of the importance of the issues at stake. He suggested an approach that would rely instead on a complementary qualitative analysis that integrated information about voting behavior while being attuned to the relative importance of the different policies. "It would be more illuminating," he argued, "to go back fifty years and study the voting record of the Southern delegation in Congress on some one hundred outstanding measures of policy" than to focus on only a small sample of roll calls across a limited number of years. Moreover, he noted, a full accounting of southern politics required attention to the multiple ways by which the South might have influenced the content of national policy, some of which were "not too amenable to study by quantitative methods." In short, a more specifically historical approach might more fully evaluate the importance and consequences of southern influence in Congress.[35]

Tacking between two modes of analysis, the strategy we have adopted aims to fulfill this task. Following Key, we deploy indices of voting behavior, but across a much longer time frame and with more systematic attention to issue substance. Key's analysis led him to suggest that the substance of issues under debate played an important role in structuring the behavior of southern lawmakers, with race producing a near-unanimous solidarity while other issues, such as agriculture, labor, relief, or price controls, generated varying patterns of internal divergence or defection toward the Republicans. Yet, while there is an episodic attention to policy substance in *Southern Politics*, the book does not classify votes according to their policy substance, a move that is necessary for that suggestion to be fully developed. We remedy this limitation by deploying a comprehensive coding scheme applied to all votes cast in Congress from 1877 that allows us to identify specific roll calls with broader issue areas. Following in the footsteps of Hofstadter, we also select a large number of policy measures and political debates for closer inspection through contextually situated legislative histories and policy debates.[36]

CASE SELECTION

The issues we probe most deeply were selected on the basis of several related criteria, including indices of congressional voting that allow us to identify specific issues and policy areas where southern lawmakers exhibited distinct preferences, as well as measures of legislative significance that generate more consideration to policies that were especially important for American political development. Thus, the book's legislation and issue areas have been chosen on the basis of (1) a measure of voting alignments, showing how southern Democrats voted vis-à-vis both Republicans and other Democrats; (2) preference-based measures that allow us to identify votes on which southerners evaluated policy beyond a simple party or economic redistribution cleavage; and (3) accounts of significant legislation, including statistical measures and historically oriented surveys of important policy areas, that facilitate a focus on especially important issue areas.

Our case selection begins with an analysis derived from an intuitive metric introduced by Ira Katznelson and Quinn Mulroy that distinguishes roll calls into categories based on the constellation of party and regional support. Each roll call in Congress is assigned a series of scores indicating the similarity in the voting patterns of different predefined blocs, known as a "likeness" score. The larger the number, the more the two blocs resembled each other on a given roll call. In particular, we look at the likeness score for southern Democrats and Republicans, and for southern and other Democrats. When southern Democrats aligned with their non-southern Democratic colleagues but not with Republicans, the vote is coded as a "partisan" roll call. When they aligned with both Democrats and Republicans, the vote is coded as "cross-partisan," as it indicates a broad degree of similarity across these three principal voting blocs. When southerners stood apart, with relatively low levels of similarity with either Republicans or northern Democrats, the vote is coded as "sectional." And when southern Democrats voted in alignment with Republicans rather than with non-southern Democrats, the vote is coded as "disloyal."[37]

The result of this classification for the House of Representatives, from 1877 to 1932, is shown in figure 2.8. During the period we examine in this project, only 3.9 percent and 6.4 percent of votes in the House and Senate, respectively, fell into the "disloyal" category. In both chambers, a majority of roll calls were partisan, followed by cross-partisan votes and then sectional votes—when southern Democrats, either as a cohesive unit or as a majority of the region's members, stood alone.

Because each dot represents a single roll call, its location in one of the four quadrants provides an initial basis for characterizing voting alignments on a given issue area. By classifying votes according to policy content, we can select certain issue areas for closer attention. Figure 2.9 shows the proportion of votes in a given issue area that fell into one of the four quadrants. The y-axes are not on the same scale in order to better see differences across issue areas.

Civil rights, not surprisingly, was by far the issue area most likely to produce sectional voting, followed by military pensions—that is, pensions to Civil War veterans, from which much of the South was effectively excluded—and labor policy, which implicated the region's commitment to its particular racial and economic ordering. Education, immigration, and social policy were issue areas that saw an elevated degree of disloyal voting as southern Democrats

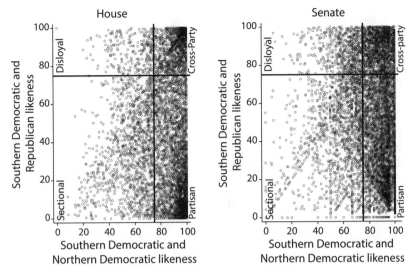

FIGURE 2.8. Distribution of Roll Calls across Sectional, Disloyal, Cross-Party, and Partisan Likeness Quadrants

aligned with Republicans. The bulk of the social policy votes that produced this particular alignment concerned prohibition. We break out this category for closer analysis in chapters 6 through 8, when it was an issue of heightened importance on the political agenda. Similarly, constitutional amendments, which produced a substantial number of cross-party as well as sectional votes, can be broken out into women's suffrage, the direct election of senators, the income tax, and other proposals. For the moment, however, it suffices to note that party lines were especially likely to break down on these matters.

State-supported infrastructure spending for internal improvements tended to be cross-partisan, but so too were a large number of votes on immigration, labor, and economic regulations. Finally, there was an important set of subjects that regularly produced high levels of partisan voting, including policies with a potential to change partisan representation in Congress, such as state admission and contested elections, and also the tariff, one of the key economic issues of the period and a policy that clearly separated most Democrats from most Republicans. It is worth noting, however, that the issue that most persistently produced a partisan voting alignment was African American voting rights, a subject central to the organization of the Solid South as well as to the continued national viability of the Democratic Party.

We first identify issues for closer analysis by selecting roll calls and bills that were especially likely to exhibit "sectional" or "disloyal" voting. These distinctive roll call patterns are especially pertinent to our overarching questions, for they allow us to identify policy areas on which a core of southern members stood alone against both Republicans and other Democrats, as well

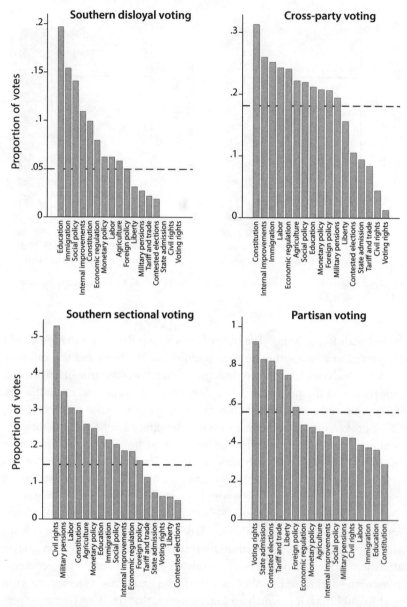

FIGURE 2.9. Alignments of Roll Call Voting, 1877–1932. Dashed line is the average proportion of all other votes.

as those policy areas that presented an alternative to southern solidarity within the Democratic Party. These, however, might not have been the only issues on which southerners had distinctive preferences. For some matters at particular historical moments, a southern-specific evaluation of policy could result in a tighter alignment of party and region rather than a coalition with

Republicans or sectional voting. The issue of African American voting rights, for instance, clearly animated concerted southern action in national politics, yet for much of the period under analysis the southern position gained near-unanimous support from the northern wing of the Democratic Party. Votes on this issue did not separate out southerners or push them into alignment with Republicans, but produced highly partisan voting.

To accommodate this possibility, we estimate a statistical model of legislator preferences that allows us to identify votes in which southerners were especially interested and use the results from this analysis as part of our selection process. To do this, we incorporate into the statistical model the possibility that southern legislators experienced a common inducement, unique to their region, that made them more likely to vote together for or against a policy than their estimated preferences would otherwise imply. If southern Democrats evaluated a policy along an additional dimension, such as the implication of policy for local racial hierarchies, but one that correlated closely with the party divide, the resulting voting pattern would neither place them in a coalition with groups they otherwise did not support nor even isolate them from their northern copartisans. Rather, it might result in making them appear even *more* Democratic in their voting behavior. By incorporating this possibility into the model, we can identify issue areas where voting might have been partisan but where the South nonetheless had a distinctive set of preferences.[38]

Figure 2.10 shows the proportion of votes, across different issue areas, from 1877 to 1900—a period in which the South tended to constitute the bulk of the Democratic Party and northern Democrats gave their strong support to many issues of concern to the South—that show evidence of a southern-specific inducement to vote with the South (left panel), as well as the issues on which the proportion of votes shows evidence of such an inducement distinct from any inducement that might have operated equally for all Democrats (right panel).

The issue areas on which there was a high probability of an inducement specific to southern Democrats closely map the pattern of partisan voting shown in figure 2.9, but figure 2.10 also captures the extent to which the South not only was supported by northern Democrats but voted with a degree of solidarity beyond what we would expect from the preferences of southern members on other issues. Voting rights was not simply a partisan issue, although it was undeniably that; it was also an issue area that witnessed an extreme degree of southern Democratic solidarity. Across the fifty-five years we examine, not a single southern Democrat voted in favor of any measure that would have continued or restored Washington's involvement in supervising federal elections and protecting voting rights. Civil rights for African Americans—especially the question of equal accommodations in interstate travel—is clearly marked out as an issue that saw heightened southern solidarity, but it

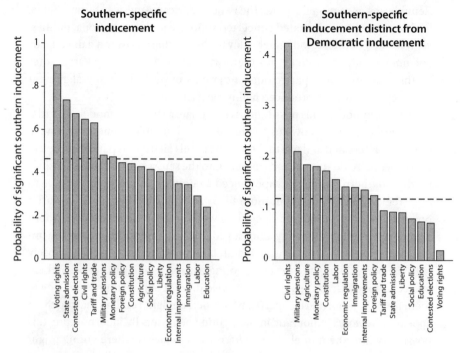

FIGURE 2.10. Issue Areas with Southern Regional Inducement. Dashed line is the average proportion of all other votes.

is also one on which their northern copartisans were more likely to defect and vote with the Republican Party.

Working this way with roll call information is insufficient. For one, this approach is likely to undersample the issues on which southerners' voting patterns resulted less from specific regional considerations than from the sort of constituency and partisan matters that often are emphasized in the congressional literature. We might also be missing instances of southerners acting on distinct preferences but not being included in the roll call record or not producing distinctive regional patterns of voting. Finally, on their own, the roll call measures we utilize do not address the importance of southern legislative behavior for national policy.

To remedy some of these evidentiary problems, we draw on a variety of sources to identify significant issue areas and legislation across time. We begin with a statistical ranking of each of the 15,232 public laws passed by Congress between 1877 and 1932, which draws on the expert ratings of historians and contemporaneous observers to generate estimates of legislative significance, not all of which have roll call votes attached to them. In addition to examining issues and legislative debates that produced distinctive patterns of southern voting, we also sample legislation from the top 500 most important statutes

TABLE 2.3. Policy Areas Selected for Closer Analysis

1877–1900		1900–1932	
Political Economy	*Civil Rights and Democracy*	*Political Economy*	*Civil Rights and Democracy*
Tariff and trade	Voting rights and election	Tariff and trade	Enforcement of Four-
Taxation	law	Income tax	teenth Amendment
Monetary policy	Accommodations in trans-	Monetary policy	Women's suffrage
Interstate commerce	portation	Interstate commerce	Segregation
and antitrust	Contested elections	and antitrust	Direct election of senators
	"Exodusters"	Price controls	Anti-lynching
Federal Support			
Education	*Labor Policy*	*Federal Support*	*Labor Policy*
Internal im-	Labor arbitration	Education	Railroad workers' com-
provements	The Eight-Hour Law	Agricultural loans	pensation
Civil War		Internal improvements	Child labor
pensions			The Eight-Hour Law
		Foreign Policy	
		Imperial policy	*Immigration*
		World War I	Exclusion of "undesir-
		Treaty of Versailles	ables"
			Literacy test
		Social Policy	National-origins quotas
		"White slavery"	
		Prohibition	

enacted during this period in order to attend closely to those laws that defined the American state and the content of its public policies. Additionally, we complement the statistical ranking of legislative importance by applying findings and insights from groundbreaking works by Lawrence Chamberlain, Elizabeth Sanders, and Richard Bensel, each of whom has tracked policy-making across relatively discrete issue areas. These texts are especially useful not only in identifying important legislative enactments but in organizing the policy agenda across different periods according to the *issue areas* that animated public attention during the half-century with which we are concerned. This allows us to extend the analysis to issues that were important but did not always get expressed in roll calls or public laws. After all, an analysis of southern politics limited to actually enacted legislation or bills that received a roll call vote would undervalue a mechanism vital to southern influence—the ability to keep issues off the agenda or to defeat them through obstruction.[39]

Table 2.3 provides a summary of the policy areas that received the most attention in the decades we analyze. These different policy strands and issues were chosen to capture variation in the different configurations of southern voting behavior discussed here, but also to ensure that the most important legislation and issue areas were covered.

ASSESSING SOUTHERN INFLUENCE

We examine these issue areas through contextually situated case studies of legislation, both proposed and enacted, drawing on a range of methods to map the contours of debate, examine ways in which the policies were interpreted by southern members, and trace the process and identify the specific mechanisms by which they sought to secure their policy objectives.

V. O. Key studied the role of the South in Congress by examining voting patterns in a sample of roll calls; so doing, he helped inaugurate the quantitative study of the institution's national lawmaking. There are important limits, however, to his pioneering analysis. For one, the measures he relied upon, both likeness scores and what is known among political scientists as "Rice cohesion," simply summarize how often a given bloc voted together or voted with other blocs. Although these measures convey important information about aggregate voting patterns, they can tell us little about individual members or their preferences. Key, for example, could report that Senator Hugo Black (D-AL) tended to vote with non-southern Democrats on issues that a majority of southerners voted on with the Republican Party, but he could not rank southern senators from liberal to conservative, nor could he identify the issues Black and other southerners might have supported along a liberal-to-conservative continuum. For our purposes, an important limitation is that these measures do not tell us which members are likely to be in the pivotal median position in a given policy domain.[40]

Just as important is that Key's near-exclusive reliance on roll calls, as he himself noted, did not reveal "the tactical advantage that the South enjoys through the capacity of its committee chairmen to bottle up measures." Neither could his roll call analysis tap into an important element of southern members' influence in lawmaking: the intensity of their distinctive preferences. If we are to examine the full range of mechanisms by which southerners might have shaped the content of public policy, we need to go beyond the question of whether they voted with or against northern Democrats or Republicans to more directly evaluate the reasons for their voting as well as the other ways in which they might have influenced the legislative agenda and the terms of national policy.[41]

We address the first of these concerns by means of new measures specifically designed to provide a fine-grained account of the structure of political conflict and individual preferences over time. These computations, in turn, allow us to identify some of the likely pivotal members across different policy areas, as we have done in figure 2.2. We address the second of these limitations through situated case studies, drawing on a range of historical and secondary sources to better understand how a given policy was interpreted by southern legislators and attentive publics, how these legislators sought to shape, advance, or impede policy proposals in accordance with their preferences, and to evaluate the success of any such efforts.

Our account of southern influence in Congress emphasizes the ability of key actors to impede or advance legislation, by occupying either critical agenda-setting offices or pivotal locations in the overall distribution of preferences. It is relatively straightforward to identify southerners who occupied important committee, party, or institutional offices; it is more difficult to identify occasions when southerners occupied the median or filibuster location.[42]

This effort requires some measure of individual preferences by which we can array members according to their voting behavior on policy issues. These measures, depending on the policy at issue, can sometimes be thought of as ordering members on a liberal-to-conservative dimension. For many issues, however, roll call scales for members cannot readily be interpreted on a liberal-to-conservative continuum because the policy issue maps onto such a scale only with difficulty. In those instances, we interpret scales substantively according to the policy being considered. Fortunately, the last few decades have seen significant advances in the estimation of individual preferences, commonly referred to as "ideal points." We estimate aggregate and issue-specific ideal points for each member of the House of Representatives using the item-response model of Clinton, Jackman, and Rivers, estimating both aggregate ideal points based on every roll call across a defined period of time and issue-specific ideal points based on a subset of roll calls in a given policy area.[43]

These preference-based measures allow us to map political conflict across time, an exercise that proves especially valuable in identifying trends or moments of sharp voting pattern change. Figure 2.11 shows the location of the median southern and northern member of both parties, from 1877 to 1932. These scores were estimated using all roll call votes cast during a six-month period, centered on the date. What is evident in figure 2.11 is that when considered as an aggregate measure of political preferences, southern Democrats anchored the Democratic coalition.[44]

These measures allow us to identify the likely pivotal members for a given issue area at a particular moment, information that can then be used to assess the likelihood that the South was able to exercise influence in this way. The panels in figure 2.12 simply rank all senators from most liberal to most conservative, with each dot representing a single member and the light gray bars indicating the confidence intervals for our estimate of their ideal point—that is, their estimated location on this dimension. The right panel zooms in on the likely location of the median senator. More often than not, the precise determination of an individual pivotal member is less important than the set of like-minded legislators whose collective votes are pivotal. The technique used to estimate member ideal points allows us not only to identify the location of

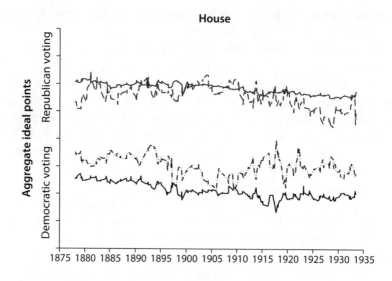

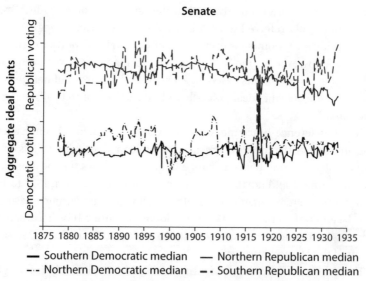

FIGURE 2.11. Development of Party and Regional Positions, 1877–1932. Ideal points are estimated across a six-month interval centered on the date.

the preference pivots with a reasonable degree of certainty but also to say that there was a 47 percent chance that the median member in the Senate was a Democrat from one of the seventeen southern states, or a 32 percent chance that they were from the former Confederacy (figure 2.13).

Though these measures are an important source of information about southern preferences and potential influence, on their own they are insuffi-

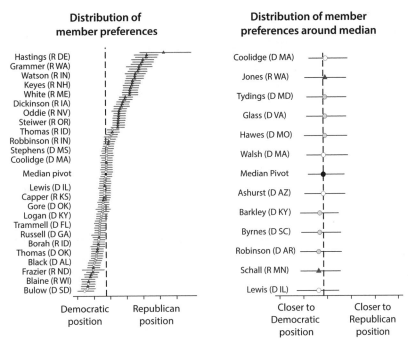

Distribution of member preferences

Hastings (R DE)
Grammer (R WA)
Watson (R IN)
Keyes (R NH)
White (R ME)
Dickinson (R IA)
Oddie (R NV)
Steiwer (R OR)
Thomas (R ID)
Robbinson (R IN)
Stephens (D MS)
Coolidge (D MA)

Median pivot

Lewis (D IL)
Capper (R KS)
Gore (D OK)
Logan (D KY)
Trammell (D FL)
Russell (D GA)
Borah (R ID)
Thomas (D OK)
Black (D AL)
Frazier (R ND)
Blaine (R WI)
Bulow (D SD)

Democratic position   Republican position

Distribution of member preferences around median

Coolidge (D MA)
Jones (R WA)
Tydings (D MD)
Glass (D VA)
Hawes (D MO)
Walsh (D MA)
Median Pivot
Ashurst (D AZ)
Barkley (D KY)
Byrnes (D SC)
Robinson (D AR)
Schall (R MN)
Lewis (D IL)

Closer to Democratic position   Closer to Republican position

FIGURE 2.12. Distribution of Members around the Median Position, 72nd Senate, 1931–1933. Dashed line is the location of the median senator.

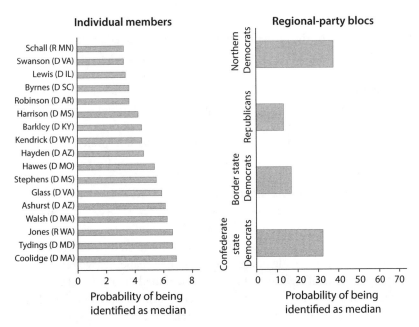

Individual members

Schall (R MN)
Swanson (D VA)
Lewis (D IL)
Byrnes (D SC)
Robinson (D AR)
Harrison (D MS)
Barkley (D KY)
Kendrick (D WY)
Hayden (D AZ)
Hawes (D MO)
Stephens (D MS)
Glass (D VA)
Ashurst (D AZ)
Walsh (D MA)
Jones (R WA)
Tydings (D MD)
Coolidge (D MA)

0   2   4   6   8

Probability of being identified as median

Regional-party blocs

Northern Democrats
Republicans
Border state Democrats
Confederate state Democrats

0   10 20 30 40 50 60 70

Probability of being identified as median

FIGURE 2.13. Probability of Members Being Pivotal, 72nd Senate, 1931–1933

cient to make reliable inferences about the ways in which the South might have exercised a consequential influence on national policy. Accordingly, our legislative case studies draw on an extensive range of secondary sources, including policy histories and histories of southern politics and society at specific moments, and on primary sources that allow us to measure preferences in a more nuanced way and gauge intensity in ways that are not possible through quantitative analysis alone.

A key question for our analysis is how legislative fights and the political agenda were interpreted by the different "attentive publics" in the South. There are no surveys of southern attitudes or policy preferences for us to recover. And while we rely heavily on the historical literature to understand the broader currents of southern opinion at a given moment, this literature often has little to say about specific legislative fights. To supplement the historical literature, we draw extensively on a wide variety of newspapers—primarily from the South but also some with national scope, such as the *New York Times*, the *Chicago Tribune*, and the *Washington Post*, and newspapers of importance to a particular region—in order to get a sense of how contemporary legislative debates and politics were presented and interpreted. For each of our case studies, we examined contemporary newspaper reports from across the region, as well as a more limited number of non-southern newspapers, to get a better sense of how policy was interpreted within different communities at different times.

To be clear, we do not believe that this is a reliable measure of southern attitudes, especially for the millions who rarely read newspapers and who were unlikely to be the principal audience for papers needing a steady stream of subscriptions and advertisements to stay afloat. Indeed, we believe it likely that southern newspapers generally were more conservative on matters of economics than public opinion in the broader region. But even if newspapers do not provide an entirely reliable guide to southern attitudes, especially outside of more elite and urban constituencies, this type of source provides valuable information on how national politics was being interpreted by attentive communities and framed to a broader public. Papers also provide some sense of the diversity, and the moments of unity, in the expression of southern public opinion. Some, like the *Atlanta Constitution*, were New South boosters; others, such as the *Macon Telegraph*, were consistently conservative, opposed to all but the most mundane and clearly established federal activities and suspicious that even these were probably part of a plot to enforce "negro supremacy." By drawing on a wide range of southern newspapers as well as an extensive historical literature, we are better able to embed the statistical analyses of southern legislative behavior within particular historical, political, and institutional contexts and thus to pay close attention to how shifts in context—

whether caused by war, economic depression, or civil rights activism—might have altered how southerners evaluated policy options.

Our coverage is not exhaustive: we have not examined every policy debate, nor do we discuss every instance for which we found evidence of the South having distinctive preferences or playing an important role in shaping public policy. For the large number of cases we do study, however, these sources facilitate reasonable inferences about how southerners interpreted policy debates—as well as, crucially, whether they believed a given policy was implicated in the question of white supremacy, whether southern Democrats showed distinctive patterns of legislative behavior on this issue, whether southern legislators sought to shape the policy so that it would reflect their concerns, and, if so, through which legislative mechanisms they made this effort.

Conclusion

In 1913, on the occasion of Woodrow Wilson's inauguration, Judson C. Welliver, who later served as President Harding's "literary clerk," the nation's first speechwriter, noted that the victory of the Democratic Party had brought a defining southern influence to national affairs. "Note a few details," he wrote: "The President is a native of Virginia. The Speaker of the House is a native of Kentucky" and a representative from Missouri; "the leader of the House is a native of Virginia" and a representative of Alabama.

> The leader of the Senate is a native of Virginia. The ten members of the Cabinet include one native of Texas, one of Georgia, two of North Carolina, one of Kentucky. . . . The chairmen of most of the important committees of both Senate and House are native of the South, and elected from it. The Chief Justice of the Supreme Court is a native of Louisiana. Aside from all this, the South is getting, in the general personnel of executive positions that are filled by appointment, a vastly larger proportion of big and influential posts than it has held since the Civil War.

When "you hear strange names of men to whom leadership and importance are attributed," he concluded, "if you ask, you almost invariably learn that they are from the South."[45]

Like Welliver's, our study of southern influence will engage in a fair amount of counting—of the southerners who occupied leadership positions, of the number of votes cast by southerners for and against important laws, and even of the frequency with which a southerner was likely to be in the pivotal median position for a particular issue at a given time. "The real, final test, however," as Welliver noted, "is the one that cannot be deduced from any mathematical

analysis." It was whether "the spirit and disposition, the purpose and inspiration, the tendency and direction which we note in the guiding forces of affairs"
was shaped by southern priorities and southern lawmakers.[46]

To assess this more subtle characterization of southern influence, we have
reworked leading theories of legislative influence to account for the distinctive
character of southern representation. We have offered a theory of southern
lawmaking that accommodates the great diversity of the region while also
emphasizing when and how this diversity was subordinated to the defense of
white supremacy. And we have outlined a combination of quantitative and
qualitative approaches to the study of southern politics in Congress that allows
us to now move beyond summaries of voting patterns to examine the legislative process in closer detail.

PART II

Union Restored

3

Uncertain Combinations

> The highest goal of the southern people, which is the southern democracy,
> should be and will be the husbanding of her own resources that she may attain
> in the union that most precious of boons—perfect independence.[1]

"The South only is solid," declared the *Daily Picayune* in 1877, "and while it
has the political sagacity to remain so it will carry victory to whatever side it
may espouse." The writer had good reason for optimism. The Democratic
Party in the South had dramatically reconstituted itself as a capable political
force, reconquering the region's legislatures and governor's offices as well as
a majority of its congressional delegations. In state after state, the tenuous
biracial coalition that had supported the Republican Party was fractured and
reduced through the re-enfranchisement of former Confederates, economic
intimidation, violent "bull-dozing" of Republican voters, and race-baiting
campaigns intended to consolidate white support for the Democratic Party.
So long as white solidarity could be maintained, an imposing "Solid South"
would confront the rest of the nation in Congress and in presidential elections.
This feature would be the most important fact of political life during the last
quarter of the twentieth century, the fulcrum around which Gilded Age politics would turn.[2]

Recognition of the region's potentially pivotal role emboldened the South's
white political elite. "Now that we hold the balance of power," the *Picayune*
continued, "we are in a position to demand our rights, and our Senators and
Representatives will not deserve well of us if they do not make their weight
felt whenever a question arises which affects the material interests of this section." At least with respect to issues that most animated regional solidarity,

southern members of Congress seemed to be well placed to ensure that southern priorities would be accommodated in national policy.[3]

The persisting and durable solidarity of the white South after Reconstruction is well known. But it was not preordained or inescapable. As C. Vann
Woodward observed some time ago, this was a period of "forgotten alternatives," a time of "experiment, testing, and uncertainty—quite different from
the time of repression and rigid uniformity that was to come toward the end
of the century." As the South grappled with the consequences of the Thirteenth, Fourteenth, and Fifteenth Amendments, political struggles across and
within racial boundaries erupted. Taking a wide range of forms, mass politics
contested what kind of South, and with it what kind of nation, would close
out the nineteenth century and enter the twentieth.[4]

Central to these fights was an assertive black political consciousness, born
in part out of the role that African American troops had played in the Union
Army, advanced by the bittersweet experiences of Reconstruction, and
marked not only by revolutionary enfranchisement but by the acquisition of
new levels of schooling, literacy, and skill. With the protections offered by the
Military Reconstruction Acts of 1867, former slaves became political actors en
masse. Some nine in ten eligible black men registered to vote, overwhelmingly
as Republican supporters. As blacks continued to organize political clubs and
leagues after the withdrawal of Union troops, their activities generated what
Steven Hahn has described as a "white counterattack" that was "sweeping and
ferocious." It was an unstable, liminal moment when the most challenging
issues of citizenship and membership, labor and land, mores and safety, remained to be defined through political competition, legal jurisprudence, and
adjudication from among the array of available policy choices.[5]

But for all the boasting of white solidarity, deep divisions and considerable variation in hierarchies of preferences and practices threatened to fracture white southern unity, potentially even blunting the full force of white
supremacy. These divisions, as Woodward noted, were "eventually resolved
at the expense of the Negro." By the end of the nineteenth century, a regnant,
officially racist, white South had successfully safeguarded its ability to enact
Jim Crow without interference of any consequence from the national government. What followed was a dramatic constriction of black political rights as
the vast majority of African Americans lost the right to vote in local, state,
and national elections, to serve on juries, and to receive equal protection
under the law, as well as the social standing and economic opportunities that
only the ballot and the equal enjoyment of civil rights could have secured.
But Woodward's suggestion that there were alternatives to this story presses
us to explore their possible content more closely and to identify the individuals and issues in national politics from which such alternatives could have
been formed.[6]

By focusing our story in Washington, we inevitably pay less attention to the means by which white supremacy in the South was restored and secured at the state and local levels. This is an important limitation to our story, for the alternatives we trace were starkly posed in southern elections and organizing campaigns, just as the violence, intimidation, and electoral fraud indexed in debates and testimony in Washington were carried out by individuals and groups with an eye to local ascendancy. The insurrections against federal supervision in the 1870s, as with the disfranchising conventions of the 1890s, were organized and carried out in states and local communities, with southern members of Congress playing a supporting role. Fortunately, these developments have been chronicled in exquisite detail and fine complexity by many historians and social scientists.[7]

With a few exceptions, however, the post-Reconstruction story of the South as a coherent and determined actor in national politics has not received the same close and systematic attention. While the restoration of white domination and racial exploitation was accomplished in southern state legislatures and county courts, in its cities and small towns, it was also defended in Congress by a phalanx of legislators who subordinated their priorities on a range of policies to the paramount issue of "home rule" and white supremacy. If not for the legislative victories won by southern Democrats in Congress, the repertoires of political possibilities in the region would probably have widened considerably.

Paradoxically, these victories radically curtailed possibilities that could have advanced the region's collective well-being. By 1900, the South was securely racist in its institutions, economic organization, and social practices. It also was mired in poverty and underdevelopment, unable to match the quickening pace of growth in the North. Our contribution, then, lies in demonstrating not only the means used in Congress to protect southern states as they fashioned segregated white hegemony, but the quite profound price this victory entailed.

Looking at the South in Congress reveals how these outcomes were entwined as southern legislators navigated the choices posed by their dual commitment to defend white supremacy and rebalance the political economic order built up by twenty years of Republican government. Almost since its founding, the Republican Party had been pursuing an ambitious program focused on the integration of a national market, federal support for industry and infrastructure, and the creation of a financial system that could mobilize capital and maintain exchange rate stability, while guaranteeing that political and civil rights would be allocated without distinctions of race or color. Each of these commitments had dramatic consequences for the South. While white southern legislators desperately wanted reforms that would better reflect their constituents' economic interests and their own visions of how their region's political economy should be organized, they had to order these priorities and weigh them against the need to defend white supremacy. Though this was the paramount priority of southern Democrats, this fact did not fully determine their legislative and political choices. In some cases, southern lawmakers were willing to make surprising compromises.[8]

Republicans in Congress also were operating under conditions of constrained agency and were forced to weigh their priorities. During Reconstruction, southern Republicans had been supported by powerful national allies in embracing "a vision of civil and political society that was altogether new in the South," premised on the enfranchisement and mass mobilization of black Americans. As Richard Valelly has shown, the democratic politics the Republican Party inaugurated in the region relied on both local political organizations and national institutions that could sustain political engagement and constrain efforts aimed at its suppression. The confrontation with an emboldened white South, however, compelled the national Republican Party to establish its own ordering of priorities and to choose whether it would buttress the institutions needed to protect black enfranchisement or leave these in a weakened state.[9]

The violent resistance to Reconstruction first compelled Congress and Republican administrations to decide on the military and political resources to deploy in defending black political and civil rights and to consider whether this effort would be worth the cost of alienating northern electorates tired of war and ready to believe that their obligations to freed black southerners had been fulfilled. Later in the century, the coordinated opposition of Democratic legislators to Republican policy proposals would force the party to decide at what cost they would pursue their goal to restore federal supervision of elections. For William Chandler of New Hampshire, Republican industrial policies such as the tariff had "been only an incident of [the] great labors" of resisting slavery, winning the war, freeing the slaves, and securing black political and civil rights, and he urged the party's leadership not to forget this fact. For James Clarkson, the influential editor of the Des Moines *Iowa State Register*, it was imperative to deemphasize black political rights in favor of Republican support for industry. "The seaboard cities," he wrote in a widely reprinted article, "are determined to have good relations re-established with the South, and are as determined in this respect as they were in the days before the war. It is also clear that there is no longer a majority in the North to respond to the nobler issues on which the Republican party has so long stood." He argued that the party should instead emphasize a broad tariff encompassing both northern and southern industries.[10]

There was no unique or obvious ordering to these priorities, which were weighed differently by legislators' different constituencies. In theory, moreover, it was possible to pursue them simultaneously. Indeed, between 1889 and 1891, Republicans tried to do just that in the remarkable 51st Congress, which debated tariff legislation, currency legislation, a massive expenditure program, and a proposal to renew the federal supervision of elections.

By century's end, a rough settlement had been worked out. The Republican goal of an industrial economy organized around an integrated national market, adherence to the gold standard, and trade protectionism had been firmly established in law. Simultaneously, the Democratic South had entrenched the right of state governments to regulate the region's social, political, and labor relations without any external control or supervision. By prioritizing white supremacy, southern legislators had forced Republicans to make stark choices in the 1890s that led to the abandonment of legislative efforts to secure the rights of black Americans and to a focus instead on consolidating the new American industrial order and expanding its access to foreign markets. No formal deal or compromise was hashed out. Rather, a gradual definition of sectional and partisan priorities and a tacit acquiescence were worked out by specific choices with attendant costs, risks, and benefits in concrete political fights, administrative decisions, and legislative processes.[11]

The triumph of white supremacy imposed considerable costs on the whole region. For sure, many whites benefited from discrimination against African Americans—in the allocation of school funds, in the provision of infrastructure, in access to skilled trades, and in the gradual appearance of a racial wage gap. But overall, the South cohered as a low-wage, undereducated, and underdeveloped section in part because the commitments of its representatives to racial hierarchy and regional autonomy dramatically limited their ability to secure federal support on terms they could accept or to block fiscal policies that disproportionately burdened the South. As Woodward argued in his classic synthesis, by 1900, "the great majority of Southerners were confined to the worn grooves of a tributary economy." Not just the black but the white majority was "cut off from the better-paying jobs and the higher opportunities," stuck in "farming, mining, forestry, or some low-wage industry, whether they liked it or not," within what many southerners (and Woodward) labeled a colonial economy.[12]

This chapter charts these developments through a consideration of southern politics from the return of the region to Congress to century's end. We begin by detailing the process of "redemption," in which the Democratic Party across the South wrested control of state legislatures and national representation from biracial coalitions organized primarily within the Republican Party. Different policy priorities and ideological orientations, as well as a varying willingness to accept the formal legitimacy of the Reconstruction Amendments, were ultimately subordinated to the cause of home rule. But these options were not erased, and their continued relevance helped sculpt the politics of the post-Reconstruction era. We then examine the structure of political conflict in Congress, the site where southern diversity was transformed into regional solidarity, to show that the familiar story of the Black Belt as the core of southern solidarity must be revised. At least for this period, there was a considerable diversity of preferences among southern members, and in fact Black Belt legislators often were more open to compromise than their fellow southern representatives.

Turning to the substantive bases for southern unity and diversity, we identify the issue areas that implicated distinctively southern priorities and arrayed the region's members in diverse coalitions with northern Democrats and Republicans. From this set, we select for detailed examination legislation that reflected competing intraregional priorities: a reconfiguration of the political economy that had grown up under twenty years of Republican rule; a reorientation of spending that would allow the South to gain a greater share of federal disbursements; and the defeat and repeal of federal authority to protect the civil and political rights of African Americans, a policy objective to which all southern Democrats were pledged.

Reconstruction, Redemption, and the Solid South

Black voting in the former Confederate states was inaugurated with passage of the Reconstruction Acts in 1867 and 1868. These federal laws turned southern politics and society upside down. Massive black voting brought about a political revolution as state conventions elected by manhood suffrage redrafted their constitutions. These were revolutionary gatherings. These state constitutional conventions were the first representative assemblies in which whites and blacks participated together. The delegates, Hahn writes,

> set out to do something that no other society in the world, let alone state in the South or the Union, had so much as attempted. They would inscribe into fundamental law the enfranchisement and full civil standing of a very large social group—one making up nearly half of the population and much more of the labor force, and held for over two centuries in the condition of slavery—thereby reconstructing the body politic of the South and potentially reordering the politics and society of the nation.

The conventions were buttressed by the remarkable political engagement of black Americans, whose Union Leagues galvanized grassroots participation and advanced a new class of black political activists and politicians who connected black community and kin networks to political life.

Together with progressive and investment-minded white southerners, and briefly advantaged by the disfranchisement of former Confederate rebels and by white abstention, the Republican Party came to power in every former Confederate state except Virginia and Georgia. In 1870, the Fifteenth Amend-

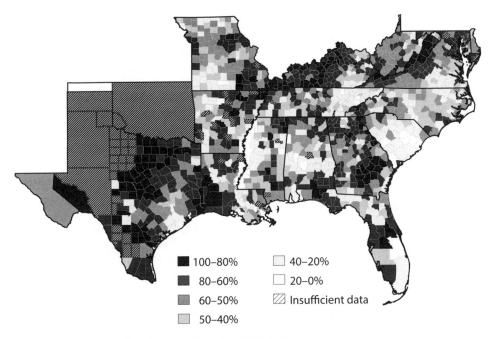

■ 100–80%	▫ 40–20%
■ 80–60%	▫ 20–0%
▨ 60–50%	▨ Insufficient data
▨ 50–40%	

FIGURE 3.1. Party Vote Share in National Elections, 1867–1875

ment extended racial democracy to the rest of the South and the country at large by providing a national guarantee that voting, the foundational right of democratic citizenship, would be protected.[13]

Figure 3.1 records the distribution of Democratic and Republican support in the South during the years 1868 to 1875. The darker regions show strong Democratic support, while the lighter regions are counties where the Republicans were in the majority. We have insufficient voting data for those counties marked by diagonal dashes. The Republican Party was strongest in the region's Black Belt; support there rested on an often tenuous coalition between African Americans and backcountry whites. In Tennessee the party was a loose alliance between the staunch Republicans in the eastern mountains, whose deep wounds suffered as Unionists during the Civil War would make the region a long-enduring bedrock of white Republicanism, and African Americans and some old Whigs in the center and west of the state, the heartland of the cotton and tobacco economy. A similar coalition between African Americans in the east and upcountry whites was evident in North Carolina. In Missouri, Republican strength rested on the "small farmers and the poor whites of the Ozark area," Germans settlers, St. Louis merchants, and, after the Fifteenth Amendment, African American voters concentrated along the Missouri River. The large black majority of South Carolina enabled a Republicanism that was strong throughout the state, especially in the coastal regions, where most of the freed slaves lived, while Georgia—evenly divided between black and white voters—failed to develop a stable biracial coalition.[14]

Despite the fact that the Republican Party's strength rested heavily on black voters, a majority of every state legislature except South Carolina's remained white. Still, more than 600 African Americans served in statehouses across the reconstructed states, the vast majority of them former slaves. In 1872, free-born P. B. S. Pinchback became the first (and until 1990 the only) black governor of an American state, taking office in Louisiana after the impeachment of the sitting governor. As southern states were readmitted to the Union, beginning with Tennessee in 1866 and concluding with Georgia in 1870, a small contingent of black legislators was sent to Congress to represent states and districts with black majorities. In February 1870, Republican Hiram Revels of Mississippi became the first black senator, followed in the House by Joseph Rainey of South Carolina, the first directly elected African American to be seated by Congress. In the Congress that sat from 1871 to 1873, there were five African Americans in the House, a number that would increase to seven in the next two Congresses. The election of African American officials at the local, state, and national levels marked a radical reconfiguration of the face of southern political power as the political halls in "white man's country" were populated by vocal black legations assertively pressing the concerns of their constituents onto the political agenda.[15]

For what W. E. B. Du Bois called "the few years of an eternal second," biracial governments in the southern states established public education systems; exempted homesteads from debt collectors; established more equitable tax structures based more on property than poll taxes and license fees; founded hospitals, penitentiaries, asylums, and orphanages; and in many states passed equal accommodations laws. South Carolina, whose black majority helped make it perhaps the most radical state, went so far as to fund medical care for poor citizens, enact sweeping equal accommodations legislation, and embark on "a path-breaking program of land distribution," which by 1879 had settled 14,000 African American families on homesteads. But the "most dramatic transformation," writes Eric Foner, "concerned labor relations." Restrictions on labor mobility were repealed and a rich array of social and labor legislation was passed into law, designed to protect the region's wage laborers, to provide protection against nonpayment of wages or denial of their share of the harvest, and to produce a collective commitment to the education and well-being of the poor and working classes. For the first time in history, planters in the reconstructed southern states were unable to rely on public coercion to control their labor force; Republican governors' hesitation, or even refusal, to use the state militias to break strikes by cotton workers dramatically laid bare the reversal of social and economic hierarchies.[16]

Reaction arrived almost as soon as the revolution began, starting in the border states that had not been subject to Congress's reconstruction program and where military rule had been only a temporary wartime measure. After 1866, it was Kentucky, wrote Woodward, that "presented a more solidly Confederate-Democratic front" than any other southern state. Delaware preserved its Democratic majority after ratification of the Fifteenth Amendment with a violent race-baiting campaign intended to consolidate the white vote and limit black voting. One report claimed that the U.S. senator Willard Saulsbury drunkenly opened his election campaign by exhorting dispirited Democrats, who knew full well that black voting could shift the balance in the state, to "go home and yell White Man's Party!" U.S. deputy marshals were attacked and driven from the polls. African Americans were physically blocked from voting or saw the ballot box rushed away as they approached. When Democrats were found guilty of violating the Federal Enforcement Acts, the Democratic legislature passed a tax collection law "clearly designed to make it difficult to get colored men qualified as voters," a disfranchising measure that was both highly successful—it was the subject of a special investigation by the *North American Review* in 1885—and ahead of its time. Missouri's Republican majority was defeated in 1870 by its own factionalism and a Democratic Party that consolidated around white supremacy and the re-enfranchisement of Confederates, inaugurating nearly a quarter-century of Democratic rule. Maryland, whose pro-secession legislators had been arrested in 1861, saw Democrats in power from 1866 until 1895, while West Virginia was reconquered for the Democratic Party in 1870, with former Confederates taking an outsized role in the new government.[17]

The worst violence, however, appeared in the former Confederate states. In 1866, white veterans, led by the mayor of New Orleans, massacred over 200 New Orleans black residents who had supported a constitutional convention intent on establishing manhood suffrage. After Radical Republicans won in Tennessee in 1867, the state was home to the formation of the Ku Klux Klan, whose members led a wave of violence against Republican voters. Two years later, with Republican factionalism at its height and black turnout dropping precipitously, Tennessee returned a Democratic majority that immediately set to work revising the constitution and re-enfranchising former Confederates. Violence helped Democrats carry Georgia in the 1868 presidential elections; the precarious situation of black legislators had been made clear earlier that year when white Republicans in the legislature expelled the body's black members. Although the Republican governor appealed to Congress to renew military reconstruction and the military commander of the region expelled the ex-Confederates from the General Assembly, Georgia's Democrats managed to hold on to power. Alabama Democrats regained control of the state in 1874 and swiftly revised the constitution to severely restrict opportunities for state-supported economic development and to vest power in the hands of Black Belt planters.

With the return of state legislatures to Democratic rule, black voting strength was frequently diminished by gerrymandering, the passage of laws that gave local officials a great deal of discretion in registering voters, the placement of Democrats on election returning boards, and, in some cases, the passage of poll tax qualifications for voting. As J. Morgan Kousser has detailed in his classic study *The Shaping of Southern Politics*, black turnout declined significantly in response to these changes, but it persisted nonetheless. Biracial politics became more fragile as the suppression of southern black voting made it harder to build statewide Republican majorities, and black officeholding declined, though here, too, there was considerable variation across the South. Black political strength was confined increasingly to particular localities, but black voting would remain a potent factor in southern politics for the remainder of the century.[18]

The Democratic Party gained strength in the South as a result of the worldwide depression that began in 1873; the backlash against Republican efforts to pass a robust civil rights bill that in its initial form would have outlawed segregated schools; sporadic terror campaigns against black and white Republicans; and the limits of the southern Republican strategy to build political support through debt-driven economic development. In 1874, the Republican Party lost control of the House of Representatives, for the first time since 1859, when a narrow Democratic victory in the North was buttressed by new southern majorities. In the closing weeks of the lame-duck congressional session, an enforcement bill accompanying the 1875 Civil Rights Act was defeated by a filibuster, a Democratic victory that, for southern Democrats, would long serve as a source of inspiration as well as gratitude for their northern allies who helped organize and carry it out. By 1876, only Louisiana and South Carolina remained under Republican control. In the congressional elections that year, Republicans won only 14 of 106 southern seats in the House and just 6 of 34 in the Senate.

That year's presidential election most clearly exhibited the scale of the Republican Party's decline in the South. The party was defeated everywhere outside of Florida, Louisiana, and South Carolina, where both parties claimed victory. The U.S. military was deployed to guard Republicans in the state capitol in Charleston and the returning board and Republican governor in the Louisiana statehouse in New Orleans. Shortly after an electoral commission had awarded him the electoral college votes of the three contested states, the new president, Rutherford B. Hayes, wrote the Secretary of War in April 1877 that there did not exist "such domestic violence as is contemplated by the Constitution" to justify the use of the Army, and thus federal troops were being

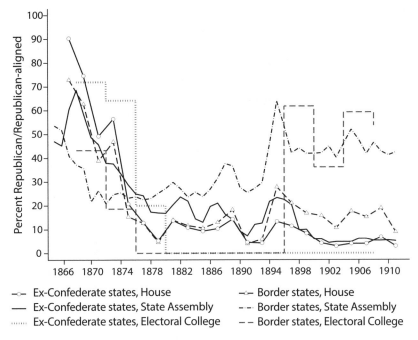

FIGURE 3.2. Southern Republican Officeholding, 1866–1912

ordered to stand down. The Republican governors conceded defeat, leaving all southern states under Democratic Party control.[19]

The result of this "redemption" from Republican government was the Solid South, a massive phalanx of Democratic representatives, senators, and electoral college votes. The sheer size of the South gave the region a disproportionate role in national politics. Rather than encompass only the states of the former Confederacy, the region's politics reached out to cover the entire territory in which slavery had been established before the Civil War. In these circumstances, Republican Party strategists came to believe that "it was nearly impossible," in the words of one historian, "to make sufficient gains elsewhere," while northern Democrats understood that any break in the Solid South would make the national party a struggling minority.[20]

Figure 3.2 provides a measure of the Solid South's breadth, tracking the proportion of congressional, state legislative, and Electoral College votes won by Republicans in the former Confederacy and the border states from the end of the Civil War to the beginning of the Wilson administration. Before 1877, a capable and competitive Republican Party organization could win seats in state legislatures and secure Electoral College votes. From time to time, as after 1896, competitive politics in the border states returned, leading the *Savannah Tribune,* a black Georgia newspaper, to proclaim that the " 'Solid

South' is at last broken." But overall, the Solid South encompassed the entire area of the former slaveholding states, enabling southern Democrats to hold an average of 31 percent of seats in the House and 40 percent in the Senate. To carry presidential elections the Democratic Party needed only to expand on its reestablished southern base by winning the very closely contested states of New York and Indiana. Had Democratic solidarity extended only through the former Confederacy, the proportions would have been 22 and 25 percent for the House and Senate, respectively, and the party would have needed to find between thirty-three and forty-six more Electoral College votes—an extremely heavy lift given Republican strength in New England and the Midwest.[21]

The very factors that secured the South's 'redemption' paradoxically ensured that the Solid South simultaneously presented itself as an imposing unified bloc in opposition to much of the rest of the country but also as a fragile configuration of diverse interests and ideas ripe for Republican appeal. Southerners throughout this period would repeatedly insist that sectional cohesion had been achieved by the voluntary unity of nearly the entire white population in a spontaneous expression of opposition to "negro rule." The Democratic Party had provided the organization for redeeming the region from Republican misrule, and "the white element of the south, almost to a man, embraced it." "There is only one party with the whites of to-day," wrote the *Dallas Weekly Herald* in 1877.[22]

This type of claim masked more complex and contingent patterns of coalition-building marked by often tenuous alliances between different agricultural and industrial sectors. If southern solidarity defined the politics of the period, so too did its brittleness. Alternative possibilities for orderings of political life were not foreclosed. Though Republican officeholding collapsed throughout most of the region, Republican Party candidates, as well as third parties aligned with the Republicans, continued to win an important share of the southern vote. Figure 3.3 indicates the proportion of votes cast for Republican or Republican-aligned candidates for Congress and the presidency. Even in the Deep South, Republicans continued to win an important share of ballots well into the late 1880s, the majority cast by African Americans still able to vote and have their votes counted. In the Upper South and border states, Republicans often came within striking distance of statewide majorities. Benjamin Harrison, for instance, lost Virginia in 1888 by only 2,000 votes, and Republican candidates regularly polled between 40 and 50 percent of that state's vote.

On occasion, a configuration of Republican and third-party support displaced Democratic governments. In 1880, for example, divisions within the Tennessee Democratic Party brought a Republican governor to power and, with the assistance of the Greenback Party, Republican control of the General

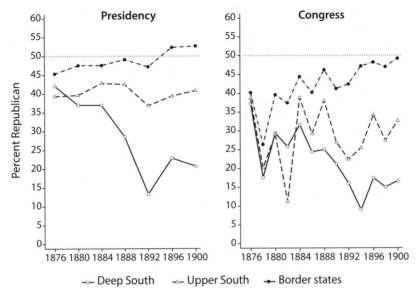

FIGURE 3.3. Republican Party Vote Share across South, 1876–1900

Assembly. The following year a third party backed by black and white voters gained majority status in Virginia. The persistence of African American voting in some counties also could result in fusion arrangements that ceded local offices in exchange for African Americans not contesting state or national positions. In some states, black officeholding at the local level actually peaked in the 1880s.[23]

Democrats' electoral anxieties were hardly uniform across the region, but there was a shared recognition that the party's electoral successes rested on a tenuous foundation and that the Republican Party could come to power either by making further inroads among the white population or when divisions within Democratic ranks offered black voters the balance of power. Neither prospect was difficult to imagine. One correspondent in the South noted that "every where I have been I have found a division of opinion among the intelligent white people sufficiently radical to work out in a division in party action." This belief was reinforced by an awareness that the South had been contested political terrain before the war; in many cases, moreover, former Whigs had been the ascendant force within southern Democratic Party organizations during Reconstruction, and thus "a great many of the most efficient and faithful members of the Democratic party are men who were once opposed to it." After twenty-five years, a declining number of southerners could claim to have been active members of the Whig Party, which had ceased to have an organized existence in the region after 1852. The most prominent was Alexander Stephens, the vice president of the Confederacy and afterwards a

Democratic representative from Georgia who died in 1883. As the *Charleston Republican* noted in 1875, "it is a favorite theory with some that a successful republican party can be organized in the south by uniting the old line Whigs with colored voters. No proposition could be more chimerical." The party was "defeated, dead and buried," in the words of the *Pilot* in Jackson, Mississippi. And it could not be resurrected, not least because the radicalism of the southern Republican parties made affiliation with it by upper-class planters "an abandonment of both political principle and class loyalty." The Republican Party, after all, was "emphatically the poor man's party" in the South.[24]

But the idea of persistent Whiggery endured, as it encapsulated the possibility of "a floating detachable bloc of voters" who could be persuaded to break with the solid Democratic front. "The real tendency of the Old Line Whigs, and also of all the conservative men who have been forced by past circumstances to act with the Democracy, is toward the Republican party," wrote the *Houston Daily Union* in 1871. "Nothing is needed to bring about this result but wise and liberal management on the part of the Republican Party." This was certainly an exaggeration, and Michael Perman has clearly shown that in fact it was the Democrats who in the early 1870s had the upper hand in courting former Whig notables. But many national Republican strategists remained convinced into the 1880s that they could appeal to "those men in the South who now accept the tariff views of Clay and the constitutional expositions of Webster," while white southerners upset with northern Democrats or their own state leadership would frequently remind listeners that "half of the whites of the south were once Whigs, and half of the white people now entertain the old Whig doctrines upon economic subjects." This was a testament less to the endurance of a party that had been buried a generation before than to the unsettled character of the southern Democratic coalition during this period.[25]

While some Republicans appealed to southern Whiggery, others saw brighter prospects in fragmenting Democratic supporters into third parties. Instead of appealing to conservative Whigs, they would appeal to constituencies chafing under the leadership of conservative Democrats, including former Unionists who resented the prominence of Confederates among the leadership of the Democratic Party by the late 1870s. The decades after the Civil War saw a flourishing of third-party movements as the coalitions that had been built up around slavery and the conduct of the war came under increasing strain. The Radical Republicans in Missouri split in 1870 over the question of ending the disfranchisement of former Confederates, and the quickly organized Liberals took 30 percent of the seats in the state legislature. The next few decades saw the spread of Liberal or reform factions to other states, but also the spread of the inflationary Greenback Party, the organization of the Union Labor Party in Arkansas, the quasi-military "Readjuster" movement in Virginia, the appearance of independent third parties in Florida and Alabama, and the dramatic rise of the People's Party by the 1890s. Arkansas in particular became a hotbed of third-party activism as former Unionists bitterly recoiled against the control of local government and national representation by "the bitterest, rebels, mostly confederate Soldiers," and as groups such as the Brothers of Freedom and the Agricultural Wheel organized white farmers in the formerly Unionist northwest and the Knights of Labor made deep inroads into the region despite intense opposition from the Democratic government. When Democratic state and county officials crushed a strike in 1886, the Wheel and a biracial committee of Little Rock Knights began to explore running a third-party Union Labor ticket.[26]

To be sure, only a few third parties came to power, but when combined with Republicans, they posed significant challenges to Democratic rule in several states. Whether through the vehicle of a revitalized Republican Party or a coalition, white solidarity in the Democratic Party thus was widely believed to be burdened with tensions that made the party vulnerable to splits. The South, in short, was both solid yet potentially ripe for a division into parties arrayed along different lines than the "appeals to issues buried in the dead past." The insecure cohesion of the Democratic Party thus raised questions about the content of the legislative program southern representatives might successfully advance.[27]

Over and again, southern politicians and editors emphasized that the South's "great object since the war has been restoration to the Union on a footing of perfect equality with other sections," by which they meant first and foremost the maintenance of local self-government and white supremacy, but also the reconfiguration of the emerging political economy so that it would no longer work to the region's detriment. That economic goal implied lowering and rebalancing the tariff and internal revenue taxes, as well as support for internal improvements in the South; on the latter issue, even the most committed advocates of states' rights principles believed that the South should cease being content with the North getting "all the money, while [we] accepted the honors" of constitutional consistency. These southern voices also advocated a range of fresh policies to regulate interstate commerce, establish a more elastic currency, and even promote federal support for public schools.[28]

These issues divided white southerners. Those who supported greater investment in the region objected to "a stupid Bourbonism which would sacrifice the hopes and material advancement" of the South "to satisfy some Procrustean theory of the past." The Democratic Party, complained others, had no desire to consider the issues of vital importance to the country, such as the currency, or "relief of the people," but instead tried constantly to "force a discussion of topics which may serve to unite the two parties in bitter, sectional quarrel," namely, the threat of "negro domination" and the loss of home rule.[29]

   Such criticisms were leveled at many southern Democratic legislators, but also were accompanied by an explicit warning to northern copartisans. "Is it not high time for us to say to Northern Democrats," asked the Vicksburg *Daily Commercial*, "that we shall have no more 'one-sided reciprocity,'" that the region would "sever our coalition with Northern Democrats, and look to others for the aid and fair treatment which they refuse us." "The Northern Democracy," another white southerner insisted, "must begin to give us something more than sweet words." So long as "home rule in their several States" was in doubt, observed the *Daily Picayune*, southerners were bound to the Democratic Party, despite "just ground of complaint against the Northern wing of the party, on account of its indisposition to advance the material development of this neglected section." It was only because the northern "friends and defenders" of the South in its defense of home rule were "found in the Democratic ranks" that "the Southern Conservative feels himself most congenially situated" in that party. But if ever home rule were secured, southerners would then be "at leisure, so to speak, to prepare themselves to select with intelligence their side."[30]

Sectional Politics in the Gilded Age

Southern complaints about northern Democratic perfidy reflected the basic structure of political conflict, which arrayed not just Democrats against Republicans but northerners against southerners, with northern Democrats torn between their partisan commitments and sectional interests. By empirically probing these historical observations, we can see how tensions within the Democratic coalition were manifested in divergent patterns of voting in the national legislature.[31]

   Figure 3.4 shows the location of the party and sectional medians in the House and the Senate, with the median member of southern members of third parties—the National Greenbackers, the Readjusters, and the Populists—labeled. In both chambers the Democratic Party was divided between southerners and a band of northern legislators who generally voted with their copartisans, but who also could break away to vote with Republicans. With such "one-sided reciprocity," in the language of complaining southerners, southern support for northern Democrats' priorities failed to be returned when questions relating to the South's "material advancement" were under consideration. This lament was a persistent, at times marked, feature of congressional debates.

   Although both party and sectional polarization were high, a closer examination of member preferences suggests possible alternatives to southern solidarity. In the 1940s, V. O. Key Jr. found that the extreme sectional center of

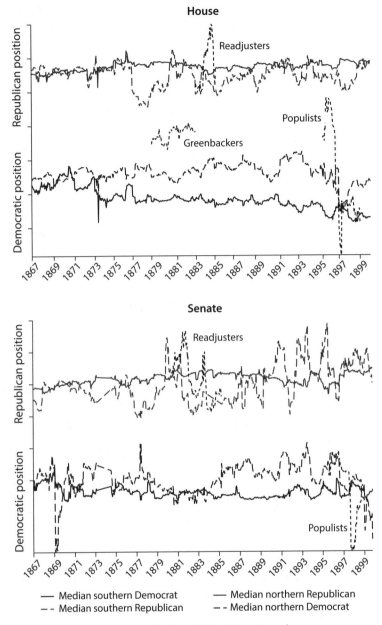

House

Republican position

Readjusters

Populists

Greenbackers

Democratic position

1867 1869 1871 1873 1875 1877 1879 1881 1883 1885 1887 1889 1891 1893 1895 1897 1899

Senate

Republican position

Readjusters

Democratic position

Populists

1867 1869 1871 1873 1875 1877 1879 1881 1883 1885 1887 1889 1891 1893 1895 1897 1899

—— Median southern Democrat   —— Median northern Republican
-- Median southern Republican   -- Median northern Democrat

FIGURE 3.4. Party and Sectional Medians, 1866–1900. Estimated across twenty-week interval. Third parties with southern representation are labeled.

the South was located in the Black Belt, the "hard core of the political South—and the backbone of southern political unity." When we disaggregate the Democratic representatives of the Gilded Age into their regional groupings, however, we witness a surprising inversion. Figure 3.5 shows the predicted ideal point location of Democrats according to their region and state.[32] In the House, the non–Black Belt districts of the former Confederacy were the most extreme, followed by Black Belt representatives, those from the border states, and finally, Democrats from outside the South. But representatives from Louisiana, South Carolina, and, to a lesser extent, Florida were more like northern Democrats in their willingness to vote with Republicans than were other southerners outside the border states. In the Senate, the Black Belt states—Louisiana, Mississippi, South Carolina, Florida, Georgia, and Alabama—consistently voted with other "centrist" Democrats, insofar as centrism is conceptualized as the willingness to vote with the other party against their own. In both chambers, southerners from the Black Belt were relatively more independent in their voting than southerners from the former Confederacy outside the Black Belt, especially Democrats from Arkansas, Tennessee, and Texas, who were especially likely to stake out a staunchly partisan position.[33]

We can examine this variation in more detail by mapping members' preferences onto the districts and counties from which they were elected. In figure 3.6, we assign each county or state the average ideal point of all the Democratic representatives or senators who represented it in Congress across a particular period, with lighter counties and states being those represented by the most moderate Democratic lawmakers (i.e., those that voted most frequently with Republicans), and darker ones those represented by the most extreme and partisan. The sectional cleavage separating northern from southern Democrats is clearly apparent. Yet so too is a significant degree of heterogeneity within the Democratic South. The relative moderation of Louisiana's congressional delegations, for instance, was rooted in and around New Orleans, along the sugar-producing Gulf Coast, and in the Mississippi Delta, while the South Carolina delegation most likely to break party ranks came from coastal counties with large black populations. The bipartisan voting patterns of representatives from along the Rio Grande in Texas, where wool was a major economic sector, on Louisiana's sugar-producing coast, and in the coal-producing hills of West Virginia points to the appeal of Republican tariff policy, which at times heavily subsidized each of these industries.

The role of Deep South senators in particular suggests an alternative set of political configurations in which southern support for the Republican Party's developmental agenda could be rendered compatible with commitments to white supremacy. Mississippi's Lucius Quintus Cincinnatus Lamar II famously eulogized Charles Sumner in the House of Representatives, a speech whose

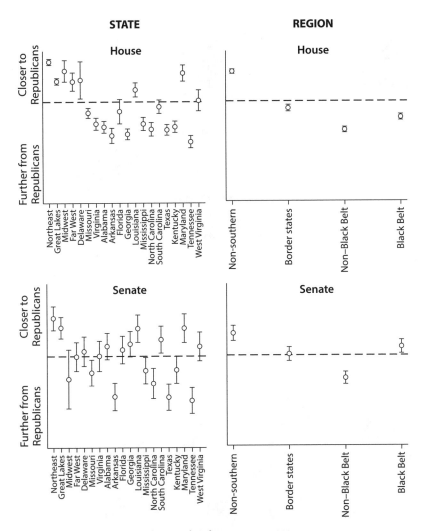

FIGURE 3.5. Geographic Distribution of Preferences, 1877–1900

core message—that the North should place its trust in the white South and abandon Sumner's civil rights bill—has often been forgotten amid accolades for Lamar's "profile in courage." The Mississippi senator, who was quite possibly the "Grand Dragon" of his state's Ku Klux Klan in the early 1870s, defended KKK members in court, attacked US deputy marshals, toured the state delivering incendiary speeches with Georgia's Grand Dragon John Gordon, and ultimately played an important role—while a member of Congress—leading the "Red Shirts" in the violent campaign of intimidation and economic coercion that overturned the Republican government in his state. But Lamar also was a proponent of federal investment; he cast the only vote

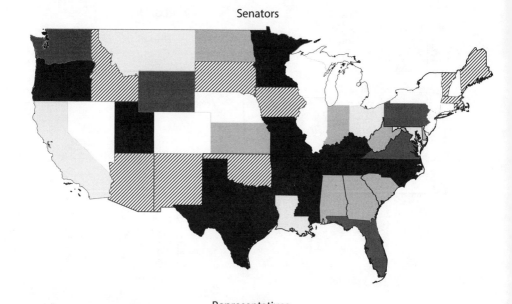

Senators

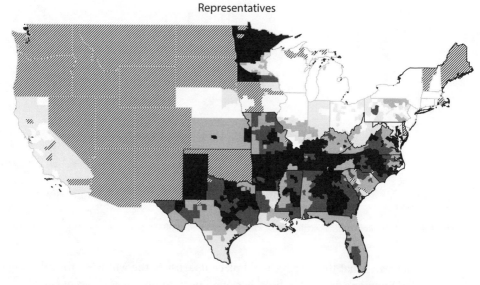

Representatives

■ Least likely to vote   ▦ Average levels of voting   □ Most likely to vote
  with Republicans   with Republicans   with Republicans

■ Below-average voting   ▫ Above-average voting   ▨ Too few Democrats
  with Republicans   with Republicans   or missing data

FIGURE 3.6. Relative Moderation of Democratic Members of Congress, 1877–1900

in the state legislature dissenting from support for a silver currency and was accused, with Matthew Butler of South Carolina, of having "voted, and, worked for, Wall Street, like nice little men."[34]

Likewise, Wade Hampton III, South Carolina's governor and senator, strongly supported developing the state's education system and insisted that he had been "the first man at the South" to support black suffrage—a claim that was at odds with his reliance on paramilitary violence to suppress black voting in 1876 but that reflected the widespread belief among Black Belt legislators that their rhetoric had to be pitched for northern consumption. In later years, senators such as Samuel McEnery of Louisiana and John Morgan of Alabama would strongly support the Republican industrial program; though both came from primarily rural states, their bases of support lay primarily in New Orleans and Birmingham, respectively, and the populations of these two cities were deeply affected by Republican economic and financial policies. These legislators presented a possible alternative to white solidarity within the Democratic Party. They supported Republican policy priorities, sometimes quite strongly. Were it not for the overwhelming issue of white supremacy they likely would have been comfortable within the Republican fold.[35]

The Bases of Southern Unity and Division

"Were it not for the race question," wrote the Republican *Daily Inter-Ocean*, "the solidity of the South would crumble in a day." This belief in a fragile South, premised exclusively on the maintenance of racial hegemony and subject to disruption once other issues came to the fore, was widespread during the late nineteenth century. But if we are to identify alternatives to southern solidarity, then we need to do more than simply find the relatively more moderate southerners who might have been willing to break with the Democratic Party. We must also identify the particular issues around which any alternative coalitions could have been built—issues that strained existing coalitions and were understood by contemporaries to be promising avenues for reordering political loyalties. By systematically cataloging issue areas according to the type of political alignment they produced, we can select specific policies and issue areas to analyze more closely.[36]

Following this course, we calculate the percentage of roll calls from different issue areas that can be categorized as revealing cross-party, partisan, sectional, or disloyal southern voting alignments, following the approach identified in chapter 2. The proportion of roll calls that fall within each of these four categories for the Senate and the House, from 1877 to 1900, is shown in figure 3.7, with disloyal, cross-party, partisan, and sectional votes displayed in the four panels. The dashed line shows the proportion of all other issue areas that fall within the specified category. The *y*-axis for the category of partisan voting

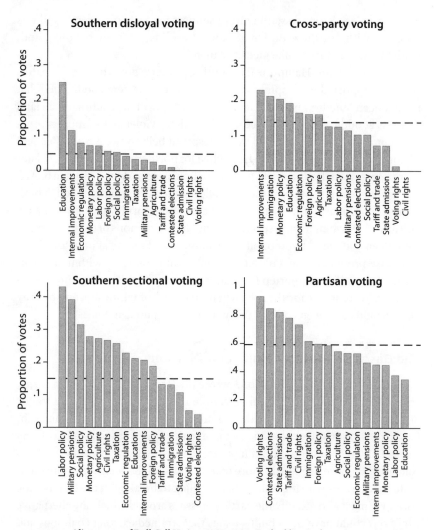

FIGURE 3.7. Alignments of Roll Call Voting, 1877–1900. Dashed line is the average proportion of all other votes in the specified category.

is not set to the same scale as the other categories: most issue areas saw southern and northern Democrats voting together, and so the bottom-right panel of figure 3.7 runs the full range from zero to one.

Some issues immediately stand out, demanding greater attention. In the top-left panel, we see that it was relatively common for votes on education and internal improvements to array southerners with Republicans against their northern copartisans. Voting alliances between Republicans and southern Democrats were especially common on the Blair education bill, which would have entailed a massive investment of federal funds disproportionately targeted at the South. But such alliances also were common on internal improvements, a substantive issue area that produced a considerable degree of cross-party voting (top-right panel of figure 3.7).

Education and internal improvements occasioned repeated complaints among white southerners about the meanness of northern Democrats. As one southerner complained that "we are good enough to furnish a congressional majority or a majority of the electoral college" for the Democratic Party, but when "congressional aid to public schools in the south is suggested," the region's representatives could find little support from their northern allies. "We must vote for vast outlays on New York and New England harbors, but content ourselves with pittances for the south Atlantic and Gulf harbors." In turn, these issues led many Republican strategists to believe that they could serve as legislative vehicles to lure southerners into their party. "The republicans," wrote the *New York Herald* in an appeal for the party to appeal more vigorously to the South, "favor liberal appropriations for internal improvements, and this policy has great, and indeed overwhelming strength in almost all the southern districts," and thus was a highly promising avenue for expanding the party in the region.[37]

On another set of policies, however, the South stood apart, with large numbers of its representatives voting against both Republicans and northern Democrats. These issues are shown in the bottom-left panel of figure 3.7. The most important of these was labor, an issue central to southern redemption and to the profound economic and social changes that were occurring during the Gilded Age. Southern lawmakers could take what seem to be contradictory positions concerning the era's massive labor struggles: they offered verbal support for striking railroad workers in 1877—a strike that extended across several states, choked commercial traffic, and was ended only with the intervention of the Army—while providing the only major opposition to minimum hours or binding arbitration laws. These positions were less inconsistent than might appear. Southern sympathy for the Knights of Labor, for example, declined considerably in the wake of reports that the Knights were organizing cotton-pickers in Arkansas and Texas, while southern lawmakers from states with significant black populations were generally more hostile than other Democrats to any federal intervention in the area of labor policy. Southern Democrats also were likely to stand apart on the question of military pensions, opposing further expansions of Union Civil War pensions; by the 1890s, these pensions constituted one of the single largest categories of federal spending, and the vast majority were allocated to non-southerners. These issues impinged on distinctively southern concerns in such a way that left the region's lawmakers more likely to stand alone, with little support from either northern Democrats or Republicans, and that sometimes divided the region itself along lines defined by race and the Civil War.[38]

In the top-right panel of figure 3.7, we observe that issues relating to internal improvements, economic regulation, monetary policy, and education were likely to induce high levels of cross-party voting. Such votes sometimes reflected a high level of consensus, but they could also be the result of internal divisions within the parties. For instance, half of southern Democrats, half of northern Democrats, and half of Republicans voted to reduce the appropriations made for the improvement of the Missouri River in 1893, while each of these blocs strongly supported a bill to resolve mining claims in the same year.

Finally, a set of issue areas divided consistently along partisan lines, as seen in the bottom-right panel of figure 3.7. Partisan voting was the most common pattern on every issue with the notable exception of labor, where sectionalism was slightly more common. Both because there was some sorting of members and constituencies into supporting one party or the other on the basis of its issue positions, and because the complexities of the legislative process were often reduced to a political choice over alternatives defined by partisan actors, it hardly is surprising that party affiliation structured a substantial portion of congressional roll call behavior. Still, a few issues were especially likely to divide the parties from each other and to persuade southern legislators to line up with their northern copartisans against Republicans: voting rights and election laws, votes on contested election cases in the House, and the tariff. More than any others, these substantive and political issues divided the parties from each other in the last quarter of the twentieth century.

———

Table 3.1 enumerates these issues both by the partisan configuration of southerners' positions and by whether they generally produced a solid or divided South in congressional voting. This typology further points toward different possible political alignments in the late nineteenth century between a Solid South supported by northern Democrats on questions of voting rights and the country's financial and industrial policies and an internally divided region that sometimes stood alone and other times joined with the Republican Party.

These seemingly disparate policy areas hung together in relatively coherent and compact categories. Based on our reading of the secondary literature and a rich array of historical sources, we have identified the categories within which the diverse and disparate policy debates of the Gilded Age were understood by southerners, who used this classification to fashion an overarching narrative of sectional interest and a corresponding lexical ordering of policy priorities. Table 3.2 arrays the issue areas identified here, as well as specific policies we have selected for closer study, into three broad groupings through which southerners tended to interpret national policy debates. The first, in the left-most column, is the question of home rule and the political conditions

TABLE 3.1. Issue Areas and Sectional-Party Configuration

Party Alignment	Solid South	Divided South
Aligned with northern Democrats	Voting rights Contested elections Tariff and revenue	
Divided from northern Democrats	Civil rights (*segregation in interstate travel*) Military pensions Monetary policy	Labor policy
Aligned with faction of Republicans		Education policy Internal improvements Economic regulation

TABLE 3.2. Gilded Age Policy Areas as Understood by Southern Lawmakers

Home Rule	Political Economy	Regional Investment
Voting Rights –Repeal election laws –Posse Comitatus Act –Federal elections bill –Soldier voting bill	*Tariff and Revenue* –Proposed and enacted tariff revisions	*Internal Improvements* –Rivers and harbors and roads bills
Civil Rights –Equal accommodations in interstate commerce –"Exodusters" investigations	*Taxation* –Internal revenue –Income tax –Restriction of federal enforcement authority	*Military Pensions* –Civil War pensions –Pensions for veterans of Mexican-American War
Contested Elections –Investigations into elections to House and Senate	*Economic Regulation* –Interstate Commerce Act –Sherman Anti-Trust Act	*Education* –The Blair Bill –Agricultural experiment stations –1890 land grant
Labor Policy –Eight-hour bills –Arbitration bills	*Monetary Policy* –Silver bills	*Taxation* –Reimbursement of direct and cotton taxes

required to secure white control over the region's political and economic order. This group importantly included the different forms in which questions of elections and civil rights for black Americans came onto the congressional agenda, as well as national labor policy, which concerned both the political-economic order of the late nineteenth century and the ability of southerners to regulate the region's labor practices. The middle column concerns the persistent demands of southern lawmakers that the period's emerging political economy be reorganized to reduce the disproportionate burden borne by southern agriculture by reducing the tariff, regulating northern railroad corporations, whose economic dominance was increasingly felt in southern communities, and providing for a more flexible currency that could expand the money in circulation in the region. The right-most column involves federal spending, and the issue areas reflect a broadly shared—though not unanimous—desire to secure more economic investment in the South.

Elections and civil rights provided the principal terrain upon which southern home rule was contested in national politics. The region's lawmakers fought to secure control over the South's racial hierarchy by white-dominated state governments in fights about the repeal of the federal election laws, the proposed federal elections bill of 1890, whether to seat Republicans or Democrats chosen in contested southern elections, the scope of federal authority in enforcing the law, and the causes of the migration of black southerners out of the South in the late 1870s. These issues had formed the basis for white solidarity during redemption and, following Reconstruction, continued to be paramount among southern policy priorities.

The tariff, taxation policy, monetary policy, and efforts to rein in the increasingly sprawling and powerful corporations were issue areas seen by southern members as falling within a category concerned with reconfiguring the economic order that had emerged during the period of Republican ascendancy. Perhaps no sentiment was as widely shared among southern lawmakers and newspaper editorial writers than that the political economy that had been advanced during the twenty years of Republican control unfairly burdened the South and other agricultural areas in favor of the manufacturing regions of the country. Internal taxes, for instance, were crushingly raised on agricultural products, especially tobacco, while the tariff was explicitly designed to transfer income from consumers and agricultural producers to manufacturing employers and workers. Southerners repeatedly sought to build national majorities to support a reconfiguration of the revenue system to lessen this burden by lowering internal revenue taxes, reestablishing an income tax, and reducing tariff rates. They also took the lead in supporting the regulation of corporations in interstate commerce.[39]

Republicans believed that some of these policies could be calibrated to appeal to southern constituencies, though there were inherent limits to how far they could go without abandoning the protective tariff and the gold standard, their core economic priorities. Although tariffs on cotton products, for example, might protect southern cotton mills, lowering tariffs would help cotton growers who wanted to secure the best price in international markets and gain cheaper tools and consumer goods. On some of these issues, the South stood united: particular forms of agricultural production across the region led to common trade, tax, and regulatory priorities. On others, however, the region could divide, either because southern preferences cut different ways or because southerners differed in their evaluation of the costs of harnessing the power of the federal government for their own purposes. Far-reaching regulation of corporations, after all, carried a potential to magnify the authority of the national government, which it might use once again to contest the region's racial hierarchy.

By contrast with the redistributive and regulatory nature of these policies, another set of issues were more distributive in nature, presenting less of a zero-sum game among regions and economic sectors than possibilities to secure broadly shared gains. These policies included internal improvements and other spending programs that largely had been targeted toward northern states since the outbreak of the Civil War; the largesse directed to the North was a persistent source of southern grievance. "The South," went a frequent complaint, "remains simply the step-child of the Federal system, and her only office is to cross her arms every week or so before some fresh Yankee accusation and humbly protest that she is loyal, that she was whipped in the war, and will never ask a dollar from the Federal Treasury for any purpose if she can only be pardoned and suffered to pay taxes."[40]

In turn, Republicans were more willing and able to reconfigure spending patterns in ways that would appeal to southern constituencies without abandoning their core policy commitments. Internal improvements and education were explicitly viewed by Republican strategists as opportunities to win southern support for the broader Republican program of state-supported economic development and thus wean some legislators and states away from the Democratic Party. Soon after the Democrats gained the majority in the House, southern Democrats joined with Republicans—against northern Democrats—to pass a Rivers and Harbors bill over the veto of a Republican president that was more generous to the South than previous legislation. Such issues had the potential to divide the region's lawmakers, as federal spending in these areas tended to cut against Democratic orthodoxy but were highly desired by the southern voting public. As federal money brought with it dangers of control and regulation, so southern lawmakers were tasked with doing what was necessary to secure the former but limit the latter.

Southerners often referred to these categories when evaluating policy proposals, allowing individual legislators as well as attentive public opinion to assess the value of a given policy to the South and weigh the gains against possible costs. Support for increased expenditures, for instance, might make tariff reform more difficult by allocating the surplus generated by the high tariff rates; support for a more active federal labor policy might help protect workers from the corporations empowered by Republican "class legislation," but could threaten to legitimize the national regulation of local labor markets; and southern demands for tariff reform might alienate them from important factions of the northern Democrats who had proved to be vital and essential allies in blocking and rolling back federal supervision of southern elections.

Each category of policy tended to produce different political alignments. Both southerners and Republicans attended to the substantive bases that presented possibilities to build alternative policy coalitions, but with inherent constraints, as the parties could not readily pursue their priorities within each arena simultaneously. Indeed, southern priorities on these distinct issues were not straightforwardly compatible: their achievement required making evaluations concerning which policies were more important, as well as when decisions might deserve the sacrifice of sectional and partisan unity. Southern lawmakers were repeatedly forced to choose among policy objectives to prioritize as they were repeatedly confronted with the need to subordinate preferences on a range of issues in order to secure their paramount interest in protecting white supremacy.

Conclusion

In *Reunion and Reaction* and *Origins of the New South,* C. Vann Woodward argued that southern lawmakers in the late nineteenth century were confronted with the choice of aligning either with the Northeast and its policy of state-supported industrial development or with the West and a more agrarian-oriented set of policy priorities, based on easy credit for farmers, rigid regulation of corporations and trusts, and state support for farmers rather than manufacturers. Throughout the 1880s, he argued, the region's conservative leadership was able to herd "the mass of Southerners up the right fork" and to ensure a commitment to the industrial and economic policies supported by the Northeast, at least until the revolt of the People's Party resulted in a reorganization of the Democratic Party along lines favored by the agrarians.[41]

This interpretation has long been subject to criticism, especially by questioning whether there was ever any broad support in the South for Republican political economic priorities. Lucius Lamar, who served in Grover Cleveland's cabinet and was appointed to the Supreme Court in 1888, might have been an enthusiastic supporter of the commercial and economic policies of the Northeast, but he was hardly typical of most southern Democratic elected officials. Instead, most of the South's congressional delegation opposed not only Republicans but the northeastern Democrats who led the conservative wing of their party. Southern Democrats constituted the core of any agrarian voting bloc in Congress, and most of their legislative efforts during this period were focused on advancing policies that historians and political scientists generally associate with the agrarian agenda.[42]

The most important political question in the Gilded Age, however, was not whether the South would go right or left, but whether it would remain a solid bloc within the Democratic Party. If not, on what terms might a small but stable Republican party rebuild in the region? As envisioned by Republican strategists, there were opportunities for the party to expand in the South by making issue-specific appeals to conservative and moderate constituencies, by renewing federal protection of African American voting rights, or by supporting the independent and fusion movements that posed a perennial threat to Democratic ascendancy. In hindsight, these visions might seem hopelessly naive, and certainly they were in tension with one another.

In point of fact, the end of the century did bring about the breakup of the Solid South, though perhaps not in the form once anticipated. Although it had been the conservative Deep South states that seemed to offer the most potential for renewed southern Republicanism, ultimately it was the border states that broke ranks with southern solidarity.

Southern Democrats, after all, had their own agendas to advance. Their wishes certainly included the reconfiguration of the country's political economic order and the redirection of federal funds into the region, but above all they sought to maintain southern autonomy about race. Although the Democratic Party may have been a constraining factor impeding some of the region's political economy and spending objectives, the party was universally recognized in the South as the most effective vehicle to ensure that the national government would not interfere with the prerogatives of their state governments to define the region's civic and social hierarchies.

When the different goals of the white South came into conflict, southern lawmakers had to weigh possible material gains against the threat to the racial order. How, we now ask, did southern lawmakers evaluate alternatives, weigh priorities, and strategically intervene in national politics to pursue their objectives?

4

Tests of Priority

The South can never catch up with the North in the march of progress, when hundreds of millions are annually expended in the latter section, of which the South is compelled to pay her proportion. . . . We had best take all the Blair bill can give, all that the rivers and harbors legislation can draw out of the Treasury, and Southern representatives [should] join all the jobs on hand and all that may be proposed.[1]

The Southern people, sensible of their unfortunate condition at best, have exhausted their ingenuity to imagine some way by which they could use their political influence without injury to themselves.[2]

Having stopped short of a fundamental reorganization of southern relations of property and race, congressional Reconstruction concluded with African Americans in a condition of vulnerability to the political resurgence of Confederate nationalists and the withdrawal of northern protection. Concurrently, the return of southern Democrats to Congress required them to confront the economic devastation wrought by the Civil War. Long-standing financial markets and patterns of labor relations had been disrupted, and the reorganization of American capitalism left the South both absolutely and relatively poor, enmeshed within a postwar political economy that drained money from the region with little to show in return.

During the last quarter of the nineteenth century, southern Democratic lawmakers tried to use their influence in Congress to guarantee the right of their state governments to regulate matters of race without federal oversight, and to advocate a framework for American commercial development in which the South could recover the economic agency and wealth it had known before the war. These goals, however, posed fundamental dilemmas for southern legislators. Should they press their demands for a reconfigured political economic order even at the risk of rupturing their alliance with northern Democrats, whose support would be essential to defeat any renewed efforts to protect black civil and political rights and whose numbers were needed to forestall a return to unified Republican government? If they were able to forge temporary coalitions with western and midwestern Republicans or with conservative Republicans from the Northeast, how should they weigh the value of new spending and regulation against insistent Republican demands for some measure of protection for the rights of black southerners? Could they forge alternative political coalitions that did not force this choice and in which their situational allies would accept the bedrock premise of white Democratic politics in the South—the maintenance of home rule and white supremacy?

How southern members of Congress navigated these dilemmas fundamentally shaped the course of American political development. In the end, they were able to make only modest headway in moderating the terms of the nation's economic policies by reducing internal taxes, securing access to federal infrastructure spending, and beginning the process of regulating interstate corporations. Overall, the nineteenth century closed with the economic priorities of the South almost as neglected in national public policy as they had been before 1877. The tariff was as high as ever, the gold standard was firmly established, the spending patterns of the federal government were even more biased toward the non-South, and the new Interstate Commerce Commission (ICC) and the income taxes that southern lawmakers had helped establish and impose had been rendered ineffective or nullified by Supreme Court decisions.

As the twentieth century began, southern legislators had failed to reconfigure or substantially modify an economic order that reinforced a dependent, even colonized, region. By contrast to this catalog of economic failure, the white South had enjoyed stunning political success in the area of race and home rule, which we detail in chapter 5. Its congressional representatives had not only defeated renewed efforts to establish the federal supervision of elections but managed to repeal almost all remaining Reconstruction legislation, reshaping the priorities of the Republican Party in the process. As a result, southern legislators could make fresh choices at the turn of the century that redefined the Democratic Party without having to worry about how the potential loss of support in the Northeast might open the South to the threat of a new Reconstruction.

On November 10, 1860, James Chestnut of South Carolina withdrew from the U.S. Senate in order to participate in his state's secession convention. By the close of the congressional session four months later, thirteen southern senators had withdrawn, along with twenty-nine representatives. More would follow as Virginia, Arkansas, North Carolina, and Tennessee withdrew from the Union. The result of this sectional absence in Washington was exaggerated power for the Republican Party, which occupied approximately 60 percent of the votes in each chamber, enough to easily overrun the remaining Democratic minority.

Republicans took full advantage of the situation. They passed an ambitious legislative program directed at not only winning the war but enacting policies long supported by the different constituencies of former Whigs and western Democrats who made up the party's base. As soon as southern Democrats began to withdraw, Congress passed the Morrill Tariff, which sharply increased import duties with the explicit purpose of providing economic protection to particular industries. Congress next asserted federal control over the country's currency and financial system, assuming an authority that had long been opposed by the southern-dominated Democratic Party. A series of Revenue Acts established the country's first income tax, imposed a direct tax on property and excise taxes on a wide range of products, and established the Office of the Commissioner of Internal Revenue to administer and enforce the new tax laws.

Republican majorities also passed legislation to directly support the economic activities and investments of individuals, states, and private corporations. The Homestead Act and the Morrill Act, both passed in 1862, provided land to small farmers and to state-established agricultural colleges, setting a precedent for federal support for education while greatly expanding opportunities for citizens and immigrants to acquire productive property. The Pacific Railroad Acts, passed between 1862 and 1865, authorized the construction of a transcontinental railroad, subsidized by land grants to private corporations, and helped revitalize a system of federal support for internal improvements that had been left moribund after decades of Democratic rule. Shortly after the war, with southern states still out of Congress, the Republican Congress passed a Rivers and Harbors bill that appropriated over $8 million to improve the country's coastal and internal waterways, twice what had been spent for this purpose in the previous twenty years, inaugurating a new era in federal support for infrastructure.[3]

The overall impact of these policies on American industrial development is still debated, but it was a widely held belief in the late nineteenth century that they provided the institutional basis for a remarkable economic transformation. "The damnable policy that shaped itself financially from Republican hands is wearing the energy, the enterprise, the very life out of the labor element in this country," declared *Pomeroy's Democrat*. "It made two millions of men to be Bondholding lords over thirty-eight millions of laborers."[4]

The cost of the federal government's fiscal policy, organized without input from southern lawmakers and going against their long-held preferences, was heavily biased against the South. After the war, white southerners complained with good reason that money raised primarily on southern agriculture, grown by black and white labor, was being spent principally in the North on internal improvements that neglected the South, or on military pensions that were available only to those who had fought for the Union. The federal government's policy of actively supporting discrete interests also was widely believed to have contributed to the overweening dominance of railroad companies and monopolistic trusts. By providing support to select industries through the tariff, land grants, and subsidized internal improvements, the nation's government was charged by Democrats with having impeded the operation of the free market to advantage a select few, with the consequence of widening economic inequality and advancing an eruption of labor activism in the form of local and regional strikes.

These disruptions and the variety of problems introduced by the new political economy could be tackled only by congressional action. The core economic concerns of southern constituencies could not be addressed without efforts by their lawmakers to reconfigure this political economic order and the sectional and class conflicts they believed it engendered. Many doctrinaire Democrats insisted that simply reversing these policies would be enough, while others believed that some form of federal regulation was required. "The people of the United States," declared *Pomeroy's Democrat*, "intend to have a new deal." With the end of Reconstruction, the return of the Democratic South to national influence was seen to be the vehicle by which this purpose could be achieved.[5]

Congressional responses to these challenges of the late nineteenth century, however, threatened to separate the South from its Democratic allies and to divide the South into subregions defined by race, geography, and integration into the new political economy. The choices confronting the South had more far-reaching implications than could be contained within the region's desire for a new economic order, since the decisions taken by southern legislators were conditioned by an awareness that federal money and regulations came with the danger of new intrusions. The South's defense of white control did not impinge equally on all issues, nor was it raised at all times. But on key policies related to the revenue, interstate commerce, and the terms of federal spending, these concerns vitally shaped southern preferences, forcing the region's white Democratic legislators to subordinate their economic preferences to stand together to defend home rule, no matter the pecuniary cost. To be acceptable to the region, federal policy, wrote one newspaper, would have to be "liberal in its monetary provisions and well-guarded against Federal interference." "The people of the South," warned the *Macon Telegraph*, should reject the motto "put Federal money in thy purse," as they had a particularly strong interest in ensuring that the "constitutional barriers against centralization" not be swept away.[6]

Efforts to reconfigure the national economy also revealed the limits of southern influence. When southern legislators were able to cultivate nonsouthern allies, Democratic or Republican, they were able to achieve modest policy gains, often while revealing a willingness to compromise that might surprise later observers. When the region was isolated, however, the only tool at their disposal was sustained obstruction, an uncertain strategy when the rules of debate could be changed by majority vote, and one of less use in advancing their own policies against a Republican-crafted status quo.

Here, we examine how southern members of Congress balanced and selected among their contending priorities, how they sought to change legislative institutions to achieve their goals, and how their choices and actions shaped national policy in enduring ways. We examine southern lawmaking across three broad issues: revenue, economic regulation, and spending. In each issue area, the South hoped to achieve changes that would make policy more equitable across the country's regions. Each confronted the South with a set of unpalatable choices, options that the region's representatives ultimately were unable to reconcile.

We look first at the politics of revenue, an issue on which southern Democrats had to make common cause with often unreliable northern allies. Complaints about northern Democratic perfidy had to be balanced, however, against the recognition that pro-tariff Democrats of the North had provided— and might provide again—the critical margin needed to defeat Republican efforts to protect black political and civil rights.

Second, we turn to market regulation and finance, particularly efforts to regulate interstate commerce, break up trusts, and establish a more locally responsive financial system. Although the region's lawmakers could look for support from some factions of the Republican Party, such cross-party alliances were vulnerable to the possibility that Republicans might use the expansion of federal authority desired by the South to mandate civil rights protections or further entrench the power of sprawling interstate corporations.

The final issue area concerns national spending policies. Southern lawmakers agreed that spending patterns were biased against the South, but they often disagreed about whether retrenchment or compensation through new spending programs would be the better way to remedy the imbalance. The former would leave the region impoverished, having paid for northern development with little to show in return; the second could bring a needed infusion of money and investment, but with it the possibility of dividing the white South and legitimizing a new role for the federal government in areas that had long been within the purview of state legislatures.

In sometimes subtle and ambiguous ways, each of these policy areas eventually was implicated in questions of home rule and white supremacy. As much as some white southerners tried to insist that a particular policy position carried no unmanageable danger to regional autonomy, they were forced repeatedly to choose between desired policy goals and the defense of home rule. By the end of the century, southerners in Congress had secured some modest gains in taxation and infrastructure spending, but otherwise had failed to recalibrate the Gilded Age's political economy, having elected at critical moments to defend white supremacy at the cost of their section's underdevelopment.

The Dilemmas of Tariff and Taxation

"New England and the North," complained the *Wheeling Daily Register*, "with their immense wealth, barely feel the burthens of government, whilst the South and the West, bankrupt and overwhelmed, carry all the load." This was a persistent refrain in the southern press in the decades after the Civil War as southern publics excoriated the protective tariff for redistributing money from agricultural exporters to manufacturing sectors of the economy. Because the most important export during this period was cotton, the cost of protection fell disproportionately on southern farmers and laborers, both white and black. Compounding the problem was the fact that 35 percent of the country's internal revenue was raised on tobacco, 75 percent of which was grown in a handful of southern states, and that the "enormous" tax on whiskey and other fermented liquors, though drawn from across the country, was "exacted of an industry of the South and West almost exclusively." Despite holding only 20 percent of the country's wealth, the South paid nearly 25 percent of the internal taxes by 1880: for every $100,000 of wealth, including all property and investments, southerners paid $20 while non-southerners paid $16. This imbalance was especially pronounced in tobacco-growing states such as Kentucky, Virginia, and North Carolina, whose residents respectively paid $758, $670, and $402 per $100,000, more than any northern state other than Ohio.[7]

The disproportionate tax burden was only made worse by postwar policy changes: the Republican Congresses during Reconstruction had committed the federal government to resume specie payment, a measure that reduced the availability of money in the South and West, and it had repealed the inheritance, income, and excise taxes on manufacturing by 1872. Three years later, with Republicans about to lose control over a congressional chamber for the first time since the Civil War, Congress dramatically increased tariff rates and raised the internal revenue tax on tobacco by 20 percent. This "bold, even audacious, defiance of the opposing party," in the words of the New England journalist Edward Stanwood, ensured that the status quo during the next decade of divided government was strongly tilted toward the preferences of Republicans and the industrial Northeast. "In the eyes of southern Democrats," the historian Carl Harris has noted, the changes "perfected a brazenly sectional revenue system, which funneled profits from all consumers into the pockets of northeastern industrialists," while taxing the "southern tobacco farmer and harass[ing] him with obnoxious internal-revenue agents."[8]

Reducing the burden was a core priority of the South's legislators. Yet by the end of the nineteenth century, they generally had not done so, having lowered tax rates modestly on tobacco but having failed to secure a more favorable tariff. The most significant tax bills passed between 1877 and 1901 were the four tariffs passed between 1883 and 1897; the reduction of internal taxes in 1879, 1883, and 1890; the imposition of an income tax in 1894; and the war revenue bills of 1898 and 1901. Three of the four tariff schedules were strongly tilted toward Republican priorities, and the income tax, which southern Democrats had strongly supported for decades, was quickly struck down by the Supreme Court. The South was able to win an important lessening of internal taxes in 1879, but further reductions divided the region's legislators, who debated whether lowering tax rates further would open space for an increase in the tariff. Near century's end, revenue legislation for the Spanish-American War largely undid the region's earlier gains.

What explains this uneven but broadly poor showing? For one, it was northern Democrats whose votes were most likely to be pivotal, and they were more supportive of the Republicans' revenue system. Combined with their aggressive use of agenda-setting offices in Congress, northern Democratic votes stymied most reforms desired by the South. In any case, with Republican dominance of the Senate and the Supreme Court, even when the Democratic House could enact policy changes to the advantage of the South, the final legislation was either unlikely to take the form preferred by southern representatives or vulnerable to challenge from the other branches. One other factor was absolutely essential to why the South did not make greater gains in this area: as important as it was to southern interests to rebalance the revenue system, it never became the paramount priority of southern Democratic members, who repeatedly subordinated their preferences on this issue to the cause of white supremacy.

The Democratic Party in Congress was divided between southern legislators who wanted steep reductions in tariff and tax rates and a faction of northern Democrats who were open to reductions in internal taxes but generally favored the protective tariff. Crucially, these pro-tariff Democrats were frequently pivotal and well situated in congressional positions to block reform.

The top two panels of figure 4.1 plot the distribution of member preferences on the tariff from 1877 to 1887, when President Cleveland tried to make the tariff a matter of party discipline. A large bloc of pro-tariff northern Democrats were located between southern Democrats who desired steep reductions in rates, if not outright free trade, and Republicans who supported either a modest reduction or even more protection.

Although the pro-tariff bloc was only ever slightly more than half the northern party in the House—and about one-third of the small northern Democratic delegation in the Senate—it could exercise disproportionate influence over the content of legislation—effectively deciding which tariff measures would, or would not, pass—because it straddled the party divide. The two panels of figure 4.2 show the probability that the pivotal median voter was drawn from a particular bloc of members in the House of Representatives and in the Senate. Despite the House having a Democratic majority in most of these years, the South had little likelihood of being pivotal.

From 1876 until 1881, moreover, the Democratic speaker of the House of Representatives was Pennsylvania's Samuel Jackson Randall, a staunch protectionist who used his position as speaker, and later as chair of the Appropriations Committee, to block tariff reform. In the 45th Congress, Randall named the moderate protectionist Fernando Wood as chair of the Ways and Means Committee, which crafted a bill that was framed by the principle of retaining protection while modestly reducing rates. Even this proposal was defeated when seventeen northern Democrats voted with almost all Republicans to strike the enacting clause, defeating the bill 145 to 136. When Wood's committee killed tariff revision in the next Congress, the blame was quickly cast on Randall for having formed the committee with "an eye to protection for Pennsylvania." "There will never be any tariff reform while Samuel J. Randall is Speaker of the House and Fernando Wood chairman of the Ways and Means Committee," complained the *Augusta Chronicle*, and Randall made sure that efforts to send tariff bills to a more favorable committee were defeated.[9]

Despite his support for the protective tariff, Randall owed his position as speaker to the support of southern representatives, backing he had earned by organizing the party behind a filibuster that killed the enforcement bill to accompany the 1875 Civil Rights Act. "There never was a minority led with more skill," wrote Virginia Democrat Eppa Hunton in his autobiography, "than the minority [Randall] led in that fight." When it came time to choose a speaker, many southern representatives felt that they could not "vote against the man who had led us so persistently and ably in the filibuster against the Force Bill." In a letter to his constituents explaining why he had supported Randall for the speakership even though they desired free trade, Texas Democrat John Reagan

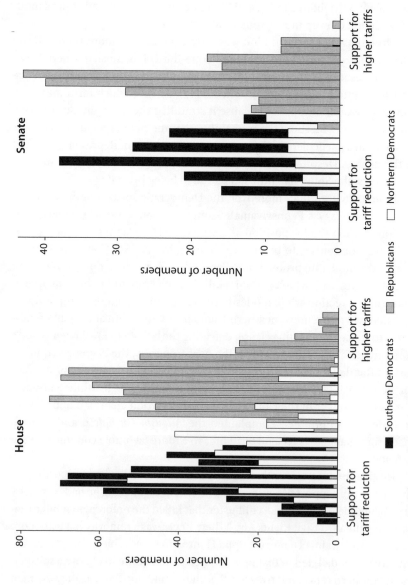

FIGURE 4.1. Distribution of Tariff Preferences, 1877–1887

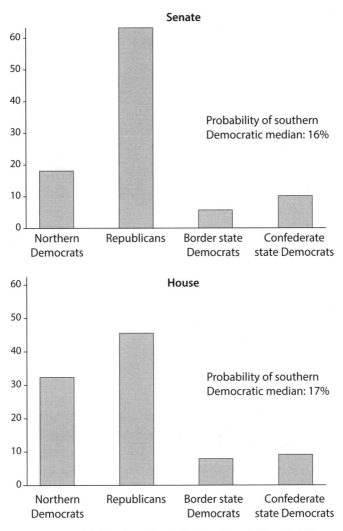

FIGURE 4.2. Probability of Members Being Pivotal on Tariff, 1877–1887

cited Randall's "courage and consummate ability" in organizing the filibuster. Randall, he argued, had "saved the South from untold sufferings and wrongs, and our whole people were profoundly grateful to him for it."[10]

Southern opinion, however, was torn between the need for northern allies and the desire for tariff reform. Many southern Democrats wanted to continue supporting Randall, but believed that "the tariff sentiment in their districts is so strong" that they could "not dare to." In editorials and letters, southerners debated whether tariff reform was worth the risks, with many arguing that maintaining the sympathy of northern Democrats was vital for the South's broader interests and warning that it would be "political folly" for "a solid South to overthrow a Northern Democrat on this issue." So long as Republicans were eager to "revive the sectional issue," the region had to support Randall and give leeway to northern Democrats. The *Daily Picayune* warned that any effort to defeat Randall would be paired with recent election violence in Danville, Virginia, to revive support for federal intervention. When a pro-tariff Pennsylvanian was accused of party disloyalty by a southern representative, he sternly pointed out to his colleague that he "had seen the time when the Southern Democracy needed his vote," a reminder that was repeated by southerners who asked how any southern Democrat could "cast his vote against Randall when he remembers . . . the gallant fight he has always made in our behalf when our interests were involved." It was the South's role, the *Macon Telegraph* remarked resentfully, "to assure Democratic ascendancy in her State governments" and to follow "the lead of Northern Democrats who have helped her in this respect."[11]

It was only by persuading white southerners that the threat to white supremacy had receded that southern lawmakers were able to open space to assert their policy preferences and demand that the congressional party be responsive to their tariff priorities. Tariff reformers sought to rally support in the region to depose Speaker Randall in 1882 in favor of conservative southerner John Carlisle as speaker. "Sectionalism was dead," Carlisle reassured anxious southern Democrats, and "no effort could revive it." In this changed context, he argued, the South could assert its policy priorities within the Democratic Party without needing to worry too much about provoking northern animosity. As southerners grew more confident that they could secure regional autonomy in matters of race, they felt a diminishing loyalty to Randall, whose support for an economic program they considered to be colonial in nature grated.[12]

With the strong support of southern representatives, Carlisle was elected speaker in 1883. He quickly assembled a reformist Ways and Means Committee that reported a proposal to reduce rates. Given that Republicans controlled the Senate, prospects for passage were always slim, and soon they were dashed completely when the House voted to strike out the enacting clause, 159 to 155, with 37 northern Democrats led by Randall voting with nearly every Republican. Despite having a majority of nearly 80 votes in the 48th House and the backing of most of the House leadership, the Democratic Party could not pass a relatively moderate bill of intense significance to the party's southern majority.[13]

The South's inability to build a stable majority for tariff reform can be juxtaposed to the region's relative success in reducing internal revenue taxes in 1879, 1882, and again in 1890. Crucially, these were not southern Democratic victories alone. The 1879 reduction of the tobacco tax was supported by every southern Democrat, but also by every voting southern Republican, a rare instance of bipartisan sectional unity. With a unanimous South in favor of the reduction and a "powerful tobacco lobby ... from all sections" watching the vote closely, additional votes of northern Democrats were unnecessary to defeat the 90 percent of non-southern Republicans who voted against the reduction. The lowering of the tobacco tax, declared the *Daily Picayune*, was a "simple act of justice" to the "Southern and Western interests." Tobacco taxes were reduced further in 1882, when southern representatives secured an amendment to a Republican revenue bill reducing taxes on manufactured tobacco; southern senators from both parties voted unanimously to include a substantial tax reduction on unprocessed tobacco, which passed 34 to 32. All Democrats, North and South, voted with Republican senator William Kellogg of Louisiana, the Readjuster senator William Mahone of Virginia, and John P. Jones of Nevada against every other Republican. When Mahone subsequently proposed lowering the tax even further, the South was divided, with many believing that this would cost it the support of the pivotal Republican senators and, in changing the whole character of the bill—"making it a bill to relieve farmers as well as capitalists"—would have been too much for northern Democrats to support. This legislation passed the House, with most northern Republicans voting against a small majority that included almost all southerners of both parties plus a handful of northern Democrats. A cohesive region, with the support of northern Democrats, in short, was able to secure policy change against the opposition of non-southern Republicans.[14]

After the tax reductions of 1879 and 1882, the South became less uniformly supportive of reducing internal revenue. In June 1884, 70 percent of southern Democrats voted to block consideration of a bill that would have eliminated the tax on tobacco entirely, while substantial majorities voted against similar proposals in 1885 and 1886. A key reason for this shift was the fact that internal revenue had become yoked to tariff reform: the strongest case the Democrats had for reducing the tariff was the ballooning surplus in the Treasury, an argument that would have been undercut by internal revenue reductions. Proposals for tax relief came increasingly from Republicans, while even "high protectionists" were reported as having become "quite as inimical as the South" to internal revenue taxes, "since the large income thus obtained caused the treasury to be less dependent upon the import duties." The Republican platform of 1888 advocated repealing the tobacco taxes as "an annoyance and burden to agriculture," and if this measure proved insufficient to ending the surplus, they proposed "the entire repeal of internal taxes [over] the surrender of any part of our protective system." While a large contingent of southern Democrats continued to support reductions in internal taxes, especially on tobacco, the party's southern leadership decided to prioritize the tariff. Accordingly,

Speaker John Carlisle of Kentucky began to "strangle every bill to reduce or repeal the tobacco taxes, refusing even to allow the House to consider them." In the 49th Congress, the House Ways and Means Committee simply refused to report internal revenue bills, leading Republicans—and some southern Democrats—to support sending such bills to the Appropriations Committee or even the War Claims Committee. Although Carlisle justified his position by noting that he supported taxing luxury items, such as alcohol and tobacco, before the essentials taxed by the tariff, it was widely acknowledged that he did so because he was "a free-trader" and "for no other reason."[15]

Southern political leaders now began to use their growing control over House organization to enforce some measure of party discipline on the tariff. In 1885, Randall's Appropriations Committee was divested of its authority over most appropriation bills, depriving him "of the influence he is supposed to have had over that committee in favoring measures of protection" and sending a "clear signal to protectionists that there was no room for them in the Democratic party." The "Solid South" was credited with having "compelled the Northern Democrats to declare for 'a tariff for revenue only'" in the party's platform of 1880, and an even clearer signal came when President Grover Cleveland endorsed a "radical reduction" of the tariff in his annual address to Congress in December 1887. This speech, frequently credited with inducing heightened levels of party unity on this issue, was drafted with the close assistance of southern Democratic leaders. The commitment to far-reaching tariff reform that it embodied reflected the persistent efforts by southern Democrats to win the adhesion of their party.[16]

Upon his reelection to the speakership in 1887, Carlisle appointed Roger Q. Mills of Texas, an "avowed free trader," chair of the Ways and Means Committee, and he stacked the rest of the committee with a disproportionately southern membership. The tariff advanced by the Democratic leadership proposed sharply lower rates, and marked the party's clear commitment to fight the upcoming presidential election on the question of tariff reform. In the Committee of the Whole, Democrats traded votes and raised rates on some items, but despite hundreds of amendments, every Republican proposal was defeated. The bill passed the House 163 to 152, with only four Democrats dissenting. Although the bill was radically transformed by the Republican Senate and died in an interchamber stalemate, the Democratic Party finally was united.[17]

One measure of the emerging Democratic unity on this issue is shown in figure 4.3, the standard deviation in individual ideal points for both parties, centered on each tariff roll call and divided between the period before and after Cleveland's December 1887 speech. The impact of Cleveland's intervention was nearly immediate, although Democrats would remain more heterogeneous than Republicans on the tariff until the number of northerners in the

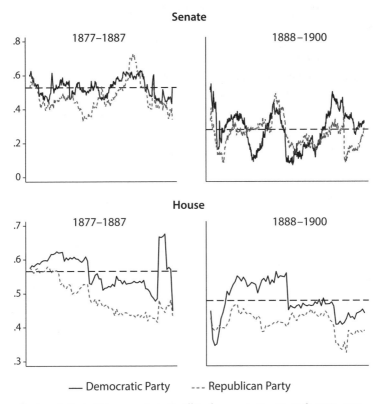

FIGURE 4.3. Party Heterogeneity in Tariff Preferences in Four Periods, 1877–1900. Dashed horizontal line is the average for the Democratic Party during a given period.

party was reduced considerably in the mid-1890s. But from 1888 onward, both parties were more united in their voting on the tariff, which increasingly came to define the party cleavage.

There was a second factor limiting the ability of the South to secure policy change on this issue. The region's lawmakers were intensely committed to reduce the tariff, but it never was their paramount policy priority: unlike Republicans, who ranked the tariff first in an ordering of their priorities, southern Democrats prioritized the race question above all else. The Republican preference to retain the protective tariff, modified as necessary to accommodate changed economic and political conditions, was at least as strong as the South's desire for a "tariff for revenue only," and Republicans were not hampered by the existence of a higher-priority concern to which they would subordinate this objective. This asymmetry gave Republicans a distinct advantage in legislative maneuvering: because they were more willing to change the rules to offer control over the agenda to the pro-tariff party leadership, they could effectively counter southern Democratic obstruction.[18]

During the dying days of the 47th Congress, the Republican majority in the House made aggressive use of the Rules Committee to modestly reduce tariff rates while favoring Republican constituencies, alleviating public pressure for reform without sacrificing protection while making more extensive revisions more difficult for the incoming Democratic House. The Republican House leadership had been struggling to pass a tariff bill, and southern obstruction had made the prospects for success increasingly slim as the session was quickly coming to a close. The Senate, near equally matched between the parties, with Virginia's Readjuster senator William Mahone providing the Republicans with a pivotal vote, had successfully passed a tariff revision, but southern Democrats, by staying unified across over two hundred amendments, had substantially recrafted the bill to be much more in line with their priorities. The Senate bill was unacceptable to the Republican leadership, and the House was unable to pass a bill of its own.

To resolve this dilemma, Republicans agreed on a strategy by which the Rules Committee would report a special order allowing the House to suspend the rules by majority vote and bring up the Senate bill for consideration, which in a very different form had already passed the House the previous session. The House thus could vote to disagree with the Senate and request a conference, where the Republicans would be empowered to rework the tariff to their liking. The rule change, operative for this bill only, would effectively end the possibility of southern obstruction. It would also set the precedent that the Rules Committee could modify the rules for individual bills, a precedent that would eventually became essential to the operation of the House.[19]

When the Republicans were in charge of a unified government from 1889 to 1891, they again made aggressive use of the Rules Committee to advance a protective agenda. Future president William McKinley of Ohio had the committee report a rule opening the bill to amendment for one week, after which debate would be cut off and all pending amendments abandoned. The ostensible purpose of the rule was to deny opponents an opportunity to delay, but everyone recognized that its practical effect would be to ensure that few if any Democratic amendments would be considered. The rule worked as intended. A series of amendments were quickly offered by McKinley, who as chair of the reporting committee had priority to offer amendments. These and a few others were all that could be considered when the allotted time ran out. The one feature of the tariff to draw substantial southern support was yet a further reduction of the tobacco taxes, a provision included in the bill by McKinley and supported by a majority of southern members. In most other respects, however, the Republican House leadership was able to pass a bill that moved policy even further from the preferences of southern Democrats.[20]

As we discuss in chapter 5, southern obstruction was much more effective in the Senate, where southern lawmakers engaged aggressively in a new Republican proposal to safeguard elections. As debate over the bill stretched out over more and more months, Republicans began to threaten southern Democrats with changes to the rules that would considerably limit the ability to obstruct, or even abolish the filibuster outright by creating a procedure for cutting off debate by majority vote. In early August, the Republican conference debated whether they should change the rules to end debate, and Henry Blair of New Hampshire and others began introducing cloture proposals to this effect. "A bad rule," wrote the *Philadelphia Inquirer* in support of the Blair proposal, "is best broken, and it is plainly the duty of the Senate to provide once and for all for a limitation to filibustering debate."[21]

Ultimately, however, the rule change would not be necessary. After seven weeks, the Senate agreed by unanimous consent to end debate on the tariff. For the South, this decision, by which it effectively accepted passage of a rate-increasing tariff bill, was framed by the paramount goal of defeating the federal elections bill, which would have established a permanent system of federal supervision of congressional elections across the country. In a deal worked out by Matthew Quay of Pennsylvania, the Democrats agreed to end debate on the tariff in exchange for a delay in the consideration of the federal elections bill until the next session, which would lessen the bill's chance for passage. As one senator remarked, "There has been an agreement here whereby the Democratic party agrees to forego practically its opposition" to the tariff, "and of course we are bound to presume that that was done in order that something else might be had which was desirable." Others were less oblique: Republican senator Orville Platt called Quay's proposal "a weak and cowardly surrender," while the *Philadelphia Press* would later attack Quay in an editorial cartoon showing him striking the bargain with a southern senator, while African Americans were being shot and lynched in the background: the federal elections bill, noted the *Press*, "will be killed as thoroughly as the Southern colored vote."[22]

Republican senator Nelson Aldrich gave notice that if the Democrats reneged on the agreement, he would move to amend the rules to close debate. The South was confronted with a stark choice—either continue to delay a vote on the tariff and risk uniting the Republicans behind a rule change that would greatly facilitate enactment of a law that directly threatened white supremacy, or accept a tariff bill that would further commit the federal government to a protectionist policy paid for largely by southern agriculture. The choice was made. Faced with the peril of renewed federal supervision of elections, south-

ern Democrats allowed the tariff to come to a vote, trading their policy preferences concerning the tariff for better odds to preserve white supremacy.[23]

The final reason the Democratic South was unable to achieve and sustain
policy gains in this issue area was its inability to muster regional unanimity.
This failure was largely a reflection of the perceived need to not fracture the
white vote by imposing a strict party orthodoxy on economic issues. At various moments, Republican strategists came to believe that the tariff as an
issue could be crafted to build a new Republican Party in the South. The *New
York Herald*, for instance, mapped out the potential terrain of southern support, seeing in "Louisiana and parts of Alabama, North Carolina, Georgia,
Tennessee, Arkansas, Missouri, Maryland, Virginia, and even of South Carolina . . . congressional districts favorable to the protection policy," while the
election of a Republican from that "stubbornly democratic little state, West
Virginia, show[ed] the tendency of opinion in the south." Indeed, representatives from districts with southern industries that might benefit from the
tariff were keen to secure accommodations, with Alabama's representatives
supporting higher tariffs on pig iron and lumber, Louisiana's committed to
tariff support for sugar, Mississippi senators wanting support for unprocessed jute, and South Carolina, Arkansas, Texas, and Louisiana supporting
tariffs on rice.[24]

Figures 4.4 and 4.5 sketch out some of the variation in southern Democratic positions on the tariff and internal revenue. Figure 4.4 shows the estimated ideal point on tariff and taxation policy among Democrats, by state and
region, with the dashed line showing the mean Democratic position. The
higher the score, the more a region's representatives voted with the Republicans. Figure 4.5 projects these scores onto a map of the country, for both the
Senate and House, with dark gray indicating strong support for the tariff or
the revenue system relative to the mean Democratic position and light gray
showing strong support for reducing tariff and taxation rates.

With some exceptions, the base of southern Democratic opposition to the
revenue system lay in the Cotton Belt, especially the Mississippi Delta. For
their own reasons, including an important manufacturing sector and specific
agricultural products that could be easily accommodated by a protective tariff,
Louisiana, Maryland, and West Virginia were generally more supportive. And
though South Carolina may have sought to nullify the tariff in the 1830s, by
the 1890s its representatives were generally more pro-tariff than the rest of the
region: "If we are to have this stealing from the people by protected interests,"
argued Senator Ben Tillman, "I want my share for South Carolina, and I am
not ashamed to say it."[25]

The Republican Party also found evidence that it could foster a cross-
sectional coalition in the election of Republicans from Louisiana and Alabama
on pro-tariff platforms. Republicans Hamilton Coleman of Louisiana and

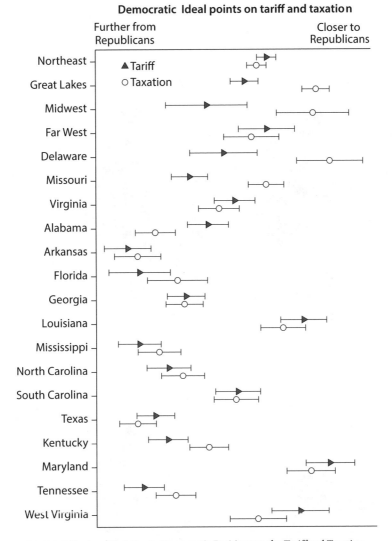

FIGURE 4.4. Regional Variation in Democratic Positions on the Tariff and Taxation

George H. Craig, John McDuffie, and William Aldrich of Alabama each suggested a route toward an alternative Republican Party in the region based on appeals to local industries rather than on a national commitment to the region's African American population. Coleman, for instance, was elected on a tariff platform and strongly opposed the federal elections bill, which he denounced as liable to raise the specter of "negro supremacy." In this spirit, white Republicans in Birmingham organized the White Protective Tariff League to wrest control of Alabama's Republican Party away from a biracial group that

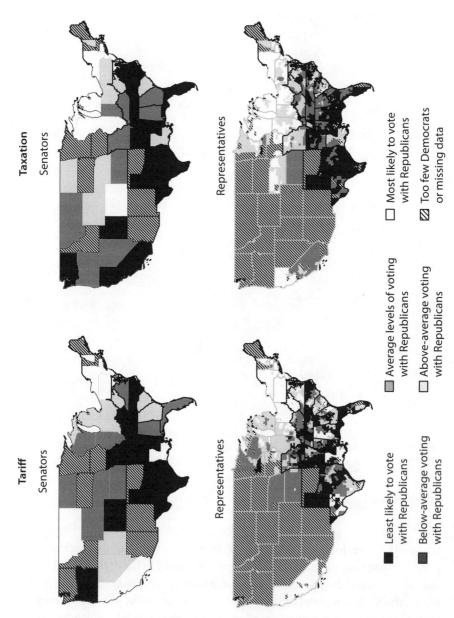

Tariff

Senators

Representatives

Taxation

Senators

Representatives

☐ Least likely to vote
    with Republicans

▨ Below-average voting
    with Republicans

▨ Average levels of voting
    with Republicans

☐ Above-average voting
    with Republicans

☐ Most likely to vote
    with Republicans

▨ Too few Democrats
    or missing data

FIGURE 4.5. Map of Variation in Democratic Positions on the Tariff and Taxation

supported the cause of African American civil and political rights; the league ultimately sent several representatives to Congress.[26]

Republican hopes of a bisectional party founded on the tariff were ultimately dashed, as outside of the border states only a handful of Louisiana and Alabama constituencies would actually return Republicans on a tariff platform. Yet precisely because there was at least some threat to the unity of the region's white vote, the southern Democratic Party was flexible on what otherwise would have been party orthodoxy. Democrats who supported Republican tariff positions were generally unwilling to break with the Democratic Party as the necessary guarantor of white supremacy, and there was little effort by other southern Democrats to oppose them. Precisely because the Democratic Party relied on the solidarity of the white vote, they were unwilling to enforce the strictures of a "tariff for revenue only" on deviant representatives. As Louisiana governor—and future pro-tariff senator—Samuel McEnery remarked in endorsing President Cleveland in 1888, "Louisiana will cast its vote by a large majority for him without reference to any tariff issue raised in the campaign. Democracy means with us white supremacy, and this we will not yield for any other issue."[27]

The resulting freedom of southern Democrats to vote with the Republicans on the tariff undermined the legislative effectiveness of the region at key moments. In 1894, Maryland senator Arthur Pue Gorman organized a bloc of Democratic senators from both the North and South to oppose the tariff bill passed by the Democratic House. While the House passed a bill that reflected "Southern public opinion on the great question," southern defectors in the Senate, "mainly spokesmen for Alabama and West Virginia coal and iron and for Louisiana sugar," joined with Gorman to radically revise the bill and "[scuttle] meaningful tariff reduction." House Democrats reluctantly passed the Senate bill, while President Cleveland denounced the "communism of pelf" that had made a Democratic reform a measure of "Republican protection." Although rates were generally reduced, it was seen as an abysmal failure for a party that had been committed to a revenue tariff since the 1870s and for the first time in decades controlled the Senate, the House, and the presidency.[28]

The South would lose the little it had won a few years later when a unified Republican Congress passed the Dingley tariff of 1897, raising rates to their highest level ever. Ironically, this was one of the few times when there was a high likelihood that the pivotal median senator on the tariff would be from the South. The left panel of figure 4.6 shows the estimated location of the median pivot, as well as the several senators surrounding this pivot. The right panel shows the likelihood that a given senator was pivotal. Because of a single senator, Samuel McEnery of Louisiana—the politician whose Democratic affiliation was almost exclusively based on his support for white supremacy but who otherwise was a mainstream Republican—the 55th Congress had a 73 percent

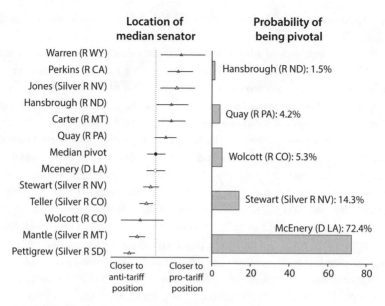

FIGURE 4.6. Median Senators on the 1897 Tariff

chance of having a southern median member in the Senate. McEnery supported the tariff increase, and the bill was enacted into law.

As the twentieth century began, tariff rates were higher even than when they had provided a key source of income for the Union government during the Civil War. The successful reduction in tobacco taxes was an important gain, although it was most important to communities in North Carolina, Kentucky, Virginia, and Tennessee. A more meaningful rebalancing of the tax burden would require more dramatic measures.

The South found such a vehicle in the income tax. Only "the income tax would equalize the burden," argued the *Atlanta Daily Constitution*, "nothing more." Although not all southerners supported renewing the tax—"part of the reconstruction timber that the republicans gave years ago"—the region's representatives generally gave the measure their full support. When all but four southern Democrats in the House joined eight of ten southern Republicans in instructing the Ways and Means Committee to report a graduated income tax in 1878, northern newspapers remarked that "at last the North is beginning to feel the effect of the power of the solid South, organized and aimed at the wealth of the large cities and the North generally." Again in 1879, all but three southern Democrats would vote for an income tax, voting to suspend the rules and pass a bill reestablishing the measure. Finally, in response to southern representatives' demands, an income tax was included in the tariff bill of 1894. While some southern conservatives remarked that "they knew of no scheme more thoroughly antagonistic to Democratic principles" than the "socialistic" graduated income tax, they were forced to acknowledge that it had broad support in a region that was carrying an unfair burden of the tax load and whose citizens increasingly were attracted to the Populist movement.[29]

Southern senators defended the tax against both northern Democratic and Republican opponents, defeating efforts to lower the deduction—which would have made it less likely to pass—to exempt income from federal, state, or local bonds, to exempt corporations, to allow corporations to deduct dividends paid to individual stockholders, to exempt lineal inheritances or inheritances between husband and wife, to exempt gifts, and to exempt income gained from rental of real estate; they also voted unanimously against a motion to strike the tax altogether. Despite the opposition of key northern Democratic constituencies and the skepticism of President Cleveland, southern lawmakers succeeded in retaining the income tax in the final law. While northerners "complained that the income tax is a sectional tax," southern lawmakers and newspapers responded by saying it was the only measure that could help balance the fiscal burden, as "over fifty millions are drained from the South each year to pay pensions." If the tax bore more heavily on the North, it was only "because the protective system dictated by the North and East had concentrated the wealth of the country in those sections."[30]

Success would be short-lived. In 1895, the Supreme Court ruled the income tax to be unconstitutional. Other than tariff reform, the income tax was the South's most consistently promoted and demanded fiscal policy in the late nineteenth century. Unable to build a stable national majority in support of the former, southern legislators had to watch in vain as their tax success was overturned in a sectional five-to-four decision: five northern justices lined up in opposition to the tax, voting against the three southern justices, joined by one non-southern justice.[31]

Northern Capital and National Regulation

"Mill fires were lighted at the funeral pile of slavery," declared Benjamin Harrison in his inaugural address in 1889. "The emancipation proclamation was heard in the depths of the earth as well as in the sky; men were made free, and material things became our better servants." For many Americans, particularly in the South, the material things had instead become the masters, as the railroads came to dominate commerce and constitute the material face of the exploitation of their region by the industrial Northeast, the "hydra-headed monster" that had placed "its iron heels" on the region, the "vampire that is feeding on the life blood of our industries and trade." In response to growing anger among their constituents, southern lawmakers pushed for legislation to restrain the economic and political power of the sprawling corporations, taking the lead in opposing the legislative subsidies and benefits provided to railroads but also in trying to regulate interstate railroad companies and using the power of the federal government to rein in monopolistic trusts.[32]

Southerners had several complaints against the railroads, most of which they shared with other farmers in the "peripheral" regions of the United States. In response to competition, railroads had begun to enter into pooling arrangements, cartelizing the market and creating local monopolies through which they could extract more favorable terms from small farmers. They were also offering rebates and discounts to large producers, subsidized by small producers, and they were discriminating between long and short haul rates, favoring "competitively situated shippers and receivers at major transportation nodes against 'captive' shippers" in the interior. But southerners' grievances went well beyond the railroads. A process of vertical integration was under way that soon would result in a radically different industrial landscape, one in which over one hundred distinct sectors were each dominated by a single firm. Through trust agreements, and later through the institution of the holding company, the new monopolies of the Gilded Age were slowly coming to dominate markets and politics. "This age of corporation trusts and combines in which we live," announced one former Democrat turned Populist, "is debauching our politics, corrupting our laws and destroying our government; making a wreck of our liberties and paupers of our people."[33]

The regulation of the national economy was a central plank in the southern Democratic policy agenda. Notwithstanding that most southern Democrats continued to insist on "states' rights" principles, they also were increasingly willing to see the federal government assert a more active role in regulating the railroads and prohibiting the formation of monopolistic combinations. This activism was fraught with dangerous potential. By clothing the federal government with the authority to regulate the national economy, the door might open to mandates that would prohibit discrimination in accommodations on the basis of race, or even regulate the type of combinations that southern planters routinely engaged in to suppress the wages of their largely black workforce. Despite this fear, southern lawmakers did not simply oppose any and all enlargements of federal authority. Instead, they championed federal regulations that might further the specific concerns of the region's farmers, consumers, and small shippers even as they sought to carefully define their scope to preserve control over the South's agricultural workforce and its system of racial domination.[34]

From his position as chair of the House Commerce Committee, John Reagan of Texas came to be one of the most important policy entrepreneurs regarding the regulation of interstate commerce. He drafted legislation, assembled bipartisan and cross-sectional coalitions, and negotiated compromises between supporters of a federal commission empowered to arbitrate cases and supporters of his own preferred measure of statutory prohibitions with criminal and civil liability. Coming from a cotton district in his state's Black Belt, Reagan had served as postmaster general of the Confederacy, a position that often had placed him in an antagonistic relationship to the railroads, but in which he also encouraged the building of new lines that would more effectively penetrate the southern countryside. An early advocate for a new departure by the Democratic Party after the Civil War, he had urged his fellow Texans to retrospectively denounce secession, to extend limited voting rights to African Americans—a move that would "save us from universal negro suffrage"—and to rally behind a coalition of moderate Democrats and Republicans who could avoid the imposition of military government.

From 1875 to 1891, Reagan led the fight in Congress for legislation to "control the powers for evil of the seventy-five thousand miles of railroad in this country"; these powers, he argued, had been used to corrupt the legislative process in the states and the nation and dominate over the productive classes. Controlling these powers, in his view, required strict prohibition of the various activities that gave the railroads an unfair advantage in their dealings with small farmers and shippers. These limits included outlawing the so-called pooling agreements that cartelized the market; prohibiting rebates and rate discrimination, for both similar or long-haul/short-haul services; mandating the public posting of all rate schedules; and making the officers and directors of the railroads personally liable for violating the regulations.[35]

The vision of regulation drafted by Reagan—a position characterized by statutory prohibitions with little room for executive or judicial discretion—would inform southern demands for the remainder of the century and into the next. It looked to impose regulations on railways involved in interstate commerce without simultaneously establishing a federal commission with an open-ended mandate to coordinate industry and arbitrate differences between railroads and shippers. Enforcement was to be accomplished not through appointed supervisors or a national bureaucracy, but by citizens empowered "on the basis of clear prohibitions, to take railroads to federal district courts . . . and to sue before local jurors to recover damages."[36]

Figure 4.7 shows the probability that the legislators of different states and regions would support the different Reagan versions of the interstate commerce bill, either on final passage or in preference to weaker measures originating in the Senate. Democrats from the Northeast were out of step with their party, but the only southern representatives to join them in opposition were from South Carolina, who objected to the expansion of federal authority. In every region, Democrats were more supportive of the bill than Republicans, and southern Republicans were more favorably inclined toward Reagan's bill than many of their copartisans from other regions.

Over the course of the 1880s, however, southern lawmakers were forced to accept a potentially more expansive bureaucratic agency than Reagan and

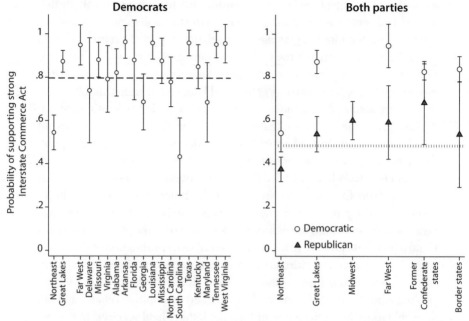

FIGURE 4.7. Support for a Strong Interstate Commerce Act by State and Region. Dashed line is the probability for Democrats, dotted line for Republicans.

other southern Democrats had envisioned. Forging a legislative majority in support of regulations required bringing on board conservative and moderate Republicans in the Senate who worried that strict regulations would "destroy the commerce of New York, Boston, Philadelphia and Baltimore." Charles Francis Adams Jr., the conservative son of the former Free Soil vice presidential candidate, grandson of former president John Quincy Adams, and director of the Massachusetts railroad commission, drafted legislation that would create a federal commission authorized to regulate the railroad industry through admonitions and legislative oversight. Its overarching purpose was to help manage and reduce the heightened competition that had roiled the industry, and it quickly found favor with business interests and Republicans in both chambers.[37]

Given the Senate's preference for an administrative agency, southerners were forced to choose between prioritizing their desire for effective control over the railroads and their anxieties over the dangers implicit in empowering a central authority that could exercise discretion in regulating interstate commerce. One danger, emphasized repeatedly by Reagan, was that discretionary agencies would become heavily reliant on expert opinion, which the railroads would be able to muster in abundance. The economists and lawyers who worked on behalf of the railroads, he worried, would overwhelm the commissioners and advocates for stricter regulations.

FIGURE 4.8. John Reagan (left) and James O'Hara (right). Courtesy of the Brady-Handy Collection, Library of Congress and the Special Collections Research Center, University of Chicago Library.

But there was another danger that weighed on the minds of southern lawmakers, one that had long informed, without strictly dictating, southern opposition to centralized federal authority. Reagan's initial bill narrowly defined interstate commerce as that which was "wholly or partly carried on any railway or other means of transportation as a part of one continuous carriage from or to any foreign nation or country, or from one State or Territory into another State or Territory of the United States." This definition, said Reagan reassuringly, "leaves nothing to be guessed at."[38]

But if the white South could use federal authority over interstate commerce for its own purposes, so too might black southerners. In 1883, the Supreme Court struck down the 1875 Civil Rights Act, which had prohibited the denial of equal accommodations in inns, public conveyances, and places of public amusement, as not authorized by either the Thirteenth or Fourteenth Amendment. The Court had left open, however, the question of whether Congress, "in the exercise of its power to regulate commerce amongst the several States, might or might not pass a law regulating rights in public conveyances passing from one State to another."[39]

During consideration of Reagan's interstate commerce bill the next year, African American representative James O'Hara, Republican of North Carolina, would call on the Congress to do just that. O'Hara introduced an amendment to the interstate commerce bill that would have required any person who purchased a passenger ticket to travel across state lines to receive "the same treatment and be afforded equal facilities and accommodations as are furnished all other persons holding tickets of the same class without discrimination." It was the last two words that provoked southern opposition, as it suggested that railroads could not separate passengers by race even if the accommodations were equal. O'Hara argued that the authority for his proposal was the same as that which southern Democrats claimed for their bill, that "if Congress has the right to regulate the using of the vessel, it certainly has the right to regulate the using of the cars, and if it has the right to regulate the using of the freight cars . . . then it must certainly follow that it unqualifiedly has the same right to regulate the use of passenger cars."[40]

Although Reagan had to concede that Congress had the power to prohibit discrimination or the segregation of passengers, other southern Democrats did not. Charles Crisp, a Georgia Democrat who later would become speaker of the House, warned that the O'Hara amendment "goes even further" than the "civil-rights bill or social-equality law" struck down by the Court. Ethelbert Barksdale of Mississippi argued that if the amendment did not bar separate accommodations, then it was irrelevant, but that if it was interpreted as doing so, it would be struck down by the Supreme Court. Clifton Breckinridge distinguished between a right to have the same accommodations for the same fare and the right of railroads, for public convenience and safety, to segregate on the basis of race. The first, he insisted "is commerce. The other is society." A broad prohibition of discrimination, argued Hilary Herbert of Alabama, would be a deprivation "of the natural right to give equal accommodations in separate cars."[41]

Reagan insisted that the amendment was not germane, as it concerned passenger rail rather than freight. But he also seems to have initially been confident that it would be defeated by a House with a Democratic majority, and so he did not raise a point of order against its consideration. His mistake became clear when, to "the utter horror of Reagan and the other Southern Democrats," their northern copartisans started voting with the Republicans. Reagan became sufficiently alarmed to rush over to the clerk's desk to follow the count and was left stunned when it became clear that the amendment was going to pass. Recognizing that the bill was now in a form that was no longer acceptable to its southern supporters, Reagan moved to adjourn.[42]

The next day, after an effort to reconsider the vote was defeated, Crisp proposed an amendment stating that nothing in the act would be "construed as to prevent any railroad company from providing separate accommodations for white and colored persons." Robert Smalls, an African American representative, former slave, and Civil War hero, provided a quick response. Smalls remarked that he was pleased that this amendment was being offered by a representative from Georgia, because while his own state of South Carolina provided genuinely equal accommodations, he wanted the House to know "that colored men and women do have trouble in riding through the State of Georgia." African Americans, insisted Smalls, had "no objection to riding in a separate car when the car is of the same character as that provided for the white people." But when an African American traveler "reaches the State of Georgia," the train would stop on some pretense and "we always find a crowd coming into the cars and asking us, not very politely, to go out; and if we do not go out peaceably we are put out by force."[43]

A number of southern Democrats regretted that the Crisp amendment—unlike that offered by O'Hara—explicitly mentioned race and color; they preferred a substitute that would allow railroads to "classify passengers as they may deem best for the public comfort and safety." The substitute was supported by most southern and northern Democrats, and when this passed the South was almost unanimous, with only two white southerners from Baltimore and St. Louis dissenting. Northern Democrats, who had split 43 to 19 in favor of the O'Hara amendment, now voted 48 to 23 to allow segregation in interstate commerce, with no mention of race. Nathan Goff, a Republican from West Virginia, next proposed to add to the substitute the proviso that no discrimination could be made on account of race or color. "We sit here as their equals," he said, referring to O'Hara and Smalls, "and before the law and Constitution of our land they are our equals." This too passed, with a handful of representatives from Baltimore, St. Louis, and New Orleans and one from Georgia providing the only southern Democratic votes in support: whether these votes were sincere is unclear, but John Nicholls of Georgia voted for the amendment and against final passage. Again, thirty-nine northern Democrats provided the needed votes, and again Reagan moved to adjourn.[44]

The next day brought the fight over the O'Hara amendment to a conclusion. Barksdale offered a final provision stating that provision of "equal accommodations" would not constitute discrimination, prompting laughter from Republicans. This passed with only four southern and eighteen northern Democrats voting nay, alongside every Republican. Forty-six northern Democrats provided the eight-vote margin for victory. Again, the only southern Democrats willing to support equal accommodations were from urban areas, and only two of them would ultimately support the bill's passage. A final amendment was offered providing that separate and equal facilities would not be related to race and color, which failed 114 to 121, with only northern Democrats and Republicans voting for it. An additional measure of security was assured a few weeks later when National Hammond of Georgia proposed an amendment that no case brought under the act could be removed from state to federal courts. As the amendment was "in the interest of the Jim Crow car," Robert Smalls insisted upon a quorum call and upon the yeas and nays. Ham-

mond's amendment passed 128 to 89 and was supported by all but three southern Democrats and opposed by every southern Republican but William Cul-
bertson of Kentucky. Hammond would nonetheless vote against the bill,
which he attacked for being "the first effort ever made by Congress to legislate
as to the transportation of passengers on land, except in the civil-rights bill,
which has lately been declared unconstitutional."[45]

Often treated as a cynical effort to kill the bill—Reagan's biographer called
it the railroad companies' "ace in the hole"—O'Hara's amendment in fact reflected a sincere effort by its author to reestablish some measure of protection
for African Americans in the wake of the recent Supreme Court ruling. A year
earlier he had introduced a proposed constitutional amendment to empower
Congress to "protect citizens of the United states in the exercise and enjoyment of their rights, privileges, and immunities, and to assure them the equal
protection of the laws," and soon after he introduced bills requiring equal
treatment in pensions for blacks and whites and regulating restaurants and
other public places in the District of Columbia. A few years later, O'Hara
would request a congressional investigation into the Carrolton Massacre, in
which dozens of African Americans in Mississippi were killed. What was surprising was not that O'Hara would offer such an amendment, nor even that it
would find broad favor with Republicans. What was surprising was that his
proposal would find support among northern Democrats, most of whom
would ultimately vote for the bill's passage: twenty-five of the forty-three
northern Democrats who voted for the O'Hara amendment also voted for the
bill to pass, while only nine who had voted for the amendment voted against
the bill.[46]

Although there were probably some Democrats, North and South, who
supported the amendment in order to kill the bill, contemporaries mostly
understood northern Democratic support as an extension of their recent efforts during the 1884 presidential campaign to cultivate support among northern black voters. Robert Smalls urged those northern Democrats "crying out
that they are going to be the best friends of the colored man" to continue
supporting the substance of the O'Hara amendment. Republican Roswell Horr
mocked northern Democrats for the dilemma of following through on their
campaign commitments and voting their partisan loyalties and personal
preferences:

> Instead of adopting such measures with cheerful countenances they sit here
> and look like men going to a funeral. Why this despondency? Why this
> feeling that takes possession of you gentlemen in reference to this great
> question upon which you claim to have taken such advanced ground? You
> are certainly the best friends of these people, are you not? You all meant
> what you said, did you not?

Whether they meant to do so or not, pivotal northern Democrats provided the votes needed for passage of both the O'Hara amendment and the bill itself a few weeks later. As expected, the bill as amended was radically altered in the Senate committee, with Reagan's scheme of explicit legal prohibitions replaced by an administrative commission. On the first amendment, southern senators unsuccessfully tried to remove the entire section pertaining to "Jim Crow" cars, and the next day Republicans—with the support of two northern and two southern Democrats, the latter probably looking to kill the bill—were able to strike the clause establishing that separate cars would not constitute discrimination. The O'Hara amendment was restored to its initial form, making it all but impossible that the bill would pass the southern Democratic–dominated House.[47]

The Interstate Commerce Act eventually would become law two years later, with an empowered commission that the South opposed; the legislation retained, however, the specific prohibitions on rate discrimination and rebates that they strongly championed. Reagan's version of the bill was silent on passengers, but in conference he was forced to accept a broad and vague prohibition in the Senate bill against giving "any undue or unreasonable preference or advantage" or to subject any person, company, firm, corporation, or locality to "undue or unreasonable prejudice or disadvantage," a clause that covered rate discrimination as much if not more than race discrimination. In all, southern lawmakers had achieved a large share of what they had demanded, and they had ultimately succeeded in passing an interstate commerce bill that did not carry a clear prohibition on racial segregation and hierarchy. But they had been put on notice of the dangers implicit in their efforts to authorize a more active role for the federal government in regulating interstate commerce. This would not be the last time that the white South's lawmakers had to weigh their desire to restrain the corporate power of the railroads against the cause of white supremacy.

The effort to rein in corporate domination of the national economy had a close parallel in efforts to reconfigure the nation's financial system, which southerners claimed had been arranged by the Republican Party to operate "in the interests of the money power and the monopolists, and against the working people, against the productive enterprise of the country, against the interests of the multiplied millions of the South." The American financial system of the post–Civil War era rested on the massive bond issues that had financed the war. Federal bonds, in turn, sustained a new system of national banks in which nationally chartered banks were authorized to issue currency backed by bonds deposited in the U.S. Treasury. To ensure that the new nationally backed currency displaced the older system of state-bank-issued money, a tax on state bank notes was imposed that worked to gradually push these notes out of circulation. During the war, these moves toward centralizing the financial system ironically had been accompanied by a fracturing of the country into three separate monetary regions: the Pacific coast remained on the gold standard, the Northeast and Midwest moved to the fiat standard based on the greenback, and the South adopted the Confederacy currency. But beginning in 1873, the federal government was committed to resuming the gold standard, a decision that was widely blamed for a profound contraction of the currency and deflation that hit southern and western states most severely. "That money is scarce in the whole country and more particularly in the south and west," complained the *Dallas Morning News*, is "admitted by every one," and the "withdrawal of greenbacks and demonetization of silver in favor of the banks and bondholders" had brought "financial distress and ruin upon the people."[48]

Almost every facet of the system provoked southern resentment. As contemporaries recognized and numerous economic historians have confirmed, federal banking policy, even if not wholly responsible for the South not being reintegrated into the country's capital markets after the Civil War, did not encourage reintegration. Capital had flowed freely between the two regions before the war, but afterwards southern interest rates "generally exceeded northern rates and at times were twice as high as rates in New York City," while the economic shocks that accompanied failures in the cotton crop or lower-than-expected international demand led to capital flight from the region. By requiring payment in U.S. currency for obligations contracted in Confederate currency, southern banks were almost all forced to close after the war, "while the statutory requirements for erecting national banks and the dearth of capital in the region severely restricted the reemergence of banking institutions." Particularly hated was the state-bank tax, which southerners perceived as impeding the reemergence of a regional banking system. As one prominent Virginian noted in 1875, by destroying the state banks, "the national banking law has virtually deprived the South" of the resources it needed to extend credit. "Had the south been able to substitute national banks in their place as was done in the North, the evil would have been slight. But under a system which requires heavy deposits of federal bonds the Southern people, who were not the owners of such bonds, were deprived of the ordinary facilities of credit." Only in 1900, when capital requirements were introduced for national banks, would monetary policy encourage the expansion of credit in the region.[49]

Given that bonds were held primarily in the Northeast, southern opposition to federal banking policy tended to stress the injustice of channeling the country's currency toward one section of the country. Table 4.1 shows the amount of federal bonds of all classes held in different regions in 1882. New York clearly possessed the lion's share, although on a per capita basis the District of Columbia was more important. But the South, especially the former Confederate states, and the Midwest owned relatively few bonds, either in the

TABLE 4.1. Distribution of Federal Bonds, 1882

Region	Amount	Per Capita	Bondholders per 100,000 Persons	Average Holding	Percent with More Than $10,000	Percent with Less Than $500
New York State	$210,264,250	$41.37	291	$14,204	8.5	23.5
New England	$70,862,059	$17.67	664	$2,662	2.7	40.7
Mid-Atlantic	$48,327,210	$8.93	242	$3,683	3.9	37.4
Great Lakes	$32,818,409	$2.93	79	$3,719	3.8	40.8
West and territories	$14,673,506	$7.71	39	$5,465	7.3	27.0
Border states	$14,198,009	$2.57	47	$29,114	5.4	28.6
District of Columbia	$12,419,050	$69.92	1,327	$5,269	2.7	46.2
Former Confederacy	$10,678,650	$0.82	15	$5,366	7.9	22.6
Midwest	$3,143,250	$0.82	20	$4,147	4.4	26.8

Source: Robert Porter, *Report of the Valuation, Taxation, and Public Indebtedness in the United States, Tenth Census* (Washington, DC: U.S. Government Printing Office, 1884), 492–501.

aggregate or on a per capita basis. In the former Confederacy, there were only two thousand bondholders, with some states having as few as sixty. Ownership of bonds in the South was even more concentrated than it was in the rest of the country, reflecting the fact that much of the debt had been taken on to pay for the Civil War. As a result, a relatively small number of southerners, often recent migrants to the region, owned a disproportionate share of the federal bonds held in the region. The debt that had financed the defeat of the Confederate South now posed an obstacle to the region's economic development as well as the access of the region's small farmers to credit. "In this contest," wrote the *Georgia Weekly Telegraph*, "the South will join hands heartily with the West, and for the following palpable reason: In the East the government bonds are principally held."[50]

For southern Democrats, this was a clear case of class legislation, especially since the hated tariff and revenue policies were used principally to make payments on this debt. But these arrangements also provoked deeper worries about the corruption of democratic government among Democrats in the North and South. The two thousand national banks, complained Allen Thurman of Ohio, were located in every state and in most districts, and "acting openly or in secret," they were able "to influence legislatures, Congresses, and thousands of voters."[51]

Southern, midwestern, and western politicians and public figures offered a variety of solutions to what they saw as the pathologies of Republican finance. Democrats, for instance, insisted on the need for fiscal retrenchment in order to create space for reducing tax payments without necessitating new bond issues, while southern Democrats frequently demanded that interest payments on bonds be taxed and called for repealing the tax on state bank notes. Some Democrats were even willing to accept greater expenditures to avoid paying a penalty for early repayment to bondholders.

The most important policy proposals centered on expanding the currency supply by returning to unbacked greenbacks or the free coinage of silver, an issue that had broad support in the South and in western regions but was anathema to the industrial and commercial Northeast. When 70 percent of southern Democrats and 83 percent of the still-important contingent of southern Republicans helped passed the so-called Inflation Bill of 1874, it was met with a prompt veto by President Ulysses S. Grant. Southern Democrats unsuccessfully supported remonetizing silver in 1876, failed to defeat the Specie Resumption Act in January 1875, and were defeated in their efforts to block the rechartering of the national banks in 1882. Their frequent efforts to repeal the tax on state bank notes "won support from only a few western Democrats and never came near success." But southern Democrats did successfully support the Bland-Allison Silver Coinage Act in 1878, which did not allow for free coinage but nonetheless roughly doubled the currency base during the 1880s and brought about a much-needed infusion of money into the region. "The principal strength of the silver faction," regretted *The Nation*, "is in the South," which consistently supported legislation to expand the currency for the next two decades.[52]

With some exceptions, positions on financial questions were closely related to those on regulating corporations. Both issues brought the South into a voting alignment with western and midwestern Republicans, while modestly dampening the degree of partisan voting with northeastern Democrats. The left panel of figure 4.9 shows the similarity in voting on three issue areas for four regional-partisan pairings. The right panel shows the ideal points of Democratic representatives and senators on the issues of monetary policy and business regulation. While the South voted more like the West than the Midwest on money, and vice versa for business regulation, both issue areas saw the region voting at high rates with Republicans from outside the Northeast.

Economic regulations had required southern Democrats to try to balance their support for more active federal involvement against the priority of resisting possible federal encroachments on white supremacy, but debates about the financial system did not have the same implications. Repeal of the state bank tax or modifications to the National Bank Act largely aligned with a traditional states' rights position but did not obviously impinge on the region's racial hierarchy, nor did an expansion of the currency bear in any clear way on the scope of federal authority in local affairs. As a result, southern papers were relieved to report, the Republicans could not reasonably expect to be "in the least assisted by denouncing the secession leaders, or by charging the Southern Democrats with inhumanity" for their position on this issue. It was an issue

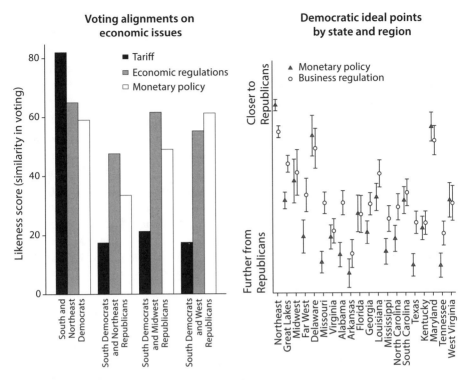

FIGURE 4.9. Voting Alignments and Democratic Ideal Points on Economic Issues

on which they could safely take a position without worrying about a "bloody shirt" backlash. Southern Democrats also saw in an expanded currency a policy issue that not only would benefit their constituents but might allow them to deflect the appeals of the third parties that threatened to make inroads in the region. A growing number of Democrats were arguing that the financial demands of the Greenbackers and Populists were "perfectly sound Democratic planks" that could be achieved without consenting "to the surrender of States' rights and to the initiation of a great commune." The conservative *New Orleans Daily Picayune* adamantly opposed the policies of the Greenbackers, but even this paper suggested that some common ground could be found.[53]

Even though the financial system seemed to be an issue that did not directly threaten the South's racial order, the region's lawmakers nonetheless had to weigh these priorities against each other. The need to retain northern Democratic support once again limited the leeway within which they could maneuver. As Richard Bensel has written, "Democratic platforms tacitly endorsed the gold standard as a concession to the eastern wing of the party while Democrats in Congress consistently provided heavy majorities for its abandonment." The Democratic Party nominated Grover Cleveland for president despite his having been excoriated by Democratic and white Republican papers in the South for signing a school integration act as governor of New York. Shortly after his election, Cleveland revealed himself to be a strict supporter of the gold standard and ignored pleas from pro-silver Democrats, led by John Reagan, who were urging him not to make his position known until he had weighed their arguments.[54]

Once Cleveland's views became known, gold Democrats tried to circumvent Missourian Richard Bland's Committee on Coinage, Weights, and Measures. Bland, who served as chair or ranking minority member of the committee from 1883 to 1895, had steadfastly refused to advance any bills to limit silver. With the support of President Cleveland and other gold Democrats, Samuel Randall carefully drew up an amendment to suspend silver coinage in the Sundry Civil Appropriation Bill of 1885, an amendment that he believed—with the help of a sympathetic presiding officer—would not be ruled out of order. Bland argued that "it is too near the end of the session" and that he and other silver members could easily "filibuster until after the 4th of March." By a large majority, the amendment was struck, and Randall beat a hasty retreat, leaving Reagan to complain that "Cleveland is preparing to defeat himself before his inauguration" and to worry that the president's cabinet would be totally in the control of the "gold-bugs." "Reagan, Bland, Blount, Mills, and [other silver men] will stand on the defensive. They expect war from the start." The next year, Bland proposed a measure to allow unlimited coinage of silver, which he knew could not pass given Cleveland's now open and vociferous hostility. Samuel Dibble, a South Carolinian gold Democrat from the port town of Charleston, proposed an amendment suspending free coinage, which failed by an overwhelming margin. And when the Senate authorized the coinage of silver to take the place of retired national bank notes, the administration intervened to guarantee that it would be "smothered in the Committee of Ways and Means."[55]

Cleveland's stance on the tariff helped him retain his southern allies in 1888, but the reported "hostility to him among the older Democrats of the Bourbon sort" was said to be "decided and unforgiving," with the party having to fear "the existence of a Southern element which will not vote at all which does not like Cleveland." But the need to nominate a presidential candidate who could carry the pivotal state of New York meant that the majority of southern Democrats who supported silver were stuck with an anti-silver candidate. Free to support silver bills in Congress, they could not afford to make it a matter of party discipline or to displace anti-silver northern Democratic lawmakers from positions of influence. Despite a vague commitment to bimetallism in the platform of 1884, the convention of 1888 avoided even mentioning the currency so as not to offend Cleveland, "the autocrat of the party."[56]

As long as the Northeast, and New York State in particular, was needed for the Democratic Party to win national majorities, pro-silver southern lawmakers were obliged to accept these constraints. While gold-standard southern Democrats such as Thomas Bayard, Lucius Lamar, and John Carlisle were unable to hold back "the great mob of half-baked statesmen in the House," the opposition of the administration and the recognition that free coinage would hurt the party's electoral chances helped rally a sufficient number of southerners to defeat Bland's bill. Thirty percent of southern Democrats voted against free coinage, the highest level of opposition from the region's lawmakers during this period. Articulating this position, Hilary Herbert of Alabama asked how any southerner could doubt that "in the President and in the success of his administration lay the hope of Democratic ascendance," admonishing "Democrats who seem to think that the hope of the Democracy lay in the destruction of the present administration."[57]

But if the South was tied to the Democratic Party, and thus forced to subordinate the preferences of a majority of its legislators and constituents to the interests of their northeastern copartisans, congressional voting alignments repeatedly signaled the possibility of an alternative coalition with western Republicans and Democrats who strongly supported the remonetization and free coinage of silver. This possibility began to loom larger in southern political debates after the entry of six new western states in 1889 and 1890, with their additional twelve senators and twenty Electoral College votes. Though initially represented by Republicans, at least two of the new states had important silver mining industries, and all of them were suffering from the same shortage of currency as the rest of the West. The entry into Congress of silver Republicans, combined with a mounting wave of foreclosures on farms throughout the plains states, led to renewed pressure for unconditional silver coinage. Instead, Congress took a difference course, passing the Silver Purchase Act of 1890. As desired by the silver-producing states, the law required the government to purchase the silver by issuing special Treasury notes that could be redeemed in silver or gold, depending on the discretion of the treasurer and the request of the redeemer, but it did not provide any means by which this design would expand the money supply.[58]

Western Republicans gave notice, however, that the Silver Purchase Act did not go far enough. Almost as soon as it passed they demanded new legislation to require the free coining of silver. Although most southern Democrats supported this position, an influential minority were adamantly opposed to it, yet nonetheless chose to form an alliance with silver Republicans in order to help defeat the federal elections bill that was being debated simultaneously. After the new silver bill had passed the Senate, the silver Republicans quickly threw their support behind the effort to defeat the elections bill. This coalition of western Republicans and Democrats was vital to the defeat of the bill and would constitute the nucleus around Democratic efforts to make inroads among western voters in the years ahead.[59]

The Silver Purchase Act resulted in a quickening movement of gold out of the country, causing bank runs and the suspension of specie payments, the depletion of the Treasury's gold stock, and the flight of capital from the South and interior to the country's financial centers in the Northeast. The crisis reached a critical stage in the first year of the second Cleveland administration. In the summer of 1893, he called for an emergency session to repeal the act. Pressed by a rapidly deteriorating economic climate, the House quickly acquiesced, although the South was divided and a majority of southern Democrats opposed passage. The situation was dramatically different in the Senate, where southern and western senators launched a filibuster against the bill that would last nearly two months. "There was a belief," reported the *Times-Democrat*, "that certain Southern Senators, not silverites, would either be compelled to vote with the silver Senators now, or at least not to vote against them, in liquidation of Southern indebtedness to the Republican silver Senators who helped defeat the Force bill."[60]

This belief was reinforced by southern senators, who loudly expressed their debt to the western Republicans. Senators from the South could not forget, declared William B. Bate of Tennessee, that "when the Force Bill was lately threatening to dissolve southern society and the forces of sectional passion and prejudice were seeking to upheave our civilization and place all political power under the control of the lowest strata of society," it had been the "Senators from the silver states" who rose up and "and stood manfully firm, an impregnable defense to southern civilization and southern society." He continued:

> Now when the great vital interests of the states whose senators then protected and defended the South are threatened, I know that the grateful and generous people I represent in part of this Chamber, expect that reciprocation of favor and defense, when it can be rightfully and consistently done, which we received from the silver State Senators. For one, I acknowledge the obligation.

The administration demanded the unconditional repeal of the silver purchase law and promised to withhold all patronage from any Democrat who failed to conform, while Gorman assured southerners that "the obligation, which was confessedly incurred, was wiped out by the Southern Democrats when the free coinage bill was passed through the Senate last Congress."[61]

As the filibuster dragged on it became clear that the pro-silver southern Democrats would not vote for repeal unless they were provided with some other legislative accomplishment they could take home to their constituents. In late September, Charles Crisp, the Democratic speaker from Georgia, allowed a bill repealing the remaining federal elections laws to be brought up, infuriating Cleveland, who had promised Republicans that if they supported the repeal of the Sherman Act they could then adjourn the special session without any new legislation. When the president asked him to desist, Crisp is said to have told Cleveland that

> a good many of our Southern friends have voted for your policy to please the bankers and money interests of the East, and we now propose to introduce and pass a bill in which our people in the South are particularly interested. What arrangements your New York friends made with the republican leaders I know not, nor do I care. Our Southern friends are determined that this bill shall go through and that a vote shall be had on it at an early day, whether the republicans like it or not.[62]

On October 10, 1893, the repeal of the election laws passed the House. It was a small but symbolically important victory, one that would do more to help legislators trumpet their having repealed the last of the Reconstruction statutes than it would to prevent any federal supervision of southern elections, outside of the few cities large enough to fall under the law's coverage. Two weeks later, with all hopes of passing a compromise measure dashed by President Cleveland, silverite southern Democrats abruptly abandoned the filibuster, informing their Republican partners that they could no longer continue.[63]

The South had sacrificed its hopes for an expansion of the currency in order to salvage party unity. In the process, they won expanded security regarding home rule and white supremacy, albeit in the form of repealing laws that protected black voting rights that no longer were of consequence. That proved to be the only compensation they would receive for the loss of silver. Despite intimations that the party might support the abolition of the state bank tax, a proposal to do that would be defeated a year later, with 91 percent of southern Democrats and only eleven northern Democrats in favor, against sixty-seven northern Democrats and all but one Republican. When the South supported a new silver bill, it was promptly vetoed by Cleveland, leading to immediate warnings by southern Democrats that this rejection would produce new converts to Populism and encourage demands to form a new party that would "repudiate once and forever eastern domination on financial policies." Perhaps even worse from the perspective of the South, John Carlisle, the conservative former speaker, now Secretary of the Treasury, announced in early 1894 that the country would need to float its first ever peacetime bond issue in order to avoid default. The financial system of the Republican Party, first erected during the Civil War, had not only been preserved but was being consolidated by a Democratic administration.[64]

The demands of the South on the currency were fundamentally at odds with those of the Northeast states, whose votes were pivotal in national elections and whose elected Democratic representatives long had provided the support needed to push back federal civil rights or elections laws. So long as there was a possibility of renewed federal intervention, the South found itself trapped in a coalition with a region that had starkly different economic and financial priorities. After the repeal of the election laws, however, newspapers throughout the South warned that an expansion of the currency "should and will be presented as the ultimatum of the South," with a readiness to overthrow the Cleveland and northeastern wing of the party if necessary.[65]

Alternative Souths

Other coalitional configurations were advanced by the question of who would benefit from federal government spending. The South desperately needed money. While northeastern Republicans were loath to expand the currency, they were eager to spend down the surplus accumulating behind the tariff wall.[66]

Despite the dangers inherent in federal spending, southern lawmakers could not reject federal expenditures out of hand. The stark economic deprivation, widespread poverty, and illiteracy in the South posed deep-rooted dilemmas and opened significant possibilities. One of the period's most ambitious proposals for federal intervention in local affairs, the Federal Educational Bill—more commonly referred to as the Blair bill, after its sponsor, New Hampshire Republican Henry W. Blair—put the South in the surprising situation of disproportionately finding itself aligned with the former Radical wing of the Republican Party; in this position, southern legislators were potentially willing to accept compromises that stipulated how states would spend federal money and even to accept conditions for its equal allocation between the races. This legislative history suggests the possibility of an alternative South in which coalitions with northern Republicans could have been organized around specific issues that struck a compromise between a fading, but still real, national concern for the condition of southern blacks and the local autonomy that was the overarching purpose of white Democratic politics.

The Blair bill was among the most important and far-reaching of several proposals that would have provided temporary and conditional federal funding to states for the purpose of supporting public elementary schools. A more radical proposal had been offered by George Hoar of Massachusetts that would have authorized the federal government to establish local public schools, operating without distinction of race, where such schools had not already been established by the states, to be paid for by the states through a direct tax of real estate valued at more than $1,000. Even during the heady days of Reconstruction, there had been little support for the national government to take on such a direct role in education, and subsequent proposals had exclusively focused on federal money being used to support state public schools. In the 1870s, several proposals were put forward to set up an education fund based on land sales, the investments from which would eventually provide a steady funding stream for state public schools. These ideas were widely recognized as insufficient to meet the educational crisis in the South, where a slowly maturing fund would be of little use given the magnitude of the underinvestment in schools. The white South, insisted one Kentucky representative, would not "educate the negro children" just so that it could "receive the small sum of six or eight dollars to each of our free schools."[67]

Illinois representative John Sherwin introduced a proposal in the 47th Congress to appropriate $50 million over five years to support education, conditional on a state allocating the funds across school systems and districts without distinctions of race. To ensure compliance, an annual state report was to be prepared and sent to the U.S. Commissioner of Education. A state would be excluded from subsequent payments if it was found to have violated these conditions.[68] The Blair bill was introduced for the first time in the same Congress. It offered more money—$105 million over ten years, with $15 million the first year, declining by $1 million each year thereafter—but a more substantial role for the federal government, with supervisors appointed in each state and all expenditures requiring joint approval of the state and federal governments. Both proposals would have allocated money on the basis of illiteracy rates, which would have ensured that the funds would disproportionately be directed to the South. Republicans favored the Blair bill, but the supervisory provision led white southern members of Congress to generally prefer the Sherwin bill. Neither came to a vote.[69]

After the 1882 elections returned a Democratic House majority, Blair recognized that there was no chance that a bill with an extensive supervisory system could pass. He indicated a willingness to drop this feature and set about cultivating support for the bill among southern lawmakers. The controversy over earlier proposals had made clear that southern Democratic support would be conditioned on an acceptance of segregation and on Washington having no direct authority over local schools. Otherwise, the duties of implementing officials would eventually be "prescribed by Congress, and a school system utterly variant from the State school system may be adopted; mixed schools may be established, different books used, a different standard for teachers, and a different course of study for the scholars." "It would be an independent system from the one we have now," complained Henry McHenry in 1872, "for we do not intend to establish a system of mixed schools, leading to a social equality." Republican support would be equally conditional upon there being some means by which the government could ensure that the money was disbursed equally across race.[70]

In 1883, Blair and James Pugh of Alabama undertook an investigation into labor conditions in the South. Black witnesses, as well as a number of white public officials and schoolteachers, expressed strong support for federal government aid to education; African Americans favored greater federal involvement as well, by contrast to whites, who were adamant that any direct role for the federal government would lead the proposal to be opposed even by otherwise supportive southerners. Drawing on this experience, Blair and Pugh drafted a plan to spend $120 million over ten years, allocated equally by race but without any supervision or enforcement mechanism. After Republicans in the Senate objected to the cost and the absence of protection, Blair reduced the sum to $77 million over eight years, inserted more precise language concerning allocation, and added a requirement that the states file annual reports with the Secretary of the Interior, who was additionally allowed to hear complaints that the equal allocation conditions were being violated.[71]

The threat that southerners might withdraw their support led Blair and most Republicans to oppose efforts to strengthen the bill's assurances that the money would be allocated equally by race. When Republican John Sherman of Ohio introduced an amendment to distribute the funds directly to counties, cities, and townships to provide an additional check against states violating the condition of proportional funding, Democrat Lucius Lamar made clear that this would scuttle southern support. He audaciously suggested that this approach would amount to reverse discrimination, evidence that while the federal government "is animated with a desire to benefit and improve and elevate and edify one race, it looks upon the other as an object of distrust and suspicion. It would be the enactment of the color line." Blair and all but seven Republican senators joined with a unanimous South to defeat Sherman's amendment.[72]

Southern senators also did not want to yield responsibility to the executive branch, where they would have less influence than in Congress. Every southern senator supported an amendment to restrict the authority of the Secretary of the Interior to that of simply receiving complaints and reporting these to Congress. Though this proposal failed on a tie vote, the right of states to appeal to Congress against the secretary's decisions was retained. With the support of all but one southern senator, the bill was amended to restrict the scope of information that the Secretary of the Interior could require of states. The bill passed the Senate on April 7, 1884, with the one southern Republican and eighteen southern Democrats voting for and ten southern Democrats against. Southern support was especially strong in the former Confederacy, which voted sixteen to five in favor.

The Blair bill is not usually thought of as a civil rights measure. For its supporters, however, it was understood to be an essential accompaniment to the civil and political rights extended after the Civil War. To "guard the sacred truth of equal rights," wrote Rutherford Hayes, "we must . . . furnish to all our countrymen the means for that instruction and knowledge without which wise and honest self-government is impossible." "In putting the ballot in one hand," argued the *Christian Union*, "we obliged ourselves to put the school-book into the other." The measure was expressly intended to assist southern blacks and secure them in the exercise of their voting rights, described by Mississippi's Lucius Lamar as "the most important step that this government has ever taken in the direction of the solution of what is called the race problem . . . the logical sequence and practical continuation" of the Reconstruction amendments.[73]

But it was a deeply ambivalent and uneven civil rights measure. It retained Republican commitments to nondiscrimination, in the sense of equal treatment, even as it explicitly accommodated segregation and relied on white officials in southern states to achieve the intended result. Making compromises to secure southern support, a majority of the Senate and the Republican Party effectively conceded that school segregation was an acceptable practice within the constraints of the Fourteenth Amendment. The concession, some Republicans acknowledged, had been won through "the superior tact and subtlety of Southern politicians."[74]

Alone among civil rights measures, the Blair bill achieved substantial support in the white South. As such, it presented an alternative route to rebuilding the Republican Party in the region, one that would accommodate white supremacy while furnishing material benefits to southern blacks and whites. According to Albion Tourgée, a North Carolina Republican who later served as lead counsel for Homer Plessy in the *Plessy v. Ferguson* case, "a large party of the very best men—I mean truly best and not pseudo best—will break away and go with us on the 'educational' idea. They need an excuse and that gives them one." Some southern Democrats did just this. Patrick Winston of North Carolina became a Republican in 1883 after the defeat of the Sherwin bill, charging Democrats with "not only fail[ing] to educate our children but refus[ing] to let others furnish the money." As we have seen with the tariff, the southern Democratic Party could be flexible regarding policy choices. Instead of any substantial conversion of white southerners to the Republican Party, what emerged was a cross-party coalition in which the racial egalitarian commitments of Republicans were tamed and confined by compromise with white supremacist Democrats.[75]

Black southerners were emphatic in their support for federal funding and, eager for the expanded educational opportunities the bill promised, proved willing to compromise on the question of segregated schools. White southerners were more guarded, but all evidence suggests that the bill had the support of a majority of this group as well. The bill, it is important to note, received the support of "prominent Redeemer Senators, including Augustus H. Garland of Arkansas, Joseph E. Brown of Georgia, Zebulon B. Vance of North Carolina, [and] Wade Hampton of South Carolina," and was advanced in the

House of Representatives by Albert S. Willis, Democrat from Kentucky. It was repeatedly voted for by a majority of southern senators and endorsed on several occasions by the legislatures of North and South Carolina, Louisiana, Georgia, Mississippi, Virginia, Alabama, and Florida, as well as several state Democratic platforms.[76]

The central reasons for the breadth of southern support was the scale of the problem and the amount of money at stake. The 1880 census indicated that fully 80 percent of illiterate Americans above the age of ten were found in southern states, with 70 percent of southern blacks and 20 percent of southern whites unable to read. By contrast, only 6 percent of the non-southern white population was illiterate. Clearly, the great majority of funds would have flowed to the South. Such funding would have made education an exceptional domain for national spending, prompting a significant redistribution from wealthier to poorer parts of the country rather than the other way around.

Since the return of the South to Congress, southern legislators—Republican as well as Democrat—had tried to secure money for the region through several avenues, most of which failed. Their support for the Blair bill thus reflected the relatively constrained options available to them. The largest spending categories in 1875 were interest payments on the debt and pensions for military veterans (35 and 10 percent of expenditures, respectively), which were distributed disproportionately to non-southerners. We already have seen how the sectional patterning of bond payments troubled many southerners. Even southern conservatives who considered this arrangement to be an unfortunate but unavoidable consequence of having lost the war and who opposed proposals to adjust the debt or pay for it in silver-backed currency, together with more radical southerners, opposed Republican efforts to dramatically expand the pension program to include veterans who had received a disability after the war or to include dependent veterans and their families. Despite the sustained disapproval of a solid South, by 1890 a succession of Republican-sponsored and northern Democrat–supported policy legislative initiatives had produced a dramatically expanded system of Civil War pensions, with sums amounting to nearly 30 percent of the total budget, an increase from $29 million to $107 million.[77]

Moreover, southern efforts to gain a very modest portion of the pension money were beset by sectional animosity. Southern soldiers who had fought in the antebellum war against Mexico had been entitled to very modest pensions if they had incurred a disability. In 1862, Congress struck persons from these pension rolls who had "in any manner encouraged the rebels or manifested a sympathy with their cause." Upon the accession of the Democratic Party to the majority, southern legislators sought to re-enroll their region's veterans to this pension list and provide them with a service pension regardless of their Civil War status, a policy that would have covered fifty thousand southerners. Republicans went on the attack, aggressively accusing Democrats of trying to secure a pension for Jefferson Davis, who had served in Mexico three decades earlier. Otho R. Singleton of Mississippi read a letter from Davis in which the former president of the Confederate states asked "for the adoption of an amendment forever excluding him from the benefits of the bill, if that would aid its speedy passage." This proposal failed amid considerable sectional acrimony, as some southerners leapt to Davis's defense and attacked the amendment as an insult to the South, while others acquiesced to Republican demands that former traitors not receive government support. "We have lost all," despaired James Bailey of Tennessee. "We are poor . . . [and] we will submit to anything that you say rather than to have further enmity or further hostility."[78]

A modest service pension for veterans of the Mexican War was eventually passed in 1887. As southern Democrats secured this small victory, they were unable to prevent passage of the Civil War Dependent Pension Bill, which authorized a disability pension for all injured Union veterans regardless of when they sustained their injury. The bill was vetoed by President Cleveland but passed again by the next Congress, with a majority of northern Democrats siding with the Republicans against all but one southern Democrat in the House and all but five southern senators. This expansion was the single largest increase of the Civil War pension system, a key source of its swelling costs.[79]

The South's lawmakers also were unable to block other fiscal policies that disadvantaged the region, including refunding the direct tax that had been imposed during the Civil War. Backed by most northern Democrats and brought up by Samuel Randall in order to delay action on tariff legislation, the bill proposed to refund states for the direct tax they had been obliged to collect for the federal government in 1861. States that had paid their full share of the obligation would receive a complete refund, while those that had not would be forgiven the remaining debt. Most of the loyal states, South and North, had paid their share of the tax in full, though there were exceptions. Some of the Confederate states also had paid nearly three-quarters of their share, including Virginia, Arkansas, and Louisiana, while South Carolina had paid its entire obligation, largely by the forced expropriation of property during the war. By contrast, Georgia, Mississippi, Alabama, and Texas had all paid less than 40 percent of their apportionment, with Georgia having only paid 18 percent.[80]

Led by William Oates of Alabama, southern Democratic representatives launched a prolonged filibuster against what they considered to be a starkly sectional bill, noting that the South would receive only 28 percent of the funds while the bill was to be paid for by the tariff-generated surplus, which bore disproportionately on southerners. They also insisted that if the direct tax was to be refunded, so too should the cotton tax, which had been requisitioned during and after the war; amounting to over $70 million, the cotton tax had been raised almost exclusively from southern states, compared to the much smaller $17 million obtained by the direct tax. Although northern Democrats initially offered some support to the South, as the filibuster wore on they became increasingly adamant that the direct tax pass without any payment of the cotton tax. Southern Democrats, for their part, were not united in support of the filibuster; representatives from states that had paid a significant portion of the tax broke ranks to oppose it. The obstruction eventually ended, and the bill was passed with all Republicans, as well as nearly 40 percent of northern Democrats and one-quarter of southern Democrats, voting in favor. Though vetoed by Cleveland, the bill, like the pension bill, was passed in the next Congress after an amendment to refund the cotton tax was defeated, with all but two southern Democrats voting in favor against all Republicans and northern Democrats.[81]

A more promising source of federal money was the potential expansion of internal improvements. Federal spending to improve rivers and harbors and build roads, lighthouses, and public buildings never was as starkly sectional as pension spending, but there was a strong distributional tilt nonetheless. During the early 1870s, the bulk of federal spending supported projects in the Midwest, with less than 20 percent of funded projects allocated to the South. "It is a matter of notoriety," claimed the *Picayune*, "that the South has been shamefully neglected heretofore in the matter of internal improvements," and its editorial listed rectification as the top priority that the newly empowered southern congressional delegation should pursue in 1877.[82]

When Democrats gained control of the House in 1875, the South's share of projects and funds improved considerably. For the next several years, the Commerce Committee was "made up in favor of Southern schemes for rebuilding the commerce of the South," with southern chairs assembling large coalitions of western and southern legislators able to command supermajorities and pass these bills via suspension of the rules. Subsequently, the region usually received a proportional share of the funds, and in some years the South was able to carve out a considerably larger share by securing funds for the improvement of the Mississippi River system. In 1882, after extensive flooding of the Mississippi left tens of thousands homeless, Congress passed the most expensive rivers and harbors bill to date, appropriating $19 million, much of which was dedicated to improving the Mississippi below Cairo, Illinois. When added to the more than $5 million appropriated for other regional projects, the South now would receive more than half of the appropriated funds. President Chester A. Arthur's veto was quickly overridden by a coalition of southern Democrats and western Republicans.[83]

Like education, internal improvements was an issue on which an alternative configuration of parties and sections proved possible, with the South achieving substantial gains by cultivating a series of cross-sectional and bipartisan coalitions. Up to 1884, northern Democrats tended to vote most frequently with northern Republicans, and southern Republicans with southern Democrats. But roll call voting was never starkly sectional, for the decisions of southern members reflected how local priorities could cut across sectional boundaries. After 1884, voting became more clearly aligned by party, at least in the aggregate. But on distributive logrolls, including annual rivers and harbors appropriations bills, the South was a consistent—if not always cohesive—ally of the southern, western, and midwestern wings of the Republican Party. Southern Democrats regularly voted with more than 70 percent favoring the bill's passage, while northeastern Democrats were consistently opposed and Republicans, especially from the West, were broadly supportive.[84]

Southern Democrats also pushed to alter the rules to insulate rivers and harbors legislation from the cost-cutting priorities of their northern Democratic copartisans on the House Appropriations Committee. When the House Rules Committee tried to rein in spending by strengthening Appropriations' oversight, requiring a three-quarters vote rather than two-thirds to pass appropriations bills under suspension of the rules, Reagan maneuvered for his Commerce Committee to be allowed to report rivers and harbors bills at any time to the House directly, bypassing the Appropriations Committee altogether. Freed from its oversight, the southern-dominated Commerce Committee could organize cross-sectional and bipartisan logrolls that ensured stable majorities for rivers and harbors bills, thus securing much-needed improvements for the South's infrastructure. Southerners chaired the Commerce Committee and the subsequent Rivers and Harbors Committee in every year the House was controlled by the Democratic Party between 1875 and 1894; in many years, southern Democrats constituted a near-majority of the committee. Undergirded by these institutional developments, internal improvements came to be the one issue on which "the returning southern Democrats truly became and remained a major bulwark of the Republican economic program, avidly supporting the appropriations and hungrily demanding their share."[85]

Despite these legislative successes in winning infrastructure spending for the South, the amount appropriated in most years was relatively small—$3 million in 1878, and $5.7 million in 1896. But with the growing universalism of the sum's distribution—most members were able to receive at least some targeted spending for their districts—internal improvement dollars hardly compensated for the much more substantial aspects of the nation's fiscal policy, which effectively transferred money from agricultural producers to pay for pensions, bond payments, protection, and infrastructure that advantaged other parts of the country. It thus was common to find southern observers despairing that the "the South [could] never catch up with the North in the march of progress, when hundreds of millions are annually expended in the latter section, of which the South is compelled to pay her proportion."[86]

Only a retrenchment of the pension system, its extension to Confederate soldiers on the basis of their service in the Civil War, or an equally generous alternative source of spending could have alleviated these burdens. This uneven distribution of national largesse made the Blair bill, in particular, attractive enough to overcome the anxieties many southerners had regarding a federal role in local education.

The top panel of figure 4.10 shows the amount of money distributed annually to pensioners in 1887. What is immediately apparent is the extent to which these funds were sent to the Northeast and the Great Lakes region compared with the paltry amount distributed to the South, especially outside of the border states. The bottom panel, by way of comparison, shows the likely allocation of Blair bill funds, using the conservative assumption that southern states would not have distributed the money at greater rates to the Black Belt counties where illiteracy was highest. Of the $105 million first proposed by Blair, the South would have received approximately $84 million over ten years. Although this would not have compensated the region for the more than $50 million spent yearly on pensions outside the South, it was the only seriously considered measure that would have alleviated some of the unevenness of U.S. fiscal policy.[87]

Some of the same factors working in favor of the South's congressional delegation in internal improvements also were in play regarding education. Although the region was divided internally, a substantial majority supported aid for education, and both ideological conviction and the prospect of getting some "cherry worth distributing"—"one hundred and five million dollars," Missouri Democrat George Vest observed wryly, "has been thrown into this council of state and the monkeys are grabbing in every direction"—underlay substantial support among Republicans and even northern Democrats.[88]

Figure 4.11 indicates the location of different party and sectional means regarding education in the Senate, from the end of the Civil War to the ultimate defeat of the Blair bill in 1890. During debates about agricultural colleges and establishing an education fund in the 1870s, the average southern representative was located between the Republicans and the northern Democrats. Education policy again became polarized during debates about the Civil Rights Act of 1875, when the desegregation of public schools was on the agenda. By the time of the Blair bill's introduction in the 1880s, the South again strongly supported federal funding for schools, as party lines on this issue had largely collapsed.

The left panel of figure 4.12 shows the relative location of Democratic preferences on education by region and state. The right panel displays the probability that the median member was from a different regional-party bloc in the Senate. Lawmakers from states with large African American populations—the states that would later be said to constitute the "hard core" of the Solid South—

Pension spending by county, 1887

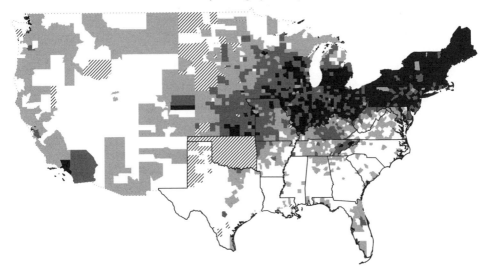

Proposed education spending by county, 10-year period

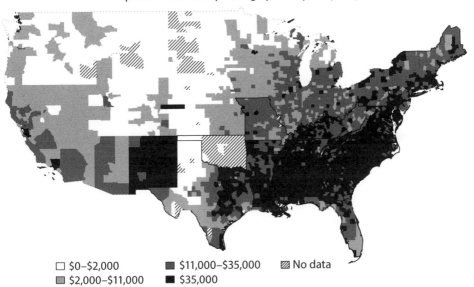

□ $0–$2,000   ■ $11,000–$35,000   ▨ No data
■ $2,000–$11,000   ■ $35,000

FIGURE 4.10. Spending on Pensions and Proposed Spending on Education

were especially likely to vote with Republicans to support the Blair bill. These legislators, along with Republicans, were especially likely to be pivotal. Opponents argued that the bill cost too much, that it was unconstitutional, and that the involvement of federal supervision, no matter how unobtrusive at first, would invite a return to more active federal involvement in southern race

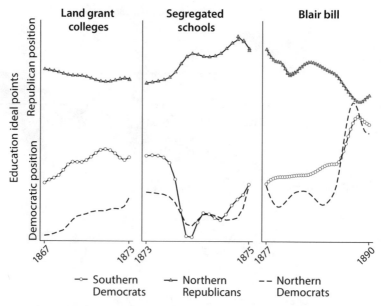

FIGURE 4.11. Development of Senators' Preferences on Education, 1867–1890

relations. James Beck of Kentucky, warning that "Troy fell when her leaders accepted the fatal gift from the Greeks," argued that mixed schools, racial strife, and the return of "Radical tyranny in the South" would be the result of accepting the Blair bill. Senator Ephraim Wilson of Maryland worried that any substantial education of African Americans would reduce their value as laborers, while John Morgan fretted that the extended school term required by the bill would limit the availability of children, black and white, for picking the cotton harvest. But southern opponents of federal aid were in a distinct minority in Congress, and when the bill was reconsidered in 1886 and 1888, southern support either stayed the same or increased.[89]

After several attempts at passage, the Blair bill was finally abandoned in 1890. Supporters of federal aid to education had assembled a bipartisan majority, but it was never large enough to bypass the regular order. By contrast, the institutional changes allowing the Commerce Committee to directly report internal improvements legislation greatly facilitated passage in a House that was otherwise dominated by cost-cutters. Supporters of education were left dependent on the chairs of the House Education, Labor, and Rules Committees, as well as the speaker, to advance the bill. During the 1880s, this support was mostly absent. Thus, although the median members of the House and Senate were supportive, and despite repeated passage in the Senate, opponents who filled key House offices were able to bar the legislation from receiving consideration.

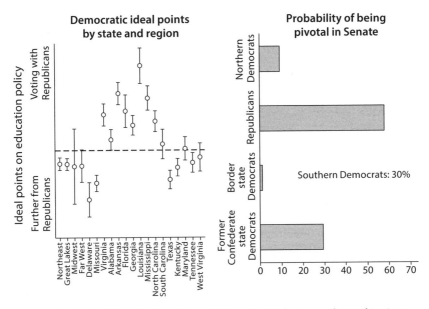

FIGURE 4.12. Regional Variation in the Senate in Education Preferences and Pivotal Regions. Dashed line is the Democratic average.

The bill thus passed the Senate but was never brought up in the House in 1886 and 1888 because of the opposition of the Democratic leadership. In the 48th Congress, Speaker Carlisle, anxious to avoid any reduction of the surplus that might alleviate pressure for tariff reform, successfully resisted attempts by the Education Committee to bring the bill to the floor, and the legislation was left "buried under [the] infamous system of rules on the Speaker's table." In the 49th Congress, Carlisle put together a House Education Committee that was largely hostile to the bill, with only three southern members. As Blair complained in a letter to Frederick Douglass,

> In the last congress power to prevent consideration was vested under the rules of the House in one man unless there was a two-thirds majority. Now that power is placed in committees & what [William] Morrison [(D-IL),] [Samuel] Randall [(D-PA),] or Carlisle could do alone, they now accomplish by constituting an *Education* Committee adverse to the bill by a two-thirds vote.

As expected, the committee refused to report on the bill. Unwilling to concede, an alternative strategy was devised. An identical bill was introduced that was referred to the more sympathetic Labor Committee by majority vote. This committee did not act on the Blair bill until very late in the session, apparently because Carlisle had promised speedy action on a labor arbitration bill that was a higher priority for its members. When supporters sought to bring up the Labor Committee's version during the morning hour, they were defeated by obstruction; when supporters on the Rules Committee sought to fix a date for a consideration of the bill, the leadership of the committee refused to report any rules at all. So long as the Democratic leadership remained hostile, and so long as southern Democrats were unwilling to make a more decisive break with the party over the issue, the Blair bill could not be considered by the House.[90]

By the time Republicans took charge of both chambers in the 51st Congress, southern support had begun to wane because the bill increasingly came to be evaluated in light of the vivid prospect of renewed federal intervention in southern elections. Supporters of federal aid to the South had been careful to stress that the Blair bill would not enable Washington to control local schools, and that there was no danger of children being taught that "old John Brown was a saint or that Lee and Jackson were evil men," despite many southern suspicions to the contrary. But as Republicans campaigned on a platform of more aggressively protecting African American voting rights, support for the bill suffered. By 1890, a "remarkable falling off in the support of the Blair Bill" in the South was being widely reported.[91]

"The Blair bill is losing support all along the line," noted the *Macon Telegraph*. "This is the natural result of the fact that the intent and possibilities of the scheme are being generally apprehended." After he was burned in effigy and accused of enabling a return to Reconstruction, the governor of Tennessee, who had been a supporter, was forced to clarify that his backing could last only so long as it was "stripped and freed of every possible condition of Federal supervision and control" or of any "conditions prejudicial to the local government of the states." The "Bad Blair Bill," it was argued, would provide "in effect for the absolute surrender by the states of the right to control their own schools in their own way"; it also constituted "a means for a new republican crusade in the South." The claim that southerners needed to defeat the bill to "keep their autonomous state governments" became increasingly prominent after the election of 1888. In an article titled "Why the South Rejects the Blair Bill," the *Charleston News and Courier* noted that, were it to support the legislation, it could not "consistently oppose the Chandler, Sherman, Hoar and Lodge bills for the polls." More bluntly, the *Louisville Courier-Journal* argued that "the bill was never intended as a means of education. The purpose of it is the destruction of local institutions, to make way for the further extension of federal power. Back of Mr. Blair—the Greek bearing gifts—stand Mr. Chandler, with his bludgeon, Mr. Ingalls with his torch, and Mr. Sherman with his shot-gun." These men were the principal supporters of the elections bill in the Senate.[92]

As the education bill became increasingly contentious in the South, it also was losing support among Republicans, in part as a consequence of how clear it was becoming that school funds in the Deep South were being unfairly allocated by race. The *Dallas Morning News* noted that "republicans assume that democrats in the south are keeping the negro down" and asked whether they believed the "democratic supporters of the Blair bill [were] less eager or resolute than its opponents to maintain white supremacy . . . ? If the Virginia democrats would take the federal appropriation they must have made their calculations that it will not or shall not lead to negro supremacy." Other Republicans became skeptical of the whole project of federal aid to education, especially as the Treasury surplus significantly declined.[93]

The bill could have survived the loss of some Republicans, just as it could have survived the loss of some Democrats. It could not survive losses from both wings of their uneasy coalition. In 1890, much to the shock and dismay of Blair, the bill failed to pass the Senate after having passed with large majorities on several earlier occasions. A majority of southern Democrats now opposed the bill, and while opposition remained concentrated in the border states, it now included both Tennessee senators, one senator each from Alabama, Louisiana, Mississippi, and North Carolina, and both senators from Arkansas. While the Virginia senators and a few other Deep South senators continued to offer support, the southern coalition fractured. After two months of debate, thirty-two senators voted for a third reading and thirty-six voted against, with a dejected Blair changing his vote to nay so that he might later move to reconsider. A measure that promised considerable benefits to the region became difficult for southern Democrats to defend, for it came to be seen as part of a broader package of reforms intended to renew the active involvement of the nation in southern racial affairs.

Nonetheless, some compromises reached in pursuit of the Blair effort for public education survived the bill's defeat. The Morrill Act of 1890, the second Morrill land-grant college act, was passed into law, providing new money and imposing new conditions on states for support of agricultural colleges. The Morrill Act was intended to place the nation's land-grant colleges "upon a basis of assured support for all time" by providing $25,000 a year to each. Although concerned with higher education, particularly agricultural and industrial education, the law largely followed the lines of compromise laid down in the Blair bill: receipt of funds was conditioned either on the institution not discriminating on the basis of race or on the state maintaining a separate college for African Americans that would receive an equitable division of funds.

But while the 1890 land-grant colleges act had a more detailed and extensive role for federal supervision than had been provided in the 1862 act, which had not included a provision for nondiscrimination by race, it also was considerably less extensive than even the compromised Blair bill supported by southern senators. Blair had required that money received by states with separate schools be apportioned according to each race's proportion of the school-age population, and receipt of funds was conditional upon there being a system of public schools free for all children without distinction of race, "either in the raising or distributing of school revenues or in the school facilities afforded." The Morrill Act required simply that the state legislature propose and report to the Secretary of the Interior a just and equitable division of the funds; the secretary would be entitled to determine whether the state was in compliance, a decision that could be appealed to Congress. The Morrill Act traded less money and a more narrow objective—the provision of higher education facilities for southern blacks rather than support for elementary public schools—for less federal supervision. The bill passed both chambers by large majorities, and with little opposition. With it, the principle of "separate but equal" in education was established in federal law.[94]

Conclusion

During the lead-up to the 1896 Democratic National Convention, New York Democrats warned southern lawmakers not to adopt a silver platform, "to avert the possibility of a Force bill by uniting with the Democrats of the East and the West in framing a platform on which all Democrats can stand." Although not usually framed in such explicit terms, southern lawmakers had been confronting this choice since their return to Congress in the late 1870s. Should they pursue policies that would materially benefit their region or subordinate such efforts to the controlling exigencies of white supremacy?[95]

Benjamin Tillman, the vitriolic one-eyed governor of South Carolina, gave expression to southern resentment at having been repeatedly forced to subordinate his region's racial and economic priorities to the Democrats' northern coalition. To the cheers and hisses of his fellow southerners, as well as Democrats from other regions, Tillman stood before the 1896 convention and, alluding to the secessionist fracturing of the Union in 1860, warned that South Carolina's delegates were "willing to see the Democratic party disrupt[ed] again" in order to "emancipate the white slaves" who had been oppressed by bondholders and the country's economic policy. The South was grateful to northeastern Democrats, he said, but had come to realize that "we were but mere hewers of wood and drawers of water, tied in bondage, all our substance being eaten out." He compared the growth in population and wealth between the North and the South, arguing that the former was developing at the cost of the latter because of the "financial system that the misgovernment of the Republican party has fastened on it." "It is," he said to prolonged hissing, "a sectional issue," and "we of the South have burned our bridges as far as the Northeastern Democracy is concerned."[96]

Tillman was perhaps the most extreme, and certainly the most belligerent, orator at the convention. But the great majority of southern lawmakers and delegates joined him to support a candidate and a platform that explicitly contravened the leadership and priorities of northeastern Democrats. Ninety-two percent of southern delegates voted against commending the Cleveland administration, and the region provided more than half the votes for the convention's extraordinary repudiation of the party's sitting president.

As we discuss in more detail in chapter 6, the South's decision to go with the West left it a beleaguered and isolated minority in national politics and compounded its earlier failure to substantially revise the terms of the nation's political economy. Although the region's white lawmakers had had some success in advancing the material interests of their section in Congress, they had also been repeatedly forced to set aside central economic priorities in order to preserve southern autonomy in matters of race and maintain a national coalition that would sustain home rule. The choices made by southern lawmakers during this period were of extraordinary consequence for American politics, the American state, and its racial orders.

One scholar estimates that the late-nineteenth- and early-twentieth-century tariffs amounted to an implicit tax of 11 percent on exports—a transfer of around 3 percent of GDP, primarily from the South and from consumers, to the industrialists of the Northeast. Given the commitment of the Republican Party, and the lack of support from pivotal northeastern Democrats, it is unlikely that the South could have dramatically altered the country's tariff policy, whether by establishing a tariff for revenue only or by going further toward free trade. But nothing about the specific tariff rates was predetermined, and it is certainly likely that the region could have secured both lower rates—as the 1894 tariff had done—and greater attention to its specific concerns had its representatives not been defeated so handily in 1896. Their subsequent exclusion from national office left the region considerably poorer; unable to revise the tariff in line with the needs of the South; unable to reinstitute an income tax, which had been struck down but which many believed could be resuscitated through slight modifications; and unable to curtail—let alone retrench—the massive growth of the pension system, almost all of which went to recipients outside of the former Confederacy, with only a few migrants, some former black soldiers, and border state veterans included.[97]

But it was the defeat of the Blair bill—the only legislative vehicle that could have realistically begun to compensate the region for the costs it was forced to bear—that perhaps most encapsulated the dilemma facing white southern legislators. Moreover, the costs of its defeat were not borne equally by all southerners: even though southern education systems would generally be underfunded relative to their non-southern counterparts, middle-class white schools would be relatively advantaged, working-class and poor white schools would be disadvantaged, and black schools would be deeply deprived.[98]

Nor was the Morrill Act of 1890, despite its importance, anywhere close to compensation. Between 1890 and 1920, all seventeen southern states would establish or designate a black college or institute as a land-grant college, supporting eighteen of what would become the nation's Historically Black Colleges and Universities (HBCU). These institutions exemplified the opportunities and costs for southern African Americans implicit in the Republican and southern Democratic coalition on education, the coalition that had fought and failed to pass the Blair bill, settling for the Morrill Act instead. The colleges provided an important route for individual advancement, but were hampered from the beginning by unequal funding and unequal status in federal and state law. The Hatch Act of 1887, for example, funded agricultural research stations attached to the 1862 land-grant colleges and was an important source of funding for those schools, but was never ~~was~~ extended to include the 1890 black colleges. Though the 1890 Morrill Act did put all the land-grant colleges on a firmer footing and encouraged greater investment in the institutions by the states, the law required only that states equitably allocate money received from the federal government and made no such stipulation on any additional appropriations they might make. As a result, many states provided the black colleges with the minimum the law required—many did not even do this—while nearly all provided much more to the 1862 colleges. As Robert Jenkins has noted, "genuine state interest was lacking in the colleges' development," and the South would "do only the barest minimum, whatever it had to do to receive its share of the Morrill Act's funds."[99]

Perhaps most telling was the limited scope of the law in its implications for education. The law abandoned the terrain of elementary education entirely. Instead of a broad measure intended to reinforce citizenship—to "guard the sacred truth of equal rights"—federal support for black education would be oriented toward a small class of graduates who mainly would be given practical training in agricultural techniques; meanwhile, efforts by black colleges to teach a broader curriculum were hampered by state legislatures and meager resources. The 1890 Morrill Act, moreover, also restricted the terms of the 1862 act, which had explicitly allowed for liberal arts instruction. When black land-grant colleges sought to provide a collegiate or liberal arts education, they often found themselves forced by state legislatures to back down. Such was the case in 1902 when the Virginia Normal and Collegiate Institute was forced by the legislature to change its name and mission by abandoning collegiate education. The discrimination against black colleges in favor of industrial institutes was implicit in the 1890 law, which referred to "one college for white students and one institution for colored students."[100]

The terms of Republican and southern conciliation endorsed school segregation, effectively accepting unequal allocations in state funding by race with only a minimal constraint on funding decisions; encompassed only a small number of southern blacks; and was intended, if anything, to complement rather than challenge the racial and economic priorities of the region's white population.

By the end of the century, it had become clear that the party of Lincoln no longer would place black rights front and center or maintain the prior generation's broad antislavery and civil rights coalition. Southern Democrats after 1896 might have been an isolated minority, but for the first time since 1860 they would also be secure in the knowledge that they alone would be empowered to set the terms of racial hierarchy and labor practices in their region. For all the defeats they had experienced in the fight to reconfigure the national political economy, for all the concessions they had been forced to make, and notwithstanding the subordination of their priorities to party unity, the region's legislators had been able to secure one overwhelmingly important victory. To this subject we now turn.

5

Racial Rule

There is only one party with the whites of the south to-day. . . . Together we felt the galling chains of the usurper; together we have been the prey of thieves; together we have been relentlessly pursued by the disciples of hatred and vindictiveness, and together we have a score to settle.[1]

"In 1877 we lost all hopes." In his testimony before a Senate committee investigating the emigration of black agricultural workers into Missouri and Kansas, the twenty-seven-year-old farmworker Henry Adams recounted some of the information that he and a committee of black laborers had gathered on working conditions across the southern states. He described how black southerners had endured the Ku Klux Klan, the White Leagues, the "bulldozing" campaigns against black voters, the regular theft of wages and crops by employers and landlords, high rents, increasing taxes, and even "whippings by the old owners." He then discussed the course of action that had been decided by the committee: an appeal to Congress and the president to "help us out of our distress and protect us in our lives and property, and pass some law or provide some way that we might get our rights in the South." If this plea failed, they would instead ask for territory to which southern black Americans could emigrate in order to live "in peace and quiet." Soon the hopes they had for congressional action gave way to a firm determination to leave the South entirely, based on the decided conviction that the "redemption" of the region by the Democratic Party meant that "there was no way on earth" black Americans could hope to better their condition below the Mason-Dixon Line.[2]

Planter control over southern labor and Democratic control over southern elections were closely connected and mutually reinforcing. As the historian

Michael Perman has described this relationship, "with control over the political apparatus" came the possibility of "restoring order and discipline to the black labor force that had been unsettled and agitated because of Reconstruction and its promises." Surveying the political landscape in 1877, Adams saw clearly how Democratic victories were bringing to power a party committed to using the full power of the state to tame black farmworkers: "The whole South—every State in the South—had got into the hands of the very men that held us slaves—from one thing to another—and we thought that the men that held us slaves was holding the reins of government over our heads in every respect almost, even the constable up to the governor. We felt we had almost as well be slaves under these men." Exit seemed the only option.[3]

The willingness of national political actors to intervene in the South's labor system on behalf of black workers through the supervision of contracts or mediation between employers and workers largely had ended when the Freedmen's Bureau was closed in 1872. Afterward, Republicans within and outside of Congress repeatedly drew attention to southern exploitative and racist labor practices as part of a general indictment of Democratic government in the region. Like Adams, they connected southern elections with the oppression of southern labor. As William Hepburn of Iowa noted, the economy of the South depended on access to cheap and tractable labor; thus, black voting was "not altogether a political question" for southern Democrats. "It is an economic question," he explained, "the question of how you can maintain the cheap labor that is necessary to enable you to produce cotton in competition with the cheap labor of other parts of the world."[4]

But it was never just an economic issue. The Democratic Party was winning elections in southern states where the black proportion of the population was small, in states that had seceded and those that had not, and with votes from backcountry whites who had supported the Republican Party during Reconstruction. Democratic gains in the elections of 1874 were attributed by both Republican and Democratic observers to white opposition to the civil rights bill then under debate in Congress, which would have banned segregation in public accommodations and initially prohibited segregated schools. Democratic gains in North Carolina and Tennessee were attributed "to a very general antagonism in those States (as elsewhere in the South) to the Civil Rights bill." The staunchly Republican "mountaineers" of East Tennessee, wrote the *Macon Telegraph*, had accepted "negro suffrage simply because its influence was practically unfelt," but the civil rights bill proposed to "compel personal and social equality, and to begin the process with the children of the poor—of those who can only educate their children in public schools." There was "no proper conception of the depth of violence of popular rage" felt by these Republicans against the bill. The newspaper predicted that "eastern Tennessee, which broke the backbone of the Confederacy, will now resist the North as fiercely as it did the South." Even the Republican *Detroit Tribune* frankly admitted that "there are a large class of white voters in the South who have heretofore acted with the Republican party, but who are averse to what they stigmatize as 'nigger equality,' and who have abandoned the Republican party because it proposed to enforce by the law the provisions of the Fourteenth Amendment to the Constitution."[5]

Restoring and maintaining white Democratic control over state governments, then, was an issue that mobilized geographically diffuse but highly influential economic interests and attracted support from whites of all social strata in opposition to any substantial leveling in the region's racial hierarchy. This was the context in which the "Solid South," based on economic, social, and political white supremacy, mobilized the great majority of white southern voters behind the Democratic Party. With white Democratic control over state governments restored, black claims to equality could be effectively resisted and denied.

Federal intervention, a possibility heightened by the black franchise, threatened these arrangements. During the last quarter of the nineteenth century, black men throughout the South continued to vote and mostly have their votes counted. In some states there was a sufficiently large body of white voters willing to either support the Republican ticket or at least vote against the Democrats. As the persistence of black voting hovered over the white South like a specter, it was widely recognized that any substantial division among whites or any renewal of federal supervision would significantly boost both Republicans and third-party organizing in the region.

Political white supremacy triumphed by century's end. "Home rule" was restored, and the white population could shape public policy without supervision or interference by the federal government. With the defeat of the federal elections bill and the repeal of the remaining Reconstruction-era election laws in the early 1890s, southern Democrats in Congress effectively removed the question of southern elections from the national agenda.

During the pre–New Deal twentieth century, Republican legislators occasionally would raise the prospect of reducing southern representation in Congress under the terms of the Fourteenth Amendment, or the Supreme Court would issue a decision that limited the means by which southern states could restrict their electorate on racial lines, as they did in striking down the Oklahoma grandfather clause in 1915. Overall, however, Republican Party leaders were induced to acquiesce in the consolidation of the southern racial order as a direct consequence of successful strategic behavior by southern political leaders, who persuaded broad public opinion that any renewal of federal supervision would be steadfastly rejected by southern whites and only produce more violence and instability. Whether it agreed or not, the Republican Party had been chastened, and its politicians saw little political advantage in fighting disfranchisement or defending black rights in the South.[6]

These developments emboldened the region's white elite to seek a more severe and permanent solution: the systematic disfranchisement of southern blacks. Black political activism in no way disappeared, but for the first time since before the Civil War, African Americans lacked an influential partner in national politics. They were left alone, without an organized vehicle by which the country's attention and action could be brought to bear on their worsening material conditions, subjection to tightening social control, and near-total exclusion from political power.[7]

Home Rule and the Labor Question

Reestablishing control over the region's black labor force was a central goal of the "redeemer" project. African American organizing and mobility, undergirded by the civil rights and social policies of Reconstruction governments, had threatened planter dominance over the supply of labor by allowing black workers to seek better wages, strike at vital moments in the planting and harvest seasons, and pursue legal and political remedies for the exactions of planters and merchants. Redemption did not, however, "settle the daily contest over labor, as many planters had hoped." Black laborers continued to seek better wages, moving to new employment and participating in strikes for higher payer and better working conditions, and southern planters continued to complain that "the demands of the negro [were] yearly increasing," that "once the farmer controlled labor, now labor controls him."[8]

What "redemption" secured was a transformed political context in which state legislation could be crafted to strengthen the hand of white planters and the coercive authority of the state could be relied upon to come to their assistance. Southern blacks, observed Frederick Douglass in 1879, possessed "a monopoly on the labor market" that gave them the "power to say, 'Give us fair wages or your fields will go untilled.'" To counter this possibility, planters urged the Grange and other farmers' organizations to disseminate strict adherence to the principle, "never interfere with your neighbor's hands." With the restoration of Democratic control in southern legislatures, planters turned to lawmaking and state action to achieve what voluntary compacts could not. After the Civil War, southern states had passed anti-enticement and vagrancy laws as part of the infamous Black Codes. Most of these laws had been repealed during congressional Reconstruction, but modified versions were passed in more than a half-dozen southern states by 1877. It was made a crime, for instance, for agents or employers to entice workers "away from their employers under promises of better wages and treatment." The theft of agricultural produce and livestock was recategorized as grand larceny punishable by a prison term of two to five years, penalties for trespassing and vagrancy were considerably toughened, and "deadfall" sales of produce or cotton before it had been harvested and registered with the landowner were criminalized.[9]

This punitive turn supplemented an increasing reliance on convict labor for public and private purposes. "Only in the South," writes Alex Lichtenstein, "did the state entirely give up its control of the convict population to the contractor; and only in the South did the physical 'penitentiary' become virtually synonymous with the various private enterprises in which convicts labored." The joke about "Old Ned" Richardson of Mississippi, reputed to be the largest cotton planter in the South and said to be "constantly after convict labor," was that when he died the statue on his tomb would have "one eye on the penitentiary and the other on the capitol."[10]

Southern legislatures also erected a legal infrastructure that enabled planters to secure labor on favorable terms, backed, if needed, by legal compulsion. Contract enforcement statutes criminalized entering into a contract with the intention of violating it and treated the refusal to do the demanded work as prima facie evidence of intent, effectively criminalizing any work stoppage. The system of credit that had developed early in the postbellum South, based on liens on a farmer's crop given to merchants in exchange for an advance of supplies, was modified to give top priority to claims by landlords for rent, while legislation granted the landlord "undisputed control over the crops growing in the fields owned by him." With the process firmly under the control of landlords, with work stoppages criminalized, and with tenants and croppers unable to dispose of their crops before they were divided, few options remained for them but to accept the terms offered.[11]

Under Democratic governments, planters and other large employers also could rely on state police and militias to "intervene unequivocally on their behalf," while turning a blind eye to extralegal violence employed by white employers against black workers. In the 1880s, a sheriff's posse shot a black strike leader on a plantation outside Little Rock, allegedly for resisting arrest, while local black union activists and prominent citizens complained about systematic persecution by "armed troops" and "armed men, without the shadow of law or authority." After a strike of cotton pickers in Lee County, Arkansas, was suppressed by a sheriff's posse, the strike leaders were lynched by a masked mob. The state militia was called out to repress strikes in Louisiana's sugar districts on several occasions. In 1877, southern newspapers complained that the "violent Republican" press was seeking to "make political capital out of the recent labor troubles in the sugar districts of Louisiana," insisting that the strike was "devoid of political significance" and thus did not merit national attention. When ten thousand workers, 90 percent of whom were black, went out on strike a decade later, Governor Sam McEnery sent ten infantry companies and artillery to suppress their action, and the state district judge set himself up as the head of a "Peace and Order Committee" that unleashed a series of massacres that killed dozens of black workers and their families. During the following year, the headquarters of the Knights of

Labor was attacked and several of its organizers "disappeared." As one witness remarked, "I think this will settle the question who is to rule, the nigger or the white man for the next fifty years."[12]

A reliance on state and private violence to suppress strike action by no means was unique to the South. The *New Orleans Picayune*, for example, accused Governor Joseph Foraker of Ohio of hypocrisy for his denunciation of Louisiana's suppression of striking black workers given his own use of the militia for the same purposes. But such violence was unquestionably more pervasive and extensive in the South, where it was backed by the tightening web of restrictions, legal and otherwise, on black laborers' ability to change employment or organize for higher wages and better working conditions. Outside the region, striking workers often could find support among local politicians or a sympathetic press. Within the South, by contrast, practically "all elements of white society" cooperated with planters in their efforts "to maintain control of their cheap labor supply." It seems to have been a widely shared view among southern whites that black laborers must be "compelled to work now, just as they did when they were slaves."[13]

The extent of white success in controlling black labor has been a matter of historical controversy. The judgment by the historian William Cohen to the effect that this labor system "alternated between free and forced labor in time to the rhythm of the southern labor market," with the omnipresent threat of force and legal compulsion having a "pervasive effect upon the tone" of southern labor, has been characterized as exaggerating "white ability to manipulate blacks." For sure, there always was substantial movement among black southerners post-slavery, and this generated complaints by southern planters and employers who wanted a more docile workforce. But if southern legislation and labor practices were not always able to guarantee that black laborers would not strike or leave when the harvest was due, they did reflect the pressing desire of the region's planters to gain more control over their labor force. Anti-enticement laws, for instance, had a modest effect on black mobility and wages, not by limiting the right or ability of black southerners to move to new employment but by restricting the opportunity to be approached by prospective employers. And though the number of persons caught up in the web of convict labor was relatively small, the institution nonetheless helped reduce wages and acted "as a check on free labor, in keeping down strikes."[14]

This was the background against which southern members of Congress evaluated labor conflict and weighed possible national responses to the labor question in the final decades of the nineteenth century. Southern Democrats were not reflexively opposed to the labor movement or to what were the emerging lines of a limited national labor policy, but instead considered the degree to which national action would impinge upon—or serve as a precedent for impinging upon—the region's racial labor hierarchy. Two distinct crises brought the labor question to the sustained attention of Congress: the Great Strike of 1877, and the exodus of black agricultural workers out of the South two years later. Analysis of these developments helps reveal the complex ways in which southern congressional representatives evaluated labor strife and national policy responses.

In 1877, a wave of strikes spread along the country's rail network. They began in Martinsburg, West Virginia, then spread to Maryland, Pennsylvania, and Illinois, and ultimately produced a general strike of workers in St. Louis demanding wage protections, an eight-hour day, and a ban on child labor. Although initially a wildcat response to a reduction in pay by the Baltimore & Ohio Railroad, the stoppage extended quickly to other lines and other industries and at least initially seemed to find widespread support in many of the affected towns and cities.[15]

Although the strikes spared most of the South outside the heavily impacted border states, newspapers across the region denounced the "rule of anarchy" and placed blame for the violence in Pittsburgh and Chicago and the general strike in St. Louis on the Communist International. The *Macon Telegraph and Messenger*, declaring that the strike was a "war against property," deplored the spreading "infection" of "communism in the United States." The *New Orleans Times* called for the violent suppression of the strike lest revolution overtake the country, lectured workingmen against embracing the un-American act of striking for wages, and reminded readers that "if the scattered forces of protesting labor unite, there must result a commune most disastrous to the interests of the country." For Georgia's *Columbus Daily Enquirer*, the strike was the "work of communists" who, its editors warned, were now "coming South." Emissaries of the strikers, they announced, "have gone through the States of North Carolina and Virginia, attempting to poison the minds of the workmen and produce disorder at Alexandria, Richmond, Lynchburg, Charlotte and other points." So far these efforts had "entirely failed," commented the *Daily Picayune*, because "the population of these States have no sympathy with Communism and lawlessness." The newspaper warned that any uprising in New Orleans would be met by a "military and police" who were "a little too well disciplined to stand any communistic pranks long." The paper also noted that a leader of the workingmen's clubs was arrested for attempting to excite a disturbance, but that "the arrest was not recorded on the policy books, for obvious reasons."[16]

After a month of violence between state militias and striking workers, President Rutherford B. Hayes ordered the Army to restore peace in the affected cities. Troops en route to the midwestern frontier, where they were to quell a threatened uprising of the Indian nations, were delayed in Chicago in case they would be needed closer to the industrial heartland. Many of the frontier posts saw their allotment of soldiers sent east, and some of the Army regiments stationed in the South were temporarily deployed to quell the walk-out in the Ohio Valley. By early September, the strike was over.[17]

At the height of the strike, with editorial writers drawing a direct parallel between St. Louis and the Paris Commune of 1871, there seems to have been broad bipartisan and cross-sectional agreement that something urgently had to be done. In the months that followed, southern and border state Democrats leapt at the opportunity to attack the Republican administration for how it had handled the crisis, arguing that the growing conflict between labor and capital had been caused by the Republican Party's financial and economic policies. Joseph Blackburn of Kentucky, for instance, denounced what he called a policy of "shoot[ing] down the impoverished laborers of the land who dare to complain of the robbery of which they are the victims, by reason of the persistent class financial legislation of the dominant party for the last fifteen years." William Felton of Georgia opposed the resumption of specie payments by arguing that it had been the class legislation of the Republican Party, whose purpose was to "protect and enrich the creditor class and those having fixed incomes," that had antagonized labor, leading it to form combinations that were "wrong and criminal" in their objectives and actions. But if labor had been mistaken, the fault lay with the Republicans and the creditor class, who together had formed a "colossal combination which has for the last few years waged an exterminating war upon the labor of this country."[18]

A number of border state newspapers chastised the railroads for attempt-ing to reduce wages and hoped that the strike would persuade them that this was a ruinous policy. "None," noted the *Wheeling Daily Register*, "not even the monopolists themselves, have thus far dared to deny that the prices they now pay are starvation and not living wages." And some southerners argued that the laborers were not doing the "work of the Commune," nor was the fight one "between capital and labor in the European sense, but between honest but poor and hard-working citizens and swindling speculators and financial thieves." Southern Democrats had even voted disproportionately in favor of an 1871 resolution expressing regret at the severity with which the French government was persecuting former Parisian Communards, and a number of Democrats suggested that in the coming struggle between "the interests of labor and the oppressive demands of capital," they would enlist as "in the ranks of that mighty phalanx that shall come up and exact equal justice."[19]

Most southern Democratic newspapers reserved their fire for the Repub-licans' economic policies, claiming that the eruption of class conflict was the "inevitable progeny of the system of class legislation which has so long been working the conversion of this whole republic into a vast mass of organized distemper." The "true cause of the conflict between labor and capital" was the "class legislation" that had made "capital in *money* more valuable than capital in *labor*." Class conflict was said to be the "necessary culmination" of

Republican policies, which used the fiscal system to protect and reward certain industries and regions and restricted the money supply in order to protect the interests of capital. Since the advent of Republican rule, a "powerful combination of capital" had been able to secure favorable legislation, dictating "its own terms to every interest and every class."[20]

These also were the terms in which southern Democratic papers denounced the Workingmen's Party, which had helped organize the St. Louis general strike and appeared poised to make inroads in Louisville, Baltimore, and other southern cities. Class conflict could be relieved only by "the resurrection of the genuine, simon pure, old time Democracy," which alone could "restore the land to its *ante-bellum* prosperity and progressiveness." "We are opposed to class legislation," declared the *Memphis Appeal* in celebration of the defeat of Workingmen's candidates in Baltimore. "Exclusive legislation," the paper argued, whether "for either white or black" or "for lawyers, physicians, artisans, mechanics, or for workingmen," would sooner or later bring "communism, socialism and the overthrow of the rights of person and property." The *Appeal* argued that the Democratic Party was the appropriate vehicle for the working class, as "intelligent workingmen do not ask or expect class legislation in their behalf" but want only "equal laws, equal privileges, equal taxation, equal protection." Democratic newspapers insisted that what labor wanted was for the government to be "wrested from the hands of those who manipulate it to their own aggrandizement and to the oppression of the masses," for it to be "extricated from the corner into which it has been forced by the bondholding and money capitalists, who through it are wringing the property of the masses into their own treasuries." In short, the strikers were perhaps misled, but their fundamental complaints were valid, and the appropriate response would be to support the Democratic Party.[21]

The second crisis of the late 1870s was the mass "exodus" of thousands of southern blacks from Louisiana, Mississippi, and Texas to St. Louis, and from there to Kansas and beyond. In late December 1878, newspapers in Louisiana and Mississippi were reporting that thousands of African Americans were planning to leave for Kansas. By February, the "African hegira" was in full swing, with hundreds of migrants arriving in the city "on nearly every boat from the South" and hundreds more congregating along the banks of the Mississippi trying to secure passage. By 1880, more than fifteen thousand African Americans had successfully made the journey to Kansas. Thousands more were defeated by poverty, the discouragement of St. Louis officials, and the opposition of white southerners, who combined persuasion, violence, and legal compulsion to hold on to their black labor force. In Louisiana, a delegate was sent from the redeemer constitutional convention to plead with the migrants to return, and the convention took the extraordinary step of passing a resolution to not reenslave the black population or strip them of their rights in order to persuade them to return. Elsewhere, migrants were threatened with "imprisonment for debt and brute force," arrest for breach of contract, and a denial of transport by river steamboats.[22]

During April and May, as the exodus crested, many white steamboat operators simply refused to pick up the so-called exodusters and did not relent until they were threatened with lawsuits over racial discrimination and threats to have their boats seized. Black migrants reminded hostile boat captains that they were operating common carriers under the terms of the 1875 Civil Rights Act and thus could not deny service on account of race. "I am a man who was a United States soldier," John Solomon Lewis told one such captain, "and I know my rights, and if I and my family gets put off, I will go in the United States Court and sue for damages." The captain turned to his officer and said, "Better take that nigger or he will make trouble." But the refusal of service kept thousands of others from reaching their destination.[23]

Almost from the outset, the exodus brought national attention to the laboring conditions of southern workers. In interviews, black newcomers to St. Louis repeatedly emphasized the tightening screws of post-redemption labor laws as well as electoral "bulldozing" as their central motivations for fleeing the South. "The National government," noted one Mississippian, "has stood idly by and refused to protect us against lawlessness, and to-day the blood of 5,000 innocent colored martyrs calls from the ground and arouses us to action." Black refugees complained of persistent abuse and violence and an inability to secure equal protection of the laws in southern courts; arguing that "all claims to a just recompense for labor rendered or honorable dealings between planter and laborer" were "disallowed," these refugees emphasized the "ever-present fear" of many southern blacks that "slavery in the horrible form of peonage is approaching." Henry Adams noted that "a great many" southern black laborers would explain their desire to migrate by stating that "'I have been working ever since I pretended to be free'—some would say 'pretended to be free,' and others would say 'ever since I have been free'—and I never have got nothing of any account, but every year I come out in debt." Another migrant noted that "we never realize a nickel from our cotton" because "the white folks take all."[24]

The emphasis on laboring conditions and on political oppression was picked up by Republicans, who noted that the reasons for the exodus were the same that had led to slaves to flee northward before the Civil War: "having no rights of citizenship," on account of the "refusal of the whites to allow them to have the rights guaranteed them by the Constitution," black southerners were "at the mercy of their employers." The *Chicago Tribune* criticized southern planters for their "total inability to account for what [they] [regard] as little less than lunacy on the part of the blacks," and argued that black laborers would continue to leave so long as they did not own the land they worked, the only guarantee of economic and political independence: "these planters at the South must open their eyes to the inevitable fact that free labor must own the land it cultivates."[25]

In many ways, the *Tribune* was envisioning an earlier period in southern agriculture, when the large plantation dominated the southern landscape. In fact, the dislocations of the post-emancipation period were the result of a radically changing organization of southern agriculture. Large landholdings were broken up, and a growing number of black Americans were able to purchase small plots of land. There was much variation in these changes across the South; patterns varied considerably between the upper and deep South. In 1875, only 10 percent of the acreage under cultivation in the Black Belt and 7 percent of farms were owned by black southerners, despite constituting more than 50 percent of the agricultural population; by contrast, the proportion of black farmers who owned land in the upper South reached 40 percent only a few years later.[26]

The refugees were generally not included in this small but growing class of black landowners. More important than landownership, however, was what Kansas Republican senator John James Ingalls noted from his meetings with the refugees. None had given any indication of being attracted by " 'forty acres and a mule,' " he claimed, but they had been nearly unanimous in their desire to "secure a fair day's pay for an honest day's work and equal political and civil rights." He also noted that the refugees had repeatedly referred to the convict lease system, "which amounted to practical slavery, under which a negro who stole a biscuit was imprisoned ten years while a white man who killed a negro got only two years." Northern Republican papers, warned the *Vicksburg Daily Commercial*, were using the crisis to argue that "it is the duty of the Federal government to regulate the wages which are paid to negro laborers in the South."[27]

White southerners consistently put the onus for the migration on unscrupulous demagogues, but its sheer scale generated calls for a national response. The Democratic majorities in both chambers initially showed little inclination to open an investigation, but in late 1879, when a few hundred African American migrants from North Carolina arrived in Indiana, local Democrats quickly charged the Republican Party with trying to lure black voters to a pivotal northern state in preparation for the upcoming elections. Despite the small number of refugees entering Indiana, it was this "exodus" that swiftly drew congressional attention. Indiana's Democratic senator Daniel Voorhees, who took the lead in demanding an investigation, was explicit about his purpose: "to find out who these infernal damned political scoundrels are, who are trying to flood our State with a lot of worthless negroes. We propose to get at the bottom facts and expose those rascals. I asked Senator Vance [D-NC] about it, and he told me that those negroes had no reason for leaving their homes, that they have been treated very well by the whites in their native State, North Carolina."[28]

Voorhees's attempt to keep the focus on Indiana was clearly recognized as a partisan gambit, intended to frame the issue in terms that would be favorable to the Democrats. Republican William Windom of Minnesota moved that the scope of the investigation be expanded to include the entirety of the exodus, and that if an investigatory committee were to find that "the colored citizens have been deprived of their rights," they should report to the Senate "what action of Congress is necessary to secure to every citizen the full enjoyment of all rights guaranteed by the Constitution," including the possibility of setting aside territory in the West to which African Americans could emigrate "from their present homes in order to secure their enjoyment of constitutional rights." Although this suggestion was defeated—only one Democrat, Benjamin Hill of Georgia, voted with all Republicans in favor—Voorhees stated that he did not object to widening the scope of the investigation beyond North Carolina.[29]

Southern senators were divided about the wisdom of Voorhees's proposal. Many expressed reservations or opposition to any congressional investigation of southern affairs. The resolution, after all, was "opposed to the ground formerly taken by Democratic Congressmen, that these investigations of the Southern States are impertinent and offensive, and its introduction was deprecated by some Democratic Senators who did not like to vote with Republicans against it." The "whole proceeding was a blunder and is condemned by Democrats," reported one southern correspondent. Benjamin Jonas of Louisiana did not "consider it a proper and legitimate subject for congressional inquiry," and Georgia's Senator Hill spoke about how well southern blacks were treated and made clear that he "opposed the idea of investigating the question and thought it ought to be left to settle itself." Still, he recognized that "if we vote against it gentlemen will say that we are afraid of the investigation," a point that was also made by George Vest of Missouri: "I know full well if the democratic party votes down that resolution the partisan press of the North in the interest of the republican party will immediately charge that it is voted to suppress investigation." Southern Democrats divided almost equally on the question of appointing an investigating committee; even the Republican senator from Louisiana, William Kellogg, voted against it.[30]

While some southern Democrats were hesitant and anxious about the possibility of another investigation, others believed that an inquiry would provide an important opportunity to frame the national record. "It is doubtless true," noted the *Daily Picayune*, "that most of the Republican inquests were impertinent interferences in matters which did not concern Congress, and that the Democrats were, as a rule, opposed to them." They had been directed "to no other purpose than that of suppressing the truth, and of crystalizing calumny and falsehood into the form of an official record." But white southerners also expected "better things of inquiries controlled by the Democratic majority in Congress." If national attention was going to be placed on southern labor practices, better that the record be prepared by southern Democrats and their northern allies, who would give the region "a fair showing in the official reports of Congressional committees."[31]

The Democratic majority on the committee delivered. Working diligently to advance the favored interpretation of white southerners, it dismissed southern laborers' complaints of coercion and political violence and frequently cut them off in their testimony or cast doubt on their claims. The majority focused on the theory that the migration had been caused by Republicans seeking to import black voters into Indiana to sway the presidential election; as the minority charged, witnesses were selected "mainly with reference to their supposed willingness to prove said theory." The majority report underscored that much of the testimony about southern violence or labor practices was hearsay, and it insisted that the migration from North Carolina had been "undoubtedly induced in a great degree by Northern politicians, and by negro leaders in their employ, and in the employ of railroad lines." The political violence brought up by many of the refugees and witnesses had "formed the staple of complaint for many years against the people of the South," the majority noted, and consisted of "nothing or almost nothing new." "It was all hearsay," the report charged, "and nothing but hearsay, with rare exceptions." "In justice to the planters of the South," it concluded, any abuse occurring was "not at all general nor frequent"; moreover, "while exorbitant prices are exacted sometimes from men in the situation of the blacks," it was justified by the risk carried by the planter. "Any further attempts at legislation," the majority concluded, "or agitation of the subject [of black political and civil rights] will but excite them in the hopes of exterior aid that will be disappointing to them, and will prevent them from working out diligently and with care their own salvation. . . . The sooner they are taught to know that their true interest is promoted by cultivating the friendship of their white neighbors instead of their enmity, the sooner they will gain that friendship."[32]

The different southern responses to these two crises suggest the complex considerations involved in southern evaluations of a national role in investigating and defining labor policy. As long as southern Democrats understood labor strife to be a war by the northeastern trusts against the producing sections and classes of the country and were able to tie it to a broader critique of Republican legislation, they had some sympathy for labor unions and white strikers and could even support federal legislation. This supportive view was strongest in the border states, but also found advocates in Texas, Louisiana, and Mississippi.

When the complaints of labor were interpreted as the product of the "general system of robbery of the great mass of the people for the benefit of the few," southern Democrats could endorse unions as a "counterpoise to the overmastering growth of monopoly" and offer as a policy remedy the end of "the protective tariff and the monopoly of the national banks" and a promise to "control these great corporations by law." Some framed the suppression of labor unrest as part of the Reconstruction policy of denying home rule. Otho Singleton of Mississippi, for example, was opposed to the use of "a standing Army" in "putting down labor strikes in the States," complaining that "we have had enough of United States troops stationed in the States to interfere with local affairs, intimidating citizens and to control elections." A few years later, John Reagan reminded his fellow representatives that "the first impulse" of capital in 1877 was "to appeal to the Federal Government, the next was to enlarge the standing Army, in order that it might be used as a police force to answer the complaints and murmurings of the people by shot and shell." To many southerners, the parallels with Reconstruction were clear. The Republican Party in both instances was said to be willing to use the army "for the destruction of our own people who combine for the assertion and maintenance of what they conceive to be their rights." These interpretations allowed many southern members to see in successive labor conflicts a manifestation of their own struggles with northern capital, thus facilitating an identification and sympathy with striking workers.[33]

But the position of many white southerners on labor questions was conditioned by the fact that the workers whose interests were most directly at stake in federal labor policy were primarily white men who worked in occupations removed from the labor-intensive sectors of southern agriculture—the economic sector, by contrast, where policy demands were more likely to impinge on the region's racial hierarchy. When southern black labor was at issue, as it was during the national debate over the "exodus," southern lawmakers worked diligently either to keep the issue off the national agenda or to shape how questions and solutions were framed. In the case of the black migration, for instance, southern Democrats split on the wisdom of an investigation and were willing to support it only if they could be confident that it would be orchestrated by a Democratic majority and would reflect Democratic priorities and perspectives. The distinctions upon which this calculation rested— between white and black labor, between agricultural and manufacturing work, between local and interstate commerce, and even between investigations run by a Democratic Congress and those run by Republican-appointed commissions—were never stable; these different categories and alternatives bled into each other to complicate southern positions on national labor policy.

One recurring proposal was to establish a department or bureau to collect information on wages, hours, and the relations between labor and capital. This

initiative had the strong backing of the Knights of Labor, which had successfully lobbied for the creation of similar bodies across a number of northern
states, and the proposal was championed in Congress by a number of activist
Republicans, such as George Frisbie Hoar and Henry Blair, as well as by northern Democrats such as James Hopkins and Martin Foran.

Southern senators joined with conservative Republicans in 1872 to defeat
a proposal by Hoar to establish a labor commission, complaining that it would
be an intrusion by the federal government into an area where they had no jurisdiction and would intrude into the private relationships between employer
and employee. When it passed by a large majority in the House, twenty-three
southern Democrats voted against it and just thirteen in favor, the only substantial bloc of opposition. The general tenor of debate suggested that most
representatives considered white non-agricultural labor to be the principal
subject for such a commission, but Hoar suggested that it would embrace the
entire question of labor in the United States. When Benjamin Biggs of Delaware
accused the Republican Party of being enemies of the laboring man, Hoar asked
him whether he had not just recently "advocate[d] the policy of the capitalists
owning the workingmen; in other words, slaves?" "Slavery has been 'wiped
out,'" Biggs responded, "and Massachusetts, so fond of meddling with other
people's business, cannot rest satisfied." Its representatives were now going to
try to delude the white laboring classes in the same way that they had deluded
newly freed blacks, with the promise of "forty acres of land and a mule."[34]

In the Senate, the bill was opposed by Joshua Hill, a Georgia Republican
and former Whig and Know-Nothing. "Shall we not have a commission to
oversee the entire people of this country," asked Hill, "the proprietors of workshops and of lands, the laborers in workshops, the tillers of the soil, and every
other class that we have throughout this broad land?" He blamed the new interest in labor legislation on the 1868 Eight-Hour Law, which had supposedly
led "demagogues" to "perambulate the country and persuade the laborers,
even in the corn and cotton-fields, that they are not half paid, although you
should give them everything they make." "What is there in private life," he
asked, "that shall be sacred from the intrusion of government?" Although Hill
was nominally a Republican, he was a cotton planter whose elevation to the
Senate had been engineered by conservatives in order to defeat the Radical
Republican candidate. In Congress, he had been a notable Republican opponent of a civil rights bill, insisting that it was not desired by Georgia's black
population, although one constituent believed that Hill's position did not "express the desire of fifty colored men in Georgia." The labor commission proposal was defeated with all southern Democrats but one voting no. Seven
southern Republican senators voted in favor, while Hill was joined by two
others and most northern Republicans in opposition. For the rest of the de-

cade, the South would provide the bulk of the votes against any investigation, whether by commission or federal agency, of the condition of labor in the United States.[35]

The strikes of the 1870s and early 1880s, however, opened space for southern Democrats to support inquiries into their causes, which they expected would prove that labor strife was the product of Republican class legislation. Responding to labor conflict in the ironworks of his state, John Morgan of Alabama proposed in 1882 that the Senate authorize a special committee to investigate the cause of strikes in the United States. He was pleased to see that "recently the strikers have confined themselves to what might be called legal operations," but this only caused him additional worries that something much more important than sporadic conflict over wages and working conditions was going on. "There is some deep-seated politico-economical question involved in this," he admitted, "which I do not understand." His proposal was seconded by James George of Mississippi, who worried that capital was "in danger from a leveling and communistic spirit," but who also decried the "enormous growth of corporate power and corporate privileges and the aggregation of immense wealth in the hands of a few fortunate and favored persons." George was especially insistent that Republican legislation was to blame: "there are wrongs which should be righted," he declared, and "there are inequalities which should be removed."[36]

Morgan's proposal was modified by Henry Blair to authorize an expanded investigation, one entitled to travel and hold meetings throughout the country, that would look not only at the causes of strikes but at the full set of relations between labor and capital. The amended resolution passed the Senate by unanimous consent. The southern leg of the investigation, chaired by Senator Blair and Senator James Pugh of Alabama, a former Whig and leading figure in the "redemption" of the state, was drastically different from Reconstruction-era investigations in the region and even had little in common with the contemporaneous investigations being held in Washington on the subject of election outrages and contested elections. In each town where the so-called Blair Committee held a hearing—the major sites in the South were Augusta, Atlanta, and Columbus in Georgia; Birmingham and Opelika in Alabama; and Washington, DC—they were met with prominent citizens and elected officials who sought to use the committee to attract capital to the region and solicit public investments. The hearings were generally well received in the region's newspapers, and Blair and Pugh repeatedly described the warm and friendly welcome they were given.[37]

In many ways, however, the hearings presented an opportunity to define the question of labor relations from the perspective of white factory owners and planters, who were disproportionately represented on the witness lists.

Although the hearings were mostly concerned with manufacturing and mining, a considerable number of questions were raised about southern agriculture, and considerable attention was paid to black labor. White witnesses insisted that the young black men and women raised since the war did not want to work, that the free black laborer did "not work so constantly as the slave did when he was forced to do it." This discovery apparently had come as "a great disappointment to our planters." "Beyond a certain point these free laborers will not be driven, and the payment of wages will not induce them to do the constant hard work which they were forced to do when they were slaves." The former governor of Alabama complained that black men and women were "not willing to be controlled or guided by their employers, because they have an idea that that is submitting to slavery again," to which Blair—ever eager to promote education as the cure for industrial conflict—responded that the difficulty seemed to be an intellectual one, a failure to appreciate that being compelled against one's wishes to work for contracted wages was different from being compelled to work against one's wishes for no wages. But he supposed that sooner or later black workers would "butt their heads against necessity, and that will teach them." Others argued that the experience of slavery, or the teachings of Republican politicians, had led black workers to have little regard for contracts, and they urged passage of state or even federal laws to require their strict enforcement. "The great secret of the industrial trouble here," remarked one witness, "is the uncertainty of labor and the fact that when your laborers desert you have no remedy." Others remarked that "I am not afraid of the war between labor and capital as long as we have the colored laborer," as even the younger generation was more easily managed and cheaper than white labor.[38]

This perspective was contested by the 30 percent of witnesses who were African American, all of whom agreed that, despite many hardships, life was better as freemen than as slaves. Black witnesses, who placed considerable emphasis on the gains made by the black community despite laboring under considerable difficulties, were underrepresented relative to the cities and states where the hearings were held; they generally appeared in delegations organized by prominent members of the community in order to advocate for aid to education. The black witnesses were hardly representative: one-third were either independent contractors or large landowners, and another 40 percent were clergy, educators, or newspaper editors. Although a few black witnesses were porters, independent farmers, carpenters, and, in one case, a convict leased out to work in the mines, most were drawn from the precarious middle classes: they owned small contracting firms in construction or painting or were pursuing uncertain careers in newspaper publishing or the church. None were sharecroppers, tenants, or agricultural wage earners. As one remarked, "I don't know very much about the condition of the laboring class of people, because I never was out among them very much." All that held back black business owners, one black witness argued, was that "we go entirely upon energy and self-will and no capital. The white men have the capital." White witnesses were disproportionately presidents of iron, coal, and railroad companies, bank presidents, or owners of manufacturing firms. Living wholly separate lives from black business owners, they exhibited virtually no sympathy for the argument that opportunities for African American business were slight and access to capital was lacking.[39]

Some black witnesses raised the issue of equal accommodations on the railroads; the recent overturning of the Civil Rights Act was an issue of clear concern for many. Many argued that the act had been ineffective. One witness described his reliance on his sister's ability to pass for white in order to receive a measure of equal accommodations: "Whenever I took a notion to exercise my 'civil rights' without the risk of any trouble I would be her 'servant' and go on to Macon with her and ride behind her and take care of her baggage. I have got more sense now than I had then. I just thought I wanted to ride in a first-class car." But there was general agreement among the witnesses that something needed to be done to ensure that, "if a colored man is paying the same fare on the railroad that a white man pays, he has just as much right as the white man has to proper accommodations." The complaints of discrimination in Alabama were met with a confident statement by Blair that the issue would be resolved at the local level without federal involvement. With few exceptions, the witnesses stressed that state governments, particularly the new state railroad commission in Alabama, would be the target of organized efforts to secure equal accommodations.[40]

Most black witnesses pressed for federal education funds while stressing, perhaps to support this position, that good relations between the races and steady material improvements had been achieved since Reconstruction. Throughout, black witnesses emphasized the support and consideration they had received from the "better class" of the community; one reverend even remarked that "the colored people sustained an intimate and profitable relation to the white people of the South previous to the war" and claimed that this relation was gradually being rebuilt. Interpretation of tone in historical documents is inevitably a tricky affair, but it is not far-fetched to imagine that it was difficult for the reverend to make this statement.[41]

A number of black witnesses noted that they could not speak freely in a public hearing held in their local community with prominent citizens in attendance. After one witness accidentally ventured into the question of civil rights and social equality, he quickly backed off. "That is a very delicate matter," he explained, "and I do not care very much about going into it. It might create some unpleasantness. I do not want to testify to anything but that which is pleasant." Another testified that most of the people of color who had appeared before the committee "want to say things, but they are afraid of the white people; afraid that the white people will say to them afterwards, 'Look here, John, you remember the sort of remarks you made before that commit-tee. I am done with you now.'" As owners of small contracting firms who were by and large dependent on being hired by white capital, they were in a precari-ous position. "A white man is a white man," this witness remarked, "I don't care where he is. If it is in a manger a white man looks for a colored man to look up to him as a white man and to respect him as a white man."[42]

Still, the conversation could not wholly remain within the bounds that the prominent white southern citizens and senators would have liked. Even before the committee reached the South, the issue of southern labor practices caused tension. When one white witness in New York, a member of the Brotherhood of Carpenters and Joiners, argued that the black exodus from the South had been the result of "social intimidation"—namely, the "truck system practiced by the storekeepers, who had mortgages on the crops even before the crops were raised, so that the poor negroes were used up"—Senator Wilkinson Call of Florida intervened to demand that the record state that the witness was wrong. Standing his ground, the witness reported that he had chaired a work-ingman's committee in St. Louis during the exodus that "went among them and assisted them with provisions, and made inquiries, and found out the cause of the exodus to be largely that truck system." Another southern senator at the hearings, James George of Mississippi, did not interrupt this testimony, but likewise wanted it noted that the witness was misinformed. When Blair, during a hearing in New York, remarked that the "wages of the colored work-men in the South were thirty cents a day," Senator Pugh was inflamed. "Where did you get that information," he demanded, to which Blair responded, "I got it from yourself, I believe." Growing red in the face, Pugh lashed out: "I don't think any other man but you would make that statement," and insisted that he had been making nothing but a "jocular remark" that "was not intended to be repeated here nor elsewhere." Once it became clear that the conversation was going to veer into the subject of the wages of "the colored laborer in the South" relative to "his brother in the North," Senator Call broke in to "protest against the committee going into any questions that are foreign to the inquiry."[43]

During the southern leg of the hearings, white witnesses occasionally would argue that southern blacks were willing to vote the "Southern ticket"—that is, for white Democrats—because they "now have come to realize the fact that the intelligent white man is a safer and better representative or governor than one of their own people." Black witnesses repeatedly disagreed. One for-mer member of the Alabama House of Representatives complained that he would not buy property in the state because he was unsure whether his invest-ment could be safe: "I was afraid that you folks were going to keep out count-ing us, and I want to have my rights at the ballot box," he told Pugh. When pressed, he agreed that black southerners were less committed to the Republican Party than they had been before, and he even signaled that he might vote for Democrats. "I am now like all the rest of the colored men," he stated. "If you say you are my friend, and prove it, I am with you. We don't care now for 'Democrat' or 'Republican' or anybody else." But he would consider voting only for Democrats who supported aid to black schools; otherwise, when "the Democratic party wants to carry the election they create prejudice between the poor white man and the nigger. . . . Senator Pugh well knows it. But if they will give us schools, we will agree to let them keep on counting us out, so that we don't have no more confusion and fuss."[44]

The complaint of being "counted out" and the suggestion that black southerners might withdraw from politics or begin voting with Democrats were repeatedly brought up. "Our white friends down here think this is a 'white man's' country," noted one witness. "They say they are going to rule it, and they are ruling it, there is no doubt about that; and the better class of our colored people have about made up their minds to let politics alone; at least, I have. I am going to try and be a good quiet citizen." When asked whether he would vote for Democrats "if they will give you your rights," another witness responded, "Yes, sir. But the way the matter stands now we are afraid to trust them in the whole matter; we will just take a half hitch on them and watch them." This witness noted that it had become nearly impossible to elect black candidates; despite being "in a majority here," he said, "you may vote until your eyes drop out or your tongue drops out, and you can't count your colored man in out of them boxes; there's a hole gets in the bottom of the boxes some way and lets out our votes." When Reverend Welch of the African Methodist Episcopal Church (AME) testified about the growing good spirit between the races, Blair jokingly asked whether eventually the "white race will get so by and by, that they will vote the Republican ticket?" "Well," Reverend Welch responded, they might vote for "the principles without the name." Pugh jumped in at this point, pressing the witness to admit that "the colored people are just as likely to vote the Democratic ticket as the whites are to vote the Republican ticket." Reverend Welch responded that some did, and that the black vote was likely to become more divided in coming years, especially as black voters expressed their frustration with a Republican Supreme Court overturning the Civil Rights Act. Southern blacks were "a little divided since the decision on the civil rights bill, and I am afraid they will be more divided. It is hard to determine the political sentiment among our people now; a very difficult matter." But he also remarked that while African Americans intended to divide politically in the future, they would do so only "if the vote is only counted as it is cast." When Blair joked that education would eventually help the whites do better "counting," Pugh unrepentingly responded that "education will obviate the necessity of resorting to false counting to avoid other evils" and "remedy the evils by keeping bad men out of office." "Of course," remarked another witness, white Democrats "might go to work and do as they said of the Republican party, disfranchise the colored man from voting because he is not able to read and write. They might go to work and fix up something like that, but I do not expect any such thing."[45]

When another witness remarked sarcastically that "there is no difference of opinion between the white and colored voters, for instance, if the colored men all go up and vote the Democratic ticket," but insisted that there was "considerable friction" when black men tried to vote for the Republicans, Pugh tried to suggest that such friction was natural and entirely unconnected with race: "Is there not considerable friction between whites where they belong to different parties and want to vote differently?" The witness responded that it was not the same, that "the white people calculate on differing with each other, and they do not mind those differences, but they have never been used to being differed with by the darky, and they just cannot stand it." He then explained that whites had resorted to "desperate measures" to regain political control, and that many black men were now scared of voting lest there be a repeat of the violence that accompanied Democratic "redemption." The witness, who suggested that he was fifteen-sixteenths white, was well respected in the community, and when he went to vote he was given a guard of four policemen to accompany him. Nevertheless, Pugh pressed the witness to admit that black voters should not be the "sole element controlling the government."

> Q. This white power which you speak of as exercised here is the power of morality and intelligence, in which, as you admit, the white race is superior to yours?
>
> A. Well, that is so to a certain extent, but I cannot justify the manner in which this morality and intelligence have sometimes asserted themselves. I think that the man who has intellectual power can afford to assert that power without committing violence of any kind upon other men.
>
> Q. Don't you find, as a rule, what the intelligent colored people who have testified before us have stated to be their experience, that the intelligent and cultivated white men are the most friendly to the colored man? . . .
>
> A. Yes, sir; that is largely so, but at the same time I think the intelligent, cultivated white people adapt themselves to surrounding circumstances. . . . In remote sections of the country the intelligent and cultivated white people, while they may not themselves take any part in this kind of violence, they tolerate it and do not try and prevent it when they could.

Q. Do you not find frequently that the condition of public feeling has been caused by the wicked leadership of bad white men misleading and deceiving these poor colored people?

A. I think it is the result of wicked leadership on both sides. I think the white people have a great many bad leaders.

When Pugh dared the witness to indict the "white men here who control public sentiment and opinion in politics," such as the state governor or the U.S. senator, he responded by deftly attributing wickedness to those "local leaders in counties, men who never come to the surface in any national sense at all, and men that you don't know anything about."[46]

By the end of the hearings, Pugh had been convinced that federal funds for education would be a cause worth pursuing, and he believed that the testimony of southern whites against federal supervision had persuaded Blair to accept compromises on this point. With the other southerners on the committee, James George of Mississippi and Wilkinson Call of Florida, he formed a "middle-of-the-road coalition in Congress" in favor of modest interventions by the federal government into labor policy, in particular the establishment of a permanent agency tasked with collecting statistics on the condition of labor.[47]

They would have a hard time, however, convincing their fellow southerners. When Morgan first proposed the committee, the *Montgomery Advertiser* warned that the "investigation is not within the legitimate sphere of congressional duty" and suggested that the senator had erred in proposing it.[48] Whether because he had received similar warnings, because he had believed a temporary committee on strikes was a limited and acceptable federal intervention, or because he had seen the ways in which the Blair Committee had gone off track while interviewing black witnesses, Morgan was now vociferously opposed to a bureau of labor statistics. The principal difference, he suggested, between his proposed commission and the proposed bureau was the scope of its authority. He pressed Senator George of Mississippi, who supported a proposed bureau, on what kind of labor would fall under its jurisdiction:

MR. MORGAN. Does the Senator refer to agricultural laborers at all?

MR. GEORGE. So far as I know I have heard no complaint from them.

MR. MORGAN. This bill, then, does not apply to them?

MR. GEORGE. Yes; it applies to all.

MR. MORGAN. It applies to alien laborers also?

MR. GEORGE. It applies to all laborers in the United States.

MR. MORGAN. And the negro laborers in the South?

MR. GEORGE. Of course; but I say I have not heard the complaint urged by that class that I have heard from others.

George wanted reports on the condition of black laborers to be kept distinct from those on white labor, but was not willing to sink the bill on this account. Blair insisted that black workers in the South had expressed the same demands as northern workers: "a desire for increased opportunities for education, industrial as well as common-school education, and for the diffusion of further information as to their general condition among the legislators and what they look upon as the ruling classes in the country."[49]

Morgan went on the attack, framing his critique of the bureau in terms calculated to raise the hackles of southern senators. "This commissioner," he began, "I suppose will send his emissaries, his agents, into my State among the people who live in the hill country, the white people who own the land and work it themselves, and who would not allow a negro to come within sight of a fence if they could help it. Not only are they not colaborers, they are not associates with them." The federal inquisitors—"for it is intended to be nothing else" than an inquisition, he insisted—would then say to the head of the family:

> "I want to know the moral condition of your wife, this laboring lady, and of your daughter; and I want to know your condition as to material prosperity, and I want to know your social condition. I want to know whether you are in the habit of recognizing as equals the colored people that live in your neighborhood; I want to inquire whether it is in accordance with your views of social duty that you should associate with every person that you meet. What is the rule of social intercourse between you and your neighbor? What do you do if a colored man or colored woman wants to come and sit down at your table and the like?"

When another senator suggested that this line of inquiry would require a huge staff, Morgan supposed that "it would take as large an army as General Grant commanded at the time of the surrender." Morgan proposed that the bill should strictly demarcate wage laborers from farmers, sharecroppers, and business owners. Although David Aiken, the head of the South Carolina Grange, and James Blount of Georgia had raised similar points in the House, it was Morgan who most effectively framed the dangers of the bureau in terms that were easily recognizable to southern members of Congress. He was, in the words of one contemporary, the South's "watchful genius," who would use his considerable talents to defend white supremacy in the South against any interference.[50]

With the exception of Pugh, George, and Call—the three southerners who had served on the Blair Committee—the region was unanimous in supporting amendments to weaken the bill, and they provided the bulk of votes for recommittal. Congress later would elevate the bureau to a department in 1888, albeit without cabinet status; again, opposition came primarily from southern Democrats. At the state level, the region's Democrats hardly were more supportive. Most southern states established bureaus of labor statistics years after they were established in the North, and these showed a persistent "disinterest in black and women's labor."[51]

Along with the proposal to gather information, the other major policy ideas to gain traction in Congress during the last quarter of the century were proposals to enforce and expand the scope of the 1868 Eight-Hour Law and to provide for some means of arbitrating differences between capital and labor. The Eight-Hour Law read simply that "eight hours shall constitute a day's work for all laborers, workmen, and mechanics who may be employed by or on behalf of the Government of the United States." Under President Andrew Johnson, it had been accompanied by a reduction in pay, and though the Grant administration instructed all government officials to strictly enforce the law and not reduce pay, this directive was only varyingly adhered to by executive branch officials. In 1876, the Supreme Court ruled the law to simply be a definition of the workday for government employment, not a limitation on contracts, effectively leaving it without effect.[52]

Even in the most expansive form that it would be debated in Congress, the federal Eight-Hour Law would have regulated wages and hours for only a very small number of employees and had little to no direct or indirect effect on southern agricultural labor. So long as the proposals occupying congressional attention were confined to a narrow band of the economy, there was no necessary conflict between southern Democrats' priority of maintaining control over the region's agricultural workforce and supporting pro-labor legislation. White southern anxieties nonetheless inclined the region's representatives to consider federal policy in light of its potential to reach beyond its intended recipients. Thus, even within the narrow set of proposals actually considered by Congress or in national debates about labor, southern Democrats consistently emerged as the voting faction most likely to oppose protective legislative action. When the Republican candidate for governor in Ohio suggested establishing a minimum, living wage in railroads and mining as a response to labor conflict, southern members asked whether this proposal did not imply extending the benefits of a minimum wage to "farm-laborers, mill and factory operatives, shoe-makers, carpenters, marines and sailors?" In similar terms, John Reagan attacked the federal Eight-Hour Law: it "may do in factories; it may do in Government employment," but there were some, he warned, who "advocate it indiscriminately. Adopt it generally, and what will be the result in this agricultural country of ours?"[53]

Although the position of southern Democrats on the Eight-Hour Law was never unanimous, the region consistently provided the bulk of votes against its enforcement or extension. All but one southern Democratic senator voted on June 12, 1878, against considering a resolution to enforce the law; by contrast, most northern Democrats and Republicans voted in favor. In 1879, a majority of southern Democrats in the House voted against considering another resolution implementing the law. A majority of southern representatives would vote to pass an enforcement resolution in the run-up to the presidential election of 1880, but eight years later southern Democrats would vote against a clause to an appropriations bill requiring the public printer to "rigidly enforce" the Eight-Hour Law. A vote to strike out the clause had the unanimous backing of southern Democratic senators and over 60 percent of southern Democratic representatives, but was opposed by only three northern Democratic senators, two-thirds of Republican senators, and nearly 90 percent of northern Democratic and Republican representatives. Almost all southern senators also voted against considering a bill to settle accounts with workers who had been made to work longer than eight hours since 1868.

Some measure of the South's distinctiveness on labor issues, as well as the variation within the region, is illustrated in figure 5.1, which displays the probability that a given state's delegation in the House or Senate would vote from 1877 to 1900 to enforce or extend the application of the Eight-Hour Law. The left panel shows the probability for Democrats and the right panel shows the same for Republicans, with the dashed line showing the total percentage who voted the pro-labor position for the party as a whole. Lawmakers from Georgia, Mississippi, the Carolinas, and Texas were especially likely to stand in opposition, and it was primarily in the former Confederacy that southern Democrats showed the strongest opposition to strengthening or enforcing the Eight-Hour Law.

Proposals to initiate a role for the federal government to manage labor conflict likewise received a colder reception from southern Democrats than from other regions. Responding to the Great Southwestern Strike of 1886, the House Committee on Labor proposed a voluntary arbitration bill for disputes between railway companies involved in interstate commerce and their employees, a measure that even the committee chairman recognized as being highly circumscribed in its application. A succession of southern lawmakers attacked the proposal as "the foundation of a new and indefinite and dangerous jurisprudence." If "labor organizations are unwisely" led to support federal arbitration, warned John Rogers of Arkansas, "why should we not extend it to every class of laborers in this country? Why not extend it to the printers, the steamboat men, the factory men and women, the miners, the day laborers on the farms, ay, the farmers themselves, who have their complaints and their grievances against these very same corporations." Federal arbitration would be the "beginning of an unseen ending," warned Virginia Democrat John Tucker, and would ensure that "all the labor troubles of railroads and on the fields, on the sea and the land, will be dealt with here" rather than in the states, where solutions would be more responsive to local concerns. John Reagan, who was busy trying to pass his interstate commerce bill, insisted that the

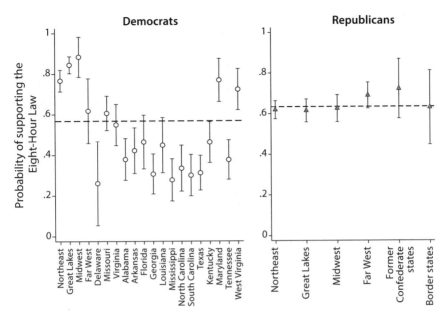

FIGURE 5.1. Probability of Supporting Eight-Hour Law. Dashed line is the probability for each party.

arbitration proposal was "not a bill regulating commerce" but one "regulating labor contracts between parties." Its passage would endorse, he argued, an expansive definition of the federal government's authority that "would take from local tribunals the adjustment and settlement of local questions, that is to say, questions between the hirer or employer and the laborer." John Daniel of Virginia derisively suggested that the authority of the federal government to arbitrate differences between classes was to be found "under some other occult and unnamed clause" in the Constitution, and he warned that the federal government would now be empowered "to penetrate society, drag people from their homes, put them in jail for contempt, fine him if need be, and unearth everything that is private in correspondence or business record."[54]

Not all southerners opposed the bill; some even wanted to make it stronger. Missouri Democrat John Glover offered a substitute that would make the decision of the arbitration board legally binding, while Texas Democrat William Crain, whose Seventh District included Galveston, accused Reagan of hypocrisy for pushing the interstate commerce bill while opposing the arbitration measure. Perhaps most worrisome, however, was that the bill had the eager support of Republican James O'Hara of North Carolina. "I represent," said O'Hara, "a constituency . . . composing a large class of unorganized labor, but which must in the very near future be organized for its own protection." When that time came, he was hopeful that the black farmworkers in his district would receive the same support for federal arbitration "in its clash with other great interests" as rail workers were now receiving. Northern Democrats appealed to their copartisans to vote for a popular but toothless proposal, arguing that the bill's limited scope foreclosed any possibility that the federal government would claim "the power or the right to say to a railroad company or to a laborer so many hours shall constitute a day's work or so many dollars shall constitute a month's wages." This appeal helped sway a number of southern Democrats, who voted 46 to 30 in favor of final passage, but the region provided the only substantial opposition to the proposal, as just three representatives outside the South voted against it. As often was the case, voting varied considerably across the region's racial landscape, with 57 percent of Black Belt representatives voting against passage compared to 22 percent from outside the Black Belt. The bill passed the House but died in the Senate. Not until the 1890s would a weak arbitration bill pass.[55]

The threat raised by O'Hara was hardly an idle one: black workers throughout the South were organizing into labor unions, both in agricultural regions and in manufacturing, trades, and mines. A question that was repeatedly raised during the Blair Committee's inquiry in the South was whether black workers "show some inclination to organize" into labor unions: "They have a great many associations of their own," replied one employer, "and they have some labor unions. The stevedores have organized." When Edward King of the Central Labor Union in New York suggested the importance of organizing agricultural labor, as had recently been accomplished in England, it was Blair who seemed most taken aback: "Then you would organize the agricultural labor of the South and of the North and of the whole country into trades unions, so that the agricultural laborers might be under the control of those unions instead of under the control of the planters?" King agreed with the goal of organizing southern and northern labor, but stressed that the workers would not be "under the *control* of the trades unions." At this point, Pugh intervened, asking whether "anybody suggested anything of that sort to you?" "No, sir," the witness replied. Efforts to organize black agricultural labor in common with the emerging trade union movement remained mostly speculative in the fall of 1883, and it was commonly observed that the unions were making it increasingly difficult for black workers to gain access to skilled positions.[56]

The possibility gained renewed attention during the Strike of 1886, in which the Knights of Labor took a prominent role. Although the strike was targeted primarily against Jay Gould's Union Pacific and Missouri Pacific railway lines, with more than two hundred thousand workers on strike in Arkansas, Illinois, Kansas, Missouri, and Texas, it threatened to spill over into agricultural sectors when black workers reportedly affiliated with the Knights also went on strike on "Tate's Plantation" outside Little Rock. The *Texarkana Independent* and other southern newspapers warned that "adventurers and meddlers are at work organizing some kind of secret societies amongst the colored men in the country," while John Reagan, whose district was 40 percent African American, attacked those "friends of labor, so called, who never work, but go about through the country agitating." Denouncing the Knights as trying to array black strikers "against the white citizens as a class," the *Arkansas Gazette* printed panicked stories predicting an impending "uprising" by a thousand "armed negroes" who had been stockpiling weapons for the occasion.[57]

The prospect of black organizing called into question whatever sympathy southern Democratic representatives and newspapers had for labor unions. Black union workers were said to be especially susceptible to becoming the "blind instruments of some bold Communist," and supposedly more liable than white workers to radicalism: they were "an element far more dangerous . . . than the white brotherhood of the Knights." Southern newspapers argued that support for unions among black workers was the product of the "war system of attempting to establish prices by the mere arbitrary fiat of one of the parties to the bargain," and suggested that such support was another pernicious legacy of the Freedmen's Bureau's efforts to intervene in southern labor relations by mediating contract disputes. When informed that a black woman was organizing a cooks' union, the *Telegraph* remarked that "there can be no doubt of the fact that what are called 'Labor unions' will become very popular with the negroes," and it asked how southern papers, which, "generally, indorse the 'strikes' of the white men," would then respond. "Will not the same logic force them to justify the strikes of negroes?" The *Telegraph*'s conclusion was that, rather than carve out a racial exception, labor unions were to be rejected altogether. Although some southern papers viewed the formation of the Colored Farmers' Union as a positive thing—especially given its emphasis on "withdraw[ing] their attention from political partisanship"—they also repeatedly warned that the new organization would "have to be narrowly watched," and that "if it is suffered to degenerate into a mere political machine, or a secret society for the accomplishment of unlawful ends, it would be well to strangle it at the start." Watching the ongoing crackdown against black labor activism, the Republican *Daily Inter-Ocean* noted that under slavery it had been a crime for a Negro "to run away," but "now it is a crime in South Carolina for him to join the Knights of Labor or organize for the purpose of securing better wages."[58]

Home Rule and the Federal Election Laws

None of the policy proposals that received serious congressional consideration during this period would have substantially undermined state authority over labor regulations and practices. But southern labor practices, especially in

agriculture, rested on the dominance of the Democratic Party in state legislatures and the influence of southern planters secured by this partisanship. In
turn, Democratic control rested on the maintenance of "home rule," the right
of the white population of the southern states to govern themselves without
federal interference.

"As long as the negro shows himself politically hostile to the property owners and intelligence among the whites," wrote the *Wilmington Northern Star*,
"he will be a source of absolute danger to society and all the educational
schemes in the universe can not cure it." It had been opposition to black political influence that had galvanized so many white southerners to align with the
Democratic Party and subordinate differences of political opinion on a range
of questions to the paramount objective of restoring and maintaining white
supremacy. When asked by the *Boston Herald* to identify the basis for the
"solid South," southern governors responded that it was "the result of the false
reconstruction policy of the Republican party," the "massing" of black voters
against the "wealth and intelligence" of the state, and the denial of "self-
government" to the region's white population. Any break in the southern national front was objected to on account of the "fear that their State governments will return to the condition of things existing under the scallawag and
carpetbag governments." White southerners who addressed this question
repeatedly argued that "perforce" Democrats were united to a party they otherwise disdained solely by the "paramount necessity of rescuing and preserving [their] State from the ruinous rule of carpet-baggers and the negroes."
"The white people," argued Governor Fitzhugh Lee of Virginia, "will not practically divide until the colored people do," because only then could they be
certain that white southern men committed to the region's racial hierarchy
and labor practices would be empowered. Before any "large body of whites
will withdraw from the Democratic party," there would have to be "a thorough
conviction, reenforced by experience, that no further danger need be apprehended of the massing of the black vote." The main purpose of white southerners' allegiance to the Democratic Party, repeated in some form by almost every
white southerner who ventured an opinion, was "to hold on to local self-
government and to insure themselves against Federal interference."[59]

This commitment translated into an unparalleled commonality of purpose
in Congress on the question of elections and voting rights. Figure 5.2 shows
the probability that southern Democrats would be more likely to vote with
their region than their preferences alone would predict on a given roll call in
the House or Senate across a number of issue areas. Unlike labor policy, where
the region divided between representatives from the border states and those
from the former Confederacy, and to a lesser extent between Black Belt and
non–Black Belt legislators, on nearly every roll call relating to black voting

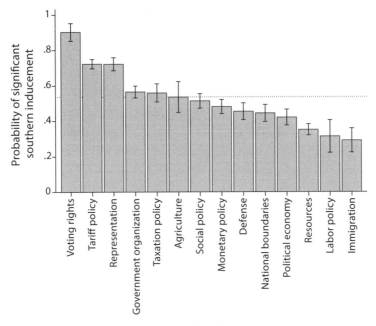

FIGURE 5.2. Probability of Southern-Specific Inducement in Issue Areas

rights or to the authority of Congress to supervise elections, southern Democrats were unanimous, voting with their region at rates much higher than
would be predicted by their estimated preferences alone. The result was a level
of agreement unmatched across any of the other issue areas that animated
southern or national politics during this period.

When addressing northern audiences, many white southerners stressed
that home rule did not necessarily require eliminating black suffrage. Southern
Democrats were more likely, at least in the late 1870s and 1880s, to be focused
on protecting existing electoral gains than pursuing the wholesale disfranchisement of black voters. Mississippi representative, and future senator and
Secretary of the Interior, Lucius Q. C. Lamar insisted that with local self-
government, "all the rights of the black man" could be protected without
"abridging universal suffrage or subjecting either race to the control of the
other." Wade Hampton, who led the Red Shirts terror campaign of 1876, argued that while African Americans should never have been enfranchised, it
would be impossible and wrong to disfranchise them; "the South," he maintained, "does not desire to see this done." Augustus Bacon of Georgia agreed
and, with many others, stressed that "we would not re-enslave [the African
American] if we could, and we would not take away from him the right to vote
if we had the power to do so."[60]

Though we should not take these speakers at their word, their rhetorical insistence on the inviolability of black suffrage speaks to the unsteady equilibrium that characterized the period. Large numbers of southern black men continued to vote after 1877, and much of the legal framework for federal protection of voting rights remained in place. Southern black political activism remained an important part of state and national politics, and in some states black officeholding actually peaked in the 1880s. This situation in part reflected local "fusion" arrangements—blacks gaining local offices in exchange for ceding higher-level ones—as well as the strategic manipulation of district lines by southern Democratic legislatures in order to pack black voters into a small number of districts. It also was the result of efforts by congressional Republicans to support the southern wing of the party by recognizing black representatives as the winners of contested southern elections. Black representatives would be returned to Congress on thirteen occasions between 1881 and 1900, and the presence of men such as James O'Hara, Robert Smalls, Henry Cheatham, Thomas Miller, George W. Murray, George Henry White, and John Mercer Langston spoke to both the continued importance of black voting in the South and the commitment of many northern Republicans to its defense.[61]

Notwithstanding the fact that many white southerners were willing to rhetorically accept the legitimacy of the Reconstruction Amendments, southern Democrats were unanimous in their belief that the continued existence of legislation authorizing the federal government to protect political rights posed a danger to white supremacy that had to be dismantled. The legal authority of the federal government to secure the right to vote had been curtailed by Supreme Court decisions in the 1870s and constrained in its practical effects by Democratic control over state election boards after redemption. In 1876, the Court had ruled that the Fourteenth Amendment applied only to state actions, and that the federal government had no authority to prosecute members of a white militia who had killed dozens of African Americans in Colfax, Louisiana. The same year, the Court ruled that the Fifteenth Amendment had not conferred suffrage on anyone and struck down a section of the Enforcement Act of 1870 providing that if the preliminaries to voting, such as payment of a poll tax, had been conducted in a racially discriminatory fashion, the right to register to vote could not be denied. What remained was the authority of the federal government to closely supervise congressional elections in cities with more than twenty thousand inhabitants, as well as the authority of the president or deputy marshals to use the Army to preserve the peace at polls.

Democratic efforts to overturn the remaining laws began in the 44th Congress. The party had recently pushed through the Holman Rule, which allowed including substantive legislation in appropriations bills. The Democratic strategy was now to attach legislative riders repealing the election laws to "must-pass" appropriations bills. In the immediate aftermath of the contested presidential election of 1876, but before its resolution, the Democratic House attached a rider to the Army appropriations bill requiring that no part of the money be spent for the purpose of sustaining any state government that had not been recognized by Congress. The appropriations bill itself mandated a reduction in the army from twenty-five thousand to seventeen thousand soldiers, and both measures were defended as necessary to restore the "rights of self-government" to the South and end the Republican Party's "policy of vengeance and remorseless hate" toward the region. After the Republican Senate refused to pass the restriction, Congress adjourned; enlisted men were left without pay for a year, while a syndicate of bankers led by J. P. Morgan arranged for officers to cash their pay vouchers at a modest discount.[62]

This first effort to limit federal authority was overshadowed by the unresolved presidential election crisis. By 1876, only three thousand troops continued to be stationed in the former Confederacy outside of Texas. (Ongoing wars against the Indian nations necessitated a larger force in that state.) But while the Republican candidate, Rutherford B. Hayes, had campaigned on a pledge to restore southern home rule, his claim to the presidency effectively depended on the continued use of the Army to protect the election boards and Republican legislatures of Louisiana and South Carolina, the two states whose electoral votes could provide Hayes with an Electoral College majority. After a hastily organized electoral commission decided in favor of Hayes, an agreement was hashed out between Republicans and certain Democrats in which the latter would complete the count of the Electoral College votes, along the lines decided by the commission, on the understanding that Hayes would "adopt such a policy as will give to the people of the States of South Carolina and Louisiana the right to control their own affairs in their own way, subject only to the Constitution of the United States and the laws made in pursuance thereof." The dwindling ranks of the Army would not be withdrawn from the region, but they would no longer be employed to defend the Republican state governments of these two states.[63]

A determined faction of southern and northern Democrats had been filibustering to delay counting the Electoral College votes, but once the outlines of an agreement were decided, the Democratic leadership in the House helped guide the count to completion, with the newly installed Speaker Randall ruling that he would not entertain dilatory motions. His decision was sustained by thirty-six of sixty-eight southern Democrats, by all Republicans, and by forty-six of seventy-five northern Democrats. Although the filibuster did not prevent the election of Hayes, it did ensure that Democrats and the South received some compensation: a southern Democrat was to be given the patronage-distributing post of postmaster general, while Louisiana's and South Carolina's Republican governments were to be abandoned. As the political scientist Gregory Koger notes, "To the extent that the Compromise of 1877 shifted Reconstruction policy, this change is the result of a filibuster in the U.S. House." House Democrats could not have successfully challenged the returns without the concurrence of the Republican Senate, but their ability to "credibly threaten a descent into chaos empowered them to extort an apparent shift in federal policy toward the South."[64]

After the crisis had been resolved, southern Democrats decided to back away from their legislative efforts, and new appropriations bills passed without the restrictive riders. The president, argued one southern Democrat, had shown a "determination to allow the people of the States to regulate their own affairs in their own way," and it would be unwise to "express a want of confidence in his policy" and precipitate further conflict unless there was good cause.[65]

Southern Democratic legislators remained committed to repealing the election laws and restricting federal authority; while the party leadership counseled a cautious accommodation to Hayes's conciliation strategy, they also wanted to show progress in their pledge to roll back Reconstruction-era enforcement powers. In early summer 1878, shortly before Congress adjourned for the upcoming elections, southern Democrats in the House voted to attach a legislative provision to the Army appropriations bill, prohibiting the Army from being used as a *posse comitatus* to enforce the laws. This in part was a response to a memorandum circulated in the run-up to the 1876 elections by Attorney General Alphonso Taft, who instructed federal marshals to form posses of citizens, state militias, or U.S. soldiers to protect voters. Given white hostility to federal authority and black voters, the first two options were difficult to actually enforce, and so deputy marshals and federal agents on occasion turned to the Army to assist them in enforcing U.S. laws in the region. The use of the Army as a posse was widely disliked among southern whites, not only because of its use in elections but also because of their more general opposition to the expanded scope and role of federal authority. The amendment passed both chambers, and the appropriations bill was signed into law.[66]

Urging the amendment's passage, North Carolina senator Augustus Merrimon explained that it was not intended as a sign that Democrats distrusted Hayes to continue his conciliation policy, but that it provided necessary insurance should their hopes prove misplaced. He "trusted the President would not use the army" to supervise elections, but he had believed Grant earlier only to have been gravely disappointed. Even though passage of the *posse comitatus* law is occasionally treated as marking the definitive end to federal authority to protect voters in southern elections, its significance is somewhat ambiguous. It did restrict the coercive authority that Washington could bring to bear, but it also included a proviso allowing the Army to be used as a posse whenever expressly provided by an act of Congress or the Constitution. General

William Sherman considered the law to have been "dictated by the people whom we have whipped and who do not want to see Union soldiers" or even "to see the American flag among them," and in an order he circulated among Army officers, he made clear that he took a broad view of what was included in the exceptions. Civil rights laws, noted Sherman, provided for the use of the Army "as may be necessary to aid in the execution of judicial process, or as shall be necessary to prevent the violation and enforce the due execution of civil rights," while the Ku Klux Klan Act as well as the Constitution authorized the Army to suppress insurrections or enforce the laws whenever the execution of the laws of the United States was impeded "by reason of unlawful obstructions or assemblages of persons, or rebellion against the authority of the Government of the United States." The federal election laws already prohibited persons "engaged in the civil, military, or naval service of the United States" to bring troops or armed men to the polls, but had the vital caveat that they could be used if needed to "keep the peace at the polls." Sherman suggested further that a variety of other laws, concerning American Indian nations, timber on public lands, and even the Guano Islands Act, provided authorization for the Army to be deployed for enforcement purposes.[67]

Given the extensive list of exceptions, many Republicans believed the *posse comitatus*'s restriction of federal authority was "certainly irrelevant" to southern elections, "and may be left out or kept in the bill without doing any harm." It was this expectation—to the effect that the express authorization of the civil rights and enforcement statutes exempted these laws from the curtailment of federal authority—that made the bill acceptable to a Republican Senate, a Republican president, and even the Republican representative from North Carolina's disproportionately black Second Congressional District, who joined other southerners in voting for its passage. With this understanding, the Democratic *Baltimore Sun* noted that "every intelligent officer and citizen knows that the section in the appropriation bill makes no change in the law regulating the employment of troops."[68]

The law was far from meaningless, however. For one, it gave southern Democrats an opportunity to highlight their efforts to roll back federal authority. James Chalmers of Mississippi, for example, extolled the act as the "magna charta of our people," which had been "secured to them by the fidelity and determination of our Congressional representatives." But the statute was not simply an occasion for showing results to constituents; it imposed new limitations on the procedures by which the Army could be employed. As Sherman noted, all requests to use the Army as a posse would now have to be "forwarded through the military channel to the Adjutant-General for the consideration of the President." Deputy marshals and revenue agents in the field no longer would be authorized to mobilize the Army on their own initiative, thus placing sharp limits on their ability to respond quickly. When outlaws in Texas took advantage of the new law to attack American Indians, ranchers, and travelers, the president and cabinet debated the scope of the act's restrictions and ultimately decided that unless there was a threatened insurrection, a danger to the public property of the United States, or an attack on the mails, the Army would be restricted from intervening.[69]

In fact, most Republicans and southern Democrats seem to have understood the primary purpose of the *posse comitatus* clause as intending to constrain the authority of the federal government to use the Army to aid revenue officers in tax collection, "chiefly so that the army could not be used to collect the whisky tax in the South." The "principal and most onerous and disagreeable duty" of the Army in the South, writes one historian, was to "assist revenue officers," a task that was widely disliked among Army officials but also necessitated by the fact that local resistance to internal revenue collection was much more extensive in this region than elsewhere. And in contrast to revenue collection in the rest of the country, opposition to the taxes in the South often received the sanction of state prosecutors, judges, and juries.[70]

Internal revenue employees serving in the South were the only agents in the country supplied with weapons for self-defense, necessitated by the frequency with which they were ambushed or violently resisted. For their actions, revenue agents regularly were indicted in state courts on charges ranging from possession of a concealed weapon to murder. To counter these local nullification efforts, Congress had authorized the government to remove cases against revenue officers to federal courts.[71]

After passage of *posse comitatus*, southern representatives secured an amendment to a revenue bill that would have ended the removal authority altogether, arguing that this amounted to "an oppression . . . used to rob the people of [their] section"; in any case, they claimed, it was one of the "war measures" that a pledge had been made to overturn. The amendment was defeated in the Senate, but it underscored the sustained commitment of southern Democrats to reducing the means by which the federal government could defend its authority in the states. The relation between the *posse comitatus* act and removal authority is perhaps best illustrated by a controversy that broke out between South Carolina and the federal government within a month of the law's passage, when state prosecutors arrested several revenue officers and, with state judges, openly dared the federal government to raise a posse of civilians to enforce the removal law. While Republican newspapers insisted that the Army should be used to secure removal, "delicate handling" of the issue by the president and local authorities eventually dampened the controversy. When the U.S. marshal served a writ of *habeas corpus*, the local sheriff refused to recognize it, but instead pointed the marshal to the keys of the cell and allowed him to unlock it, take control of the prisoners, and relock the cell on his own.[72]

Neither the *posse comitatus* nor southern opposition to removal authority for U.S. revenue agents was reducible to white supremacy. Indeed, southern Democratic efforts to restrict federal authority in enforcing the revenue laws could often find support among black Republican lawmakers. But they were not altogether separate matters. The Civil Rights Act of 1866 had established a similar authority to remove cases to U.S. courts if defendants could show that they would not be able to secure their civil rights in state or local courts, either because of discriminatory procedures in jury selection or because of more vaguely defined local prejudices. Writing about a revenue agent who had shot and killed a man, as well as the grant of removal authority in the Civil Rights Act on account of "*prejudice against color or race*," the *Raleigh Observer* complained that "not a man who has moved his case to the Federal Courts has been punished, and removal now means exemption from the criminal laws of the land." By ending removal authority for revenue officers, or the ability to use the Army to collect the revenue, southern lawmakers could reduce federal authority in an issue area where it would not provoke as strong a Republican reaction, for undoubtedly more Republicans were willing to vote to roll back revenue collection than to repeal the remaining election, Ku Klux Klan, and civil rights laws, especially given that many of them saw reductions in the internal revenue as an opportunity to expand the tariff. By curtailing federal authority in this area, however, the scope of authority over civil rights or elections became even more anomalous.[73]

Posse comitatus passed a few months before a new election campaign, one that witnessed new outrages—including violence and fraud—in a number of southern states. As news of the atrocities made its way northward during the election, Republicans called on the president to employ the Army to protect voters at the polls. But Hayes was determined to maintain his conciliation policy. Northern newspapers reported that "it was thought best, in view of the approaching elections . . . to give [the *posse comitatus* law] as literal an interpretation as can be, so that there may be no excuse to complain." After the election, Ohio representative John Sherman complained that "it is difficult for the executive officers of the United States, crippled as they are by recent legislation, to meet this formidable opposition to the execution of the laws," and he detailed the assaults on voters during the elections and the resistance that federal authority revealed by the recent controversy over removal in South Carolina.[74]

The conciliatory sentiments of 1877 did not last. The 1878 elections were bloody and fraudulent, and an indignant Hayes wrote in his diary that the southern states were attempting by "legislation, by frauds, by intimidation, and by violence of the most atrocious character," to deprive black southern citizens of the right to vote, "despite the promises and assurances given . . . by Southern leaders" and the "[solemn] pledge" of the southern people. South

Carolina had indeed been at the forefront of offering such promises, with Wade Hampton writing, "I pledge my faith, and I pledge it for those gentlemen who are on the ticket with me, that if we are elected, as far as in us lies, we will observe, protect, and defend the rights of the colored man as quickly as of any man in South Carolina." Perhaps it was the ambiguity implied by the last clause that allowed him to make such a pledge. In any case, emboldened by their electoral gains, and perhaps recognizing that Hayes would no longer be deceived by southern assurances, southern Democrats in the lame-duck session of the 45th Congress launched a much more ambitious effort to secure the repeal of the election laws. Announcing that "we do not propose to stop until every vestige of the War-legislation is torn from the statute books," Democrats again attached a rider repealing the election laws, this time to the legislative, executive, and judicial appropriations bill. Conciliation or not, argued the *Baltimore Sun*, "there are acts still upon the statute books . . . which authorise the use of Federal troops as a posse in aid of United States marshals and supervisors at elections." The subject was too important "to be regulated according to the different temperaments and policy of a Grant and a Hayes." The Senate again refused to accept the bill, and Congress adjourned without action.[75]

The incoming Congress, however, held Democratic majorities in both chambers. During a special session in March 1879, Democrats quickly passed an Army appropriations bill with riders that repealed the Army's authority to maintain peace at the polls as well as the juror's test oath, which required jurors to swear to have neither engaged in nor incited rebellion, nor to have resisted the execution of the laws of the United States. With 250 "ballot-box stuffers" awaiting trial in federal court in South Carolina, the *Chicago Tribune* suggested that the real motivation for repeal of the juror law was that "Southern jury-boxes might be filled up with ex-Confederates who sympathize with that class of criminals." In anger at what he now saw as a personal betrayal as well as a concerted attack on the Constitution, President Hayes promptly vetoed the bill on April 29, 1879. Republicans who had been suspicious of his conciliation policy were delighted by the emphasis he placed in his veto message on the necessity for national legislation to "secure the right to vote to the enfranchised race at the South" and prevent fraud in "the large cities of the North."[76]

Regrouping, Democrats passed separate legislation repealing the election laws, which Hayes promptly vetoed. Returning to the appropriations tactic, Democrats included a provision in the legislative, executive, and judicial bill that allowed only civil supervisors to be present at the polls, barring U.S. marshals and their deputies and thereby restricting the government's authority to prevent violence or prosecute fraud. This too was vetoed. Democrats then divided the government appropriations bill into two, the first providing funds for the legislature and executive without any legislative riders and the second providing funds for the judiciary, which both repealed the juror's oath and forbade payments to deputy marshals for enforcing the election laws. Hayes signed the first and vetoed the second.

The Democrats next passed a judicial appropriations bill that repealed the juror's oath and simply omitted any provision for deputy marshals. Throughout the debate, most Republicans had signaled their willingness to repeal the juror's oath—part of which had already been repealed, only to be re-included during the revision of the statutes in 1874—and even to accept a new juror selection process that Democrats believed was necessary to ensure that federal juries were not disproportionately composed of Republicans. Hayes signed the new judicial appropriations bill.[77]

With a small, but potentially important victory, Democrats now passed a final appropriations bill; exclusively concerned with federal marshals, it prohibited their use in elections. This effort also was vetoed by Hayes. The authority of federal officials to preserve the peace during elections was maintained, but left the marshals without funds. A year later, with the elections of 1880 looming, Congress again tried to pass an appropriations bill for U.S. marshals that would have limited their deployment during elections; Hayes sent his veto, and Democrats, conceding the fight, passed appropriations for the marshals without any restriction on their use.

"There is certainly no law," remarked the *Tribune* once the conflict was over, "against Democrats making asses of themselves." Had there been, "the Democratic majority in the present Congress would undoubtedly have repealed it." If Republicans had successfully defended the principle of federal protection of voting rights, the Democrats had managed to secure an important change in the juror selection process. Although the Republicans were willing from the outset to abandon the oath requirement, they were opposed to the Democrats' proposed revision of the selection procedures, and it is likely that Hayes would have vetoed this legislation had it not been a means by which he could signal his willingness to accommodate some southern Democratic demands. Far from being irrelevant, however, these new procedures were of considerable consequence for the South. As one historian of the jury selection process notes, before the revision southern Republicans had been somewhat overrepresented on juries while African Americans had been included at rates roughly approximating their share of the population; after 1879, federal juries were dominated by Democrats, and the participation of black men was "reduced to an insignificant level."[78]

Throughout the fight over repeal, the Democratic Party had been perfectly united, a reflection in part of the fact that most of the money that was spent on election supervisors was being disbursed in cities, primarily in the North, where the laws authorized a more extensive supervisory role. Allen Thurman of Ohio, who would be the vice presidential nominee in 1888, argued that the laws had been passed not "to protect the freedmen against the kuklux," but to "oppress voters at the North, and especially to disfranchise, nay, worse than disfranchise, to imprison and persecute the naturalized citizens of the North." But Democratic unity reflected not just the fact that both sections might be covered by its provisions, but also the inescapable fact that the "solid South" was essential for Democratic political success. "Northern Democrats," argued one Michigan Republican, "realized that without the solid South it was nothing, and the South could not be kept solid by honesty at the polls." In turn, he continued, the "Southern Democrats had served notice on the Northern Democracy that unless it stood by the members sent from the south the partnership would be dissolved."[79]

As the conflict progressed, the sectional character of the fight became increasingly pronounced, leading southern Democrats to attack Hayes for abandoning regional conciliation. The *Daily Picayune*, for instance, reported after the first veto message that "the few southern Democrats who have been disposed to place as favorable a construction as possible on Hayes's [conciliation] policy are bitterly disappointed. . . . The great point and animus of the President is to hold on to the power to appoint Radical supervisors and deputy marshals at the elections." Hayes himself was becoming even more convinced that this policy had come to little: "I tried an experiment in Southern matters," he noted to a Republican critic, "but it failed. From this time on I intend to be radical enough to suit our people."[80]

Democratic efforts to repeal the election laws, combined with the fraud and violence of the 1878 elections, prompted a backlash, emboldening Republicans once again to make southern elections a campaign centerpiece. The Republican platform of 1880 prominently asserted the responsibility of the nation to defend the rights of citizenship, protect "honest voters" from "terrorism, violence, or fraud," and divide the Solid South through the peaceful agency of the ballot, and President Garfield would give considerable emphasis to this theme in his inaugural address. The Department of Justice renewed a modest level of supervision of southern elections, prosecuting more than twice as many cases during the four years of the Garfield and Arthur administrations than during the entire term of Hayes.[81]

During the final session of the 45th Congress, the Republican majority in the Senate passed a resolution appointing a committee to investigate fraud and violence in recent elections. After inquiring into abuses in Louisiana, Mississippi, and South Carolina, the committee concluded that Congress was empowered under Article I of the Constitution to protect voters in the election of members to the House of Representatives: "The time has come when the Congress should exercise the power it clearly possesses of providing by law for fair and free elections of members of Congress."[82]

Over the course of the next decade, Republicans used contested election cases to publicize violence in the conduct of southern elections: when the Republicans held the majority in the House of Representatives in the 47th Congress, they used several contested election cases to seat black members, including Robert Smalls, and to highlight the continued role of violence in southern elections and the systematic efforts to deny political rights to southern African Americans. The reliance on contested election cases in the House came to an end when the Democrats regained control in 1883, but the Republican Senate took up the slack. After an 1883 riot in Danville, Virginia, resulted in the deaths of at least four black men and helped defeat the coalition government of Readjusters and Republicans, the Senate again held an investigation. The majority report concluded that the violence had been a deliberate scheme by Democrats to "intimidate the colored voters in localities where they are strong" and, more importantly, to "produce such a frenzy of feeling in the State as would induce the white electors to join with their own race and escape the contumely and reproach to which they would otherwise be subjected for fraternizing politically with 'niggers.'" The Constitution provided a remedy: reducing the representation of those states where the use of the ballot was effectively being denied. William Chandler, who had already begun to canvass Republicans in Louisiana, Florida, Mississippi, and South Carolina for advice on how to strengthen the election laws, suggested that "when we get ready we can open the southern question with good effect on a new line." In 1887, he introduced a bill to regulate the election of members of Congress from these four states. Though the bill never reached the floor, it served notice that Republicans were looking into the possibility of new legislative action. Chandler then moved successfully for the Committee on the Judiciary to examine whether black electors had been denied the right to vote in a Jackson, Mississippi, municipal election, and he accused the Democratic-appointed U.S. deputy marshals and revenue collectors of participating in vote suppression. This proposal passed with every Republican in favor and only Democrats and Harrison Riddleberger, a Virginia Readjuster, voting against. An earlier investigation that had examined elections in Mississippi and another inquiring into election violations in Texas had both concluded that these two states possibly should see their representation reduced, that the president should take a more aggressive role in protecting the right to vote, and that Congress should revise the laws regulating elections "with a view of providing for a more complete protection of the elective franchise, and for the punishment of offences against it."[83]

Home Rule Defended

Though violence remained an important part of the repertoire used by southern Democrats to suppress voting, it became less important than fraud after the accession of Democratic governments enabled state-appointed election boards to simply "count out" black votes or tally them for the Democratic Party. Some states, including Virginia, Georgia, and South Carolina, passed legislation or revised their constitutions to disfranchise many black voters, through poll tax requirements (abolished by the Readjuster coalition in Virginia in 1882) and, in South Carolina, through the notorious Eight-Box Law. That law required that each ballot be deposited in a separate box; the boxes were periodically rearranged, and only the white election officials were allowed to tell illiterate voters which box was for which contest. Any mistakenly deposited ballot was ruled inadmissible. Because curtailment of black voting in the South now was primarily accomplished through fraud—the "counting out" that witnesses to the Blair Committee had identified—or the discriminatory application of registration and voting procedures, the existing authority of the federal government to protect southern elections was limited. Even if U.S. marshals had taken on a more active role to protect the right of black men to vote, they would have had no ability to prosecute fraud outside of the major cities, nor could they have supervised the process to ensure that it was not racially discriminatory. If the right to vote was to be meaningfully defended, new legislation would be needed.[84]

In 1889, the Republican Party took control of the House, Senate, and presidency for the first time since 1876 and immediately began to draft legislation for a more extensive and regular supervision of congressional elections. The federal elections bill was a compromise between different proposals put forward by Republicans Harrison Kelley of Kansas, Henry Cabot Lodge and George Frisbie Hoar of Massachusetts, and Jonathan Rowell of Illinois, with Kelley's being the most extreme, for it would have fully nationalized all congressional election procedures. The president was widely rumored to favor less extreme measures, to avoid the remainder of the administration becoming "exceedingly unpleasant"; Kelley's version was rejected by a divided party caucus. A slight majority favored the more moderate proposals, and "only a relatively small minority of Republicans [were] opposed to any bill at all." The basic outlines of the final proposal enabled three supervisors to oversee the registration and election process of any congressional district upon the petition of one hundred qualified voters or fifty voters in any individual county. These supervisors would be empowered to inspect registration lists, challenge the registration of voters, supervise naturalization procedures, keep a list of rejected voters, receive their ballots in a separate envelope, inform all voters who asked about the proper ballot box in which to place their votes, and even prepare their own election returns. State-imposed qualifications, such as lit-eracy tests, were not to be altered. Still, the presence of federal supervisors would enhance the prospects for nondiscriminatory elections.[85]

Southern Democrats quickly "served notice that they will never consent to the passage of such a measure" and intended to "resist it in debate until the close of Congress." The threat that the South would use all opportunities for procedural delay across the entire congressional term fundamentally shaped Republican strategy. In the House, which heretofore had been the chamber in which obstruction could most effectively be exercised, Speaker Thomas Brackett Reed decided to carry out a plan to reduce delay and curtail the abil-ity of the minority to filibuster. Instead of simply adopting the rules of the previous Congress, Reed operated during the first few weeks of the session under general parliamentary law, which provided the speaker with consider-able discretion in recognizing dilatory motions and in counting votes. (There was no provision for teller voting for instance, by which the members them-selves could check the count and delay proceedings.) This authority would be crucial when, during a contested election case from West Virginia, Reed began counting as present Democrats who were in the chamber but had refused to vote, thereby seeking to deny the existence of a chamber quorum, a crucial means of coordinated delay. The next day Reed was sustained in his decision by a majority of the House; the following day he was sustained in a decision to ignore dilatory motions.[86]

Soon, new rules were passed that enshrined the right of the speaker to count members as present and ignore dilatory motions, to reduce the quorum in the Committee of the Whole from a majority of the chamber to one hun-dred members, and to allow the speaker to refer all bills and resolutions to an appropriate committee without debate. Although Reed had long wanted a reform of the rules to achieve these purposes, his decision to do so at this juncture was fundamentally related to the party's goal of passing a new elec-tions law. Members repeatedly framed the fight over the rules in the same terms as their argument for new election legislation. As William McKinley put it, the question was whether the minority or majority should rule; explicitly referring to the Civil War, he announced that "we settled one question at a great deal of cost—that the minority could not rule in this country [applause] and we intend to settle, if we can, in broad light of public opinion and in the presence of 60,000,000 of people whether a constitutional majority in this house shall do the business of this house." Benjamin Butterworth of Ohio made a similar point, highlighting the nationalization of citizenship and gov-ernment that had followed the Civil War: the argument that each representa-tive was responsible to his constituents alone might "have done when it was held that members were ambassadors from the states. It would not do in Janu-ary 1890." "The members must determine to-day whether the constitution contained in itself the element of suicide," which he defined as the ability for the minority to rule and impede the authority of the nation.[87]

On a near-straight party vote on June 25, the House adopted a resolution providing for a weeklong consideration of the federal elections bill, to be followed immediately by a vote. Democrats, recalling the recent fight over the McKinley tariff, complained that "no one except a favored few were to be given the opportunity to have their amendments considered." Reed was praised by Republicans for carrying out the wishes of the caucus and ensuring both that a contingency was prepared for "every emergency that was likely to arise" and that all efforts "were made to guard against any line of tactics the opposition might employ." After a week of "red hot debate," the House voted 155 to 149 to pass the bill, with Herman Lehlbach of New Jersey and Hamilton Coleman of Louisiana the only Republicans voting against; Coleman was a very different type of southern Republican from those who had been returned to Congress since the war, having built his electoral coalition primarily around the issue of the tariff; he relied almost as much on white as on black voters. Another Republican opponent of the bill, Hamilton Ewart of North Carolina, who also hoped to build a white Republican Party in the South, absented himself from Congress during the bill's consideration. "He lacked the grit to face the music," claimed the *Columbus Enquirer-Sun*.[88]

Half a year later, the federal elections bill was dead, defeated in the Senate by sustained Democratic obstruction that fatally eroded pivotal Republican support. The Republicans in the 51st Congress had several major legislative priorities, including the elections bill, the McKinley tariff, multiple appropriations bills, and a host of other policies prioritized by one or another faction of the party, the most important of which was new currency legislation desired by western Republicans. The intensity of southern preferences on the issue of elections fundamentally shaped the calculations of the different Republican factions in the Senate. As soon as an elections bill was introduced in April, James Pugh gave notice that it would be resisted by every method "allowed by the Constitution of the United States." Just as importantly, southern Democrats suggested that they might filibuster not just the elections bill but "the tariff bill and any other measure" so long as the specter of federal supervision of elections loomed on the horizon. The promise of an extended obstruction campaign on all issues raised the possibility that some portion of the Republican agenda would have to be abandoned, making the order in which issues were considered crucial for different Republican factions, for whichever issue was pushed back would likely be brought up only in the short session after the midterm elections, when the ability of southern Democrats to run out the clock through obstruction and delay would be much higher.[89]

Faced with a growing Populist Party revolt, a large number of members from both parties in the House and Senate were eager to pass some form of silver currency legislation before the midterms to undercut support for the new party. Congressional action on the tariff would help calm markets before the upcoming elections—a point stressed by Republican representative Nelson Aldrich in particular—but it would also facilitate Democratic delay; even at the best of times, tariff revision was a laborious and time-consuming task, and Democrats would now have the incentive and opportunity to extensively debate every one of its many provisions. This development could push the session into the late summer and early fall, when members of Congress would be eager to return home to engage in the election campaign. If the Senate moved first on the elections bill, however, Democratic delay would almost certainly ensure that, unless drastic measures were taken, action on the currency or tariff would have to wait until after the midterm elections, thus prolonging market instability while raising the likelihood of legislative defeat. Given a promise by each southern senator to speak for twenty days on the elections bill, it had been apparent from the outset that passing the entirety of the Republican agenda would probably require that the Senate "adopt a new code of rules limiting debate," lest it be "impossible to pass a Federal election law or any other important measure to which the minority might take exception." There was "almost unanimity" in the Republican Senate conference "that it would be absolutely necessary to adopt a cloture rule in order to pass the bill," but many of the western supporters of free silver, concerned about not antagonizing Democrats whose support might be needed, were opposed. Support for a rule change seems to have been strongest among those who wanted quick action on the elections bill and who detailed a list of precedents that had been utilized to pass the Reconstruction Amendments and, they believed, would presently allow them to overcome Democratic delay.[90]

After considerable debate, the Republican conference decided to move first on the currency, then on the tariff, with the promise to bring up the elections bill as soon as work on the tariff was completed and before adjourning for the summer and fall. They also decided to change the rules only after ample evidence had been accumulated that the Democrats were engaged in a filibuster; Republicans preferred "to await for a pretext which will stand public scrutiny before resorting to arbitrary measures." The decision to deal with the currency issue first raised the prospect of the party fracturing, as "pronounced silver men" voted with the Democratic minority against bringing up the tariff bill until the currency bill was passed. Even more ominous, however, was that a provision passed by the Senate for the free coinage of silver, with a minority of Republicans voting with a majority of Democrats, was struck out in conference with the House in early July; the most committed "silver men themselves declare that they accept it only because it is all they can get this session and serve notice that they will continue the battle for free coinage indefinitely."[91]

The decision to consider the tariff before the elections bill was hugely advantageous to the Democrats, as they were able to drag debate out into late August. Southern Democratic senators stayed in Washington rather than return to their states to attend to their reelection. The bill "surpasses anything the audacity of the Republican party ever produced," argued James Pugh in a letter explaining why he could not return to Alabama; it was designed, he wrote, to "insure the subjugation of the Democratic white people of the South to the domination of the Republican party on the basis of negro suffrage." What little hope was "left of defeating this diabolical scheme is in the Senate, where the rights and powers of the minority have heretofore had ample recognition and protection in parliamentary procedure. I know you will agree with me that under these circumstances no Democratic Senator can leave his post without subjecting himself to the disgrace of desertion in the face of the enemy."[92]

"Congress has entered upon another week of time wasting," complained the *Inter-Ocean*. "Seldom has a legislative body presented so discreditable a spectacle," as the minority "is openly and persistently engaged in the one occupation of blocking the wheels of legislation of all kinds." What made this obstruction campaign unique, the paper noted, was that "the entire range of legislation has at last been included." But Democrats were careful: their delaying action against the tariff did not primarily take the form of dilatory motions or endless speeches, but rather sustained interrogation and discussion of each provision and each item on the duty rolls, leading the *Baltimore American* to note that "there is a big difference between tariff discussion and tariff obstruction. And the Senate should recognize it."[93]

After months of debating the tariff, the Pennsylvania Republican Matthew Quay, who admitted to not having read or cared much about the elections bill, worked out a deal with Democrats in which they agreed to end debate by unanimous consent in exchange for pushing off consideration of the elections bill until the next session. Speaker Reed, among other Republicans who had prioritized the elections bill, was furious: he had been trying to keep his members in Washington precisely that they might be present to quickly act on the elections bill once it was passed by the Senate. The passage of Quay's resolution would make it "impossible for him to keep the Congressmen here, and he would be d——d if he was going to try it." As discussed in chapter 4, a slight majority of the Republican conference was more concerned with passing the tariff than the elections bill, whose defeat was the paramount priority of southern Democrats: they were willing to subordinate any other policy goal to this objective. The plan agreed to by Quay, for which he was castigated as a traitor and a stooge of Andrew Carnegie by much of the party press, had been the southern objective all along. In the early summer, it had been widely reported that the Democrats were going to filibuster the tariff precisely to tire "the republican senators into an agreement to a compromise by which the federal elections bill will be allowed to go over until the next session." Although Quay had initially wanted to abandon the elections bill altogether, Senator Hoar was adamant that it pass, and he secured a written commitment from every Republican senator that the bill would be made the paramount issue when the Senate reconvened in December.[94]

The election campaign in the North and South focused heavily on the elections bill, and the southern Democratic position was buttressed by a full-throated appeal to northern public opinion, including industrialists, journalists, and readers of literary and contemporary affairs magazines. A series of essays written by southern lawmakers was quickly published under the title *Why the Solid South? or Reconstruction and Its Results*. Dedicated to the "Business Men of the North," this volume made the case that any renewal of federal protection of voting rights would undermine property and investments in the region, and that the ensuing political crises and misrule by black voters and white demagogues would send the entire country's economy into a tailspin. John Morgan threw himself entirely into the campaign, authoring "Shall Negro Majorities Rule?" and "Federal Control of Elections" in *The Forum* in 1889 and 1890, respectively, and "The Race Question in the United States" in *The Arena*. Morgan would later write a preface to a new edition of Tocqueville's *Democracy in America*. Tocqueville, wrote Morgan, had been primarily concerned with "the white race, who are described as 'We, the people,' in the opening sentence of the Constitution." He decried the enfranchisement of black Americans as "a political party movement, intended to be radical and revolutionary," and suggested that Tocqueville would have applauded "that elementary feature of our political organization which, in the end, will render harmless this wide departure from the original plan and purpose of American Democracy. 'Local Self-Government,' independent of general control, except for general purposes," was the fundamental guarantor of American democracy.[95]

Republicans responded in kind. Albion Tourgée, asking Morgan "Shall White Minorities Rule?," noted that "deterrent violence or neutralizing fraud" is "what southern writers mean when they insist that white minorities at the South shall be left to deal with the Negro question in their own way. This was the demand which Slavery always made." Robert Smalls, who to his great disgust had found himself compelled to endorse the "straight out" Democratic nominee Alexander Haskell in order to defeat Benjamin Tillman, called "upon the true Representatives who are in favor of honest elections and a fair count to give their undivided support to the Lodge Election Bill." But the divisions within the Republican ranks, as well the economic crisis induced by the months-long uncertainty over the tariff and currency, limited the impact of their counterarguments.[96]

The landslide Democratic victory in November was attributed in no small part to their aggressive campaigning against the "Force bill." The Republicans lost ninety-three seats in the House; Democrats would occupy 70 percent of the seats in the new Congress meeting in December 1891. Still, the Republican conference remained determined to pass the elections bill in the lame-duck session and brought the bill up for debate in the Senate on the first day of the short session. At this point, the filibuster began in earnest, even as the obstruction campaign had already begun months earlier. All through December the "daily profitless debate on the Force bill went on," with Democrats led by Maryland senator Arthur Pue Gorman engaging in "endless digressions and oratorical diversions and utiliz[ing] every parliamentary device that could be remembered or invented."[97]

Republican restlessness grew as the filibuster continued. When the election of two Populist senators and eight Populist representatives further convinced silver Republicans of the inadequacy of the Silver Purchase Act, they demanded legislation that would allow the free coinage of silver without reference to gold. In early December, the Republican conference agreed to introduce a rule change to limit debate for the remainder of the legislative session, and on December 23, Senator Nelson Aldrich announced that he was authorized by the Committee on Rules to report a resolution, introduced by Hoar in August, to this effect, finally playing "the high card so long reserved by Republican Senators." In addition, Aldrich presented a resolution authorizing a vote to be held at a defined moment on House Bill 11045, the federal elections bill. These proposals were to lie on the table to be called up when Republicans saw fit. Southern newspapers complained that "the last hope has about gone," and that "the Election bill will in all probability pass." While there was still some possibility that an amended bill might not pass the House—where a lot of the defeated Republicans were unwilling to return to vote on it—President Harrison was reported saying that any Republican who failed "to do their full duty in working for its passage . . . should not expect favors from him," and that "no more patronage would be distributed until the election bill had passed through the house."[98]

On January 5, however, eight Republicans from the West and Midwest—California's Leland Stanford, Colorado's Henry Teller and Edward Wolcott, Minnesota's William Washburn, Nevada's John Jones and William Stewart, and William McConnell and George Shoup from the new state of Idaho—voted with every Democrat to put the elections bill aside and begin consideration of a new currency proposal. Democrats had been paying close attention to the demand of the western and silver Republicans for a more liberal silver law, and they leapt at the opportunity to further delay the elections bill. Although a majority of southern Democrats supported free silver, many did not, including the de facto Senate minority leader, Arthur Pue Gorman, who later would remark that he "would have voted for the free coinage of lead to preserve the liberties of the American people." As had happened with the tariff, a pivotal group of southerners were willing to subordinate their preferences on the currency in order to defend white supremacy.[99]

Some silver senators were hopeful that both measures could be adopted before the end of the Congress if there was "a proper spirit of determination on the part of the majority," but Republican senators "were all surprised at the displacement of the election bill," and one western senator who was indifferent but wanted it to pass as a party measure reported that "the friends of the bill did not know what to think or do now, for they had been so surprised they had not had time to consider the situation." Senator Hoar was particularly furious. He carefully preserved the written agreement to prioritize the elections bill over other matters that had been signed by silver Republicans who now voted to consider their preferred bill. It was, he wrote, "inexplicable perfidy."[100]

Senate Democrats could not filibuster the silver bill, which so many had committed to supporting, and thereby delay proceedings even further; doing so would have deeply antagonized the silver Republicans, driving them back into the arms of their party. "In tolerably rapid succession," a series of amendments were debated and passed before a Democratic senator, George Vest from Missouri, proposed as a substitute a simple free silver bill. The substitute passed without a roll call, and the bill was approved 39 to 27, with conservative Republicans confident that this legislation either would not pass the House—which had rejected just such a proposal in July—or would be vetoed by the president. The Republican leadership was eager to get back to work on the elections bill, and immediately after passage of free silver, Hoar moved to bring it up. This motion passed 34 to 33, with the vice president casting the tie-breaking vote. The silver Republicans, whether out of indifference, conviction, or gratitude to the Democrats, now were in open opposition.[101]

"It was at this point," writes Gorman's biographer John Lambert, "that the ceaseless opposition of the Democratic minority achieved the peak of perfection." They disappeared the quorum, talked relentlessly, and offered repeated dilatory motions. If the rules were to be changed, it would have to be now. On January 22, after an extraordinary effort at obstruction, the vice president determined that the reading and correction of the *Journal* could be disposed of without unanimous consent, and a motion was brought up to change the rules. "Parliamentary law, the rules of the Senate and the rights of the minority," complained the Democratic *Boston Post*, "were ruthlessly trampled under foot today." The Senate then voted 36 to 32 to consider a motion to change the rules to allow for cloture, with four western Republicans in opposition. To limit Democratic opportunities for delay, Republicans kept the Senate in session, extending the legislative day for almost a week. But by now even staunchly Republican newspapers began calling on the party to make a "grace-ful retreat." The *Philadelphia Inquirer* remarked that "nearly two months have been wasted—worse than wasted," by the party's insistence on passing the elections bill over the intense opposition of the South.[102]

On January 26, Republican senator Edward Wolcott of Colorado moved that the Senate take up an apportionment bill, thereby setting aside the rule change. This passed 35 to 34. "The gag-rule," wrote the *Baltimore Sun* the next day, "which was to have been the weapon with which to force the passage of the elections bill was successfully displaced," delivering a "fatal setback" to both. Without a majority and without much more time, Republican support-ers of the bill conceded defeat. The rules and procedures of the House had been dramatically reworked, obstructionist tactics in the Senate had been pushed further than ever before, and the authority of the majority had been put to the test, with the vice president overruling the rules and precedent in order to advance the cause of majority control. In the end, the filibuster had been preserved, and the Democratic Party had—possibly for the first time ever—defeated a central legislative priority of the majority party through a campaign of sustained obstruction.[103]

The defeat of the elections bill was not so much a failure of Republican will as it was a victory for southern Democratic commitments. The central diffi-culty for the bill's supporters was that the South's members were unanimously and intensely opposed to it, while Republican backing, though genuine, was unevenly passionate. Newspapers reported that, while "there was a decided majority for a federal elections bill" in the Republican Senate conference, "and it is said that no one strongly objected to it . . . a fairly good number showed a great deal of lukewarmness on the subject." "From a party standpoint," noted one observer, western Republicans and other lukewarm supporters "would probably feel obliged to vote for the passage of the elections bill" if it could be brought to a vote on final passage. But some were also hopeful that they might not "be compelled to show their hand." What defeated the bill was the extraor-dinary filibuster, which began effectively in the early summer of 1890 when the tariff bill was brought up and then continued with intermittent truces until January. It was this opposition strategy that forced the various Republican factions to choose between their different legislative priorities and decide which should go first and whether or not to agree on rule changes to limit obstruction. Those Republicans who would have supported the elections bill so long as it did not impinge on their other priorities were denied this luxury.[104]

Some measure of the success of this Democratic strategy can be gleaned from figure 5.3. The left panel shows the location of Republican senators from the beginning to the end of the 51st Congress, as these developed over the course of the period. The right panel shows the estimated location of the me-

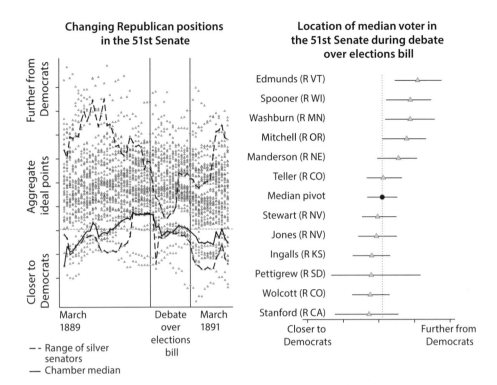

Changing Republican positions in the 51st Senate

Location of median voter in the 51st Senate during debate over elections bill

FIGURE 5.3. Preference Development and Median in the 51st Senate. Dotted line is average location of median during debate over elections bill.

dian voter during the two months when the elections bill was under debate, when there was a high likelihood that the pivotal member would be a silver Republican. It was less the case that the silver Republicans were the median voters in the Senate because of some stable preferences across all issue areas, and more that they were pushed away from the Republican mainstream by their frustration with a majority of their fellow Republicans who refused to support the free coinage of silver. For the first half of this Congress, the voting patterns of silver Republicans ranged across the entire spectrum of Republican positions, but by December and January further progress on their legislative priority was being impeded by their party's decision to finish up with the elections bill. It was only when this choice was forced that they began to cluster around the median as they cast more votes with Democrats who were eager to cultivate their support. The Republican senators who voted to set aside the rule changes were Jones, Stewart, Teller, Washburn, and Wolcott, all of whom by now were clustered around the median despite having earlier ranged the spectrum of Republican voting. They were joined by James Cameron of Pennsylvania, the "recruit whose vote made the coup successful." Cameron, whose voting record on black Americans' political rights would have predicted his support for the bill, came under intense criticism in the succeeding days and months amid allegations that he had sold his vote to avoid the disclosure of embarrassing financial investments.[105]

With the defeat of the federal elections bill—the most forceful Republican effort to protect black voting rights since the end of congressional Reconstruction—congressional Republicans effectively abandoned the cause. Recognition of this relinquishment opened up political space within the South for the systematic disfranchisement of black voters, not because the legal context had changed but because southern political leaders now believed that they could act without fear of legislative retaliation.

Black rights further declined. Two years after the defeat of the federal elections bill, the Democratic Party gained unified control over the government for the first time in thirty-four years and soon acted to repeal any remaining Reconstruction-era election laws. When, in 1894, Virginia Democrat Henry St. George Tucker III introduced a repeal bill, he realistically boasted that "every trace of the reconstruction measures" would now be "wiped from the statute books."[106]

The remaining laws themselves had failed to protect the integrity of elections in the South. Absent sufficiently high levels of election day violence to justify the use of the Army or the formation of a posse by deputy marshals, and lacking the ability to police elections outside cities with more than twenty thousand residents where supervisors with the power to arrest voters or mark ballots for later inspection could be requested, the still-existing election laws clearly were ineffective. There were only twenty-five cities of this size in the South in 1890. Only in Baltimore, New Orleans, Little Rock, Memphis, St. Louis, and Wilmington were supervisors regularly used in the region, although they were often present in rural congressional districts to watch over the process, despite being able only to attend, witness, and report on violations of state electoral laws. The *Dallas Morning News* complained that repeal was simply a distraction, asking, "Who cares anything about the federal election laws? Who does not know that those which are now in the statute books could not have been strengthened even if the republicans had won? Who does not know that as they now stand, they amount to nothing except in communities where the people want them enforced." Harrison's administration had been even less involved in prosecuting election offenses under the existing laws than Hayes's had been, a tangible sign of the withdrawal of Republican commitments.[107]

For white southerners, the election laws thus were mainly significant in symbolic terms, for the claim they represented to the effect that the national government possessed the constitutional authority to regulate congressional elections and thereby intervene in local affairs. Josiah Patterson, a Tennessee

Democrat whose district included Memphis, which continued to be subject to federal supervision, recounted the travails of Reconstruction and insisted that the Anglo-Saxon race would always do what it must to retain its supremacy, up to and including fraud and violence. A parade of southern representatives repeated the same basic themes, arguing that the "people had thrust the Democratic party in power in order to enable it to repeal these laws." Debate in the House lasted nearly two weeks, with sessions sparsely attended.[108]

There was renewed turnout, however, when George Murray of South Carolina, the only African American Republican in the House, rose to speak. "Everything" in the South, he argued, "economics, finances, laws, customs, morality, and religion—is subordinated to the false teachings of white supremacy." Its principles "permeate and breathe their poisonous breath throughout the whole of society." So long as it was possible that "persons armed with knives, revolvers, shotguns, or rifles, occupying places near the polls or within their sacred precincts," would kill or intimidate "the rulers of the land," then the federal election laws were needed and should not be repealed. Murray explained that the men of his district had tried to register but were denied by the state-appointed official; he concluded by calling on "my people everywhere to take the roll," to "mark the name of every man casting an affirmative vote, and regard him as their perpetual enemy." It was an elegant speech met with prolonged applause on the Republican side; at least a few southern Democrats insisted that he could not have written it himself. The repeal bill passed a week later, on a straight party-line vote.[109]

The Republicans attempted nothing like the sort of obstruction campaign that had been waged by the Democrats against the federal elections bill in 1890. In the Senate, Republican leaders conceded that the repeal bill would pass, being "impossible to prevent." They recognized that even as the first session of Congress had "only fairly begun . . . the majority [was] united upon the policy of passing the bill," making "any effort on the part of the republicans to attempt to accomplish its defeat by dilatory tactics . . . foolhardy." Senate Democrats in fact had already considered whether to impose cloture in order to pass the bill repealing the Sherman Silver Act, and it seems reasonable that any sustained obstruction campaign against the repeal of the election laws would have had an even greater number of Democrats supporting some type of limited cloture measure. Given the strength of Democratic commitments on this issue, as well as the timing of the repeal effort, the Republicans understood the degree of disadvantage they would face should they mount an obstruction campaign.[110]

Still, as Richard Valelly persuasively points out, the decision not to filibuster was less a calculation of odds than an acquiescence to changed political circumstances. "They called off the fight," he writes. Republicans reportedly believed that the election laws were a "dead letter," while the minority report on the bill frankly conceded that a Republican effort to supervise national elections was not likely to "ever be revived. The control of national legislation in this country will be for some time beyond the reach of the republican party, and we believe that that is the desire of a majority of the people that the experiment should be fully tried whether existing laws and an improving public sentiment will not cure the evils complained of." Even Senator Hoar—who had been steadfast in his commitment to the federal elections bill—would recall that "so far as I was concerned, and so far as I had the right to express the opinion of Northern Republicans, I thought the attempts to secure the rights of the colored people by national legislation would be abandoned until there was a considerable change of opinion in the country, and especially in the South, and until it had ceased to become a matter of party strife." Republicans conceded that they would "attempt nothing more" than "some speeches on the subject" and framed repeal as "one of the legitimate results of the democratic victory."[111]

But not without one last remonstration. The minority report provided a record of southern misrule, highlighting that "when the repeal takes place elections according to the principle of 'home rule'" would be held under the auspices of southern state electoral laws that were designed to enable Democratic Party fraud. The report detailed the laws of the southern states, showing how they concentrated power in the Democratic governor or general assembly, and argued that they constituted the "means of which, year after year, unscrupulous oligarchies perpetuate their absolute political control of the States." The authors of the report conceded that existing laws and their degree of enforcement were inadequate to the task, but insisted on recounting "how the South has been made solid" through murder, intimidation, and deceit, so that "the young men and women of America, by obtaining and reading the annals of these atrocities, may learn some of the reasons why the national election laws were enacted and have been kept upon the statute book, and also discover if they can see the reasons why they should be repealed."[112]

When the secretary of the Senate came to the House to announce that repeal had passed that chamber, Democrats burst into applause. Representative Tucker had even purchased a golden pen for the occasion, which he asked the vice president, the speaker of the House, and the president to use when signing the bill. He kept the pen as a cherished memento. "It Is Finished," proclaimed the front-page headline of the *Knoxville Journal*, one of relatively few remaining Republican papers in the South. "Fraud is now legalized," and "ballot box stuffing may now be engaged in with beautiful impunity."[113]

This retraction signified "the close of an era in the nation's legislative history," although its actual impact was limited. Ironically, the repeal soon was accompanied by a dramatic increase in the Republican share of the vote in the border states and the upper South. The congressional elections of 1894 saw

Republicans pick up seats in Delaware, Maryland, West Virginia, Kentucky, Missouri, Tennessee, Virginia, North Carolina, Alabama, and Texas. Republican gains at the state level between 1894 and 1896 were almost as pronounced, with the party winning a majority of the state legislatures of West Virginia, Delaware, and Missouri for the first time since the 1860s, and of Kentucky and Maryland for the first time ever. Together, Republicans and Populists cut deeply into Democratic hegemony in Louisiana, Tennessee, Virginia, Alabama, Georgia, and, most dramatically, North Carolina.

There were numerous reasons for this drop-off in Democratic support, including the economic depression begun in 1893, the repeal of the Silver Act, and the Wilson-Gorman Tariff. Many Republican strategists emphasized instead, however, the election laws repeal, which ushered in "a new epoch" in the party's career. As one Republican wrote,

> The repeal of the federal election laws removed the specter of "negro domination," relaxed the pressure which held differences of views on economic questions in imperative subjection to the one over-mastering issue, and permitted the South to divide like the rest of the country on the living questions of the day. Nine months after the federal election laws were stricken from the national statute book, in February, 1894, the Republicans gained an overwhelming victory.[114]

Of course, repeal was unlikely to have been the principal reason for the Republican sweep, which had multiple causes. But the causal emphasis placed on repeal reflected the rise of a faction of the party that saw the defense of black political rights as irrelevant or even contrary to Republican prospects. The writer added optimistically that "the Southern States promise to be the great recruiting ground of the [Republican] party in the future," and even many of the region's African American newspapers hailed a new dawn to proclaim that the " 'Solid South' is at last broken."[115]

Paradoxically, this judgment was at once correct and deeply mistaken. The Republican Party became competitive in all the border states. But the defeat of the federal elections bill and the passage of repeal signaled a new political climate in which disfranchisement could be undertaken across the South without fear of northern retaliation. Even before the fight over the federal elections bill, some southern states had begun to look for constitutional solutions to the threat posed by black Americans' political rights. With the renewed political activism of the 1890s by African Americans, white southern Democrats vigorously embraced disfranchisement. The expectation of a new elections law in 1888 had prompted Tennessee's Democratic Party to pass legislation to "give a practical, Constitutional and happy solution of the race problem," tightening registration in select counties, providing for an effective literacy test, and only narrowly failing to authorize a poll tax; the next year, after this last means of restriction was passed by making it binding for the Democratic caucus, it was quickly pushed through. Arkansas, Florida, and Mississippi had also acted to preempt federal supervision. Florida imposed a poll tax in 1889, Arkansas established an effective literacy test in 1891, and after Senator James George had carefully tested Republican reactions to the possibility of requiring a literacy test in the spring of 1890, Mississippi held a constitutional convention while the federal elections bill sat delayed in the Senate with precisely this explicit purpose. "If the force bill now pending in Congress" were to pass, argued the *Clarion-Ledger*, "it is fortunate for Mississippi that she will be able to through her Constitutional Convention . . . put such restrictions on suffrage as to render it largely nugatory and deprive it of much of its power for evil."[116]

The combined defeat of the federal elections bill and the repeal of limited national supervisory authority eliminated any worry about federal retaliation. Governor Benjamin Tillman was obsessed by the possibility that black South Carolinians would be "brought in as the balance of power between the contending white factions," and the state in 1895 passed a new constitution explicitly designed to disfranchise black voters. An 1892 general strike in New Orleans had raised the prospect of black and white laborers working together, although subsequent strikes and violence in the city showed the working-class communities to be deeply divided; more worrisome, that year the Republicans and Populists put forward a joint ticket for that year's presidential election. By 1896, a newly organized "National" Republican Party, whose primary purpose was to support the tariff, had begun making inroads among white voters, and only through a heavy reliance on fraud—counting black votes for the Democratic candidate—was the Democratic Party able to defeat a coalition of regular Republicans, National Republicans, and Populists. The Populist-Republican candidate won in almost every majority-white district as well as in East Baton Rouge, the only black-majority district where it was widely acknowledged that black voters could cast a free and fair vote. Two years later, Louisiana Democrats revised the state constitution and enacted a byzantine and severely disfranchising voter qualification law. North Carolina revised its constitution in 1900 after Democrats defeated the Republican-Populist fusion party that had governed from 1894 to 1898. They were followed by Alabama in 1901, which built upon an 1893 election law's voter registration and effective literacy test, and by Texas and Virginia in 1902. Georgia had curtailed black voting through its poll tax since 1877, but the rise of the Populists had been accompanied by a considerable increase in black voting; legislation was passed in 1894 to strengthen Democratic control over the voting process, and in 1907 the state agreed to finally get "rid of the negro even as a *political potentiality*" through a combined property and literacy qualification.[117]

The impact of disfranchisement was devastating. Turnout, especially black turnout, collapsed. Disfranchisement was most pronounced in the Black Belt

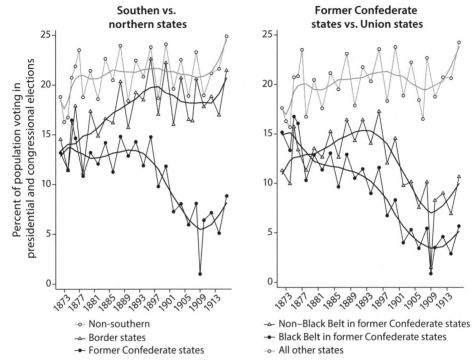

FIGURE 5.4. Turnout in National Elections, 1873–1915. Turnout is based on total populations and includes presidential and congressional elections as well as special elections.

counties, which would become the undisputed hard core of southern politics for the next half-century (figure 5.4).

It is difficult to assess what might have happened had the federal elections bill passed. Certainly some disfranchisement mechanisms, including literacy tests and poll taxes, still would have been acceptable under the bill, and some states would have followed Tennessee's example of separating out their procedures for federal elections from those for state and local ones, thus limiting the extent to which the bill would have been able to protect voting rights for the offices of most immediate importance to southern communities. But as Robert Smalls made clear, the voter suppression laws already in place in the South depended "upon the unfair methods of its enforcement for its effectiveness. The poor whites who form the bulk of the Democratic voters could no more vote intelligently under its provisions than the ignorant colored voter." Passage of the elections bill would by no means have ensured manhood suffrage in the South, but it would have made racially discriminatory restrictions or evasions of voting registration and balloting procedures more difficult and thus would probably have preserved a role, however diminished, for black voters. And it would most likely have limited the ability of Democrats to "count out" the votes cast by black southerners, or to count these for Democratic candidates. Given the role these means played in defeating the Populist insurgency, it is at least conceivable that had the elections bill passed, either a Populist-Republican coalition would have been a viable option in more states or white conservative Democrats would have had to make genuine appeals on policy and appointment grounds to middle-class black voters.[118]

Conclusion

The United States declared war on Spain in April 1898. The war was skeptically received by many southerners; the region's representatives provided fifteen of the nineteen votes cast against the initial war resolution in the House. Yet despite the region's anti-imperialist sentiment, the war with Spain became an occasion to affirm the South's definitive return to the Union. "To Americans of that era," writes Richard Wood, the war "meant the triumph of a reconciled Union," and southern governors and representatives loudly proclaimed the region's eagerness to once again "march together under Old Glory" with their northern countrymen. When former Confederates Fitzhugh Lee and Joseph Wheeler were given commissions as major generals of volunteers, the *Nashville American* remarked that it showed "the complete abolition of all rancor growing out of the civil conflict," although the aging General Wheeler would be transported to an earlier time when, during the Battle of San Juan Hill, he rallied his men by yelling, "We've got the Yankees on the run."[119]

This reconciliation was enacted symbolically in countless speeches, newspaper articles, and songs, especially after it was learned that the first American to die after war had been declared was a southerner. But it was also enacted in public policy. In 1896, the Supreme Court had established the legality of "separate but equal" in *Plessy v. Ferguson*. This decision was followed two years later by a unanimous Court judgment that the conviction of a black man by an all-white jury did not demonstrate that Mississippi's new suffrage law determining juror eligibility discriminated against African Americans. Further, this case had been preceded by a decision to uphold registration requirements that the circuit court had considered "close to the border land that divides outrage from crime," and would be followed by a series of decisions culminating in *Giles v. Harris* in 1903—the "nadir of black rights in the Supreme Court," according to J. Morgan Kousser—when the justices decided that the scale of disfranchisement was so extreme that no judicial remedy could be found. A Court that was "decidedly 'activist'" in overturning economic regulations gradually eliminated the opportunity for black plaintiffs to assert their right to vote under the Fifteenth Amendment.[120]

In early June 1898, John Lacey, an Iowa Republican best known for his environmental interests, proposed a bill to enable volunteers in the Army to vote in congressional elections. The bill's introduction and debate over a few days was closely watched by southern representatives, who questioned whether the bill might be authorizing too much, especially its provision that the "requirements of the State laws as to registration and places of election shall not apply" for Army volunteers. Lacey conceded at the outset the limited authority of Congress, which could not in any way change the qualifications required of voters. Southerners stressed that they wanted to support the bill, but could not as long as it interfered with state registration requirements; "strike out the words 'registration and,' and your bill is right," they said. "Just strike out those words." Southern lawmakers warned that if Congress "has the power to pass such a law during a war, it has the same power to pass it in a time of peace." It would be "dangerous to pass such a measure," warned the *Lexington Herald*, precisely because it would open the door to future federal activism. Lacey and other Republicans, however, recalled the "very acrimonious debate" over the repeal of the election laws and were anxious to "avoid having anything of that kind in this bill." The bill's supporters made clear that they were ready to drop the section in order to accommodate the concerns of southerners. The bill passed the House, but no action was taken in the Senate.[121]

Months later, as Democrats orchestrated a pogrom against the black residents of Wilmington, North Carolina, southern blacks appealed to President McKinley, who, like his party, had earlier supported black rights. Now prioritizing the tariff and the need for the "goodwill of the Southern white congressional delegation in order to obtain ratification of the Treaty of Paris," the president decided to leave the citizens of Wilmington to the gun and the noose. "We have made friends with the Southerners," wrote William Graham Sumner, "they and we are hugging each other. . . . The negro's day is over. He is out of fashion."[122]

In 1900, George Henry White, the African American representative of North Carolina's Second District, delivered his parting address to Congress. Black representatives such as White and George Murray long had pushed for federal protection of the civil and political rights of southern blacks, providing a counternarrative to the white southern story of racial harmony and respect for equal rights under white supremacy. In a widely reprinted interview, White explained why he was not seeking reelection and why he had chosen to leave the South behind. "I cannot live in North Carolina," he said, "and be a man and be treated as a man." Now speaking before his colleagues, he sought to "enter a plea for the colored man, the colored woman, the colored boy, and the colored girl of this country." He praised labor unions for bettering the condition of workers but attacked their racial exclusions. He criticized "lily-white" Republicans who had benefited from the black vote but now "feel that they have grown a little too good for association with him politically, and are disposed to dump him overboard." And he recounted the attainments of African Americans in the decades since slavery, gains that had been achieved "in the face of lynching, burning at the stake, with the humiliation of 'Jim Crow' cars, the disfranchisement of our male citizens, slander and degradation of our women," and with all good jobs closed. "This," he concluded, "is perhaps the negroes' temporary farewell to the American Congress; but let me say, Phoenix-like he will rise up some day and come again. . . . The only apology that I have to make for the earnestness with which I have spoken is that I am pleading for the life, the liberty, the future happiness, and manhood suffrage for one-eighth of the entire population of the United States. [Loud applause.]"[123]

This farewell reflected how southern lawmakers had fundamentally shaped American policy during this period—by playing a central role in advancing and defeating legislation that defined the course of American political development. The impact, however, cannot be simply tallied by counting bills passed or defeated by southern votes and initiative. The coordinated opposition of the region's white Democratic legislators fundamentally recast expectations about what could be achieved through congressional action. As Henry Clayton of Alabama noted in 1897, the Senate had become the citadel of white supremacy, the institution where the final effort to guard and advance black political rights for over half a century had been defeated: "It is the Senate which stands to-day as the one deliberative body of the Congress; that Senate which has in the past, when all else failed, been the last refuge of the people of my beloved Southland when political passion and persecution sought to nullify their self-government." The ability of southern senators not only to delay or modify but undermine support for civil rights legislation through their coordinated opposition represented the white South's singular triumph. No other accomplishment in the last quarter of the nineteenth century would do as much to make the United States a southern nation.[124]

PART III

Egalitarian Whiteness

6

Limited Progressivism

The South has had its will, has won its fight. . . . Henceforth, though we be Southerners, and would not cease to be Southerners, we shall also be, in the fullest sense, Americans. Though we be, and must be, guides and guardians and therefore, for a time at least, rulers of this backward race which dwells among us, we will not ourselves be ruled by our own rulership. Henceforth we will ourselves be free.[1]

A southern Democrat surveying the election returns of 1900 would have had little reason for optimism. The country's Republican president, William McKinley, had been reelected with only four states outside the South supporting the Democratic candidate, William Jennings Bryan. The divisions in the Solid South that had opened up in 1896 persisted. Delaware, Kentucky, Maryland, and West Virginia had voted Republican. The Democratic Party, the region's vehicle for influence in national politics, was "at about the lowest point in power and influence it has been in one hundred years." During a period of tight party control over the legislative agenda, the large majority of southern representatives were effectively excluded from national policymaking. "The South is now completely at the mercy of Congress," worried the *Charlotte Observer*, "which has not since 1868 been so heavily Republican," a configuration of national politics that was "fraught with danger" for the region.[2]

For the white South, there were silver linings. The economy was doing well, and it must have seemed as though the oft-promised "New South" finally was emerging. The country had just gone through a war that ended with a quick victory and was widely interpreted as marking a national reconciliation. Crucially, the long threat to white supremacy had finally abated. The 57th

Congress convened in December 1901 without a single black representative present and with "the prospect of any negro being elected to congress in the near future" bleaker than "it has been at any time in the last third of a century." In turn, the "public mood" among white southerners, according to Dewey Grantham, seemed to have become "more relaxed," as many grew comfortable in the belief that the "threat to the integrity of the 'Southern' community had faded away."[3]

This mood was hardly shared by black Americans. "The south has asked to be let alone," noted the African American *Cleveland Gazette*, "and the administration says 'Let the south alone in its encroachment upon the liberties of the people.'" Some few saw a glimmer of hope in McKinley's speaking out against lynching, though even they "looked in vain" for him to speak out against disfranchisement. "McKinley cannot help the negro," wrote one black correspondent to the *Birmingham Age-Herald*, "and has not the backbone to aid him if he could." Black southerners did not acquiesce, as a wealth of new historical writing has shown. They had been abandoned by their most important political ally. No longer did a reliable institutional vehicle exist to exercise local influence or force public officials to take black priorities into account. "Strictly as a race man," the correspondent to the *Age-Herald* concluded, "I would not vote for William McKinley for a dog-catcher."[4]

In this environment, white southern Democrats could craft public policies that they hoped would recompense their region's poor and peripheral status with a new confidence that doing so would not impinge upon white supremacy or force difficult choices among priorities. The trade-off between protecting southern racial autonomy and gaining resources for the South no longer was starkly posed. Southern lawmakers soon explored the possibilities this new freedom of action allowed.

This chapter charts areas in which the dampening of white southerners' anxieties opened new space for the region's "progressives" by empowering political leaders who wanted to organize politics around a more active federal role in the economy and society while consolidating the subordinate status of black Americans. As the rich literature in American political development has demonstrated, the "qualitatively different kind of state" that emerged out of the Progressive era embedded populist and agrarian policy objectives within an administrative state that could be rendered responsive to the different interests of the emerging industrial, commercial, and financial economy. What is less commonly recognized, however, is that the southerners who helped push progressive reforms through Congress not only expanded the scope of federal activity but also ensured that this activism would be premised on its compatibility with white supremacy.[5]

Although the South was no longer confronted with a painful choice between desired policy reforms and maintaining home rule, it did face new problems that stemmed from the consolidation of Democratic control in most of the region and the minority status that followed the defeats of the 1890s. The defining feature of southern politics outside the border states in the early twentieth century was the suppression of meaningful competition between the political parties, with representation largely confined to the Democratic Party. The situation posed a dilemma for southern lawmakers. During a period in which congressional procedures were dominated by the majority party, they needed the Democratic Party to win nationally if they were to secure their policy goals, thus empowering the party leadership to decide which of the South's divergent goals and diverse priorities to pursue. Even were Democrats to regain the majority, there perhaps would be just as much to divide southern lawmakers as to unite them around a common legislative program. This reality only became more pronounced as the agrarian and progressive tides began to ebb during and after America's entry into the Great War, and especially after the policy victories of Woodrow Wilson's first term removed from the legislative agenda many issues on which southern Democrats had been able to cohere.

Southern Democratic lawmakers acted strategically to resolve this dilemma by crafting changes to the rules and institutional practices of Congress to enhance their role in lawmaking over both the short and long term. Instead of only attempting to displace the Republican majority, they sought to develop alternative mechanisms of influence by allying with dissident Republican factions and supporting the diffusion of policymaking authority away from the majority's leadership. Upon regaining the majority, they consolidated institutional changes that decentralized legislative influence even as they empowered their own party caucus to facilitate intraparty coordination. Perhaps most surprising, southern Democratic senators helped design rule changes that limited the ability of small minorities to obstruct legislation even as they formalized the right of more substantial minorities to do so.

These rule changes had a durable impact. Congress gradually was transformed into a legislature in which more and more legislation was passed by policy-specific, cross-party coalitions, a development that accommodated the increasing heterogeneity within the country's political parties and enhanced the South's ability to block legislation that threatened its paramount priority. Despite being in the minority, southern Democrats fashioned an institution that would facilitate the considerable range and variety of their preferences to be represented without imperiling their ability to act as a cohesive and determined bloc to defend white supremacy.

The Abandonment of Black Americans

At the Democratic National Convention of 1896, southern states threw their support behind William Jennings Bryan and the cause of free silver, refused to endorse the Cleveland administration, and split the Democratic coalition.

The results were disastrous. A few western states were added to the Democratic column, but the loss of New York, Connecticut, New Jersey, and Indiana produced a landslide defeat. Conservative southern Democrats urged the region not to make the same mistake in 1900, pleading with the party to drop the "silver question," to pledge to "uphold the Constitution, to oppose imperialism, to put hooks in the noses of the leviathan trusts," and most importantly, to focus on rebuilding support in the Northeast and reconstituting the Solid South. Nevertheless, southern delegates again supported Bryan, free silver, and a Democratic platform that called for more economic regulations. Once more, the party was left without the support of the Northeast and most border states. "If the South is without power in Congress it is her own fault and folly," complained the *Lexington Morning-Herald*. "The division of the Democratic party could have been prevented if the Southern men had not forced it" by making free silver the "fatal Shibboleth of party life."[6]

It was not just silver that weighed against the Democratic Party. In 1904, southern and northeastern conservatives succeeded briefly in "reorganizing the party along conservative lines," supporting the nomination of Alton B. Parker of New York—eminently acceptable to the northeastern wing of the party—as part of an effort to rehabilitate "Southern influence in the national councils." The platform that emerged from the national convention's drafting committee made no mention of the currency, and Parker—who to the fury of southern delegates quickly announced that the gold standard was "irrevocably established"—was awarded the nomination unencumbered by many of the more progressive measures promised by the platforms of 1896 and 1900. Again the party was defeated. Suffering its worst loss since the Civil War, the Democratic Party carried no state outside the South while losing Missouri, West Virginia, and Delaware.[7]

As the Democratic Party entered "a state of demoralization throughout the north," the white South was "gradually tightening its hold" over elections and acting to effectively destroy opportunities for competitive elections. The resulting pattern of Democratic collapse in the North and conquest in the South is shown in figure 6.1, which maps the average two-party vote margin in congressional districts between the reapportionments of 1902 and 1912. The figure highlights the few seats that on average were decided with less than ten percentage points separating the winner from the runner-up. In all, only a thin band of the country—concentrated in the border regions of West Virginia, Kentucky, southern Indiana and Illinois, northern Oklahoma, western North Carolina, Colorado, and Missouri—was politically competitive.[8]

The central fact of politics in the first decade of the twentieth century was the geographic division of the country into two opposed sections within which competition was often only sporadic and localized. The "solid North" as well as a solid but reduced South came to define the politics of the period,

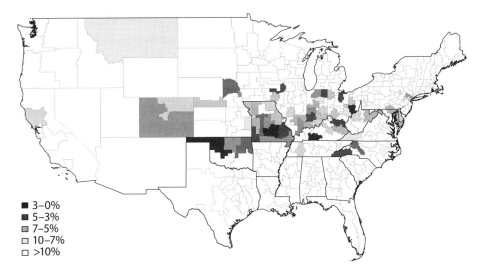

3–0%
5–3%
7–5%
10–7%
>10%

FIGURE 6.1. Average Margin of Victory in the Two-Party Vote Share, 1902–1910

and the interests and preferences of the pivotal midwestern and border states carried outsized policymaking influence.

This electoral map had several profoundly important consequences for twentieth-century American political development. Most important, Republican ascendancy eroded the union of principle and electoral interest that had underpinned the party's commitment to black political rights since the Civil War. Republican electoral victories after the repeal of the election laws were understood to show "a disposition on the part of the people that elections should be regulated by the several States" without interference by the federal government. That the Republican Party leadership had acquiesced to this judgment was described by some white southern Republicans as the "most significant" event since the defeat of the federal elections bill, a clear commitment that the party would not try to build support in the region on the basis of black votes.[9]

Acquiescence did not mean that national Republican Party leaders were entirely silent on the question of disfranchisement. Many denounced the new state suffrage qualifications as "the most un-American, undemocratic provisions that can be imagined." But with lopsided national majorities, Republicans could safely condemn disfranchisement without supporting legislative action against it. Wisconsin Republican senator John Spooner, "the Senate's most fervent spokesman for the southern Negro," regularly denounced disfranchisement and called the murder of black voters "a wrong" that had "yet to be righted." At the same time, he insisted that no one denied that southern states should be free to "disfranchise in a uniform and constitutional way," through literacy, property, and heavy taxation requirements that did not explicitly mention race.[10]

Southern success in defeating the federal elections bill conditioned the expectations of Republican political leaders, who came to believe that any further effort in this vein would be defeated while exposing the country to sustained instability. Equally important was the crumbling of racial equality as an attainable ideal not only under the influence of southern intransigence but as a consequence of what was understood to be scientific progress. There had been "a great change of opinion" in the North, reported Charles Francis Adams to an audience in Richmond, Virginia. "In the light" of Darwin's major works, "and the inferences necessarily drawn from them, the Afro-American Race Problem [had] assumed a new shape," one that denied the "'glittering generalities' of the Declaration of Independence." Adams in some sense was not saying anything new, as he and many other prominent northerners had been staking out explicitly racist positions since at least 1870, when these liberal Republicans had called for an end to Reconstruction and the withdrawal of national support for black political and civil rights in the South.[11]

For sure, there was no single or uniform direction to northern attitudes on race. While a number of northern states passed so-called antimiscegenation laws, others continued to enact legislation that responded to black Americans' demands for antidiscrimination statues. But shifting attitudes toward racial equality were the subject of frequent commentary in northern papers, which noted that Republicans who had once insisted on defending a belief in common and equal humanity now either embraced or were silent in the face of claims about black inferiority. As the country annexed Hawaii, conquered and repressed the Philippines, and claimed sovereignty over Puerto Rico, such arguments found defenders among Republican imperialists. William Taft, for example, the former governor of the Philippines, attacked William Jennings Bryan for his ostensible assertion "that the Filipinos are entirely capable of self-government." Instead, he asked "the whole Southern people, whether we can safely trust a people, the great majority of whom are without political experience, to govern themselves and produce a modern civilization." "Do the people of the South contend that the difficult science of self-government is so implanted in the breast of every human being, be he Hottentot, Esquimaux or any of the uncivilized races, or even one of those partly civilized or those having no experience in government, that he ought not to be assisted in the maintenance of a government which shall secure law and right?" A few years earlier, the *New York Evening Post* had reflected on the change in northern public opinion about racial equality, observing that while there were "various other reasons," the "one which comes home to most editors just now grows out of the scheme to annex Hawaii."[12]

Southern Democrats took pleasure in taunting Republicans for their seeming changes in sentiment, as the former champions of racial equality now were taking "the position that the general principles of the Declaration of Independence are applicable only to white, and not to colored men . . . that the brown man in the Philippines has no right that the white man in the United States is bound to respect." Tillman waved the "bloody shirt" "like a red flag to a bull," mocking Republicans for their abandonment of egalitarian ideals: "You deal with the Filipinos just as we deal with the negroes, only you treat them a whole heap worse. You deal with the Puerto Ricans, just as we deal with the negroes, only you treat them a whole heap worse." Republicans responded with evasion, silence, and occasional defenses of racial inferiority.[13]

The growing prominence of racialist thought provided terms by which many expressions of Republican opinion could conclude, as did the *New York Sun*, that the enfranchisement of black Americans had been "one of the most deplorable mistakes in our history," the result of "an ignorant overestimate of the possibilities of the development inherent in race." The policy implications were clear, at least so far as they concerned mass voting by black majorities in the South: "Local expedients in evasion of the spirit, if not of the letter, of the Fifteenth Amendment" should be supported as a necessity. The article, which urged "American common sense" to go "fearlessly to the root of the matter" and repeal the amendment, was reprinted favorably in southern newspapers that underscored the *Sun*'s Republican affiliation. The South, declared the *New York Times*, had "carried the question of negro equality far toward a settlement in which practically the whole country has acquiesced," an implicit recognition the Fifteenth Amendment had been a "mistake" that no African American, no matter how well qualified, should be given federal office, no matter how insignificant, and the white South should be left alone to determine its racial ordering. "The solution" to the race problem, Adams concluded before his Virginia audience, "must be worked out in the South," and the North now recognized that interference would do more harm than good. President William Taft would go even further, announcing in his inaugural address that the electoral restrictions passed by southern states were "square" with the Fifteenth Amendment and praising these states for removing the threat of "domination" by "an ignorant, irresponsible element." It was "not the disposition or within the province of the Federal Government," Taft assured white southerners, "to interfere with the regulation by Southern States of their domestic affairs."[14]

The belief that white southerners' sensibilities had to be accommodated shaped, to varying degrees, the decisions of every Republican president during this period. None of the three Republican presidents from McKinley to Taft "made any effort to challenge the political and racial hegemony of white southerners," and all three actively encouraged the development of "lily-white" factions of the southern Republican Party. The few exceptions to this policy came during Theodore Roosevelt's administration; for example, he chose to appoint an African American physician, William D. Crum, as customs collector for Charleston, South Carolina, despite the refusal of the Senate to confirm the appointment out of deference to Benjamin Tillman. Crum had been born free in 1859 to a German-African slave-owning family, and as a respectable physician who followed the region's racial mores, he was among the most well-regarded African Americans in Charleston society. But many in the white community nonetheless were bitterly opposed to his appointment. Taft worried that any effort to renew Crum's position would undermine Republican efforts to appeal to the white South. Instead, he arranged for Crum to retire. "One of the race's leading and best men," complained the *Cleveland Gazette*, had been sacrificed "upon the altar of that baneful Southern prejudice."[15]

On a few other occasions, Roosevelt took a stand against specific acts of southern racism. He insisted on closing the post office at Indianola, Mississippi, after the black female postmaster was harassed and threatened by the town's residents, a decision that led to considerable uproar in the region. He also was bitterly denounced for his "studied insult to the South" when he invited Booker T. Washington for dinner in the White House. Overall, however, Roosevelt's public acts and pronouncements tended to converge on his privately expressed belief in black racial inferiority. On a tour of the South after his reelection, Roosevelt repeatedly expressed the need for sectional reconciliation and made clear that he "would not fight for negro rights." He ordered the dishonorable discharge of the alleged perpetrators of the Brownsville raid, which "brought widespread approval from white southerners," and even when speaking out against lynching, he argued that "the greatest existing cause of lynching is the perpetration, especially by black men, of the hideous crime of rape."[16]

Following the lead of these presidents, the Republican congressional leadership made clear that they no longer would support action to protect southern black voting rights. Though there was some support among Republicans for enforcing the Fourteenth Amendment, which required Congress to reduce the representation of states disfranchising male voters, the leadership generally ensured that such proposals would not be brought to the floor, at least not unless there was some momentary political advantage to be gained. In 1901, however, Pennsylvania Republican Marlin Olmsted managed to catch an irritated party leadership off guard. Introducing a privileged resolution instructing the census committee to investigate the abridgement of the vote in southern states, Olmsted's action provoked a "sensation" and induced Alabama's Oscar Underwood to vow to fight "to the bitter end." His organization of a

brief filibuster led some southerners to observe that his "influence and importance in the House" were "steadily gaining." With the leadership, the president, and most of the Republican Party "secretly in sympathy" with the South,
Olmstead was forced to abandon the effort, receiving nothing more than an
annoyed and vague commitment from the committee chair to seriously consider the proposal, a proposition met with laughter from Democrats. Newspapers reported that Republican "indifference to the fate of the Olmsted resolution in the end gave the opposition the victory."[17]

The Olmsted resolution is notable in part because it was brought up without support by the party leadership. More commonly, Republicans were allowed to advance civil rights proposals only when the leaders believed that
these initiatives could be used to cynically derail legislation they opposed. A
campaign finance bill, for example, was defeated in April 1908 when Edgar
Crumpacker, an Indiana Republican who long had championed enforcing the
Fourteenth Amendment, was recognized for the purpose of suspending the
rules and passing the bill with amendments that would reenact the federal
election laws and reduce southern representation. The Democratic leader in
the House, Mississippian John Sharp Williams, angrily denounced the Republicans for supporting a reduction of southern representation at the same time
as it tried to gain seats by "holding out to white men in the South the hope of
ignoring the fifteenth amendment," a not-too-subtle reference to President
Taft's southern outreach. As was true whenever the issue of black civil and
political rights was broached, southerners vividly communicated the intensity
of their commitments, insisting that they would do whatever it took to "protect ourselves" and demanding that "the world must understand this." The
amendment passed, followed quickly by the campaign finance bill to which it
had been attached, which would have required all political committees to disclose their lists of contributors. Republicans had recently supported a temporary change in the rules of the House to allow a bare majority to suspend the
rules, a move that was needed to expedite passage of legislation at the end of
the session and avoid Democratic filibusters. But they now had no chance to
guide the bill through the Senate given that it was sufficiently late in the session that, as one southern representative put it, "even a half dead Senator from
the South could easily speak it to death." The elimination of minority influence
in the House of Representatives continued apace, while the Senate was gradually becoming the citadel of southern protection.[18]

Even when the Republican leadership did bring up the issue of disfranchisement, they were usually careful to make clear that they were not opposed
to judicious restrictions on the right of black men to vote. In March 1901, Olmsted's resolution was reintroduced with the support of the party leadership
after the Democratic governor of Maryland, taking "advantage of our kindness
and leniency," according to one Republican, called a special session of the state

legislature to pass a new election law that would impose an effective literacy test and "disfranchise many of the negro voters of the state." This development came just as Virginia, West Virginia, and Kentucky also were moving to reform their suffrage laws, each of these being states in which Republicans had already made gains or were counting on making new inroads. William Chandler, chair of the Senate Committee on Privileges and Elections, produced a resolution authorizing an investigation by the Justice Department into southern disfranchisement, backed by a $25,000 appropriation. But Republican leaders, even long-standing defenders of black rights such as Joseph Foraker, were highly sensitive to the changing state of public opinion, noting that when "the ostensible object of a disfranchisement law is to prevent negro domination, as has been the case to the present time, there is great disinclination on the part of the Northern states to take any action." Republicans believed that Maryland's proposed disfranchisement was worth opposing precisely because it was supposedly motivated not just by white supremacy but by partisanship. The *Chicago Tribune* was explicit that Maryland should be able to purge its electorate of ignorant voters, but that this law was simply a "Democratic party measure, to be put through by a party vote for partisan purposes." As Michael Perman notes, "The national Republicans' growing tolerance, even endorsement, of the disfranchisement of African Americans did not go unnoticed by Maryland's Democrats," who calculated that Congress would not act to stop them. Senator Arthur Pue Gorman coordinated with state Democrats to make sure that the extra session of the state legislature was not called until after Congress had adjourned and the brief threat of a national response had disappeared.[19]

The defeat of the campaign finance bill after Crumpacker's amendment had passed reflected a continuation of the pattern we observed in the late nineteenth century, in which southern Democrats were forced to subordinate policy objectives to defeat threats to the racial order. What was different by the early twentieth century, however, was the level of cynicism involved. The speaker's control over the legislative agenda usually enabled the Republican Party leaders in the House to keep race off the agenda unless it served their purpose. It was widely understood that the party had no appetite for a serious fight over the issue. As the *Chicago Tribune* noted, the use of Crumpacker's amendment to kill the campaign finance bill "was the best joke of the season." In 1911, when Crumpacker chaired the Census Committee and was in charge of drafting a new reapportionment bill, he rejected as "impracticable" a proposal to reduce southern representation.[20]

Some Republicans continued to be concerned about the plight of southern blacks, but few were willing to support federal action on civil rights. In the main, they reflected the attitude of what the essayist and editor Hamilton Wright Mabie in 1905 called the "New North," which "does not believe that the door of citizenship should be closed in any man's face because of race or color; but it also believes that all the conditions of citizenship, save this, belong to the States for settlement." The emerging national consensus was that the South no longer should be threatened with federal intervention to pursue a hopeless and fatally flawed ideal. Black Americans were now peculiar citizens, with their rights and privileges to be determined by southern whites rather than by the terms of the national constitution and legislature.[21]

The Transformation of Southern Politics

These changes opened space for southern Democrats to support a more activist federal government in order to provide greater security and assistance to white farmers and small producers and regulate the terms by which northern corporations engaged in the southern economy. White support for the Solid South always had rested on the fear that black voters would support the inversion of local property, class, and race hierarchies, both through public policies favoring the tenant and farm laborer and by occupying the local offices that were the face of public authority in southern communities. This threat had been contained, without disfranchisement, under the conservative Democrats who dominated the politics of most southern states during the late 1870s and 1880s. But it had once again burst into public attention with the rise of the People's Party and its potential for a cross-race alliance, a prospect that threatened both Democratic rule and the ascendancy of the planters who had come to power after Reconstruction.

The exact terms and dynamics of disfranchisement varied from state to state, but certain broad patterns were shared. In defeating the Populist threat, southern Democrats in some states had relied on black votes, either sincerely appealed to or, more commonly, counted for the Democratic candidate regardless of how the actual vote was cast. The Bourbon, conservative faction of the Democratic Party was usually the prime mover in disfranchisement, seeing in this a policy means to suppress once and for all the threat of losing their ascendancy. But in some states, most notably Georgia, former Populists came to support disfranchisement in order to prevent the manipulation of black ballots that had contributed to their defeat. The outcome was largely the same: the threat to white supremacy was muted. As a result, former white Populists and populist-inclined constituencies had a bit of room to maneuver, so long as they remained in the Democratic Party and reassured conservatives that their reform program had been stripped of its more threatening aspects.[22]

Southern Democrats, then, could continue to harness the reform impulse—as they had done at key moments throughout the "Long Agrarian Moment" of the 1870s to the 1910s—while dampening its more extreme aspects. This pattern was especially evident with free silver, a "safe" program often given exaggerated importance by southern Democrats precisely because, unlike the subtreasury and other more radical Populist programs, "it required no extension of federal power into local affairs." The People's Party was defeated as an organized threat to Democratic rule, but the spirit of agrarian revolt that had animated the movement continued to infuse southern politics, albeit in muted and constrained form within the Democratic Party.[23]

Southern progressives were not, by any means, Populists in a new guise. Progressivism, as C. Vann Woodward argued and as subsequent historical work has largely supported, was "essentially urban and middle class in nature," in stark contrast to the rural concerns of the People's Party. But while southern progressivism was not the lineal descendant of Populism, its advocates were willing to adopt some of the core planks of this more radical movement. "Under the growing pressure of monopoly," Woodward wrote, "the small businessmen and urban middle class overcame their fear of reform and joined hands with the discontented farmers." Although southern progressive Democrats were "not motivated by a desire merely to propitiate Populists," added Dewey Grantham, they did adapt themselves to the demands made by former Populists and their constituencies: "Populist proposals for stringent railroad regulation, liberal agricultural credit, abolition of convict leasing, and support of public education became part of the reform agenda of the region's progressives," while a good "number of former Populists became leaders in the Democratic party, and agrarian radicals often discovered compatible allies in the Bryanized wing of the party." State governments had always been a more acceptable site for regulating the economy than the national government, and so what was perhaps most striking about the change in southerners' political demands was the degree to which Democrats had become willing to advocate for a more active federal role to regulate the economy and assist submerged groups. Populism and the agrarian revolt of the 1890s had left a legacy of organized constituent sentiment around a set of activist policy proposals at the federal level, and "since there were a great many small farmers in the South," key planks from the Populist program would remain "an important part of the Southern political scene" even after the movement's defeat.[24]

This increased support for federal activism was premised on the effective disfranchisement of black voters and the withdrawal of northern concern with the region's racial order, which made "threats at the North to settle the negro question for the South on certain so-called philanthropic lines" no longer so pressing. If diversification of the southern economy, urbanization, and increased social differentiation along lines of wealth, education, and professional occupation were crucial for creating a southern constituency for progressivism, disfranchisement facilitated the acceptance by middle-class constituencies of reformist proposals. The staunchly conservative *Macon Telegraph* had envisioned just this possibility when it warned against disfranchisement:

"Can't you read between the lines that this is a Populistic catch? As soon as the negro is disfranchised, you will see the Populists unfurl their tattered banners emblazoned with more resplendent inscriptions than they had on them in their palmiest days." The new mottos of southern Democrats were hardly as far-reaching as those of the Populists, nor were the preoccupations of southern progressives with social order and paternalistic reform the same as the earlier movement's concerns. But contemporaries and historians have recognized that the increased willingness of middle-class southern opinion "to use the power of the state government in more active ways than it had been used before" was the product of "the new political environment of disfranchisement and [white] primaries." "Once the political aspect of the Negro problem had been solved by abolishing the Negro's political rights, and the rights of plenty of poor whites in the bargain," writes Sheldon Hackney, "the way was open for the Progressives to assemble from the purged electorate a winning coalition." Or as the former Populist leader Tom Watson wrote about William Jennings Bryan's popularity in the region, Bryan had *no everlasting and overshadowing Negro Question to hamper and handicap his progress: I HAD.* Disfranchisement dampened the fears of the upper classes, and the emergence of factional politics within the Democratic Party as the key site of political competition created new opportunities for the "emergence of interest-group politics" and for an enhanced political influence of "middle-class organizations and professional groups," both of which helped explain why southern Democrats "increasingly accepted the Populist concept of the positive state."[25]

We provide some empirical details of this "transformation of Southern politics" in figures 6.2 through 6.9. Figures 6.2 and 6.3 show the changed location of the average Democratic ideal points from the end of Reconstruction to the beginning of the New Deal for the House and the Senate and across different regional specifications. The bars along the bottom designate the proportion of the total chamber from each of these regions, while the dashed line shows the cross-chamber Democratic average. A leftward shift beginning in the 1890s and intensifying in the following two decades is immediately evident in the House. Although this seems to have occurred for all House Democrats, in the border states and the North it was driven primarily by the defeat of moderate representatives, who more regularly voted Republican. In the Black Belt, however, representatives both continued to be returned in large numbers and became more partisan in their voting patterns, while members from the former Confederate states outside the Black Belt stayed relatively constant in their voting patterns. In the Senate, there was more constancy in the voting patterns of Democrats from all regions, although the Black Belt senators from Alabama, Florida, Georgia, Louisiana, Mississippi, and South Carolina displayed increased partisanship during the Wilson administration.

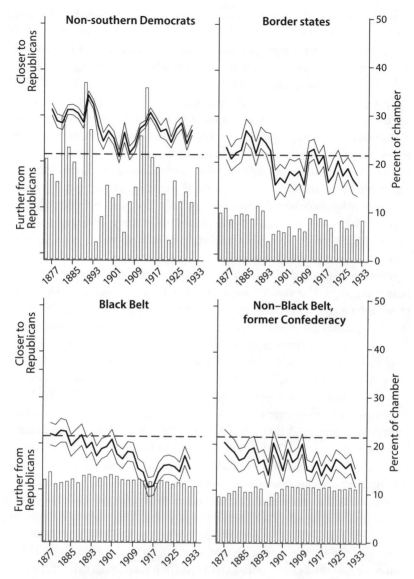

FIGURE 6.2. Changes in Democratic Voting Patterns in the House, 1875–1932. Bars are the proportion of the chamber. Dashed line is the cross-chamber Democratic mean ideal point. Ninety-five percent confidence interval is shown.

Figures 6.4 through 6.6 map changes in voting patterns. Figure 6.4 shows the estimated location of the average Democrat from the North and different subregions of the South, the black circle showing the period from 1877 to 1900, the gray triangle covering the Progressive era to the last years of the Wilson administration, and the white circle the 1920s. In the Senate, the modest shift

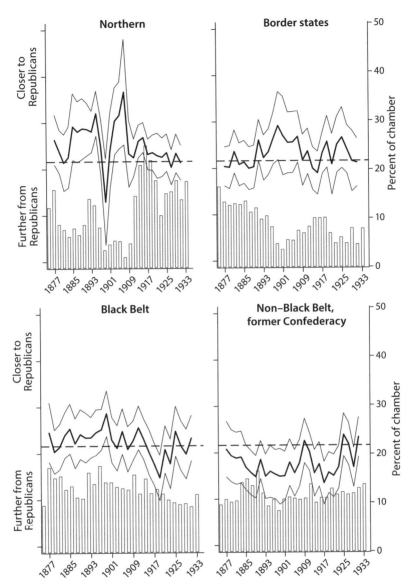

FIGURE 6.3. Changes in Democratic Voting Patterns in the Senate, 1875–1932. Dashed line is the cross-chamber Democratic mean ideal point. Ninety-five percent confidence interval is shown.

toward more partisan voting in the early century was concentrated among senators from the Black Belt. In South Carolina in particular, Benjamin Tillman's rise brought a dramatic move away from the politics of conciliation and distributive logrolling that had characterized aspects of the state's politics under Wade Hampton and more conservative factions. This shift occurred

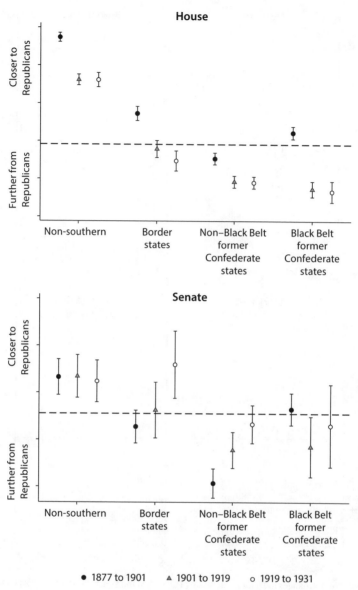

FIGURE 6.4. Change in Southern Democratic Preferences, by Region, 1877–1931. Dashed line is the Democratic mean for 1900 to 1930.

even as non–Black Belt states such as Tennessee began moving to the center, a trend that would continue into the 1920s.

The suppression of black voting coincided with the emergence of a pattern that would become more familiar by the time of the early New Deal, a hard core of Black Belt representatives and senators who constituted the most loyal

partisans and extreme faction of the Democratic Party. While Black Belt senators in the late nineteenth century had generally been more accommodating
of Republican positions, by the onset of the Wilson administration this distinctive position had largely disappeared. If we convert the preferences of legislators into county-level averages (figures 6.5 and 6.6), we see that outside of a
few districts in Virginia and Tennessee, almost the only counties in the former
Confederacy that continued to elect moderate legislators were those few that
had an important manufacturing or commercial basis, such as New Orleans,
Birmingham, and Charleston, or that relied heavily on Republican tariffs or
bipartisan infrastructure programs, such as the Mississippi Delta or parts of
Louisiana.

The increased partisan voting among Black Belt southern Democrats in
the House was largely the product of the replacement of the earlier generation
of southern representatives who had dominated the region's politics in the
1870s and 1880s. Figure 6.7 shows the aggregate ideal points of southern representatives by the decade in which they were elected. Democrats elected
from the Black Belt in the 1890s and 1900s were significantly more partisan
than those who preceded them. Although there was a noticeable shift away
from the center outside the Black Belt as well, there was no significant difference between incoming representatives and those who came before them;
only in the 1890s was there any noticeable discontinuity in the preferences of
those members elected in the decade before and after, and this was driven
almost entirely by southern Democrats elected from the border states, a moment of heightened political competition in this region.

The representatives the South was sending to Congress were more partisan
in their voting patterns than those who had been elected in the immediate
post-1877 period, but they were also younger and less likely to have fought for
the Confederacy (figure 6.8). This was not just a steady process of generational
change, although that was the driving factor. In the congressional elections of
1892 and 1894, nearly 50 percent of southern Democrats—upwards of 60 percent in the border states but also around 40 percent in the former Confederacy—were defeated, chose not to seek reelection, or were denied renomina-
tion by their party (figure 6.9). As Arthur Link noted in 1946, even where the
Populist Party had not made electoral gains the movement split the Democrats
and "forced the retirement of many of the old conservative leaders." Not incidentally, these elections were marked by a sharp jump in the number of members who listed "farmer" as their occupation, reflecting both the success of
Populists in electing some of their own and a tactical decision on the part of
some Democrats to better fit their electoral profile to the times. The South,
for example, was the only region of the country where more of the "farmer"
legislators had attended college than had nonfarmer legislators, and the farmers elected in the 1890s in the South also tended to be more moderate than

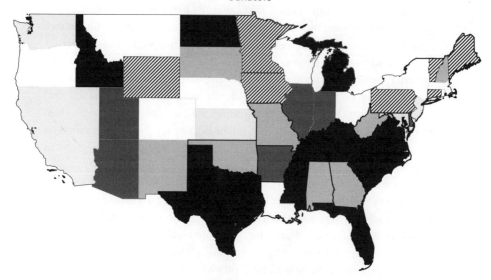

Senators

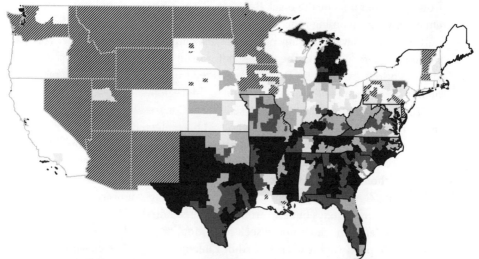

Representatives

| ■ Least likely to vote with Republicans | □ Average levels of voting with Republicans | □ Most likely to vote with Republicans |
| ■ Below-average voting with Republicans | □ Above-average voting with Republicans | ▨ Too few Democrats or missing data |

FIGURE 6.5. Distribution of Partisan Voting among Democrats, 1900–1917

Senators

Representatives

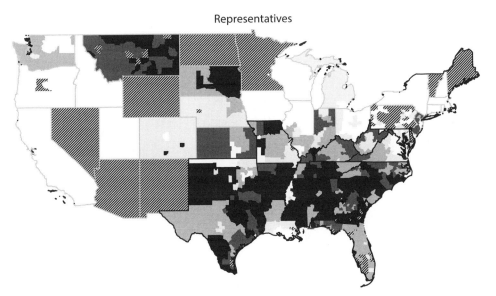

- ■ Least likely to vote with Republicans
- ▦ Below-average voting with Republicans
- ▨ Average levels of voting with Republicans
- ▢ Above-average voting with Republicans
- □ Most likely to vote with Republicans
- ▨ Too few Democrats or missing data

FIGURE 6.6. Distribution of Partisan Voting among Democrats, 1917–1932

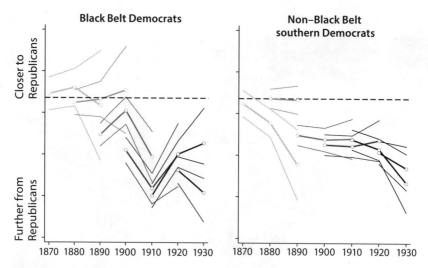

FIGURE 6.7. Ideal Points of Southern Democratic Representatives, 1870–1930, by Decade of Election. Dashed line is the Democratic average. Ninety-five percent confidence interval is shown. Only cohorts with twenty representatives are included.

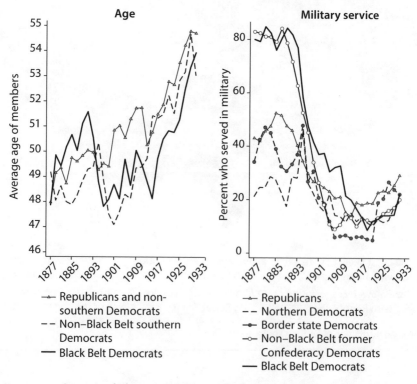

FIGURE 6.8. Generational Change in Southern Politics by Age and Military Service, 1877–1930

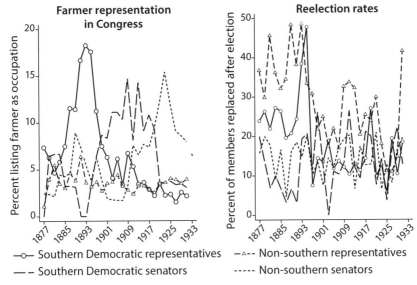

FIGURE 6.9. Impact of the Populist Revolt, 1877–1930

their nonfarmer southern Democratic colleagues. The farmers quickly disappeared in the House as the South returned to its long-standing pattern of being the region most likely to elect lawyers and least likely to elect businessmen, but in the first two decades of the twentieth century, a relatively large share of southern senators continued to identify their principal occupation as farmer or planter.[26]

Many southern political leaders insisted in the first decades of the new century that what the South wanted was simple. "Just let us alone," declared Clark Howell of the *Atlanta Constitution*, "generally recognized as the brainiest and most progressive of the younger element in the new south." "That is the whole story. Let us alone to settle this matter" (the "race question") "ourselves without interference." For Howell, being "let alone" included not only abandoning any effort to secure black voting rights, but "that there should be no appointment of negroes to any important Federal position in white communities."[27]

A large majority of the white South and their Democratic legislators also wanted positive federal action on a range of issues, varying across class and regional subgroups. "Railroad regulation, a graduated income tax, rural credits, rural free delivery, parcel post, direct election of senators—all these progressive causes were also Southern causes," noted the historian Anne Firor Scott. Southern progressives in the early twentieth century were insistent that "it was government's duty to intervene directly in economic affairs in order to benefit submerged or politically impotent economic interests," such as farmers and adult white labor. Simultaneous demands to be left alone and for new federal activism were not contradictory but complementary—not logical correlates but mutually implicated given the development of southern politics since Reconstruction. The southern successes in the 1890s that helped ensure that the region would be "let alone" on race had, in turn, created room for a more "respectable" public opinion to support federal activism in other areas. This fact would condition southern politics in Congress and be of fundamental importance in shaping national policies.[28]

The Contours of Southern Progressivism

Although disfranchisement helped empower the leftward shift of the Democratic Party, southern Democrats in the early twentieth century were not all of one stripe, nor had they all abandoned their traditional belief in states' rights principles. There was no purge of conservatives, and wariness about an active federal state remained an important feature of the region's political landscape. The coexistence of these tendencies—in favor of reform and in opposition to centralization, for government intervention to assist farmers and for the Jeffersonian position of "special privileges for none"—perhaps explains the persistence of radically different interpretations of the political character of the South during this period, ranging from "radical agrarianism" to "monolithic conservatism." To the extent that these were distinct and coherent political tendencies, they were both contained within the Democratic Party and given form in national politics by representatives whose policy positions reflected in part their efforts to mediate between small and large farmers, middle-class professionals, New South industrialists, and merchants.[29]

Southern Democratic parties had been characterized since Reconstruction by a degree of policy ecumenicalism on all issues but white supremacy. Beginning in the 1890s, this doctrinal flexibility was buttressed by the white primary, hailed as the salvation of the South for its effectiveness in neutralizing black electoral importance. One result of making the Democratic primary the almost exclusive forum for allocating political power, however, was a brand of politics peculiar to the South: often indecipherable to the rest of the country, it simultaneously could be conservative and radical, populist and demagogic. As E. Culpepper Clark argued, "Southern demagogues seemed singularly without ideological moorings." They were neither liberal Democrats nor conservatives of the Republican or even old-line Jeffersonian southern mold. They spoke some of the language of populism, but eschewed its "cooperative-democratic vision." "Pitchfork" Ben Tillman, his fellow South Carolina senator "Cotton Ed" Smith, Arkansas's Jeff Davis, Mississippi's James K. Vardaman, and a host of others whose careers never made it beyond their state coupled occasionally populist programs with an aggressive emphasis on corrupt elites, a celebration of violence, and, above all, the determination to preserve white supremacy.[30]

In part for this reason, the contours of southern progressivism have always been difficult to pin down. There was a relatively clear progressive mold in the North—middle-class urban reformers looking to government, either state or federal, for the regulation of social and economic problems, either to assist groups hurt by the period's dislocations or to purify government and provide a stable ordering to society. But this characterization only very imperfectly characterizes the southern Democrats who would provide support for much of the progressive legislation of the Wilson era. Although middle-class reformers may have "articulated the progressive rationale and mission" in the South, political support for activist federal and state policies was provided by the large majority of legislators who were elected from overwhelmingly rural constituencies. Benjamin Tillman, for one, claimed that "properly interpreted," the term "progressive" "in its essence is the Chicago platform and nothing else"—that is, the platform adopted by the Democratic Convention in 1896 that heralded the triumph of the rural activist wing against Cleveland conservatives. Southern members of Congress were often seen by "many northerners . . . as reactionary and anachronistic," both in style and in substance, more of a throwback than a progressive vanguard.[31]

The uncertain progressivism of the South was in part a reflection of the extremism of the region's political leaders on race. The progressivism of southern Democrats "was shaped by a belief that federal power would have to forswear racial equality and escape the clutches of the money power before it could be trusted"; whenever the "race question" was raised, either it was met by a wall of vitriol from the South or it had been raised by southern legislators demanding national fealty to white supremacy. Northern progressives were hardly unanimous believers in racial equality. But even within the terms of a confining national consensus, the white South stood out for its extremism. Tillman, for instance, proposed a nationwide passport system in 1906 that would require black southerners to have a "fixed domicile" or the endorsement of a white employer in order to travel freely. Similar state-level proposals were considered across the South, while Georgia revived a proposal from the 1880s to make any white person who taught colored students punishable by service on a chain gang. At the local level, "progressive" reforms in the South often "either excluded blacks or were directed against them." Segregation and the white primary were framed as progressive reforms, intended to either purify the ballot or ease the problem of "race friction." As the African American *Atlanta Independent* observed, "Reform legislation used to mean remedial and helpful legislation for all the people, and special privileges to none; but under the present regime at the state capitol it means special favors for white people and the downright outlawry of the black man's rights."[32]

Partly for this reason, northern progressives such as Robert La Follette often remarked that they did not "know of any progressive sentiment or legislation in the South." For others, the intensity of southern racism did not vitiate its claim to being progressive, but constituted a distinct and separate question. "It is a curious and regrettable thing," noted *The Public*, a Democratic reform magazine, "that the politicians of the South who are progressive on economic issues are reactionary on the race question."[33]

In retrospect, neither of these assessments was quite right. Southern politics in fact was increasingly marked by progressive policy reform at the state level. The border states went furthest in providing bans on child labor, compulsory education, pure food and drug safety oversight, workers' compensation, and eight-hour labor laws, as well as regulatory commissions and antitrust legislation. In these states, there was a renewal of competitive politics, and both Republicans and Democrats could compete for support by offering policies that appealed to progressives and were tailored to meet the needs of their primary constituencies. But progressive reforms were not limited to the border states. Throughout the South, state legislatures curtailed the activities of corporations. Railroads, seen as "firmly controlled by 'northern men, money, and management,'" faced state-led campaigns that strengthened state railroad commissions, attempted to lower passenger and freight rates, and forced the railroads to adhere to a uniform rate classification. The regulatory surge subsided after 1909 only because the railroads successfully turned to federal courts for protection; in turn, however, these legal victories invigorated calls for action among southern Democrats in Congress.[34]

But far from being a separate question, race fundamentally inflected the terms of southern progressivism. Not only had disfranchisement opened up space for middle-class white southerners to support a more active federal government, but the region's persistent anxieties over the possible consequences of centralization shaped the types of policies that southern progressives preferred. Reflecting a worry that federal administrative agencies would protect the interests of northeastern industrial elites and that the expansion of the federal bureaucracy would result in Republican appointments of black officials, southern Democrats had always been more likely to support clear legal prohibitions, backed by criminal penalties, as distinct from new administrative agencies authorized to exercise discretion. This was never a hard distinction, and southern progressives generally accepted expanding federal regulatory authority if the alternative was inaction. But as Elizabeth Sanders has shown, southern Democrats in Congress persistently preferred regulating through explicit legal prohibitions rather than by empowering federal administrative agencies. Southern progressives tended to believe that laws should be written and enforced to break up the concentrated economic and political power of large corporations and had little sympathy for the distinction between "good" and "bad" trusts drawn by Roosevelt and many other northern progressives.[35]

In one sense, the parameters of southern progressivism could be said to reflect an ongoing conservative commitment to the tenets of Jeffersonian democracy, including opposition to monopolies, an organization of the economy and social life around agriculture, and an intense suspicion of centralization, inflected by the concern with maintaining the local hierarchies that always had informed this tradition. But the program supported by a large and active portion of southern lawmakers in the early twentieth century was much more radical than anything old-line Jeffersonian democrats would have countenanced. John Reagan, who had led the fight for strong interstate commerce antitrust laws, had been adamantly opposed to direct ownership of the railroads by state or national governments, a cause that Bryan raised to prominence upon his return from Europe in 1906. Although Tillman and others warned that "nationalizing the railroads would create a political army to be used by the party in power and would undermine the hard-won political autonomy of the former Confederate states," the idea nonetheless found some favor among southern Democratic legislators and publics. Reagan had also opposed labor arbitration and eight-hour legislation on the ground that they would open the door to federal regulations that would threaten southern agricultural labor practices, yet these measures were supported by southern Democrats in the early twentieth century, as were a host of other policy proposals that both southern conservatives and earlier reformers had opposed.[36]

Although it is important to recognize the force and content of southern progressivism, we do not want to create the perception that progressives dominated unopposed. Even as a growing number of southern legislators became willing to support federal regulations, old-line states' rights conservatives continued to be an important force in the region; in fact, many of the legislators who supported progressive policies also either identified with or were characterized as believing in the Democratic Party's traditional stance based on states' rights and Jeffersonianism. As one progressive Democrat from Nevada remarked while defending a broad interpretation of the federal government's power to regulate interstate commerce, "I have reason to believe that there are a few, and only a few, upon this side of the House who shared this view," with his "friends from the Southern States" being "particularly tenacious of state rights."[37]

But outside the border states, conservative politicians were simultaneously pressed by a varyingly progressive public opinion and trapped within a Democratic Party that since 1896 had provided an organized political vehicle for the expression of these views. One southern legislator reportedly admitted, for example, that "he was only advocating Bryan because the people behind him demanded it." It was his opinion that "the majority of Southern Congressmen stood exactly where he did, anxious to give up Bryan and free silver if only the people would consent." Southern progressives occasionally worried that the region's newspapers, which they argued were more conservative than the population, might be able to shape public opinion. But they remained confident that the mass of the people were on their side. Conservative newspapers in the South, since the rise of Bryan, "have been apart from the people; the proof of which is that year after year State conventions in the South have without exception elected delegates and adopted platforms opposed by them. For whom then, do these newspapers speak? Whom do they represent? Certainly not the masses of the Democratic people. Who remains? The answer is that they stand for the views of the city bankers, merchants and corporation managers who surround them."[38]

In turn, southern conservatives frequently bemoaned their fate and complained that "the South does not seem to understand," that if the region's public "really perceived the situation and understood the issues," they would never consent to the abandonment of the states' rights principles necessary for the protection of the "weaker section." But in the changed political climate, even states' rights principles were being refashioned into an argument for federal regulation. Democratic leader Williams, for instance, repeatedly distinguished between two types of states' rights: the right to "insist that its reserved rights shall not be usurped," but also a "coordinate and coequal States right" for the federal government to carry out its delegated responsibility to promote the general welfare of the people. With the South being "the most thoroughly 'Bryanized' part of the country," the region's conservatives found their voices at least temporarily eclipsed; they were left to complain that in "no other part of the country have the Socialistic tendencies" of the day gained so much traction as "in the Southern States." But they also recognized that however much the conservative white man "may be disgusted at with the leading policies now advocated by the leaders of their party, he is likely, after arguing the questions at issue and shaking his head in sorrow, to go and vote as heretofore."[39]

The different faces of southern politics during the Progressive Era can be seen in Oklahoma, the South's newest state. Figure 6.10 shows a few measures of its southern character. The top-left panel indicates the proportion of the population in 1910 who were either born in or had parents who were born in one of the sixteen other southern states.[40] A majority of the settler population came from the South, many of them hoping to escape the poverty that had spread across the region. A significant share of Oklahoma's population was African American (shown in the top-right panel): they were either descended from slaves held by the Indian Nations or migrants themselves. Promoters of

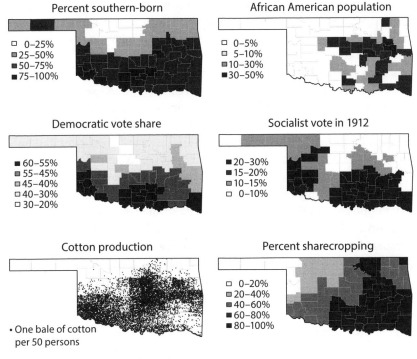

Percent southern-born

□ 0–25%
■ 25–50%
■ 50–75%
■ 75–100%

African American population

□ 0–5%
□ 5–10%
▣ 10–30%
■ 30–50%

Democratic vote share

■ 60–55%
▣ 55–45%
□ 45–40%
□ 40–30%
□ 30–20%

Socialist vote in 1912

■ 20–30%
■ 15–20%
▣ 10–15%
□ 0–10%

Cotton production

• One bale of cotton
per 50 persons

Percent sharecropping

□ 0–20%
▣ 20–40%
▣ 40–60%
■ 60–80%
■ 80–100%

FIGURE 6.10. Oklahoma's Southern Character.

black migration, many of them "exodusters," founded the Oklahoma Immigration Organization and the First Colored Real Estate Homestead, organizations that encouraged the acquisition of land by black settlers and helped establish communities of all-black towns where migrants might be free from the racial persecutions and economic hardships they faced in the rest of the South.

While many white southerners brought their Democratic partisanship with them to Oklahoma, a substantial minority of the new state's population migrated from deeply Republican states in the Midwest, ensuring that Oklahoma would be competitive in national politics. In the areas where southerners were disproportionately located, the Socialist Party drew impressive levels of support, well above the national average. The Socialists were a serious irritant to the state's Democratic Party; at one point, they publicized the fact that Senator Robert Owen, the famed progressive reformer, was one of the largest proprietors of farms sublet to tenants in the state. During the campaign of 1916, they extracted a promise from him to subdivide and sell the property. The Socialist-voting tenant farmer, complained the *Johnson County Capital Democrat*, was "a goose that wants a new mate every spring, and had soon have a black one as a white one. . . . He persuades himself that he has been robbed by the rich when he never had enough to buy a negroe's supper."[41]

In some ways, the hopes of both white and black southerners outpaced reality. By the first decade of the twentieth century, more farms were operating on a sharecropping basis in Oklahoma than in neighboring non-southern states, and there were only slightly fewer than in the Deep South states. In 1910, only one-quarter of all farms were owned outright and free of encumbrances, against a national average of 50 percent; only Mississippi had a lower rate, although the value of farms and crops in Oklahoma was higher and the percentage of nonfarm homes owned outright was slightly above the national average. For black Oklahomans, the picture was a little bit better, but only relative to the extreme deprivation in the rest of the South: the rate of landownership among black farmers, at 54 percent, was higher than in most other southern states—only Missouri, Maryland, and Virginia had higher rates. The exact opposite was the case for white farmers in Oklahoma, whose rate of landownership was not only the lowest in the South but in the entire country: compared to a national average of 73 percent and a southern average of 63 percent, only 44 percent of white Oklahoman farmers owned their land.[42]

Perhaps for this reason, when the Oklahoma and Indian Territories were finally authorized to draft a constitution in 1907, the convention prepared what was widely regarded as a radically progressive document. There were constitutional provisions regulating banks and corporations, providing for the initiative and the referendum, prohibiting corporations from buying land, breaking up monopolies, and restricting landownership to citizens. Newspapers either attacked or praised this constitution as the "most radical organic law ever developed in the Union," and it earned praise from Samuel Gompers and Charles Beard for its "fierce opposition to monopolies." William Jennings Bryan endorsed the "cornfield lawyers of Oklahoma" for writing the best constitution in the country.[43]

But if there was a strong radical streak to Oklahoma's politics, there was also an equally strong commitment to white supremacy. To avoid a presidential veto, the convention had decided not to enshrine Jim Crow or black disfranchisement in the new constitution, although the document did require segregated schools and provided that persons of Indian descent would be considered white. But the first statute passed by the new state legislature mandated racial segregation on railroads and streetcars and was quickly followed by legislation outlawing interracial marriage. In 1910, the Democratic legislature proposed a constitutional amendment that required a literacy test for voting rights, though its stipulations were waived for those who could show that they or their lineal ancestor had been able to vote in 1866 or had been resident of "some foreign nation." The chair of the Republican Central Committee warned President Taft that the law's intent was to "deprive ninety per cent of the African race of the right of suffrage," but the administration refused to intervene lest it "stir up the South." U.S. Attorney John Embry, a former

Kentuckian, nonetheless went ahead and indicted election officials J. J. Beal and Frank Guinn under one of the few pieces of Reconstruction-era election legislation that remained on the books, part of the old Ku Klux Klan Act prohibiting conspiracies to deny the exercise of constitutional rights. When his superiors in Washington called him to task, Embry threatened to resign and leave the administration in an embarrassing situation. Attorney General George Wickersham ultimately decided to let the case proceed, apparently because he was convinced that the judge and jury would not convict. To his surprise, an Oklahoma jury found both officials guilty. Needing the votes of black delegates to the Republican National Convention, President Taft changed his mind and endorsed further prosecutions, although once he had secured the nomination he encouraged local U.S. attorneys to tone down the rising temperature over the issue.[44]

Though Taft's loss in 1912 led many Republicans to worry that the case against Beal and Guinn would be abandoned upon appeal, the incoming solicitor general decided to defend the case before the Supreme Court. It was, in many ways, an intrasouthern affair. The solicitor general was John W. Davis, a former West Virginia representative and later a Democratic presidential nominee. Four decades later, in the 1950s, Davis would defend South Carolina's school segregation law in a companion case to *Brown v. Board of Education*. He squared off against conservative senator Joseph Bailey from Texas, who was representing the defendants, before a Court whose chief justice, Edward White, had been a member of the conservative Democratic faction that opposed the version of a grandfather clause used in his home state of Louisiana. The two justices who subsequently were reported to have been most likely to dissent were Justices Joseph Lamar and Horace Lurton, from Georgia and Kentucky, respectively.

Justice White's majority opinion—while scathing in its evaluation that Oklahoma's grandfather clause represented barely concealed racial disfranchisement—was careful to insist that literacy tests were unquestionably constitutional and that the Court need not consider whether they were being discriminatorily applied, but could make a simple evaluation of intent based on a simple reading of the provision. White, writes J. Morgan Kousser, wanted to "rule that escape clause unconstitutional, but he did not want to endanger white Democratic supremacy in the South." The majority decision, written by White, struck down the grandfather clause as a violation of the Fifteenth Amendment, but was careful to sidestep earlier cases that might have broadened the scope of his decision. Beal and Guinn were pardoned by President Wilson, and southern state newspapers generally suggested that the decision was merely a "temporary embarrassment," the removal of an expedient whose time had passed. Some even expressed their gratitude that White had clearly identified the "line a State may follow in restricting its franchise" while remaining within the constitutional limits of the Fifteenth Amendment. The Oklahoma state legislature responded by creating a perpetual register of all persons who had voted before 1914—that is, most adult white men—and allowing only a twelve-day window in 1916 for those who had not previously been registered to do so. Any Oklahoman who missed registering during this period lost suffrage rights forever. Although voters rejected a new literacy test—which was opposed by Republicans and Socialists and defended by Democrats as needed to "continue Oklahoma as a white man's state"—the registration law accomplished a similar purpose.[45]

Oklahoma blended radicalism and racism. It also had a pronounced conservative streak, which became more prominent as Socialists gained adherents and defended black voting rights and as World War I helped kick off a boom in the oil industry that promised new opportunities for economic advancement outside of land reform or support for farmers. During the war, a network of local defense councils was organized to whip up patriotic sentiment, oppose Socialism, and suppress the so-called green corn rebellion: the threat by white, black, and Indian tenant farmers opposed to conscription to march east and force a repeal of the draft. After the defeat of the rebellion, the defense councils began targeting farm and labor unions for repression and later served as a training ground for the new Ku Klux Klan, which would become so important in the state's politics in the early 1920s that Governor John Walton would declare martial law and try to block the Klan-dominated state legislature from meeting. With the Democratic Party deeply divided between supporters of the Klan and supporters of the newly organized Farmer-Labor Reconstruction League, the Republican Party was able to make inroads in the state, even outpacing the gains made in the 1920s in other border and upper South states. With backing from the Klan, the Republican Party captured the state legislature, elected John Harreld as senator, and won the state's ten Electoral College votes in 1920. In 1925, another Republican senator was elected, William Pine, who, like Harreld, generally took conservative positions on the economy. In 1928, Republicans won 64 percent of the statewide vote for president, more than in any other southern state except Delaware.[46]

The Rise of Southern Influence

The twentieth century began with considerable momentum in the South for progressive reforms, though it was more of a tendency than a consensus view. Three decades later, there was still support for federal policy activism in the region, but also an invigorated states' rights conservatism, represented by southern Democrats as well as a considerable number of Republicans elected in 1928. Whether southerners wanted to expand the scope of federal activity or roll it back, however, their ability to do so varied with changes in the institutional environment and their own success at cultivating bipartisan coalitions. Just as southern policy priorities varied across the region and across time, so did their ability to influence the content of national policy.

We have found it useful to subdivide the Progressive era in national politics into two periods, ranging roughly from 1900 to 1916 and from 1917 to 1930. This unusual periodization is guided by attention to the dynamics of southern Democratic lawmaking, in terms of both the substantive positions taken by the region's legislators and their prospect for shaping public policy and the means by which they could do so. The first period can be characterized as one of slowly cresting momentum: after a decade in which southerners had been largely excluded from power and progressive priorities were usually defeated or substantially reworked, newly elected Democratic majorities were now rapidly able to enact most of the items on the South's legislative agenda. It is a story of rising action as southern Democrats largely maintained their cohesion on a set of shared priorities, and it culminates in reforms that were progressive in economic terms while further entrenching white supremacy in national policy.

The second period began around the time of the policy enactments that accompanied Wilson's preparedness program and America's entry into the war, and it concludes with the catastrophic crisis that global capitalism faced after 1929. The story of this period picks up at the height of Wilsonian progressivism. If in the early years of Wilson's administration the South had largely been able to maintain cohesion on core priorities, working out compromises and accommodations as needed but otherwise shepherding through Congress a reform program that reflected the region's long-standing demands, in his second term party unity collapsed, the caucus ceased to serve as an effective coordinating mechanism, and a divided South entered into shifting coalitions with progressive and conservative Republicans. The pattern of politics that followed in the 1920s bore more similarities to Wilson's second term in its unstable legislative coalitions than to the 1900s or early Wilson years. The story is of the dissipation of progressive momentum, the fragmentation of Democratic and southern unity, and the rise to prominence of a different pattern of congressional lawmaking that was organized around issue-specific legislative coalitions as much as around the majority party's agenda. Southern lawmaking in this period looked more like interest-group politics, without the unifying themes of progressive reform or the imperatives of supporting the presidential administration that earlier had induced regional cohesion.

These periods also correspond roughly with variation in the types of issues that received attention in national policymaking; generally, the shift was from financial and economic regulation to war and social issues, and finally to a renewed concern with agriculture, resource development, and a new set of economic regulatory proposals. The periods also correspond with changes in

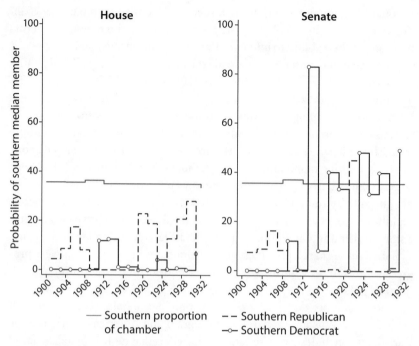

FIGURE 6.11. Southern Pivotal Politics, 1900–1930

the level and type of influence that southern Democratic legislators could exercise in national lawmaking as the South went from being excluded from most important positions in the policymaking process to being "at the helm," then back to being in the minority, but with revised institutions that facilitated the formation of cross-party coalitions.

Figure 6.11 shows the probability that a southerner of either party would be pivotal in the House or Senate from 1900 to 1930. We will see in chapters 7 and 8 that these probabilities varied across issue areas in ways that facilitated southern influence, but for the most part neither southern Democrats nor Republicans were likely to be pivotal during the first decade of the century. Southern Democrats were the likely pivotal actors in the Senate during the first two years of the Wilson administration, but in the House the advent of a Democratic majority left northern and western Democrats as the pivotal members most willing to defect from the party line. After the Democratic Party suffered substantial losses in the midterms of 1918, the Republicans were able to eke out a small majority in the Senate and a substantial majority in the House, pushing out the plurality coalition between Democrats and Progressives that had organized that chamber since 1917. Yet during the decade that followed—which included the Democratic nadir of 1921, when Republicans held 60 percent of the seats in the Senate and 70 percent of the seats in the

House—the South was more likely to be pivotal than it had been in a genera-tion. As we discuss in chapter 8, this was in part a function of the increased dissatisfaction of midwestern and western Republicans with their party's con-servative leadership, but it was also a reflection of an increased willingness among senators of both parties to build issue-specific legislative coalitions across the party divide.

Southerners' ability to influence lawmaking was also constrained by changes to the rules and practices of each chamber that increasingly concen-trated power in the leadership of the majority party. The advent of the "Reed rules" in the House in the early 1890s had rendered the minority party nearly irrelevant. In the Senate, the right of unlimited debate was maintained, but here too a small coterie of senators—centered on Nelson Aldrich of Rhode Island, William Allison of Iowa, Orville Platt of Connecticut, and John Spooner of Wisconsin, and backed by the now-regularized institution of the steering committee and party caucus—was able to exercise considerable con-trol over the legislative agenda, "arranging the legislative schedule in detail week by week." Although the Senate's centralization of agenda-setting author-ity was nowhere near as severe as in the House, it nonetheless limited oppor-tunities for the minority party to get its issues onto the agenda.[47]

Figure 6.12 shows the percentage of party leaders in the House from the South in either party, including the speaker, the majority leader, the chair of the Rules Committee, and the chairs of the ten most important legislative committees; for the Senate, we follow the ten most important legislative com-mittees. The influence that southerners could exercise through control over the legislative agenda was clearly tied to the fate of the national Democratic coalition. But between 1911 and 1919 in the House and between 1913 and 1919 in the Senate, the South was in charge. This institutional dominance was by no means inevitable; though southern Democratic seniority had increased during the period when they were increasingly protected by a restricted elec-torate and the handful of northern Democrats were regularly defeated, the allocation of committee chairs on the basis of seniority was a political choice made by a party leadership that was under considerable pressure to balance the composition of committees and committee chairs by section and ideologi-cal faction and that nonetheless choose to empower its southern members.

Southern influence whipped from the extreme of near-total exclusion to being "back in the saddle" to once again being in the minority. But the South was not simply an inert mass buffeted by changing national fortunes. Rather, southern representatives acted strategically across these different periods to carve out opportunities to play a constructive role in lawmaking and to craft reorganizations of institutional authority. As we detail in chapter 7, southern Democrats responded to their institutional exclusion by deliberately choos-ing to forgo partisan advantage in the hope of building cross-party legislative

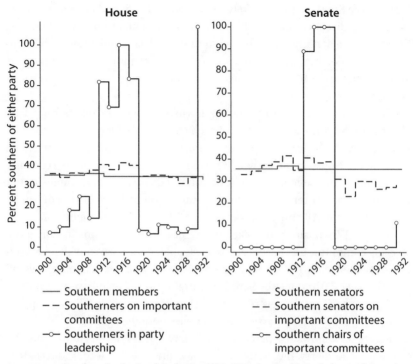

FIGURE 6.12. Southern Institutional Authority, 1900–1930. Leadership includes speaker, majority leader, and the chairmen of the Rules, Ways and Means, Appropriations, and other important committees.

coalitions—a choice that was made easier by the recognition that the party remained an embattled minority outside the South—and by cultivating support among a faction of Republicans for rules changes that would allow both groups more influence in the lawmaking process. In the 1910 revolt against Speaker Joseph Cannon in the House of Representatives, the speaker was stripped of much of his agenda-setting power and control over committee assignments and the all-important Rules Committee was returned to first the Republican conference and later the Democratic Committee on Committees. Once Democrats gained the majority, they maintained these rule changes while overlaying them with new institutional mechanisms that would allow them to act quickly on their legislative program. In the Senate, other changes, to both the rules and informal practices, had similar effects. The development of a formal mechanism for cloture—which, as we discuss in chapter 8, was crafted by southern Democrats with an eye to securing their continued ability to block legislative action—regularized the practice of seeking supermajoritarian support for legislation in that chamber. At the same time, the organization

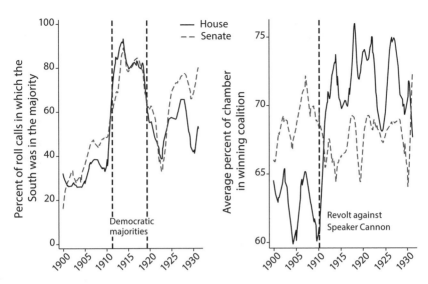

FIGURE 6.13. Shifts in Congressional Politics, 1900–1930

of nonparty coalitions such as the Farm Bloc—which briefly gained control over the legislative agenda—ensured that southern interests were more important in this chamber than they had been during the years when the Republican steering committee gave firm direction to Senate proceedings.

The impact of these changes was evident in voting patterns. The left panel of figure 6.13 displays the percentage of roll calls in which the majority of southern lawmakers voted with the majority coalition. The right panel shows the average size of the winning coalition across all roll calls from 1900 to 1932 in the House and Senate. The diffusion of authority that followed the revolt against Speaker Cannon quickly increased the size of the average winning coalition, which persisted after the Republicans returned to power. The decentralization of authority opened up space for more bipartisan and encompassing legislative coalitions as the dominance over the legislative agenda by conservative Republicans gave way first to a Democratic agenda that had some appeal to progressive Republicans, then later to a more diffuse and decentralized process that allowed a greater variety of power centers to participate in policy formation. Despite being in the minority in the 1920s, the South was more likely to vote with the majority in both chambers than ten years earlier.

These shifts in voting patterns were not solely the product of institutional changes. Both the Senate and the House were undergoing profound changes in the composition, career paths, and objectives of their members as long-term careerists selected by primary electorates replaced party-appointed loyalists.

Figure 6.14 shows the average number of years served by regional-party bloc, as well as the bloc's size in the chamber. (When there were few members from a bloc, the averages could be inflated by a handful of long-serving members.) Relative to non-southern Democrats or border state Democrats, southerners from the former Confederacy gained steadily in seniority, especially after restrictions on the franchise reduced competition in the region. This new configuration of authority in Congress, in which the locus of power lay with the senior members of important committees—who had as much power as party leaders and in some cases more—ultimately would provide southern legislators with a heightened ability to translate their diverse preferences into national policy. In this changed context, the ability of southern Democrats to cultivate shifting and overlapping coalitions with progressives and conservatives of both parties allowed them to exercise greater influence than they had during the first decade of the century.

The first three decades of the twentieth century marked a clear shift in congressional productivity. Table 6.1 lists some of the most important acts for each decade. Table 6.2 shows the number of bills passed by decade between 1877 and 1945 that ranked among the top 100, the top 250, the top 500, or the top 1,000

Although the Wilson years witnessed a remarkable burst in national lawmaking, with southern legislators playing an especially important role, they also were part of a broader shift that saw the country turn increasingly toward Washington for solutions and Congress become newly receptive to national action. The number of bills ranked among the 1,000 most important passed between 1877 and 1945 increased in the first two decades of the twentieth century and remained at heightened levels thereafter. The decade that overlaps with Democratic control of Congress and the White House saw a doubling of the most important landmark legislation, as well as large increases in the number of laws that met the lower thresholds of the top 250, top 500, and top 1,000.

Regulation of interstate commerce, labor, and the financial system, including a fundamental reorganization of the monetary system, as well as antitrust and trade legislation were among the most important bills passed in the first two decades. Issues related to agriculture and resource development became especially important during the 1920s. But Congress also addressed questions about the composition of the country, the character of its democracy, and the regulation of its society through the Mann Act and prohibition, imperial and colonial policy, immigration policy, anti-lynching legislation, the direct election of senators, and women's suffrage. These various issue areas produced not only different configurations of partisan and regional voting but also a range of opportunities for southern influence.[48]

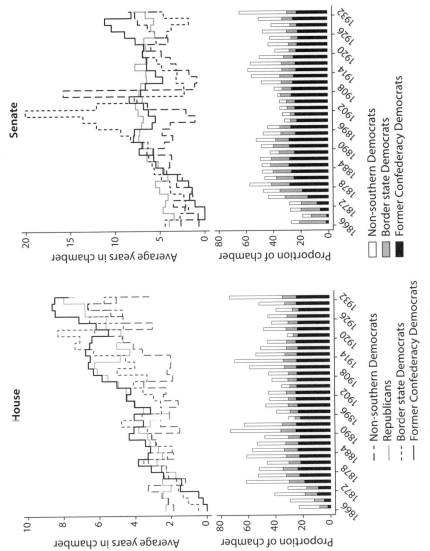

FIGURE 6.14. Seniority and Delegation Size, 1866–1932

TABLE 6.1. Highly Significant Legislation, 1900–1930

Time Period	Legislation	Issue Area
1900–1917		
Roosevelt's first term	Gold Standard Act, 1900	Finance/money
	Philippines Organic Act, 1902	Empire/colonialism
	Irrigation Act, 1902	Resources and agriculture
	Department of Commerce and Labor, 1903	Labor/economic regulation
	1887 Interstate Commerce Act Amendment (Elkins Act), 1903	Interstate commerce
Roosevelt's second term	Agricultural Appropriations (Land-Grant Colleges), 1906	Agriculture and education
	Interstate Commerce (Hepburn) Act, 1906	Economic regulation
	Pure Food Act, 1906	Economic regulation/health
Taft's first term	National Bank Circulation Act, 1908	Finance/money
	Income Tax Amendment, 1909	Taxation/Constitution
	Tariff of 1909	Tariff
	Commerce Court, 1910	Economic regulation/judiciary
	"White Slavery" (Mann) Act, 1910	Social regulation
	Direct Election of Senators, 1912	Representation/Constitution
	Department of Labor, 1913	Labor
Wilson's first term	Underwood Tariff, 1913	Tariff
	Federal Reserve Act, 1913	Finance/money
	Anti-Trust Act, 1914	Economic regulation
	Federal Trade Commission, 1914	Economic regulation
	Philippines Government Act, 1916	Empire/colonialism
	National Defense Act, 1916	Defense
	Federal Farm Loan Act, 1916	Agricultural/finance
	Revenue Act, 1916	Taxation
	Child Labor Act, 1916	Labor/social regulation
	Eight-Hour Law, 1916	Labor

1917–1930	
Wilson's second term	
Immigration Act, 1917	Immigration
Declaration of War, 1917	Diplomacy/defense
Emergency Army Increase, 1917	Defense
Food and Fuel Act, 1917	Economic regulation/price controls
War Revenue Act, 1917	Taxation
Espionage Acts, 1917 and 1918	Liberty
Prohibition Amendment, 1917, and Prohibition Act, 1918	Social regulation
Consolidation of Executive Agencies, 1918	Government organization
War Finance Corporation, 1918	Finance/defense
Women's Suffrage, 1919	Representation/Constitution
Transportation Act, 1920	Transportation/economic regulation
Federal Water Power Act, 1920	Natural resources
Harding's/Coolidge's first term	
Alien Immigration Act, 1921	Immigration
Packers and Stockyard Act, 1921	Agriculture/economic regulation
Maternity and Infant Hygiene, 1921	Social regulation/health
Cooperative Marketing Act, 1922	Agriculture
Grain Futures Act, 1921 and 1922	Agriculture/finance
Tariff of 1922	Tariff/agriculture
Immigration Act, 1924	Immigration
World War Adjusted Compensation Act (Bonus Bill), 1924	Military pensions
Hoch-Smith Resolution, 1925	Agriculture/economic regulation
Coolidge's second term	
Air Commerce Act, 1926	Transportation/economic regulation
Revenue Act, 1926	Taxation
Railway Labor Act, 1926	Labor
Radio Act, 1927	Economic regulation
Hoover's first term	
Agricultural Marketing Act, 1929	Agriculture/finance tariff
Tariff of 1930	

TABLE 6.2. Important Laws Passed, by Decade

	Top 100	Top 250	Top 500	Top 1,000
1880—1889	6	20	34	70
1890—1899	9	21	41	71
1900—1909	10	24	46	95
1910—1919	22	49	109	205
1913—1919 Unified Demo-cratic control	*16*	*32*	*58*	*110*
1920—1929	10	33	64	149
1930—1939	36	70	127	244
1940—1945	6	30	68	145

Figure 6.15 demonstrates the pattern of voting alignments across some of the main issues on the political agenda. What immediately stands out are the distinctive configurations of the politics that accompanied immigration, prohibition, women's suffrage, civil rights, and child labor, as well as constitutional amendments that were primarily concerned with establishing an income tax, providing for the direct election of senators, and attempting (unsuccessfully) to change the president's term of office. The South broke party ranks and supported conservative as well as progressive Republicans in favor of both restricting the levels of immigration and confining new immigrants to those from primarily northwestern European countries. The region also provided the most consistent support for authorizing the federal government to prohibit the manufacture and sale of alcohol, an incredible expansion of national authority over the activities of individual citizens in what had been an area of unquestioned state control. The South stood nearly alone on a set of issues that were understood as threatening the region's class, racial, and gender hierarchies, including their opposition to anti-lynching legislation and their efforts to ban both child labor and women's suffrage. And the tariff and trade policy continued to unite the parties against each other, as did issues relating to the basic balance of partisan advantage in national politics, such as state admission and contested elections.

Figures 6.16 and 6.17 break out these aggregate patterns by more closely examining the different ways in which southern voting could resemble the voting patterns of different Republican groups. Southerners were most likely to break with their northern Democratic allies on the issues concerning social regulations around which the progressive movement had mobilized; the region's legislators were sometimes pushed into alliances with the conservative northeastern Republicans and, at other times, with the progressive midwesterners. Although there was no one progressive stance on prohibition, this issue arrayed southern Democrats against their northern copartisans

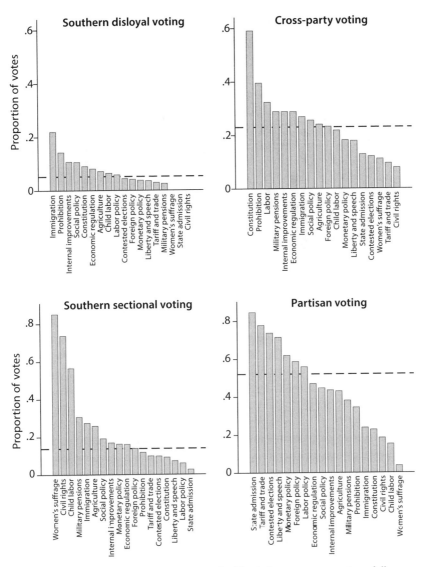

FIGURE 6.15. Voting Alignments, 1900–1930. Dashed line is the average proportion of all other votes.

and aligned them with Republicans. After 1917, the number of issues on which southern Democratic votes looked more like those of Republicans increased. On women's suffrage, southern legislators were more similar in their voting to conservative northeasterners than to their own copartisans; this was also true of child labor, while immigration was an issue area that brought southern Democrats and western and midwestern Republicans together.

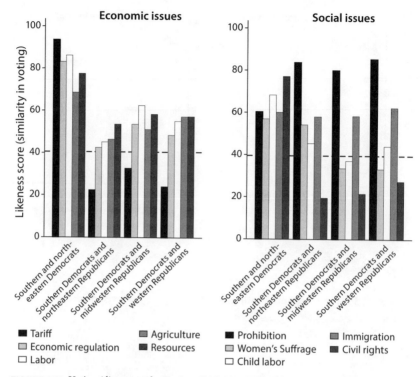

FIGURE 6.16. Voting Alignments by Region, 1900–1917. Dashed line is likeness score with Republicans on all other issues.

On issues that were more directly concerned with the regulation of the national economy or state-supported development of resources and agriculture, southern Democratic voting patterns in the first period generally were closest to those of their northern copartisans than to any of the Republican groupings. Even as the tariff continued to starkly separate the parties, most southern members could generally count on support from non-southern Democrats, as well as from progressives in the Republican Party, on other issues of importance to them. These policies included the regulation of interstate commerce to greater advantage for farmers and small producers, the aggressive use of antitrust authority to break up and curtail the market and economic power of the monopolistic corporations, the development of a system of agricultural credits, and support for agricultural education. The collapse of party lines regarding these matters only intensified after 1917, when southern Democratic voting looked less like non-southern Democratic voting and almost like midwestern Republican voting. The relatively high similarity between southern Democrats and northeastern Republicans suggests that the South itself was increasingly divided on some of these questions. On each of the major economic issues listed in figures 6.16 and 6.17, southern Democrats

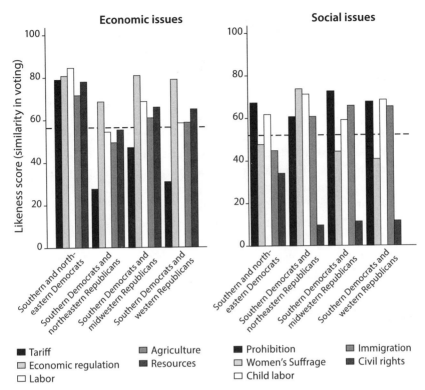

FIGURE 6.17. Voting Alignments by Region, 1917–1933. Dashed line is likeness score with Republicans on all other issues.

after 1917 voted more like Republicans than they had before, and they were more internally divided. Southern cohesion on these issues declined significantly as the region's lawmakers became more likely to break party ranks and vote inside issue-specific coalitions.

Conclusion

Historical orientations toward southern progressivism were crucially shaped by the historian Arthur Link, who influentially rejected the "popular notion" that "there was no progressive democracy in the South." Link charted the strength of southern progressivism, tying it to earlier agrarian movements and recovering the vital role played by southerners in fashioning progressive reforms in the nation's legislature. "The Southern agrarians of the Wilson period," he argued, "were the direct inheritors and now the prime articulators in the Democratic party of the philosophy underlying the Agrarian crusade—namely, that it was government's duty to intervene directly in economic affairs in order to benefit submerged or politically impotent economic interests."

Indeed, it was the large body of southern agrarian Democrats in Congress, "often far to the left" of the administration, who "helped to make Wilson an advanced progressive and helped to commit his administration to a broad program of welfare legislation," although their concerns were "aimed at benefiting the farmers almost exclusively."[49]

Link's interpretation of southern progressivism later was challenged on many fronts. He had suggested that there was an essential continuity between the progressives and the agrarian movements of the 1870s to 1890s, but C. Vann Woodward treated the Populist revolt as a sharp break in southern history. In Woodward's framing, southern progressivism had distinct social and economic origins drawn from the earlier agrarian movements, and little in the way of shared organizations or personalities connected them. Others asked whether southern Democrats in Congress had in fact played the progressive role in which Link had cast them. Richard Abrams, for instance, questioned not only the role of southern agrarian radicals but the very existence and stability of such a group: "it is clear," he argued, "that whatever there was of a coordinated radical faction, its stable core was very small (perhaps fifteen or twenty congressmen), its periphery of drifters was highly mobile, and its political position was not consistently progressive."[50]

The broad historiography on progressivism, however, tended to go in different directions—toward a characterization of national reforms as a response to the demands of northeastern capitalists, toward questioning the coherence of the concept of progressivism itself, or toward studies of progressive reforms in specific states and localities. Not until Elizabeth Sanders's *Roots of Reform* was the thesis of a progressive and consequential South in national politics recovered, indeed expanded and put on solid empirical foundations. She offered a wealth of evidence that Populism, progressivism, and other social movements in the country's agricultural regions offered a relatively coherent and consistent set of critiques and policy prescriptions in response to the period's economic dislocations, and that their efforts fundamentally shaped the new type of American state that was built in the early part of the century. Through detailed case studies, Sanders showed that the national impact of farmers—and of southerners in particular—provided considerable fuel for reform in Congress and persuaded that body to accept, however grudgingly, the compromises necessary for enactment.[51]

Largely absent from these accounts of southern progressivism was the virulent racism with which it coexisted and that it often seemed to deepen. As Howard Rabinowitz observed, "Link had noted that nothing had been done *for* blacks," but he generally "ignored what progressives helped do *to* blacks in terms of disfranchisement, legally enforced segregation, and weak opposition to lynching." Missing from this account of the role of the South in shaping national progressive reform was attention to how white supremacy shaped, and was shaped by, the exercise of southern influence in national politics. These elements, by contrast, were central to Woodward's examination of southern progressivism. As he noted, some of the defining reforms of progressivism had emerged in the South, such as the city-manager and the commission form of city government. Although the party primary did not originate in the region, Charles Merriam noted that South Carolina's mandatory primary system constituted "a new and advanced type of primary election legislation" when it was passed, marking "the transition from invitation to command." At the heart of each of these reforms was the goal of reducing the influence of black residents and the white working classes on city or state government or in congressional elections. As the Trades and Labor Assembly of Des Moines, Iowa, was warned when that city was debating the commission system, "This is the Galveston [Texas] system pure and simple to keep the so-called white trash and colored vote of the south from exerting itself in participation of the affairs of the city."[52]

"I think one of the great and pathetic ironies of our history," Woodward told a congressional hearing in 1981 on extending the Voting Rights Act, "is that the most reactionary period of racial legislation got tied with the name of 'progressivism.' That was the period when the great bulk of the discriminatory laws about voting and civil rights were put on the books, when the northern opinion was most lax and permissive about those laws." Since Woodward, historians have detailed how the legal architecture for white supremacy helped constitute progressive reform; how white southern progressives accepted and reinforced many defining features of Jim Crow by reframing the issue of racial inequality as one of managing "race relations" or "adjusting social differences"; and how the radical curtailment of joint black and working-class politics provided the social and political conditions for southern progressivism to emerge.[53]

These rich accounts of the intersection of white racism and progressive reform for the most part have followed Woodward in their attention to local and state-level politics, but they have continued to pay insufficient attention to Congress. Such a focus is essential to recover the importance of the South in shaping progressive reforms while embedding white supremacy inside a transformed American state.[54]

7

Ascendancy

One section of the country is denied responsibility for the Government and through its political representatives must content itself with obstruction and opposition instead of being permitted to take part in constructive legislation by being able to bring forward measures that will command the support of the majority.[1]

The southern men now in public life have not risen to the national occasion. They seem never quite to lose sectional consciousness.[2]

No longer hampered and held back by insecurity at home, our leaders of all parties may and should prove themselves at Washington as national, as American, as any others they shall there encounter. The South may and should rise again at least to equality with other sections in the Union, and confidently and hopefully assume at least an equal share of the noble burden of the destinies of the Republic.[3]

On March 2, 1913, Josephus Daniels shared a stage in Raleigh, North Carolina, with a man introduced as "the greatest apostle of The Prince of Peace on earth today, the world's foremost citizen and the highest example of real statesmanship." Daniels, a few months shy of his fifty-first birthday, was the publisher of the *News and Observer* and probably the most influential political operative in North Carolina; he had long championed progressive causes in his state and recently had played a pivotal role in rallying southern progressives around the candidacy of Woodrow Wilson, their party's presidential nomination. Daniels listened closely and with evident approval as the speaker, William Jennings

Bryan, the "great commoner" and three-time presidential candidate, told a crowd of thousands that a millennium of "universal peace" could be secured if the United States would accept the mantle of global leadership. After rousing applause from the assembled members of the North Carolina chapter of the American Peace Society, the two men boarded the Seaboard Air Line train, which took them "through the heart of the South" to Washington, DC, where they were to serve in the cabinet of Woodrow Wilson, Bryan as Secretary of State and Daniels as Secretary of the Navy.[4]

As a Bryanite, Daniels had long been a leader in the progressive wing of the party. He led calls for regulation of the trusts and railroads, support for public schools and public works, and the prohibition of alcohol. Serving as Secretary of the Navy, Daniels came to know Franklin Delano Roosevelt, whose later rise to political prominence he would actively promote. Roosevelt's New Deal, in turn, would find few southerners as supportive as Daniels, who saw in the new president's program a muscular continuation of the very progressive policies he had long endorsed.[5]

Throughout Daniels's long career, he also was a steadfast defender of white supremacy. He had grown up in the "second district," the disproportionately African American constituency that had elected James O'Hara and George Henry White to Congress in the 1880s and 1890s—Daniels believed that his mother had been removed as postmaster to make way for a Republican appointee at the request of O'Hara—and both his progressive and white supremacist politics would be rooted in the anxieties and priorities of the Black Belt. In the late 1890s, he had played a critical role in coordinating violence against black Americans and "fusionist" politicians in North Carolina, which culminated in the arson of a black newspaper in Wilmington and spread from there to a massacre of the city's black residents. Daniels publicly praised the rioters and murderers for having manfully defended the virtue of white women, and he insisted that they had only responded to the violent provocations of Wilmington's black residents. His political star rose considerably as a result of his involvement in the violence of 1898 and the disfranchisement campaigns that followed. Subsequently, he effectively backed the localization of education finance, which greatly increased inequality in the allocation of funds, both between white and black residents and between upper-, middle-, and working-class whites.[6]

It was in part through Daniels's influence that the state Democratic Party became the party of "white men and white metal," as he put it, the champions of free silver and progressivism in addition to its established role as the guarantor of racial hierarchy. As the state Democratic Party moved left, Daniels leveraged his influence to become a key broker in the national party, a position that allowed him to help shape the party's national policy commitments. He was an ardent promoter of William Jennings Bryan in the state and would later play a key role in persuading Bryan to get behind the candidacy of Woodrow Wilson, whom he had met in 1909 when the Princeton president was on his way to Chapel Hill to deliver a speech commemorating the birth of Robert E. Lee.[7]

Across the South there were hundreds of Democrats like Daniels, though few who could match the reach of his influence. Many more pressed their political leadership and officeholders to support the aggressive use of state and federal authority to regulate or break up trusts, provide for a more elastic currency, facilitate the provision of credit to farmers, prohibit or regulate the production and consumption of alcohol, invest in public schools, and even, in some cases, to prohibit the use of child labor. These activists set the tenor for many state Democratic parties, as well as the actions of the region's congressional legislators.

Like Daniels, they expected their candidates for national office to do more than simply recognize the reality of white supremacy in southern states. They wanted it to be actively embraced as national policy. "Out of a bitter experience," Daniels wrote in a widely reprinted 1912 editorial, "the South has evolved certain convictions on the race question; and she takes her place in the Nation with those convictions."

> They are paramount convictions. It is not conceivable that any man or any party that is not clear upon those convictions will ever receive her support: She is seeking not merely a sectional but a national policy on this subject; for she knows that short of a national policy on the race question, she will never be secure. . . . The subjection of the negro politically, and the separation of the negro socially, are paramount to all other considerations in the South short of the preservation of the Republic itself. And we shall recognize no emancipation, nor shall we proclaim any deliverer that falls short of these essentials to the peace and the welfare of our part of the country.

Of the three candidates for president in 1912, he argued, only Woodrow Wilson could be trusted to bring about the progressive reforms that the South desired while extending white supremacy into all corners of national policy.[8]

This chapter examines the period from the turn of the century to the outbreak of World War I, a time when southern influence over national policy went from its lowest point in history to heights unmatched since before the Civil War. We begin by examining the limits of southern influence in the first decade of the twentieth century, when southern Democrats struggled to advance a legislative agenda that accommodated their multiple, at times conflicting, priorities. Operating in an unfavorable institutional context and unlikely to win a national majority outright, southern Democrats chose to act strategically and forgo partisan advantage in favor of substantive policy gains, all the while probing for opportunities to change the rules and enhance their role in lawmaking over the long term. We follow the story of southern lawmaking through to the dramatic reconfiguration of authority and influence that followed the elections of 1912, when southern Democratic influence over national policy jumped dramatically and the region's sometimes fractious body of legislators managed to forge and pass an ambitious progressive policy agenda. We conclude by elaborating how southern priorities were accommodated in the construction of the new American state as a southern-led Congress recognized and affirmed the power of southern states and local white elites to regulate the region's racial and class hierarchies.

The Limits of Southern Influence

Southern legislators and constituencies had a long list of policy priorities at the beginning of the twentieth century. The "Bryan wing" of the party wanted a progressive income tax, further regulation of railroads, a system of agricultural credit, free rural delivery of mail and packages, and monetary reform so that the "vastly valuable privilege of issuing paper notes as money" would no longer "be turned over bodily to private corporations." The "New South" advocates of industrial progress, including many economically conservative southern Democrats with support in the region's growing commercial and manufacturing centers, wanted construction of an isthmian canal connecting the Caribbean to the Pacific Ocean and aggressive pursuit of the "open-door" policy of trade with China. And both progressive and conservative southern Democrats looked for government support for internal improvements in their states and districts. The South should "stop giving its entire time to the study of the constitution, and pay some attention to appropriations," complained George Burgess of Texas. "Those Yankees have been getting the money while we have been talking about the constitution. Put good men in congress and keep them there. It takes about five years for a man to find the way into the crib. Just keep us there and we'll get your appropriations—we'll grab everything in sight." In fact, the South continued to receive its proportionate share of rivers and harbors funding, reflecting the enduring success of John Reagan's efforts in the late nineteenth century. But their political marginalization had also led to southern Democrats being "almost totally excluded from the benefits of legislation and the special favors and opportunities emanating from government"—that is, they had been denied "equal opportunities for wealth making" through patronage appointments.[9]

It was the task of John Sharp Williams, who was occasionally lauded as "the modern Democrat," to develop a strategy to remedy this situation. Williams's responsibility, as the leader of the minority party in the House, was to detail a policy agenda that could reconcile the party's warring factions and craft a legislative strategy that would either facilitate the restoration of majority status or carve out some other means to exercise influence. The platform he wrote in 1904 for Mississippi Democrats called for an "open-door" foreign economic policy and the cessation of the partnership between the Treasury and favored national banks. It opposed new bond issues, supported liberal appropriations for public works, and called for a reduction in Army expenses, the development of a merchant marine (but not at public expense), and impartial dealings between capital and labor. Answering the call that "the Democrats of the south can, and should, take the lead" in uniting the party, Williams played a key role in 1904 in drafting the national platform, which neither repudiated earlier campaigns nor reaffirmed the losing principles. Instead, Williams artfully suggested that recent gold discoveries that had expanded the currency vindicated the Bryan wing of the party while allowing the Democrats to not press the issue of the gold standard. "For ten or more years," wrote one paper in 1909, "the Democrats of the House have formed a sort of political mob that idolized William Jennings Bryan and John Sharp Williams—the one for his dreams and the other for his charming personality, his courage, his daring, his eloquence and his splendid fighting ability."[10]

Williams had gained favor in the party by cultivating progressive support in the South, regularly introducing legislation for an income tax, and calling for the dissolution of all trusts as well as "drastic federal regulations" on interstate corporations. But as minority leader, he also worked to reassure conservatives in the party by directing his "attention straight to the only issue that absolutely distinguishes democracy from republicanism, the only issue on which a campaign can be fought between the democrats and the republicans, the tariff issue." His role as party leader also led him to tack strategically between vitriol and a form of moderation on matters of race. In the election campaign of 1904, he and other southerners had advocated attacks against Roosevelt and the Republicans for threatening the southern racial hierarchy on the basis of Roosevelt's nomination of a few African Americans to southern offices and the inclusion of a proposal to look into reducing southern representation in that year's party platform. But facing off against the race-baiting James K. Vardaman for a Senate seat, he wrote that "the South ought to take its part in solving the great questions of the tariff, trusts, transportation, colonialism, et id omnus genus, and not occupy itself in 'baying at the moon,' or in a thing equally useless and much more dangerous." Williams, like other southern Democratic party leaders, was perfectly willing to play the "race card" when it suited his purposes, but was more than a bit peeved when it was used against him or used indiscriminately in such a way that might undermine the party's national ambitions. Southern Democratic leaders wanted to make absolutely clear how intensely they would oppose federal interference, but also wanted to avoid giving Republicans an issue that might limit Democratic opportunities in the North. For example, when Benjamin Tillman launched one of his periodic and widely reported tirades in defense of murdering south-

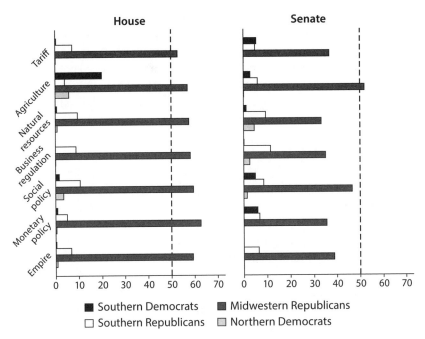

FIGURE 7.1. Probability of Members Being in Median by Region and Party, 1900–1910

ern blacks for daring to try to vote, the entire Democratic conference—North and South—left the chamber to wait in the cloak room until he was done.[11]

Williams's hope that the South would "take its part in solving the great questions" of the day was curtailed by Democrats' minority status and the dominance of the Republican House leadership. With heightened polarization during this period, there was little likelihood of southern Democrats being pivotal. Figure 7.1 shows the probability of a different region-party group being pivotal, in the House and Senate, across a range of important issue areas. On only one issue, agriculture, did the probability of southerners being pivotal rise above 10 percent, despite the fact that the South could claim, between both parties, approximately 35 percent of the seats in the House and Senate. Between 1901 and 1911, had southern votes been entirely reversed, they could have changed the outcome on only 12 percent of roll calls, most of which concerned relatively small matters or private bills. The main exceptions were a series of amendments to agricultural appropriations acts, including the establishment of a feed-seed provision, an increase in appropriations for the Bureau of Soils, and passage of Republican Knute Nelson's amendment to double the yearly funding given to the land-grant colleges to train agricultural teachers—for which all but five southern representatives voted in favor. Only James Ollie and Joseph Sherley of Kentucky, Finis Garrett of Tennessee, Oscar Gillespie of Texas, and John Lamb of Virginia voted against the Nelson amendment. But if southern votes were essential to passage of these progressive provisions, they also were the key factor in weakening a child labor law for the District of Columbia. An amendment to allow boys over the age of fourteen to work in mercantile establishments passed only because southern Democrats broke party ranks to support it. Each of these votes reflected a rare moment when divisions among Republicans allowed southern legislators to play a pivotal role.[12]

In addition to their weak floor position, southern Democrats were constrained by the high concentration of agenda authority in the House and Senate in the party leadership. This was especially true in the House, where Speaker Joseph Cannon arguably exercised more control over the legislative agenda than any of his predecessors for more than a century. Cannon had come to power with a promise to enhance the prestige of the House, which he aimed to do by fully exploiting the speaker's power to set the agenda through the Rules Committee, committee appointments, and floor recognition to allow only legislation that had the support of the majority of Republicans to be brought up. When Democrats tried in 1906 to pass an eight-hour law for railroad workers, Republicans on the House Committee on Labor were "practically forbidden" by Cannon to report the bill; when Democrats took advantage of the temporary absence of three Republicans on the committee to report the bill, Cannon simply refused to recognize any member he thought might move to consider it on the floor. In the Senate, party leadership was more informal and exercised by a handful of leaders through a combination of coordination, personal persuasion, and control over committee assignments. But the result was broadly similar, with the majority party able to effectively control the legislative process with little attention to southern Democratic priorities.[13]

Even when issues of importance to the South were brought up, majority party agenda control gave southern lawmakers little chance to refashion proposed reforms to their taste. Substitute bills could be kept off the agenda, floor amendments could be blocked through restrictive rules, time limits on considering amendments, or refusal to recognize members. If southern amendments passed, they could be dropped by conference committees appointed by the party leadership. When President Roosevelt called for a bill regulating railroad rates, a core priority of the South, the Republican leadership devised a special rule with the "purpose of preventing a majority of this House"—that is, Democrats and the minority of progressive Republicans—from passing a stronger version. In 1903, the House had considered another railroad bill under a rule that foreclosed the option of substituting a more far-reaching and popular measure. And in 1909, when the House debated a new tariff, the Rules Committee, for the sole purpose of preserving the bill in the form reported by the Conference Committee, which was much more conservative than what had passed the House, temporarily suspended the right of representatives to raise points of order. Operating under rules that greatly empowered the majority party leadership, southern lawmakers found their ability to advance their priorities greatly hampered. As Williams remarked, "The minority can initiate nothing, can accomplish by its own votes nothing, and can only vote."[14]

Southern lawmakers did retain some ability to obstruct legislation, in the Senate especially. In 1903, southern-led or -supported filibusters defeated a statehood bill, a Philippines tariff bill, and a finance bill proposed by Senator Aldrich, while ship subsidy bills were defeated in 1901 and 1907 and Tillman was able to deny the black physician William Crum reappointment by the Senate to the office of customs collector for Charleston. But with the exception of the fight against Crum, none of these battles was waged exclusively by a solid South. The filibuster against the statehood bill had initially been waged by Republicans opposed to the admission of Arizona, New Mexico, Oklahoma, and the Indian Territory as four separate (and likely Democratic) states, but after a compromise was reached to combine New Mexico and Arizona into one state and Oklahoma and the Indian Territory into another ("only four Democratic Senators, instead of eight," announced the *Chicago Tribune*), the filibuster was picked up by southern Democrats. The ship subsidy bills were generally opposed by the South, but opposition was concentrated among agricultural state lawmakers from both parties. The Farmers' Non-Partisan League, which wanted government-owned ships, proudly noted that it was "farmers" who had "fought the ship subsidy bill to a finish."[15]

On occasion, southern lawmakers could use the filibuster to force action on their own agenda. Tillman was able to secure funds for South Carolina by threatening to deny unanimous consent to an appropriations bill on the last day of the 57th Congress. Even in the House, southern Democrats could sometimes leverage the large amount of time required for a roll call vote to delay legislation and extract some modest concessions. Led by Williams, House Democrats in 1906 were able to force consideration of a bill to make railroads liable for injury or death resulting from the negligence of any of their officers, agents, or employees. By threatening to withhold unanimous consent and demand a roll call on every proposition—"as it required three-fourths of an hour to call the roll," noted the *Dallas Morning News*, "the progress of legislation during the rest of session would not be very rapid"—they forced the Republicans, with multiple appropriations bills looming, to concede. After the Liability Act was held unconstitutional by the Supreme Court, Williams resorted to the same tactics in early 1908 to force consideration of a revised bill, as well as proposals to prohibit injunctions in labor disputes, Tillman's campaign contributions publicity bill, a measure removing the tariff on wood pulp, and federal support for state highways. The majority now responded with special rules that temporarily curtailed the right to demand a roll call vote and allowed the House to recess rather than adjourn at the end of the day, stretching out the "legislative day" over several days or weeks and limiting the opportunity for dilatory motions.[16]

Perhaps the most symbolically important southern filibuster was the partially successful effort in 1909 to remove a few remaining Reconstruction-era provisions from the penal code. Taking advantage of the fact that several senators from "dry" states wanted to clarify the right of state governments to enforce local prohibition laws, a group of southerners led by James Clarke demanded that provisions forbidding racial discrimination in the selection of jurors, regulating the use of troops at the polls, and imposing criminal penalties for conspiracy to deny federal rights—part of the original Ku Klux legislation—be dropped from the revised code. Reflecting the shift in Republican priorities, the opposition to the filibuster by "Republican leaders was perfunctory"—Aldrich and Hale were reported as obviously being "in sympathy with the Democratic filibuster, inasmuch as there is little desire on the Republican side" to retain the legislation in the revised code—and Clarke successfully got them to agree to drop the provisions for peace at the polls and all reference to the jurors statute, and to add the word "willfully" to the intent to deny civil rights in the Ku Klux Klan bill.[17]

The South was willing to filibuster almost any "measure in which Negroes are interested," including a strenuous filibuster in the House against paying a meager allowance to the estate of Samuel Lee, a black South Carolinian who had been elected to the 47th Congress but denied his seat by a successful southern filibuster! The expectation that almost any issue in which the civil or political status of African Americans was involved would meet with a wall of southern opposition had the effect of conditioning Republican calculations about the utility of pursuing civil rights legislation.[18]

A successful filibuster relied on common purpose and a willingness to sacrifice desired legislation as the legislative session wound down. It also relied on parliamentary acumen, which at times was lacking. A filibuster against a monetary bill proposed by Nelson Aldrich failed in part because the chair of the Senate Democratic caucus and de facto party leader, the relative rookie Charles Culberson of Texas, did not notice that his fellow filibusterers, Robert La Follette of Wisconsin and William Stone of Missouri, were absent. When the blind Senator Thomas Gore from Oklahoma sat down without the floor being taken by one of his partners, Aldrich moved that the roll be called. "The Democratic leader of the Senate," complained the *Charlotte Daily Observer*, "has lost what many of his friends consider the opportunity of his life and is discredited as a leader." Although the waning of the legislative session expanded the opportunity to defeat legislation, the defeat of the majority party's legislative priorities generally required a level of determination and breadth of support that few groups could muster. With the dampening of southern racial anxieties, there were few issues that could inspire the region's lawmakers to the level of coordinated action they had displayed in the fight against the federal elections bill. In 1907, an immigration bill was proposed that would prohibit the importation of contract labor. In recent years, however, a number of southern states had established commissions that raised private money from cotton manufacturers to pay for passage to the region, relieving wage pressure on southern agriculture and helping to preserve the South's racial labor hierarchy by averting further hires of African Americans in the factories. Despite the argument of Tillman and Augustus Bacon of Georgia that the bill effectively outlawed such commissions, making it "objectionable to the South," and that the "South's interests are as usual ignored," the filibuster was abandoned after other southern senators announced that "they would not follow them" in obstruction. Williams's 1906 threat to filibuster all legislation unless the Employers' Liability Act was passed was met with "murmurings and mutterings against his course" by southern Democrats eager to pass a public buildings bill. Even the filibuster to remove the Reconstruction-era provisions of the penal code was met with annoyance by some southerners who argued "that Federal troops are not now used" at the polls, and who were eager for the laws to be revised to accommodate state prohibition efforts. After a majority of the Democrats failed to back him in calling for the yeas and nays, Clarke reminded his colleagues of the stakes.[19]

Not only were filibusters uncertain, but they risked a backlash, which southerners in particular were anxious to avoid. Southern lawmakers abandoned several filibusters in order to stave off "the growing sentiment in favor of having cloture in the Senate," a danger they believed could "not be regarded lightly." More important than any individual bill, after all, was the preservation of institutional rules that enabled determined minorities to defeat legislation, a real concern as Republicans often indicated their willingness to alter these rules in consequential ways. During the debate about Aldrich's monetary bill, Republicans adopted three interpretations that considerably weakened the opportunity to filibuster: allowing the chair to count a quorum regardless of whether the senator responded by name, requiring more than "mere debate" to occur between quorum calls, and allowing enforcement of the rules that barred senators from speaking on the same subject twice in the same day. The *Charlotte Daily Observer* warned, with some hyperbole, that "the result of these three interpretations of the rules makes it absolutely impossible to prolong debate indefinitely, and thus makes filibuster impossible where the end is indeterminate." Recognizing the possibility of more drastic measures, and knowing that waiting in the wings was a bill passed by the House that would have reduced southern representation and reenacted the federal election laws (see chapter 6), most southern Democratic senators chose not to participate

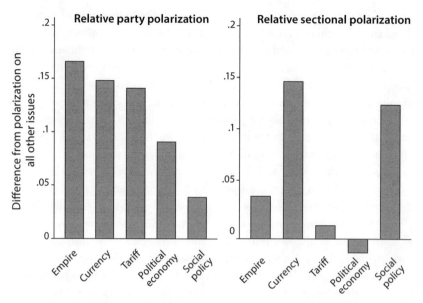

FIGURE 7.2. Polarization across Select Issue Areas

in the currency filibuster. As the *Washington Times* described it, "the threat of a cloture rule in the Senate," combined with the "force bill" passed by the House, "served the purpose of passing the currency bill. At least, that threat made the Democrats fear to come to the re-enforcement of the filibusters, and was at least useful to the extent of ending the filibuster sooner than would otherwise have been possible." Southern senators repeatedly prioritized the defeat of "any change of Senate rules" over whatever objections they had to individual legislation. As long as changes could be averted, noted the *Dallas Morning News*, "the Crumpackers and Olmsteads [*sic*]," and other Republicans who wanted to restore a federal commitment to southern black voting rights, "are effectually squelched."[20]

Our case studies generally bear out the claims of historians and contemporaries that the South was excluded from influence over national policy during this period. Consider the cases of the currency and imperial expansion, two of the most highly polarized issues in the first decade of the twentieth century (figure 7.2). Figures 7.3 and 7.4 show the party medians on the currency in the Senate and House from the mid-1880s to 1910. The pattern was largely the same in the House and the Senate: a gradual shift left among southern Democrats and a burst of northern Democratic support for Republican positions during the financial crisis of 1893 and debates on the repeal of the Sherman Silver Purchase Act. After the elections of 1894 and 1896, the ranks of gold Democrats and silver Republicans were greatly reduced, and polarization between the parties on these issues spiked.

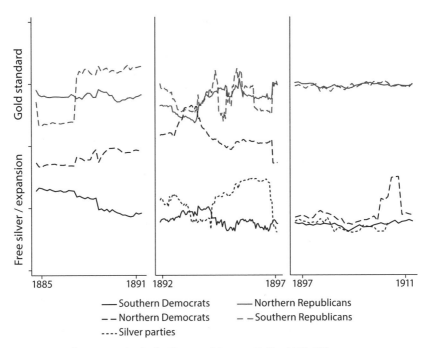

FIGURE 7.3. Change in Voting in the House on Monetary Policy, 1885–1911

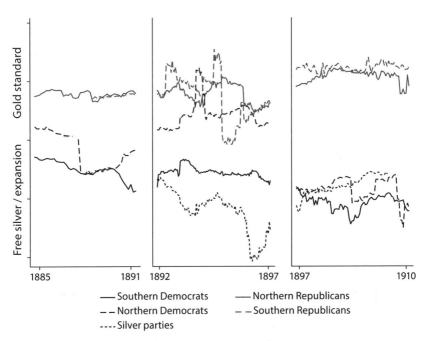

FIGURE 7.4. Change in Voting in the Senate on Monetary Policy, 1885–1911

With little prospect of reaching across the aisle, the South was unable to make much headway in securing a more accommodative national monetary policy. The passage of the Gold Standard Act of 1900, under a rule barring a motion to recommit or a vote on a substitute, saw only twelve Democrats in either chamber, and only three from the South—Representative James Denny of Maryland and Senators William Lindsay of Kentucky and Donelson Caffery of Louisiana—vote with almost all regular Republicans. Although the act did lower the capital requirements needed for opening a national bank, it was insufficient to accommodate the region's needs. The South continued to stand as the "counter example" to the gradual integration of both short-term and long-term national capital markets between 1870 and 1914. Southerners' hopes for currency reform were dashed with the defeat of Bryan in 1900 and the recognition that the South no longer had "friends in the North" on this issue. Even many free silver Democrats were forced to admit that "the silver question has been eliminated," and many of the region's newspapers implored the South to "have sense enough to form alliances that will give them political strength and advantage," to abandon the West and embrace the Northeast. After the passage of the Gold Standard Act, there was little significant change in American monetary policy for over a decade. Even the emergency Aldrich-Vreeland Act of 1908, which sought to expand the money supply in response to the Panic of 1907, was largely ineffective in facilitating access to credit in the region, in part because of a tax imposed on the currency during the first month that it was issued, but also because it required ten or more national banks with a defined, and relatively large, surplus to form currency associations that would be authorized to issue the emergency currency. Although a number of southern banks responded to the opportunity—which Stone of Missouri and Gore of Oklahoma denounced as a shifting of public resources and responsibilities onto corporations—there were only seventeen associations in the entire country by 1910. It was not until the Federal Reserve Act in the first years of the Wilson administration that the nation's monetary policy would be rendered more responsive to southern needs.[21]

The South was similarly limited in its ability to influence the national policy of imperialism. Although there were many in the South who looked excitedly on a "commercial conquest" that would create new markets for tobacco, raw cotton, and textiles, and a few who believed that imperial conquests might provide a place to send the South's "surplus" black population, southern sentiment generally opposed the annexation or possession of new territories. Not only might this antagonize cotton-purchasing European powers, but it would bring under American authority a large population of nonwhites and the danger of a "collective nationalization," the sort of mass grant of citizenship that had occurred after the Civil War. It also did not take much historical imagina-

tion to perceive, in Dewey Grantham's words, "that the most likely consequences of the new imperialism would be militarism and the political suppression of peripheral territory." Indeed, the repeatedly floated possibility of
reducing southern representation in line with the Fourteenth Amendment
was denounced as "evidence of the 'imperialism' in domestic affairs which we
may expect to be adopted along with 'imperialism' in the Philippines."[22]

Southerners were able to achieve only two successes in their fight against
imperialism: they allied with a faction of Republicans at the outset of the
Spanish-American War to pass a resolution denying any intent to retain Cuba,
and they secured a restriction on American property ownership in the Philippines Organic Act. The first success depended on a level of Republican support
that was not usually forthcoming. The restriction on property ownership by
Americans was advantaged by the fact that congressional debate coincided
with the revelation of extreme cruelty against Filipinos by the U.S. Army,
which so undermined support for the bill that its sponsor was forced to make
concessions.[23]

Otherwise, the turn-of-the-century fight against imperialism generated a
succession of defeats. Southern Democrats failed to modify the terms of the
treaty ending the Spanish-American War, failed in repeated efforts to recognize the independence of the Philippines—one proposal by Augustus Bacon
was defeated only on the tie-breaking vote of the vice president—and failed
to defeat or amend the Spooner Amendment establishing an executive-
controlled government for the Philippines. Democratic threats to filibuster
the Philippines Organic Act failed when it became clear that the bill was the
highest priority for the leadership and administration. Threats to filibuster the
Platt and Spooner Amendments came to nothing after President McKinley
promised to call an extra session, during which, southerners worried, Republicans would "almost certainly have changed the rules of the senate and established a cloture." Tillman, who had been leading the opposition to the amendments with Republican Richard Pettigrew, now declared himself satisfied with
"some immaterial modification." Not incidentally, the Republican leadership
in the House announced that they would allow appropriations for Charleston
Harbor to be included in the pending rivers and harbors bill.

Southern Democrats "lost their battle against empire" and were left denouncing imperial policy, emphasizing their opposition in campaign literature, and ultimately conceding that they were unlikely to have much of an
impact. They also lost their fight against the gold standard. Thus, regarding the
two most important issues at the turn of the century, the currency and imperialism, the South was unable to achieve any substantial accommodation to its
preferences in national policy. As the *Lexington Morning Herald* declared,
"The two issues of [imperial] expansion and sound money are settled," and
counseled the South to turn attention to new matters.[24]

The South responded to institutional exclusion by strategically choosing to forgo chances for partisan advantage in order to cultivate support from well-placed institutional actors and by repeatedly looking for opportunities to change the rules of the House. When President Roosevelt began articulating a vision for greater national regulation of the economy, southern lawmakers saw a chance to achieve substantial progress on some of their core priorities. This meant, however, that they would have to side with their partisan opponent, which threatened to both undercut their own claim to the popular progressive agenda—southern Democrats went to considerable pains to point out that much of the agenda Roosevelt was endorsing came straight out of the Democratic platforms—and to strengthen the political position of the rival party. Had southern Democrats instead "endeavored to secure partisan advantage," noted the *Herald*, "they might have wrecked his whole program by supporting his opponents in his own party." Instead, they followed the injunction of John Sharp Williams: "whenever anything comes from the other side of the Chamber that is right," he said, "vote for it." The result was the extraordinary spectacle of a Republican president finding more support from congressional Democrats than from his own party.[25]

With Roosevelt's issue advocacy, southern proposals that otherwise would have been bottled up in committee were more likely to be considered, but it did not mean the legislation ultimately reflected the region's collectively preferred terms. This limitation was exemplified by the Hepburn Railroad Rate Act of 1906. The regulation of railroad rates had been one of the most important demands of southern lawmakers since the late 1870s; a central impetus behind the Interstate Commerce Act of 1887, it had been a southern-demanded plank of the Democratic platforms of 1896, 1900, and 1904. Regulating railroad rates was especially popular among the region's farmers and former Populist constituencies. The progressive opponent of monopolies Augustus Stanley, for example, mocked the opponents of railroad rate regulation for saying, " 'Ah, my God, you can not afford to do it because Bryan is not dead and the country is full of Populists.' [Applause on the Democratic side.]" Had it not been through the "tender nurturing care of that long-haired anarchist, William J. Bryan, it would have been run over by a train long ago." But Bryan, "the idol of the Democracy and the defender of the poor," the "winged Nemesis of graft and plunder everywhere," was simply carrying out the principles of the Democratic Party: "It is the dogma of Jefferson applied to present conditions. It is equal rights to all and special privileges to none [applause on the Democratic side], uttered in a way that the common carriers shall understand."[26]

An anti-rebate bill was passed in 1903, sponsored by Republican senator Stephen Elkins of West Virginia. The Elkins Act prohibited railroads from providing preferential rebates to shippers; this practice had flourished as a way of getting around the prohibition on rate discrimination and was opposed as much by the railroads—who were being pressured to provide rebates by large shipping corporations—as by small shippers. It was widely regarded as a very modest effort at regulation. When a slightly more progressive measure sponsored by Republican Charles Littlefield of Maine had passed the House, it was denied consideration in the Senate by a vote of 28 to 38, with all southern Democrats and only three Republicans voting in favor. When the House then took up the Elkins bill, Republicans united in support of a rule blocking any possibility of substituting the Littlefield bill. Southern Democrats lacked sufficient support in the Senate to advance their priorities, and any Republican support they had gained in the House was not committed enough to provoke a fight with the party leadership.[27]

The issue was brought up again two years later in the form of a bill, sponsored by Charles Townsend of Michigan, that would restore the right of the Interstate Commerce Commission to set railroad rates but also create a special transportation court to hear appeals from the ICC. Even though a majority of the Republican caucus was "opposed to railroad rate legislation," Cannon implored them to support their president's program, despite the fact that it was being denounced as "revolutionary" and "insane" by railroad lobbyists. "We've got to pass this bill," he reportedly told the caucus, "or we've got to pass some other bill. We've got to pass some kind of a bill and we've got to pass it right away." After a Democratic substitute that removed the court provision was defeated on a partisan vote, the Townsend bill passed with only ten Republicans and six non-southern Democrats in opposition. The bill would languish and die in the Senate, never making it out of committee.[28]

Under growing pressure from shippers—over five hundred businesses had recently met in convention in Chicago and endorsed rate-setting legislation—Roosevelt pushed for renewed action in 1906. Cannon "openly traded" with the president, agreeing to pass a railroad bill on the condition that the president abandon any plan to revise the tariff. One Republican leader estimated that fewer than twenty of his members would have supported the bill on a secret ballot. Although this was likely a "wild understatement" of Republican support for the bill, it is indicative of the degree to which the tariff was their most important priority and rate-setting regulations a more divisive issue for the party.[29]

A railroad bill was introduced by Republican William Hepburn of Iowa in the House that would allow the ICC to set a maximum reasonable rate and would also extend the commission's authority over several classes of private cars. Though southern Democrats were generally unsuccessful in strengthening the bill on the floor, they voted unanimously for passage in the House. The Senate Republican leadership, however, delayed consideration in the hope that they could weaken it sufficiently to secure a "general agreement" within the party. Senate Democrats now "made an unreserved offer of their support" for the bill, and Senator Tillman and Senator Francis Newlands of Nevada convinced their fellow Democrats on the Commerce Committee to "present a solid front," forgo the opportunity to oppose the president and his party, and vote with three midwestern Republicans to wrest control of the bill and report it unamended. Stung by this rebuke, Nelson Aldrich had Tillman named as the bill's floor manager, counting on the fact that Tillman was a highly polarizing figure who was not on speaking terms with Roosevelt.[30]

A bill encompassing reforms long desired by the South had passed the House near-unanimously and been reported to the Senate floor under the management of one of the region's most dynamic and controversial legislators. The bill, as contemporaries noted, was "really more [a] Democratic than Republican" measure, and John Sharp Williams could reasonably boast that despite being "in a minority, by constant driving and reiteration, a very much cherished Democratic policy is about to triumph under a Republican administration."[31]

Despite these good auspices, the South was unable to ensure the passage of its preferred policy design. The critical difference between Republicans and southern Democrats was on the scope of judicial review. Most southern lawmakers wanted review to be narrowly circumscribed to determining the constitutionality of the law and preferred that rates be set aside only upon a final decision of the Court, lest a preliminary injunction leave the old rates in place during the protracted process of litigation. Conservative Republicans wanted an explicit right for the judiciary to evaluate any decision of the commission; progressive Republicans were torn between a desire to maintain party harmony, a slight preference for a weaker role for the judiciary, and worries that restrictions on judicial review might be ruled unconstitutional.[32]

After more than a month of delay and vacillation, Roosevelt announced his acceptance of a broad judicial review amendment. Despite being in charge of the legislation in the Senate, southern lawmakers were forced to make concessions to the pivotal bloc of progressive Republicans, who quickly cohered around a common party position once Roosevelt had made his position clear. The bill passed in this form in May 1906.[33]

Figure 7.5 shows the median members in the Senate on political economy issues and the probability that the median came from a particular regional-partisan grouping. Midwestern Republicans were most likely to be pivotal. They had been gradually persuaded that judicial review was "a power that inheres in the court that need not be conferred by statute and probably cannot be taken away by statute." Alfred Kittredge of South Dakota announced his support for the bill without judicial review, but seemed to back away from it over the next few months. Republican Moses Clapp supported the House bill, but acknowledged that his support was not conditional on the inclusion of a judicial review clause. Newspapers had begun reporting in March that "infor-

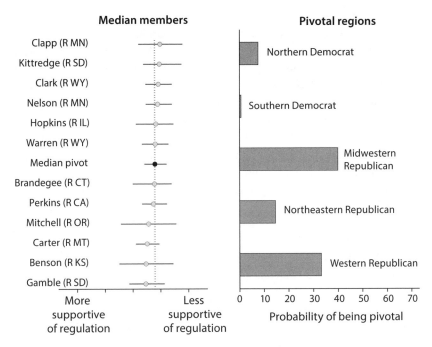

Median members

Clapp (R MN)
Kittredge (R SD)
Clark (R WY)
Nelson (R MN)
Hopkins (R IL)
Warren (R WY)
Median pivot
Brandegee (R CT)
Perkins (R CA)
Mitchell (R OR)
Carter (R MT)
Benson (R KS)
Gamble (R SD)

More supportive of regulation — Less supportive of regulation

Pivotal regions

Northern Democrat
Southern Democrat
Midwestern Republican
Northeastern Republican
Western Republican

0 10 20 30 40 50 60 70
Probability of being pivotal

FIGURE 7.5. Median Senators on Political Economy, 1905–1907

mal poll[s] show a majority of the senate in favor of a court review feature," and Aldrich announced that he was ready to provide unanimous consent for a vote. Tillman sparred for time, rejecting the offer at first, but was ultimately forced to concede that he no longer had the votes to pass the bill in the form he desired and he endorsed final passage with a broad judicial review clause. Had Tillman led the South in pulling support, the bill would have been defeated amid acrimonious Republican divisions.[34]

Tillman and Joseph Bailey of Texas, who chaired the Democratic caucus and was de facto leader, did have some success strengthening the bill on the Senate floor. With the help of the pivotal progressive Republicans, they passed amendments that restricted the ability of railroads to engage in the production and distribution of goods they produced, such as coal, extended the ICC's authority to include pipelines, and restricted the use of the free passes by which the railroads sought to influence local and state officials. Southern Democrats pressed for an amendment that would have prohibited the judiciary from issuing injunctions suspending ICC rulings, for restoring clauses of the 1887 bill that had been removed by subsequent legislation or by Supreme Court interpretation, and for a physical valuation of railroad property in order to determine reasonable rates. In their zeal to strengthen the bill, southern Democrats came up against the limits of their conception of the proper role of the federal government in regulating interstate commerce. An amendment to prohibit carriers from transporting their own goods, for instance, had to be rewritten by anxious Democrats to ensure that it did not interfere with state jurisdiction over the production of any commodity within a state, which would have been too extensive a broadening of the commerce clause for them to accept.[35]

Although certainly more limited than what most southern Democrats would have preferred, the Hepburn Act represented a dramatic extension of federal regulation of interstate commerce. Along with other legislation, such as the Pure Food Act, this Congress was seen as inaugurating "a new epoch in federal legislation," one in which governmental regulation would "stay the hand of private greed and protect the pocketbook and the health and general welfare of the masses." Contemporary observers recognized that "the whole Roosevelt program would have been wrecked" had it not been for the "support of Southern Democrats." By strategically prioritizing legislative accomplishments over partisan advantage, the South had been able to make some progress on its various policy priorities. But the dynamics revealed in the fight over the Hepburn Act exemplified the limits of southern influence during this period. Unable to control proceedings in committees or on the chamber floor, and wanting more progressive policy than the conservative Republicans were willing to offer, the South could provide votes for reforms but had to accept accommodations worked out among Republicans.[36]

Changing the Rules

If southern members were to exercise greater influence over national policy, they would need to change the rules to restore the influence of minority legislators or regain the majority. During the first two years of the Taft administration, an opportunity appeared to accomplish both. Williams had for several years led House Democrats in repeated efforts to revise the rules of the chamber so as to require that special rules from the Rules Committee receive a two-thirds vote. As long as the majority leadership could use the rules to limit the influence of both the minority Democrats and the minority of progressive Republicans willing to work with them, the chamber, he believed, would be the "House of so-called Representatives of the American people."[37]

Williams had been unable to persuade progressive Republicans to break ranks with their party on this issue, but the election of William Howard Taft fundamentally shifted the calculus. The progressives had been increasingly dissatisfied with the party leadership, but so long as Roosevelt was in the White House they had an important ally who could help place their priorities on the agenda and whose veto precluded most conservative reforms. Taft, however, gradually made it clear that he was willing to break with Roosevelt progressivism, inflaming tensions between conservatives and progressives and thus creating a unique opportunity for southern Democrats.[38]

In the opening days of the 61st Congress, during a special session called by Taft to revise the tariff, an alliance of progressive Republicans and Democrats in the House defeated a motion to adopt the previous rules. This alliance had been carefully cultivated by Albert Burleson of Texas, who persuaded the incoming Democratic minority leader, Champ Clark of Missouri, that the dissident Republicans were serious about their intent to pursue rules changes and could be trusted not to abandon the Democrats. The clear implication of the vote was that there was majority support for revising the rules. Yet, within a few hours, a Democratic proposal to do so was defeated when twenty-three Democrats broke ranks; nearly half of these were from the South, mostly from Georgia. After a few modest amendments, such as the establishment of a unanimous consent calendar so that such requests would proceed in a less arbitrary fashion than the scramble to gain recognition by the speaker, the rules of the previous session were adopted.[39]

A few days later, the Payne-Aldrich tariff was brought up. Southern Democratic defectors were revealed to have supported the speaker in exchange for local accommodations on lumber, sugar, and citrus fruits. The failure to maintain a united front carried over to the tariff bill itself, which saw a number of Democrats sacrificing party commitments for local advantage: eight southern Democratic senators voted with all Republicans against placing lumber on the free list, in direct opposition to their party's platform, prompting especially severe criticism. In the end, only Senator McEnery and Representatives Estopinal and Broussard from Louisiana voted in favor of the conference report, and Champ Clark insisted that the Democrats had come out of the fight "more united than they have been in a generation."[40]

One possible reason for Clark's optimism is that southern Democrats had secured one important victory, although it was neither immediately evident as such nor entirely in the form that they desired. Ever since it had been ruled unconstitutional, southern lawmakers had been demanding a reinstatement of the income tax. The initial decision had been quite close; in the meantime, the composition of the Supreme Court had changed. More important, the Court had not ruled an income tax unconstitutional so long as it was a tax on wages and salaries and not on the rent or proceeds of property, stock dividends, or the income from state, county, and municipal bonds. Joseph Bailey introduced an income tax amendment to the tariff bill, which included the tax on rents and interest but not on state or local bonds. As Democrats and progressive Republicans began meeting to draft a proposal they could mutually support, Republican leaders were forced to concede that some compromise would have to be reached with the pivotal midwesterners, who supported an income tax in principle but had doubts about its constitutionality. Republicans repeatedly delayed considering Bailey's amendment in order to provide time for the party leaders to work out an acceptable compromise, but despite several attempts, Aldrich's count showed that it was too risky to hold a roll call.[41]

President Taft intervened with a compromise acceptable to most Republicans. The tariff would include a corporate income tax, which most believed to be perfectly constitutional, paired with a separate proposal to amend the Constitution to authorize the federal government to levy a personal income tax. The corporate tax substitute was guided through the Senate by Aldrich, against the votes of southern Democrats and seven progressive Republicans who desired both a corporate tax and the immediate imposition of an income tax. The major concern of the South and the progressive Republicans was that Republican-controlled state legislatures would simply refuse to ratify the amendment. Still, a corporate tax was a step in the right direction. After it was substituted for Bailey's proposal by a vote of 45 to 31, with all Democrats against, the substitute passed 59 to 11, with all southern Democrats in favor. The constitutional amendment passed the Senate unanimously a few days later, but only after a southern-led effort to have the amendment ratified by state conventions rather than legislatures was defeated, 30 to 46. Only two southern senators voted against the convention amendment, John Daniel and Thomas Martin, both from Virginia.

The Sixteenth Amendment was quickly ratified by almost all southern states: Alabama within a month, followed quickly by Kentucky, South Carolina, Mississippi, Oklahoma, Maryland, Georgia, and Texas. But while the income tax had broad support in the region, it was not uncontested. The region's conservatives, though constrained by the progressive bent of public opinion in the region, urged the white South to "stand by what your fathers fought for" and protect state sovereignty against the centralization that would follow if the federal government were to gain new sources of revenue. In classic form, they appealed to white supremacy, arguing that the tax would create an army of federal officials empowered to inquire into the affairs of white citizens. Virginia saw the debate decided by appeals "to the memories of the Federal intrusion in the days of the Civil War and reconstruction." Charles Champe Taliaferro, a Confederate veteran, invoked the period when "the North had sent satraps to the South to enter every home and go to every crossroads," while Stephen Henry Love—another veteran—warned about the possibility of a "South-hating man" being elected president and naming African Americans as tax collectors—just as Roosevelt had persisted in his appointments of Crum and a few black postmasters. According to the *Times-Dispatch*, he "drew a pathetic picture of a negro entering his home and assessing the income from the sale of eggs and butter." What "forebearance has the Federal government ever exercised toward Virginia," asked Richard Byrd, father of the future U.S. senator and leader of the conservative coalition Harry Byrd. "Virginia gave the government an empire and in return she gave us dismemberment. West Virginia is a beacon light to show us to what forebearance leads." He recalled that his family had been killed in the Civil War and he had vowed to never give any more power to the federal government. James New Stubbs, who recalled bitterly that he had cast his vote against the Fifteenth Amendment forty-one years before, appealed to legislators "as sons of the men who followed Lee." Supporters of the amendment urged the legislature not to be scared by the "bugaboo of the reconstruction period" or the "bloody shirt" being waved by conservatives and to recognize that the amendment "discriminates only in favor of the poor." They insisted that times had changed, that while they deeply respected the Confederacy, northern "fanaticism has passed away." "The war is over, and for God's sake let us not bring these things into the practical problems of the day." Virginia was the only southern state besides Florida not to ratify the amendment.[42]

As Robin Einhorn has demonstrated, southern anxieties over the dangers of the income tax varied with how they evaluated the possibility that it might enable Republicans to intervene once again in the region's racial hierarchy. For the most part, southern legislators recognized that Republicans had moved on. "The conclusion is inescapable," writes Einhorn, that "Southern politicians supported the Sixteenth Amendment because they believed that the South would benefit . . . but they also, critically, felt secure in supporting it because of a new confidence that increasing the power of the federal government would not tempt Northerners to interfere with their oppression of African Americans." So long as national progressive reforms "promised subsidy without interference," southern conservatives' warnings were less persuasive, opening space for southern progressives to support reform.[43]

The Payne-Aldrich bill failed to significantly lower tariff rates, pushing progressive Republicans closer to Democrats. Further, Taft's seeming alignment with the conservative wing of the party threatened progressive Republicans with seeing the policy gains of the last few years rolled back or future reforms embodying more conservative principles than they wanted. It was in this context that the long-standing southern priority of revising the rules could be achieved. The revolt against Speaker Cannon, a transformative moment in congressional development, was planned primarily by the informal Republican Insurgent Committee on Procedure, with Burleson serving as the Democratic emissary to the insurgents and Champ Clark, Oscar Underwood, and the newly elected John Nance Garner of Texas helping to clarify the terms of the fight and organize the Democratic minority in support. After the Democratic defections of the year before, Clark and his team worked assiduously to ensure that the votes would be there the next time a rules change was offered. This would be crucial, as the insurgents could not have acted on their own. As Ruth Bloch Rubin has shown, the pivotability of the "insurgent" Republicans depended on the organizational scaffold that they had built up as well as the mutual willingness of insurgents and Democrats to work together.[44]

On March 17, 1910, the House voted to support Cannon's claim that a bill for the census enumeration involved a privileged constitutional question. George Norris of Nebraska quickly seized the opening and presented his resolution to change the rules, arguing that these now also fell within the scope of the new interpretation of which measures were privileged under the rules. After several hours of debate, Norris substituted his resolution for a revised version drafted by Underwood, which removed a requirement that the Committee on Rules be geographically representative and continued the speaker's power to appoint members to other committees. According to Champ Clark, Norris insisted that he rather than Underwood offer the substitute, leading Henry Clayton of Alabama to fume about the insurgent "tail wagging the [Democratic] dog."[45]

The Norris-Underwood proposal would make the House responsible for electing the members of the Rules Committee rather than vest this power in the speaker, increase the size of this committee from five to ten (a reduction from the fifteen-member committee proposed by Norris), and, most important, remove the speaker from the committee. Underwood argued that while majority party leadership was necessary, it should be exercised by the chair of the House Rules Committee rather than the speaker, who should play a nonpartisan role as a simple "presiding officer who wields the scales of justice between . . . the two contending political parties."[46]

The removal of proportional geographic representation on the Rules Committee and the continuing ability of the speaker to appoint members to committees is usually attributed to Democrats' expectation that they would soon be in the majority. As we discuss later in the chapter, when Democrats came to power, they did not continue speaker control over committee appointments, and so their opposition to this decentralization of power could hardly have been a matter of political importance. Norris's proposal, however, would have had a committee divide the states into nine and six groups, for the majority and minority, respectively. Each regional group would then select a member to represent them on the Rules Committee. This option would almost certainly have limited the number of southern representatives on the committee, despite the fact that the region would have been subdivided. When the Democrats did gain power in the next Congress, the South took all but two of the majority party's allocation seats on the Rules Committee.[47]

Republicans sought a compromise within the party, but Cannon would not budge on the position of the speaker on the Rules Committee. The insurgents then joined with a unanimous Democratic Party to change the rules. Clark's efforts to rally his party behind the rule changes had been successful, and one of the bolters from the year before announced his readiness to "subordinate any individual views I may have, and to stand here harmoniously and unitedly with my party associates at this time."[48]

The victory inspired southern Democrats and signaled a new flexibility in congressional procedures that might allow the party to once again exercise a meaningful role in national affairs. As the *Atlanta Journal* remarked, "Whatever reform the progressive Republicans hope to achieve must be won through the aid of Democratic representatives. Hence it is really the Democratic minority which is making history at Washington today and bringing to birth a new and better era of national politics." In the remaining months of the 61st Congress, southern Democrats in the House were able to leverage the support of insurgent Republicans to reshape a proposed railroad bill that brought telephone and telegraph rates under the authority of the ICC (a long-standing demand of southerners sponsored by Charles Bartlett of Georgia), removed provisions that would have allowed traffic agreements and railroads to purchase stock in other railroads, added strengthening amendments, and ensured that the ICC would have a role in any hearings that went before the Commerce Court proposed by the bill. In the Senate, where the lack of a unifying experience made Democrats and progressive Republicans less trusting of each other, Democrats decided to lie low, to just "say enough to keep you irritated." But southern Democratic senators nonetheless provided most of the votes needed to retain most of the House amendments, although they failed to save Robert La Follette's proposal to require a physical valuation of railroad property.[49]

The only two consequential issues on which the Senate alliance between southerners and progressive Republicans broke were on the regulation of stock and bond issues and the establishment of a Commerce Court; the latter was central to Taft's proposal but strongly opposed by southerners, who suspected the federal judiciary was even more susceptible to corporate influence than the ICC. On the question of the Commerce Court, southerners were defeated by midwestern Republicans who sided with the Taft administration and their conservative copartisans. On the question of regulating stock and bond issues, both southern Democrats and the insurgents supported increased regulation, but differed on whether the regulatory authority should lie with the federal government or the states. On May 26, 1910, a large majority of the Senate struck the provisions regulating stock and bond issues, uniting conservatives with states' rights southern Democrats. The only southern Democrat to vote for the measure was William Stone of Missouri, although James Clarke of Arkansas, Alexander Clay of Florida, and Robert Owen of Oklahoma announced that they would have so voted had they not been paired. Francis Newlands critiqued the southerners for their narrow constitutional construction and urged them to "cut loose" from party traditions that had developed "when the Democratic party was allied to the protection of human slavery, and when the protection of that institution required a jealous attitude toward the exercise of national power." Conservative southerners responded that once "you admit that the power of the Federal Government descends to a regulation of stocks and bonds, the power of the States over the question disappears at once and forever," ultimately authorizing the federal government to "regulate the wages of the railroad employees."[50]

The 61st Congress closed by passing a campaign publicity bill sponsored by Tillman, the Postal Savings Bank Act—another long-standing demand of southern populists, but which passed over southern opposition when it was amended to allow the banks to invest their deposits in U.S. bonds—and the Mann "White Slavery" Act. Although southerners on the House Interstate and Foreign Commerce Committee opposed this last bill as an invasion of states' rights—Bartlett reminded southerners that if the federal government could prohibit transporting women across state lines for immoral purposes, it could also overturn the "enticement laws" used by Georgia and other southern states to "prevent her laborers from being enticed away and the farms from being depopulated and the laborers carried off"—most were unwilling to have their opposition recorded. The legislation passed on a voice vote.[51]

———

With the limits on southern influence, the region's legislators had to look either to regain the majority or to change the rules to enable the minority to play a greater role. The revolt against Cannon had provided an opportunity to pursue both goals at once. As Champ Clark recalled years later, "The rules, in my opinion, needed liberalizing," but there was also an opportunity "for political advantage." He had "seized with delight the growing dissatisfaction among the Republicans in the House over the rules, as a wedge with which to weaken and finally split the Republican party wide open."[52]

The midterm elections of 1910 seemed to validate Clark. Northeastern conservatives who had supported Cannon were defeated in large numbers. Republican divisions enabled state Democratic parties to recruit strong reformist candidates in Ohio, New York, and New Jersey. For the first time since 1892, the Democrats won a plurality of representatives from every southern state except Delaware, as well as a majority in the House and an increase of eleven members in the Senate. The new Democratic House majority moved to further decentralize authority by divesting the new speaker, Champ Clark, of the power to make committee appointments, the responsibility for which was given to the Democratic members of the Ways and Means Committee, a proposal that John Sharp Williams had made almost a decade earlier. The Democratic members of this committee, in turn, were to be elected by the party caucus, which, with an eye on sectional and ideological balance, selected seven southerners and seven northerners. Democrats were not abandoning party control over the agenda, but they were ensuring that this would now be vested in a broader cross-section of the party. In fact, the Committee on Rules actually increased its use of special orders and restrictive rules in the next few sessions, as well as rules that temporarily allowed certain committees to report specific items of legislation at any time to the floor, including a bill requiring the valuation of railroad property and a bill for agricultural extension stations to be established at land-grant colleges. The difference was that they did so less at the behest of the speaker than by discrete accommodations with the multiplying centers of authority, namely, the empowered committee chairs.[53]

The Democrats also empowered their party caucus. The Democratic caucus had already adopted new rules after the failure of 1909, including one that allowed two-thirds of the representatives voting in caucus, constituting a majority of the Democrats in the House, to make a caucus decision binding on all its members. Only explicit contrary pledges to constituents or issues that concerned a matter of constitutional interpretation were exempted. If representatives wanted to be excused from caucus discipline, they had to explicitly file an exemption. In theory, such discipline was to be enforced by the automatic expulsion of party defectors. But as Matthew Green has pointed out, the caucus was not primarily important as a means to bind members but as a site where the party could build support for a measure through persuasion, legislative side deals, or the construction of compromise legislation outside of the committee system. To this end, Democrats passed new internal rules that authorized the caucus to forbid committees to report bills without approval.[54]

Both the diffusion of influence and the strengthening of the caucus empowered southern legislators. The majority of southern Democrats were elected in what effectively were uncontested elections. As a result, they had accumulated years of seniority over their northern Democratic colleagues. With Democrats in the majority, there was considerable pressure to abandon the seniority rule or at least to be flexible in its application, lest it "give to the south the chairmanships of all of the great committees and leave unrecognized the new Democratic membership from the northern and western states." The party instead chose to adhere rigidly to the seniority rule, knowing full well that this would advantage the South over the North and West. Further, the new requirement that no one on the Ways and Means Committee could chair another committee—to reduce conflicts of interest in committee assignment—eliminated a few northern Democrats "from chairmanships despite their rank." "The South," complained one progressive Republican, "took the chairmanships of 40 of [the standing committees] and gave the Northern Democrats 16. Not only that, but they took the chairmanships of practically all the great working committees." The result was that "practically all the important legislation must pass through one or another of the committees" chaired by southerners, and that every "measure submitted to the house at

this session . . . first passed through a Democratic caucus" dominated by southern members. It was the "first time since the war when matters have been so
adjusted as to leave Southern Democrats in absolute control," and it was
widely expected that all the legislation that would "come before the next congress is to be dominated by the political thought of southern Democrats."[55]

The southern-dominated House majority now moved quickly to pass a
succession of bills high on the list of progressive demands. In a special session
from April to August 1911, the House passed the Seventeenth Amendment
requiring the direct election of senators, a campaign finance bill, a reciprocity
act with Canada and other bills that would reduce tariff rates, a statehood bill
for New Mexico and Arizona, a congressional apportionment act stripped of
any suggestion of reducing southern representation, and a committee to investigate violations of the antitrust laws. In the regular session, the House
passed bills establishing a Department of Labor and a Children's Bureau
within the department, providing an eight-hour workday for workers on government contracts, limiting the use of injunctions against labor unions, establishing a system of workers' compensation for railroad workers, improving the
conditions of American seamen, and excluding convict-made goods from
interstate commerce.

The Senate and President Taft stopped much of this agenda, blocking a
reduction of tariff rates on wool, cotton products, and agricultural imple-
ments, a literacy test for immigrants, and the seamen's labor bill. The bill authorizing Arizona and New Mexico to draft state constitutions was vetoed on
the grounds that Arizona's constitution was excessively radical (New Mexico's,
by contrast, was highly conservative), but this was overridden. In the Senate,
close margins and the deepening divisions between the Republican factions
allowed southern Democrats to exercise a pivotal role. As the new senator
from Mississippi, John Sharp Williams, remarked, "We will continue to change
partners every time we can dance better by it." The Democrats were able to
showcase their progressive credentials and further the split in the Republican
ranks just in time for the 1912 presidential elections.[56]

The South in the Saddle

On March 4, 1913, Woodrow Wilson was inaugurated, the first southern-
born president since Andrew Johnson. He was sworn in by Chief Justice
Edward Douglass White, a former Confederate, while crowds of white
southerners hooted rebel yells and sang "Dixie." Wilson's cabinet included
more southerners than any since Cleveland's of 1895. Southerners dominated
the Democratic majorities in the House and Senate. The South was not only
" 'back in the Union,' " wrote Judson Welliver, but "at the helm of the ship
of state."[57]

During the Wilson years, southern Democrats were able to realize much of the ambitious legislative agenda they had been advancing, including substantial tariff reform, an extensive reorganization of the banking and currency system, a strengthening of antitrust legislation, and various measures of federal support for farmers. These accomplishments were tempered by the need to secure support within a diverse caucus and by an awareness that the party's majority rested as much on Republican divisions as on Democratic popularity. Some of the party's legislative compromises resulted in a level of administrative centralization that was viewed with deep suspicion by southern conservatives, and even by many of the region's progressives and former Populists. It was "the New South," complained southern conservatives, that was in "the van in the assault upon the ideals and standards so long and ably defended by the Old South." But compromises were worked out and supported by southern committee chairs and party leaders. Whether they were "New" or "Old" South, progressive or conservative, whether they represented rural or commercial districts, they wanted their party to succeed and their constituents to be prioritized in public policy.[58]

In the 63rd Congress, the powerful Ways and Means Committee was chaired by Oscar Underwood, who by virtue of this position also was made majority leader. Robert Henry of Texas chaired the Rules Committee, Henry Clayton of Alabama the Judiciary Committee, and William Adamson of Georgia the Interstate Commerce Committee; William C. Houston, Lemuel Padgett, and John Moon of Tennessee were in charge of Territories, Naval Affairs, and the Post Office Committees, respectively; Henry Flood of Virginia chaired Foreign Affairs, Stephen Sparkman of Florida Rivers and Harbors, Asbury Lever of South Carolina Agriculture, and Carter Glass of Virginia Banking and Currency. The only significant House committee not chaired by a southern Democrat was Appropriations, which was led by John J. Fitzgerald, head of New York's Tammany Hall delegation. Some southerners urged the party to provide more chairs to the North and West in order "to overcome the prejudice against Democratic control on the ground that it means Southern control." But generally there was agreement that the important committees should be chaired by experienced legislators—in other words, southerners.[59]

The challenge for the new Democratic majority in the Senate would be to coordinate their diverse conference around legislation desired by the more progressive House and president. In early 1913, the new caucus chair, John Kern of Indiana, appointed a steering committee largely dominated by young progressives like himself: James O'Gorman of New York, Robert Owen of Oklahoma, Luke Lea of Tennessee—the youngest member of the Senate in a generation—and Hoke Smith, the former progressive governor of Georgia and an architect of that state's disfranchisement of black voters. Of the committee's eight members, four were from the South, including the two most conservative members, Thomas Martin of Virginia and James P. Clarke of Arkansas. In making its committee assignments, the steering committee worked to reconcile more conservative members, such as Furnifold Simmons of North Carolina and Augustus Bacon of Georgia—who, "had they been so disposed, could easily have wrecked the whole party programme"—by giving them and other conservative senators "all the chairmanships to which they were entitled" but placing "upon every one of the great committees a working majority of 'new' men." To preserve seniority while maintaining "unity of action," Democrats placed inexperienced but progressive senators on many of the most important committees. Power within the decentralized Senate was to be shared between relatively more conservative southerners and more progressive members, from the South and Midwest, who could outvote the chair if he were to "show a wicked tendency." The one exception to the maintenance of the seniority rule was Benjamin Tillman, who was entitled to be chair of the Appropriations Committee but whose severe stroke a few years before would have made him an inexpedient choice.[60]

The extent to which southerners dominated legislative committees was "the most complete proof that the South is in truth in charge of the nation's business." Southern lawmakers used the influence these positions provided to fundamentally "shape the character of Wilsonian reform." Southern-dominated legislative committees guided through Congress a succession of progressive laws that radically reshaped the American state. The region's lawmakers played a central role in establishing institutions that could regulate capital and help sustain a more egalitarian economic order, even as they expanded the scope of racial inequality in the federal government and ensured that the new national commitments only minimally disrupted the South's racial hierarchy.[61]

Immediately upon the convening of the 63rd Congress, Oscar Underwood introduced a bill that provided the largest reduction in tariff rates since the Civil War. This bill passed 281 to 139, with three Louisiana representatives being the only Democrats in opposition. In a move to secure party unity, the Ways and Means Committee delayed making committee appointments until the bill had passed. In the Senate, Democrats took the unusual step of first debating the bill in conference, then binding their members to support it. Despite a summer of debate on the floor, the party was unanimous on nearly every roll call and the bill passed, with the two Louisiana senators the only Democrats in opposition.[62]

On February 25, 1913, the Sixteenth Amendment was declared ratified. To make up for the revenue lost by lowering import duties, the tariff bill included an income tax. Although the tax was progressive in structure, its rates were set relatively low and the exemptions high, leading to a revolt among progressive Republicans and southern Democrats, led by the racist demagogue

James K. Vardaman of Mississippi. With the backing of a majority of the Senate's Democratic caucus, supporters of a more progressive tax threatened to introduce a new income tax schedule and thus forced the conservative Simmons to agree to revisions that placed a heavier burden on larger incomes. The plan to reconcile older conservatives by giving them chairmanships while stacking the important committees with progressives had its intended effect. The "insurgent democrats" tried to force the party caucus to agree to raise rates further, but only Gilbert Hitchcock of Nebraska broke ranks to try to amend the bill on the floor. While southern Democrats stuck with the party, their continued dissatisfaction ultimately compelled President Wilson and William Jennings Bryan to intervene, and another compromise was drafted by Simmons and John Sharp Williams. Although hardly radical, given the growing strength of the Socialist Party and the widespread organizing of radical unions such as the Industrial Workers of the World, the income tax of 1913 was relatively steep in its progressive rate structure: the tax was set at 1 percent for incomes up to $20,000, with a $3,000 individual deduction, and gradually increased to 7 percent for incomes over $500,000, for a ratio of seven-to-one from the top bracket to the lowest. In 2016, by contrast, the ratio for federal income taxes was 3.9-to-one.[63]

Having finally achieved their long-standing goal of rebalancing the country's revenue system, southern Democrats moved to reorganize its banking system. The question of the currency had fatally divided the Democrats in the 1890s, but after almost a decade of congressional inaction, the issue had gained new urgency after the financial crisis of 1907. Congress had established the National Monetary Commission, headed by Senator Nelson Aldrich, which proposed to charter a privately owned central bank that would hold the deposits of the federal government. In the eyes of southern Democrats, according to Arthur Link, Aldrich was proposing nothing less than "a resurrection of the second Bank of the United States, which Jackson had destroyed." Although Democrats almost unanimously opposed the Aldrich plan in favor of a network of regional banks, they differed on the number of banks that should be established and the degree to which they should be placed under public control. A large number of southern Democrats, supported by some progressive Republicans, demanded that the entire system be controlled by the public, and also that issuance of currency should be restricted to public institutions, that interlocking bank directorates should be prohibited, and that the government should establish a system of agricultural credits.[64]

The relatively conservative chair of the House Banking and Currency Committee, Carter Glass, supported a decentralized network but insisted on private ownership. His draft plan was forcefully rejected by the progressive wing of the party, supported by Bryan, the Rules Committee chair Robert Henry, and the chair of the Senate Currency Committee, Robert Owen. With progressive Republicans, the supporters of public control had a majority on the House Banking and Currency Committee. Once again forced to intervene, Wilson insisted on government control as "the absolute minimum that would satisfy the Bryan element."[65]

The Democrats on the committee had initially considered the bill in secret sessions, but on July 9, progressives on the committee voted against Glass to open its hearings to the public. A few days later, proposals to prohibit interlocking directorates and provide for agricultural credits were made by J. Willard Ragsdale of South Carolina and Otis Wingo of Arkansas, who insisted that the South required "easier and more direct methods of getting emergency money during the moving period"—that is, the period from September to January when cotton was moved from plantations to cotton factors before being sent overseas or to domestic producers. "Can the Democratic party in the hour of its victory," asked Wingo, "afford to turn its back on the South?" Wilson, who now had to promise that a prohibition on interlocking directorates would be included in a separate antitrust bill, offered his support for short-term agricultural credit as a compromise, and he successfully persuaded the committee to send the bill to the party caucus, where it could be debated confidentially. By late August, most of the southern farmer contingent had been reconciled, and the party voted in caucus 163 to 9 to bring the bill to the House floor. Five southerners voted against it, including Robert Henry, Joe Eagle, and Oscar Callaway of Texas, Thomas Hardwick of Georgia, and Thomas Sisson of Mississippi.[66]

The chair of the Senate Currency Committee, Robert Owen—who had suggested that the "Treasury Department should directly control the entire banking system"—temporarily lost control over the committee proceedings as O'Gorman of New York, Reed of Missouri, and Hitchcock of Nebraska joined Republicans to delay the legislation by holding hearings throughout September and October. The Senate Currency Committee eventually decided to report three separate bills: the version that had been passed by the House; a slightly amended bill that compromised between the southern demand for decentralization and the worries of the administration and others that this would undermine the purpose of a central bank; and a highly centralized alternative, supported by Hitchcock, that expanded public ownership. The Democratic Senate caucus voted to bind its members to support the second bill. After a few additional concessions were made expanding the role of the private sector and increasing the gold reserve behind the new Federal Reserve notes, the bill passed the Senate, and after a brief conference and amendments, the bill was signed into law.[67]

So far southern Democrats had been able to cohere on proposals that accommodated their diverse policy priorities, either directly or with a promise of future action. The antitrust issue, however, proved more complicated. In the fall of 1913, Democrats from the Midwest and South had combined to abolish the Commerce Court established a few years earlier, but developing a positive antitrust policy would be delayed while the party debated the tariff and currency. As chair of the Judiciary Committee, Henry Clayton was initially tasked with developing antitrust legislation. He proposed a series of measures that would prohibit interlocking directorates, define unlawful restrictions of trade, give private parties the benefit of decisions in suits originated by the government, establish an interstate trade commission, and empower the ICC to control the issuance of railroad securities. The last of these was Texas Democrat Sam Rayburn's first legislative initiative. Although modeled on a Texas measure endorsed by John Reagan, it resembled a bill that Senator Bailey and southern Democrats had opposed for states' rights reasons in 1910. Although Clayton's "five brothers" largely reflected the policy preferences of southern Democrats, his proposal would be drastically revised before final passage. In its final form, the bill would mark the "adoption by the Wilson administration of Roosevelt's program" for regulating the economy through administrative agencies rather than clear legal prohibitions.[68]

The first substantial change was the inclusion of a provision intended to relieve labor and farm organizations from prosecution under the Sherman Act, a measure Democrats had supported several times while in the minority. Wilson opposed this as class legislation, but he was forced to make a modest concession: Henry and Claude Kitchin of North Carolina drafted a compromise stating that labor and farm organizations were not to be considered illegal combinations in restraint of trade. The compromise was given different interpretations. The president and Edwin Webb of North Carolina, the bill's floor leader, suggested that it simply held that farm and labor organizations should not be considered illegal so long as "they lawfully sought to obtain legitimate objectives." Other labor provisions in the bill, however, included a guarantee of jury trials in contempt of court cases and a restriction on the use of injunctions to situations needed to prevent loss of life or property.[69]

In March 1914, control of the interstate trade commission was removed from Clayton's Judiciary Committee and given to the Interstate Commerce Committee, where it would be rewritten substantially by William Adamson of Georgia and James Covington of Maryland. Adamson in particular was "violently opposed to all plans for a strong commission." He modified the proposal to restrict the number of corporations over which it would have jurisdiction and to remove its power of independent initiative. Soon after, the definitions bill was dropped at the request of Wilson. The remaining features were combined into an omnibus antitrust bill, with specific statutory prohibitions on trade activity and defined criminal penalties. This version passed the House in early June 1914, along with the modified interstate trade commission and Sam Rayburn's bill to have the ICC regulate railroad stock and bond issuances.

This provision would soon be dropped, and when Rayburn tried to have it reintroduced the next year, Wilson asked Adamson "to pigeon-hole the bill in his committee" in order to stave off Republican charges that the Democrats were hostile to business.[70]

The antitrust program was subject to further revision in the Senate, where the southern brand of progressivism "was not as strong." Francis Newlands, chair of a committee with relatively few southern Democrats, rewrote the trade commission bill to provide for a much stronger bureaucratic agency empowered to investigate alleged antitrust violations and to issue cease-and-desist orders against corporations that it found to be engaged in unfair methods of competition. The Senate Judiciary Committee, chaired by Culberson, rewrote the Clayton antitrust bill at Wilson's request, dropping its clear proscriptions and stiff penalties in favor of deliberately open-ended prohibitions that could be flexibly interpreted by the new commission. Newlands drew considerably on a bill sponsored by Raymond Stevens, a New Hampshire Democrat, which had been prepared by a New York attorney and drew heavily on the regulatory plans of the Progressive Party. The Culberson bill greatly weakened the protections for labor. The result was an antitrust program that was progressive but out of step with the type of reform preferred by most southern lawmakers. Some southerners even denounced the proposals as "a betrayal of the Democratic party and of the country," an embrace of Roosevelt's doctrine of regulating rather than destroying monopolies. Southern conservatives, in turn, found it to be exemplary of a Wilsonian progressivism that they did not like or trust. "The Federal income tax, the new currency law with its supreme Federal Reserve Board, the government-owned railroad in Alaska to be built under Executive direction," and especially the bills "for a Federal trade commission, and for the Federal regulation of the issuance of railroad securities" amounted to "a vast expansion of Federal authority and activity, and go a long way toward putting Mr. Roosevelt's theoretical 'new nationalism' into actual practice" and disregarding the "State-rights view" of national problems. Wilson, complained the *Macon Daily Telegraph*, "has made it perfectly clear that he is Hamiltonian rather than Jeffersonian in his views." A shifting combination of Republicans and Democrats, including Vardaman and Reed, sought to amend both bills to impose criminal liabilities for restraining competition and to prohibit holding companies, but most southerners sided with the administration and opposed further alterations on the chamber floor.[71]

Although southern Democrats had been demanding antitrust reform for more than a decade, and it was southern lawmakers who shepherded the Wilson program through Congress, the final policy details reflected a political need to accommodate non-southern Democrats and northern progressives, who were convinced that the statutory restrictions envisioned by the initial

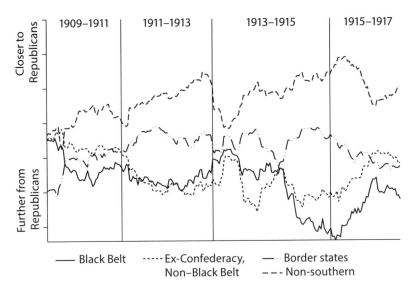

FIGURE 7.6. Democratic Party Medians in the House, 1909–1917

legislation would be unworkable and severely constrain trade. Despite misgivings among many southern Democrats—Williams, doing his best to support the administration, tried to rework the legislation on the floor but told confidants that "privately I am disgusted and tired all at once"—more of them were willing, after so many years in the wilderness, to subordinate their own preferences to the guidance of a Democratic president.[72]

Figures 7.6 and 7.7 show the location of the median member of different factions of the Democratic Party from 1909 to 1917. In both chambers, the majority of Democratic lawmakers moved gradually to an extreme position that reflected their loyalty to Wilson and to the decisions of the Democratic caucus. As legislative attention in the Senate turned to the antitrust program, however, a clear divide opened up between southern Democrats who sought to carry out the administration's policy—including, in addition to Culberson and Simmons, Duncan Fletcher of Florida, Hoke Smith of Georgia, John Bankhead of Alabama, and Lee Overman of North Carolina—and the primarily non-southern Democrats who were willing to break with the party and try to remake the bill on the chamber floor.[73]

The variation in this pattern across issue areas was itself a reflection of the varying degree to which the committee process had resulted in a bill compatible with divergent southern preferences. Figure 7.8 shows the estimated location of southern Democrats on monetary policy in the House and antitrust policy in the Senate, relative to all other issues. Names are shown for those members whose differences across these two sets of estimates were statistically significant. In the House, a small contingent of southern Democrats,

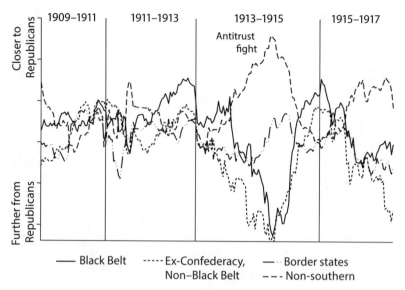

FIGURE 7.7. Democratic Party Medians in the Senate, 1909–1917

including Oscar Callaway—who opposed the centralization and executive control of the Federal Reserve and denounced the bill as a gift to Wall Street—Wingo, Henry, and Samuel Witherspoon of Mississippi—who vowed never to vote for a bill that included a gold standard, a "gratuitous insult to four-fifths of the Democratic party"—had been willing to carry the fight over the Federal Reserve to the floor. In the Senate, however, the South held solid on this issue and voted unanimously against all amendments except those exempting the appointees from the civil service requirements. It was on antitrust where a faction of southern senators were willing to carry the fight to the floor of the chamber, with Vardaman, Reed, Williams, Morris Sheppard of Texas, and John Shields of Tennessee against the majority of the southern Democrats who stuck with the bills preferred by the administration across dozens of roll calls. Southerners were the group most likely to vote in favor of the policy proposals that came out of committees and caucus, but substantial and shifting groups of them also contributed to the efforts to rework these on the chamber floors.[74]

But the region's influence during Wilson's first term did not rest on whether southern lawmakers were pivotal in roll call votes. On only one issue, the tariff in the Senate, do our estimates show that southern Democrats had a greater than even chance of being pivotal. On most other issues, the success of floor amendments depended largely on the decisions of non-southern Democrats, whose preferences had often been taken into account for legislation to pass. Southern influence was exercised primarily through the ability of southern

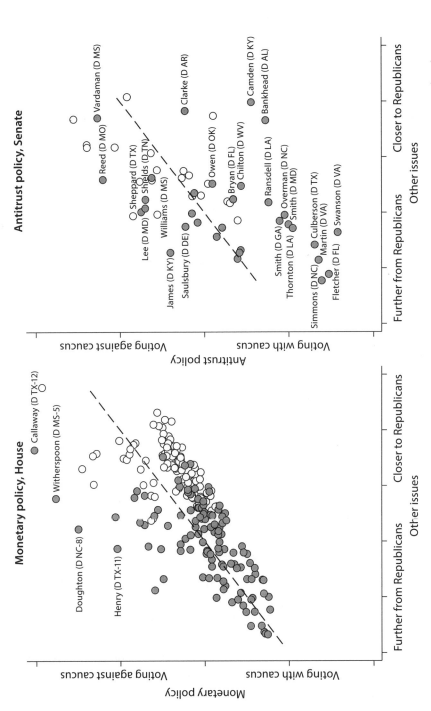

FIGURE 7.8. Democratic Loyalists and "Intransigents." Dashed diagonal line shows the 45-degree angle. Gray dots are southern Democrats, white dots are northern Democrats.

lawmakers to craft legislation in committees and in caucus and to put policy proposals onto the agenda that reflected southern priorities.

According to Link, it was on the issue of agricultural policy that southern Democrats were most consistently "far to the left" of the president; agriculture policy was also the issue area where southerners "had the greatest influence in the shaping of the later Wilsonian program." Our research supports this conclusion, but our analysis also suggests that insofar as this was the case it was rooted principally in the economic needs of cotton agriculture. Figure 7.9 shows the relationship between agricultural ideal points and those for other issues. In both the House and the Senate, it was members from cotton-growing districts, and especially those from the Black Belt, who were consistently furthest away from Republicans. Tobacco districts from Virginia, North Carolina, Tennessee, or Kentucky, including some in the Black Belt, were consistently more like non-southern Democrats in their voting patterns, and more willing to vote against legislative provisions tailored to the needs of cotton.

In August 1915, Wilson wrote to a friend complaining of "southern congressmen with wild schemes, preposterous and impossible schemes to valorize cotton and help the cotton planter out of the Reserve Banks or out of the national Treasury—out of anything, if only they can make themselves solid with their constituents and seem to be 'on the job.'" With the outbreak of world war in 1914, the demands on southern members of Congress for legislative action to aid cotton farmers reached a fever pitch, especially once the belligerent European countries placed cotton on the list of interdicted items subject to the embargoes. The "Farmers' Union men" threatened to quit the Democratic Party if Congress did not provide money for the cotton crop; southern members of Congress were reported to be "frightened out of their wits." Robert Henry introduced legislation for the Treasury to deposit $500 million in southern reserve banks, and under increasing pressure, the Georgia-born Secretary of the Treasury, William Gibbs McAdoo, announced that the Treasury would deposit $30 million in gold in the new reserve banks of Atlanta, Dallas, and Richmond. This investment would assist cotton farmers in gaining low-interest loans secured by the receipts from cotton warehouses, which in turn would allow them to hold back some of their crop from the market. At the same time, the new Federal Reserve board's southern representative, W. P. G. Harding, entered into secret negotiation for Britain to buy enough cotton to stabilize the market. The infusion of money was attacked by Republicans as a giveaway to the South but viewed more optimistically by at least some non-southerners. "Confronted with the uprising of his [the president's] loyal supporters in the South," wrote the former North Dakota Populist Henry Loucks, the government was willing to loan money "to aid the farmers to hold, or move, their crop." Loucks wanted the program to be made permanent and extended to the entire country, with private banks cut out of the

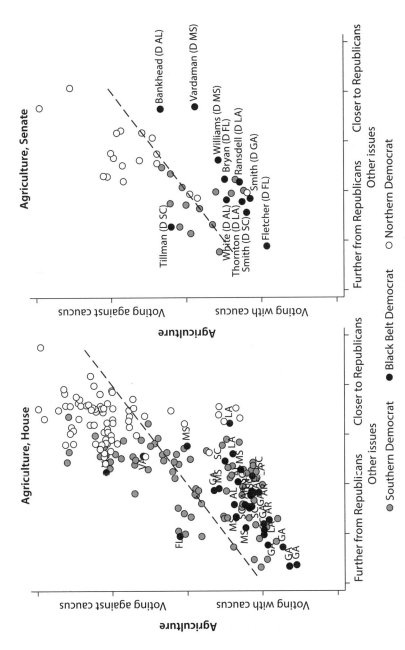

FIGURE 7.9. Agriculture and the Black Belt. Dashed diagonal line shows the 45-degree angle.

process. "Had our Representatives from the Northwest and West been as faithful to their constituents as were the majority from the South to their constituents, I firmly believe that our farmers would have benefited as much in the sale of their grain as [did] the Southern farmers in the sale of their cotton."[75]

A year later, Asbury F. Lever's cotton warehouse bill passed into law, with southern Democratic senators voting unanimously to establish a system of federal licensing for cotton and tobacco warehouses that would enable them to use their receipts for credit and help farmers hold some of their crop back from the market in order to raise the price. The bill had broad support among southern Democrats, although it met with some opposition by some who worried that it authorized too much federal involvement in regulating crop storage. An earlier version had been opposed by at least eighteen southern representatives, including a mix of conservatives and progressives. Versions of a cotton warehouse bill were now being sponsored by Lever, Hoke Smith, Adamson, and Sheppard. "When there is a great general good to be accomplished by legislation," declared Lever, "I am not so squeamish about the Constitution." Some southerners were even calling on the federal government to mandate a reduction of acreage, a proposal that pushed even progressive southern newspapers to worry about the sheriff "going to arrest Bill Jones who has planted, forsooth, a half acre too much of cotton."[76]

A federal system of long-term agricultural credit also was a core priority of southern representatives. By 1916, over one hundred separate bills had been introduced, ranging from "those who believe the Government should lend directly to the farmer to those who merely want the Government to supervise the farm mortgage business." From his position as chair of the House Committee on Agriculture, Asbury Lever continued his legislative efforts on behalf of farmers by introducing a bill for a decentralized system of federal farm loan banks, which would contract out with national farm loan associations to provide long-term credit. Denounced by many progressives as insufficient and by conservatives as socialism, Lever's bill passed the Senate in 1916 with only five northeastern Republicans in opposition and the House with only ten votes against. Despite his earlier opposition, Wilson signed the bill as part of a broader shift toward a progressive agenda that directly supported specific classes and acknowledged the political imperative that cash-strapped farmers of the Midwest would be needed in the upcoming elections.[77]

Although agriculture was the main animating concern of southern progressives, the years of southern ascendancy in Congress showed that an emerging alliance between the Democratic Party and the labor movement was beginning to take root. Throughout the first decade of the century, southern Democrats had regularly supported amendments to the antitrust laws that would exempt labor unions. They supported a bill regulating hours on railroads engaged in interstate commerce, and in 1912 nearly 90 percent of southern Democrats in the Senate voted in favor of an eight-hour law for laborers and mechanics employed by the United States, with only the conservative planter LeRoy Percy of Mississippi (paired with Bailey) against. A workers' compensation bill for railroad workers had divided southern Democrats in 1912 and 1913; although a slight majority of them voted for it in the Senate, a majority of the region's lawmakers opposed it in the House. In 1916, however, they largely supported the administration-backed Kern-McGillicuddy workers' compensation bill for federal workers. The year before, the region's legislators had also voted for passage of La Follette's seamen's bill, which protected workers at sea whose rights continued to be defined by "ancient feudal relationships embedded in the common law and treaties." Perhaps more significantly, despite long-standing warnings by southern Democrats that regulating hours for railroad workers would open up a dangerous Pandora's box, the Adamson eight-hour bill for railroad workers was supported with "practically no southern opposition," at the urging of an administration desperate to avoid a pending nationwide strike. The eight-hour law and the seamen's law were the first to provide for federal regulation of working conditions in private industry—exactly what southern conservatives, as well as reformers like John Reagan, had long warned against. Nevertheless, they passed with large majorities of southern lawmakers in support.[78]

These tentative moves to define a national labor policy did not, for the most part, reflect the policy priorities of southern Democrats. But southern legislators were willing to work with the national labor movement, so long as their collaboration was effected through the mediating institution of the Democratic Party and the movement's policy demands did not impinge on agricultural labor. Figure 7.10 shows the probability that Democratic lawmakers from different regions and economic areas would vote in favor of national labor legislation, for both the period from 1877 to 1900 and the period from 1900 to 1920. The border state districts and states are divided into agricultural and manufacturing based on whether they were above or below the national median for percent employed in manufacturing. There were too few manufacturing districts in the former Confederacy, and so these were divided into more "urban" districts—where over 30 percent of the population lived in a city with more than 25,000 people—and rural districts, which were subdivided into Black Belt and "white" agricultural districts.

In many ways, the issues of the twentieth century were not only a continuation but an amplification of the issues that had been placed on the legislative agenda by the late nineteenth century: eight-hour laws, a department of labor, distinct institutions for railroad workers, exemptions from antitrust laws, and limits on injunctions. The South continued to be the region whose Democratic representatives were most likely to oppose labor legislation, as happened in

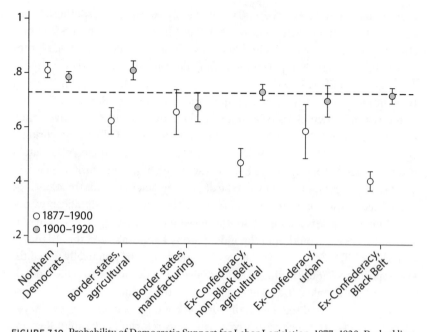

FIGURE 7.10. Probability of Democratic Support for Labor Legislation, 1877–1920. Dashed line is the Democratic mean for 1900 to 1920.

January 1918 when southern Democrats voted against establishing a commission to inquire into the advisability of a national unemployment insurance scheme. But there had also been a profound change in their willingness to support federal regulation of labor conditions. While northern Democrats remained relatively consistent in their propensity to vote in favor of labor reforms, most regions of the South became more supportive, some dramatically so. This shift was especially pronounced for agricultural constituencies, which had been the bastion of conservatism on labor in the nineteenth century but whose legislators were now almost as supportive of reform as northern Democrats. Whether because they were willing to subordinate their preferences to the needs of the national party or because of the success or even residue of efforts to build "farm-labor" coalitions in places such as Oklahoma and Arkansas, or because the American Federation of Labor (AFL) did not seek to organize agricultural workers and not only respected but helped reinforce segregation, the South in the early twentieth century showed a historically unique willingness to support federal labor policy. The major exception came in an area of special importance to the region—the effort to prohibit child labor, which we discuss in more detail in chapter 8.

The bills the southern leadership guided through Congress during this period rank among the most significant in modern American history. The list of highly consequential legislation passed between 1900 and the beginning of 1917, ranked by the measure of legislative significance we discussed in chapter 2, is extremely impressive, an indication of the profound alteration in the relationship between the federal government, the national economy, and the individual states. The Federal Trade Commission is one of the single most important bills passed before 1945, but it is statistically indistinguishable from the Federal Reserve Act of 1913 and the Pure Food Act of 1906. Also passed during this period were the Hepburn Act of 1906, the Anti-Trust Act of 1914, the Underwood Tariff of 1913, the Mann-Elkins Act of 1910—which southerners had helped pass and then helped repeal its controversial Commerce Court—the Federal Farm Loan Act of 1916, the Eight-Hour Act of 1916, and the 1909 income tax amendment.

Although some consequential legislation, such as the Gold Standard Act of 1900 and the Aldrich-Vreeland Act of 1908, passed over sustained southern objections, and although the South rarely got all it wanted, much of this legislative output reflected long-standing southern priorities that they had sustained and built support for against the opposition of the northeastern conservative Republicans who long had dominated congressional procedures. Even when they were empowered, southern lawmakers had to compromise. The Federal Trade Commission, for instance, did not reflect the southern preference for avoiding grants of power to administrative bodies, but it did reflect long-standing southern opposition to the monopolistic power of American business; likewise, the Hepburn Act reaffirmed the southern goal of regulating railroad rates even as it was paired with a power of judicial review that the region opposed. Both the Underwood Tariff, with its imposition of an income tax, and the Federal Farm Loan Act clearly reflected the interests of southerners and were shaped primarily, if never exclusively, by southern legislative action.

Perhaps most important, the Federal Reserve Act was deeply informed at every stage of the legislative process by southern priorities. Both in its broad contours and in many of its specific features, it made the nation's financial system more responsive to southern interests. The national banking system established by Republicans during the Civil War, and reinforced by the financial legislation of the first decade of the twentieth century, was deeply unresponsive to the unique features of the southern economy. The intense investment of the South in cotton—which only increased after the Civil War—made the region's economy subject to extreme seasonal variations, while the fragmentation of large plantations and the national system's legislated bias against small, agricultural banks kept the region very poorly integrated into national capital markets. The Federal Reserve system was designed in large measure to allay these problems. The committee charged with deciding where to place the new Federal Reserve banks ultimately decided that four of the twelve would be allocated to the South—five counting Kansas City, Missouri—despite the region's smaller economy. "South to rule system," complained the *Chicago Tribune*, noting that it would be "southern men" who would "undertake the responsible duty of designating not less than eight nor more than twelve cities as federal reserve cities." By placing banks in places such as Dallas, Texas, outside of established financial centers, the committee aimed to carry out the party's goal of "breaking up the Northeast's monopoly on the levers of credit."[79]

These legislative reforms cannot be understood apart from the other face of southern progressivism—the shared priority and common assumption that united most white southern politicians, progressive and conservative, into the Democratic Party. For if the South had begun to remake national policy to be more accommodating of its particular economic priorities, it also acted to shape policy in ways that would mute the potential dangers of centralization and further embed white supremacy in the structure of the new American state.

Progressivism and White Supremacy

Discussing the progressive movement in the southern states, C. Vann Woodward aptly described its accomplishments as "progressivism—for whites only." The same was true of many of the national progressive achievements. Southern legislators and administrators constricted the parameters of the new progressive state; extended Jim Crow segregation into the federal government; ensured local control over the developing "agricultural welfare state," thereby enabling either the exclusion of African Americans or their inclusion on terms defined by the local white elite; and further defined the terms of American citizenship along racial lines.[80]

A shared commitment to racial hierarchy shaped the terms of southern reform, limiting the scope of policy change that southern progressives were willing to support, providing the region's conservatives with a potentially resonant argument, and occasionally driving a wedge between southern lawmakers and their potential allies among midwestern and western Republicans. At times this orientation was manifested in a diffuse and shifting commitment to "states' rights," neither separable from nor entirely reducible to commitments to racial hierarchy. The Pure Food Act of 1906, for instance, was initially opposed by the southern members of the House Interstate Commerce Committee on the grounds that it would represent a federal usurpation of the state's police powers. Southern opposition had a number of different motivations, including the worry that the bill as written would preempt state labeling and content regulations that were essential to state and local prohibition laws. Inflecting these concerns was a recognition that racial hierarchy, like manufacturing, was a local matter that might be touched through an expansive interpretation of the interstate commerce clause. One Texas candidate for Congress pledged to vote for the "pure food bill" only if it respected "the right of local self-government in the liquor traffic or any other local issue," to which he immediately added, "the Federal government should keep its hands off the south in the settlement of the race issue." Another indication of how race inflected southerners' evaluations of the issue can be found in the House minority report, prepared by Adamson and Bartlett of Georgia and Russell of Texas, which denied the right of Congress to pass any law for the purpose of "exercising the police power within the States." The report concluded by favorably quoting a conservative Republican who had warned that the tendency to look to the federal government for relief had recently led a governor of a northern state to request national legislation to ensure that the people of his state could "have equal and fair treatment under similar conditions with other favored citizens"—in short, passage of a law prohibiting Jim Crow on the railroads. It was "southerners in particular," notes Kimberley Johnson, who "pressed the constitutional issue, arguing that national regulation would inevitably lead to a centralization of power and a diminution of state power." Sixteen of the seventeen votes cast against the bill in the House were from the South.[81]

Although southerners provided the bulk of opposition to the pure food bill, most nonetheless voted in its favor, making clear during debate that they strongly supported the principle of federal regulation of food and drug labeling. One conservative southern Democrat, "who fancied that states' rights were jeopardized" by the proposal, despaired that "those who formerly had stood with him in combating such legislation had now become converts and ardent proselytes." He was not mistaken. In 1884, 81 percent of southern Democratic representatives had voted to table a resolution authorizing an investigation into adulterated food and drugs, and Senator John Morgan had denounced the Blair education bill as setting a precedent for "national prohibition, pure food and drug laws, abolition of penitentiaries, requirements of higher wages for workers, and socialized medicine," believing that this would help turn southerners against the legislation. By the twentieth century, the argument that the Republican Party would once again intervene in southern labor practices without accommodations that preserved whites' control over the region's racial hierarchy were less salient, and more Democrats were willing to stake out a progressive position.[82]

The question of government ownership of the railroads also invoked southern anxieties over centralization, executive aggrandizement, and racial hierarchy. When Bryan began talking about the virtues of public ownership during his extended European tour in 1906, John Sharp Williams traveled to meet him and persuade the presumptive Democratic nominee to drop the issue. Government ownership "will doubtless be very acceptable to the grangers of the west," reported the *Biloxi Herald*. But "southern politicians say it will not go in their part of the country," as it would mean "an end of the 'Jim Crow' car, the continuance of which is imperative." Southern conservatives, insisting that the region "regards government ownership very much as it regarded the Force bills," sought to persuade their fellow southern Democrats that it would "inevitably lead to negro officials throughout the service." Although Bryan came out in favor of government ownership upon his return to the United States, southern Democrats continued to impress upon him the necessity to drop the issue, whose racial implications made it unacceptable. The hopes of many conservative white southerners were deflated every time Bryan brought up the issue, but even Furnifold Simmons had to report that "the Democrats of the South . . . were still loyal to the Nebraskan." Bryan would slowly back away from his position, conceding that while it was a good idea, it remained unacceptable to the party's core constituencies in the South.[83]

The issue came up again during the Wilson administration. The president decided to support a measure that would have the federal government build and operate a railroad in Alaska. Southerners in Congress were deeply split on the issue: pressed by their western allies and the administration, they nevertheless were worried about "wiping out the 'twilight zone' between the states and the federal government." The bill passed against the opposition of forty-nine of the ninety southern Democrats in the House; seven of sixteen southerners voted against it in the Senate. Figure 7.11 shows the probability of southern Democrats supporting the railroad across different regional specifications. Southern Democrats with a significant urban component to their district were highly likely to support the railroad project. Those from Black Belt districts, by contrast, were especially likely to be opposed, followed by members from white agricultural districts in both the border states and the former Confederacy. Observers noted that, on this issue at least, "the southern president is progressive; the southern congressmen are conservative," but it would be more accurate to say that the region was split, and that this split mapped onto both an urban-rural and racial divide.[84]

But if commitments to white supremacy placed limits on southern progressivism, it was perhaps just as common to see southern concerns eagerly accommodated by northern progressives looking to advance shared policy goals without provoking a sectional rift. Where a particular feature of policy might impinge on state control over the social and economic institutions necessary for preserving racial hierarchy, southern preferences were often taken into account by progressive Republicans. During consideration of the Hepburn railroad bill, for example, James Mann of Illinois explained that the initial proposal did not cover sleeping and Pullman cars because Republicans "did

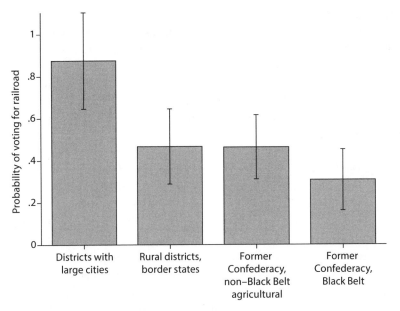

FIGURE 7.11. Southern Democratic Support for the Alaska Railroad

not want to array southern senators against the bill and open up in this body the question of separate cars for whites and blacks in the south." The inclusion of sleeping cars had been recognized as constitutional but undesirable by John Reagan in the 1880s for precisely the reason that it would provide an opening for Republicans to reinstate provisions of the Civil Rights Act. In this case, Mann's forbearance was unnecessary, for southern Democrats were among those who most supported the inclusion of sleeping cars in the bill.[85]

When George Southwick of Albany proposed an amendment to the effect that "no railroad subject to the provisions of this act shall be allowed to discriminate in accommodations or otherwise between persons on account of their race, color, or previous condition of servitude," it was resoundingly defeated by a margin of 143 to 11. When Joseph Foraker later offered an amendment in the Senate to restrict "Jim Crow" cars, progressive Republicans threw their support to the South. Foraker, who had a record of defending black rights in Ohio, also was making an appeal to southern conservatives, warning them that, so long as it was the railroads setting the rates, "we can stand by and see a great many things done," but once "we put the Government into that business, the Government becomes responsible for the rates that are made and for the treatment of the passengers who pay those rates." In short, regulation of rates would make rates and accommodations subject to the Fourteenth Amendment. "If anything could have been designed to kill this bill," warned Hernando Money of Mississippi, "this is the very instrument to do it. I say very frankly I will not vote for any rate bill with this provision in it." Texan Charles Culberson instead offered a substitute amendment without an equal accommodations provision, which, "after an intricate maze of filibustering," passed 38 to 35, with twelve Republicans and all Democrats in favor, "all because someone of the fascinating Southland alleged that there was presumably 'a nigger in the wood pile.'" The Afro-American *Indianapolis Freeman* described the congressional proceedings, with considerable disgust, as watching the "old parties join hands on the color line."[86]

Reflecting the changed political and ideological context of the twentieth century, even Foraker made clear that he did not want to interfere with segregation, but only require an equality of services. Tillman congratulated Foraker—who he said had been known as "Fire Alarm" because of his adamancy on the question of race—for his recognition "that there are conditions in the South which make it imperative that we should be allowed to deal with that question in our own way." Bailey pointed out, as George White had, that in fact Foraker's amendment might reinforce southern segregation laws, and he argued that if this was true, "surely those of us from the South, where we try to enforce the separation of passengers, could find no possible objection to it." Clarke of Arkansas suggested that with some amendments the proposal would be acceptable and would amount to a "substantial step in recognition of the fact that experience in my section of the country has shown that this class of legislation has been necessary; and it is that which has created that impression here. Such legislation would not have been possible a few years ago. I am disposed to meet the proposition in a friendly spirit and to do justice to the motives which induce Senators on the other side to make these concessions." To the laughter of the galleries, Tillman concluded that so long as the amendment recognized segregation he had no problem with it, especially since the railroads "are owned in the North, anyhow, and I want no discrimination by northern capitalists against southern negroes." A new version of the Foraker proposal would be passed a few days later by Republican William Warner of Missouri, apparently at the request of the black voters of his state. But it had been reworded to exactly meet the stipulations laid down by Clarke—to require only that "equally good" accommodations be provided. Southern Democrats did not oppose it because it did not require integration if equal accommodations were unavailable, while a delegation of black citizens, led by George White, warned that, with worsening racism in the North, the amendment might supersede state anti–Jim Crow laws outside the South and lead some railroads there to begin "to separate the negro passengers from the whites." A few prominent black voices were more hopeful, but stressed that all would depend on the composition of the ICC and where the members stood on the "race question." But with William Monroe Trotter's *Boston Guardian* fiercely against the provision, there was little Republican appetite for pushing it further, and the amendment was struck in conference.[87]

Foraker and Warner had modified their proposals to meet southern objections and to effectively recognize the validity of "separate but equal." This type of solicitousness was not uncommon among non-southern progressives during this period and should be understood as largely a result of southern intensity on this issue. Robert La Follette, for instance, redesigned his proposed eight-hour bill for railroad employees to meet southern concerns that the measure treated all railroads as subject to federal authority, regardless of whether they operated in interstate commerce. To stave off a southern rebellion La Follette accepted an amendment that limited the application of the bill, explaining later that, "unless I accepted Culberson's amendment, I knew I would lose the over sensitive states rights votes among the Democrats." Once the amendment was passed, southern opposition evaporated. On the pure foods bill as well, progressives sought to accommodate southern preferences, amending the conference report so that it would not preempt state regulations. Williams had been "very anxious to vote for the bill" and was delighted to report that he was now "able to do just that." The South dropped its opposition, and the conference report passed unanimously.[88]

Accommodations from non-southern progressives were welcomed, but many southern Democrats wanted more. Like Josephus Daniels, they wanted not simply a begrudging recognition of segregation but its positive affirmation and extension. Almost immediately upon attaining a majority in the House, southern legislators began introducing bills that would establish white supremacy as national policy, a goal they pursued across multiple issue areas, with varying success. Bills outlawing racial intermarriage and requiring Jim Crow street cars in the District of Columbia, segregating government employees on the basis of race, prohibiting the enlistment of African Americans in the armed services, and repealing the Fifteenth Amendment were introduced on several occasions during the years of Democratic majorities, while the House Committee on the Judiciary heard the argument of Thomas Sisson of Mississippi that the Fourteenth and Fifteenth Amendments had not been legally ratified—long a complaint of the South but hardly an effective use of the committee's time. To the great irritation of many southern Democrats, perhaps especially its conservative wing, James Vardaman of Mississippi had whipped up public support for his senatorial candidacy by promising to repeal the Fifteenth Amendment. Although Williams and other prominent figures had denounced this goal as hopeless and misguided—one that, at best, would not go anywhere and, at worst, was liable to provoke a northern reaction—resolutions to repeal the amendment were introduced in the 61st Congress by Underwood, Hardwick, and Ezekiel Candler (D-MS-1), who were probably taking advantage of the opening offered by Taft's inaugural address while offering a cheap crowd-pleaser to white southern constituencies. The resolutions were reintroduced in the 62nd Congress by Hardwick and Candler, in the 63rd by Hardwick, and in the 64th by Carl Vinson of Georgia.[89]

Southerners were hardly successful in all of these endeavors. In 1902, a constitutional amendment for the direct election of senators—an important policy objective of progressives—had passed the House, only for the Senate Committee on Privileges and Elections to attach a provision proposed by Republican senator Chauncey Depew of New York that "the qualifications of citizens entitled to vote . . . shall be uniform in all states, and Congress shall have the power to enforce this article by appropriate legislation and to provide for the registration of citizens entitled to vote, the conduct of such elections, and the certification of the result." In short, Depew proposed to provide a clear constitutional authority for the federal government to assume responsibility for federal elections, for the registration of voters, and even for voting qualifications. This was enough to kill support among southern Democrats, who "were in favor of the resolution, but could not go before their constituents as in favor of anything smacking of 'force legislation.'" There had probably not been a Senate majority in favor of the constitutional amendment, and while Depew himself was a sincere defender of black political rights he was not "above trying to defeat the proposal by offering an amendment unacceptable to the South." As Bailey noted, were the amendment ever to reach the floor of "the Senate, the Depew amendment would be put on it, and that would mean its defeat."[90]

In the 61st Congress, a Senate committee had reported a constitutional amendment for direct election of senators that would have effectively repealed congressional authority over national elections, which Isidor Rayner of Maryland declared to be the price of southern support. When this provision was struck in the Senate and replaced with a version of the Depew amendment sponsored by George Sutherland, southern senators from the former Confederacy voted against the constitutional amendment, depriving it of the two-thirds vote required. In the next Congress, southern Democrats, "mindful of the malodorous Force bill and reconstruction days," again insisted on a measure that would repeal constitutional authority for Congress to regulate national elections. When this was narrowly rejected by the Senate, the constitutional amendment was stalemated for a year. Under pressure from William Jennings Bryan and others anxious that further delay might imperil the party's chances in the upcoming presidential election, the House leadership met and decided to bring up the measure as passed by the Senate. "Better to accept what they could get than sacrifice the whole movement." Still, only 40 percent of southern Democrats supported the constitutional amendment, and a large majority voted for an alteration that would have explicitly banned sending federal officials to monitor elections.[91]

With southern Democrats in control of both chambers, efforts to extend the principle of white supremacy across the nation took on a new importance. Frank Clark of Florida introduced a succession of bills to outlaw interracial marriage in the District of Columbia, as did Georgians Hardwick, Vinson, and Samuel Tribble, as well as John Hall Stephens of Texas. The southern-dominated Committee on the District of Columbia urged the House to pass intermarriage bills in the 62nd and 63rd Congresses, believing that "the District should be in line with the general sentiment of the States of the Union upon this subject." A bill to segregate street cars was introduced by Joseph Thompson of Oklahoma, while Charles Edwards, Vinson, and James Aswell of Louisiana introduced bills requiring the segregation of government employees. In the Senate, southern legislators were a little more circumspect. But they were unwilling to accept Wilson's appointment of Oklahoma's Adam Patterson, an African American, to be register of the Treasury, despite the support for the nominee from his home state senator, Thomas P. Gore, and the fact that this position had traditionally gone to an African American. Thomas Dixon, author of *The Clansman*, wrote Wilson that it was one thing for Grover Cleveland to have appointed African Americans to positions of authority, but "that we have travelled many leagues from the Negro equality ideas that were in vogue" when Cleveland had done "this thing." "I think that the defeat of this appointment of a Negro," announced Vardaman, "is of more importance than the passage of the tariff bill and the enactment of currency legislation. It rises like a mountain peak above the other questions of the day." Patterson withdrew his nomination when it became clear that the Wilson administration, in providing no vocal support, was serving "notice that even the most innocuous and traditional of African American appointments would fail" and that the "patronage machine" for black Democrats would be "deliberately dismantled."[92]

Most of the proposed segregationist legislation never made it out of committee. Chairs saw little advantage in placing northern Democrats in an awkward position. Many of the proposals represented simple position-taking by members who had campaigned on a platform of establishing segregation as national policy or who did not want to be seen as lax when it came to the suppression of black political standing. Hoke Smith insisted that his vote against Robert H. Terrell, an African American renominated by Wilson to be a municipal judge in the District of Columbia, be made public even though such votes made in executive session were generally closed to the public. Explaining that "political opponents back in Georgia had accused him of favoring the nomination of a Negro over a white man," he wanted to have proof of his absolute commitment to white supremacy in appointments. Maryland Democrat Charles Coady's bill limiting marriage rights did, however, pass the House, 238 to 60, with all southern Democrats in favor and only seven northern

Democrats and a bare majority of voting Republicans in opposition. The Senate did not consider it, but the constant threat of adverse laws led the NAACP to assign paid agents "just to keep up with all the pending anti-Negro legislation."[93]

The influx of southerners into the cabinet resulted in a new level of scrutiny of the racial hierarchy in federal workplaces. The exclusion of blacks from important offices had already been a feature of federal employment under the Roosevelt and Taft administrations, but it became explicit, widespread, and durable during the Wilson administration, the result of pressures both inside and outside of Congress. With Democrats in charge, racist white workers felt empowered to demand the extension of segregation into the national government, reversing what they claimed had been Republican discrimination against white southerners, on the grounds that hiring African Americans made the workplace "noxious to 'Negrophobic' Democrats." Wilson received letters counseling him to solve the "negro question" by firing all black workers, which one writer hoped would force a test of the Fourteenth Amendment: "It can only be by testing these Amendments that this problem can be solved." When African American women workers complained about the lunchroom of the Bureau of Printing and Engraving being segregated, at the request it seems of Woodrow Wilson's wife, a white woman responded indignantly, "Do you know that we Democrats are in power."[94]

When Albert S. Burleson, the U.S. postmaster general and a Texas Democrat, broached the subject of segregating the federal bureaucracy at a cabinet meeting in 1913, the proposal met with no objection. Wilson simply noted that he wanted to avoid friction—the supposed problem that many progressives believed segregation would solve. Within a few months, segregation was instituted in the Bureau of Engraving and Printing, the Post Office Department, the Auditor of the Post Office, the Treasury, and the Auditor of the Navy. By 1914, the Civil Service Commission required photo identification of all new applicants for federal jobs; though this was purportedly a measure to prevent impersonation, African Americans believed that the intent was to screen them out. The "world of many black Americans fell apart" as they lost stable working- and middle-class jobs or were demoted to menial positions at much lower pay. Within a few years, "virtually all blacks had been removed from managerial positions." Even Robert Smalls, a Civil War hero and former member of Congress, was stripped of his collectorship in South Carolina on the urging of Senator Tillman, who urged that Smalls's "negro deputy" also be fired: "Do cut off the negro's head instanter, and I will sleep easier."[95]

As racial discrimination in the nation's capital deepened, Wilson and the southern Democrats in Congress made sure that white supremacy's newly gained political influence would reverberate throughout the federal service. Of particular symbolic and substantive importance were southern efforts to make the military draft compatible with their region's labor needs and racial code. As the drums of war grew louder in 1915, Wilson requested that Congress prepare for the possibility of becoming entangled in the world war by enlarging the Army and Navy and establishing a peacetime draft. A central plank of his early preparedness program was the creation of a new national reserve force that would fall under the exclusive control of the federal government and displace the state militias, which, despite recent reforms, were widely regarded as lacking in training and coherence. James Hay, the Virginian chair of the House Military Affairs Committee, successfully blocked any action on this proposal and forced the administration to back down and accept a compromise that kept intact the system of state militias that had been put to extensive work in the South—indeed throughout the country—to put down labor unrest in the preceding decades. The bill would have expanded the authority of the president to "federalize" the National Guard in emergencies, but Hay worried that a reserve force under the exclusive control of the federal government might allow "a President hostile to their racial system" to enlist African American soldiers, removing needed laborers and increasing racial tensions, and prohibit segregation in the ranks. After Wilson accepted this limitation, Secretary of War Lindley M. Garrison tendered his resignation.[96]

The question of national conscription divided many southern Democrats from the administration, both because of the South's strong pacifist and isolationist sentiment and because of the region's pervasive worry that a draft would lead to the "arrogant strutting representatives of black soldiery in every community." Many white southerners opposed any conscription that included African Americans because it would strain their ability to retain cheap labor. Some even proposed that southern blacks should be conscripted into forced service as agricultural laborers, a proposal that Asbury Lever believed went too far and could be avoided by vigorous enforcement of state vagrancy laws: "There are a lot of darkies hanging around towns and cities, and on farms even, that should be put to work either on the farms and in places where they are needed or on the public works of the State."[97]

Conscription of whites or blacks was highly controversial, and many southern Democrats argued that it was a plot of northeastern monopolists to repress dissent. "They say, 'we have too much discontent, too many Socialists, too many I.W.W.'s, too many strikes, too much industrial disorder, too much freedom of speech, too many ranting demagogues and labor agitators,'" roared George Huddleston of Birmingham. "They would suppress all this with the iron hand of the military." But conscription was a top priority of the administration, and in the end southern Democrats helped shepherd the legislation through. Although southern lawmakers who opposed the conscription of black Americans were unable to carve out an exemption, Wilson and the new

Secretary of War, Newton Baker, addressed their concerns with circumspec-tion. The draft form required registrants to indicate their race, ensuring that they could be segregated once enlisted, and Wilson promised that essential agricultural labor, along with essential industrial labor, would be exempted. After a deadly riot in Houston occasioned by the strict enforcement of Jim Crow ordinances against black soldiers, Baker tried to accommodate white southern fury—Vardaman in particular made great hay out of it—by attempt-ing to limit the training of black soldiers to the North, although he would have to abandon this policy as deeply impractical. But the riot also led "authorities to keep loaded arms from African American combat troops for as long as possible."[98]

The draft did not explicitly exclude black Americans, nor did it conscript them into agricultural labor, as some had hoped. Baker's efforts to accommo-date the South by restricting the presence of black soldiers in the region was effectively abandoned. But the design of the draft nonetheless provided white southern elites with the crucial ability to protect the racial order. Instead of universal conscription, induction into military service was to be selective, partly to exempt workers in essential economic sectors. But this required some means of determining who would be exempted, and the legislation left this decision to local draft boards composed of local elites. The boards were to be staffed by the president, who would rely on names submitted by state governors; they, in turn, would draw on elected officials and prominent local citizens. The decision to decentralize implementation and registration was deliberate, reflecting the anxieties of the Wilson administration about avoid-ing a repeat of the kind of resistance to the draft, both North and South, that occurred during the Civil War, and also the recognition that passing the policy through Congress required that it win the support of southern Democratic committee chairs.[99]

The result, however, was a highly decentralized system housed within a War Department where commitments to segregation were deeply entrenched. "In the entire country," writes Paul T. Murray, "there were only five or six black members of local draft boards." In practice, the boards tended to side more with middle- and upper-class white farmers opposed to sending their children to war than they did with the white planters anxious about the in-ability to secure cheap labor. Both black and white working-class registrants were inducted at higher rates than their numbers warranted. "Tenant farmers of both races," notes Jeanette Keith, "neither owned their land nor completely controlled what crops were planted there. Only the wealthiest southern 'farm-ers,' such as the planters who still dominated agriculture in the Deep South, could hope to obtain an agricultural exemption under Selective Service regu-lations." One of the main standards for exemption was whether a family de-pended on the earnings of the potential inductee. The fact that a potential draftee's wife worked in domestic service, which was especially common among married black men, was taken as evidence that the family was not dependent on his labor. And since the Army pay was often more than the wages earned by blacks or working-class whites in the South, their poverty paradoxically worked against an exemption. Black southerners who were deemed ineligible for combat duty because of age, disability, or other factors often were inducted all the same, as the boards believed, usually correctly, that they would be used as conscripted laborers, not as soldiers. The cost to black southerners of white local control over the draft was not so much that they were prevented from enlisting, but that they were too commonly enlisted. In some cases, the bias against African Americans was so severe that Baker had to step in and suspend or disband the local exemption board. In Fulton County, Georgia, for example, deferments had been given to 526 of 618 whites, but only to 6 of 212 African Americans.[100]

As segregation was extended to the federal bureaucracy and reinforced in the "nation's service," southerners were ensuring that the country's new agricultural policies would not undermine white supremacy. The Smith-Lever Act of 1914 considerably extended the country's emerging services-based agricultural welfare state, establishing a system of agricultural demonstration projects organized through the nation's land-grant colleges, with an appropriations disbursement formula that heavily advantaged the South. Funds were allocated on the basis of rural population rather than the improved acreage in a state or total population, which Senator Albert Cummins of Iowa would denounce as discriminatory against the West and Midwest in favor of the South. The bill was unanimously approved by the Agriculture Committee and passed the House under suspension of the rules on January 19, 1914, with only nine votes cast against. Southerners argued that the benefits of the bill merited flexibility on constitutional interpretation. In response to one northern Democrat who opposed the bill, invoking the opposition of "men who calmly study and familiarize themselves with our form of government," Lever interjected, "Men who are inhuman." In the Senate, Vardaman noted his belief that lawmakers should live within the limits set by the Constitution, but as "the highest end of Government is the improvement of man," he would be willing to make an exception.[101]

Agricultural legislation passed under Republican governments, including the Nelson amendment that the South had enthusiastically backed in 1906, had maintained the 1890 Morrill Act's explicit requirement for equal provision across black and white land colleges. They recognized segregated education but stipulated that there should be equal allocation by race, which in practice was adhered to by allocating the federal portion of the money equally but restricting the matching state funds to white schools. The Smith-Lever bill, however, did not even make this concession to racial equality, for it simply provided that states with two or more land-grant colleges—largely southern states that had used the 1890 Morrill Act to create a black college—would have the appropriation "administered by such college or colleges as the legislature of such State may direct." "Our enemies," bemoaned Moorfield Storey of the NAACP, "seem to gain in audacity constantly."[102]

In the Senate, Republican Wesley Jones of Washington provided evidence that the "17 Southern States" were already circumventing the Morrill Act's requirements for equal funding of black and white land-grant colleges. He introduced an amendment requiring states to submit periodic reports to the Secretary of Agriculture to confirm that the money was being equitably allocated. The Jones amendment was a relatively weak measure, reaffirming existing law's embrace of "separate but equal" while simply requiring that states report how the money was being spent. But it went too far for southerners. Two of the region's most outspoken "progressives," Hoke Smith and James Vardaman, insisted that the region's whites alone could manage "the negro problem" and frankly stated that state legislatures would not appropriate a single dollar for the black colleges to administer the extension work. There was no pretense that the money would be equally allotted. After a few days of debate, Democrat John Shafroth of Colorado proposed a compromise that did not include any mention of equal allocation; it passed without a roll call. Immediately afterwards, Jones's amendment was defeated, 23 to 32. Four progressive Republicans, James Brady of Idaho, Cummins and William Kenyon of Iowa, and Albert Fall of Arizona, cast their votes with the South. The only southern senator to support the Jones amendment was William Bradley, a Republican from Kentucky, while only two Democrats—Gilbert Hitchcock of Nebraska and Atlee Pomerene of Ohio—voted for it. Hitchcock then moved to include a provision that the program would be carried on without discrimination as to race, which passed without a roll call.[103]

The debate provided an opportunity for racist diatribes from Vardaman and others, as well as an elaboration by southerners on the ostensibly compassionate treatment that African Americans had received as slaves. But even with these provocations, most Republicans who spoke were willing to accept the core southern claim that the question of regulating the racial hierarchy should be left to the southern states, even if they believed that there should be some accounting for how federal money was being spent. "I believe the Senator from Georgia," noted Senator Porter McCumber of North Dakota, "is better able to determine, and the legislature of his State can probably better determine, what is for the interest of both the colored population and the white population of Georgia than I, who have never been in that State."[104]

The conference committee provided the southern committee chairs with a final opportunity to make the bill more acceptable to white southern Democrats. The conference report dropped the Shafroth amendment, which itself had been a very weakened compromise, as well as the Hitchcock amendment, which they now concluded was "unnecessary." This shift passed without debate in the Senate, with Republican supporters of the Jones amendment either absent or under the mistaken impression that the Shafroth and Hitchcock compromises had been retained. When they learned that these provisions had been dropped, they took the rare step of voting to recall the bill from the House of Representatives to reconsider the report's adoption. After Smith informed the Senate that Lever and the House conferees insisted that state legislatures retain the sole power of distributing the money, and that no bill could pass with anything like the Shafroth or Hitchcock amendments, the Senate voted against reconsideration and thus left the conference report as adopted. Party control in the House of Representatives had kept the issue of equal allocation off the agenda in that chamber, while control over the key offices in the legislative process—in particular the committee chairs' right to name conferees—ensured that the South would get what it wanted in the Senate.[105]

In 1917, Congress passed the Smith-Hughes Act, which established a matching program of federal funding for vocational training. Although conservative southerners opposed the measure as an "assault upon the prerogatives and the high duties of the States," it again did not include a provision for equitable allocation of money. Instead, the funds would be administered by state boards working in coordination with a federal board for vocational education. As critics had anticipated, the result of local control was that African Americans rarely received an equitable share of federal funds, and even where they did, it was because states used the federal money alone to pay for black educational programs; for white students, federal and state funds were combined. Moreover, when state and local boards did equally allocate Smith-Hughes funding, black students tended to be pushed into segregated occupations deemed appropriate. Oscar B. Martin, a former South Carolina school superintendent who became the director of the cooperative extension program for the southern states, opposed the use of federal funds to subsidize 4-H clubs for African American girls and insisted that black recipients be marked off by uniform and club name and not be trained in commercial activities—such as canning—that might bring them into competition with the white girls' clubs.[106]

As the political scientist Kimberley Johnson has shown, the parameters of American agricultural policy during the period of southern ascendancy were constructed to "reflect the interests of the Jim Crow southern racial order." This aim was accomplished not primarily by explicit racial proscriptions in federal law, although the education programs explicitly or implicitly affirmed segregation; such proscriptions would have been subject to Fourteenth Amendment challenges and would also have caused potential political problems for northern Democrats. Instead, southern white supremacy was secured by vesting considerable discretion over the allocation of resources and implementation of policy in state legislatures; in white land-grant colleges and their attached agricultural experiment stations; in state vocational boards composed of white officials; in the white directors of state extension services; in the regional agents of the Department of Agriculture, who managed the sponsored agricultural club work; in the network of federal farm banks and national farm loan associations created by the Federal Farm Loan Act; and even in the 4-H club. The disproportionate exclusion of black Americans from the benefits of the agricultural welfare state was achieved by southern members of Congress who designed legislation so that national policy would be implemented in a highly decentralized fashion, with state and local elites able to limit the potential threat of these new federal programs to the region's racial order.[107]

The Federal Farm Loan Act, for example, was quiet about racial discrimination. Many of the regional banks set up under the act made a point of declaring, regardless of the act's omissions, that they would not discriminate on the basis of race. But the law required that loan recipients be members of a national farm loan association, and membership in these associations was granted only upon a two-thirds vote of the directors. As observers were quick to note, the result was that "the negro would probably be denied this vote by the directors of a white association, and an immigrant might be treated in the same arbitrary fashion by a board of directors composed of nativists." With some exceptions, experience tended to bear out this expectation. The farm loan banks generally discouraged the formation of separate associations for African Americans, although when federal regional coordinators were sympathetic to black concerns, separate associations were authorized. Some black farmers even were offered membership in largely white associations. But while there was no explicit prohibition, and some black farmers did benefit from the program, the control vested in white directors together with the requirement that recipients be creditworthy—in other words, financially secure—put extreme limitations on black access to credit. As Lorenzo Green and Carter Woodson noted in 1933, the difficulties imposed on black farmers by the program's design should compel them to begin organizing, so as to "bargain collectively instead of individually," in order to "derive the maximum benefit" from the program.[108]

Southern blacks could participate in the education extension programs, and could even serve as demonstrators. But by denying black institutions the right to control the funds or select the extension program demonstrators, lawmakers ensured that the program's operation would not unsettle the South's racial hierarchy. Martin would even write that black demonstrators were especially eager to be extension officers, not because of the money or the opportunity to serve their community, but because "negroes are very susceptible to commendation and praise" and so were proud to wear the button "Demonstrator." So long as this opportunity was restricted to areas with large black majorities, and so long as white farmers would not be taught by black demonstrators, the arrangement was compatible with white supremacy. Black southerners were legally eligible to receive the farm loans supported by the federal government. But only the most successful black farmers and relatively well-off communities, who could either gain the backing of white directors or were sufficiently organized that they were authorized to form black associations, and who also met the race-blind but certainly not poverty-blind requirements for credit, could gain loans under the new program.[109]

Conclusion

A few months after the opening of the first Democratic majority in the House of Representatives in almost twenty years, one progressive Republican, reflecting on the changed priorities and politics he had seen, expressed his anxiety for the future. "The country takes on the spirit of its rulers," he suggested, and "if the South controls this government we will have southern civilization." The ascendancy of the Republican Party, he argued, had organized the country's political and economic life to reflect the best of the North and West. "Can any one predict with reasonable certainty," he asked, "what the effect upon our civilization will be to have the South absolutely dominate our financial, industrial, educational, and social policies for the next 50 years?"[110]

His projection was cut short, at least for a time, by the return of Republicans to power in the 1920s. Notwithstanding, by the close of Wilson's first term, southerners could confidently claim to be successfully remaking the country in their image. Claude Kitchin of North Carolina, for one, pointed to a list of reform policies that southern lawmakers had been demanding for decades and remarked with great satisfaction that "in every detail they had been carried into effect." The basic thrust of southern legislation during the Wilson years reconfigured the national economy, placing it on a more democratic and egalitarian basis by diffusing capital, providing aid to farmers, enacting modest legislation that favored the industrial working classes, and decisively reconfiguring the balance of the federal tax burden, which had long been regressive and deeply imbalanced across sections. The fight to retain these policies against conservative reaction would be a key struggle in the last years of the Wilson administration and the decade that followed.[111]

Concurrently, as the South advanced the cause of progressive reform, its legislators deftly secured local control over policy implementation in areas of critical interest to the region's enfranchised constituencies. The decentralized and federal structure they demanded and secured across a range of policies had been the condition for southern support. It also placed a limit on the impact of these reforms, by states and local elites to regulate implementation in a manner that muted, even if it did not entirely contain, any threat to local racial hierarchies.

8

Minority Power

The South is thickly sown with contradictions. . . . Think of Cole Blease and
Carter Glass, Jim Heflin and Oscar Underwood, Pastor Norris and Dr. Poteat,
magnolias and billboards, colonial mansions and real estate developments,
paved roads and pig tracks, horse races and Methodist conferences—and you
have symbols that are a rebuke to quick conclusions.[1]

Forces are at work, which if not checked soon, will split the Solid South from
flank to dewlap.[2]

On Thanksgiving evening in 1915, thirty-four men in white robes met at Stone
Mountain, Georgia. This first meeting of the resurrected Ku Klux Klan had
been called by William Joseph Simmons, an Alabaman and "inveterate joiner
and promoter of fraternal societies," in anticipation of the premiere of D. W.
Griffith's *The Birth of a Nation* and in response to calls for its revival during the
trial of Leo Frank, a Jewish factory manager who was lynched for the alleged
murder of a young girl. For the next few years, Simmons would struggle to
keep his new society afloat, but a rising tide of nativism, red scares, labor
strikes, and race riots would eventually provide a context in which its membership would swell. By the early 1920s, the Klan had spread throughout the
South, with just under 60 percent of its membership found in Arkansas, Oklahoma, Louisiana, and Texas, and an additional 20 percent east of the Mississippi and south of the Ohio.[3]

The Klan now moved into politics. When the governor of Georgia, former
senator Thomas Hardwick, demanded that Klansmen unmask and cease
acts of violence, the Klan responded by throwing its influence behind his

opponent, Clifford Walker. In 1922, Walker defeated Hardwick in the white Democratic primary. That year the Klan helped elect Earle Mayfield of Texas to the U.S. Senate, and Klan-backed candidates won a majority of seats in the Oklahoma legislature. Across the South, writes George Tindall, "thousands of local officeholders owed their places to the Klan." Membership was seen by many aspiring politicians as a promising vehicle for their political careers.[4]

The national Klan or its local affiliates endorsed immigration restriction, health and hygiene reforms, prohibition, and even child labor laws. *The Fiery Cross* praised "Cotton Tom" Heflin of Alabama, Park Trammell of Florida, and Morris Sheppard of Texas for their progressivism and denounced "reactionaries" such as Oscar Underwood. In the border states and the Midwest, Klan-backed legislators included members from both parties, while in the one-party Deep South its involvement in Democratic politics threatened many established officeholders and helped gird some prominent voices to take a stand against them. In Texas, "Ma" Ferguson easily defeated a Klan-backed candidate in a gubernatorial election watched closely across the country. When the Louisiana Klan bragged of murdering the son of a wealthy planter, the state's governor declared martial law and sent in the National Guard. The conservative Oscar Underwood of Alabama denounced the Klan's growing influence as a "national menace." "It's either the Ku Klux Klan or the United States of America," he declared. "Both cannot survive. Between the two, I choose my country." In 1926, he ended his political career "in disgust when it became apparent that his opposition to the Klan would prevent him from being re-elected." He was replaced by Hugo Black, future New Dealer, Supreme Court justice, and Klansman.[5]

The fight against the Klan was not, for the most part, replicated in Congress. The House of Representatives declined to act on legislation to combat the organization, and beyond considering the Klan's involvement in a Texas election, the Senate took even less interest. "It seems to me that it is largely a state matter," noted Philip Campbell, the Republican chair of the Rules Committee in 1922.[6]

But the Klan's revival was indicative of broader changers in southern congressional politics. For one, the fights over the Klan were telegraphed onto the national stage during the party conventions of 1924. While the Klan became "quite cozy" with the Republican Party leadership and easily defeated a proposal to denounce it, there was a protracted fight in the Democratic National Convention over whether the party should pledge to oppose "any effort on the part of the Ku Klux Klan or any organization to interfere in the religious liberty or political freedom of any citizen, or to limit the civic rights of any citizen or body of citizens because of religion, birthplace, or racial origin." Underwood's Alabama delegation was the only southern state delegation to unanimously support the pledge, which was narrowly defeated. It was one of

many acrimonious divisions that resulted in the Democrats "literally ceas[ing]
to be a national party."[7]

The Klan also embodied the fragmentation of southern political cohesion.
In Mississippi in 1911, James Vardaman's campaign of class antagonism, what
Albert Kirwan summarized as "the revolt of the rednecks," had threatened the
ascendancy of the state's planter class. Campaigning against Vardaman, Senator LeRoy Percy told an audience in Brookhaven, Mississippi, that "the cost
of white supremacy is white solidarity. Is it too great a cost for you to pay?"
When a Klan organizer came to recruit in Greenville, Mississippi, eleven years
later, Percy returned to this theme. He praised the original Klan for helping
restore white supremacy, but denounced its successor for driving away labor
and creating religious dissension. "With the white man in control of every
department of government, of the courts, judges and juries," with thousands
of acres now left untilled for want of labor, with black southerners daily moving north for "better opportunity," with white religious communities standing
"shoulder to shoulder," the Ku Klux Klan was to be "dragged from its grave
and revamped for profit," with the inevitable outcome of fracturing white solidarity. The Greenville crowd voted to denounce the Klan, but its growth in
the region was emblematic of how white solidarity could unravel in the absence of an imminent threat to white supremacy.[8]

By the 1920s, the threat to white supremacy was much less dire, and the
impulse toward solidarity less pressing. The Republican Party had become
more sympathetic to southern control over the region's racial hierarchy, while
southern Democratic lawmakers in Washington seemed confident in their
ability to preserve white supremacy against external threat. The white primary
and disfranchisement continued to work to keep most black men and women
out of state and local politics, and for many younger politicians the days of
black voting were little more than a memory. At the same time, changes to the
rules and institutional practices of Congress, especially in the Senate, were
making party a less important factor in organizing politics and influence in
policymaking. Southerners remained united on issues that impinged upon
white supremacy, but on a growing number of issues, the region's lawmakers
were drifting apart, forming new coalitions that addressed the particular priorities of their different white constituencies.[9]

Instead of a "return to normalcy," the 1920s saw the emergence of new
patterns of congressional politics, characterized by more issue-specific legislative coalitions and a significant dissipation of party unity. This development
first became evident in the resurgence of southern conservatism after World
War I, perhaps best embodied in the rise of John Nance Garner, whose eventual candidacy for the Democratic Party's presidential nomination was rooted
in the "desire of the rank and file Democrats to get away from everything the
East implies and to find a good, safe politician with an innocuous record who

knows the game and how to play it. Unconsciously, what they want is a Democratic Coolidge, and they instinctively feel that Garner is their man. They are not wrong."[10]

But while conservatism was an increasing force in the region, the contours of what would eventually be the New Deal realignment were gradually being etched. Shifting coalitions of southern Democrats and Republicans were organized around specific legislative policies, including agriculture, resource development, immigration, prohibition, and taxation, and constituted in new legislative blocs that aspired to play a direct role in setting the congressional agenda. By the end of the decade, a progressive coalition uniting the large majority of southern Democrats with western and midwestern legislators had been organized, and it would form the basis for the early New Deal Democratic majorities.[11]

The War and Its Disruptions

"Why should not war serve as a pretext to foist innovations upon the country?" This was the question many progressives were asking in 1917, including the southern Democrats in Congress who would be responsible for mobilizing the country's resources. Ironically, one of the first innovations that the South would foist upon the country was one that they had always feared and resisted—a rule to cut off debate in the Senate.[12]

For two decades, proposals for the federal government to support the construction and purchase of merchant ships had provoked bitter divisions in Congress and been subject to repeated defeats at the hands of southern and western filibusters. In 1915, a merchant marine bill supported by the Wilson administration as part of a broader preparedness program was again defeated by a Senate filibuster. Wilson was furious, and the pressure to pass a bill now pushed Senate Democrats to seriously consider changing the rules to provide a way to end debate. Senate Democrats debated several proposed cloture rules, and from the caucus minutes it can be inferred that the ranks of southerners who supported a rule change included a mix of administration loyalists who viewed Wilson as one of their own, such as Duncan Fletcher of Florida and Blair Lee of Maryland, progressives Luke Lea of Tennessee, Robert Owen of Oklahoma, Morris Sheppard of Texas, and William Stone and James Reed of Missouri, but also conservative Thomas Martin of Virginia, "who rarely agreed with President Wilson except on the desirability of getting things done." Owen was the most supportive of a cloture rule that would allow a majority to cut off debate, while South Carolinians Ellison Smith and Ben Tillman and James Clarke of Arkansas were the most vocally opposed to any change. The caucus ultimately decided to support "a modified cloture rule," limited only to the shipping bill, and on February 12, 1915, a motion to consider a resolution changing the rules was brought up in the chamber.[13]

Smith and Tillman ultimately voted to consider the resolution, but Clarke, James Vardaman, John Bankhead of Alabama, Thomas Hardwick of Georgia, and Johnson Camden of Kentucky broke ranks and voted no, forcing the vice president to provide the tie-breaking vote. The Democrats abandoned the effort, and with it the ship bill, after it became apparent that the proposed rule would be amended to apply in all cases except where a party caucus had bound its members. To remind his colleagues of the stakes, Jacob Gallinger, a New Hampshire Republican, had read into the record an editorial from the *Lexington Herald* entitled "Remember the Force Bill," which beseeched southerners to recall that the "only salvation of the South from the enactment of the force bill rested with those Democratic Senators who, day after day, week after week, with watchless vigilence [*sic*], check-mated every move of the Republican majority." In 1916, a modified version of the shipping bill, made more palatable to progressive Democrats by providing for increased government regulation, passed the Senate on a party line vote.[14]

The next year, as Germany escalated its submarine warfare in the Atlantic, the administration proposed a plan to arm American merchant ships. When the administration released an intercepted telegram from the German foreign minister proposing an alliance between Germany and Mexico, the House responded immediately by passing the Armed Ships Bill, 403 to 13, with two Missouri Democrats the only southerners to vote no. But the congressional session was in its final days, and a small group led by Robert La Follette, but including southerners James Vardaman, William Kirby of Arkansas, and William Stone of Missouri, filibustered it to death.[15]

The president and party leaders in the Senate were outraged, not just at the defeat of the armed ships bill but at the simultaneous loss of the Army appropriations bill, the civil appropriations bill, the general deficiency bill, and a conservation bill that would have opened up protected natural resources for immediate exploitation. Wilson immediately insisted on establishing some means to close off in order to meet the emergency; in the interim, he ordered the Navy—without statutory authority—to begin supplying weapons to civilian merchant ships. Robert Owen had previously arranged for forty-two Democratic senators to sign a petition in favor of cloture, and he now got thirty-three senators, most of them Democrats, to renew their demand.

The irony of a southern-led Democratic Party proposing a cloture procedure was not lost on contemporary observers. Their very willingness to consider such a change reflected not only their investment in the administration's success but their dampened worry that Republicans would seek to advance civil rights legislation while in the majority. Even James Vardaman announced that he did not "share the apprehension of some of my southern senatorial brethren that there is any possibility of limited cloture being used by any majority, however great that majority may be, of northern Republicans to put the ignorant and incompetent negro over the white people of the South." Vardaman suggested that Republicans had moved on and were now infused with a broad patriotism and "disposition to do the right thing," but he also insisted that sooner or later the Fourteenth and Fifteenth Amendments would have to be repealed.[16]

Few southern Democrats were as confident that the danger could never again arise, noting that a Pennsylvania Republican, Boies Penrose, recently had introduced a proposal to reduce southern representation in line with the Fourteenth Amendment, that Republicans had endorsed this in their national convention, and that "the more rabid members wished to pledge the party to the more drastic program" of the former federal elections bill. Ellison Smith warned of the "possibility of a force bill under republican domination of the senate if a cloture rule is put in effect," while newspapers reported that the "southerners particularly are strong against the cloture plan for fear a 'force bill' might be used against them later." "The hobgoblin that arises in their minds whenever cloture is discussed," noted one observer, "is the danger that it will permit the passage of a force bill." Whenever a cloture rule was debated, the point was raised that the filibuster against the elections bill "has never been forgotten" among the region's lawmakers, that "the single weapon against [measures] touching the black and white question has been in past times a filibuster."[17]

Southerners persuaded of the need for cloture were anxious to limit its application. The conservative *Macon Daily Telegraph*, which saw a threat to white supremacy behind every federal initiative, applauded the adoption of cloture, but urged that it be limited to the duration of the war or clearly restricted to matters relating to international affairs. The full consequences of cloture, "not only for the immediate future but far into the years to come," had to be weighed and balanced: "In our domestic affairs, at least, we must conserve some body that may with propriety" delay and block legislation. Others suggested that any cloture rule should be designed to not apply to "political question[s] such as the Force Bill," thereby ensuring that such measures could be "talked to death if time of the Congress permitted it."[18]

Ultimately, a committee of five Democrats and five Republicans was appointed to draft a rule. Unsurprisingly, the Democrats on the committee were almost all from the South: James Reed of Missouri, Claude Swanson of Virginia, Robert Owen of Oklahoma, Ollie James of Kentucky, and Hoke Smith of Georgia. (Thomas Walsh of Montana subsequently was added.) This was not, however, a committee opposed to cloture. Owen favored a majority cloture rule, Walsh supported some form of revision, and Reed and Smith had both called for a limited measure. The proposal that was ultimately agreed to had already been drafted and approved months before by the Senate Rules Committee, chaired by Lee Overman of North Carolina; southerners held four of the committee's ten seats. The rule required a motion to be made to end debate, signed by sixteen senators, after which two calendar days would pass before the presiding officer would ask whether it was the sense of the Senate that debate should be brought to a close. For the question to be decided in the affirmative would require the support of two-thirds of senators voting. Even after cloture had been invoked, every senator was guaranteed an hour of speechmaking, which could impair the probability of passage if time was pressing. The rule did nothing to impede the use of dilatory motions and was drawn up to apply only on debatable motions. The requirement of a supermajority, as well as the ample opportunities for delay, largely reflected the preferences of the southerners.[19]

In a special session of Congress called for the express purpose of changing the rules, the Senate voted 76 to 3 in favor of the proposal, with all southern Democrats in favor and only La Follette, Asle Gronna of North Dakota, and Lawrence Sherman of Illinois opposing.

Most observers seem to have agreed with Senator William Borah of Idaho that the rule "was not a cloture rule in the usual sense, and that it probably would be seldom invoked and then only to prevent defeat of legislation by a very few men." One important reason why the committee decided on such a limited measure, as contemporaries recognized, was the need "to induce Southern Democrats who have always feared a 'force bill,' if cloture were possible with Republicans in control, not to oppose this change." Still, the new rule did change lawmaking in the Senate in subtle but important ways. One consequence was that the conditions for successfully defeating a filibuster were now explicit and predictable. As Eric Schickler and Greg Wawro have argued, senators effectively accepted a need to build supermajority legislative coalitions in exchange for a greater degree of confidence in passage. But the two-thirds requirement also institutionalized the power of large minorities to obstruct legislation, almost perfectly calibrated to empower the South. If all senators were present and voting, then cloture required thirty-two senators to be invoked—two fewer than the number of southern senators. Not only would committed, large minorities—as the South was on issues that impinged upon white supremacy—be able to obstruct legislation, but their ability to do so was if anything strengthened. The cloture rule, then, charted a clear path to successful obstruction of issues of significant importance to both parties, but only the South could be regularly expected to be capable of such obstruction. In short, southerners had successfully maneuvered an institutional change that did not, as the *Macon Telegraph* reassured its readers, amount to a "bona-fide cloture rule," at least not where southern priorities were concerned.[20]

Campaigning on a platform of having kept the country out of war, Wilson won reelection in a decision that seemed to herald a new configuration of partisan voting in the country. For the first time, the Democratic Party had won the presidency without carrying either Indiana or New York, and for the first time since 1856 it had won without the support of the Empire State. It was now California's four-thousand-vote margin, and thirteen electoral votes, that had been pivotal to Democratic success, a fact that western Democrats were quick to point out. Immediately after the results were in, they began dropping hints in public that the region should be rewarded with greater recognition on important committees. Other overlapping divisions also threatened the cohesion of the Democratic Party. Democrats opposed to prohibition, primarily from the Northeast, warned that they would ally with Republicans to deprive "dry" Democrats of seats on important committee chairs. With neither party having an outright majority in the House, the Democratic leadership in that chamber was pulled between the need to appeal to the independents and the rebellious "wets." Champ Clark was reelected speaker with the support of the progressives, the one prohibitionist, and Meyer London, the Socialist representative from New York, but only after a few extra committee seats were given to northern Democrats and the Ways and Means Committee was temporarily increased to be more representative.[21]

On March 21, the American ship the *Healdton* was sunk by the Germany navy, without warning or time to evacuate, despite sailing in a designated safe zone and bearing clear American markings. On April 2, Wilson asked the newly reconvened Congress to declare that a state of war existed between the United States and Germany.

Since the outbreak of the conflict, the South's posture toward the possibility of American involvement had been shaped by the shifting influence of administration loyalists who supported the policy of preparedness, isolationists who worried that preparedness was a prelude to participating in war, and a smaller contingent of interventionist lawmakers. Although isolationism in the South was perhaps not as strong or consistent a tendency as in the Midwest and Northeast, it was far from a fringe position. A poll of newspaper editors in 1914 showed that a higher proportion of the population in the South favored neutrality than was the case in any other section; constituent letters suggested that non-interventionism was strongest in the region's "rural counties and in the back country."[22]

Worried that Wilson was too aggressively asserting the rights of American neutrals—including the right to travel on armed enemy ships within the blockaded zone—Thomas Gore and Jeff: McLemore (the colon was part of his name) introduced a resolution prohibiting Americans from traveling on armed enemy ships. Under pressure from the administration, the House and Senate each voted to table it. Southerners both led the charge in favor of the resolution—including Gore, McLemore, Claude Kitchin, Robert Page, Edwin Webb of North Carolina, Hoke Smith, and William Stone, chair of the Senate Foreign Relations Committee—and also carried out the "cloakroom struggle" to table it and support Wilson. Georgia members of Congress prepared their own resolution, stating their full confidence in the administration, while Carter Glass, Byron Harrison of Mississippi, Thomas Heflin of Alabama, Thetus Sims of Tennessee, and Edward Pou of North Carolina organized Democratic support for the administration. "Shall I exclaim 'America first,'" asked John Sharp Williams, "or shall I sing 'Deutschland Uber Alles?'"[23]

Frank Park of Georgia voted to table the resolution, but insisted that this meant only that he was unwilling to encroach upon the executive's authority to conduct foreign relations: he asserted that he "would never be willing to vote for war, which would hurl the sons of the South to death and destruction." Avoiding entry into the conflict, argued Eugene Black of Texas, was an issue that demanded loyalty to country above loyalty to party. When Wilson requested a declaration of war, Claude Kitchin of North Carolina—majority leader since Underwood's accession to the Senate—prayed for guidance and concluded that it would be a "crime against civilization and humanity for this Christian nation to plunge into the war and make a slaughterhouse of the whole world." "No invasion is threatened," he noted in casting his vote against the war resolution, "not a foot of our territory is demanded or coveted. No essential honor is required to be sacrificed." Kitchin was joined by two Democratic representatives from Alabama, four from Missouri, one from South Carolina, and another from Texas—nine of the sixteen Democrats breaking ranks. Only six senators voted against war: James Vardaman, William Stone, Harry Lane of Oregon, and three Republicans from the Midwest.[24]

With the entry of the United States into the war, party lines collapsed almost completely on the floor of the Senate. Figures 8.1 and 8.2 trace the location of the party and regional medians across the three Congresses that sat between 1913 and 1919. Southern Democrats and other legislators divided over the terms of military enlistment, over a revenue bill to pay for national mobilization, over a price controls bill intended to rein in inflation as the nation geared up for war, and—somehow implicated in all of these issues—over the prohibition of the manufacture and sale of alcohol. In the House, there was more stability in partisan voting, but contemporary reports detailed a breakdown of party lines in committees, and a significant amount of within-party disagreement was kept out of sight only by the majority party's ability to set the agenda and keep divisive amendments from being considered.[25]

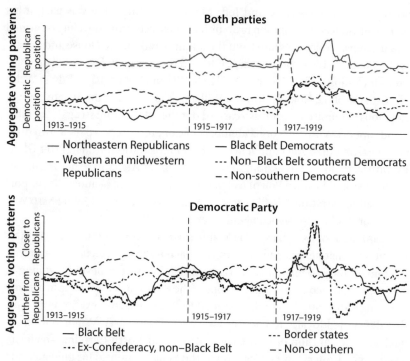

FIGURE 8.1. Location of Party and Regional Medians in the Senate, 1913–1919

When William McAdoo, the Secretary of the Treasury, requested an increase in revenues to fund the preparedness program in 1916, Kitchin used his position as chair of the Ways and Means Committee to draft a tax bill that doubled the top income tax rate, imposed the first inheritance tax since the Civil War, and placed an excess profits tax on munitions manufacturers, going well beyond what the administration had requested. Kitchin was reported as saying that since it was the North that wanted preparedness, it should be the North that paid for it. Although he denied saying these exact words, he was adamant that preparedness should be paid for by the firms most likely to profit.[26]

A year later, Kitchin proposed what he called "the greatest tax bill in the history of the world" to pay for the extraordinary projected costs of mobilizing the country for war. McAdoo had requested a 40 percent tax on all incomes over $1 million, but the Ways and Means Committee set it at 33 percent on all incomes over $500,000, made it retroactive, lowered the exemption, and made the overall structure more steeply progressive. At Kitchen's insistence, the revenue bill also included a large tax on excess profits, "an approach Republicans derisively labeled 'Kitchinism,'" and one they deemed "particularly appealing to the nation's large rural constituencies." The excess profits tax was

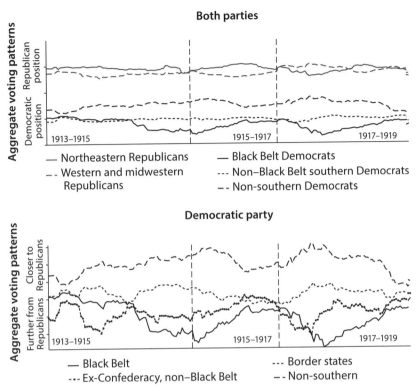

Both parties

— Northeastern Republicans
_ . Western and midwestern Republicans
— Black Belt Democrats
--- Non–Black Belt southern Democrats
_ . Non-southern Democrats

Democratic party

— Black Belt
... Ex-Confederacy, non–Black Belt
--- Border states
_ . Non-southern

FIGURE 8.2. Location of Party and Regional Medians in the House, 1913–1919

not aimed just at war profits: it was also seen as a way to tax "the profits accruing to monopoly power." Party lines in the Ways and Means Committee broke down almost completely. After a fight in which income tax rates were raised further, the revenue bill passed unanimously. On the floor, a proposal by Democrat Edward Keating of Colorado to simply confiscate all income above $150,000 was rejected, as was an effort by Joseph Sherley of Kentucky to broaden the base and increase the rates. When Irvine Lenroot, a Wisconsin Republican, proposed to increase the rates for each tax bracket and to create a new bracket for incomes over $1 million, to be taxed at 55 percent, Kitchin announced that the Treasury was now requesting even more money, and he dropped his opposition to further amend the bill on the floor. On May 23, the legislation passed, 329 to 76, with primarily northeastern Republicans in opposition and with all southerners except the region's nine Republicans in favor.[27]

Before the revenue bill could be considered on the floor, however, the Senate had to complete the food price control bill. The war, combined with smaller than anticipated crops, was wreaking havoc on agricultural markets.

Trading on the American grain futures market was suspended, as there was insufficient grain to fill existing contracts. In February, women in northeastern cities rioted in response to the steep increase in prices. The hungry "wives, mothers, and daughters" of striking workers in Philadelphia, unable to afford the high prices, attacked police officers and black strikebreakers. After a few days of riots in New York, women began organizing picket lines to enforce a boycott of merchants. While government sources suggested that the riots were the work of German provocateurs, newspapers across the country demanded quick action by the government to stamp out the speculators, fix prices, or—as one Louisiana paper suggested—"seize food stores and sell them at their actual value."[28]

Wilson's food administration bill proposed a sweeping grant of executive authority, although it was deliberately vague on details. The chair of the Senate Agriculture Committee, the old Populist Thomas Gore of Oklahoma, reportedly "flew the coop." He became obsessed with reducing government expenditures and condemned the administration's plan to regulate the country's food supply. Unwilling to impede a core component of Wilson's emergency legislation, he left Asbury Lever of South Carolina, the chair of the House Committee on Agriculture, to play the most important role in defining the administration's proposal. Presenting what he called a "war measure pure and simple," Lever warned that "the wrath of the people is not going to be appeased by the screams and squalls about conferring autocratic powers on the President."[29]

Of course, opponents stressed exactly this, highlighting the dangers of stretching the war power, misusing the interstate commerce clause, or going beyond the enumerated powers of the Constitution. Hardwick urged the administration to use the Clayton antitrust bill to rein in food speculators, arguing that the constitutional power of Congress was being "stretched until it covered, like a blanket, every business and every industry in this Republic, until it covered every enterprise that human ingenuity could devise and operate." Senators Gore and Reed were opposed to the creation of a single administrative agency charged with managing agricultural prices, while McLemore and Slayden of Texas, as well as Vardaman, worried that it established an authority without clear foundation in the Constitution and not necessarily tied to the war effort. Lever probably undercut his own efforts when he was reported to say that "if I should ever meet the world leader of socialism I would say to him, 'take off your hat to me for I give you a measure that is more socialistic than any you ever dreamed of.' "[30]

Others were less concerned with constitutional issues than with the costs the law would impose on farmers. The *South Alabamian* commented that "it is not for the southern farmer to bother his head over the terrible strain of wage earners to buy foods. That is the wage earner's trouble, not the farmers. . . . It is for our farmers to make money and plenty of it while the making is good." Members of Congress usually had more tact, with Young of Texas warning Congress not to "tie the hands that feed us." "The farmers are being driven off the farms because they are not prospering on the farms," he noted, but claimed that were they left alone, unhampered by class legislation and allowed to profit off the rise in prices, they would "feed not only our Army and our allies but [also] . . . the starving nations." Although Young did "not want to do anything that will make me get down on my knees to the socialists of this country," he supported extreme measures to curb speculation: instead of price controls, he wanted Congress to "control exchanges, boards of trade, speculators, and your hoarders, and when you have done that the farmer is satisfied and happy."[31]

The bill passed the House 365 to 5, with only three Texas representatives voting against it.

Lever had been very careful to make sure that the bill's exclusive focus would be food supplies, not a broader range of commodities. Most important, the measure covered wheat—the major agricultural product of the Midwest and much of Texas and Oklahoma—but not cotton. Southern cotton farmers, who barely had recovered from the price depression of 1914, were especially worried by the prospect of price controls, and Young tried to turn southerners against the proposal by insinuating that it would empower the food administrator to reduce the cotton price:

> I want to burn this into you gentlemen who represent this committee from the Southern States: You have got to answer it to your constituencies in the States you come from, and I want especially to refer to my friend from Alabama, [Mr. Heflin], who talks so eloquently in season and out of season about cotton—I want to burn this into him: In the year 1914 his people were absolutely driven to starvation by reason of the prices of cotton going to nothing on account of this war. Cotton is now worth 25 cents a pound. Let my eloquent friend explain to the Alabama farmer about cotton; Let him explain why this Government in 1914 was asked to give the cotton farmers relief, and why in 1917, with the war still on, when cotton is selling at 25 cents a pound, you now say we give you a dictator to cut down that price. The cotton farmer still owes his debts of 1914. Now he has a chance to get even with his losses of 1914.—Explain that to him in the South.[32]

Westerners demanded that the issue be revisited in the Senate. An amendment to include cotton passed with eight southern senators, including two Republicans, in favor and with fourteen opposed. Immediately there was an uproar across the region. Many southern members of Congress pressed Wilson to intervene to ensure that the provision would be struck from the final bill, as it was. Party lines broke down entirely, and the final bill passed almost unanimously.[33]

As a concession to the wheat representatives, the administration agreed to set a minimum price for wheat, now the main commodity subject to price controls. But the price set by the administration was lower than the market rate and quickly eroded as prices for other goods rose dramatically. For the remainder of the war, westerners would introduce legislation fixing the price of cotton, only for these to be sent to Lever's committee to die. Subsequent efforts to raise the minimum price for wheat were cut down by the Senate Agriculture Committee, then cut down further by the House; when one did pass Congress, it promptly was vetoed by Wilson, despite "frantic appeals from western Democratic congressmen that such a course would be ruinous to them in the coming election." The veto was sustained, with two representatives from Oklahoma and one from Virginia providing the only southern Democratic votes in support of the majority of midwesterners.[34]

The Senate could now take up the House revenue bill, which had been pulled apart in Furnifold Simmons's conservative Finance Committee. "Manufacturers, jobbers and retailers in many lines," reported the *Wilmington Morning Star*, "flocked to the Senate committee hearings to protest" against the excise taxes and tax on stock dividends. Under Simmons's guidance, the committee decided against raising anything near what the Treasury had requested, struck out the tariff increases, the inheritance tax increases, changed the income surtax rates, and replaced the excess profits tax with a war profits tax. Gore, Thomas, and La Follette voted against reporting the bill because they preferred raising more revenue through taxes on corporations and excess profits rather than on small incomes or consumption.[35]

When it reached the floor, the southern senatorial leadership found itself unable to "counteract the influence of several little cliques." A progressive faction led by La Follette, Gore, Hollis, and Borah proposed to further increase taxes on the rich. A coterie of southern members led by Underwood and Bankhead wanted "to make audible the distress of the cotton planter and manufacturer." Stone and James Reed of Missouri, as well as Vardaman, seemed to engage in obstruction solely for the purpose of opposing the president and any war measure. Under pressure from La Follette and Hardwick, Simmons relented and agreed to restore the higher House rates and implement an excess profits tax.[36]

The Revenue Act was a dramatic reconfiguration of the tax burden, broadening the base while imposing heavy burdens on corporations and the wealthy. The top rate, which applied to incomes over $2 million, was increased from

15 to 67 percent, while the deduction was lowered from $20,000 to $2,000; a year later, the top rate would be increased even further, to 77 percent.

The result of these conflicting priorities was that party lines in the Senate in the opening months of the 65th Congress effectively disappeared as a factor structuring members' votes. There was no sharp division between progressives and conservatives, however, but rather different regional alignments depending on the issue at stake. Figure 8.3 shows the location of party and region medians on political economy issues, largely taxes, and on planning and resources issues, namely, the price control bill. Figure 8.4 traces the median location of five regional-party blocs, from the beginning until the end of the 65th Congress, across the issue areas of political economy and resources and planning. On the issue of price controls, southern Democrats generally aligned with the urban Northeast in defense of a policy that would control food prices—which was especially important in the cities—while leaving cotton farmers free to sell at the market price. On taxation, the South was more likely to vote with progressive Republicans, generally from the Midwest, and to support higher income taxes, excess profit taxes, and a more progressive tax structure. On both policies, the South was divided, with its lawmakers appearing on each side of the crucial divisions.

One of the more remarkable innovations was the nationalization of the country's railroads, first by presidential decree and then by southern Democrats who lined up to back Wilson's actions. Not a single southern Democrat voted against legislation authorizing public control in the House, and only Thomas Hardwick and Hoke Smith voted against it in the Senate. "Cotton" Ed Smith guided the route to passage, while Vardaman called for permanent public control over all railroads. William McAdoo, who was popular in the South, boasted in 1917 that government control of the railroads during the war necessarily would lead to public ownership: "We have it now," he said, "the eggs are being scrambled; after the war no railway management will be able to say 'This is my egg.' "[37]

In part because of fears over its impact on their region's racial order, southerners long had been opposed to government ownership of railroads, and this still was the case. Most probably took the position of Joseph Robinson, or the newly elected Martin Dies of Texas, who disavowed "government ownership in principle" but were willing to support it as an emergency measure. A bloc of southern Democrats joined with conservative Republicans to block McAdoo's proposal that the government be allowed to maintain control indefinitely. Instead, the House Committee on Interstate Commerce voted to return the roads to private ownership two years after ratification of a peace treaty. The committee chair, Thetus Sims of Tennessee, and five other Democrats, including three southerners, had supported McAdoo's proposal, but they were

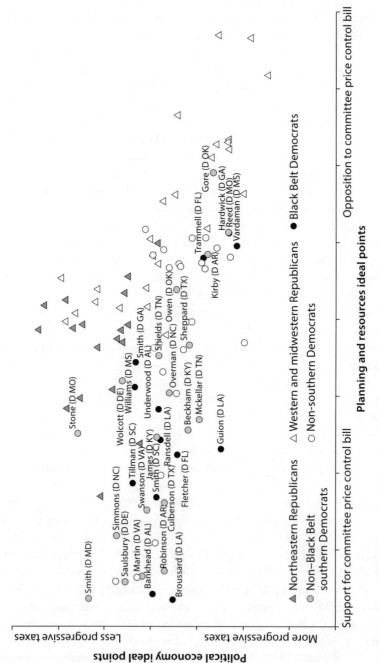

FIGURE 8.3. Senate Ideal Points on Political Economy and on Resources and Planning, 65th Congress

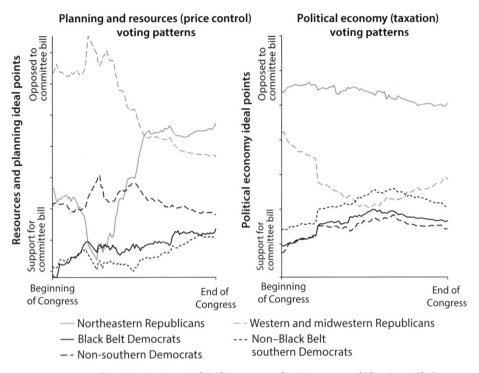

FIGURE 8.4. Regional-Partisan Voting on Political Economy and on Resources and Planning, 65th Congress

defeated by five Democrats, including Sam Rayburn, who voted with all Republicans to impose a time limit.[38]

———

Wilson had been outraged at the willingness of some southern Democrats to oppose his administration's preparedness and mobilization policies. He would take his revenge in the midterm elections of 1918 by embarking on a campaign to "purge antiwar southern Democrats" from the party. In primary elections in Georgia, South Carolina, Texas, and Mississippi, Wilson used the patriotic fervor that accompanied entry into the war to call for the defeat of legislators who had opposed him. In Georgia, former Populist Tom Watson—whose magazine had been denied access to the mail on the grounds of its opposition to the war—was defeated in his primary election bid by Carl Vinson. Thomas Hardwick lost his seat after Wilson wrote a letter to the *Atlanta Constitution* urging his defeat. The former governor of South Carolina, Cole Blease, a demagogue even too vitriolic for Tillman to stomach, was beaten in the primary because of his opposition to the war, as was Jeff: McLemore of Texas. James

Slayden, who served as president of the American Peace Society, saw the writing on the wall and withdrew from the race, having served in Congress since 1897. Wilson's "most impressive victory," however, came in Mississippi, where the issue of unquestioning loyalty rallied opponents of James Vardaman, the vicious white supremacist who had dominated the state's politics for almost two decades. Of those southerners who had taken the most aggressive position against Wilson and the war, only Claude Kitchin and Edward Almon of Alabama survived the summer.[39]

Wilson scored important victories in his southern purge, but he was unable to hold together the progressive coalition that had sustained Democrats in power since the House elections of 1910. Republicans picked up seats across the country, taking a slim two-seat majority in the Senate and a forty-eight-seat majority in the House. A week later, the armistice ending hostilities in Europe went into effect. The years of southern control were over, and the international and domestic conditions that had provided the context for progressive reforms were coming to an end.

Southern Reaction

The end of the war brought a resurgence of conservatism among southern Democrats, as a backlash against some of the extraordinary powers granted to the federal government began to set in. Sam Rayburn, for instance, whose first legislative proposal had been for the federal government to directly regulate the issue of all railroad stocks and bonds, now expressed his desire to "see all of these war powers repealed and the Government get out of these expensive and socialistic businesses. I want to get back to normal."[40]

Addressing Congress in December 1919, Wilson offered a message that generally pleased southern conservatives. He called for a reduction in taxes, but not so far as would necessitate a return to high tariff levels. "American business is full grown," he wrote, "and America is the greatest capitalist in the world." He called for a "genuine democratization of industry, based upon the full recognition of the right of those who work, in whatever rank, to participate in some organic way in every decision which directly affects their welfare." But he warned strikers that "there is a predominant right" over their right to strike, "and that is the right of the Government to protect all of its people and to assert its power and majesty against the challenge of any class." The administration, led by Attorney General A. Mitchell Palmer, recently had secured an injunction against striking coal and steel workers under the Lever Price Control Act's prohibition of interference with the production of necessities, which Wilson had promised would not be applied to labor. The strike was repressed when four thousand troops were sent to the coal fields, and a railroad strike was averted when the administration made clear that the government would use all means available to defeat it. With over three thousand ongoing strikes, Wilson's message to Congress cheered southern conservatives.[41]

Still, on most labor issues southern Democrats continued to align with their northern copartisans and with the American Federation of Labor, reflecting a mix of progressivism with the recognition that the labor movement was a potentially pivotal constituency for the national Democratic Party. Alben Barkley of Kentucky, for instance, was the cosponsor of the Howell-Barkley bill, which proposed to enforce a closed shop on the railroads with the sixteen national railroad unions, making them the exclusive contractual agents of the railroad workers. On May 5, 1924, the House voted 194 to 181 to discharge the bill out of the Interstate and Foreign Commerce Committee, with only twenty-four southern Democrats not siding with the majority. Still, the South provided all but four of the Democratic votes against discharge, as well as a considerable number of votes in favor of the remarkable Republican filibuster effort that followed and ultimately defeated the proposal.[42]

When questions of labor regulation would have had a direct impact in the region, southern lawmakers were even more likely to stake out a conservative position. This was especially true on the question of child labor, which saw many southern Democrats join with conservative Republicans who were opposed to further regulation of private industry. In 1912, southern Democrats had provided the bulk of opposition to establishing a Children's Bureau in the Department of Labor as well as to a bill prohibiting child labor in the District of Columbia, both of which were seen as entering wedges to national regulation. Progressive Hoke Smith pled in vain with his fellow southerners to support the bureau, arguing that it would not in any way impinge on states' rights. Southern senators tried to amend the District child labor bill in order to prohibit officials from entering private homes, and they divided evenly on final passage, with its defenders arguing that the bill took into account the unique relationship of Congress to the District and did not imply support for regulating labor in the states.[43]

Soon after the District bill passed, members of Congress began advocating for national legislation. In 1914, a small band of southerners had waged a filibuster in the House and threatened to keep the Senate in session all summer if a national child labor bill was not abandoned. In early 1915, the House Labor Committee voted unanimously to report a bill drafted by Robert Owen of Oklahoma and A. Mitchell Palmer of Pennsylvania, which passed 233 to 43 under suspension of the rules. Only two of the opposing votes came from outside of the South. Unanimous consent was denied in the Senate, and the bill died with adjournment. "We of the South oppose this measure," remarked the agrarian pacifist, and advocate of high taxes, Claude Kitchin, "because we believe our people who have to work should be permitted to do so." Wilson

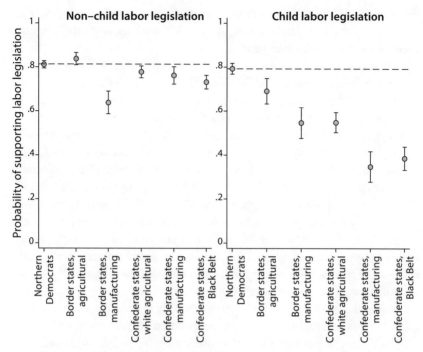

FIGURE 8.5. Probability of Democratic Support for Labor Legislation, 1900–1932. Dashed line is the northern Democratic average.

adamantly insisted on a vote before the 1916 elections, and his intervention was decisive. Some southerners, recognizing that the bill was likely to pass sooner or later, urged the party to "take advantage of [the bill's] possible political effect." Brought up, it passed the Senate with only twelve votes in opposition, all but two of them from the South.[44]

In a 1918 case originating in North Carolina, the Supreme Court struck down the child labor law on the grounds that it was an unconstitutional use of the commerce clause. Later that year, progressives renewed their efforts by passing legislation that imposed a punitive tax on companies employing children under the age of sixteen (in mines) or fourteen (in factories and mills). Again, the bulk of opposition came from the South, combined with a few northeastern conservative Republicans. This statute, too, was struck down by the Court in another North Carolina case. In consequence, progressives tried in 1924 to amend the Constitution, with most of the opposition coming from southern lawmakers.

As George Tindall and others have noted, "The child labor controversy revealed a division in Southern opinion." Figure 8.5 shows the probability that Democratic members of Congress between 1900 and 1932 would support legislation regulating labor conditions and prohibiting child labor by region and

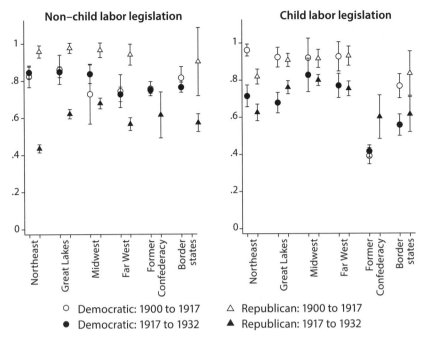

FIGURE 8.6. Probability of Support for Labor Legislation, Both Parties, 1900–1932

state. Figure 8.6 looks at patterns of support for labor legislation across the two parties and across two distinct time periods: from 1900 to the beginning of Wilson's second term in 1917 (white markers), and from then until the end of the Hoover administration (black markers).[45]

On most labor legislation, the South was distinctive but not radically out of step with non-southern Democrats. Delaware Democrats voted more like Republicans from the industrial Northeast, while Maryland and Mississippi voted in line with Republicans in general; Arkansas and Oklahoma voted in favor of labor legislation at roughly the rates of northeastern or Great Lakes Democrats. In 1917, Democratic levels of support remained relatively constant, while Republicans moved sharply against labor; though southern voting patterns had not changed, the region's members now were voting more frequently with Republicans on labor policy than before.

On the issue of child labor, the South clearly was distinctive. The section's growing manufacturing and mining sectors employed thousands of children, and the depth of southern poverty made many families dependent on the income provided by their laboring children. Moreover, the proposals advanced by progressives—to prohibit entry into interstate commerce of products made by child labor, or to impose punitive excise taxes on employers using children under certain ages or at certain times—relied on a broad interpretation of the

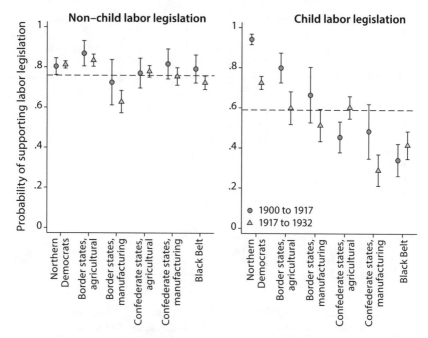

FIGURE 8.7. Probability of Democratic Support in Regional Subgroups for Labor and Child Labor Legislation, 1900–1932. Dashed lines are the Democratic average.

federal government's regulatory authority and thus perhaps posed a greater threat to the constitutional safeguards that protected southern labor practices and the region's racial hierarchy. Unsurprisingly, the states most reliant on child labor—North Carolina, South Carolina, Florida, and Georgia—were most opposed to its prohibition.

Figure 8.7 breaks down southern opposition into specific subregions. The Democratic lawmakers most likely to oppose labor legislation came from manufacturing districts in the border states, where a growing industrial base and a sharpening of union demands during and after the war led to a higher than usual level of opposition among southern Democrats. The Democrats most opposed to child labor laws likewise came from southern districts with substantial manufacturing bases, especially in the former Confederacy, and from Black Belt districts. After 1919, southern Democrats from the white agricultural regions of the former Confederacy became more likely to support child labor legislation, while members who represented the growing manufacturing base in the former Confederacy became especially opposed.

The proposed constitutional amendment passed Congress but was not ratified by the states. Arkansas was the first to ratify the amendment, in 1924, but few others followed suit; by 1938, when it was rendered moot by passage of the Fair Labor Standards Act, the amendment had been ratified by only

twenty-eight states, with Oklahoma, Kentucky, and West Virginia the only
southern states to join Arkansas. The only non-southern states to reject the
amendment were conservative New York, Massachusetts, Connecticut, and
Vermont, plus the generally progressive South Dakota and Nebraska.

When child labor first appeared on the congressional agenda, conservative
Texan Joseph Bailey had complained that its very consideration was a trou-
bling reflection of the insidious feminization of politics: "The more a woman
knows about the things she ought to know about, the less she knows about
things we are doing here." The coalition that had been evident on child labor
was also apparent on the issue of women's suffrage, which either isolated
southern Democrats from the rest of the country or aligned them with conservative Republicans from the Northeast and the Great Lakes region.[46]

As was true across the country, suffrage for women was decried as threatening patriarchy. But opponents in the South could also draw on reasons more
particular to their region, arguing that a suffrage amendment would undermine white supremacy by reopening the question of federal involvement in
voting regulations and making it more difficult to resort to the extreme methods sometimes used to keep blacks from the polls. Frank Clark of Florida
pointed out that the proposed amendment included the same dangerous
clause that had appeared in the Reconstruction Amendments, giving "Congress the full, absolute, unrestricted, and exclusive power to 'enforce this article,' and to enforce it by 'appropriate legislation.'" "This opens up anew the
negro question in all the Southern States," he warned, a "Pandora's box" that
would inevitably produce "another 'reconstruction' conflagration in our
Southland." He also suggested to his northern colleagues that the potential
radicalism of black voters now had an analogue in the North, with "your Bolsheviki, with your anarchists, with your I.W.W.'s." Indeed, it was the potential
intersection of black voting and radicalism that he found most threatening,
the danger that the "negro women of the Southern States, under the tutelage
of the fast-growing socialistic element of our common country," would insist
on political participation and social equality, thereby reawakening "in the
negro men an intense and not easily quenched desire to again become a political factor." There would, as a result of the immigration that was sure to resume
after the conclusion of the war, be "white Bolsheviki" readily available to organize black men and women into politics.[47]

Nathan Bryan of Florida insisted that Calhoun's "concurrent majority"
should continue to apply, that the right of local communities to arrange their
own "internal affairs" was an essential bulwark of political liberty, and that
since the amendment threatened this protection, it should be subject to a
southern veto. "If the Democratic party stands for one thing above all others,"
conservative southerners argued, "it is the right of local self-government and
that the right of franchise should be governed by the States of the Union and

not by the national government." Southern opposition defeated the amendment on several occasions before it finally passed in 1919.[48]

Suffrage for women never was an issue that unanimously arrayed white southerners against other regions. There was a suffrage movement in every southern state, although they varied in its size and level of activism. Both the southern suffrage movement and its opponents stressed the importance of maintaining white supremacy. In 1916, the Alabama Anti-Suffrage Society was organized around "the motto of 'Home rule, states' rights, and white supremacy,'" with Nellie V. Baker, "one of the wealthiest women of Selma," elected president. The suffragist movement in the South focused more on state than national action and defended women's suffrage as needed to buttress white supremacy, while southern legislators often conditioned their support for a national amendment on the simultaneous repeal of the Fifteenth Amendment or on limiting the proposed suffrage amendment to white women only.[49]

Patterns of white southern opposition to women's suffrage followed clear regional lines, in many ways mirroring the patterns of opposition to national child labor laws. Figures 8.8 and 8.9 show the probability that representatives and senators from different states and subregions supported a women's suffrage amendment. Legislators from West Virginia, Missouri, Oklahoma, and Arkansas were most consistently supportive, followed by those from Tennessee, Texas, Maryland, and Kentucky. These states had relatively small African American populations, making the maintenance of white supremacy at the ballot box a less resonant worry. Arkansas and Oklahoma also had a tradition of radicalism that produced strong support for other progressive priorities. These would be the only southern states to ratify the amendment before 1923, when they were joined by Delaware. Opposition was strongest in the Deep South and the Black Belt. Democratic support increased across the board as the decade progressed, leaving southern anti-suffrage representatives complaining that their allies were abandoning a principled position in favor of states' rights to the "shifting sands of expediency."[50]

Southern conservatism generally left the region isolated or in a contingent alliance with a scattered cluster of northeastern Republicans. But it could also be manifested in alliances with Republicans from the West and Midwest, as issues on which the South was distinctively conservative dovetailed with a broader rural and small-town reaction to the growing influence of cities. For decades, southern lawmakers had joined with the rest of the country to support restrictions on immigration, in particular immigration from China. Anarchists and epileptics were excluded by the Immigration Act of 1903, which passed with only a few southerners voting nay, on the grounds that the legislation had been "emasculated" in the Senate. The Immigration Act of 1907 imposed additional restrictions on persons judged to be "defective," as well as prohibiting certain arrangements for soliciting or financing the immigration

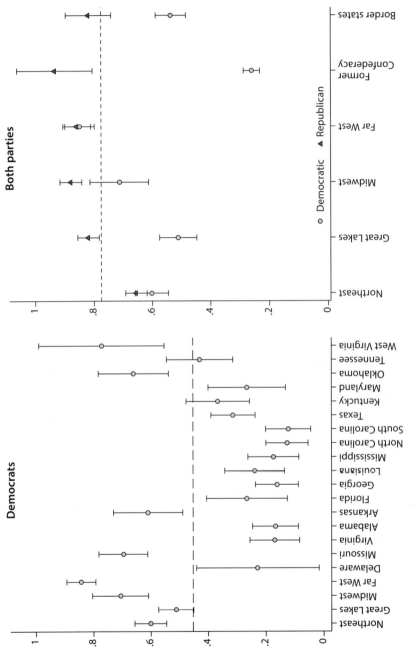

FIGURE 8.8. Support for Women's Suffrage, 1913–1921. Dashed line in the left panel is the Republican average. Dashed line in the right panel is the Democratic average.

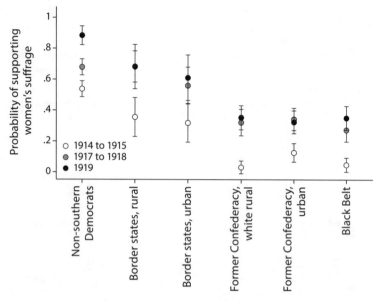

FIGURE 8.9. Support for Women's Suffrage in Regional Subgroups, 1914–1919

of laborers. With a few exceptions, most southern lawmakers supported these restrictions, and what opposition there was centered on Roosevelt's insistence that the law accommodate the famous "Gentlemen's Agreement of 1907" by allowing but not requiring the exclusion of Japanese laborers. Simmons announced that he would vote for the measure "because I believe the South will not suffer under its provisions," and because—as the *Times-Democrat* put it— he placed "a higher importance on maintaining the amity and good feeling which he said had always existed between the South and the Pacific coast on labor and other questions." In the House, John Sharp Williams announced his solidarity "with the California delegation in antagonism to the admission of Japanese coolies, and this not on the ground of race inferiority, but solely for the reason that the two races were different and unassimilable."[51]

The Immigration Restriction League had been arguing for years that only immigrants who could pass a literacy test should be allowed into the country. The implications were profound; to that date there had been no provision for "materially reducing the volume of immigration," as the restrictions had been limited in their scope or targeted against populations who amounted to a small proportion of the total, especially outside of the West. A literacy test, however, would lead to a massive reduction in the number of European immigrants accepted into the United States. In part because of the opposition of their northeastern copartisans, and in part because many localities in the South were looking to attract European immigrants, literacy restriction initially had only divided support in the region. In 1897, Grover Cleveland vetoed a literacy test bill; just a small majority of southern Democrats had supported the conference report in the House, and a considerable majority opposed it in the Senate.[52]

In the subsequent decades, southern support for immigration restrictions become more pronounced. Southerners extolled the supposedly Anglo-Saxon origins of the region's population, its ostensible racial purity, its "genuine" American-ness. "The southern people for the most part are a homogeneous people," claimed one southerner, excluding from his definition of the people the large African American population: "There are Mexicans on the southwestern border; there are French-speaking Americans in Louisiana; there are Italians along the Gulf Coast; there are other foreigners in comparatively small numbers scattered here and there. But for the most part the southern people are a homogeneous people descended from early American settlers, preserving in large measure the ideals, the traditions of their fathers." The *Wilmington Weekly Star* noted with relief that since most immigrants were headed to the North, the South would remain "conspicuously the section of the least mixture and the most genuinely American, which in the long run will be a good thing for the South, because it means less friction and fewer conflicting elements." "The Southerners, as a race," declared Ellison Smith, "believe in restricting immigration. They do not care for illiterate foreigners." "By the 1920's," writes Tindall, "nativism in the South had become a peculiar expression of sectionalism in terms of nationalism." White southerners often claimed that they alone maintained American ideals and traditions in their unadulterated Anglo-Saxon form, even making the extraordinary claim that because of this only the "southern states have never rebelled against the Constitution of the United States."[53]

Non-southern Democrats, however, were becoming increasingly responsive to the concerns of immigrant communities, including their fear that the restrictions, besides explicitly marking them as racially inferior and distinctive, would limit their ability to bring family and friends to America. Each new restriction caused great stress in the Democratic Party. When Congress again passed a literacy test in the final years of the Taft administration, the South was nearly unanimous in favor while non-southern Democrats largely were opposed. In 1915 and 1917, literacy tests were passed by Congress; both times they were met with a veto by President Wilson. In the latter year, however, the veto was overturned, with strong southern support.[54]

Figure 8.10 conveys the development of voting patterns on this issue. The y-axes are labeled according to whether legislators tended to be more or less supportive of restrictions. In the earlier years, party was such an important factor that many of the votes were partisan even when there was broad agreement over basic principles. Over the course of the period, however, party lines

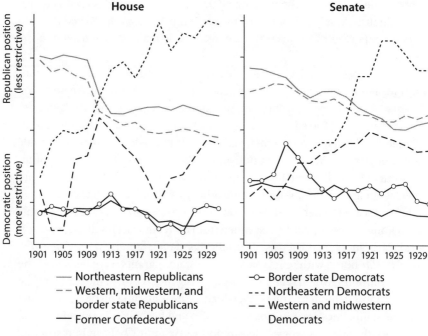

FIGURE 8.10. Development of Party Positions on Immigration, 1900–1930

broke down entirely. Legislators' voting records mapped more closely with the underlying question of how far restrictions should go. By approximately 1910, the southern and non-southern wings of the Democratic Party in the House clearly had separated; this division was muted in the Senate only because more of the non-southern Democratic senators came from the rural West than from northeastern or heavily urbanized states. The Republican Party also was shifting toward a more restrictive position, a movement evident in the positions of progressives and conservatives, westerners and northeasterners. Immigration restriction long had been advocated by many progressives in order to "substitute a so-called scientific and planned policy for a policy of laissez faire," but its appeal rested not so much on the promise of a more deliberate immigration policy, but on a promise to end the influx of persons who were seen as racially inferior, culturally dangerous, and religiously suspect. This appeal resonated in every region and locale across the country, but varied in strength; it was strongest in the South, the Midwest, and the West. Between 1921 and 1933, southern Democrats' similarity scores with northeastern Democrats, northeastern Republicans, western and midwestern Democrats, and western and midwestern Republicans were 42, 60, 76, and 65, respectively, with the South the region most consistently opposed to immigration.[55]

The nativist movement gained new strength and urgency after the war, buttressed by the Klan and also by the Anti-Saloon League. The Russian Revolution led to widespread panic that foreign agitators would foment revolution in the United States. Just as the strikes of the 1870s had been interpreted through the lens of the Commune, those of the postwar years were portrayed as part of a broader scheme to overthrow capitalism and America's government. The *Macon Daily Telegraph* claimed that a "New York negro was high in command" of the Bolshevik Party in Russia, and that the majority of its leaders were New York and Philadelphia Jews, either former members or "great believer[s] in the I.W.W. of the United States." Russia, it explained to its southern readers, "is experiencing now what each Southern State experienced during the period of 'Reconstruction.'"[56]

An emergency quota bill was passed in the final weeks of Wilson's presidency, with over 95 percent of southern Democratic representatives and senators and only 15 percent of northern Democratic representatives voting in favor. Wilson proceeded with a pocket veto, but the new president, Warren Harding, who had made immigration restriction a central theme of his campaign, oversaw the quick passage of the legislation in an even more exclusionary form. The Quota Act of 1921 passed with broad cross-party support, even though a majority of southern lawmakers had repeatedly voted against other regions to strengthen its exclusions, supporting a two-year prohibition on all immigration and opposing an amendment to exempt persecuted religious minorities. The act established what would become the basic framework for American immigration law until 1965. It restricted the number of immigrants from any country to 3 percent of the number of persons from that country resident in the United States in 1910, and when it went into effect, annual immigration levels were reduced by more than half, most of the reduction coming from southern and eastern Europe. The Immigration Act of 1924 made the national-origins quota system permanent, reducing the quota to 2 percent and using the 1890 census as the benchmark. For the rest of the decade, southern Democrats would vote consistently in favor of further restricting immigration and against measures that would liberalize existing law in any way.[57]

On none of these issues was the South unanimous; nor were southern lawmakers always successful. Their inability to block child labor legislation was redeemed only by a Supreme Court that was even more conservative and by supermajority requirements for constitutional amendments, but even these proved insufficient to protect the South from the perils of women voting. Immigration restriction was successful only because the priorities of southern Democrats were shared by pivotal blocs of Republicans from the West and Midwest, where the organizing of the Klan was helping to give local force to nativism.

But on the most important issue, the foundational issue of the southern Democratic Party, the region was unified and triumphantly successful. World War I had profoundly disrupted every region of the country, perhaps none more so than the South, and the stress placed on American racial hierarchies was significant. White racist sensitivities were further irritated by black veterans who refused to submit to the elaborate display of submission and humiliation often demanded of them. At least thirteen black veterans of the Great War were lynched. Others were stripped of their uniforms by angry mobs, the act of wearing their country's uniform being too grave a threat to their country's racial order. One returning soldier, Daniel Mack, was sentenced to a chain gang after a white man pushed him off a sidewalk. In his defense, Mack demanded his rights as a soldier-citizen of the United States: "I fought for you in France to make the world safe for democracy. I don't think you've treated me right in putting me in jail and keeping me there, because I've got as much right as anyone to walk on the sidewalk." To this, the judge responded that "this is a white man's country and you don't want to forget it."[58]

This was the context for the summer of 1919, a season of violence that amounted, in John Hope Franklin's estimation, to the "greatest period of interracial strife the nation had ever witnessed." When middle-class black residents of Ocoee, Florida, began organizing a voter registration drive, the Klan helped guide a mob to massacre the town's African American residents and raze it to the ground. Hundreds of farm laborers were killed in Elaine, Arkansas. The violence that most gripped the attention of the nation broke out in East St. Louis, Illinois. Black migration into the city had been accompanied by growing animosity among politicians, who complained that black voters had fraudulently swung local elections; trade unions and white workers who complained that migrants were being brought in to act as strikebreakers; real estate agents and property owners who complained that black residents were undermining home values; and a broad array of citizens who were led to believe by a sensational press that black migration was responsible for a local crime wave. First in May, then much more violently in early July, mobs of whites attacked black communities and individuals throughout the city, killing at least thirty-nine African Americans, leaving six thousand homeless, and forcing thousands to flee across the river to St. Louis. There was "no law or rule or anything else to curb mob violence," boasted Alexander Flannigan of Belleville, an attorney and local Republican politician who was one of the most active in calling for vigilantism. Never slow to sense opportunity, the Ku Klux Klan announced the establishment of an East St. Louis branch within a few weeks of the massacre.[59]

Black Americans had been organizing against lynching for decades, gaining national prominence with Ida Wells's pioneering articles in *Free Speech* and the *New York Age*. Black members of Congress had introduced anti-lynching legislation at the turn of the century, and the newly formed National Association for the Advancement of Colored People (NAACP) made lynching a central theme in its publication, *The Crisis*.[60]

The violence in East St. Louis provided an opening for activists to push anti-lynching onto the political agenda. In April 1918, Leonidas Dyer, a St. Louis Republican whose district had seen a large influx of African American migrants and refugees, introduced legislation to make lynching a federal felony, imposing penalties on local law enforcement and counties in which a lynching occurred. Dyer argued that the legislation was constitutionally justified on the same grounds as the ambitious legislative program supported and passed by southern Democrats under Wilson, including its price control legislation as well as child labor laws and the Eighteenth Amendment. He also based it on the Fourteenth Amendment and the police power of the United States. Still, influential Republicans doubted its constitutionality. Others suggested a different approach: Major J. E. Spingarn and Captain George S. Hornblower of the Army's Military Intelligence Branch testified before the House Committee that the issue of lynching was causing an enormous problem in the armed forces: "There is no question, so far as we are concerned, of the disloyalty of the colored people, but there is an unusual amount of bitterness which is spread by some 200 colored newspapers, most of which are absolutely unknown to the white people of the country; but these newspapers are read not only by colored civilians, but also in the Army camps by the colored soldiers." They recognized that the Dyer proposal "involves a large question of permanent public policy, with which the military can have no concern." Accordingly, Spingarn and Hornblower offered a substitute that was limited to the duration of the war and primarily concerned with black veterans and soldiers.[61]

In any case, southern Democratic control over the House Judiciary and Rules Committees ensured that no anti-lynching legislation would make any progress. When Republicans gained control over Congress in 1919, Dyer won the support of the Republican majority on the Judiciary Committee, only to see his bill languish on the House calendar. In June 1921, a race riot erupted in Tulsa, Oklahoma, that, like the massacre in East St. Louis, amounted to a mass pogrom of black residents. The lobbying campaign of the NAACP shifted into high gear as activists in the National Association of Colored Women "generated a stream of letters to congressmen" and the Harriet Tubman Club of Pennsylvania sent letters urging the state's Judiciary Committee members to vote to favorably report the anti-lynching bill. In the fall of 1921, with Republicans firmly in control of the House, the Senate, and the presidency, the anti-lynching bill passed the committee and was sent to the House.[62]

On December 19, it was brought up under a special rule providing for ten hours of general debate and amendments, after which the previous question would be considered as ordered and there would be a vote with no intervening motions but the motion to recommit. Southern Democrats succeeded in first delaying a vote on the resolution, and when the House was to go into the Committee of the Whole, enough of them were left to deny a quorum. When the presiding officer ordered the sergeant-at-arms to bring in the missing members, the Democratic minority leader—Finis Garrett of Tennessee—raised a point of order that this required a vote of the House. Overruled, Garrett pointed out that the sergeant-at-arms was away at the funeral of a deceased representative and that there was no deputy sergeant in the city. This too was overruled. Southern representatives repeatedly moved to adjourn, requested divisions, called for the yeas and nays, and suggested the absence of a quorum. They also yelled, "Sit down, niggers," at the black Americans in the galleries. The obstruction campaign forced Republican House leaders to delay consideration of the bill until after Christmas, when finally, on January 26, with hundreds of black Americans watching, the bill passed the House, 230 to 120.[63]

Despite a unanimous party caucus vote to oppose, seven northern Democrats supported passage, as did Ben Johnson of Kentucky, the first southern Democrat to break ranks on a civil rights measure. Two non-southern Democrats voted with the South, while ten more abstained or were absent. Southern Democrats were supported by seventeen Republicans, including six from the South, and a scattering of progressives and conservatives from the Northeast and West. But southern Republicans John Robison of Kentucky, Frederick Zihlman of Maryland, Henry Wurzbach of Texas, Brazilla Reece and James Taylor of Tennessee, Joseph Pringley and Lorraine Gensman of Oklahoma, and the entire Republican delegations from Missouri and West Virginia voted for passage, while Kentuckians John Langley and Charles Ogden—the latter elected with the overwhelming support of black voters in Louisville—made themselves scarce.[64]

The Dyer bill traveled to the Senate, since the 1890s the citadel of white supremacy, and the last institutional site in which the Democratic South could defeat civil rights legislation. Despite the new cloture rule, the Senate would continue in this role.

The Judiciary Committee reported the legislation in April 1922, but Republicans delayed bringing it up over the summer, and southerners were able to block consideration before the session's adjournment in September. After the November elections, Republicans tried once more in a special session called by Harding for this purpose, but again were defeated by southern senators. Their tactics highlight the weakness of a cloture rule they had helped design. Rather than filibuster during debate, which Underwood made clear would happen if the bill was actually made the issue under consideration, southerners proposed dilatory motions before the reading of the *Senate Journal*. Thus, by expanding a loophole in the rule that they had designed, they were able to ensure that the issue was never made the pending business of the chamber.[65]

On December 2, the Republican caucus voted to take up other business. Despite an extraordinary effort on the part of the NAACP, the supporters were defeated by the Senate's rules. The new cloture arrangement enabled thirty-two senators to obstruct legislation indefinitely, making the thirty-four southern senators all but certain of their prospects for success. Standing nearly alone, southern senators, in George Rable's account, had "stopped federal legislation against lynching simply by displaying greater determination and resolution than their opponents." The belief that the South could unilaterally, and relatively easily, defeat civil rights legislation would endure for decades.[66]

Even on this issue, the single most important legislative priority of the NAACP and the broader network of black activists, the Republican Party's support was half-hearted. It was widely observed among contemporaries that the legislation was supported by the Republican leadership in part for position-taking purposes in the run-up to the congressional elections of 1922. "Democrats do not hesitate," noted the *New York Times*, "to charge that the bill is a political move to solidify the negro vote for the Republicans, particularly in Massachusetts, where Senator Lodge is up for re-election." Although the support of the party leadership was not perfunctory, their legislative choices were hardly calculated to maximize chances for passage. For example, responsibility for the legislation in the Senate was given to a relative novice, Samuel Shortridge of California, who quickly lost control of the floor in September and allowed southern senators to delay consideration.[67]

There was even less support from the Republican leadership on other civil rights questions, as seen in the repeated effort to reduce southern representation as mandated by the Fourteenth Amendment. In 1920, Republican George Holden Tinkham of Boston introduced an amendment to a proposed congressional apportionment bill authorizing the Census Committee to inquire into the extent of disfranchisement in the United States. At a meeting of the Republican caucus, after Virginia representative Campbell Slemp warned that this initiative would undercut potential Republican gains in the region, it was shelved by a vote of 42 to 95. Tinkham's proposal did receive strong support from George H. Murray of the Colored American Council, James Weldon Johnson and Walter White of the NAACP, and Monroe Trotter of the *Boston Guardian* and National Equal Rights League. Their testimony in a heated committee hearing was repeatedly interrupted by the southern Democratic members of the Census Committee, who accused them of slandering southern states, of "sending secret agents all through the South" to conduct a propaganda campaign. These members generally insisted on referring to black Americans as "niggers" and brazenly denied that any persons were disfranchised on account of race. Still, the Republican majority on the committee "gave little heed to the Fourteenth Amendment," with Horace Mann Towner suggesting that it did not have jurisdiction over the question and the majority report indicating that it simply did not have the time or expertise to demonstrate that black southerners were being denied the right to vote. Even this was too much for Samuel Brinson of North Carolina, who claimed that there "was no evidence presented to the committee, valid in a court of law, to show that Negroes in the South had been denied the right to vote because of their race. Unsupported statements of colored people charging that the white people of the South have denied the colored people their constitutional rights ought not to be placed in the record."[68]

Republicans were not just indifferent—the leadership was actively hostile to Tinkham's efforts. The floor managers, for instance, conspired to deny Tinkham time to speak, and he was able to defend his resolution only after working out an arrangement with the chair of the Appropriations Committee to speak on a separate occasion. Tinkham did manage to offer an amendment to the apportionment bill, but this move led to a protracted fight over whether or not it was in order, with Republicans Nicholas Longworth, Horace Towner, and Isaac Siegel insisting that it was not. The chair agreed: a proposal to reduce the congressional apportionment of certain states was not germane to a congressional apportionment bill.[69]

Tinkham would have several more opportunities over the next decade, as Congress proved incapable of passing any apportionment bill at all. In the next Congress, Tinkham again tried to build support for his amendment, and Siegel—clearly annoyed—allowed him time to speak on the understanding that it was "a subject which [Tinkham] desires to discuss but which is not related to this bill." Tinkham's proposed amendment, which would have had eleven southern states lose a total of twenty-eight seats, relative to an expanded chamber, was easily rejected, and only Wells Goodykoontz, a Republican from West Virginia, offered it any explicit support in the House. But the overall apportionment bill was defeated by a vote of 146 to 142, as representatives from primarily rural regions—southern Democrats in particular—worried about their states losing seats.[70]

By the 1924 elections, California had more voters than Missouri, but four fewer representatives; Los Angeles alone cast more votes for president than Alabama, Georgia, and Mississippi combined, and yet had only two representatives to the thirty sent by Congress from these states. In 1928, when the Census Committee again tried to pass an apportionment bill, Tinkham again proposed a reduction in southern representation; neither his amendment nor the larger bill was adopted. In January 1929, Tinkham took another stab at it, but the Republican presiding officer again decided that it was not germane. When the House considered a new bill in June, Tinkham dutifully proposed his amendment and John Rankin of Mississippi moved that it was out of order. This time the chair sided with Tinkham, and the amendment came to a vote: despite a more than 100-member Republican majority in the House, the amendment was defeated 94 to 103 on a division vote and then 109 to 122 on a teller vote.

Only a few hours later, however, a version of his amendment passed. The reason for this reversal was that a measure to no longer count alien residents for purposes of apportionment, supported by the Klan, had been passed in the time between the defeat of Tinkham's first amendment and the introduction of his second. As the *Hartford Courant* noted, Northerners, including some Democrats, "spurred on by cries of 'come on' from Tinkham's Bay State colleagues, realized that here was a chance to get back at the southerners and westerners who had passed the alien change." "For a moment there was silence and then the Republicans broke into cheers," while "the little round Massachusetts member [Tinkham] jumped up and down in the well of the House, his black, full beard bobbling like a cork on the water." Southern Democrats were stunned. "House Votes to Rob South for Robbing Blacks," declared the *Chicago Tribune* the next day.[71]

While backbench Republicans cheered, the party leadership fumed. The success of both the anti-immigrant and Tinkham measures guaranteed failure: "Now all the South will vote against the bill if it carries the Tinkham provisions, and the Northern Democrats to a man will oppose the measure if it is freighted with the amendments aimed at aliens." Since both of these provisions had support from a different Republican faction, they could not easily be scrubbed: only by combining them could they be struck, and the leadership initially seemed chary about how this could be done under the rules. The next day, however, Speaker Longworth, in likely contravention of parliamentary procedure, decided to allow an amendment, which he had helped write, that simply replaced the amendments with the text as it had stood before. This passed, and the apportionment bill was saved at the cost of continued nonenforcement of the Fourteenth Amendment.

The priorities of the Republican leadership were clear. As James Wolcott Wadsworth, a member of the Republican leadership, put it when another member raised the possibility of investigating the election practices of the states in order to ensure that they conformed with the Fourteenth and Fifteenth Amendments

The people in the various sections of the country have their especial troubles. It is not the fault of the people; it is the fault of circumstances which have arisen over which they have no control. Their handicaps and troubles have been handed down to them for generations. I assume that the people of every State in this Union are trying to work out their political salvation to the best of their ability, and I think the more we leave them alone the better.[72]

Southern hostility to black rights obviously was nothing new. But southern racism could intersect with a broader resurgence of conservatism on issues that were not immediately concerned with race, thus producing different political patterns depending on how closely the issues were connected in the minds of southern lawmakers and attentive public opinion. With the end of the war, Congress had to decide what it would do with the railroads. The railroad brotherhoods proposed a plan for continued national ownership, and Director General of Railroad Administration William McAdoo supported continued government ownership for five years.[73]

Conservative southern Democrats, worried that Wilson might support a continuation of public ownership, began threatening a fundamental break with the Democratic Party on the issue. "There are scores of Democrats from the South holding office under the administration or in Congress," noted a correspondent for the *Macon Daily Telegraph*, "who are equally frank to say that the moment the Democratic party comes out openly in support of Government ownership of the railroads, ship lines, telegraph, telephone, and express companies, they will join in a movement for the creation of an opposition Democratic party that will stand against federation and centralization and in favor of state sovereignty."[74]

Southern conservatives long had tried to undermine support for public ownership of the railroads with the argument that it would threaten white supremacy by making the railroads subject to the strictures of the Fourteenth Amendment and by empowering a Republican administration to place African Americans in important local or regional positions. In an effort to maintain public sympathy and labor peace, McAdoo had tried to assuage such fears. Under pressure from the unions, and in response to "a reign of terror against Negro employees," the Railroad Administration had revised working rules to reduce or eliminate the employment of black Americans in skilled positions. Still, the Southern Traffic League complained that the administration had been "altogether too generous in the disposition of wage increases," noting in particular that "the rate accorded to negro labor has caused an anomalous and peculiar situation without any corresponding improvement in the living conditions of the negro. In numerous instances negro labor is paid more than their white supervisors." The postwar South, complained several commentators, was confronted by the grave difficulty of "the servant situation . . . with which the national government, principally government ownership has much to do." The problem, argued conservative newspapers, was that the government did not distinguish between black and white labor and was overly responsive to the demands of the railroad brotherhoods for wage increases. As a result, black labor had been able to earn higher wages, putting new burdens on employers and undermining the racial hierarchy. "Since the government has been in control of the railroads the negro fireman and others draw the same pay as a white man, the government making no distinction," and so wages had been pushed up "for the lowest kind of labor in all other lines."[75]

Whether because of these concerns or as part of a broader conservative shift, contemporaries soon were noting that "a profound reaction has set in" against public control across the South. After a conference of southern shippers voted in favor of a resumption of private ownership, a representative of the Southern Traffic League could tell Congress that this position had the support of 95 percent of its members. In the face of an increasingly conservative public mood, Woodrow Wilson began to back off from his earlier support for either continued public control over the railroads or a "modified public control." When McAdoo resigned in January 1919, Wilson named as his successor Walker D. Hines of Kentucky, who was distrusted by many progressives because of his "past efforts to thwart Progressive Era railroad regulation." The fight over the future of the country's railroad and transportation policies moved to the newly Republican Congress.[76]

As if to underscore the dangers of federal control, Republican representative Martin Madden of Illinois introduced an amendment, drafted by the Colored American Council, to the proposed transportation bill that would prohibit Jim Crow cars. Madden's proposal, however, not only met with the unanimous opposition of southern members but found very little favor among Republicans. The chair of the Commerce Committee, John Jacob Esch, suggested that there was no clear constitutional authority to outlaw Jim Crow cars, and he declared himself personally against such a radical policy: "Members of the House declare positively there will be no attempt made to eliminate the 'Jim Crow' cars in the Southern States." One Republican even insisted, against all organized expression of black opinion, that African Americans did not demand this step. Perhaps more important, he argued, "the north doesn't realize what it means to the people of the South." The amendment was defeated by a vote of 142 to 12 in the House, with the *Mississippi Daily Herald* noting with pleasure that "many northern Republicans [were] joining with southern Democrats."[77]

Southern conservatives nonetheless pointed to Madden's proposal as illustrating the "danger of the growing tendency of centering authority at Washington":

There were twelve Congressmen who thought it ought to be done and some day there may be a majority. The point is that the principle involved is the same as is involved in numerous other questions which some Democrats do not seem to regard as dangerous. It is the principle of local self-government. The present tendency to centralize all power in Washington is making that principle almost obsolete and it is time to ask where this sort of thing is going to go. The Esch bill, for example, practically nullifies the anti-trust laws of the State of Texas so far as they apply to railroads, why should it not abolish "Jim Crow" laws?

This argument long had been an important theme of southern political discourse, and it would continue to find traction in the South during the 1920s as conservatives tried to rally opposition to "socialistic" measures by warning of their threat to local self-government and white supremacy.[78]

In the end, only one southerner—the progressive Morris Sheppard of Texas—voted to maintain public control for at least two more years.

The Esch-Cummins Act repudiated the long-standing goals of southern Democrats to enforce competition in the railroad industry through law and regulations. The Interstate Commerce Commission, which had broad support in the region, was strengthened but now was given an explicit mandate to consolidate railroad lines into a few regional monopolies. The railroads were exempted from antitrust laws, including those of the states; they were provided with a government guarantee of between 5.5 and 6 percent return on investment; and a new Railroad Labor Board was established to adjudicate labor disputes and regulate wages. The Southern Traffic League organized opposition to the mandatory consolidation of lines, the exemption from anti-trust laws, and the effective displacement of state rail commissions, and southern Democrats provided thirteen of the thirty votes in the Senate against, joined by progressive Republicans. Eight conservative southern Democrats voted in favor, however, though a number of them, such as Augustus Stanley, would later say that they had done so "with much reluctance."[79]

The Senate version had mandated binding arbitration on all labor disputes and made any combination of employees that would disrupt traffic a criminal offense, effectively outlawing strikes on the railroads. The legislation's labor features represented an expansion of federal authority that received strong endorsement from southern conservatives. Oscar Underwood, the Democratic minority leader, even claimed responsibility for the anti-strike clause, telling the Birmingham Chamber of Commerce that whenever labor raised its "mailed fist" against the public, "I will say 'Here you must stop.'" The speech earned him a six-way tie for first place on the American Federation of Labor's blacklist, thrilled conservative groups in Alabama, and became a cornerstone of his reelection campaign. Empowering the federal government to regulate wages and intervene directly into labor disputes, it seemed, was not as worrying when the authority was to be used to hold down wages and limit the strength of the brotherhoods.[80]

On the two votes on the anti-strike clause, a number of southern senators voted the conservative position, including Bankhead, Underwood, Joseph Robinson, Joseph Ransdell, John Sharp Williams, Nathaniel Dial, and John Walter Smith of Maryland. But the majority of southern Democrats voted to remove it. The House rejected all but a very weak labor provision, and the anti-strike clause was dropped in conference after an extensive campaign waged by the AFL.

The Sectional Origins of the New Deal

The Democratic Party dramatically tore itself apart at its national convention in 1924. It divided over prohibition, immigration, nativism, and the Klan. But the Republican Party also was fragmenting, with its regional wings in Congress pulling further apart. The deepening divide in both parties was rooted in distinct constituency interests and priorities, roughly mapping onto a broader schism between the agricultural periphery and the industrial and urban core—"rural America," argued Arthur Schlesinger, "was digging in for its rear-guard stand in the twenties."[81]

But in Congress the growing divisions within the parties were undergirded by the changes to the rules and practices that had accumulated over the previous decade, changes that had been either supported by the South or designed to accommodate their priorities. The post-Cannon rules of the House had diffused legislative authority in that chamber away from the party leadership. In the Senate, a 1914 rule change had made unanimous consent agreements enforceable by the presiding officer, facilitating the use of more complex agreements and, by formalizing the process, necessitating broad agreement or accommodation of senators' divergent priorities. The southern-backed cloture rule likewise encouraged the construction of broad legislative coalitions, while the Seventeenth Amendment led senators to pay more attention to cultivating support among mass constituencies rather than a narrower cadre of partisan state legislators.

Upon attaining a majority, the Republican Party tried to work out a series of institutional compromises to accommodate the diversity of preferences in its caucus. In both chambers, for instance, they adopted what heretofore had been the Democratic practice of having a regionally representative committee on committees make assignments, part of a series of "'compromises' by which the G.O.P. majority has been settling its little internal difficulties." Rather than relying on conservative committee chairs to maintain control over the agenda, the party leadership began giving much greater weight to seniority in designating chairs of committees. Republican progressives tried and failed to oust some of the most conservative chairs in the Senate, but they did not carry the fight to the floor, despite the offer of Democratic support. The emulation of Democratic practices had the effect of further decentralizing legislative authority in Congress, empowering committees that were designed to represent "intraparty heterogeneity," and encouraging party leaders to act as "compromisers and bargainers, not commanders."[82]

For southern Democrats, the changed politics and institutional context presented an extraordinary opportunity. They were more likely to find themselves voting with the majority in both chambers, while a diffusion of parliamentary authority in the House, vesting power in substantive committees, limited the extent to which the majority party leadership would intervene in the legislative process. In the Senate, the deepening split between progressive and conservative Republicans enabled the South to throw its support to whichever side made it the better offer.[83]

This new pattern to congressional politics most dramatically appeared in the 67th Congress, elected in 1920, which saw the organization of a bipartisan voting and procedural coalition that wrested control of the Senate agenda in order to pursue legislation to help agricultural constituencies struggling with an ongoing economic crisis. It was the first occurrence of what would become a more common pattern over the course of the decade: distinct groups of lawmakers coming together across party lines in issue-specific coalitions.

The Farm Bloc emerged in the context of an ongoing collapse in agricultural prices that followed the end of the war. When the Federal Reserve, in an effort to fight inflation, raised rediscount rates, it was accused of engaging in a "deliberate 'credit conspiracy' to depress farm prices," which had been kept low in wheat but not in cotton. Southern Democrats tried in vain to persuade the administration to allow the War Finance Corporation to extend credit to farmers, but their pleas were rejected, and Congress only just managed to keep the Corporation alive over Wilson's veto. The "failure to do anything decisive to stem the downward plunge of farm prices," wrote Arthur Link, was a decisive factor in the splintering of the progressive coalition of the Wilson era, the crushing Democratic defeats in the 1920 elections, and the persistent distrust between westerners and southerners.[84]

Although the war years had been good to the South, cotton prices dropped precipitously, from a high of 35 cents per pound in 1919 to 16 cents in 1920. The price collapse was severely felt across the region. After riots erupted over the low prices at auctions, vigilante night riders tried to force a reduction in cotton-picking by burning gins and warehouses. Those who had taken on debt during the years of high prices often were ruined. Black farm laborers were left "begging for work at any price" as vigilantes tried to halt production. Hundreds of thousands of farmers and their families left the region every year, though many others were forced by poverty and discrimination to remain. Across the country, the ongoing crisis created a demand for government intervention in the form of creating more access to credit; reforming the Federal Reserve to make it more responsive to agriculture; and, for a growing number of farmers, forcing farmers to reduce the acreage under cultivation, securing a better price for crops on foreign markets, or providing a subsidy in the form of price floors.[85]

This was the context in which a group of six Democratic and six Republican legislators met in the Washington office of the American Farm Bureau Federation in May 1921. Dubbed the "Ken Kap Klan," in reference to Republicans William Kenyon and Arthur Capper, two of its leading figures, the Farm Bloc averaged about twenty-seven members in the Senate and ninety-five in the House. It included lawmakers from the West, Midwest, and South, but none from north of the Ohio and east of the Mississippi except Wisconsin, nor from Kentucky, West Virginia, or Tennessee. Its southern members included Ellison Smith of South Carolina, who took a leading role in its deliberations; Republican John Harreld of Oklahoma, "an impecunious lawyer ten years ago, but who is now an oil millionaire"; Morris Sheppard, "lily painter from Texas"; William Harris of Georgia; J. Thomas Heflin of Alabama, "who can recount inimitably for four hours in succession the best darky stories in the world"; Joseph Ransdell of Louisiana; Duncan Fletcher of Florida; and Nathaniel H. Dial, "the homespun Senator" from South Carolina. In the Senate, this group held regular meetings in which its diverse and loose membership debated strategy. In the House, it "functioned through 'key men' in the state delegations and on the important committees, who were responsible for focusing the attention and persuading the votes of their colleagues on pending agrarian legislation."[86]

When the Republican Party leadership moved to adjourn on July 5, 1921, the Farm Bloc successfully voted to keep it in session. By the end of the summer, the Bloc had won passage of the Packer Control Act and the Grain Futures Act, extended the life of the War Finance Corporation, and passed two measures relating to the federal farm loan system, increasing its capitalization and the interest rate on bonds sold by the farm credit system. In subsequent sessions, the Farm Bloc would secure passage of the Federal Highway Act of 1921, requiring states to designate a system of interstate and intercounty roads that would be eligible for federal funding; impose a 50 percent surtax on incomes; pass legislation to regulate grain exchanges under the commerce clause after regulation by taxation had been declared unconstitutional; provide for cooperative marketing; include a "dirt farmer" on the Federal Reserve board; supply seed for destitute farmers; and ensure favorable protection under the tariff for agricultural interests. In the final session before the congressional term expired, the Farm Bloc focused on a measure dear to southern representatives—an expansion of the intermediate credit available for farmers. The Bloc also followed the pattern of agrarian coalitions since 1901 to successfully filibuster a ship subsidy bill. Southerners did not provide most of the Farm Bloc leadership, but they did deliver "the most cohesive support for the Farm Bloc's policies" and had an especially important role in shaping the Intermediate Credits Act of 1923.[87]

The Farm Bloc dissolved after the 67th Congress, in part as a consequence of the divisions that emerged over two agricultural bills proposed by Republican George Norris of Nebraska. In the summer of 1921, Norris proposed that the government act as the buyer and seller of agricultural products for export. The bill initially seemed to have southern support, even with Underwood explaining that he would vote for it. Wanting to avoid a veto, the administration tried to peel off southern Democratic support by introducing a measure to strengthen the still-operational War Finance Corporation and authorize the corporation to lend money to banks to lend to farmers. The substitute, which also allowed the railroads to be refunded the $500 million they owed the government, was targeted at the problems faced by southern cotton and tobacco farmers, especially the diminished demand in Europe and the region's particular financial system.[88]

Furnifold Simmons, looking to persuade southern Democrats to support the substitute, explained why he had gone from an "ardent champion" of the Norris bill to a proponent of Kellogg's substitute. The substitute, he said, had been drawn up by Eugene Meyer and Angus W. McLean, the director and managing director of the War Finance Corporation, in consultation with "Democratic Senators from the South." Meyer had shown "deep interest in the southern situation," while McLean was one of the largest farmers in the South and the president of a large North Carolina bank. Simmons explained that, "scattered all over our Southland, in every little village and hamlet and in every little country town, as well as in the larger towns, there are agricultural credit stores, where our tenant farmers and our landlord farmers go and get credit for supplies with which to cultivate their crops, with the understanding that they are to be paid for in the fall when the crop is sold." These different credit agencies in turn took these papers to the local bank, but the Federal Reserve was largely unwilling to accept them for purposes of loaning money to banks. The Kellogg bill would provide southern banks with vital relief by authorizing the Corporation to extend loans to banks for advances made for any agricultural purpose, whether for export or not, including for advances that had already been made. With Simmons singing its praises, and as they insisted that it had nothing to do with refunding money to the railroads, southerners lined up in support.[89]

"A number of conservatives," complained the *Minnesota Daily Star*, "who had been virtually forced to join the agricultural bloc because of pressure from home, really opposed the Norris bill because 'it put the government in business' and wiped out the parasitical middlemen who prey upon the farmer.

These senators, most of them southerners, will welcome the opportunity to vote for the Kellogg bill, which, according to the best analysis, benefits the bankers of the country far more than it does the farmers." Norris recognized that he had lost once "the Southern agricultural men were taken away by the promise of the loaning of Federal money to cotton."[90]

The other Norris proposal that divided the Farm Bloc was a bill to create a government corporation to operate grain elevators and storage warehouses, to buy and sell agricultural products, to act as the agent of any person or co-operative organization engaged in agricultural production, and to extend credit for the sale or export of agricultural products. The bill was unanimously reported out of the Senate Committee on Agriculture in December 1922, al-though two committee members, Republican John Harreld of Oklahoma and Democrat Augustus Stanley, reserved the right to oppose it once it reached the Senate floor. John Sharp Williams—mocked as "the only old-time planta-tion owner left in the Senate"—declared that Norris had "accomplished the impossible": a bill Williams thought to be even more disgraceful than the ship subsidy bill that the Farm Bloc was trying to defeat, for it directly involved government in running a business on a permanent basis. "The old Ocala plat-form which the Populist Party adopted 30 years ago in this country was an angel of light in comparison with the Norris bill"; nobody who "believes that this is a Government of limited powers and delegated powers" could vote for it. Congress soon adjourned, and the Farm Bloc dissolved amid sectional ac-rimony. The "real progressives" of the Democratic Party, complained the *Capital Times* of Wisconsin, "are meeting the same difficulty which has always been a mill-stone around the neck of the Democratic party: the dominating group of southern Bourbons who control the party machinery and dictate its policies."[91]

The Farm Bloc, explained Senator Arthur Capper, was "not to be com-pared with the old Progressive wing of the Republican Party," because it had "no intention of break[ing] a party in two, but merely of insisting on the mea-sures that are of interest to the farmer." The next Congress did not see much legislative action on agriculture, largely because the different sectional wings of the agricultural coalition were unable to converge on a shared agenda; the major bill to receive western and midwestern support was intended to encour-age wheat farmers to diversify their crops and did nothing for the cotton farm-ers, who were even more tied to a single crop.[92]

Though the Farm Bloc ceased to act as a clearly defined organization, it persisted as an informal voting coalition and provided a template for the or-ganization of a progressive voting bloc in subsequent years. After the elections of 1924, when Robert La Follette's Progressive Party cut deeply into Demo-cratic support outside the South, a voting coalition uniting southern Demo-crats with western and midwestern Republicans became central to legislative

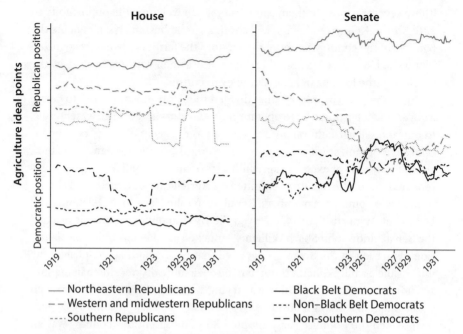

House **Senate**

Agriculture ideal points

Republican position

Democratic position

1919 1921 1923 1925 1929 1931   1919 1921 1923 1925 1927 1929 1931

——— Northeastern Republicans   ——— Black Belt Democrats
– – Western and midwestern Republicans   ---- Non–Black Belt Democrats
---- Southern Republicans   – – Non-southern Democrats

FIGURE 8.11. Development of Agriculture Ideal Points, 1919–1935. Dotted line in center is the chamber median.

proceedings in the Senate, first on agriculture and then on other issues. Figure 8.11, as well as figures 8.14 and 8.15 (pp. 371–72), show the gradual emergence of a progressive voting coalition on agriculture, political economy, and planning and resources, three areas where the South and West were gradually able to unite around specific issues across party lines.

In 1922, Secretary of Agriculture Henry C. Wallace convened a national conference to examine the condition of agriculture and recommend proposals to remedy "the severe hardships under which so important a portion of our productive citizenship is struggling." The most important recommendation to come out of the conference was the concept of "parity pricing," a guarantee for farmers of a share of national income by pegging the ratio of prices received to prices equal to those that prevailed during the "golden years" of 1910 to 1914. This goal would be achieved by dividing the total output of crops into two parts, domestic and foreign, with the first supplied in such amount as to maintain a parity of prices over this period and the second part being whatever was left over, which would be sold on the world market (and restricted from flowing back in through a tariff wall). Any losses from dumping the surplus crop abroad would be shared by producers.[93]

The McNary-Haugen bill became the most promising and controversial vehicle for achieving parity pricing. It proposed to establish a federal farm board authorized to purchase specified commodities and either keep these off the market until prices had improved or sell them on the world market and spread out the losses among producers by way of an equalization fee. Although some of the South's most progressive legislators, including Sheppard, Heflin, and Thaddeus Caraway, were strongly in favor, the proposal initially met with considerable opposition in the region because it would raise prices primarily for the domestic market while cotton was sold primarily for export, and because it would "create another great wasteful corporation" to issue bonds that would eventually have to be redeemed by the taxpayer. It was defeated in the House in June 1924, by a vote of 161 to 222, with only 28 percent of southern representatives in favor, mostly from the wheat- and corn-growing states of Oklahoma, Kentucky, and Missouri. Only New England and Mid-Atlantic members voted no at higher rates.[94]

Another version was reported favorably by the House and Senate Agricultural Committees at the end of the 68th Congress, but it died on the legislative calendar when the Congress adjourned. The next year, however, changes were made to attract southern legislative and farmer interest. Most important, the bill was adjusted so that the agricultural surplus would be handled, wherever possible, by cooperatives. This modification considerably increased the appeal of the plan to the cotton cooperatives of the South, which handled only a small portion of the cotton crop and would have been disadvantaged by any effort to hold back crops from the market that did not force all cotton producers to participate. At a conference in Memphis, the cotton cooperatives decided to join with supporters of the McNary-Haugen plan. Forty percent of southern representatives, and 30 percent of southern senators, now backed the plan, which nonetheless failed to pass either chamber.[95]

Additional changes were made to attract southern support in 1927, in the closing months of the 69th Congress, including the equalization fee, which had been delayed for corn and cotton for three years and would now be imposed immediately and used to finance the holding of large cotton crops by cooperatives. The Congress also established an advisory council for each covered commodity—thereby ensuring that the distinctive concerns of cotton exporters would inform policy—and provided new loans for cooperatives. This provision reflected the efforts by supporters to cultivate support from southern members and secured the growing interest in the region and the influence of southern members on the Senate and House Agricultural Committees, including Senators Ellison Smith, Ransdell, Heflin, Caraway, and Earle Mayfield (the Klan's man from Texas) and Representatives James Aswell of Louisiana, Marvin Jones of Texas, and Hampton Fulmer of South Carolina. Ransdell, Heflin, Caraway, Mayfield, and an aging Morris Sheppard all urged their colleagues to back the bill. An equal number of southerners spoke for and against in the House, with William Lankford of Georgia, Joseph Byrns of

Tennessee, and Eugene Black and Luther Johnson of Texas in support and Charles Edwards of Georgia, James Aswell and John O'Connor of Louisiana, and John Box and Tom Connally of Texas in opposition. The measure passed 214 to 178 in the House and 47 to 39 in the Senate, with the largest increase coming from the South: 64 percent of southerners now voted for passage in the House, as did 48 percent in the Senate, with the eight new supporting votes almost all coming from the region.[96]

The legislation was vetoed by President Coolidge. The next year its supporters tried again. Robert Doughton and John Kerr of North Carolina, as well as James Reed of Missouri, strongly favored passage, while Finis Garrett and Charles Crisp were opposed. On final passage, southern support had now increased to 72 percent in the House and 71 percent in the Senate. The bill again was vetoed by Coolidge. The next president, Herbert Hoover, was even more adamant in his opposition. After considerable debate, Congress passed his Agricultural Market Act instead.

Some features of the McNary-Haugen bill would eventually be included in one of the foundational statutes of the New Deal, the Agricultural Adjustment Act of 1933, which authorized the federal government to enter into agreements with farmers to reduce acreage devoted to basic crops, to store crops and make advances on them, to enter into marketing agreements with producers and handlers in order to stabilize prices, and to finance crop reduction by imposing taxes on processors. Although the equalization fee imposed on farmers was abandoned, the financial costs of the Adjustment Act's crop reduction subsidies were recouped by a tax on processors, with the assumption that these would then be passed on to the consumer. The goal of restoring parity in farm prices—to return to the brief golden era of 1910 to 1914, when industry and agriculture were ostensibly in a healthy equilibrium—also was a core attribute of the act. Even after this feature was abandoned in the late 1940s, the commitment of the federal government to intervene on a massive scale in agricultural markets to support prices for agriculture would endure for decades.[97]

Perhaps more important than policy legacies were the political legacies. Differential treatment of farm products had been the shoals on which an agricultural progressive coalition repeatedly shattered. One of the most important consequences of McNary-Haugen's development over the 1920s was that it provided a vehicle around which the "bipartisan alliance between South and West" could be "revived." What the historian George Tindall called its "marriage of cotton and corn" became one of the most important buttresses of a revitalized and generally progressive agricultural coalition that initially cut across party lines before being partially absorbed into the early New Deal coalition. Perhaps no one embodied this development more than Henry A. Wallace, the son of the recently deceased Secretary of Agriculture, who broke with the Republican Party over Coolidge's veto in 1928. Wallace would go on

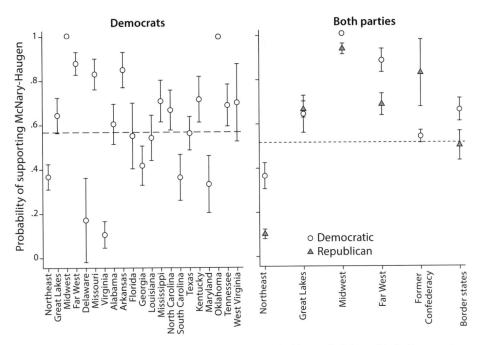

FIGURE 8.12. Probability of Supporting McNary-Haugen. Dashed line in the left panel is the Democratic average. Short-dashed line in the right panel is the Republican average.

to be Franklin Roosevelt's Secretary of Agriculture and vice president, and eventually the Progressive Party's nominee for president in 1948. One contemporary noted, "McNary-Haugenism represents an alignment, running crosswise of established party lines, which more nearly disrupts these lines than any alignment since populism." Figure 8.12 shows that the South had been the agricultural region most suspicious of the plan, with Virginia and South Carolina legislators especially hostile. And as figure 8.13 suggests, the marriage came only as southern legislators shifted from being moderately opposed to broadly—but not unanimously—supportive, largely in response to the bill's modification to accommodate their material interests. This alliance would become the "dominant influence in the development of a national farm policy" during the New Deal and for decades after.[98]

The contours of a broad progressive coalition extended beyond agriculture policy. Revenue acts in 1921, 1924, 1926, and 1928 provided for a reduction in personal and corporate income taxes, a core pledge of the Republican Party and a central goal of successive Republican administrations. But despite the efforts of Andrew Mellon, Secretary of the Treasury throughout the decade, and the consistent support of conservative Republicans for deep reductions, there was no return to the low rates and minimal progressivity that had been in effect before the war. With the expansion of federal services in recent

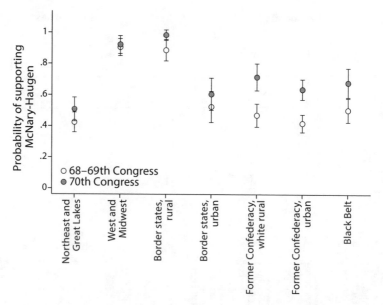

FIGURE 8.13. Probability of Democratic Support for McNary-Haugen, 68th–70th Congresses

decades, the government was in need of more revenue, especially after passage of the Bonus Bill for veterans in 1924. Just as important was the fact that a progressive voting coalition, with southerners playing a central role, generally was able to limit the extent of any tax cuts.[99]

The South, according to one historian, was "the one region that threw up a strong movement willing to use the tax power to cripple great wealth and its perpetuation through inheritance," and southerners generally sided with the progressive wing of the Republican Party in trying to maintain the tax code's progressive structure. Tax policy was one of the key sites around which a progressive coalition emerged on issues of political economy (figure 8.14). In 1921, a relatively conservative bill was able to pass the House, with all Democrats except Guy Campbell of Pennsylvania and Henry Dupré and Ladislas Lazaro of Louisiana voting against, joined by only a handful of Republican progressives. It had been a "hopeless fight" in that chamber, according to the *Raleigh News and Observer,* to stop the conservative "steam roller" in the service of "the profiteering millionaires and multi-millionaires." While the final vote of 38 to 24 in the Senate was almost as partisan as in the House, with all Democrats but Edwin Broussard of Louisiana opposed and all Republicans but Norris, George Moses, and La Follette in favor, the "progressive and agricultural bloc" generally had been able to secure changes that limited the proposed reductions and maintained much of the system's progressivity.[100]

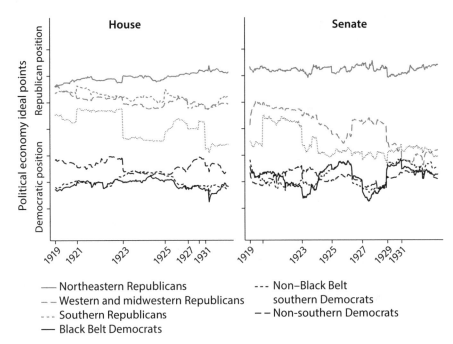

FIGURE 8.14. Development of Political Economy Ideal Points, 1919–1935. Dotted line in center is the chamber median.

Subsequent tax bills were passed by large majorities—377 to 9 and 76 to 6 in the House and Senate in 1924, and 357 to 30 and 76 to 11 in 1926. But in their drafting they occasioned considerable disagreement between progressives and conservatives, with the South and a faction of western and midwestern Republicans generally providing the votes to prevent steep reductions and maintain inheritance taxes and the progressivity of the tax code. The 1924 Mellon tax plan, for instance, would have dramatically cut rates, but it was reworked by midwestern Republicans and southern Democrats who insisted "on retaining a more progressive pattern of taxation." After progressive Republicans and Democrats were cut out of the process in the House Ways and Means Committee, they coalesced on the floor to threaten support for an alternative proposed by John Nance Garner, which would have been more costly but would have maintained a more progressive structure by increasing exemptions, raising the top surtax rate, and more aggressively lowering excise taxes. The Republican leadership was forced to offer a compromise that more closely reflected Garner's proposal than the Mellon plan. The final bill increased the estate tax from 25 percent to 40 percent, created a gift tax, and set a top surtax rate at 40 percent rather than the 25 percent proposed by Mellon.[101]

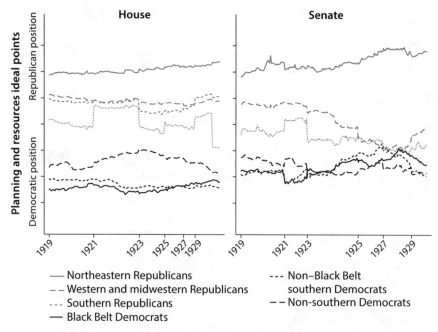

FIGURE 8.15. Development of Planning and Resources Ideal Points, 1919–1935. Dotted line in center is the chamber median.

The issue of resource development likewise saw the slow forging of a progressive coalition (figure 8.15) as midwestern Republicans and southern Democrats tried to find ways to accommodate each other's priorities. During the war, southern members of Congress had succeeded in securing war industries and military bases for the region, including a nitrate facility at Muscle Shoals, gunpowder mills in Virginia and Tennessee, naval installations in Virginia, South Carolina, and Louisiana, and thirteen of the sixteen National Guard camps. The Muscle Shoals facility would have the most enduring impact on the politics of the 1920s. By the war's end, a number of dams were under construction at Muscle Shoals, a quarry had been purchased, and several chemical plants were being built, but no nitrate had been produced. When the Republicans gained control of Congress, the site came under intense congressional scrutiny and a House investigation eventually concluded that "the entire nitrate program was a failure, that it had cost a tremendous amount of money, that it had been grossly mismanaged, and that there had been collusion with private interests who had sought to have the government build Muscle Shoals Dam so that they could secure the power." The report's criticism of the administration and congressional Democrats' spending priorities, as well as its spotlight on illicit collusion to use public land and resources for private gain, provided grist for both conservative and progressive Republicans.[102]

But it did not answer the question of what to do with Muscle Shoals. For the next decade, no other issue would absorb more time and attention in Congress. Conservatives generally wanted to sell the facility to private buyers, while Asle Gronna, George Norris, and other progressives endorsed continued government ownership and operation of the site. In any event, the initial appropriations for construction at Muscle Shoals were fast running out. In early 1921, the chair of the House Appropriations Committee reported a sundry civil appropriations bill that included no new funds for the Muscle Shoals project. Work on the Wilson Dam, the major ongoing construction site, was halted, with no obvious route to completion.[103]

In 1921, Henry Ford submitted a proposal to acquire the nitrate plant and lease the dams and electrical installations, once completed with federal funds. His promise to develop the region into the next Detroit attracted considerable support from many southerners, especially the Alabama delegation headed by Oscar Underwood. But there was considerable worry among many southern lawmakers that Ford intended to divert the facility away from its intended purpose of producing nitrates for fertilizer. Senator Norris in particular denounced the proposal as a massive giveaway of public resources to private industry, which would use the site not to produce cheap fertilizer but to obtain power-generating facilities at a "ridiculously low figure." In turn, he introduced at least one bill per Congress from 1922 to 1933 stipulating how Muscle Shoals should be owned, developed, and operated by the government. Southern Democrats were divided between those who wanted this outcome and those who preferred private ownership, or at least private operation—including conservatives such as Underwood but also the nominally progressive J. Thomas Heflin, who denounced one proposal by Norris as "Bolshevistic." The most common position, however, was to favor whichever proposal was most likely to result in the quick development of the site and the provision of cheap fertilizer to southern farmers.[104]

In July 1922, the Senate Committee on Agriculture and Forestry rejected Ford's proposal, as well as a proposal by Norris for government ownership and operation, by votes of 9 to 7 and 9 to 5, respectively. All of the committee's southern Democrats voted for the Ford proposal, with Republican John Harreld the only southerner to vote against it. Senator Caraway declared in disgust that the vote meant the fertilizer trust would be allowed to continue levying a heavy toll on farmers. Two years later, the House voted 227 to 143 to accept a modified Ford offer, which, like the other private proposals considered during this period, would not "cover most of the expenses the government had already incurred." All but two southern Democrats, John Linthicum of Maryland and Thomas Blanton of Texas, and two southern Republicans, John Hill of Maryland and Leonidas Dyer of Missouri, voted for the legislation, against large majorities of Republicans and Democrats from the Northeast. The margin of victory was provided by fifty-eight progressive Republicans.[105]

In the Senate Agriculture Committee, however, Norris substituted a bill to turn the fertilizer facilities over to the Secretary of Agriculture to operate on an experimental basis, with the power plants given to a federally owned corporation. Subsequently, the committee voted against Ford's offer, and the industrialist withdrew his proposal in disgust. When the Norris Muscle Shoals bill reached the Senate floor, Underwood introduced a substitute retaining public ownership but authorizing the president to lease the facilities to private interests, with a stipulation that the lessee had to manufacture fertilizer. Norris claimed that this would invite illicit collusion between government and private industry—it would amount to "a concession so great it will make Teapot Dome look like a pinhead"—so the Senate Republican whip, Wesley Jones, introduced an amendment to Underwood's bill to authorize leasing the facilities to private interests only after an investigatory commission determined that this course would be in the public interest. A furious Underwood attacked Norris as a "Populist" demagogue. Of these proposals, Underwood's was the most conservative, Norris's the most radical, and Jones's an attempt at compromise.[106]

On January 8, 1925, the Senate voted 48 to 37 to replace Norris's bill with Underwood's, with southern Democrats equally divided and midwestern Republicans slightly in favor of retaining public operation. There was no clear separation between southern progressives and conservatives on this vote: some of the most conservative southern senators, including Bruce of Maryland and Bayard of Delaware, voted for the Underwood proposal because it would put the site into private operation, while many progressive senators, such as Heflin, Caraway, Owen, and Dial, supported it because the production of fertilizer would be the primary economic activity and also because the Norris bill seemed less likely to pass. The Senate then voted to replace Underwood's bill with Jones's proposal for an investigatory commission, with a large majority of southerners now voting against Underwood and with Jones. Norris then proposed his initial bill, with a minor change, as a substitute, which passed 40 to 39; Underwood reoffered his proposal, which passed 46 to 33. "We are in a circle with three points in it," complained Norris. It was Jones's proposal that eventually lost out, defeated by a vote of 38 to 43. Underwood's bill then passed 50 to 30.[107]

For those southerners who voted across the different proposals, eleven preferred Norris's more progressive bill for public operation, nine preferred Underwood's bill for private leasing, and ten—composed of both groups—preferred either one of these to Jones's bill, which would have further delayed the site's operation while the investigation was conducted. The most consistent position taken by southern senators was for renewed development of the facility, whether under public or private auspices.

The Underwood bill failed to pass the House. In 1926, Norris tried again, but failed to move his proposal out of committee. In May 1928, however, a new version did pass the Senate, with the votes of western and midwestern Republicans supplemented by increased support among southerners. Over 70 percent of southern senators voted in favor of the conference report, and only seventeen representatives broke ranks to vote against it in the House. As with McNary-Haugen, a coalition in favor of Muscle Shoals was gradually forged, as accommodations were made and provisions added to increase its appeal. Southern support was necessary for the passage of the 1928 Muscle Shoals bill; pocket-vetoed by President Coolidge, it included public operation, a mandate requiring fertilizer production—not limited to nitrates, as had initially been the case—and provisions allowing the government corporation to donate a significant share of its earnings "to be fairly and equitably distributed through the agency of county demonstration agents, agricultural colleges, or otherwise as the board may direct for experimentation, education, and introduction of the use of said fertilizers, in cooperation with practical farmers." Another version was passed in 1931. As the journalist Anne O'Hare McCormick recorded, "A few days after the second passage of the Norris resolution declaring that Muscle Shoals shall be owned and operated by the government, the valley is once more stirred by the hope of action as by a fresh wind from the north." This bill was vetoed by President Hoover.[108]

Finally, on May 17, 1933, the Norris Muscle Shoals bill, dramatically expanded in scope, passed Congress. Only nine southern representatives, two of them Republicans, voted against the conference report in the House; 83 Republicans and 22 non-southern Democrats voted with them, against 243 Democrats and 12 Republicans. The next day the Tennessee Valley Authority Act was signed into law by Franklin Roosevelt.

Conclusion

In 1928, the Democrats were again unable to rally around a candidate. To the despair of southerners and many of the party's agricultural constituencies, the party nominated the "wet" Catholic Al Smith. Furnifold Simmons refused to back Smith because of his stance on prohibition, as did Robert Owen, Sidney Catts of Florida, Thomas Love of Texas, and Thaddeus Caraway. Others held their noses, with Josephus Daniels calling it a "bitter pill for me to swallow" yet choosing to obey the "moral constraints of party regularity." Carter Glass persuaded himself that he was "profoundly stirred" by Smith's stance against privilege and "his earnest stance for the government ownership, development and operation of Muscle Shoals." In any event, Hoover, he thought, would be worse. Smith did not make it easy for white southerners by insisting on a campaign intended to attract anti-prohibition and immigrant voters. Glass complained that Smith was "obviously acting on the theory that the South is obliged to vote for him regardless of anything or everything."[109]

"They talk prohibition out here in attacking Governor Smith," wrote one correspondent for the *New York Times*, "but they mean religion." Smith's Catholicism was ripe for exploitation by his opponents in the South and Midwest, and few seized on the opportunity with more alacrity than the KKK. Senator Harry Hawes of Missouri told one reporter that the Klan had been on its last leg before the campaign but was now "being reorganized, somebody is refinancing it," to use against the Democrats in the border states. "Where the Klan formerly sent out 100,000 copies of the Knights of Columbus oath"—a document that purported to show that the Knights vowed to burn Protestants at the stake—"they are now sending them out by the millions." Throughout the South, the Klan campaigned for Hoover. In Alabama, Klansmen lynched Al Smith in effigy. Among southern Democrats in Congress, none was more vituperative than Tom Heflin, a likely Klan member, who warned that Smith would bring about unrestricted immigration. "Choose ye this day whom ye will serve," he declared, "the God of white supremacy or the false god of Roman social equality."[110]

Senator Tydings of Maryland defended the region against the charge of religious bigotry, noting that Heflin's anti-Catholic tirades had been met with sharp criticism by Joseph T. Robinson of Arkansas and Senator James A. Reed of Missouri. He mocked the contention "that the South, because of these prejudices, would go to the political extreme of repudiating the Democratic Party should it place a Roman Catholic on its presidential ticket."[111]

Others were less sanguine. With the Klan and Protestant ministers whipping up anti-Catholic sentiment in Alabama—a poll of ministers in that state showed that not one would vote for Smith, and two-thirds would denounce him—and with the Republican Party organizing furiously across the region, Democrats in Mississippi began to worry about the solidarity of the white vote. They urged the party to "draw the color line" and fight the campaign on the good old "sharply-defined issue that the Democratic Party is the white man's party and the Republican Party is the Negro party." On election day, the Democratic Party fared best in the Black Belt, where the warning of the *Charleston News and Courier* was heeded: "Let the thinnest trickle of independent voting . . . be permitted, and the torrents of independent action will sweep away the solid dam which holds the white people in the same party."[112]

In the end, Herbert Hoover, who won almost every non-southern state, carried all of the border states and made deep inroads into the "solid South," winning Florida, Texas, Tennessee, North Carolina, and Virginia. Not since

Reconstruction had the Republican Party carried so many southern states. At the presidential level, the South had rarely seemed less important.

But not in Congress. Although the divisions evident in the electoral map were also present in the voting patterns of southern lawmakers, the region was much more influential there than the presidential returns would suggest. A progressive voting coalition in which the South played a major role was firmly in place in the Senate. Such was not as evidently the case in House floor voting, but the ongoing decentralization of authority over the legislative agenda in that chamber allowed for more flexibility in lawmaking and the formation of issue-specific bipartisan coalitions centered in the substantive committees. The preceding decade had seen the emergence of a new pattern of politics that was much less polarized along party lines—although ideological divisions were acute on many issues—that presented much greater opportunities for members of the minority party to influence public policy. This pattern would be even more firmly established after the 1930s and 1940s, once southern Democrats decisively began acting as an independent bloc mediating between northern Democrats and Republicans, with a resulting dampening of party polarization that eventually would become one of the defining features of mid-twentieth-century American politics.

Southern-led coalitions on several occasions had passed legislation with the potential to radically reshape America's economy and transform relationships between state and society. Under Wilson, southern Democrats presided over the construction of an extensive national state, established a cloture rule in the Senate, regulated the hours of employees in interstate commerce, and even accepted the principle of fixing the prices of agricultural commodities. During the years of Republican majorities, southern lawmakers gradually worked out a role in a progressive coalition that envisioned, among other things, sustained government intervention in the operation of the economy, managing prices for commodities, and placing the production of energy and management of the country's natural resources under public authority, even government ownership. All that was waiting was a sympathetic administration. They would soon get that, and more.

In 1918, a Georgia Democrat had worried that "forces are at work, which if not checked soon, will split the Solid South." Such anxieties were repeated often during the 1920s, rooted in a worry that government ownership of the country's productive resources and transportation system could pose a fatal threat to white supremacy, and a corollary fear that white southerners, eager to restrain northern capitalism, would fail to grasp this danger until it was too late. By the end of the 1920s, the South, by contrast, possessed a growing sense that neither major party had an interest in disturbing the region's racial patterns, and that even if they did, southern senators would be able to check such impulses. Thus, many of the region's most prominent political leaders, as well as majorities of its congressional delegation, felt liberated to endorse proposals for active government—to establish a closed union shop on the railroads, to have the government own and operate a massive hydroelectric and manufacturing facility at Muscle Shoals, or to create an agency in Washington to purchase and sell, through the intermediary of cooperatives, the country's agricultural crop. The stage was set for a New Deal actively backed by the region, just as long as its authoritarian enclave could enjoy security.[113]

Southern Nation

9

At the Edge of Democracy

It remains to be seen whether the attempt to govern the country by the power of a "Solid South," unlawfully consolidated, can be successful.[1]

When Rutherford B. Hayes was nominated as the Republican Party candidate for president in July 1876, the United States was charged with raw uncertainty about the terms under which the Confederate South would reenter the Union. Hayes sought what, in retrospect, proved impossible. Addressing the future of the South in his acceptance letter, a document that also underscored his positions on reforming the civil service, strengthening the currency, and improving common schools, Hayes maintained that what the region "most needs is peace, and peace depends upon the supremacy of law." He effectively was offering white southerners, including ex-Confederates, the ability to govern the South without federal oversight provided they would commit to uphold the provisions of the Constitution's Civil War Amendments.

As Congress was debating how to handle that year's disputed Electoral College votes, Hayes moved to withdraw the federal government's support of contested Republican claims to govern South Carolina and Louisiana, states where both parties had claimed victory, in exchange for southern leaders' recognition and acceptance of black voting rights. Negotiating on his behalf with Kentucky representative John Y. Brown, Congressman Charles Foster of Ohio stated that "Hayes would give the people of the States of South Carolina and Louisiana the right to control their own affairs in their own way" so long as they acknowledged that they were bound by "the Constitution of the United States and the laws made in pursuance thereof." The following day, Congressman William Levy of Louisiana offered the required undertaking, stating on behalf of the white people of his state their "honest acceptance of the issues of the war which resulted in the enfranchisement of the colored race and the endowment of that race with all the rights of American citizenship under the Constitution and its more recent amendments." Wade Hampton, then engaged in a contest with a Republican rival to be designated governor of South Carolina (each backed by a rival legislature), offered an even more expansive pledge. Once one of his state's most significant slave owners and a Confederate brigadier general who had taken a lead in raising defense funds for members of the Ku Klux Klan during Reconstruction, Hampton assured Hayes that if installed as governor, his state administration would "secure to every citizen, the lowest as well as the highest, black as well as white, full & equal protection in the enjoyment of all his rights under the Constitution."[2]

Something of a realist, Hayes's diary records his satisfaction at securing these assurances to the effect "that the colored people shall have equal rights to labor, education, and the privileges of citizenship," all the while noting that "time will tell."[3]

Time did tell, but not as Hayes had hoped. This book's goal has been to understand what happened during the six decades when the South originated, developed, and protected its new system of racial hierarchy, including: how the white South reentered the world of national lawmaking during this period, how this return affected lawmaking, and how the South's role in Congress reshaped the region and the nation on terms that violated Hayes's expectations.

To that end, we have systematically assessed southern preferences and behavior in congressional debate, negotiation, and decision. How, we have asked, did those who represented the states south of the Mason-Dixon Line—overwhelmingly Democrats—make legislative judgments? To what extent and regarding which issues did they possess distinctive policy wishes? What motivations were paramount to them? Which possibilities did they consider and pass by, and which did they seize upon, and why? What was the significance of these determinations, both for their region and for the country? These questions are of profound significance for American history, for they raise the possibility that the states that had practiced chattel slavery at the onset of the Civil War would seek to remake the country during the decades that followed their military defeat. Understanding how, to what extent, under which conditions, and with what consequences they were successful has been the animating focus of this book.

We have been particularly concerned to understand when and how southern representatives—sometimes acting as a unitary bloc but often internally divided, fragmented by geography, interests, and patterns of representation—made the United States a "southern nation" in policy, partisan, and institutional terms. The South itself constituted a complex and varied territory, notably marked by variations in partisan conditions and in the ordering of preferences between the eleven states that had formed the Confederacy and the six border states. This makes all the more remarkable the degree of full southern unity that was sometimes achieved. Equally fascinating and significant are the times and issues in which southern diversity was manifest. We have chronicled both.

In part as a result of the unevenness of southern solidarity and in part because of changing vectors of partisanship, southerners, as we have shown, were not always pivotal in the ways identified by the literature on pivotal politics. Nor did southern members always achieve their goals in Congress. Yet the intensity of their broadly shared position on race, marked by a fiercely held and articulated belief in a white-black hierarchy that was enforced not only by civil society but by official rules and police powers in each of the seventeen Jim Crow states, combined with a refined ability to craft policy and maneuver within congressional rules and procedures, and aided by uncommon seniority and experience, made the South a persistent and enduring force within Congress.

The United States became a southern nation in the five and a half decades following Reconstruction by reinforcing federalism and decentralization, especially in matters of education, as we saw in Congress's ultimate rejection of the Blair bill. That decision not only missed the chance for a national assault on illiteracy and the construction of a minimum threshold of learning across places and persons, but had the effect of deepening inequalities among persons, races, and school districts. The country as a whole also tilted toward the South in matters of race by permitting, at times facilitating, widespread disfranchisement and by legitimating strands of antiblack racism that hardly were confined to the South but that gained national legitimacy and potency by virtue of the hands-off policies that southern representatives helped procure for their increasingly unequal and segregated racial arrangements.

On another side of the ledger, the wide array of progressive, sometimes populist-inspired legislation enacted in the early twentieth century was deeply shaped and enacted by southern influence. Historians long have debated the degree of policy continuity with Progressive-era social and economic policies during the New Deal. What is clear are the significant continuities in dominant southern preferences that over that arc of time enlisted the federal government in new ways to regulate and sometimes check market capitalism and decisions by firms and investors, with a rhetoric of regional anticolonialism often deployed to this purpose. With direction from the country's most distressed region, the scale and scope of the national government's responsibilities were profoundly reoriented.

These legacies also included heightened racial disparities, most notably in agriculture. Policies enacted during the 1910s and 1920s that broadly excluded

African Americans from an emerging agricultural welfare state made it relatively more difficult for southern black farmers to expand or improve their operations; thus excluded, black farmers were then even more likely to be squeezed out by the consolidation of farms that began in the 1920s and accelerated during the Depression and New Deal. Concurrently, southern preferences for progressive taxation and reining in excessively wild markets reduced, if moderately at first, larger patterns of economic inequality.

Southern wishes and behavior in Congress were shaped by a constellation of commitments: to racial hierarchy, to populist and progressive commitments, and to constituency needs in a poor region. The South thus played a key role in developing the content and contours of American liberalism, including liberalism's decades-long entanglement with white supremacy, which later became an embarrassment and a source of great conflict and partisan realignment.

The partisan patterns of the country likewise were quite profoundly shaped by how the South came to behave not as a formally separate political party, but as a quasi-independent instrument within the Democratic Party. We observed the capacity of the South to forge cross-party coalitions in the 1920s, geared to substantive alliances primarily with agrarian progressive Republicans from the West and Midwest. But as early as the 1870s, southern representatives were willing to act independently as something of a third force in Congress even as they sat with non-southern Democrats. Later, beyond the time period on which we have focused, and especially from the late 1930s, southern Democrats acted in the House and Senate with growing self-determination, thus providing the basis for a significant and decades-long dampening of party polarization. As today we experience the reverse, an intensely divided ideological party system, we would do well to recall that the "golden age" of bipartisanship during the closing of the era of Jim Crow rested on a foundation of southern white supremacy.

The South, additionally, molded the United States into a southern nation by redoing how Congress proceeded as an institution. Congress, with the South in the lead, was reordered into a legislature that diffused the capacity to set agendas and make policy more than any other in the Western world. The weak form of cloture adopted in 1917 further allowed Congress to become a lawmaking body well suited to accommodating large minorities with intense preferences. Such a legislature, as we now have seen over the course of many decades, is more often than not better at providing constituency service and passing interest-group-driven legislation than at enacting broad, programmatic policy. Even with later changes, the institutional legacies of southern politics in Congress continue to affect lawmaking, most obviously in the form of the supermajority requirement for cloture in the Senate.

Enduring Dilemmas

At stake in this analytic history are two intersecting ambitions. The first places the South and congressional lawmaking front and center in order to advance our understanding of American political development at just the moment when the United States emerged with a modern financial and industrial market economy and an enlarged, increasingly capable national state. During this crucial era, a time of striking demographic change and pitched battles of ideas about the character and purpose of American democracy and society, the country made fateful decisions about the terms of southern reintegration and about the character of public law, with the often intense predilections of the region's representatives underpinning their increasing importance in the legislative process.[4]

With eleven states emerging from defeat and military occupation and, with the addition of Oklahoma in 1907, six others also developing systems of racial segregation and black disfranchisement, at issue was the role these former slave states would play in America's political life. Would they regain the status and capacity they had achieved in the early republic and maintained through much of the antebellum period? The legacies of Civil War pain and heartbreak, memories of which continued to shape political attitudes and behavior for generations, together with the enfranchisement of the large free black male population, made the restoration of the South's full membership in the Union a dense and difficult matter. Thus, it is remarkable that from the election of 1876 to the start of Franklin Delano Roosevelt's "One Hundred Days," the now overwhelmingly Democratic white South could reappear as a political actor of growing and often vital consequence.

In the years and decades that followed, the region's white representatives fought hard and ultimately won cross-party support for the right to remake the racial order on the South's terms, thus apparently providing for its long-term security. Saluting the South for having found means to protect itself against "the domination of an ignorant, irresponsible element," and declaring efforts to bring all African Americans into voting citizenship "a failure," President William Howard Taft devoted a pivotal section of his March 4, 1909, inaugural address to observing that the region's strategies of legal disfranchisement had produced a beneficial result: "the danger of control of an ignorant electorate has therefore passed." Leaving the South to its own devices, Taft argued, had enabled southern whites to finally be reconciled to the Union and increased the "feeling on the part of all the people in the South that this Government is their Government, and that its officers in their states are their officers."[5]

With both major parties distancing themselves from the advancement of black rights, white supremacy again became the region's unmistakable and unashamed hallmark. Writing in 1928, the leading southern historian of the early twentieth century, Ulrich Phillips, described his region's white population as "Americans with a difference." The entirety of this difference, he argued, lay in the degree to which the South was committed to white supremacy. "The South is a land with a unity despite its diversity," he wrote, "with a people having common joys and common sorrows, and, above all, as to the white folks a people with a common resolve indomitably maintained—that it shall be and remain a white man's country." Phillips designated this commitment as "the cardinal test of a Southerner and the central theme of Southern history," whether "expressed with the frenzy of a demagogue or maintained with a patrician's quietude."[6]

As the country moved through the Hoover years to the New Deal, Republicans and Democrats alike were unprepared and unwilling to challenge either this formulation or its consequences. Further, with gains to their electoral confidence and officeholding tenure, the increasingly experienced and safe-seat southern delegations in the House and Senate could guide Congress to reshape its institutional rules and norms, the consequences of which included enhancing sectional autonomy in matters of race, facilitating the maintenance of a diverse coalition that could nonetheless unite to defend white supremacy, and ultimately enlarging regional power to direct the course of national legislation.

This story of enlarged southern security and success, we have stressed, followed a sometimes jagged course—it was not smoothly linear. The white South itself was only intermittently "solid" and often had to grapple with its own divisions—some geographic, some ideological, some based on party. Nor, overall, did the region's representatives proceed in ways that made the South more modern and more prosperous. As we observed with respect to the Blair bill, which would have addressed their region's deep pattern of white as well as black illiteracy, the South's representatives, when confronted with the choice between money for education and a renewal of federal attention to black rights, opted for regional underdevelopment, even backwardness. Southern Democrats, it seems, were willing to accept money for education only when not accompanied by any broader effort to undermine the racial hierarchy.

Notwithstanding this unevenness, internal heterogeneity, and shifts to contexts, the overall effects of southern motivations, preferences, and behavior strengthened the region's hand regarding its most intense commitments about race and political economy. Together, the nation's withdrawal from the promise of the Civil War Amendments and the gradual transformations to the way congressional leaders, committees, parties, and deliberations could proceed created settings within which a distraught and defeated South increasingly obtained its policy wishes, many of which were grounded in populist and progressive sensibilities.

Once the South's overwhelmingly defensive late-nineteenth-century battles had concluded with the region left to govern race relations as its white population wished, and once the South had moved decisively to restrict its electorate and build barriers separating the races across the arc of economic life and civil society, its political leaders began to rebuild their legislative political power and lawmaking capacity. The consequences of their success would change the country, both for good and for ill.

This is not a simple tale of the worthy arrayed against evil. The South did more than secure white hegemony and confine black citizenship. The representatives of these states, we have seen, charted an assertive reformist course for the nation's policies in areas that included such progressive goals as the income tax, railroad regulation and antitrust, a reformed financial system, and support for farmers. They achieved their legislative ambitions in tandem with multiple allies, including Republican Theodore Roosevelt at the start of the century and progressive Republicans in the 1920s. But their greatest influence came in the 1910s with fellow Democrats in Congress and with Woodrow Wilson, a president who fully shared their values and views about race, economics, and the role of the federal government in regulating public affairs. Each of these alliances and each of these substantive achievements took as its premise the South's increasing sense of security about home rule, the key guarantee of white domination and an essential condition for both southern extremists and moderates.

Our second, more implicit, objective is to contribute to understanding the most basic conundrum within the American experience: the relationship of a democracy committed to liberal values of free citizenship, including the rule of law and individual rights, and the consequences of legal institutional white supremacy. These patterns, including slavery, have not been exclusively southern. But the South stood out for the scale and density of its slave system and, later, for its detailed system of profound racial exclusion, hierarchy, and humiliation backed by law and often secured by physical terror.

Congress has been the institutional location where this collision between liberal democracy and white supremacy most regularly occurred, and the branch of government most responsible for its adjudication. How could it be otherwise? In liberal polities, of which the United States was the world's great pioneer, the most important political mechanisms center on political representation—the means by which citizens gain the capacity to shape public outcomes by voting, lobbying, and expressing and shaping opinion. Moreover, it is in the legislature, the great buckle linking state and society, that popular sovereignty moves from an abstract and fundamental idea to tangible practice.

From the start, the United States grappled with joining in one space the world's most free citizens with its least free persons, categories defined by the imposition of color. The most pivotal compromises guiding the Founding were the three-fifths solution for southern representation, which led to the region's exaggerated presence in the House of Representatives, and a Senate whose contours were designed to secure southern slavery from outside intervention.

When these arrangements were nullified by the end of slavery, the promise of equal protection for all citizens, including freed slaves, and the ban on color-based voting restrictions, the country's most profound questions about race and liberal democracy took new form. At stake was no less than the content and character of its liberal regime. Whether and how the South would control the terms of renegotiating the connection between freedom and racial hierarchy after secession, war, and reunion depended in large measure on how these conundrums would be managed, it not fully resolved, on Capitol Hill.

The Great Debate

The fragility of both Hayes's commitment to overcome sectional strife and the meaningfulness of southern pledges to uphold the provisions of the Civil War Amendments was on display when America's most significant literary magazine, the *North American Review*, published a riveting symposium in March 1879 devoted to two questions: "Ought the Negro to Be Disenfranchised? Ought He to Have Been Enfranchised?"

This conversation was convened in the aftermath of the midterm election of 1878, an election in which the Republican Party lost its Senate majority and miscarried in its effort to recover control of the House. The campaign season had been marked by massive antiblack intimidation. "Fraud and violence," the historian Richard White has noted, "gave the Democrats sweeping victories in the South. . . . The seventy-three representatives from the old Confederacy included only three Republicans, and none from those states with a majority black population."[7]

The luminous cast assembled to consider post-slave black voting included the organizer of the discussion, James G. Blaine, then a U.S. senator from Maine who had served as speaker of the House from 1869 to 1875, later was Secretary of State for three presidents, and then waged an unsuccessful campaign in the presidential election of 1884 as the Republican candidate. Other northern contributors included Republican James A. Garfield, soon to be elected president of the United States (only to be assassinated in July 1881, just four months after his inauguration) following nine terms in the House as a Republican from Ohio; and Wendell Phillips of Massachusetts, the noted abolitionist who, after the Civil War, battled on behalf of African American and Indian rights.

Arguing, in Garfield's words, that "between slavery and full citizenship, there was not safe middle ground" and that "to leave the defense of all the rights of persons and property of the manumitted slave to those who had just voted unanimously against his freedom, would have been alike dishonorable and cruel," these northern contributors remonstrated against southern Democratic resistance to black citizenship and suffrage, what Blaine called the history of "cruel oppression" embodied in the postwar Black Codes, and the region's continuing insurrection bordering on guerrilla warfare.[8]

Arrayed on the other side were three leading Deep South figures, as well as one northern and one border state Democrat. The former Confederates included Lucius Quintus Cincinnatus Lamar, who had drafted Mississippi's Ordinance of Secession in 1860, presently represented the state in the Senate, later was appointed to the Supreme Court by President Grover Cleveland, and may have been the Grand Dragon of his state's Ku Klux Klan in the early 1870s; Wade Hampton, now a new U.S. senator, having just completed a term as South Carolina's governor; and Alexander Stephens of Georgia, the Confederacy's vice president, a member of the House from 1843 to 1859 and then again from 1873 to 1882, and later the state's governor.[9]

The southerners' essays advanced broadly common answers to the editor's two questions. Awarding the vote during Reconstruction had been a grievous error. Hampton objected "to conferring suffrage on the negro, immediately upon his emancipation," because "he was totally incompetent to exercise or even to understand the rights conferred upon him." Thus, "the injection of such a mass of ignorant and untrained voters into the body politic," he wrote, "was the most perilous strain to which our institutions have ever been subjected, and the danger arising from this experiment have not passed."[10]

Yet however regrettable black voting rights might be, "the disenfranchisement of the negro," as Lamar put the point, "is a political impossibility under any circumstances short of revolution." Having realized, Hampton recalled, as early as 1865 "that when a man had been made a citizen of the United States he could not be debarred the right of voting on account of his color," he likewise averred that "great and startling as have been the political mutations of the last few years, the disenfranchisement of the negro at this or any subsequent period would be more surprising than any political event in our history." Moreover, he added, "the South does not desire it to be done." Stephens echoed this claim by utterly denying "that the Southern States, in whole or in part, in any way in which States can act, have ever arrayed themselves against their own constitutions and laws, to say nothing of Federal obligations, on an effort to deprive the colored man of the right to vote."

Even if black voters had entered the electorate prematurely, Lamar argued, "the ballot has been educating the negro." They had been learning not to support Republicans exclusively, as that party had placed former slaves "in antagonism to the white race, with whom all his material interests are identified." "In all," he argued, "the South took him, as he was sent to her, a wild and godless barbarian, and made him such that the North has been able to give him citizenship without destruction of our institutions." Further, he concluded, "in all respects, negro freedom and negro equality before the law, security of person and property, are ample and complete."

The evidence for black electoral education, Hampton maintained, was the growing number who now voted Democratic. He celebrated the supposed fact that "in the last two general elections in this State . . . thousands of negroes voted with their white friends." This result, he claimed, was not the outcome of intimidation of any kind, but of successful endeavors by leading white Democratic Party political leaders "to teach him here how to use the vote for his own good, and the benefit of the political society in which he lives and with which his future prosperity is identified. . . . As the negro becomes more intelligent, he naturally allies himself with the more conservative of the whites, for his observation and experience both show him that his interest are identified with those of the white race here."[11]

These southerners were joined by two presumptively liminal figures. Thomas Hendricks had just concluded his term as governor of Indiana, had run in 1876 as Samuel Tilden's running mate, and had finally become vice president of the United States under Grover Cleveland; he served only from March 4 to November 25, 1885, however, because he died suddenly. The Kentucky-born Montgomery Blair, arguably the most interesting figure in this group, was a practicing lawyer in St. Louis and Maryland before the Civil War who would leap into prominence as Dred Scott's representative before the Supreme Court in 1857. Having left the Democratic Party to become a Republican, he later served in Abraham Lincoln's cabinet as postmaster-general; there he both supported emancipation and openly battled with Radical Republicans, the likely source of his dismissal by Lincoln in 1864. After the war, Blair backed Andrew Johnson's policy of reconciliation, then rejoined the Democratic Party; he had been elected to the Maryland House of Delegates in 1878.

Blair, as it turned out, did not follow the comparatively benign line of reasoning offered by the Deep South essayists. Not for Blair the felicitous story of an elective affinity between blacks educated by experience and ex-Confederate Democrats and their program of home rule. Black voting had not been designed, he claimed, for reasons of citizenship but was "inspired by the lust of sectional power." Black voting had been "established by the sword, in violation of the Constitution . . . and the fundamental principle of local self-government." Moreover, he argued, their inherent makeup made the former slaves incapable of citizenship. "The negro," he insisted, "is not of a self-governing nature," and this "nature . . . is not changed by transplanting, more than that of the orange or the banana. Hence to incorporate him into our system is to subvert it." This race has "want of every essential quality of a voter," and such "persons of the worst class," he continued, "cannot live as equals in the same government, *if that government is to be a free government.*"

Republicans, Blair averred, had deployed the federal government to "interpose" between African Americans and the white "race which takes so largely the direction of public affairs of this continent," and which "would control the negro unless the Government interposed to prevent it." Recent years had witnessed "the recovery of political power in all the Southern States," not least because, as black votes for Wade Hampton were indicating, the emancipated black "is more feeble than he was accounted." Yet unlike Hampton, Stephens, or Lamar, Blair did not see a golden future if blacks were to continue to vote. The hope of their being guided "by a class of leaders who are responsible" and the idea that "they could be trained . . . to the exercise of government" were both chimerical at best. "It would be as reasonable to expect them to develop wings by training."[12]

We should not presume that each of these writers was conveying his honest sentiments. Because Blair was from a border state where Reconstruction had not taken place, black voting power had not proved decisive in electing state governments, and leading political figures had not very recently affirmed their commitment to the Reconstruction Amendments, he was probably freer to express his real sentiments than were Hampton and Lamar. But regardless of their sincerity, political circumstances had forced the lawmakers from the Deep South to an at least putative acceptance of back voting as a permanent feature of American, and southern, life (albeit with the expectation that such voting would not prevent, and might facilitate, the regional domination of a Democratic Party led by ex-Confederates). But it would be the voice of Blair, and those like him who outshouted more measured articulations, that ultimately determined the future of southern politics. Within three decades, recurring violent intimidation, together with legal disfranchisement, largely eliminated southern blacks from the electorate.

There were many who wished otherwise, most obviously black southerners, but also some white southerners who either accepted black voting as a right or believed that it could be guided by conservative patricians; others who were attracted to a broad and sometimes biracial populist platform; and hundreds of thousands of white and black northerners who had been convinced by the trials of abolition and the Civil War that equal citizenship should be guaranteed for all. But these citizens and their representatives were outflanked in Congress and increasingly found their views to be marginal in the Supreme Court.

With a combination of naked coercion backed by horrific episodes of brutality and, from 1890, constitutional and legal changes that hard-wired Jim Crow and an array of official means to winnow the electorate, including literacy tests and poll taxes that the Supreme Court found consistent with the terms of the Fourteenth and Fifteenth Amendments, black voting in the South was almost completely eliminated. It was maintained only in a few precincts in the border states and some urban centers, where African Americans lacked decisive influence. In turn, their rights effectively disappeared from the policy agenda of Republicans and Democrats alike.

From Anxiety to Security

It was within this context that the white South emerged as an increasingly effective political actor, a formidable force that could defend home rule and recast the nation's political economy.

During and episodically following Reconstruction, sufficient numbers of Republicans had held fast to the priority of black political rights. The Enforcement Acts of 1870 and 1871, geared to the Fifteenth Amendment, the Ku Klux Klan Act of 1871, which was geared to enforce the Fourteenth Amendment and authorized presidents to suspend *habeas corpus*, and the Civil Rights Act of 1875, mandating equal treatment for all citizens in public accommodations, transportation, and juries, were all in effect when Reconstruction ended. As late as 1890, the great majority of Republicans in the House and Senate backed a federal elections bill that would have placed the right to certify national elections in the hands of canvassers and judges appointed by the president, and that reaffirmed the president's capacity to uphold the law when violence marred an election.

These various efforts to secure equal black citizenship made white southern members deeply anxious—one might say excessively anxious—as they worried about their capacity to independently and autonomously conduct the South's social, economic, and political affairs concerning white-black relations. The pledges that southern leaders had offered to President Hayes soon were violated. Investigations of the 1878 elections in South Carolina and Louisiana revealed massive bullying and coercion, including murder, that kept blacks from the polls. Publishing a massive tome on *The Existing Conflict between Republican Government and Southern Oligarchy* in 1884, Green Berry Raum, a former Republican member of Congress from Illinois who had just stepped down as commissioner of internal revenue and who later oversaw the Civil War pensions system, detailed the South's extraordinary antiblack terror and coercion. Dedicated to "a free ballot, an honest count and correct returns," and pointing out "the means by which the South is made *solid* for the Democratic Party," Raum chronicled the era's overwhelming, if increasingly routine, efforts to keep blacks from the polls, and he took note of the region's crushing climate of violence, including, at the extreme, recurring massacres, such as those in Copiah County, Mississippi, and Danville, Virginia, both in 1883.[13]

The white South's recoil against federal protection for full black citizenship, which made a mockery of the terms of sectional reconciliation, was advanced soon after the close of Reconstruction by a key Supreme Court decision and by the inability of the Republican Party to compete for office in the South and, recurrently, to maintain unitary control of the federal government. In 1883, the Court overturned key sections of the Civil Rights Act of 1875, based on the argument that the Fourteenth Amendment prohibited state action, not racist or harrying behavior by individual citizens. The winnowing of Reconstruction's gains continued, in voting rights and then in public accommodations.

Three years earlier, not without reason, Schuyler Colfax, a former House speaker and vice president, had expressed his apprehension for the "imminent danger now of being ruled by the Rebels, & becoming, after all our sacrifices, the Confederate States of America." This fear of becoming a southern nation, shared by many Republicans, had a mirror image in the southern fear of renewed federal intervention and what regularly was called "negro domination." These fears reinforced each other and pushed the different sides to the edges of the Constitution. When the Civil Rights Act of 1875 was introduced, the future president James Garfield worried that the bill's provision permitting the president to declare martial law in regions plagued by racial violence, a provision that did not stand, placed the legislation beyond that which had been done "during the wildest days of the rebellion" by providing, in effect, for "the suspension of all law" under emergency situations. But he also was aware, as he wrote four years later, that "open violence, concealed fraud, and threatened loss of employment, in many parts of the South, have virtually destroyed the suffrage and deprived the negro of all the benefits which it was intended to confer."[14]

In turn, southern practices implicitly insisted that the Fourteenth and Fifteenth Amendments did not, and should not, actually guarantee equal republican citizenship across racial lines. Shortly after his close-run loss for the presidency to Grover Cleveland in 1884, in an election in which he lost every former slave state, James Blaine, sounding like Tocqueville, remarked that "the first instinct of an American is equality—of right, equality of privilege, equality of political power." Observing how forty-two electoral votes belonged to the South by virtue of its black population, and taking note of the region's "violence and murder," Blaine lamented that "the course of affairs in the South has crushed out the political power of more than six million American citizens and has transferred it by violence to others." Former slaves thus have been "absolutely deprived of political power." A key consequence was an equally profound distortion for whites. "For not only is the negro population disenfranchised but the power which rightly and Constitutionally belongs to them is transferred to the white population of the South, enabling them to exert an electoral influence far beyond that exerted by the same number of white people in the North."[15]

Not only was the practice of equal rights that southern leaders had promised at the close of Reconstruction traduced, but the denial of black rights went hand in hand with an ever more widespread rhetoric of white supremacy, much like the language that had justified slavery in the 1850s. Such language now was deployed to argue that African Americans were premature, ignorant voters who should not have been enfranchised and certainly were not fit to govern.

In *Southern Nation*, we have witnessed the transformation of the South from a supine condition to secure and effective national capacity at three rather different partisan moments. During the McKinley, Roosevelt, and Taft presidencies, the South gained a political security that allowed many of the region's agrarian legislators to come to prominence in state and national circles. Allied nationally with parts of the labor movement through the vehicle of the Democratic Party, they developed a partially adopted program of reform to modify national capitalism by producing enhanced "public control of private economic power." During the century's second decade, southerners were ensconced in influential positions in Congress and the executive, and their preferences led a more fundamental reshaping of the federal government's abilities to supervise and regulate "the process of transportation, banking, storage and trading of commodities, business competitive practices, and labor relations," largely without building the kind of overweening bureaucratic state that southern conservatives dreaded. Thus, the United States was transformed in a progressive direction during the South-oriented presidency of Woodrow Wilson on terms that protected, reinforced, and at times affirmed and extended the section's recently organized system of legally based racial segregation.[16]

Moreover, as we have seen, the return of Republican hegemony after 1920 did not reduce southern influence in anything like a commensurate manner. During this decade, the South in effect was the Democratic Party, and the Democratic Party was a cohesive body that would seek to promote the southern agenda without much need to worry about federal action regarding race. Working within the ambit of transformed congressional rules and norms, and exploiting often stark divisions within the Republican Party, southern members surprisingly continued to notch many successes by building cross-party coalitions in which they often were dominant substantively despite their minority partisan status.

Yet even when white southern Democrats tilted toward populist and progressive policies, deeply suspicious of capitalist wealth and open markets, they often sacrificed regional goals for economic modernization on the altar of white domination. The result was a region left behind. In 1938, when Franklin Roosevelt identified the South as the nation's number-one problem, the region was dirt poor. "The long and ironic history of the despoiling of this truly American section of the country's population," he wrote, rested on an "unbalance that can and must be righted, for the sake of the South and of the Nation." Deprivation was widespread, far more than in any other part of the depression-ravaged country. The document the president commissioned that summer, *Report on Economic Conditions of the South,* noted that "the richest State in the South ranks lower in per capita income than the poorest State outside the region." Southern average income, at $314 a year, was half that of the nation. Nearly half of the South's farmers owned no land but worked as tenants or sharecroppers; only 30 percent of non-southern farmers were in a similar condition in 1940. Nearly one in ten southerners were illiterate, and over 20 percent of men and women over the age of twenty-five had received less than five years of schooling, more than twice the rate outside the South. Hunger and disease were rampant, among whites as well as blacks. Most counties lacked any doctors or health facilities. Only 6 percent of all the farmhouses in the South had piped-in water, and only in just over 3 percent of those dwellings did those pipes lead to the bathroom. Southern living conditions, the report concluded, were similar to those "of the poorest peasants in Europe." How, then, could the South's growing legislative power and commitment to egalitarian populist and progressive programs have gone hand in hand with a growing gap among regions that had left the South standing as the big loser?[17]

A crucial source of this contradictory reality, we have seen, was the unrelenting determination of southern representatives to place questions of race ahead of economic and social progress within their own seventeen states. Fateful choices were made to protect the South's racial autonomy, especially in the post-Reconstruction period, when this capacity again threatened to disappear under the impact of Republican-sponsored voting rights legislation. Faced with the chance, for example, to gain massive federal investments in primary education—a critical instrument for introducing economic modernization, creating a New South, and closing gaps with the country's increasingly industrial and urban market economy—the South divided but ultimately said no. The white South was afraid that such largesse would undermine the racial order, from both inside and outside the region. More broadly, the South opted for robust national state formation and assertive redistributive policies only when stipulations could be secured that protected the region's capacity to impose social, economic, and civic racism.

The New Deal and Beyond

As FDR swore his oath in March 1933, the qualities of the United States as a southern nation were being reinforced. During the New Deal, southern capacities in Congress deeply affected public affairs. Later, and into our own time, a profound southern party realignment following the civil rights revolution was marked by a shift toward conservative Republicanism that compromised prospects that the country would further and durably build on the achievements of the Wilson and Roosevelt administrations in economic and social policy.

When the New Deal came to power, white southern security was at its apex. Ever since the failure of the Lodge bill in 1891, no effort to protect black rights in Congress had succeeded. Even a 1922 effort to punish lynching, a year marked by fifty such gruesome killings, failed, and race quickly disappeared from the agenda of national politics even during a period of unified Republican government.

Throughout the New Deal era, the articulation of white supremacy was unafraid and unashamed, even as particular cadences varied. Mississippi's Senator Theodore Bilbo, who was the Senate's noisiest racist and a member of the Ku Klux Klan, pronounced himself "100 percent for Roosevelt . . . and the New Deal." Bilbo spoke often about black inferiority ("the difference of the intellect, in the brain, in the mind" between blacks and whites, he asserted, made "the white man throughout all time . . . the superior race, the ruling race, the race of creating power, the race of art, the race of literature, the race of music that moves the soul") and the dangers of "mongrelization" (merely "one drop of Negro blood placed in the veins of the purest Caucasian destroys the inventive genius of his mind and strikes palsied his creative faculty"), and he had no trouble justifying lynching, sometimes even encouraging it ("It is practically impossible, without great loss of life, especially at the present time, to prevent lynchings of Negro rapists when the crime is committed against the white women of the South").[18]

Other hard-edged defenders of the region's racial order talked in softer, but only slightly softer, tones. At the start of a five-term Senate career that culminated in his long chairmanship of the Judiciary Committee, Mississippi's James Eastland advanced the view in a 1944 debate about soldier voting that returning white southern soldiers "desire more than anything else to see the integrity of the social institutions of the South unimpaired. They desire to see white supremacy maintained. . . . Those boys are fighting to maintain white supremacy." Even the most liberal southern members, notably including Florida's Claude Pepper, upheld the core features of the South's racial order. During a debate about an anti-lynching bill in 1937, Pepper stated that "the colored race will not vote, because in so doing . . . they endanger the supremacy of a race to which God has committed the destiny of a continent, perhaps of the world."[19]

Segregation and black disfranchisement seemed safe. Moreover, as large Democratic majorities took hold in the 1932, 1934, and 1936 elections, southern seniority provided a perch from which southern lawmakers could exercise unparalleled influence. Members from the seventeen southern states in the 1920s nearly had been the only surviving Democrats during a period of Republican electoral success. Now, as a great influx of non-southern Democrats came to the Hill during the height of the New Deal, southern influence could depend on two features of congressional life: negatively, the House and Senate rules they had shaped, including the blocking power of the Senate filibuster, which could be deployed either in fact or in anticipation; and positively, their control and domination of key committees in both chambers.

Together with the broad indifference of Republicans as well as their own party colleagues on matters of race, southern Democrats secured extraordinary victories. The great majority of southern representatives built on the region's populist and progressive proclivities to staunchly support New Deal social and economic policies, provided southern racial home rule could be protected. Their dirt-poor region required relief from the Depression, safety-net security, and assistance to agriculture. In keeping with a long-standing analysis of Yankee capital as colonial and rapacious, they supported the regulation of Wall Street and experiments in corporatism and planning, which brought such tangible benefits as the remarkable Tennessee Valley Authority's instruments of electrification and economic advance.

These gains to the region and country were twinned with the adoption of legislative instruments that sheltered southern racial autonomy and thus reinforced Jim Crow and its system of racial humiliation and danger. As the New Deal launched and developed, southern members of Congress exploited the disparity between the intensity of their commitment to Jim Crow and the comparative indifference of other representatives as well as their committee power and mastery of rules and procedures to safeguard their region's racial organization. Effectively creating affirmative action for whites, they inserted provisions in the Wagner Act, Social Security Act, and Fair Labor Standards Act that excluded farmworkers and domestic service workers, the categories of work for most southern blacks in the labor market. Gardner Jackson, chairman of the National Committee on Rural and Social Planning, a labor-oriented advocacy organization, testifying about FLSA in 1938, stated that

> no purpose will be served by beating around the bush. You, Mr. Chairman, and all your associates on this Committee know as well as I do that agricultural laborers have been explicitly excluded from participation in any of the benefits of New Deal legislation, from the late (but not greatly

lamented) N.R.A., down through the A.A.A., the Wagner-Connery Labor Relations Act and the Social Security Act, for the simple and effective reason that it has been deemed politically certain that their inclusion would have spelled death of the legislation in Congress. And now, in this proposed Black Connery wages and hours bill, agricultural laborers are again explicitly excluded.[20]

Further, southern legislators placed the administration of these and other key laws in the hands of local officials who made sure that the southern system would not be disrupted. And they made sure that Congress would not attach antidiscrimination amendments to the era's full range of social welfare programs. The most notable example was the 1944 GI Bill, which helped veterans buy homes, attend college, get job training, and start business ventures. At southern insistence—the bill was written in a committee chaired by Mississippi's John Rankin—the allocation and management of these benefits was decentralized. Except for low-level vocational training, southern blacks were largely left out. As the Morrill bill of 1890 had done, the GI Bill accommodated segregation in higher education, while creating job ceilings imposed by regional bureaucrats and tolerating local banks' unwillingness to approve federally insured mortgages or small business loans for African Americans.[21]

Southern security did not last. By the late 1930s, and into the 1940s, the apprehensions of white southern representatives were again raised by the combination of the rapid growth of Congress of Industrial Organizations (CIO) unions and a militant labor movement under the umbrella of the Wagner Act; the northern movement of African Americans, who were emerging as pivotal voters in Illinois, New York, Ohio, and Pennsylvania; the appearance of a still-nascent but visible civil rights movement as black voices, especially during World War II, argued for "Double V," victory at home as well as victory abroad; and the reappearance of anti-lynching legislation on the docket of Congress. The Democratic Party, lamented South Carolina senator and soon to be Supreme Court Justice James Byrnes in 1938, had fallen under the sway of "the Negroes of the South." The Court itself no longer could be relied on to back southern racial preferences, as the 1944 *Smith v. Allwright* ruling that the white primary violated the Constitution indicated. In 1947, a bipartisan coalition of senators blocked Bilbo from taking his seat after African Americans from Mississippi protested that he had threatened lynchings against any black voter in the Democratic primary. Shocked southern senators mounted a filibuster in his defense, and the fight was only resolved with Bilbo's return to Mississippi for surgery and subsequent death from cancer.[22]

As that decade progressed, southern legislators became ever more nervous about losing their control of the racial agenda, a fear manifested in the creation of the Dixiecrat alternative led by Strom Thurmond in the presidential election of 1948—the year President Truman ordered the racial integration of the still-segregated armed forces. "Through recent years," complained Senator James Eastland of Mississippi, an avid Dixiecrat who urged his state legislature to break with the national Democratic Party, "the South has retreated step by step until now it is spurned from the throne which we ourselves have created."[23]

Yet, once more, the South held important congressional trump cards. After 1938, most Democrats in both the House and Senate had been elected by the limited and confined electorate of the South, and after 1940 every senator from the South—thirty-four in number—was a Democrat. "Remember," Rankin reminded the House in January 1940, "southern Democrats now have the balance of power in both Houses of Congress. By your conduct," he warned his fellow Democrats, "you may make it impossible for us to support many of you for important committee assignments, and other positions for which you aspire." By attacking the South's race system, he continued, "you Democrats . . . are destroying your usefulness here."[24]

One crucial result of growing white apprehension was the increasing willingness of representatives of the Jim Crow South to break with the Democratic Party's policy consensus, especially regarding matters that concerned labor markets and labor unions. When what became the Taft-Hartley Act, which restricted the capacity of unions to organize, extend their reach, and become a truly national political force, was being debated in 1947, Republicans controlled both the House and Senate. But with just fifty-one seats in the Senate, far short of a supermajority, they could not alone have overridden the veto of President Truman.

Of all the lawmaking in the Truman years, Taft-Hartley represented the greatest victory for Jim Crow's security by ensuring that labor unions could not successfully penetrate the region and upset its racialized, low-wage economy. Labor organizing, southern members understood, threatened to stimulate civil rights activism and level wages across the racial divide. Southern members closed ranks, offering nearly unanimous support to a bill almost no other Democrat was ready to support. Further, Republicans kept the Wagner Act's rigorous exclusions of farmworkers and domestic workers while adding an expanded definition of the agricultural carve-out to include processing and handling activities ancillary to agriculture—jobs performed primarily in the South by African Americans.

In all, "it became clear," as Richard Hofstadter observed in 1949, that southern power was capable of insisting that the country not depart from the contours of a southern nation: "Southerners still possessed, and were determined to exercise, the balance of power, which they were free to do at any time by bolting and voting with conservative Republicans; and that no legislation could be passed, on either economic affairs or race relations, which they would not accept." In this manner, the South continued to shape key aspects of the nation in its image. So doing, it helped discern ways to construct a more effective, robust, and capable national state, but it also exacted a fearful price— above all for repressed African Americans, but also for its own blighted section and for a country that was about to face a renewed difficult struggle to secure the promise of emancipation and open the doors of its liberal political tradition to all Americans.[25]

As these tensions manifested themselves both inside and outside Congress, southern rhetoric toughened. When Congress took up legislation prohibiting racial discrimination in employment in 1946, not just the Bilbos remonstrated strenuously. Senator Walter George of Georgia likened fair employment legislation to the "philosophy of totalitarian government . . . in its most extreme form and expression," like "the latest example in Nazi Germany." Eastland said that "the bill would rape the Magna Carta." South Carolina's Burnet Maybank complained that "people from other sections of the country do not know or understand the colored man," while Olin Johnson, the former governor of South Carolina, instructed his fellow senators that "racial separation is due to an inborn instinct . . . that cannot be changed by legislation."[26]

New Coalitions and Realignment

A second key development in the late 1940s was the exploration by segregationists of a potential alliance with conservative Republicans, a possibility that had been probed in the late nineteenth century on issues other than black civil rights. A leading southern intellectual, the Alabama lawyer Charles Wallace Collins, identified the northern wing of the Democratic Party, a political entity increasingly oriented to "the whole Negro program of equality," as the South's most potent enemy. Accordingly, he recommended that two strategies be explored: the creation of an independent southern force that would "hold the balance of power," and a two-party alignment, "a logical though unorganized alliance," in which the South would increasingly join forces with conservative Republicans who wished to limit the scope and capacity of the national government.[27]

In the decades since the Truman administration, the most significant shifts in American politics—the civil rights revolution and the sharp turn toward conservatism and the Republican Party—have had southern political behavior at their core. When the Roosevelt realignment nationalized the Democratic Party, the South's seemingly rock-solid one-party system provided the centerpiece of the national partisan foundation. As a consequence of the civil rights mobilization and the successes it secured in the courts and in Congress, the electoral security of Democrats in the South dissolved, and a regional re-alignment was propelled.

The white South took up the Republican Party's offer to transform into a racially conservative southern party. At first this shift did not seem possible. Leading students of southern politics David Matthews and James Prothro declared in 1964, the year the Civil Rights Act was passed, that "the Republican tide is sweeping over Dixie at glacial speed." Two years later, even after the passage of the 1965 Voting Rights Act, the great student of elections Philip Converse concluded that the "Southern Democrat is still far from ready to receive Republicans with open arms."[28]

These scholars stressed the durability of partisan loyalties, the breadth and depths of whites' attachments to the Democrats, and the absence of sufficiently attractive Republican alternatives. Though they expected southern politics to become more competitive, they thought its post-Reconstruction, Jim Crow–era features would prove durable despite the revolutionary changes in race relations that were under way.

As it turns out, they underestimated the prospects for political change. To be sure, the partisan transformation took place slowly, with a lag separating presidential and congressional electoral behavior. Between 1965 and 1985, the South gave over two-thirds of its votes to Republican presidential candidates but only about one-third to Republican candidates for the House and Senate, and even less—24 percent and 14 percent, respectively—to Republicans running for governor and state legislative office.[29]

Over the course of a process spanning decades, the region became increasingly and ever more reliably Republican. For Congress, this shift was marked most notably in 1994. Before that election, Democrats still held on to just over 60 percent of the seats in the House. That year the South went Republican for the first time since Reconstruction. The elections that November, the political scientist Walter Dean Burnham observed, were "very probably the most consequential off-year election in [exactly] one hundred years." This realignment in southern voting has been reinforced in the decades since, and it has undergirded the national prospects of the Republican Party in the manner once accomplished for Democrats. The South became a central instrument for the ascendance of conservative Republicanism in Congress and the source of a head start even for weak Republican presidential candidates.[30]

In the 115th Congress, elected in 2016, 169 members in the House represented the seventeen once–Jim Crow states. They included 24 African Americans, all Democrats, and 26 Democrats who were white or Latino; all 119 Republicans were white. Republicans occupied 25 of the region's 34 Senate seats, one of which was held by an African American. All the Democrats outside of Delaware occupied competitive seats; the same was true for fewer than a handful of the Republicans.

Taking advantage of opportunities opened by the growing schism over civil rights in the Democratic Party, Republicans skillfully motored the region's partisan shift by using race to trump other divisions in the electorate. Choosing voters, they induced voters to choose them. As early as 1991, Thomas and Mary Edsall took note of how southern Republicans were seizing opportunities by dividing the region into "a politics of black and white." The Republican Party remade itself as the voice of the white South, albeit a post–Jim Crow white South. By contrast, especially in the Deep South, blacks had moved toward majority status within the Democratic Party, with "very few whites . . . prepared to be part of a coalition in which they are a minority." In all, they concluded, racial divisions came to be "an open invitation to those seeking to build a political majority on the basis of racial polarization."[31]

Policy signals undergirded this effort's mostly soft but sometimes hard-edged appeals to white identify and implicit supremacy. Few nationally prominent Republicans have made explicitly racist appeals, and there has been no overt call for a return to the segregationist racial order. Still, southern Republicans, strategists and candidates alike, have largely abjured courting black voters and signaled that they are the white person's party, not only by objecting to race-based affirmative action but also by using wedge assaults on social welfare programs, including the Affordable Care Act, and underscoring crime, an issue with implicit racial content.

As we write, the status of the United States as a southern nation has not been put to rest. The country faces sharp conflicts about historical memory and commemoration, the character of white identity, the scope of policies of racial rectification, and intersecting dimensions of inequality. The South itself teeters between solidarity and diversity. When states resist Medicaid expansion and billions of dollars in federal funds, or enact right-to-work laws, or cut welfare benefits, or tax regressively, the South is in the lead. When Congress makes policy, the rightward tilt of most of the region's representatives often proves decisive.

Yet who would have imagined three former Confederate states, and five southern states, opting for an African American president, as occurred in 2008. Or for that matter, that South Carolina would be represented in the Senate by a conservative black Republican, elected to a seat once held by John C. Calhoun, with the support of over 70 percent of the white electorate and less than 15 percent of black voters? Or that a white mayor of New Orleans, Mitch Landrieu, would give an eloquent address on why he supported removing monuments "to the Lost Cause of the Confederacy," which he denounced "as symbols of white supremacy" and a commemoration of the Reconstruction-era suppression of biracial democratic government?

The history of white supremacy and its protean role in congressional lawmaking cannot be wished away. Yet how the country will choose to manage the many repercussions of this legacy challenge us still. Presently, the meaning of the United States as a southern nation has become more open, more malleable, more uncertain. Despite various ugly possibilities, decent opportunities beckon. "We now have a chance to create not only new symbols," Landrieu concluded, "but to do it together, as one people."[32]

NOTES

Chapter 1. Southern Politics

1. "Why Not Southern Democratic Leadership?" *World's Work* 4(4): 2367.

2. "The South's Share," *Lexington* (KY) *Morning-Herald*, November 19, 1900, 2.

3. Edmund S. Morgan, *American Slavery, American Freedom* (New York: W. W. Norton, 1975), x.

4. Richard Hofstadter, "From Calhoun to the Dixiecrats," *Social Research* 16(June 1949): 135, 137; Richard K. Crallé, ed., *The Works of John C. Calhoun*, vol. 4 (New York: D. Appleton and Co., 1854), 533.

5. Hofstadter, "From Calhoun to the Dixiecrats," 140, 141, 146, 150.

6. V. O. Key Jr., *Southern Politics in State and Nation* (New York: Alfred A. Knopf, 1949), 5; Richard Hofstadter, "The Southern Citadel," *Commentary*, January 1, 1950, 388.

7. Hofstadter, "The Southern Citadel," 389–390.

8. Richard Franklin Bensel , *Sectionalism and American Political Development, 1880–1980* (Madison: University of Wisconsin Press, 1984); Elizabeth Sanders, *Roots of Reform: Farmers, Workers, and the State, 1877–1917* (Chicago: University of Chicago Press, 1999); Robert Harrison, *Congress, Progressive Reform, and the New American State* (Cambridge: Cambridge University Press, 2010).

9. The nonrecognition by foreign governments of property rights in slaves who escaped into their territory was called by John Calhoun, with little irony, "one of the greatest outrages ever committed on the rights of individuals by a civilized nation." Don E. Fehrenbacher, *The Slaveholding Republic: An Account of the United States Government's Relations to Slavery*, completed and edited by Ward M. McAfee (New York: Oxford University Press, 2001), 106, 133.

10. Alexis de Tocqueville, *Democracy in America*, translated by Arthur Goldhammer, edited by Olivier Zunz, vol. 1 (1835; reprint, New York: Library of America, 2012), 318, 331, 613–614.

11. Steven Hahn, *A Nation under Our Feet: Black Political Struggles in the Rural South, from Slavery to the Great Migration* (Cambridge, MA: Belknap Press of Harvard University Press, 2003), 65, 102.

12. Hahn, *A Nation under Our Feet*, 198.

13. Edward King, *The Great South: A Record of Journeys in Louisiana, Texas, the Indian Territory, Missouri, Arkansas, Mississippi, Alabama, Georgia, Florida, South Carolina, North Carolina, Kentucky, Tennessee, Virginia, West Virginia, and Maryland* (Hartford, CT: American Publishing Co., 1875), 17.

14. Jürgen Osterhammel, *The Transformation of the World: A Global History of the Nineteenth Century* (Princeton, NJ: Princeton University Press, 2014), 851.

15. D. W. Meinig, *The Shaping of America: A Geographical Perspective on 500 Years of History*, vol. 3, *Transcontinental America, 1850–1919* (New Haven, CT: Yale University Press, 1998), 197.

16. Richard M. Valelly, *The Two Reconstructions: The Struggle for Black Enfranchisement* (Chicago: University of Chicago Press, 2004), 113–118; Eric Foner, *Reconstruction: America's Unfinished Revolution, 1863–1877* (New York: HarperCollins, 1988), 531.

17. Natalie Ring, *The Problem South: Region, Empire, and the New Liberal State, 1880–1930* (Athens: University of Georgia Press, 2013); Frank E. Smith, *Congressman from Mississippi* (New York: Pantheon Books, 1964), 90–91; C. Vann Woodward, *Origins of the New South, 1877–1913* (Baton Rouge: Louisiana State University Press, 1951), chap. 11; "As to the Solids," *Macon* (GA) *Telegraph and Messenger*, November 5, 1880, 2; "The South Deserves the Presidency," *Fort Worth* (TX) *Morning Register*, June 20, 1901, 4; "A Southern Man," *Washington Post*, May 22, 1907, 6; "A Southern Democrat?" *Washington Post*, June 11, 1902, 6; "Talk of a Southern Man," *Lexington* (KY) *Herald*, March 25, 1906, 7.

18. Edward Gibson, *Boundary Control: Subnational Authoritarianism in Federal Democracies* Cambridge: Cambridge University Press, 2013); Robert Mickey, *Paths Out of Dixie: The Democratization of Authoritarian Enclaves in America's Deep South, 1944–1972* (Princeton, NJ: Princeton University Press, 2015); James C. Hempgill, "The Conservatism of the South," *Charleston* (SC) *News and Courier*, January 22, 1906; C. Vann Woodward, *The Strange Career of Jim Crow* (New York: Oxford University Press, 1955); Sanders, *Roots of Reform*; Tennant S. McWilliams, *The New South Faces the World* (Tuscaloosa: University of Alabama Press, 1988); Dewey W. Grantham, *The South in Modern America: A Region at Odds* (New York: HarperCollins, 1994), xvii, 86; Joseph A. Fry, *Dixie Looks Abroad: The South and U.S. Foreign Relations, 1789–1973* (Baton Rouge: Louisiana State University Press, 2002).

19. Ira Katznelson, *Fear Itself: The New Deal and the Origins of Our Time* (New York: Liveright, 2013); Carl N. Degler, "Thesis, Antithesis, Synthesis: The South, the North, and the Nation," *Journal of Southern History* 53(February 1987): 3–18, 6.

20. William E. Leuchtenburg, *The White House Looks South: Franklin D. Roosevelt, Harry S. Truman, Lyndon B. Johnson* (Baton Rouge: Louisiana State University Press, 2007); Hahn, *A Nation under Our Feet*; Daniel T. Kryder, *Divided Arsenal: Race and the American State during World War II* (Cambridge: Cambridge University Press, 2000); Bensel, *Sectionalism and American Political Development*; Valelly, *The Two Reconstructions*; Desmond S. King, *Separate and Unequal: Black Americans and the U.S. Federal Government* (Oxford: Oxford University Press, 1997); Desmond S. King and Rogers M. Smith, *Still a House Divided: Race and Politics in Obama's America* (Princeton, NJ: Princeton University Press, 2012).

21. "No Change of View," *Macon* (GA) *Daily Telegraph*, April 16, 1906; "England and the Negro," *The State* (Columbia, SC), March 4, 1909, 4.

22. William Garrott Brown, "The South in National Politics," *South Atlantic Quarterly* 9(2, 1910): 103–115, 111, 113; W. E. B. Du Bois, "The 'Veil' of Self-Consciousness," *The Atlantic*, August 1897; W. E. B. Du Bois, *The Souls of Black Folk* (1903; reprint, New York: Oxford University Press, 2007), 6.

23. Ulrich B. Phillips, "The Central Theme of Southern History," *American Historical Review* 34(1, 1928): 30–43, 43.

24. V. O. Key, *Southern Politics in State and Nation* (New York: Alfred A. Knopf, 1949), 315.

25. The only southern states that did not vote for the GOP at some point between 1876 and 1944 were Arkansas, Alabama, Georgia, and Mississippi. If 1876 is excepted, South Carolina and Louisiana would join this list. The remainder of the former Confederacy, except Florida and Tennessee, voted for the Republican candidate only once during this period. Kentucky voted for the Republican candidate on only three occasions before 1945: in 1896, 1924, and 1928. Key, *Southern Politics*, 10–11.

26. Ibid., 16.

27. This feature not only left racial matters outside organized politics but also created a powerful upward class bias by limiting discourse to issues that could not challenge basic patterns of inequality even among whites. Curiously, as Key observed, this pattern favoring the "haves" inside

the South weakened the local business class in national terms by insulating it from challenge and competition that might have forced it to modernize. Ibid., 310.

28. Ibid., 9.

29. Ibid., 315.

30. Woodward, *Origins of the New South*, 23.

31. The principal nations in Indian Territory had treaties with the Confederacy. Slavery was legal and practiced in the territory before the end of the Civil War. Though only eleven states declared independence from the United States, Missouri and Kentucky were represented in the Confederate Congress, Maryland's attempt at secession was impeded by martial law, and support for the Confederacy was so high in Delaware that its polling stations were occupied by the U.S. Army.

32. Address by Hammond Fowler, of Rockwood, Tennessee, *Congressional Record*, March 23, 1926, 6073; Smith, *Congressman from Mississippi*, 111.

33. For Bushnell, this was because the "negro problem [was] of diminishing significance" in these four states. Albert Bushnell Hart, *The Southern South* (New York: D. Appleton & Co., 1910), 20.

34. David L. Carlton, "How American Is the American South?" in *The South as an American Problem*, edited by Larry J. Griffin and Don H. Doyle (Athens: University of Georgia Press, 1995), 33.

35. For an overview, see Katznelson, *Fear Itself*.

Chapter 2. Southern Lawmaking

1. Judson C. Welliver, "The Triumph of the South," *Munsey's Magazine* 49(5, 1913): 731–743, 739.

2. John Locke, "Second Treatise," in *Two Treatises of Government* (1689), edited by Peter Laslett (Cambridge: Cambridge University Press, 1988), 355, 364; Donald R. Wolfensberger, *Congress and the People: Deliberative Democracy on Trial* (Washington, DC: Woodrow Wilson Center Press, 1999), 10–11.

3. Degler, "Thesis, Antithesis, Synthesis," 6; Gerald Gamm and John Huber, "Legislatures as Political Institutions: Beyond the Contemporary Congress," in *Political Science: State of the Discipline*, vol. 3, edited by Ira Katznelson and Helen V. Milner (New York: American Political Science Association/W. W. Norton, 2002), 319; Ira Katznelson, "Historical Approaches to the Study of Congress: Toward a Congressional Vantage on American Political Development," in *Oxford Handbook of the American Congress*, edited by Eric Schickler and Frances Lee (New York: Oxford University Press, 2012), 112.

4. Gregory J. Wawro and Ira Katznelson, "Designing Historical Social Scientific Inquiry: How Parameter Heterogeneity Can Bridge the Methodological Divide between Quantitative and Qualitative Approaches," *American Journal of Political Science* 58(2, 2014): 526–546, 527.

5. In this we break with many other analyses of the South, which emphasize the degree to which southerners developed a purely cultural identity after the Civil War. "A Southern political nation was not to be," argues Charles Reagan Wilson, for instance, "and the people of Dixie came to accept that." The desire for an independent state was not a relevant manifestation of southern nationality in postbellum political life, but southern identity was nothing if not political. Closely imbricated in the narrative of a southern identity was the tale of how the white South had suppressed its political divisions in order to end Reconstruction, and how it would remain united to forever sustain southern institutions. W. J. Cash, *The Mind of the South* (New York: Alfred A. Knopf, 1941), 12; Charles Reagan Wilson, *Baptized in Blood: The Religion of the Lost Cause, 1865–1920* (1980; reprint, Athens: University of Georgia Press, 2009), 1, 13.

6. Clayton (D-AL-3), *Congressional Record*, May 20, 1897, 1198; McRae (D-AR-3), *Congressional Record*, June 30, 1890, 6805; Phillips, "The Central Theme of Southern History," 31.

7. This was not simply a matter of selection. During the Civil War, the Republicans moved quickly to redefine the federal circuit courts, which were the traditional basis for allocating Supreme Court seats, so that the South would have at most only three of the nine justices, rather than the four they had been likely to hold before the war. In most years before the New Deal, they had even fewer than three.

8. Richard Fenno, *Congressmen in Committees* (Boston: Little, Brown & Co., 1966), 3.

9. We outline the logic in one dimension here for the sake of simplicity, but also because the pivotal politics approach to congressional lawmaking generally focuses on a single dimension along which members of the House and Senate and the president can be arrayed. Keith Krehbiel, *Pivotal Politics: A Theory of U.S. Lawmaking* (Chicago: University of Chicago Press, 1998).

10. It is only an approximation, as the roll call data used for this analysis do not capture preference intensity, which is very important to understand for a more complete picture of southern influence over lawmaking.

11. The filibuster pivot is identified, following Krehbiel (*Pivotal Politics*), as the senator located at the two-thirds point opposite the president. The cloture requirements have changed since 1917, when cloture had to be invoked by two-thirds of senators present and voting. In 1975, the rule was amended to require that three-fifths of members elected and sworn in invoke cloture. Joshua Clinton, Simon Jackman, and Douglas Rivers, "The Statistical Analysis of Roll Call Data," *American Political Science Review 98(2, 2004): 355-370.*

12. We have conducted the same analysis for the other sections of the country. Neither the West, the Midwest, nor the Northeast experienced such large swings in the probability of being pivotal, although most of the influence that the South lost after the Civil War seems to have accrued to the Midwest.

13. This party cartel has existed, according to Cox and McCubbins, since the 1890s, when changes to the rules empowered the speaker and the members of the Rules Committee to effectively decide what issues would be brought up and when. Cox and McCubbins agree with David Rohde and John Aldrich that a grant of positive agenda–setting authority is conditional on party cohesion and interparty polarization. Gary W. Cox and Mathew D. McCubbins, *Setting the Agenda: Responsible Party Government in the U.S. House of Representatives* (Cambridge: Cambridge University Press, 2005), 18–19; David Rohde, *Parties and Leaders in the Postreform House* (Chicago: University of Chicago Press, 1991); John Aldrich, *Why Parties? A Second Look* (Chicago: University of Chicago Press, 2011).

14. The power of the party leadership in the Senate, argue Chris Hartog and Nathan Monroe, is less the power to keep issues off the agenda than the power to put onto the agenda bills that have been crafted to minimize minority opposition. David Brady, Richard Brody, and David Epstein, "Heterogeneous Parties and Political Organization: The U.S. Senate, 1880–1920," *Legislative Studies Quarterly* 14(2, 1989): 205–223, 208-209; "Passing of the Big Five Who Ruled the Senate," *New York Times*, April 24, 1910, 52; David Rothman, *Politics and Power: The U.S. Senate, 1869–1901* (Cambridge, MA: Harvard University Press, 1966), 4; Barbara Sinclair, *The Transformation of the U.S. Senate* (Baltimore: Johns Hopkins University Press, 1989), 10; Chris Den Hartog and Nathan W. Monroe, *Agenda Setting in the U.S. Senate: Costly Consideration and Majority Party Advantage* (Cambridge: Cambridge University Press, 2011).

15. For our purposes, we count the following as cartel positions: speaker, majority leader, and chair of the Rules Committee, of the Ways and Means Committee, of the Appropriations Committee, and of five of the most important remaining committees for a given period. David Canon, Garrison Nelson, and Charles Stewart III (data collectors), Historical Congressional Standing Committees, 1st to 79th Congresses, 1789–1947: House (1–37; 38–79) and Senate (1–48;

49–79) [1997], http://web.mit.edu/17.251/www/data_page.html#1. Cox and McCubbins, *Setting the Agenda*, 11, 19, 24; Ronald M. Peters Jr., *The American Speakership: The Office in Historical Perspective* (Baltimore: Johns Hopkins University Press, 1990), 109–110.

16. Paul DeWitt Hasbrouck, *Party Government in the House of Representatives* (New York: MacMillan Company, 1927), 186; Cox and McCubbins, *Setting the Agenda*, 135; Eric Schickler and Kathryn Pearson, "Agenda Control, Majority Party Power, and the House Committee on Rules, 1937–52," *Legislative Studies Quarterly* 34(4, 2011): 455–491.

17. Gregory Wawro and Eric Schickler, "Where's the Pivot? Obstruction and Lawmaking in the Pre-Cloture Senate," *American Journal of Political Science* 48(4, 2004): 758–774; Gregory Wawro and Eric Shickler, *Filibuster: Obstruction and Lawmaking in the U.S. Senate* (Princeton, NJ: Princeton University Press, 2007); Gregory Koger, *Filibustering: A Political History of Obstruction in the House and Senate* (Chicago: University of Chicago Press, 2010).

18. George Tsebelis demonstrates that policy stability is in part a function of the cohesiveness of collective veto actors, such as committees. The greater the cohesion within a collective veto actor, the smaller the space for policy change. A corollary to this, we suggest, is that highly cohesive collective actors are more influential in defining the terms of legislation. George Tsebelis, "Decision Making in Political Systems: Veto Players in Presidentialism, Parliamentarism, Multicameralism, and Multipartyism," *British Journal of Political Science* 25(3, 1995): 289–325.

19. Brown, "The South in National Politics," 107, 111; Phillips, "The Central Theme of Southern History," 31; *Raleigh* (NC) *News and Observer*, October 1, 1912; Morton Sosna, "The South in the Saddle: Racial Politics during the Wilson Year," *Wisconsin Magazine of History* 54(1, 1970): 31.

20. Of the non-southern states, New Jersey had the largest percentage of African Americans, followed by Kansas. Pennsylvania, New York, Ohio, Illinois, New Jersey, Indiana, and Kansas had had larger black populations by 1900, in absolute numbers, than Delaware, Oklahoma, and West Virginia. All census data comes from Michael R. Haines and Inter-university Consortium for Political and Social Research. Historical, Demographic, Economic, and Social Data: Bibliographic Citation: The United States, 1790-2002 [Computer file]. ICPSR02896-v3. Ann Arbor, MI: Inter-university Consortium for Political and Social Research [distributor], 2010-05-21. doi:10.3886/ICPSR02896.v3

21. Key's threshold of 35 percent reflected the potential importance of a sizable bloc of voters in the late 1940s. In practice, we have varied the definition of the Black Belt to reflect changing demographics. We limit the Black Belt to districts with a black population of more than 50 percent in the late nineteenth century, of 40 percent up to World War I, and at Key's threshold thereafter. Key, *Southern Politics*, 666.

22. Gavin Wright, *Old South, New South: Revolutions in the Southern Economy since the Civil War* (New York: Basic Books, 1986), 157.

23. "Southern Democracy," *Dallas Weekly Herald*, January 17, 1884.

24. Lee Alston, "Issues in Postbellum Southern Agriculture," in *Agriculture and National Development: Views on the Nineteenth Century*, edited by Louis Ferleger (Ames: Iowa State University Press, 1990), 207; Gavin Wright, "Cotton Competition and the Post-Bellum Recovery of the American South," *Journal of Economic History* 34(3, 1974): 610–635, 635.

25. Election data comes from ICPSR's United States Historical Election Returns Series. Inter-university Consortium for Political and Social Research. *United States Historical Election Returns, 1824-1968* [Computer File]. Bibliographic Citation: ICPSR00001-v3. Ann Arbor, MI: Inter-university Consortium for Political and Social Research [distributor], 1999-04-26. http://doi.org/10.3886/ICPSR00001.v3

26. Winston County was exceptional, although not unique; the county had earlier opposed secession, its delegate to the secession convention arrested and popular resolutions passed declaring it to have the right to secede from the state.

27. Herbert (D-AL-2), *Congressional Record*, June 30, 1890, 6766; "What Dixie Will Do in 1932," address by Dr. A. J. Barton, January 19, 1932, *Congressional Record*, March 18, 1932, 6456. See also Eastland (D-MS), *Congressional Record*, February 9, 1948, 1193; McRae (D-AR-3), *Congressional Record*, June 30, 1890, 6805.

28. "Should the Legal Status of the Negro Be Changed?" speech by Edgar Watkins to the Texas Bar Association, *Dallas Morning News*, July 19, 1907, 14; William Garrott Brown, "The South in National Politics," *South Atlantic Quarterly* 9(2, 1910): 103–115, 109.

29. Phillips, "The Central Theme of Southern History," 43.

30. Lindsay Rogers, *The American Senate* (New York: Alfred A. Knopf, 1926), 103.

31. Thomas B. Reed, "Rules of the House of Representatives," *The Century Magazine* 37(5, 1889): 792–795, 793.

32. Key, *Southern Politics*, 368.

33. This is a recurring theme in Smith's *Congressman from Mississippi*.

34. Key, *Southern Politics*, 360.

35. Hofstadter, "The Southern Citadel," 388–390.

36. See Ira Katznelson and John Lapinski, "The Substance of Representation: Studying Policy Content and Legislative Behavior," in *The Macropolitics of Congress*, edited by E. Scott Adler and John Lapinski (Princeton, NJ: Princeton University Press, 2006).

37. Likeness scores are calculated by subtracting from 100 the absolute difference between the percentage of one bloc that voted yes and the percentage of another bloc that voted yes. If all southern Democrats and all Republicans voted yea, the likeness between these blocs would be 100; if they both divided 50–50 on a vote, the likeness for this vote would also be 100. But if southern Democrats voted unanimously in favor and Republicans unanimously against, the likeness score would be 0. Ira Katznelson and Quinn Mulroy, "Was the South Pivotal? Situated Partisanship and Policy Coalitions during the New Deal and Fair Deal," *Journal of Politics* 74(April 2012), 604–620; Stuart Rice, *Quantitative Methods in Politics* (New York: Alfred A. Knopf, 1928).

38. Two-cut point models are usually used to estimate the effect of party, rather than region. They are discussed in Nolan McCarty, Keith Poole, and Howard Rosenthal, "The Hunt for Party Discipline in Congress," *American Political Science Review* 95(2001): 673-83; Clinton, Jackman, Rivers, "The Statistical Analysis of Roll Call Data," 363-366

39. The measure we use was developed by Joshua Clinton and John Lapinski, "Measuring Legislative Accomplishment, 1877–1994," *American Journal of Political Science* 50(1, 2006): 232–249. See Lawrence H. Chamberlain, *The President, Congress, and Legislation* (New York: Columbia University Press, 1946); Sanders, *Roots of Reform*; Bensel, *Sectionalism and American Political Development*.

40. Rice, *Quantitative Methods in Politics*; Key, *Southern Politics*, 366.

41. Key, *Southern Politics*, 345–346.

42. Canon, Nelson, and Stewart, Historical Congressional Standing Committees.

43. Clinton, Jackman, Rivers, "The Statistical Analysis of Roll Call Data." The pioneering work on estimating ideal points in Congress was undertaken by Keith T. Poole and Howard Rosenthal, *Congress: A Political-Economic History of Roll Call Voting.* (New York, NY: Oxford University Press, 1997)

44. Alternative measures calculated for each Congress show an equivalent image, with less noise but in some cases obscuring potentially important moments when the distribution of preferences changed dramatically. For several reasons, we reject the use of the terms "left" and "right" in an ideal point context. While extensive validation has shown that ideal point scores, such as the well-known NOMINATE series and the scores presented here, do tend to map onto some aspect of political ideology in the present, the degree to which they do changes considerably

across time. It is largely for this reason that we prefer to use issue-specific scores generated over shorter time periods. David A. Bateman and John Lapinski, "Ideal Points and the Study of American Political Development," *Studies in American Political Development* 30(2, 2016): 147-171; David A. Bateman, Joshua Clinton, and John Lapinski, "A House Divided? Roll Calls, Polarization, and Policy Differences in the U.S. House, 1877–2011," *American Journal of Political Science* 61(3, 2017): 698–714.

45. Welliver, "The Triumph of the South," 731–732, 740.

46. Ibid., 739–740.

Chapter 3. Uncertain Combinations

1. "Southern Democracy," *Dallas Weekly Herald*, January 17, 1884.

2. "The South in Congress," *New Orleans Daily Picayune*, September 9, 1877, 4; Allan Peskin, "Was There a Compromise of 1877?" *Journal of American History* 601(1, 1973): 63–75; Clarence C. Clendenen, "President Hayes' 'Withdrawal' of the Troops: An Enduring Myth," *South Carolina Historical Magazine* 70(4, 1969): 240–250.

3. "Popular Objections to Tilden as the Nominee of the Democratic Party," *Daily Arkansas Gazette*, June 4, 1879, 5; "The South in Congress," *New Orleans Daily Picayune*, September 9, 1877, 4; "Sectional Issues," *Daily Inter-Ocean* (Chicago), August 21, 1887, 4; "Southern Democracy," *Dallas Weekly Herald*, January 17, 1884, 1.

4. Woodward, *The Strange Career of Jim Crow*, 33.

5. Hahn, *A Nation under Our Feet*, 9.

6. Woodward, *The Strange Career of Jim Crow*, 6; Hahn, *A Nation under Our Feet*, 440.

7. J. Morgan Kousser, *The Shaping of Southern Politics: Suffrage Restriction and the Establishment of the One-Party South, 1880–1910* (New Haven, CT: Yale University Press, 1974); Michael Perman, *Struggle for Mastery: Disfranchisement in the South 1888–1908* (Chapel Hill: University of North Carolina Press, 2001).

8. Richard Bensel, *The Political Economy of American Industrialization* (Cambridge: Cambridge University Press, 2000).

9. Hahn, *A Nation under Our Feet*, 201; Valelly, *The Two Reconstructions*.

10. "Popular Objections to Tilden as the Nomines," *Daily Arkansas Gazette*, June 4, 1879, 5; Stanley P. Hirshson, *Farewell to the Bloody Shirt* (Bloomington: Indiana University Press, 1962), 156, 157, 159.

11. Bensel, *The Political Economy of American Industrialization*.

12. Wright, *Old South, New South*; Woodward, *Origins of the New South*, 319–320.

13. Hahn, *A Nation under Our Feet*, 206–207; Foner, *Reconstruction*, 347.

14. Thomas B. Alexander, "Political Reconstruction in Tennessee, 1865–1870," in *Radicalism, Racism, and Party Realignment: The Border States during Reconstruction*, edited by Richard Curry (Baltimore: Johns Hopkins University Press, 1969), 62; William E. Parrish, "Reconstruction Politics in Missouri, 1865–1870," in Curry, *Radicalism, Racism, and Party Realignment*, 1.

15. John Willis Menard of Louisiana had been elected earlier, but was denied his seat owing to a contested election.

16. Foner, *Reconstruction*, 328, 364, 372–375; W. E. B. Du Bois, *Black Reconstruction in America, 1860–1880* (New York: Harcourt Brace, 1935), 346; J. Mills Thornton III, "Fiscal Policy and the Failure of Radical Reconstruction in the Lower South," in *Region, Race, and Reconstruction: Essays in Honor of C. Vann Woodward*, edited by J. Morgan Kousser and James McPherson (New York: Oxford University Press, 1982).

17. Woodward, *The Strange Career of Jim Crow*, 6; Harold B. Hancock, "Reconstruction in Delaware," in Curry, *Radicalism, Racism, and Party Realignment*, 202–206.

18. Kousser, *The Shaping of Southern Politics*; Hahn, *A Nation under Our Feet*, 366–367; Valelly, *The Two Reconstructions*, chap. 3.

19. Robert W. Coakley, *The Role of Federal Military Forces in Domestic Disorders, 1789–1878* (Washington, DC: Center of Military History, 1988), 337.

20. Vincent De Santis, *Republicans Face the Southern Question: The New Departure Years, 1877–1897* (Baltimore: Johns Hopkins University Press, 1959), 24.

21. "Micah's Letter," *Savannah (GA) Tribune*, November 28, 1896.

22. "Radicalism and Whiggery," *Dallas Weekly Herald*, May 12, 1877, 2; "Sectional Issues," *Austin Dispatch*, quoted in the *Daily Inter-Ocean* (Chicago), August 21, 1887, 4.

23. For estimates of southern African American support for different parties, see Kousser, *The Shaping of Southern Politics*.

24. "No New Party South: Time Still Necessary," *New York Tribune*, June 1, 1877, 2; Michael Perman, *The Road to Redemption: Southern Politics, 1869–1879* (Chapel Hill: University of North Carolina Press, 1984), 87, 88, 91, 95, 96, 105.

25. Perman, *The Road to Redemption*, 91; "Old Line Whiggery Crops Out," *Houston Daily Union*, November 2, 1871, 2; "No New Party South," *New York Tribune*, June 1, 1877, 2; Thomas B. Alexander, "Persistent Whiggery in the Confederate South," *Journal of Southern History* 27(3, 1961): 305–329; Gerhard Peters and John T. Woolley, "Inaugural Address of Benjamin Harrison, March 4, 1889," The American Presidency Project, http://www.presidency.ucsb.edu/ws/?pid=25825; Hirshson, *Farewell to the Bloody Shirt*, 177–182; "The Southern Whig Element a Threat to Northern Democrats," *Kansas City Star*, April 17, 1886, 2.

26. William Russ Jr., "The Attempt to Create a Republican Party in Arkansas During Reconstruction," *Arkansas Historical Quarterly* 1(3, 1942): 206–222, 211; Thomas DeBlack, "'A Remarkably Strong Unionist Sentiment': Unionism in Arkansas in 1861," in *The Die Is Cast: Arkansas Goes to War in 1861*, edited by Michael Dougan (Little Rock: Butler Center Books, 2010), 75–100, 88; Matthew Hild, "Labor, Third-Party Politics, and the New South Democracy in Arkansas, 1884–1896," *Arkansas Historical Quarterly* 63(1, 2004): 24–43, 25–26, 30.

27. "Southern Democracy," *Dallas Weekly Herald*, January 17, 1884, 1.

28. "The South in Congress," *New Orleans Daily Picayune*, September 9, 1877, 4; Perman, *The Road to Redemption*, 98.

29. "Washington Letter," *New Orleans Daily Picayune*, May 11, 1878, 2; "Letter from Col. R. K. Garland," *Daily Arkansas Gazette*, August 5, 1879, 4.

30. "Mr. Cox," *Vicksburg (MS) Daily Commercial*, April 23, 1878, 2; "Why I Am an Independent" (letter from "R.M.O."), *Macon (GA) Telegraph and Messenger*, February 23, 1882, 1; "The South and the Currency," *New Orleans Daily Picayune*, August 20, 1878, 4.

31. Bensel, *Sectionalism and American Political Development*, 12.

32. This figure and others like it were generated by regressing the estimated ideal point of all members on a state or regional dummy variable, interacted by party, and calculating a predicted ideal point for each state-party. The bars do not represent the full range of variation among party members from a given state/region but rather the 0.95 confidence interval for the predicted ideal point.

33. Key, *Southern Politics*, 5.

34. Perman, *The Road to Redemption*, 153–154, 273; Du Bois, *Black Reconstruction*, 624; Michael Newton, *The Ku Klux Klan in Mississippi: A History* (Jefferson, NC: McFarland and Co., 2010), 14; *The Farmer and Mechanic* (Raleigh, NC), February 21, 1878, 1.

35. Wade Hampton, "Ought the Negro Be Disenfranchised," *North American Review* 128(268, 1879): 225–283, 241–242; "No New Party South: Time Still Necessary," *New York Tribune*, June 1, 1877, 2.

36. "Whig Doctrine in the South," *Daily Inter-Ocean*, August 8, 1887, 4.

37. "The Southern Whig Element a Threat to Northern Democrats," *Kansas City Star*, April

17, 1886, 2; "Southern States in the Next Congress," *Dallas Weekly Herald*, October 26, 1882, 5; *Georgia Weekly Telegraph* (Macon), January 20, 1882, 4.

38. Bensel, *Sectionalism and American Political Development*, 62–73; Theda Skocpol, *Protecting Soldiers and Mothers: The Political Origins of Social Policy in the United States* (Cambridge, MA: Harvard University Press, 1992), chap. 2, 102.

39. Bensel, *The Political Economy of American Industrialization*.

40. "Washington Letter. State of Business Before Congress—Prospects of the Texas Pacific and the Levees," *New Orleans Daily Picayune*, May 11, 1878, 2.

41. C. Vann Woodward, *Reunion and Reaction: The Compromise of 1877 and the End of Reconstruction* (Boston: Little, Brown, 1951), 244.

42. Carl V. Harris, "Right Fork or Left Fork? The Section-Party Alignments of Southern Democrats in Congress, 1873–1897," *Journal of Southern History* 42(4, 1976): 471–506; Sanders, *Roots of Reform*.

Chapter 4. Tests of Priority

1. "The Last Point of Resistance Passed," *Macon* (GA) *Telegraph*, March 15, 1886, 2.

2. "As to the Solids," *Macon Telegraph*, November 5, 1880, 2.

3. Emory R. Johnson, "River and Harbor Bills," *Annals of the American Academy of Political and Social Science* (1892): 55.

4. "Reform or Ruin," *Pomeroy's Democrat* (New York), September 18, 1875, 1.

5. "Editorial Correspondence," *Pomeroy's Democrat*, October 9, 1875, 1.

6. *Macon* (GA) *Telegraph and Messenger*, January 10, 1883, 1; "Southern States," *Macon Telegraph and Messenger*, May 20, 1884, 2.

7. The South, which was home to 37 percent of the U.S. population, was also much poorer than the rest of the country. "The New Tariff Bill," *Wheeling* (WV) *Daily Register*, February 2, 1878, 1; Douglas Irwin, "Tariff Incidence in America's Gilded Age," Working Paper 12162 (Cambridge, MA: National Bureau of Economic Research, 2006); "Commerce and Navigation, American," *Appleton's Annual Cyclopaedia and Register of Important Events of the Year 1883*, vol. 8 (New York: D. Appleton and Company, 1884), 146; Robert Porter, *Report on Valuation, Taxation, and Public Indebtedness*, 10th Census, vol. 7 (Washington, DC: U.S. Government Printing Office, 1884), 12; "The New Tariff Bill," *Wheeling Daily Register*, February 2, 1878, 1; *Report of the Commissioner of Internal Revenue for the Fiscal Year Ended June 30, 1897* (Washington, DC: U.S. Government Printing Office, 1897), 29.

8. Edward Stanwood, *American Tariff Controversies in the Nineteenth Century* (Boston: Houghton Mifflin, 1903), 191; Harris, "Right Fork or Left Fork?" 494; Horace Dresser, *Internal Revenue and Tariff Law (Passed July 13, 1870)* (New York: Harper Brothers, 1870); "The New Tariff Bill," *Wheeling Daily Register*, February 2, 1878, 1.

9. Charles Stewart III, *Budget Reform Politics: The Design of the Appropriations Process in the House of Representatives, 1865–1921* (Cambridge: Cambridge University Press, 1989), 64; S. Walter Poulshock, "Pennsylvania and the Politics of the Tariff, 1880–1888," *Pennsylvania History* 29(3): 291–305, 295; Walter Stilson Hutchins, quoted in "A Racy Interview," *The Million: A Politico-Economic Journal Devoted Especially to Tariff Reform* (Des Moines, IA), August 21, 1886, 192; "Mr. Randall's Ideas," *New York Times*, October 10, 1883, 4; Ida M. Tarbell, "The Tariff in Our Times: In the Hands of the Democrats," *The American Magazine* 64(2, 1907): 169–183, 174; Stanwood, *American Tariff Controversies*, 197; Ida M. Tarbell, "The Tariff in Our Times: Under Hayes and Garfield," *The American Magazine* 63(6, 1907): 641–656, 644; Ida M. Tarbell, *The Tariff in Our Times* (New York: Macmillan Co., 1911), 84; "Bushel of Bills," *Daily Inter-Ocean* (Chicago), October 30, 1877, 1; "The Tariff Men Delighted," *Wheeling* (WV) *Register*, March 4, 1880, 1; "Personal

and Political," *Philadelphia Inquirer*, March 24, 1880, 4; "Scenes in Congress," *Daily State Gazette* (Trenton, NJ), March 26, 1880, 2.

10. Eppa Hunton, *The Autobiography of Eppa Hunton* (Richmond, VA: William Byrd Press, 1933), 153–154; "Judge Reagan on Randall and the Speakership," *Macon* (GA) *Telegraph and Messenger*, November 21, 1883, 2.

11. "The Speakership," *Macon* (GA) *Telegraph and Messenger*, July 8, 1883, 2; "Counting Up Carlisle's Votes," *Wheeling* (WV) *Register*, October 6, 1883, 1; "Judge Reagan on Randall and the Speakership," *Macon Telegraph and Messenger*, November 21, 1883, 2; "The Influential Southern Newspapers Speak Out for Randall," *New Orleans Daily Picayune*, November 23, 1883, 1; "The Democratic Unhappy Family," *Daily State Gazette* (Trenton NJ), April 19, 1878, 2; "Justice," "Hon. Sam. J. Randall" (letter to the *Gazette*), *Daily Arkansas Gazette* (Little Rock), April 28, 1883, 2; "Cause of Dissatisfaction," *Macon Telegraph and Messenger*, August 17, 1884, 1.

12. "The Speakership Contest," *Macon* (GA) *Telegraph and Messenger*, November 23, 1883, 1; "Hon. Sam. J. Randall," *Daily Arkansas Gazette* (Little Rock), April 28, 1883, 2; Poulshock, "Pennsylvania and the Politics of the Tariff," 302.

13. Tarbell, "The Tariff in Our Times: In the Hands of the Democrats," 174.

14. "Latest Telegraph," *New Orleans Daily Picayune*, February 8, 1879, 1; "Washington Notes," *New Orleans Daily Picayune*, February 11, 1879, 8; "Telegraphic News," *Baltimore Sun*, February 17, 1879, 1; "Washington," *New Orleans Daily Picayune*, January 20, 1879, 1; "The Internal Revenue Bill in the Republican Caucus," *New Orleans Daily Picayune*, June 21, 1882, 2; "From Washington," *Macon* (GA) *Telegraph and Messenger*, June 22, 1888, 1; "The Caucus Tax Bill," *New Orleans Weekly Picayune*, July 29, 1882, 1.

15. Philip A. Bruce, "The South in the Economic Policies of the United States," in *The South in the Building of the Nation*, vol. 4, edited by Franklin L. Riley (Richmond, VA: Southern Historical Publication Society, 1909), 353–382, 377; Stanwood, *American Tariff Controversies*, 238; "Mr. Carlisle's Consistency," *New York Tribune*, February 5, 1890, 5; "John G. Carlisle, of Kentucky, Cincinnati Commercial Gazette (Rep.)," *Public Opinion* 3(20, August 27, 1887): 411; "The Speakership Contest," *Baltimore Sun*, November 28, 1883, 2.

16. "The Rules of the House," *Baltimore Sun*, December 7, 1885, 2; "Letter from Washington," *New-Hampshire Sentinel* (Keene), December 9, 1885, 2; "Changing the House Rules," *Dallas Morning News*, December 13, 1885, 6; D. Roderick Kiewiet and Mathew D. McCubbins, *The Logic of Delegation: Congressional Parties and the Appropriations Process* (Chicago: University of Chicago Press, 1991), 72, 64; Stanwood, *American Tariff Controversies*, 200, 228–229; "The South and the Tariff," *American Economist* 60(2, 1917): 24.

17. *Congressional Record*, December 5, 1887, 7; Stanwood, *American Tariff Controversies*, 231; "Why the Mills Bill Was Mutilated," *Chicago Tribune*, October 26, 1888, 4.

18. "Current Opinion," reprinted from the *Vicksburg* (MS) *Commercial Herald* in *St. Albans* (VT) *Messenger*, February 21, 1889, 2.

19. Frank William Taussig, *The Tariff History of the United States* (New York: G. P. Putnam's Sons, 1900), 199; Stanwood, *American Tariff Controversies*, 218; "Test Vote in the House," *Philadelphia Inquirer*, February 6, 1883, 1; "Tariff Dragging Along," *Philadelphia Inquirer*, February 2, 1883, 1.

20. Although the tobacco provision did not receive a roll call, William Cowles, Democrat of North Carolina, suggested that forty southerners in the House would vote for outright repeal of the tobacco tax. Stanwood, *American Tariff Controversies*, 262; "Will Vote To-Day," *Philadelphia Inquirer*, May 21, 1890, 2; "No Opposition Allowed," *New York Times*, May 13, 1890; McKinley (R-OH), *Congressional Record*, May 15, 1890, 4711; "Tobacco and Sugar," *New York Herald*, February 18, 1890, 4; "The New Tariff Bill," *Cleveland Plain Dealer*, April 1, 1890, 4.

21. "Ingalls and Reed," *Macon* (GA) *Telegraph*, August 10, 1890, 4; "Pass the Tariff Bill," *Phila-*

delphia Inquirer, August 2, 1890, 4; "Filibustering to Be Stopped," *Philadelphia Inquirer*, August 12, 1890, 5; *Congressional Record*, August 11, 1890, 8422.

22. James A. Kehl, *Boss Rule in the Gilded Age: Matt Quay of Pennsylvania* (Pittsburgh: University of Pittsburgh Press, 1981), 133–136; John R. Lambert, *Arthur Pue Gorman* (Baton Rouge: Louisiana State University Press, 1953), 149; "Stirred Up a Storm," *Cleveland Plain Dealer*, August 14, 1890, 2; "Nor of One Mind," *Kansas City Times*, July 11, 1890, 1; Plumb (R-KS), *Congressional Record*, August 26, 1890, 9144.

23. Aldrich (R-RI), *Congressional Record*, August 25,.1890, 9109.

24. "Southern States in the Next Congress," *Dallas Weekly Herald*, October 26, 1882, 5; Edward Hake Phillips, "The Historical Significance of the Tariff on Rice," *Agricultural History* 26(July, 1952): 89–92; Mark Wahlgren Summers, *Rum, Romanism, and Rebellion: The Making of a President, 1884* (Chapel Hill: University of North Carolina Press, 2000).

25. Francis Butler Simkins, *Pitchfork Ben Tillman, South Carolinian* (1944; reprint, Columbia: University of South Carolina Press, 2002), 346.

26. "Virginia Bourbons," *New Hampshire Sentinel* (Keene), August 28, 1889, 1; Coleman (R-LA), *Congressional Record*, June 30, 1890, 6773; "Politics in Alabama," *Columbus* (GA) *Daily Enquirer*, September 2, 1890, 3.

27. *Baltimore Sun*, February 7, 1888, 2 (supplement).

28. "The Sham Tariff Reform Bill," *Baltimore Sun*, May 10, 1894, 4; Bruce, "The South in the Economic Policies of the United States," 375; Harris, "Right Fork or Left Fork?" 489; Stanwood, *American Tariff Controversies*, 355.

29. "The Income Tax," *Macon* (GA) *Telegraph*, January 4, 1894, 4; *Atlanta Daily Constitution*, March 8, 1878; Harris, "Right Fork or Left Fork?" 491; "Open Letter to Gov. Hogg," *Dallas Morning News*, September 14, 1892, 2; "Shall Incomes Be Taxed? A Solid South," *Philadelphia Inquirer*, February 4, 1878, 1; "Inequalities of the Income Tax," *Dallas Morning News*, January 5, 1894, 6.

30. William Dunning, "Record of Political Events," *Political Science Quarterly* 9(2, 1894): 346–376, 355; "The State's Survey," *The State* (Columbia, SC), January 5, 1894, 4; "Election Bill," *Arkansas Gazette* (Little Rock), January 31, 1894, 3.

31. "The Income Tax Decision," *New Orleans Times-Picayune*, April 9, 1895, 4; "The Income Tax," *Birmingham Age-Herald*, April 9, 1895, 4; Francis R. Jones, "Pollock v. Farmers' Loan and Trust Company," *Harvard Law Review* 9(3, 1895): 198–211.

32. Joint Congressional Committee on Inaugural Ceremonies, *Inaugural Addresses of the Presidents of the United States* (Washington, DC: U.S. Government Printing Office, 1989), 175-187; Scott Reynolds Nelson, *Iron Confederacies: Southern Railways, Klan Violence, and Reconstruction* (Chapel Hill: University of North Carolina Press, 1999), 180.

33. Bensel, *Sectionalism and American Political Development*; Sanders, *Roots of Reform*, chap. 6, 185, 274; "The Political Grab Net," *Dallas Morning News*, March 29, 1892, 3.

34. See Bensel, *The Political Economy of American Industrialization*, tables 3.2 and 3.3.

35. Ben H. Procter, *Not Without Honor: The Life of John H. Reagan* (Austin: University of Texas Press, 1962), 218; John H. Reagan, *Memoirs, with Special Reference to Secession and the Civil War* (New York: Neale Publishing Co., 1906), 227; Sanders, *Roots of Reform*, 182, 187; Perman, *The Road to Redemption*, 10–11.

36. Sanders, *Roots of Reform*, 191; John Reagan, "Regulation of Interstate Commerce," Report 245, U.S. House of Representatives, 45th Cong., 2nd sess., 1878; Reagan (D-TX), *Congressional Record*, June 1, 1880, 4024.

37. Sanders, *Roots of Reform*, 187–190.

38. John Reagan, "Regulation of Interstate Commerce," Report 245, U.S. House of Representatives, 45th Cong., 2nd sess., 1878, 1; Reagan (D-TX), *Congressional Record*, May 8, 1878, 45th Cong., 2nd sess., 3280

39. *Civil Rights Cases*, 109 U.S. 3 (1883), 108.

40. O'Hara (R-NC), *Congressional Record*, December 16, 1884, 297.

41. *Congressional Record*, December 17, 1884, 316–319.

42. "Railroad Regulations," *New Haven* (CT) *Register*, December 17, 1884, 3; "Reagan Ruffled," *Philadelphia Inquirer*, December 17, 1884, 1; "Hoist with His Own Petard," *Kansas City Times*, December 17, 1884, 1.

43. Smalls (R-SC), *Congressional Record*, December 17, 1884, 316.

44. Goff (R-WV), *Congressional Record*, December 17, 1884, 323.

45. Barksdale (D-MS), *Congressional Record*, December 18, 1884, 332; *Congressional Record*, January 7, 1885, 532–533.

46. Procter, *Not Without Honor*, 254–255; H. Res. 92, 48th Cong., 1st sess.; H.R. 7939, 48th Cong., 2nd sess.; Marianne L. Lado, "A Question of Justice: African American Legal Perspectives on the 1883 Civil Rights Cases—Freedom: Constitutional Law," *Chicago-Kent Law Review* 70(3, 1995): 1123–1195.

47. "From Washington," *Macon* (GA) *Telegraph and Messenger*, December 17, 1884, 1; Lawrence Grossman, *The Negro and the Democratic Party: Northern and National Politics, 1868–92* (Urbana: University of Illinois Press, 1976); Smalls (R-SC), *Congressional Record*, December 17, 1884, 316; Horr (R-MI), *Congressional Record*, December 18, 1884, 339.

48. "The Fusion Movement in Mississippi," *Vicksburg* (MS) *Daily Commercial*, May 7, 1881, 2; "Hon. C. J. Faulkner," *Wheeling* (WV) *Daily Register*, September 23, 1876, 1; Hugh Rockoff, "How Long Did It Take for the United States to Become an Optimal Currency Area?" Working Paper on Historical Factors in Long-Run Growth, Historical Paper 124 (Cambridge, MA: National Bureau of Economic Research, 2000); "Financial Questions," *Dallas Morning News*, March 22, 1891, 7.

49. The fragmentation of large plantations had left few economic firms large enough to support concentrated marketing and credit facilities in the region, which had earlier been served by the cotton factor. John A. James, "Development of the National Money Market, 1893–1911," *Journal of Economic History* 36(4, 1976): 878–897; Howard Bodenhorn, *A History of Banking in Antebellum America: Financial Markets and Economic Development in an Era of Nation-Building* (Cambridge: Cambridge University Press, 2000), 228; John B. Legler and Richard Sylla, "Integration of U.S. Capital Markets: Southern Stock Markets and the Case of New Orleans, 1871–1913," in *Finance, Intermediaries, and Economic Development*, edited by Stanley L. Engerman, Philip T. Hoffman, Jean-Laurent Rosenthal, and Kenneth L. Sokoloff (Cambridge: Cambridge University Press, 2003), 141; Rockoff, "How Long Did It Take for the United States . . ."; Bensel, *The Political Economy of American Industrialization*, 93; "R. M. T. Hunter on Southern Finance," *Alexandria* (VA) *Gazette*, March 9, 1875, 2.

50. *New York Evening Express Almanac* (New York: New York Express Company, 1879), 280; "Remonetization of Silver," *Georgia Weekly Telegraph*, July 17, 1877, 2.

51. "State Politics," *Wheeling* (WV) *Register*, June 27, 1879, 1; "The Key Note Sounded," *Wheeling Daily Register*, August 14, 1878, 1.

52. Harris, "Right Fork or Left Fork?" 484–488.

53. "The South and the Currency," *New Orleans Daily Picayune*, August 20, 1878, 4; "Don't Give Up the Ship," *The State* (Columbia SC), June 11, 1894, 4.

54. *The Raleigh* (NC) *Signal*, September 1888, 4; *Anderson* (SC) *Intelligencer*, September 8, 1887, 2; "Cleveland and the Currency Problem," *Washington Evening Star*, February 17, 1885, 1; Bensel, *The Political Economy of American Industrialization*, 238.

55. "The Silver Question," *Daily Inter-Ocean* (Chicago), February 14, 1885, 5; *Cincinnati Enquirer*, February 27, 1885, 1; *Chicago Tribune*, February 19, 1885, 2, 6; "Cleveland and the Currency

Problem," *Washington Evening Star*, February 17, 1885, 1; *Detroit Free Press*, February 11, 1885, 8; *New York Times*, February 27, 1885, 1; "Silver Question," *Daily Nevada State Journal* (Reno), November 4, 1888, 2.

56. For instance, "the silver men" chose not to make the Bland bill of 1892 a "party measure, and hence the bill rests on its merits before the individual judgment of every member." 1892. *Denver News*, quoted in *Public Opinion* 12(23, March 12, 1892): 568; *Chicago Tribune*, February 27, 1885, 2; "Gath," *Cincinnati Enquirer*, April 24, 1888, 1; "St. Louis Platform," *San Francisco Chronicle*, June 9, 1888, 4.

57. "Cleveland's Position," *The Philadelphia Times*, February 11, 1885, 2; *Richmond* (VA) *Dispatch*, April 9, 1886, 4; Harris, "Right Fork or Left Fork?" 485.

58. Harris, "Right Fork or Left Fork?" 486; Rockoff, "How Long Did It Take for the United States . . ."; Fred Wellborn, "The Influence of the Silver-Republican Senators, 1889–1891," *Mississippi Valley Historical Review* 14(4, 1928): 462–480.

59. In 1891, after the deal on the Force bill, Stewart's free coinage act passed the Senate but was killed in the House by the Reed rules. Wellborn, "The Influence of the Silver-Republican Senators," 479; Lambert, *Arthur Pue Gorman*, 159.

60. "Against Cleveland," *Aspen* (CO) *Weekly Times*, October 7, 1893; *New Orleans Times-Democrat*, July 29, 1893, in *Public Opinion* 15(August): 425.

61. Bate (D-TN), *Congressional Record, September 25, 1893, 1749*; *New Orleans Times-Democrat*, July 29, 1893, quoted in *Public Opinion* 15(August): 425; "Silver Men Are Defeated," *New York Times*, August 25, 1893, 8; Karen Hoffman, " 'Going Public' in the Nineteenth Century: Grover Cleveland's Repeal of the Sherman Silver Purchase Act," *Rhetoric and Public Affairs* 5(1, 2002): 57–77, 59.

62. Jeannette Paddock Nichols, "The Politics and Personalities of Silver Repeal in the United States Senate," *American Historical Review* 41(1, 1935): 26–53, 32; "Against Cleveland," *Aspen* (CO) *Weekly Times*, October 7, 1893; "First Gun To-Day," *Lewiston* (ME) *Evening Journal*, September 26, 1893, 1; "They May Agree," *San Francisco Call*, October 9, 1893, 1.

63. For different accounts of the connection between the two repeal proposals, see Hicks (R-PA), *Congressional Record*, October 6, 1893, 2218–2219; *Louisville* (KY) *Courier Journal*, quoted in *Public Opinion* 15(September 30): 615; "No Drawn Battle," *Chicago Tribune*, October 11, 1893, 1; Perman, *Struggle for Mastery*, 44; Nichols, "The Politics and Personalities of Silver Repeal in the United States Senate," 34; F. W. Taussig, "The Crisis in the United States and the Repeal of Silver Purchase," *Economic Journal* 3(12, 1893): 733–745, 743; "The End in Sight," *Arkansas Gazette* (Little Rock), October 25, 1893, 1.

64. "Cannon Heard From," *Chicago Tribune*, August 24, 1893, 3; "No Course Laid Out," *Dallas Morning News*, April 1, 1894, 8; "Why Populists Are Pleased," *Columbus* (GA) *Daily Enquirer-Sun*, April 3, 1894, 2; "Told You So," *The State* (Columbia, SC), April 9, 1894.

65. "Don't Give Up the Ship," *The State* (Columbia SC), June 11, 1894, 4.

66. The federal deficit stood at $200,000 in 1879. By the next year, there was a surplus of $8.1 million, which reached a peak of $10.1 million two years later. National Bureau of Economic Research, "Total Federal Budget Surplus or Deficit for United States (M1525AUSM144NNBR)," retrieved June 13, 2015, from FRED, Federal Reserve Bank of St. Louis, https://research.stlouisfed.org/fred2/series/M1525AUSM144NNBR/ (updated August 20, 2012).

67. Daniel W. Crofts, "The Blair Bill and the Elections Bill: The Congressional Aftermath to Reconstruction," PhD diss., Yale University (1968), 8; McHenry (D-KY), *Congressional Globe*, February 2, 1872, 788–789.

68. Crofts, "The Blair Bill and the Elections Bill," 47.

69. The Sherwin bill had been waiting on the calendar until near the end of the session, when

the Republicans were anxious to finalize the tariff. After a few hours of debate, the House voted 82–80 to adjourn during consideration of the former, effectively killing the bill. Only two southern Democrats—John Tucker of Virginia and William Hatch of Missouri—and one southern Republican, James McLean of Missouri, voted with the majority.

70. McHenry (D-KY), *Congressional Globe*, February 2, 1872, 788; see also the concluding remarks of Kerr (D-IN), *Congressional Globe*, February 2, 1871, 791.

71. Crofts, "The Blair Bill and the Elections Bill," 58–70.

72. Lamar (D-MS), *Congressional Record*, March 28, 1884, 2369. Sherman and others were "not satisfied that if this money were placed in their [southern legislatures] hands it would properly be used for the education of all classes of people in those States." *Congressional Record*, March 27, 1884, 2251–2254.

73. Charles Richard Williams, ed., *Diary and Letters of Rutherford B. Hayes* (Columbus: Ohio State Archaeological and Historical Society, 1922), 621, 624; Dan M. Robison, "Governor Robert L. Taylor and the Blair Educational Bill in Tennessee," *Tennessee Historical Magazine* 2(1, 1931): 28–49, 32; *Congressional Record*, March 28, 1884, 2369.

74. Albion Tourgée, "National Education in Congress," *The Continent* 5(May, 1884): 570–571; Crofts, "The Blair Bill and the Elections Bill," 85.

75. Crofts, "The Blair Bill and Federal Elections Bill," 38; Willard B. Gatewood Jr., "North Carolina and Federal Aid to Education: Public Reaction to the Blair Bill, 1881–1890," *North Carolina Historical Review* 40(4, 1963): 465–488, 471.

76. R. T. Payne, Superintendent of Grenada County, Mississippi, quoted in J. R. Preston, *Biennial Report of the State Superintendent of Public Education to the Legislature of Mississippi for Scholastic Years 1891–'92 and 1892–'93* (Jackson: Clarion-Ledger Publishing Company, 1894), 221; Crofts, "The Blair Bill and the Elections Bill," 62, 64; Gatewood, "North Carolina and Federal Aid to Education," 475; Allen Going, "The South and the Blair Education Bill," *Mississippi Valley Historical Review* 44(2, 1957): 267–290, 278.

77. See *Annual Report of the Secretary of the Treasury on the State of the Finances for the Year 1875* (Washington, DC: U.S. Government Printing Office, 1875), table B 4.5; *Annual Report of the Secretary of the Treasury on the State of the Finances for the Year 1890* (Washington, DC: U.S. Government Printing Office, 1891), table M, CXIII–CXV, XXI.

78. *Congressional Globe*, 37th Cong., 2nd sess., 1862, 32, pt. 1: 109, 622, 666; *Congressional Record*, March 3, 1884, 1571; John W. Oliver, "History of the Civil War Pensions, 1861–1865," PhD diss., University of Wisconsin (1915), 7; Jeffrey Vogel, "Redefining Reconciliation: Confederate Veterans and the Southern Responses to Federal Civil War Pensions," *Civil War History* 51(1, 2005): 67–93, 71; "Jeff Davis and Secession," *Vicksburg* (MS) *Daily Commercial*, March 7, 1878, 2; Bailey (R-NY), *Congressional Record*, March 1, 1879, 2226.

79. Theda Skocpol, "Did the Civil War Further American Democracy? A Reflection on the Expansion of Benefits for Union Veterans," in *Democracy, Revolution, and History*, edited by Theda Skocpol (Ithaca, NY: Cornell University Press, 1998), 73–101; William H. Glasson, *Federal Military Pensions in the United States* (New York: Oxford University Press, 1918), 273.

80. "What the Filibustering Is About," *Baltimore Sun*, April 10, 1888, 2; "Direct Tax Bill," *Cleveland Plain Dealer*, April 11, 1888, 4; "The Deadlock Continues," *Dallas Morning News*, April 6, 1888, 2; John Porter Hollis, *The Early Period of Reconstruction in South Carolina* (Baltimore: Johns Hopkins University Press, 1905), 112.

81. "Washington," *Macon* (GA) *Telegraph*, April 5, 1888, 1; "An All-Night Session," *Daily Inter Ocean* (Chicago), April 5, 1888, 2; "Sad for Ohio Republicans," *Cleveland Plain Dealer*, April 3, 1888, 4; "The Deadlock Continues," *Dallas Morning News*, April 6, 1888, 2; "Washington: The Filibuster Still on and Gaining Ground," *Macon Telegraph*, April 7, 1888, 1; "What the Filibustering Is About," *Baltimore Sun*, April 10, 1888, 2; Harry Edwin Smith, *The United States Federal Internal*

Tax History from 1861 to 1871 (Boston: Houghton Mifflin, 1914), 43; "The Obstinate Deadlock to Come to an End To-Day," *Macon Telegraph*, April 12, 1888, 1.

82. *Laws of the United States Relating to the Improvement of Rivers and Harbors*, vol. 1 (Washington, DC: U.S. Government Printing Office, 1913). Spending on internal improvements tended to be around 4 percent of the government's total expenditures across the period under study. See *Annual Report of the Secretary of the Treasury on the State of the Finances for the Year 1875* (Washington, DC: U.S. Government Printing Office, 1875), table B 4.5; *Annual Report of the Secretary of the Treasury on the State of the Finances for the Year 1890*, table M, CXIII–CXV; "The South in Congress," *New-Orleans Daily Picayune*, September 9, 1877, 4; Merrimon (D-NC), *Congressional Record*, January 21, 1874, 806.

83. In each Congress from 1879 to 1883, there was a push by members from Mississippi River states to strip authority over improvements on the river away from the Commerce Committee and place it in the Committee on Levees and Improvements on the Mississippi River. This effort was always unsuccessful, but in January 1882—as the floodwaters were rising—the threat forced the Republican chair of the Commerce Committee to make a public promise that the river would be well taken care of in the next rivers and harbors bill. Stewart, *Budget Reform Politics*, 115; Harris, "Right Fork or Left Fork?" 495.

84. "The Southern Whig Element: A Threat to Northern Democrats—Significant Words from Those Who Furnish the Votes Which Now Make the South Solid," *Kansas City Star*, reprinted from the *Mobile* (AL) *Register*, April 17, 1886, 2. See also "Southern States in the Next Congress," *Dallas Weekly Herald*, October 26, 1882, 5; "Washington Letter," *New Orleans Daily Picayune*, May 11, 1878, 2.

85. Stewart, *Budget Reform Politics*, 111; Harris, "Right Fork or Left Fork?" 495.

86. "The Last Point of Resistance Passed," *Macon* (GA) *Telegraph*, March 15, 1886, 2; Kathleen Gorman, "Confederate Pensions as Southern Social Welfare," in *Before the New Deal: Social Welfare in the South, 1830–1930*, edited by Elna Green (Athens: University of Georgia Press, 1999); U.S. Department of the Interior, Commissioner of Pensions, *Annual Report of the Commissioner of Pensions*, 2542 House Executive Document 1/32 (1887); Glasson, *Federal Military Pensions*.

87. This figure is inspired by that presented in Bensel, *Sectionalism and American Political Development*, 68; *Executive Documents of the House of Representatives for the First Session of the Fiftieth Congress*, serial no. 2542.

88. Hoar (R-MA), *Congressional Record*, April 7, 1884, 2709; Vest (D-MO), *Congressional Record*, April 7, 1884, 2690.

89. *Congressional Record*, April 3, 1884, 2540; Crofts, "The Blair Bill and the Elections Bill," 11, 159.

90. Crofts, "The Blair Bill and the Elections Bill," 109, 135; Gordon McKinney, *Blair's Campaign to Reform America* (Lexington: University of Kentucky Press, 2013), 118.

91. Gatewood, "North Carolina and Federal Aid to Education," 481; "Blair Bill," *Macon* (GA) *Telegraph*, January 26, 1890, 4.

92. *Macon* (GA) *Telegraph*, January 11, 1890, 4; Robison, "Governor Robert L. Taylor," 46; "The Bad Blair Bill," *Macon Telegraph*, January 13, 1890, 4; "Blair Changing Base," *Macon Telegraph*, January 18, 1890, 2; "A Rising Opposition," *Dallas Morning News*, January 18, 1890, 6; "Why the South Rejects the Blair Bill," *Kansas City Star*, February 22, 1890, 4; "True Meaning of the Blair Bill," *Macon Telegraph*, February 18, 1890, 6.

93. "A Rising Opposition," *Dallas Morning News*, January 18, 1890, 6.

94. Henry Blair, "Report to Accompany S. 3714," U.S. Senate, 51st Cong., 1st sess., no. 1028 (1890), 1; "S. 194: A Bill to Aid in the Establishment and Temporary Support of Common Schools," U.S. Senate, 49th Cong., 1st sess., May 13, 1886, 4.

95. "Political State Platforms," in *The Tribune Almanac for 1897*, edited by Henry Eckford

Rhoades (New York: Tribune Association, 1897), 57. See also Richard Franklin Bensel, *Passion and Preferences: William Jennings Bryant and the 1896 Democratic Convention* (Cambridge: Cambridge University Press, 2008), 15.

96. Tillman was officially recorded as saying "northwestern," but the context of the speech as well as contemporary reports make clear that he meant "northeastern." See "A Sectional Issue," *The Nation*, 63 (1620, July 1896): 43–44; Edward Dickinson, *Official Proceedings of the Democratic National Convention* (Logansport, IN: Wilson, Humphreys & Co., 1896), 207.

97. Irwin, "Tariff Incidence in America's Gilded Age."

98. J. Morgan Kousser, "Progressivism for Middle-Class Whites Only: North Carolina Education, 1880–1910," *Journal of Southern History* 46(2, 1980): 169–194.

99. Alabama has two 1890 land-grant colleges, Alabama A&M and Tuskegee. Maryland was the last state to opt into the provisions of the second Morrill Act, designating a separate black college in 1919. The Hatch Act did apply to Tuskegee and black colleges, such as Alcorn, established under the terms of the 1862 act. Robert Jenkins, "The Black Land-Grant Colleges in Their Formative Years," *Agricultural History* 65(2, 1991): 63–72, 65–66.

100. Williams, *Diary and Letters of Rutherford B. Hayes*, 621, 624; Nicholas Betts, "The Struggle toward Equality in Higher Education: The Impact of the Morrill Acts on Race Relations in Virginia, 1872–1958," MA thesis in history (Virginia Commonwealth University, 2013), 5.

Chapter 5. Racial Rule

1. "Radicalism and Whiggery," *Dallas Weekly Herald*, May 12, 1877, 2.

2. *Report and Testimony of the Select Committee of the United States Senate to Investigate the Causes of the Removal of the Negroes from the Southern States to the Northern States, Part II*, Senate Report 693, 46th Cong., 2nd sess. (Washington, DC: U.S. Government Printing Office, 1880), 103–104, 108.

3. Ibid., 104; Perman, *The Road to Redemption*, 242.

4. Roberta Sue Alexandra, "Presidential Reconstruction: Ideology and Change," in *The Facts of Reconstruction: Essays in Honor of John Hope Franklin* (Baton Rouge: Louisiana State University Press, 1991), 42; Leon F. Litwack, *Been in the Storm So Long: The Aftermath of Slavery* (New York: Random House, 1979), 386; Carole Emberton, *Beyond Redemption: Race, Violence, and the American South after the Civil War* (Chicago: University of Chicago Press, 2013), 57; Bensel, *Sectionalism and American Political Development*, 83.

5. *Daily Albany* (NY) *Argus*, August 14, 1874, 3; "The Southern Troubles the Result of Unwise Republican Legislation in Congress," *Daily Albany Argus*, September 11, 1874, 2; *Macon* (GA) *Weekly Telegraph*, August 23, 1874, 2; "North Carolina and Tennessee," *Detroit Tribune*, August 13, 1874, 4.

6. In many northern states, there was evidence of both a reaction to black civil rights and a continued political and legislative effort to supplement civil rights laws by outlawing racial discrimination in insurance policies, strengthening public accommodations laws, or passing school integration laws. The consolidation of white supremacy did not receive the unanimous support of northern public opinion, although certainly it received much. But even as northerners opposed to segregation and disfranchisement looked at southern policy changes with scorn, there was little appetite in the Republican Party for opposing these through federal policy. For a discussion of northern civil rights legislation, see David A. Gerber, "A Politics of Limited Options: Northern Black Politics and the Problem of Change and Continuity in Race Relations Historiography," *Journal of Social History* 14(2, 1980): 235–255; J. Morgan Kousser, *Dead End: The Development of Nineteenth-Century Litigation on Racial Discrimination in Schools* (Oxford: Clarendon Press, 1985), 23; J. Morgan Kousser, "'The Onward March of Right Principles': State Legislative Actions

on Racial Discrimination in Schools in Nineteenth Century America," *Historical Methods* 35(4, 2002): 177–204; David A. Gerber, *Black Ohio and the Color Line, 1860–1915* (Urbana: University of Illinois Press, 1976); Grossman, *The Negro and the Democratic Party*; Franklin Johnson, *The Development of State Legislation Concerning the Free Negro* (New York: Columbia University Press, 1919); Pauli Murray, *States' Laws on Race and Color* (Athens: University of Georgia Press, 1950).

7. Rayford Logan, *The Negro in American Life and Thought: The Nadir, 1877–1901* (New York: Dial Press, 1954).

8. John C. Rodrigue, *Reconstruction in the Cane Fields: From Slavery to Free Labor in Louisiana's Sugar Parishes* (Baton Rouge: Louisiana State University Press, 2001), 177; "The Labor System of the South," *Georgia Weekly Telegraph* (Macon), December 7, 1875, 1.

9. "Fred Douglass on Whites and Blacks," *New Orleans Daily Picayune*, May 13, 1879, 4; "The Labor System of the South," *Georgia Weekly Telegraph* (Macon), December 7, 1875, 1; "Editorial Correspondence," *Macon* (GA) *Telegraph*, February 27, 1877, 7; "The Georgia Press," *Macon Telegraph*, January 22, 1878, 3.

10. Alex Lichtenstein, *Twice the Work of Free Labor: The Political Economy of Convict Labor in the New South* (London: Verso, 1996), 3; "The Biggest Cotton Planter," *Vicksburg* (MS) *Daily Commercial*, May 16, 1879, 4.

11. *Charleston* (SC) *News and Courier*, May 12, 1877; Perman, *The Road to Redemption*, 244, 251.

12. Rodrigue, *Reconstruction in the Cane Fields*, 165, 177; "The Southern States: Arkansas," *New Orleans Daily Picayune*, September 27, 1891, 2; "A Masked Mob Hangs Nine Striking Negro Cotton Pickers," *Cleveland Plain Dealer*, October 3, 1891, 3; Theresa A. Case, "The Radical Potential of the Knights' Biracialism: The 1885–1886 Gould System Strikes and Their Aftermath," in *Texas Labor History*, edited by Bruce Glasrud and James Maroney (College Station: Texas A&M University Press, 2013), 79–108, 94, 96; "Philanthropy a Long Way Off," *Daily Picayune*, December 8, 1877, 4; Eric Foner, *Reconstruction: America's Unfinished Revolution, 1863–1877* (New York: Harper & Row, 1988), 583–595; James Keith Hogue, *Uncivil War: Five New Orleans Street Battles and the Rise and Fall of Radical Reconstruction* (Baton Rouge: Louisiana State University Press, 2006), 191–192.

13. "Philanthropy a Long Way Off," *New Orleans Daily Picayune*, December 8, 1877, 4; Donald Holley, *The Second Great Emancipation: The Mechanical Cotton Picker, Black Migration, and How They Shaped the Modern South* (Fayetteville: University of Arkansas Press, 2000), 25; *Atlanta Constitution*, July 21, 1883; Charles L. Flynn Jr., *White Land, Black Labor: Caste and Class in Late Nineteenth-Century Georgia* (Baton Rouge: Louisiana State University Press, 1983), 62.

14. Estimates of the extent of convict labor, which are fairly straightforward, suggest a huge disparity in use between blacks and whites but a relatively small proportion of the aggregate population. In 1890, there were 1,688 convicts in the Georgia penitentiary, 90 percent of whom were black; the black population of Georgia at the time was over 800,000. Estimates of debt peonage are much less certain, but most evidence suggests that, even though debt was an important feature of southern labor relations, the incidence of peonage was relatively small. Perman, *The Road to Redemption*, 244, 251; William Cohen, "Negro Involuntary Servitude in the South, 1865–1940," *Journal of Southern History* 42(1, 1976): 33; Neil R. McMillen, *Dark Journey: Black Mississippians in the Age of Jim Crow* (Urbana: University of Illinois Press, 1989), 149–150; Edward Royce, *The Origins of Southern Sharecropping* (Philadelphia: Temple University Press, 1993); Suresh Naidu, "Recruitment Restrictions and Labor Markets: Evidence from the Postbellum U.S. South," *Journal of Labor Economics* 28(2, 2010): 413–445; Lichtenstein, *Twice the Work of Free Labor*, 83; Matthew Mancini, *One Dies, Get Another: Convict Leasing in the American South, 1866–1928* (Columbia: University of South Carolina Press, 1996); Price Fishback, "Debt Peonage in Postbellum Georgia," *Explorations in Economic History* 26(1989): 219–236.

15. Robert V. Bruce, *1877: Year of Violence* (Indianapolis: Bobbs-Merrill, 1959), 80; "Rule of Anarchy," *Columbus* (GA) *Daily Enquirer*, July 26, 1877, 1.

16. "The Great Railroad Strike," *Wheeling* (WV) *Daily Register*, August 1, 1877, 3; "By Telegraph, the War against Property," *Macon* (GA) *Telegraph and Messenger*, July 26, 1877, 1; *New Orleans Times*, July 26, 1877, 4; "Rule of Anarchy," *Columbus* (GA) *Daily Enquirer*, July 26, 1877, 1; "Latest by Telegraph," *New Orleans Daily Picayune*, July 27, 1877, 1; "Groundless Rumors," *Daily Picayune*, July 28, 1877, 4.

17. Clenenden, "President Hayes' 'Withdrawal' of the Troops," 249–250.

18. Blackburn (D-KY), *Congressional Record*, November 8, 1877, 297; "Felton's Boom, Speech of William M. Felton of Georgia," *Atlanta Constitution*, November 20, 1877, 1.

19. "The Great Railroad Strike," *Wheeling* (WV) *Daily Register*, August 1, 1877, 3; House vote 95, 42nd Cong., *Congressional Globe*, December 18, 1871; Campbell (D-OH), *Congressional Globe, December 20, 1871, 253.*

20. "The Great Railroad Strike," *Wheeling* (WV) *Daily Register*, August 1, 1877, 3; "Shifting Political Lines," *Dallas Morning News*, September 8, 1888, 4; "The Apple of Discord," *New Orleans Times*, July 26, 1877, 4; "Hard Times," *Raleigh* (NC) *Observer*, November 28, 1877, 2; "Notes on the Railroad War," *New Orleans Daily Picayune*, July 26, 1877, 4.

21. "Protection at Last," *New Orleans Daily Democrat*, August 14, 1877, 3; "The Decline of the Workingmen's Party," *Memphis Appeal*, November 7, 1877, 2; "Class Legislation," *Weston* (WV) *Democrat*, October 13, 1877, 1.

22. *Vicksburg* (MS) *Herald*, February 28, 1879; Neil Irvin Painter, *Exodusters: Black Migration to Kansas after Reconstruction* (New York: W. W. Norton, 1992), 186, 188, 196–197, 231, 256; Perman, *The Road to Redemption*, 259.

23. Painter, *Exodusters*, 3–4, 197–199.

24. Painter, *Exodusters*, 190, 194; *Report and Testimony of the Select Committee of the United States Senate to Investigate the Causes of the Removal of the Negroes from the Southern States to the Northern States, Part I*, Senate Report 693, 46th Cong., 2nd sess. (Washington, DC: U.S. Government Printing Office, 1880), xxii.

25. *Chicago Daily Tribune*, March 29, 1879, May 2, 1879.

26. Loren Schweninger, "A Vanishing Breed: Black Farm Owners in the South, 1651–1982," *Agricultural History* 63(3, 1989): 41–60, 48–49; Robert Higgs, "Patterns of Farm Rental in the Georgia Cotton Belt, 1880–1900," *Journal of Economic History* 34(2, 1974): 468–482.

27. Painter, *Exodusters*, 242; "Senate," *Omaha Daily Herald*, December 19, 1879, 1; "The Negro Exodus," *Daily Inter-Ocean* (Chicago), December 19, 1879, 1; *Vicksburg* (MS) *Daily Commercial*, May 13, 1879, 2.

28. *New Orleans Times*, May 23, 1879, and April 22, 1879; Painter, *Exodusters*, 240–241; "Persons and Things," *New Haven* (CT) *Register*, December 12, 1879, 2; "The Negro Exodus," *Daily Inter-Ocean*, (Chicago), December 16, 1879, 1; "The Negro Exodus," *Kalamazoo* (MI) *Gazette*, December 17, 1879, 1.

29. *Philadelphia Inquirer*, December 19, 1879, 4; *Congressional Record*, December 18, 1879, 156, 158, 169; "House," *Daily Inter-Ocean*, (Chicago), December 12, 1879, 1; "Congressional Proceedings," *Cleveland Plain Dealer*, December 16, 1879, 1; "Senator Windom's Proposition," *Daily Inter-Ocean*, December 17, 1879, 5.

30. "Washington," *New Orleans Daily Picayune*, December 19, 1879, 1; *Congressional Record*, December 18, 1879, 160, 167, 169; "The Negro Exodus," *Daily Inter-Ocean*, (Chicago), December 19, 1879, 1.

31. "The Exodus Revolution," *New Orleans Times Picayune*, December 19, 1879, 1.

32. *Report . . . the Causes of the Removal of the Negroes . . . , Part I*, xi; *Report . . . the Causes of the Removal of the Negroes . . . , Part II*, v–vii.

33. Glover (D-MO) and Reagan (D-TX), *Congressional Record*, March 31, 1886, 2971, 2975; Singleton (D-MS), *Congressional Record*, November 8, 1877, 294; Crain (D-TX), *Congressional Record*, April 1, 1886, 3012; *Congressional Record*, Appendix, March 31, 1886, 39.

34. *Congressional Globe*, December 20, 1871, 253–254.

35. Hill (R-GA), *Congressional Globe*, May 29, 1872, 4016; Stephen Ward Angell, *Bishop Henry McNeal Turner and African-American Religion in the South* (Knoxville, University of Tennessee Press, 1992), 118.

36. *Congressional Record*, June 21, 1882, 5162.

37. "The Senate Committee," *Coosa River News* (Center, AL), November 30, 1883, 2.

38. Senate Committee on Education and Labor, *Report of the Senate Committee upon the Relations between Labor and Capital*, Senate Report No. 1262, 48th Congress, 2nd Session (Washington, DC: U.S. Government Printing Office, 1885), vol. 4 (testimony), 22–24, 26–27, 31, 44, 49–51, 53, 555; *Advertiser and Mail* (Montgomery, AL), November 17, 1883, 3.

39. Senate Committee on Education and Labor, *Report . . . Labor and Capital*, vol. 4, 393, 451.

40. Ibid., vol. 4, 450, 571, 638.

41. Ibid., vol. 4, 456.

42. Ibid., vol. 4, 576, 635.

43. Ibid., vol. 1, 342–343; "Senatorial Courtesy," *New York Herald*, August 26, 1883.

44. Senate Committee on Education and Labor, *Report . . . Labor and Capital*, vol. 4, 53, 451–452, 455.

45. Ibid., vol. 4, 379–380, 571, 618–619, 638.

46. Ibid., vol. 4, 621, 788–791.

47. Williamjames Hull Hoffer, *To Enlarge the Machinery of Government: Congressional Debates and the Growth of the American State, 1858–1891* (Baltimore: Johns Hopkins University Press, 2010), 147.

48. "Another Investigation," *Montgomery* (AL) *Advertiser*, June 23, 1882, 2.

49. *Congressional Record*, May 14, 1884, 4153.

50. Morgan (D-AL), *Congressional Record*, May 14, 1884, 4156; Aiken (D-SC), *Congressional Record*, April 19, 1884, 3141; Blount (D-GA), *Congressional Record*, April 19, 1884, 31493152–31493153; Thomas Adams Upchurch, "Senator John Tyler Morgan and the Genesis of Jim Crow Ideology, 1889–1891," *Alabama Review* 57(2, 2004): 110–131, 113.

51. David Katzman, *Seven Days a Week: Women and Domestic Service in Industrializing America* (New York: Oxford University Press, 1978), 324, fn. 49.

52. U.S. Navy Department, Office of the Solicitor, *The Eight-Hour Law: Comprising the Statutes, Decisions of the Attorney General, Decisions of the Court, and the Executive Orders Suspending Its Provisions* (Washington, DC: U.S. Government Printing Office, 1918), 3–11.

53. "The Labor Question in Politics," *Macon* (GA) *Telegraph and Messenger*, August 10, 1877, 2; Reagan (D-TX), *Congressional Record*, July 17, 1888, 6407.

54. Breckinridge (D-KY), *Congressional Record*, April 2, 1886, 3038; Rogers (D-AR), *Congressional Record*, April 3, 1886, 3062; Tucker (D-VA), *Congressional Record*, Appendix, March 31, 1886, 61; Reagan (D-TX), Hammond (D-GA), and Daniel (D-VA), *Congressional Record*, March 31, 1886, 2964, 2969, 2974.

55. Crain (D-TX), *Congressional Record*, April 1, 1886, 3010; O'Hara (R-NC), *Congressional Record*, April 2, 1886, 3049; Storm (D-PA), *Congressional Record*, April 3, 1886, 3063.

56. Black witnesses testifying before the Blair Committee, as well as black newspapers, regularly treated the opposition of the white unions as one of the principal reasons why black men could not gain entry into the higher trades anywhere in the country. Senate Committee on Education and Labor, *Report . . . Labor and Capital*, vol. 1, 103, 171, 304, 306, 361, 375, 569, 712;

"The Strikes," *Washington Bee*, May 8, 1886, 2; "Mr. Durham on the Labor Union," *The Planet* (Richmond, VA), February 5, 1898, 2; *Washington Bee*, September 17, 1887, 2.

57. While most sources stressed that the black strikers were Knights of Labor, others insisted that they were not. "The Negro Strikers on Tate's Plantation Are Not Knights of Labor," *Greensboro* (NC) *North State*, July 15, 1886, 1; *Texarkana* (AR) *Independent*, April 19, 1886; *Louisville* (KY) *Commercial*, April 21, 1886; *Galveston* (TX) *Daily News*, April 6, 1886; Case, "The Radical Potential of the Knights' Biracialism," 94–95; Reagan (D-TX), *Congressional Record*, July 17, 1888, 6407; "1,000 Armed Negroes," *Macon* (GA) *Telegraph*, July 9, 1886.

58. "End of the Fall River War," *Georgia Weekly Telegraph* (Macon), September 27, 1870, 8; *Texarkana Independent*, April 21, 1886; Case, "The Radical Potential of the Knights' Biracialism," 94; Senate Committee on Education and Labor, *Relations . . . Labor and Capital,* vol. 4, 103, 140; "The Georgia Press," *Macon* (GA) *Telegraph and Messenger*, August 1, 1883, 3; *Arkansas Gazette* Little Rock), September 1, 1898; *New York Tribune*, July 2, 1887, 4; *Montgomery* (AL) *Weekly Advertiser*, May 2, 1889, 4; Albion Tourgée, "A Bystander's Notes," *Daily Inter-Ocean* (Chicago), June 16, 1888, 4.

59. Fitzhugh Lee, Governor of Virginia, "Solid South Sentiment," *Dallas Morning News*, November 16, 1885, 1; "Senator Vance on the Future of the Negro," *Wilmington* (NC) *Northern Star*, July 6, 1884, 2; "The Solid South; Current Political Sentiment and Tendencies in the Late Confederate States," *Cleveland Plain Dealer*, November 10, 1885, 5; "No New Party South: Time Still Necessary," *New York Tribune*, June 1, 1877, 2.

60. Edward Mayes, *Lucius Q. C. Lamar: His Life, Times, and Speeches, 1825–1893* (Nashville: Publishing House of the Methodist Episcopal Church, South, 1896), 697; Wade Hampton, "Ought the Negro to Be Disfranchised? Ought He to Have Been Enfranchised?" *North American Review*, 128(268, 1879): 225–283, 241; "The Solid South," *Macon* (GA) *Weekly Telegraph*, March 18, 1881, 8; Hill (D-GA), *Congressional Record*, December 18, 1879.

61. Michael Klarman, *From Jim Crow to Civil Rights: The Supreme Court and the Struggle for Racial Equality* (Oxford: Oxford University Press, 2004), 10; Valelly, *The Two Reconstructions*; Pamela Brandwein, *Rethinking the Judicial Settlement of Reconstruction* (Cambridge: Cambridge University Press, 2011); Kousser, *The Shaping of Southern Politics*.

62. Stewart, *Budget Reform Politics*, 86; Atkins (D-TN), *Congressional Record*, March 2, 1877, 2113; Coakley, *The Role of Federal Military Forces in Domestic Disorders,* 343; Clendenen, "President Hayes' 'Withdrawal' of the Troops," 241.

63. Clendenen, "President Hayes' 'Withdrawal' of the Troops," 241; William E. Chandler, *Letters of Mr. William E. Chandler Relative to the So-Called Southern Policy of President Hayes* (Concord, MA: Monitor and Statesman Office, 1878), 81; Peskin, "Was There a Compromise of 1877?" 67.

64. Koger, *Filibustering*, 71.

65. Atkins (D-TN), *Congressional Record*, November 8, 1877, 287.

66. Brandwein, *Rethinking the Judicial Settlement of Reconstruction*, 130.

67. "Congressional," *Daily Inter-Ocean* (Chicago), June 8, 1878, 3; "How General Sherman Talks," *Daily Inter-Ocean*, July 8, 1878, 2; "Important Army Order," *Philadelphia Inquirer*, July 11, 1878, 8.

68. *Philadelphia Inquirer*, June 10, 1878, 4; "The Army as a Posse Comitatus—Gen. Sherman's Order," *Baltimore Sun*, July 12, 1878, 2.

69. "The Campaign Defined," *Vicksburg* (MS) *Daily Commercial*, July 18, 1878, 1; "Important Army Order," *Philadelphia Inquirer*, July 11, 1878, 8; Clayton Laurie and Ronald Cole, *The Role of Federal Military Forces in Domestic Disorders, 1877–1945* (Washington, DC: Center of Military History, 1997), 66–68.

70. "The Posse Comitatus Clause," *Daily Inter-Ocean*, (Chicago), October 2, 1878, 4; "Con-

gressional," *Daily Inter-Ocean*, June 8, 1878, 3; Clendenen, "President Hayes' 'Withdrawal' of the Troops," 244.

71. Wilbur Miller, "The Revenue: Federal Law Enforcement in the Mountain South, 1870–1900," *Journal of Southern History* 55(2, 1989): 195–216; see also "The Great Speech of Robert G. Ingersoll, in the Cooper Union, New-York City, Saturday Evening, October 23, 1880," in *Great Republican Speeches of the Campaign of 1880* (Stapleton, NY: Staten Island Publishing Company, 1881), 54; U.S. Department of the Treasury, *Enforcement of Internal Revenue Laws* (Washington, DC: U.S. Government Printing Office, 1880); *Report of the Commissioner of Internal Revenue for the Fiscal Year Ended June 30, 1881* (Washington, DC: U.S. Government Printing Office, 1881), vii–viii.

72. Removal authority in the case of revenue officers was upheld by the U.S. Supreme Court in *Tennessee v. Davis* 100 U.S. 257 (1879). "The South in Congress," *New York Tribune*, October 4, 1879, 1; "House," *Washington Evening Star*, June 5, 1878, 1; "State and Federal Authority," *The Raleigh* (NC) *Observer*, January 18, 1879, 2; "Affairs in Wade Hampton's State," *Daily Inter-Ocean* (Chicago), July 25, 1878, 2; *Philadelphia Times*, August 12, 1878, 2; "The Administration and the Revenue Troubles in South Carolina," *Baltimore Sun*, July 30, 1878, 2; "The South Carolina Conflict," *New York Times*, July 30, 1878, 1; see also "A Conflict of Authority," *New Orleans Daily Picayune*, August 14, 1878, 8.

73. *Congressional Record*, June 2, 1886, 5163; "The South in Congress," *New York Tribune*, October 4, 1879, 2; Theodore Krieger, "Local Prejudice and Removal of Criminal Cases from State to Federal Courts," *St. John's Law Review* 19(1, 1944): 43–47; "State and Federal Authority," *Raleigh* (NC) *Observer*, January 18, 1879, 2.

74. "The President's Privilege of Using Troops in the South," *Daily Inter-Ocean*, (Chicago), October 29, 1878, 5; "The Posse Comitatus Clause," *Daily Inter-Ocean*, October 2, 1878, 4; "The President Can Use the United States Army," *Janesville* (WI) *Gazette*, October 29, 1878, 1; "The South Carolina Troubles," *Christian Union*, November 27, 1878, 448.

75. Charles R. Williams and William H. Smith, *The Life of Rutherford B. Hayes: Nineteenth President of the United States*, vol. 2 (Boston: Houghton Mifflin, 1914), 266; "The Army as a Posse Comitatus—Gen. Sherman's Order," *Baltimore Sun*, July 12, 1878, 2; *Chicago Tribune*, April 9, 1879, 6; *South Carolina in 1876; Testimony as to the Denial of the Elective Franchise in South Carolina at the Elections of 1875 and 1876*, vol. 3, Misc. Doc. 48, 44th Cong., 2nd sess. (Washington, DC: U.S. Government Printing Office, 1877), 456.

76. *Chicago Tribune*, April 9, 1879, 6; Drew Kershen, "The Jury Selection Act of 1879: Theory and Practice of Citizen Participation in the Judicial System," *University of Illinois Law Forum* 3(Fall, 1980): 707–782, 719.

77. Kershen, "The Jury Selection Act of 1879," 715, 758.

78. *Chicago Tribune*, June 25, 1879, 4; Kershen, "The Jury Selection Act of 1879," 715, 758, 765.

79. Julius Burrows (R-MI), speech in U.S. House of Representatives, June 3, 1882; "From Washington; Wheeler Ousted and Lowe Sworn In," *Macon* (GA) *Telegraph and Messenger*, June 4, 1882, 1; Thurman (D-OH), *Appendix to the Congressional Record*, May 15, 1879, 90; Scott C. James and Brian L. Lawson, "The Political Economy of Voting Rights Enforcement in America's Gilded Age: Electoral College Competition, Partisan Commitment, and the Federal Elections Law," *American Political Science Review* 93(1, 1999): 115–131; Albie Burke, "Federal Regulation of Congressional Elections in Northern Cities, 1871–94," *American Journal of Legal History* 14(1, 1970): 17–34.

80. "The Veto Message," *New Orleans Daily Picayune*, April 30, 1879, 1; "Congressional," *Arkansas Gazette*, May 16, 1879, 1; Frank P. Vazzano, "President Hayes, Congress, and the Appropriations Riders Vetoes," *Congress and the Presidency* 20(1, 1993): 25–37.

81. Xi Wang, *The Trial of Democracy: Black Suffrage and Northern Republicans, 1860–1910* (Athens: University of Georgia Press, 1997).

82. *Report of the United States Senate Committee to Inquire into Alleged Frauds and Violence in the Elections of 1878*, vol. 1, Report 855, 45th Cong., 3rd sess. (Washington, DC: U.S. Government Printing Office, 1879), xlvi.

83. Jeffrey A. Jenkins, "Partisanship and Contested Election Cases in the House of Representatives, 1789–2002," *Studies in American Political Development* 18(2, 2004): 112–135; Richard M. Valelly, "Partisan Entrepreneurship and Policy Windows: George Frisbie Hoar and the 1890 Federal Elections Bill," in *Formative Acts: American Politics in the Making*, edited by Stephen Skowronek and Matthew Glassman (Philadelphia: University of Pennsylvania Press, 2007), 136–137; U.S. Senate, Testimony on Municipal Election at Jackson, Mississippi. Misc. Doc. 166, 50th Cong., 1st sess. (Washington, DC: U.S. Government Printing Office, 1888); U.S. Senate, *Alleged Election Outrages in Washington County, Texas*, Report 2534, 50th Cong., 2nd sess. (Washington, DC: U.S. Government Printing Office, 1889), 90; U.S. Senate, *Report on Alleged Outrages in Danville, Virginia*, Report 579, 48th Cong., 1st sess. (Washington, DC: U.S. Government Printing Office, 1884), xlii; U.S. Senate, *Report of the Special Committee to Inquire into the Mississippi Election of 1883*, Report 512, 48th Cong., 1st sess. (Washington, DC: U.S. Government Printing Office, 1884), 25; U.S. Senate, *Municipal Election at Jackson, Miss.*, Report 1887, 50th Cong., 1st sess. (Washington, DC: U.S. Government Printing Office, 1888); U.S. Senate, *Testimony: Municipal Election at Jackson, Miss.*, Misc. Doc. 166, 50th Cong., 1st sess. (Washington, DC: U.S. Government Printing Office, 1888); Hirshson, *Farewell to the Bloody Shirt*, 153.

84. Robert Smalls, "Election Methods in the South," *North American Review* 151(408, 1890): 593–600, 594, 598.

85. "Mr. Harrison Opposes It," *Macon (GA) Telegraph*, June 16, 1890, 1; Crofts, "The Blair Bill and the Elections Bill," 262; Richard Valelly, "The Reed Rules and Republican Party Building: A New Look," *Studies in American Political Development* 23(October): 115–142, 134; Smalls, "Election Methods in the South," 598.

86. "Federal Elections," *Philadelphia Inquirer*, June 3, 1890, 1.

87. Valelly, "The Reed Rules and Republican Party Building"; Thomas B. Reed, "Rules of the House of Representatives," *The Century Magazine* 37(5, 1889): 792–795, 793; "In the House," *Daily Inter-Ocean* (Chicago), January 22, 1890, 2; *Galveston (TX) Daily News*, January 31, 1890, 3; Koger, *Filibustering*, 54–55; Walter Oleszek and Richard Sachs, "Speakers Reed, Cannon, and Gingrich: Catalysts of Institutional and Procedural Change," in *The Cannon Centenary Conference: The Changing Nature of the Speakership* (Washington, DC: U.S. Government Printing Office, 2004), 131–133.

88. "The Elections Fight On," *Macon (GA) Telegraph*, June 26, 1890, 1; "From Washington," *Baltimore Sun*, July 5, 1890, 1; "The Election Law," *Knoxville (TN) Journal*, June 27, 1890, 1; "The Elections Bill," *Columbus (GA) Enquirer-Sun*, July 3, 1890, 1; James M. Beeby, *The Revolt of the Tar Heels: The North Carolina Populist Movement, 1890–1901* (Jackson: University Press of Mississippi, 2008), 19.

89. "Not of One Mind," *Kansas City Times*, July 11, 1890, 1; Richard Welch, "The Federal Elections Bill of 1890: Postscripts and Preludes," *Journal of American History* 52(3, 1965): 511–526; "The Original Package Conference," *Daily Inter-Ocean* (Chicago), August 1, 1890, 4.

90. "From Washington," *Baltimore Sun*, July 12, 1890, 1; "Gag Law Sought," *Kansas City Times*, July 14, 1890, 1; "Federal Elections: Southern Democrats Anxious over the Proposed New Laws," *Philadelphia Inquirer*, June 3, 1890, 1; "Not of One Mind," *Kansas City Times*, July 11, 1890, 1.

91. "From Washington," *Baltimore Sun*, July 16, 1890, 1; "Radicals Chilly," *Kansas City Times*, July 15, 1890, 1; "The Force Bill Will Pass," *Macon (GA) Telegraph*, July 15, 1890, 4; *Philadelphia Times*, July 13, 1890, 4; *Philadelphia Times*, July 8, 1890, 4.

92. "Senator Pugh Writes a Letter," *Daily Advertiser* (Montgomery, AL), July 18, 1890, 7.

93. *Daily Inter-Ocean* (Chicago), August 5, 1890, 4; "From the *Baltimore American*," *Philadelphia Inquirer*, August 7, 1890, 4.

94. Kehl, *Boss Rule in the Gilded Age*, 133–136; Lambert, *Arthur Pue Gorman*, 149; "Stirred up a Storm," *Cleveland Plain Dealer*, August 14, 1890, 2; "What They Think of Quay," *Philadelphia Times*, August 17, 1890, 4; "Quay and the Election Bill," *Chicago Tribune*, August 20, 1890, 4; *Philadelphia Times*, August 15, 1890, 4; Plumb (R-KS), *Congressional Record*, August 26, 1890, 9144; "Not of One Mind," *Kansas City Times*, July 11, 1890, 1; Welch, "The Federal Elections Bill of 1890," 517.

95. John T. Morgan, "Shall Negro Majorities Rule?" *The Forum* 6(February, 1889): 588; John T. Morgan, "The Race Question in the United States," *The Arena* (September 1890); John T. Morgan, "Special Introduction" to Alexis de Tocqueville, *Democracy in America*, vol. 1, translated by Henry Reeve (1835; New York: The Colonial Press, 1899); John T. Morgan, "Federal Control of Elections," *The Forum* 10(September): 24–25.

96. Albion Tourgée, "Shall White Minorities Rule?" *The Forum* 7(April, 1889), 150; Smalls, "Election Methods in the South," 599.

97. "The Political Drama," *Columbus* (GA) *Enquirer-Sun*, December 17, 1890, 1; Welch, "The Federal Elections Bill of 1890," 518.

98. "Trying Their Trump," *Cleveland Plain Dealer*, December 24, 1890, 1; "Radicals Line Up," *Kansas City Times*, December 30, 1890, 1l; "Warning Unheeded," *Kansas City Times*, December 2, 1890, 1; *Chicago Daily Tribune*, December 24, 1890, 9; "The Last Resort," *Galveston* (TX) *Daily News*, December 24, 1890, 1.

99. "Warning Unheeded," *Kansas City Times*, December 2, 1890, 1; Lambert, *Arthur Pue Gorman*, 159.

100. Welch, "The Federal Elections Bill of 1890," 520; "Laid out the Election Bill," *Bremen* (IN) *Inquirer*, January 9, 1891, 2.

101. "The Senate Acts," *Dixon* (IL) *Evening Telegraph*, January 15, 1891, 2.

102. Lambert, *Arthur Pue Gorman*, 160; Welch, "The Federal Elections Bill of 1890," 521; "Congress Running Mad," *Philadelphia Inquirer*, January 23, 1891, 4; "Minority Rights Trampled," *Boston Post*, January 23, 1891, 1.

103. "The Gag-Rule Displaced," *Baltimore Sun*, January 27, 1891, 2.

104. "Not of One Mind," *Kansas City Times*, July 11, 1890, 1; "From Washington," *Baltimore Sun*, July 16, 1890, 1.

105. "The Gag-Rule Displaced," *Baltimore Sun*, January 27, 1891, 2; Wawro and Schickler, *Filibuster*, 84–85.

106. Perman, *Struggle for Mastery*, 46–47; "War of Politicians," *Knoxville* (TN) *Journal*, October 1, 1893, 7.

107. In 1892, supervisors were used in New Orleans, Little Rock, Nashville, and Baltimore, while Populists in Mississippi, Tennessee, and elsewhere requested supervisors to be present as observers in a number of counties. James and Lawson, "The Political Economy of Voting Rights Enforcement," 122; "The Tax Question," *Dallas Morning News*, January 2, 1894, 4; "Directed to Ignore the Law," *Roanoke* (VA) *Times*, October 21, 1892, 1; "Not Fully Decided," *Atlanta Constitution*, November 3, 1892, 7; "Powers of Federal Election Supervisors," *The Clarion* (Jackson, MS), November 3, 1892, 4; *The Daily American* (Nashville, TN), September 13, 1892, 4; *Daily State Ledger* (Jackson, MS), October 29, 1892, 2.

108. Perman, *Struggle for Mastery*, 46–47; "War of Politicians," *Knoxville* (TN) *Journal*, October 1, 1893, 7; Patterson (D-TN), *Congressional Record*, September 30, 1893, 1992–1993; "Southern Men Speak Out," *Macon* (GA) *Telegraph*, October 3, 1893, 1.

109. Murray (R-SC), *Congressional Record*, October 4, 1893, 2147–48; Congressional Record,

October 4, 1893, 2158, 2161; "House and Senate: The Negro Representative Gives a Bitter Speech, Which Is Loudly Applauded by Republicans," *Arkansas Gazette*, October 6, 1893, 1.

110. "There Should Be Cloture," *Daily Charlotte* (NC) *Observer*, October 27, 1893, 2; "Why Tom Reed Is Happy," *Knoxville* (TN) *Journal*, October 1, 1893, 7; Russell (D-GA), *Congressional Record*, October 5, 1893, 2161.

111. "Federal Election Bill," *Dallas Morning News*, January 3, 1894, 1; U.S. Senate, Report 113, part 2 (views of the minority), 53rd Cong., 2nd sess., 1; "Minority Has Its Say," *Omaha World Herald*, January 12, 1894, 2; Valelly, "Partisan Entrepreneurship and Policy Windows," 147–148.

112. U.S. Senate, Report 113, part 2, 23, 26–27, 33.

113. "The Tax Question," *Dallas Morning News*, January 2, 1894, 4; "The House," *New Orleans Daily Picayune*, February 9, 1894, 6; "Wiped from the Statute Books," *Daily Picayune*, February 9, 1894, 6; "It Is Finished," *Knoxville* (TN) *Journal*, February 8, 1894, 1; "Fraud Is Now Legalized," *Knoxville Journal*, February 9, 1894, 1.

114. Charles M. Harvey, *History of the Republican Party, Together with the Proceedings of the Republican National Convention at St. Louis, June 16th to 18th, 1896* (St. Louis: I. Haas Publishing and Engraving Co., 1896), 99–100.

115. "Micah's Letter," *Savannah Tribune*, November 28, 1896.

116. "Federal Election Bill," *Dallas Morning News*, January 3, 1894, 1; Dewey W. Grantham, "Tennessee and Twentieth-Century American Politics," *Tennessee Historical Quarterly* 53(3, 1996): 210–229, 211; Perman, *Struggle for Mastery*, 54–58; *Clarion-Ledger*, August 7, 1890, quoted in William A. Mabry, "Disfranchisement of the Negro in Mississippi," *Journal of Southern History* 4(3, 1938): 318–333, 322; Upchurch, "Senator John Tyler Morgan and the Genesis of Jim Crow Ideology," 129, fn.16.

117. Kousser, *The Shaping of Southern Politics*; Perman, *Struggle for Mastery*, 95, 286; Stephen Kantrowitz, *Ben Tillman and the Reconstruction of White Supremacy* (Chapel Hill: University of North Carolina Press, 2000), 225; Donna A. Barnes, *The Louisiana Populist Movement, 1881–1900* (Baton Rouge: Louisiana State University Press, 2011), 199; Omar Ali, *In the Lion's Mouth: Black Populism in the New South* (Jackson: University Press of Mississippi, 2010), 132–134.

118. On the intersection of disfranchisement and suppression of the Populist insurgency, to which it was by no means a straightforward response, see Kousser, *The Shaping of Southern Politics*; Smalls, "Election Methods in the South," 598.

119. Richard Wood, "The South and Reunion, 1898," *The Historian* 31(3, 1969): 415–430, 415, 424–426; John P. Dyer, *From Shiloh to San Juan: The Life of "Fightin' Joe" Wheeler* (Baton Rouge: Louisiana State University Press, 1961), 230.

120. *Guinn v. United States*, 238 U.S. 347 (1915); Horace Samuel Merrill and Marion Galbraith Merrill, *The Republican Command, 1897–1913* (Lexington: University Press of Kentucky, 2014), 34; *Congressional Record*, February 26, 1900, 2243–2245; *Mills v. Green*, 159 U.S. 651 (1895); *Williams v. Mississippi*, 170 U.S. 213 (1898); *Giles v. Harris*, 189 U.S. 475 (1903); *James v. Bowman*, 190 U.S. 127 (1903); *Giles v. Teasley* 193 U.S. 146 (1904); *Jones v. Montague*, 194 U.S. 147 (1904); J. Morgan Kousser, *Colorblind Injustice: Minority Voting Rights and the Undoing of the Second Reconstruction* (Chapel Hill: University of North Carolina Press, 1999), 319–23; Robert Volney Riser, *Defying Disfranchisement: Black Voting Rights Activism in the Jim Crow South, 1890–1908* (Baton Rouge: Louisiana State University Press, 2010), 208; J. Morgan Kousser, testimony before hearings of the House Subcommittee on Civil and Constitutional Rights on extension of the Voting Rights Act, Serial No. 24, part 3, 97th Cong., 1st sess. (Washington, DC: U.S. Government Printing Office, 1982), 2025.

121. H.R. 10550, sect. 4, 55th Cong., 2nd sess., June 3, 1898; Lacey (R-IA), Greene (R-MA), and Bailey (D-TX), *Congressional Record*, June 9, 1898, 5700–5708; Livingston (D-GA) and Pow-

ers (R-VT), *Congressional Record*, June 7, 1898, 5619–5620; "Shall Soldiers Vote?" *Lexington* (KY) *Morning Herald*, June 4, 1898, 4; "Votes of Volunteers," *Baltimore Sun*, June 8, 1898, 8.

122. "The Political Situation," *Macon* (GA) *Telegraph and Messenger*, August 8, 1877, 3; John Haley, "Race, Rhetoric, and Revolution," in *Democracy Betrayed: The Wilmington Race Riot of 1898 and Its Legacy* (Chapel Hill: University of North Carolina Press, 1998); William Graham Sumner, "The Conquest of the United States by Spain," *Yale Law Journal* 8(4, 1899): 168–193, 190.

123. H. R. 9757, 54th Cong., 2nd sess., December 19, 1896; H. R. 6963, 56th Cong., 1st sess., January 20, 1900; Eric Anderson, *Race and Politics in North Carolina, 1872–1901: The Black Second* (Baton Rouge: Louisiana State University Press, 1981), 308; White (R-NC), *Congressional Record*, January 29, 1901, 1635–1638.

124. Clayton (D-AL-3), *Congressional Record*, May 20, 1897, 1198.

Chapter 6. Limited Progressivism

1. William Garrott Brown, "The South in National Politics," *South Atlantic Quarterly* 9(2, 1910): 103–115, 112, 115.

2. "Democratic Possibilities," *Baltimore Sun*, March 17, 1900, 4; "The Doctrines of Thos. Jefferson Upheld," *Columbus* (GA) *Enquirer-Sun*, March 19, 1900, 1; "Democracy's Deplorable Plight," *Charlotte* (NC) *Daily Observer*, November 11, 1900, 4; "The Blow at the South's Political Power," *New Orleans Daily Picayune*, January 2, 1900, 4.

3. Edward L. Ayers, *The Promise of the New South: Life after Reconstruction* (New York: Oxford University Press, 1992), 409; Dewey W. Grantham, "The Contours of Southern Progressivism," *American Historical Review* 86(December 1981): 1035–1059, 1042; "Looking to South," *Dallas Morning News*, May 9, 1901, 6; "Without a Negro," *Fort Worth* (TX) *Register*, December 15, 1901, 23.

4. "A Desperate Play into the Hands of the South," *Cleveland Gazette*, February 2, 1901, 2; "The Thoughtful Negro Favorable to Bryan," *Birmingham* (AL) *Age Herald*, October 8, 1900, 8; "Some League Work," *The Plaindealer* (Topeka, KS), January 4, 1901, 1; Kimberly Johnson, *Reforming Jim Crow: Southern Politics and State in the Age Before* Brown (New York: Oxford University Press, 2010); Riser, *Defying Disfranchisement*; Donald DeVore, *Defying Jim Crow: African American Community Development and the Struggle for Racial Equality in New Orleans, 1900–1960* (Baton Rouge: Louisiana State University Press, 2015); Megan Ming Francis, *Civil Rights and the Making of the Modern American State* (Cambridge: Cambridge University Press, 2014); Raymond Smock, *Booker T. Washington: Black Leadership in the Age of Jim Crow* (Chicago: Ivan R. Dee, 2009); Robert J. Norell, *Up from History: The Life of Booker T. Washington* (Cambridge, MA: Harvard University Press, 2009).

5. Sanders, *Roots of Reform*; Stephen Skowronek, *Building a New American State: The Expansion of National Administrative Capacities, 1877–1920* (Cambridge: Cambridge University Press, 1982), 4.

6. "Democrats Think of Cleveland," *Charlotte* (NC) *Daily Observer*, May 4, 1900, 4; "Democratic Possibilities," *Baltimore Sun*, April 17, 1900, 4; "The South's Share," *Lexington* (KY) *Morning-Herald*, November 19, 1900, 2; "The Way out of the Wilderness," *Charlotte Daily Observer*, November 8, 1900, 4; "What Will the Democratic Party Do?" *Lexington Morning-Herald*, November 8, 1900, 2.

7. Woodward, *Origins of the New South*, 458; Richard B. Doss, "Democrats in the Doldrums: Virginia and the Democratic National Convention of 1904," *Journal of Southern History* 20(4, 1954): 511–529, 513, fn.14, 527; *Washington Star*, June 14, 1904.

8. "Forecasting Results: November Elections," *The State* (Columbia SC), June 3, 1902, 3.

9. Pearson (R-NC), *Congressional Record*, January 8, 1901, 666.

10. Charles Henry Grosvenor, "The Negro Problem in the South," *The Forum* 29(August, 1900): 720–725, 723, 721. The most important work on disfranchisement, and on opposition to it, includes Kousser's *Shaping of Southern Politics* and *Colorblind Injustice*, Valelly's *Two Reconstructions*, Riser's *Defying Disfranchisement*, and Perman's *Struggle for Mastery*.

11. Charles Francis Adams, *"The Solid South" and the Afro-American Race Problem: Speech of Charles Francis Adams at the Academy of Music, Richmond Va., Saturday Evening, 24 October, 1908* (Boston, 1908), 17.

12. *Louisville Post* editorial, reprinted in "Sectional or National? The Discussion Proceeds," *Macon* (GA) *Telegraph*, November 25, 1900, 8; William H. Taft, *Present Day Problems: A Collection of Addresses Delivered on Various Occasions* (New York: Dodd, Mead & Company, 1908), 233.

13. "Carmack Not to Raise Issue: Does Not Intend to Agitate Repeal of Fifteenth Amendment in Congress," *New York Times*, September 27, 1903; *Congressional Record*, February 26, 1900, 2243–2245; "Is the Fifteenth Amendment to Be Permanent," *New York Sun*, April 30, 1903, 8; "Indiana and Charleston," *New York Times*, January 6, 1903, 8; Joseph Bucklin Bishop, *Theodore Roosevelt and His Time*, vol. 1 (New York: Charles Scribner's Sons, 1920), 350; Wang, *The Trial of Democracy*, 262; Seth M. Scheiner, "President Roosevelt and the Negro, 1901–1908," *Journal of Negro History* 47(3, 1962): 169–182, 171; "New York Sun Favors Repeal," *Biloxi* (MS) *Daily Herald*, May 4, 1903; Eric Love, *Race over Empire: Racism and U.S. Imperialism, 1865–1900* (Chapel Hill: University of North Carolina Press, 2004).

14. "Is the Fifteenth Amendment to Be Permanent," *New York Sun*, April 30, 1903, 8; "New York Sun Favors Repeal," *Biloxi* (MS) *Daily Herald*, May 4, 1903; "Indiana and Charleston," *New York Times*, January 6, 1903, 8; Adams, *"The Solid South" and the Afro-American Race Problem*, 19–20; August Meier, "The Negro and the Democratic Party, 1875–1915," *Phylon* 17(2, 1956): 173–191, 185; Grantham, *The South in Modern America*, 42; William H. Taft, "Southern Democracy and Republican Principles," in Taft, *Present Day Problems*, 221–222.

15. Grantham, *The South in Modern America*, 33; *Cleveland Gazette*, December 14, 1912, cited in Willard B. Gatewood, "William D. Crum: A Negro in Politics," *Journal of Negro History* 53(4, 1968): 301–320.

16. *New York Times*, October 19, 1901; "Booker T. Washington's Dinner at the White House," *Literary Digest* 23(17, 1901): 486–487; Joseph Bucklin Bishop, *Theodore Roosevelt and His Time*, vol. 1 (New York: Charles Scribner's Sons, 1920), 350; Wang, *The Trial of Democracy*, 262; Seth M. Scheiner, "President Roosevelt and the Negro, 1901–1908," *Journal of Negro History* 47(3, 1962): 169–182, 171, 176, 181; Grantham, *The South in Modern America*, 42; Theodore Roosevelt: "Sixth Annual Message," December 3, 1906," The American Presidency Project, http://www.presidency.ucsb.edu/ws/?pid=29547; Rayford W. Logan, *The Betrayal of the Negro: From Rutherford B. Hayes to Woodrow Wilson* (New York: Collier Books, 1965), 96.

17. Because the resolution involved a question of constitutional interpretation, it was privileged under the rules. Olmsted's resolution was considered at the same time as the more famous amendment by Edgar Crumpacker (R-IN), which would have reduced the number of representatives from Mississippi, Louisiana, South Carolina, and North Carolina. Crumpacker's amendment did not come to a vote on this occasion because of the opposition of the Republican leadership. "Views of Mr. Crumpacker," in *Apportionment among the Several States*, Report 2130, 56th Cong., 2nd sess., December 20, 1900, 122; "Minority Won," *Indianapolis Journal*, January 4, 1901, 1; "Underwood's Fight," *Birmingham* (AL) *Age-Herald*, January 5, 1901, 8; *Congressional Record*, January 4, 1901, 559; *Times-Register and Sentinel*, (Salem VA), June 30, 1904; Doss, "Democrats in the Doldrums," 518; Perman, *Struggle for Mastery*, 225, 231; "Army Bill Has Right of Way," *Daily News-Democrat* (Belleville, IL), January 4, 1901, 1; "Effort to Reduce Representation from the

Southern States Failed," *Columbus* (GA) *Enquirer-Sun*, January 4, 1901, 2; "May Be Hit by His Own Bomb," *Philadelphia Inquirer*, January 1, 1901, 14.

18. "House Democrats Angry," *New York Times*, April 8, 1908, 6; Crumpacker (R-IN), *Congressional Record*, May 22, 1908, 6764–6765; Hardwick (D-GA), Williams (D-MS), Lassiter (D-VA), Gillespie (D-TX), *Congressional Record*, May 23, 1908, 6765–6767.

19. Perman, *Struggle for Mastery*, 230–231; *Chicago Tribune*, March 14, 1901, 6.

20. Lassiter (D-VA), *Congressional Record*, May 23, 1908, 6765; Williams, (D-MS), *Congressional Record*, May 23, 1908, 6767; Gillespie (D-TX), *Congressional Record*, May 23, 1908, 6766; "Negro Vote Bill Passed by House," *Chicago Tribune*, May 23, 1908, 1; "Georgia Will Not Gain Member by Caucus Plan," *Atlanta Georgian and News*, February 3, 1911, 1.

21. Hamilton Wright Mabrie, "The New North," *South Atlantic Quarterly* 4(2, 1905): 109–114, 111–112; Adams, *"The Solid South" and the Afro-American Race Problem*, 19–20; Grantham, *The South in Modern America*, 33, 42, 54; Grosvenor (R-OH), *Congressional Record*, January 7, 1901, 713.

22. Kousser, *The Shaping of Southern Politics*, 216, 246.

23. Robert D. Johnston, "Peasants, Pitchforks, and the (Found) Promise of Progressivism: Review of *Roots of Reform: Farmers, Workers, and the American State*," *Reviews in American History* 28(3, 2000): 393–398, 394; Robert C. McMath Jr., "C. Vann Woodward and the Burden of Southern Populism," *Journal of Southern History* 67(4, 2001): 741–768, 744; Kantrowitz, *Ben Tillman and the Reconstruction of White Supremacy*, 150.

24. Woodward, *Origins of the New South*, 371; George B. Tindall, *The Persistent Tradition in New South Politics* (Baton Rouge: Louisiana State University Press, 1975); McMath, "C. Vann Woodward and the Burden of Southern Populism," 760–764; Grantham, "The Contours of Southern Progressivism," 1037, 1040–1041; Dewey W. Grantham, *Southern Progressivism: The Reconciliation of Progress and Tradition* (Knoxville: University of Tennessee Press, 1983), 13; Grantham, *The South in Modern America*, 46; Ayers, *The Promise of the New South*, 413; Hofstadter, *The Age of Reform: From Bryan to FDR* (New York: Alfred A. Knopf, 1955), 241; Anne Firor Scott, "A Progressive Wind from the South, 1906–1913," *Journal of Southern History* 29(1, 1963): 53–70, 54.

25. "Sectional or National? The Discussion Proceeds," *Macon* (GA) *Telegraph*, November 25, 1900, 8; "Disfranchisement a Trick," *Macon Telegraph*, September 8, 1907, 4; Sheldon Hackney, *Populism to Progressivism in Alabama* (Princeton, NJ: Princeton University Press, 1969) 326; *Jeffersonian Weekly*, January 20, 1910; C. Vann Woodward, *Tom Watson: Agrarian Rebel* (New York: Macmillan, 1938), 220 (emphasis in original); Grantham, "The Contours of Southern Progressivism," 1040, 1042.

26. Grantham, "The Contours of Southern Progressivism," 1040; Arthur S. Link, "The Progressive Movement in the South, 1870–1914," *North Carolina Historical Review* 23(2, 1946): 172–195, 177.

27. "The South and the Negro Problem," *San Jose* (CA) *Evening News*, August 11, 1903, 4; "Work to Solve Negro Problem," *Chicago Tribune*, June 21, 1903, 1, 7.

28. Scott, "A Progressive Wind from the South," 54; Arthur S. Link, "The South and the 'New Freedom': An Interpretation," *The American Scholar* 20(3, 1951): 314–324, 316.

29. George B. Tindall, "Mythology: A New Frontier in Southern History," in *The Idea of the South: Pursuit of a Central Theme*, edited by Frank E. Vandiver (Chicago: University of Chicago Press, 1964); Perman, *The Road to Redemption*, 265.

30. E. Culpepper Clark, "Pitchfork Ben Tillman and the Emergence of Southern Demagoguery." *Quarterly Journal of Speech* 69(4, 1983): 423–433, 424.

31. Woodward, *Origins of the New South*, 371; Grantham, *The South in Modern America*, 45–46.

32. Kantrowitz, *Ben Tillman and the Reconstruction of White Supremacy*, 265–266; Ray Stannard Baker, *Following the Color Line: An Account of Negro Citizenship in the American Democracy* (Williamstown, MA: Corner House, 1979), 304; Philip A. Klinkner, with Rogers M. Smith, *The Unsteady March: The Rise and Decline of Racial Equality in America* (Chicago: University of Chicago Press, 1999), 108; David Southern, *The Progressive Era and Race: Reaction and Reform, 1900–1917* (Arlington Heights, IL: Harlan Davidson, 2005); John Dittmer, *Black Georgia in the Progressive Era, 1900–1920* (Urbana: University of Illinois Press, 1977), 111; "To Strangle the Glenn Bill," *Macon* (GA) *Telegraph*, August 27, 1887, 2; Ring, *The Problem South*, 184–193.

33. Benjamin DeWitt, *The Progressive Movement* (New York: Macmillan, 1915), 4–5; Link, "The Progressive Movement in the South," 173; Donald R. Richberg, *My Hero: The Indiscreet Memoirs of an Eventful but Unheroic Life* (New York: G. P. Putnam's, 1954), 81; "A Democrat, with a Capital D," *La Follete's Weekly Magazine*, January 20, 1912, 4; *The Public*, August 24, 1907, cited in David Sarasohn, *The Party of Reform: Democrats in the Progressive Era* (Jackson: University Press of Mississippi, 1989), 17.

34. Key, *Southern Politics*, 307; Kousser, *The Shaping of Southern Politics*, 236–237; Devin Caughey and Christopher Warshaw, "The Dynamics of State Policy Liberalism, 1936–2014," *American Journal of Political Science* 60(4, 2015): 899–913; Nicholas C. Burckel, "Progressive Governors in the Border States: Reform Governors of Missouri, Kentucky, West Virginia, and Maryland," PhD diss., University of Wisconsin (1971), 546; Ayers, *The Promise of the New South*, 414; Grantham, *The South in Modern America*, 47.

35. The southern preference for legal prohibitions is a central theme of Sanders, *Roots of Reform*; *Collier's Weekly*, April 4, 1914, 16; Scott C. James, *Presidents, Parties, and the State: A Party System Perspective on Democratic Regulatory Choice, 1884–1936* (Cambridge: Cambridge University Press, 2000), 174.

36. "Plan Not Practical," *Dallas Morning News*, July 25, 1904, 3; Kantrowitz, *Ben Tillman and the Reconstruction of White Supremacy*, 265; Scott, "A Progressive Wind from the South," 54; Link, "The South and the 'New Freedom,'" 316.

37. Newlands (D-NV), *Congressional Record*, April 29 and May 27, 1910, 5559, 6962, 6971.

38. "The Hope of the Democracy," *Charlotte* (NC) *Daily Observer*, December 8, 1900, 2; "Coagulated Capital," *The State* (Columbia, SC), March 17, 1910, 4.

39. "The South Does Not Understand," *Macon* (GA) *Telegraph*, May 11, 1908, 4; "The Elections," *Macon Telegraph*, November 9, 1900, 4; "Sectional or National? The Discussion Proceeds," *Macon Telegraph*, November 25, 1900, 8; "The Democratic Party's Only Means of Restoration to Power," *New Orleans Daily Picayune*, November 23, 1900, 4; Adams, *"The Solid South" and the Afro-American Race Problem*, 5–6; Taft, *Present Day Problems*, 221–222; Williams (D-MS), *Congressional Record*, February 7, 1906, 2252; James, *Presidents, Parties, and the State*, 131; Harrison, *Congress, Progressive Reform, and the New American State*, 252–253; Grantham, *The South in Modern America*, 38; Woodward, *Origins of the New South*, 469; Sarasohn, *The Party of Reform*, 18; James C. Hempgill, "The Conservatism of the South," *Charleston* (SC) *News and Courier*, January 22, 1906; Dewey W. Grantham, *The Life and Death of the Solid South: A Political History* (Lexington: University Press of Kentucky, 2015), 60; "The Blindness of the Sun," *Macon Telegraph*, April 28, 1900, 4.

40. Data on nativity is compiled from IPUMS-USA. Steven Ruggles, Katie Genadek, Ronald Goeken, Josiah Grover, and Matthew Sobek. *Integrated Public Use Microdata Series: Version 7.0* [dataset]. Minneapolis: University of Minnesota, 2017. https://doi.org/10.18128/D010.V7.0

41. The discussion of Oklahoma draws extensively on Paul Frymer, *Building an American Empire: The Era of Territorial and Political Expansion* (Princeton, NJ: Princeton University Press, 2017), 164–171; Rachel Wolters, "As Migrants and as Immigrants: African Americans Search for Land and Liberty in the Great Plains, 1890–1912," *Great Plains Quarterly* 35(4, 2015): 333–355;

Oklahoma City Times, October 16, 1916, 1; Garin Burbank, "Agrarian Socialism in Saskatchewan and Oklahoma: Short-Run Radicalism and Long-Run Conservatism," *Agricultural History* 51(1, 1977): 173–180, 176; *Johnson County Capital-Democrat* (Tishomingo, OK), May 25, 1916.

42. These numbers are taken from the census files for 1910. Michael R. Haines and Inter-university Consortium for Political and Social Research. Historical, Demographic, Economic, and Social Data: The United States, 1790–2002.

43. Rennard J. Strickland and James C. Thomas, "Most Sensibly Conservative and Safely Radical: Oklahoma's Constitutional Regulation of Economic Power, Land Ownership, and Corporate Monopoly." *Tulsa Law Review* 9(2, 1973): 167–238, 168.

44. Benno Schmidt Jr., "Principle and Prejudice: The Supreme Court and Race in the Progressive Era," *Columbia Law Review* 82(5, 1982): 835–905, 852–859.

45. Schmidt, "Principle and Prejudice," 860, 879, 881, fn. 198; Kousser, *Colorblind Injustice*, 323, 473–474; Frymer, *Building an American Empire*, 171; Amy Bridges, *Democratic Beginnings: Founding the Western States* (Lawrence: University Press of Kansas, 2015); Philip Mellinger, "Discrimination and Statehood in Oklahoma," *Chronicles of Oklahoma* 49(3, 1971): 362–371; Murray Wickett, *Contested Territory: Whites, Native Americans, and African Americans in Oklahoma, 1865–1907* (Baton Rouge: Louisiana State University Press, 2000); James Green, *Grass-Roots Socialism: Radical Movements in the Southwest* (Baton Rouge: Louisiana State University Press, 1978), 61; *Guinn v. United States*, 238 U.S. 347 (1915); *Lane v. Wilson*, 307 U.S. 268 (1939); *The Indian Journal* (Eufaula, OK), July 28, 1916, 4.

46. David R. Morgan, *Oklahoma Politics and Policies: Governing the Sooner State* (Lincoln: University of Nebraska Press, 1991), 48–53; John Thompson, *Closing the Frontier: Radical Response in Oklahoma, 1889–1923* (Norman: University of Oklahoma Press, 1986); Allan Lichtman, *White Protestant Nation: The Rise of the American Conservative Movement* (New York: Grove Press, 2008), 43; Garin Burbank, "Agrarian Radicals and Their Opponents: Political Conflict in Southern Oklahoma, 1910–1924," *Journal of American History* 58(1, 1971): 5–23, 9, fn. 10; Kenny Lee Brown, "Robert Latham Owen, Jr.: His Career as Indian Attorney and Progressive Senator," PhD diss., Oklahoma State University (1972); Carter Blue Clark, "A History of the Ku Klux Klan in Oklahoma," PhD diss., University of Oklahoma (1976).

47. Gerald Gamm and Steven S. Smith, "The Emergence of Senate Party Leadership," in *U.S. Senate Exceptionalism*, edited by Bruce I. Oppenheimer (Columbus: Ohio University Press, 2002), 212–240; Rothman, *Politics and Power*, 58–59.

48. For details on the methodology, see Clinton and Lapinski, "Measuring Legislative Accomplishment." Chamberlain, *The President, Congress, and Legislation*; Christopher Dell and Stephen Stathis, "Major Acts of Congress and Treaties Approved by the Senate, 1789–1980," *Congressional Research Service Report* (1982): 82–156; Stephen W. Stathis, *Landmark Legislation, 1774–2002: Major U.S. Acts and Treaties* (Washington, DC: CQ Press, 2003).

49. Link's focus on southern progressivism would soon be supplemented by that of Anne Firor Scott. Link, "The Progressive Movement in the South," 172; Arthur S. Link, "The South and the Democratic Campaign of 1912," PhD diss., University of North Carolina (1945); Arthur S. Link, *Wilson*, vol. 1, *The Road to the White House* (Princeton, NJ: Princeton University Press, 1947); Link, "The South and the 'New Freedom,'" 316; Anne Firor Scott, "The Southern Progressives in National Politics, 1906–1916," PhD diss., Radcliffe College (1957); Scott, "A Progressive Wind from the South."

50. McMath, "C. Vann Woodward and the Burden of Southern Populism," 748; Richard M. Abrams, "Woodrow Wilson and the Southern Congressmen, 1913–1916," *Journal of Southern History* 22 (4, 1956): 417–437, 437.

51. Sanders, *Roots of Reform*.

52. Howard N. Rabinowitz, *The First New South, 1865–1920* (Arlington Heights, IL: Harlan

Davidson, 1992), 124–125; Woodward, *Origins of the New South*, 389; Charles Edward Merriam, *Party Primaries: A Study of the History and Tendencies of Primary Election Legislation* (Chicago: University of Chicago Press, 1908), 22, 34, 298–302; Stephen Ansolabehere, John Hansen, Shigeo Hirano, and James Snyder, "The Decline of Competition in U.S. Primary Elections, 1908–2004," in *The Marketplace of Democracy: Electoral Competition and American Politics*, edited by Michael McDonald and John Samples, (Washington, DC: Brookings Institution Press, 2006), 74–101; Bradley Rice, *Progressive Cities: The Commission Government Movement in America, 1901–1920* (Austin: University of Texas Press, 1977), 5; James Weinstein, "Organized Business and the City Commission and Manager Movements," *Journal of Southern History* 28(2, 1962): 166–182; J. Morgan Kousser, testimony before hearings of the House Subcommittee on Civil and Constitutional Rights on extension of the Voting Rights Act, Serial No. 24, part 3, 97th Cong., 1st sess. (Washington, DC: U.S. Government Printing Office, 1982), 2018.

53. C. Vann Woodward, testimony before hearings of the House Subcommittee on Civil and Constitutional Rights on extension of the Voting Rights Act, Serial No. 24, part 3, 97th Cong., 1st sess. (Washington, DC: U.S. Government Printing Office, 1982), 2024; J. Morgan Kousser, "Progressivism—For Middle-Class Whites Only: North Carolina Education, 1880–1910," *Journal of Southern History* 46(2, 1980): 169–194; Jack Temple Kirby, *Darkness at the Dawning: Race and Reform in the Progressive South* (Philadelphia: Lippincott, 1972); David W. Southern, *The Progressive Era and Race: Reaction and Reform, 1900–1917* (New York: John Wiley, 2005); Steven Hoffman, *Race, Class, and Power in the Building of Richmond, 1870–1920* (Jefferson, NC: McFarland & Co., 2004); John Whitson Cell, *The Highest Stage of White Supremacy: The Origins of Segregation in South Africa and the American South* (Cambridge: Cambridge University Press, 1982), 18; Johnson, *Reforming Jim Crow*; Amy Thompson McCandless, "Progressivism and the Higher Education of Southern Women," *North Carolina Historical Review* 70(3, 1993): 302–325, 307; Edward J. Larson, *Sex, Race, and Science: Eugenics in the Deep South* (Baltimore: Johns Hopkins University Press, 1995).

54. McMath, "C. Vann Woodward and the Burden of Southern Populism," 760; Kimberley Johnson, *Governing the American State: Congress and the New Federalism, 1877–1929* (Princeton, NJ: Princeton University Press, 2007); Kimberley Johnson, "Racial Orders, Congress, and the Agricultural Welfare State, 1865–1940," *Studies in American Political Development* 25(2, 2011): 143–161; Joan Malczewski, "Philanthropy and Progressive Era State Building through Agricultural Extension Work in the Jim Crow South," *History of Education Quarterly* 53(4, 2013): 369–400; George B. Tindall, *The Emergence of the New South, 1913–1945* (Baton Rouge: Louisiana State University Press, 1967), chap. 5; Glenda Elizabeth Gilmore, *Gender and Jim Crow: Women and the Politics of White Supremacy in North Carolina, 1896–1920* (Chapel Hill: University of North Carolina Press, 1996); Robert D. Johnson, *The Radical Middle Class: Populist Democracy and the Question of Capitalism in Progressive Era Portland, Oregon* (Princeton, NJ: Princeton University Press, 2006).

Chapter 7. Ascendancy

1. Maurice Low, "The South in the Saddle," *Harper's Weekly*, February 8, 1913, 34.

2. Walter Hines Page, "Why Not Southern Democratic Leadership?" *World's Work*, 4(4, 1902): 2367.

3. Brown, "The South in National Politics," 115.

4. "The Great Commoner Pleads for Peace," *Charlotte* (NC) *Daily Observer*, March 3, 1913, 1.

5. Lee A. Craig, *Josephus Daniels: His Life and Times* (Chapel Hill: University of North Carolina Press, 2013), 213.

6. Anderson, *Race and Politics in North Carolina*, 254; Kousser, "Progressivism—For Middle-Class Whites Only."

7. Craig, *Josephus Daniels*, 184, 213.

8. *Raleigh* (NC) *News and Observer*, October 1, 1912.

9. In the 1907 Rivers and Harbors Act, the South received 36 percent of the non-Mississippi funding. Scott, "A Progressive Wind from the South," 316; "A View of the Present Situation," *The State* (Columbia, SC), December 1, 1904, 8; "Bright Things Said at Congressmen's Banquet," *Columbus* (GA) *Enquirer-Sun*, March 11, 1906, 15; "The South Deserves the Presidency," *Fort Worth* (TX) *Morning Register*, June 20, 1901, 4; "A Southern Man," *Washington Post*, May 22, 1907, 6; "A Southern Democrat?" *Washington Post*, June 11, 1902, 6; "Talk of a Southern Man," *Lexington* (KY) *Herald*, March 25, 1906, 7.

10. "Williams, the Modern Democrat," *Biloxi* (MS) *Daily Herald*, March 13, 1904, 2; "The Democratic Party and the South," *The State* (Columbia, SC), January 25, 1904, 4; "The South Will Dictate," *Kansas City Star*, July 3, 1904, 1; "Minority Party Drifting," *Charlotte* (NC) *Daily Observer*, March 22, 1909, 10.

11. Sarasohn, *The Party of Reform*, 30; "Williams, the Modern Democrat," *Biloxi* (MS) *Daily Herald*, March 13, 1904, 2; Harrison, *Congress, Progressive Reform, and the New American State*, 232; "Snub to Tillman," *Fort Worth* (TX) *Register*, May 8, 1902, 1; "Senators and the Philippines Bill," *Cleveland Plain Dealer*, May 12, 1902, 4; Noel Maurer, *The Empire Trap: The Rise and Fall of U.S. Intervention to Protect American Property Overseas, 1893–2013* (Princeton, NJ: Princeton University Press, 2013), 45.

12. Woodward, *Origins of the New South*, 457; Grantham, *The South in Modern America*, 40; Harrison, *Congress, Progressive Reform, and the New American State*, 232; Sanders, *Roots of Reform*.

13. "Speaker Cannon: Lest We Forget," *The American Federationist* 15(1, January 1908): 32–35, 34; "A Favorable 8-Hour Report," *Kansas City Star*, May 29, 1906, 1; Rothman, *Politics and Power*, 4, 58.

14. Sanders, *Roots of Reform*, 198; "The New Publicity Law," and "The New Anti-Rebate Law," *The Outlook* 73(8, February 21, 1903): 409; "Speaker Blocks the Plan," *Washington Post*, February 6, 1903, 4; Thayer (D-MA), *Congressional Record*, February 7, 1903, 1898; *Congressional Record*, February 5, 1905, 1950–1951; Charles R. Atkinson, "The Committee on Rules and the Overthrow of Speaker Cannon," PhD diss., Columbia University (1911), 64; Williams (D-MS), *Congressional Record*, January 11, 1906, 965; Harrison, *Congress, Progressive Reform, and the New American State*, 231; see also *Harper's Weekly*, February 14, 1914, 525; Scott, "A Progressive Wind from the South," 58; Maurice Low, "The South in the Saddle," *Harper's Weekly*, February 8, 1913, 34.

15. "An Extra Session More Than Probable," *Sunday State* (Columbia, SC), March 1, 1903, 13; "The Fifty-Seventh Congress," *The Great Round World* 21(330, March 7, 1903): 218–219; "Mean to Defeat Statehood," *Chicago Tribune*, February 1, 1903, 32; "Statehood Plan Agreed Upon," *Chicago Tribune*, February 6, 1903, 1; "He Would Not Dare Be a Czar," *Cleveland Plain Dealer*, March 10, 1901, 5; "Government-Owned Ships vs. Ship Subsidies," *The Farmers' Open Forum* 1(3, December 1915): 6; Gatewood, "William D. Crum."

16. Koger, *Filibustering*, 116; "The Hot Shot from Cannon Struck Senate in a Soft Spot," *Cleveland Plain Dealer*, March 6, 1903, 1; "May Force Issue," *Dallas Morning News*, March 27, 1906, 1; "Pass Labor Bill," *Dallas Morning News*, April 3, 1906, 1; Scott, "A Progressive Wind from the South," 57; "Filibuster Threat Made by Williams," *Dallas Morning News*, March 25, 1908, 1; "Agricultural Bill Goes through House," *Idaho Daily Statesman*, April 3, 1908, 2; "House Republicans Uneasy," *Kansas City Star*, April 5, 1908, 1; Robert Luce, *Legislative Procedure: Parliamentary Practices and the Course of Business in the Framing of Statutes* Boston: Houghton Mifflin, 1922), 288; Sarasohn, *The Party of Reform*, 31.

17. "Congress Makes New Penal Code," *Los Angeles Times*, March 4, 1909, 2; "Clarke Filibuster Succeeds in Senate," *Dallas Morning News*, March 4, 1909, 1; "Filibuster," *Washington Herald*, March 3, 1909, 11; *Batesville* (AL) *Daily Guard*, March 17, 1909, 1.

18. "Democrats Begin First Filibuster," *Duluth* (MN) *New Tribune*, May 19, 1906, 2.

19. Aldrich had already moved, immediately after La Follette concluded his speech—the longest speech in the Senate to that point—that the vote should be a roll call, which meant that as soon as he gained the floor when Gore sat down he could call for a vote and the clerk would have to start calling the roll. Under the rules of the Senate, once a roll call had begun, it could not be stopped. "Democrats Being Cursed," *Charlotte* (NC) *Daily Observer*, May 31, 1908, 1; *Baltimore Sun*, May 31, 1908, 2; "State Money Only for Immigration," *The State* (Columbia, SC), February 16, 1907, 1; "Senate Will Vote on Immigration Bill," *Aberdeen* (SD) *Daily American*, February 16, 1907, 1; "Not to Filibuster," *Dallas Morning News*, February 16, 1907, 4; "End May Come Tomorrow," *Dallas Morning News*, April 5, 1908, 2; "Congress Makes New Penal Code," *Los Angeles Times*, March 4, 1909, 2; "Clarke Filibuster Succeeds in Senate," *Dallas Morning News*, March 4, 1909, 1; *Batesville* (AL) *Daily Guard*, March 17, 1909, 1.

20. Congressional Research Service, "Senate Cloture Rule: Limitation of Debate in the Senate of the United States," S. Prt. 112-31, 112th Cong., 1st sess. (Washington, DC: U.S. Government Printing Office, 2011), 16; "Fight Is Certain," *Dallas Morning News*, July 14, 1901, 1; *Charlotte* (NC) *Daily Observer*, June 1, 1908, 1; "Two Eventful Days," *The Farmer and Mechanic* (Raleigh, NC), June 2, 1908, 3; "Filibuster and Force Bill," *Washington Times*, June 1, 1908, 6.

21. In 1911, there was one association each in Louisiana, Georgia, Alabama, Texas, and Maryland, one in St. Louis and another in western Missouri, and one in the District of Columbia. "House Republicans Unanimously Endorse Overstreet Act," *Helena* (MT) *Independent*, December 7, 1899, 1; "House Passes It," *Morning World-Herald* (Omaha, NE), December 19, 1899, 1; "The Hope of the Democracy," *Charlotte* (NC) *Daily Observer*, December 8, 1900, 2; "Round About Town," *Dallas Morning News*, June 29, 1901, 5; "The Democratic Party's Only Means of Restoration to Power," *New Orleans Daily Picayune*, November 23, 1900, 4; Lance Davis, "The Investment Market, 1870–1914: The Evolution of a National Market," *Journal of Economic History* 25(3, 1965): 355–399, 392; J. Laurence Laughlin, "The Aldrich-Vreeland Act," *Journal of Political Economy* 16(8, 1908): 489–513, 499; *Annual Report of the Comptroller of the Currency to the Second Session of the Sixty-Second Congress of the United States, 1911* (Washington, DC: U.S. Government Printing Office, 1912), 76.

22. Bensel, *Sectionalism and American Political Development*, 92; Daniel (D-VA), *Congressional Record*, 55th Cong., 3rd sess.,1427–1428; Edwina C. Smith, "Southerners on Empire: Southern Senators and Imperialism, 1898–1899," *Mississippi Quarterly* 31(Winter 1977): 90–107, 97, 100; Marshall Schott, "The South and American Foreign Policy, 1894–1904: Regional Concerns during the Age of Imperialism," PhD diss., Louisiana State University (1995), 269; "A Swing Round the Circle," *Kansas City Star*, October 24, 1900, 4; Tennant S. McWilliams, "The Lure of Empire: Southern Interest in the Caribbean, 1877–1900," *Mississippi Quarterly* 29(1, 1975): 43–63, 63; Joseph O. Baylen and John Hammond Moore, "Senator John Tyler Morgan and Negro Colonization in the Philippines, 1901–1902," *Phylon* 29(1, 1968): 65–75, 69; Fry, *Dixie Looks Abroad*, 110–111, 113; McWilliams, *The New South Faces the World*, 9; Grantham, *The South in Modern America*, 45; "The Blow at the South's Political Power," *Biloxi* (MS) *Daily Herald*, January 3, 1900, 4; "Senator Hoar Sings Another Song," *Baltimore Sun*, June 27, 1900, 4.

23. Paul S. Holbo, "Presidential Leadership in Foreign Affairs: William McKinley and the 'Turpie-Foraker Amendment,'" *American Historical Review* 72(4, 1967): 1321–1335, 1326; Fry, *Dixie Looks Abroad*, 125; "Snub to Tillman," *Fort Worth* (TX) *Register*, May 8, 1902, 1; "Senators and the Philippines Bill," *Cleveland Plain Dealer*, May 12, 1902, 4; Noel Maurer, *The Empire Trap: The Rise and Fall of U.S. Intervention to Protect American Property Overseas, 1893–2013* (Princeton, NJ: Princeton University Press, 2013), 45.

24. Smith, "Southerners on Empire," 90, 94, 107; *Congressional Record*, February 11, 1899, 1736; *Congressional Record*, February 14, 1899, 1834–1835, 1845–1846; "The Deed Is Done," *The*

State (Columbia, SC), March 1, 1901, 4; "Was Ben Bounced?" *The State*, March 6, 1901, 4; "The Unvertical Tillman," *The State*, March 18, 1901, 4; "Final Vote Not Before June 4," *Duluth* (MN) *News Tribune*, May 29, 1902, 9; "Philippine Government Bill," *Dallas Morning News*, May 8, 1902, 1; "Democrats Plan Long Filibuster," *Philadelphia Inquirer*, May 9, 1902, 3; "Will the Democrats Filibuster Against Philippine Bill?" *The Little Chronicle* (Chicago), May 17, 1902, 98; "Mr. McKinley's Election," *Lexington* (KY) *Morning Herald*, November 7, 1900, 2; "What Will the Democratic Party Do?" *Lexington Morning-Herald*, November 8, 1900, 2.

25. Some Democrats did persuade themselves that by allying with, rather than undercutting, a popular president, they might weaken support for the president's party. Grantham, *The South in Modern America*, 40; "Mr. Taft and the Southern Democracy," *Lexington* (KY) *Herald*, August 24, 1907, 4; Williams (D-MS), *Congressional Record*, January 11, 1906, 965; Harrison, *Congress, Progressive Reform, and the New American State*, 231; *Harper's Weekly*, February 14, 1914, 525; Scott, "A Progressive Wind from the South," 58

26. "Railroad Bill Is Warmly Debated," *Los Angeles Herald*, February 7, 1906, 2; "Let the Democrats Help," *Kansas City Star*, February 9, 1906, 10; Scott, "A Progressive Wind from the South," 55–56; Stanley (D-KY), *Congressional Record*, February 6, 1906, 2164.

27. Sanders, *Roots of Reform*, 198; "The New Publicity Law," and "The New Anti-Rebate Law," *The Outlook* 73(8, February 21, 1903): 409; "Speaker Blocks the Plan," *Washington Post*, February 6, 1903, 4; Thayer (D-MA), *Congressional Record*, February 7, 1903, 1897–1898.

28. "Regulating Transportation Rates," *Philadelphia Inquirer*, February 1, 1905, 8; "Feared to Fight the President," *Cleveland Plain Dealer*, February 4, 1905, 1; "Mr. Roosevelt's Proposed Railroad Legislation," *Dallas Morning News*, February 3, 1905, 6; Joseph Nimmo Jr., "Our Railroads: Their Growth and Beneficent Influence," *New York Times*, February 10, 1905, 6.

29. Small farmers and agricultural shippers were the least well represented in legislative testimony and in the Chicago convention, but most evidence suggests they strong supported rate-setting legislation. " 'Uncle Joe' Has Lost His Mask," *Cleveland Plain Dealer*, June 11, 1906, 1; Sarasohn, *Party of Reform*, 4; "Railroad Bill Is Warmly Debated," *Los Angeles Herald*, February 7, 1906, 2; Harrison, *Congress, Progressive Reform, and the New American State*, 62; Richard Vietor, "Businessmen and Political Economy: The Railroad Rate Controversy of 1905," *Journal of American History* 64(1, 1977): 47–66.

30. Harrison, *Congress, Progressive Reform, and the New American State*, 62; "The Railroad Rate Bill: The Point of Divergence in the Senate," *Belleville* (IL) *News-Democrat*, February 1, 1906, 3; "Let the Democrats Help," *Kansas City Star*, February 9, 1906, 10; "Causing Speculation," *Dallas Morning News*, February 23, 1906, 11; "Roosevelt to Rely on Veto," *Cleveland Plain Dealer*, February 22, 1906, 1; "To Report Hepburn Bill," *Kansas City Star*, February 23, 1906, 6; Sarasohn, *Party of Reform*, 5.

31. "Railroad Bill Is Warmly Debated," *Los Angeles Herald*, February 7, 1906, 2; "Let the Democrats Help," *Kansas City Star*, February 9, 1906, 10; Scott, "A Progressive Wind from the South," 55–56.

32. Sanders, *Roots of Reform*; Scott, "A Progressive Wind from the South," 55–56; Sarasohn, *The Party of Reform*, 4.

33. John M. Blum, "Theodore Roosevelt and the Hepburn Act: Toward a System of Orderly Control," in *The Letters of Theodore Roosevelt*, edited by Elting E. Morison (Cambridge, MA; Harvard University Press, 1952), 1568; John M. Blum, *The Republican Roosevelt* (Cambridge, MA; Harvard University Press, 1954), 99–100; "Hepburn Rate Bill," *Dallas Morning News*, May 28, 1906, 7; "Will Pass Rate Bill," *Trenton* (NJ) *Times*, May 16, 1906, 2.

34. "Kittredge Defines Position," *Aberdeen* (SD) *Daily News*, March 1, 1906, 1; *Aberdeen Daily News*, April 28, 1906, 2; "Rate Bill Talk," *Idaho Daily Statesman* (Boise), March 8, 1906, 2; "Long Introduces His Amendment," *Lexington* (KY) *Herald*, April 3, 1906, 1; "Senate at Sea on Rate Bill,"

Fort Worth (TX) *Telegram*, March 8, 1906, 8; "Senator Aldrich Challenges Vote on Rate Bill," *Wilkes-Barre* (PA) *Times*, March 14, 1906, 1.

35. Sanders, *Roots of Reform*, 201; Harrison, *Congress, Progressive Reform, and the New American State*, 70.

36. Sarasohn, treating the Hepburn Act as emblematic of Democratic progressivism, argues that despite losing on the question of judicial review, the party had much to be proud of. This is true, but speaks to the limited influence of the party and its southern majority, whose successes were entirely dependent on the support of progressive Republicans with a different set of priorities. This is a core theme, for instance, of Elizabeth Sanders's *Roots of Reform*, which shows that while progressive reforms were generally driven by the periphery, legislative imperatives required compromises with midwestern or northeastern Republicans, generally resulting in more administrative discretion and a greater role for the judiciary. Sarasohn, *Party of Reform*, 9; "A Review of the Work Accomplished by Congress," *St. Louis Palladium*, July 7, 1906, 6; "Mr. Taft and the Southern Democracy," *Lexington* (KY) *Herald*, August 24, 1907, 4.

37. Williams (D-MS), *Congressional Record*, December 4, 1905, 42; "Democrats Should Join In," *Charlotte* (NC) *Daily Observer*, December 4, 1908, 4; Sarasohn, *Party of Reform*, 63; "Plan for Session," *Dallas Morning News*, December 3, 1905, 2; Harrison, *Congress, Progressive Reform, and the New American State*, 22.

38. "'Uncle Joe' Has Lost His Mask," *Cleveland Plain Dealer*, June 11, 1906, 1; "A Fossilized Congress," *St. Albans* (VT) *Daily Messenger*, November 16, 1905, 6; Gisela Sin, *Separation of Powers and Legislative Organization: The President, the Senate, and Political Parties in the Making of House Rules* (Cambridge: Cambridge University Press, 2015).

39. Sarasohn, *Party of Reform*, 60; Claude Barfield, "'Our Share of the Booty': The Democratic Party, Cannonism, and the Payne-Aldrich Tariff," *Journal of American History* 57(2, 1970): 308–323; Champ Clark, *My Quarter Century of American Politics*, vol. 2 (New York: Harper, 1920), 268–270; "Minority Party Drifting," *Charlotte* (NC) *Daily Observer*, March 22, 1909, 10.

40. Sarasohn, *Party of Reform*, 72; Harrison, *Congress, Progressive Reform, and the New American State*, 211.

41. Sarasohn, *Party of Reform*, 64; Roy G. Blakely and Gladys Blakely, *The Federal Income Tax* (New York: Longman, Green and Co., 1940), 29, 32–35; "Republican War on Income Tax," *Urbana* (IL) *Daily Courier*, June 11, 1909, 7.

42. Robin L. Einhorn, "Look Away Dixieland: The South and the Federal Income Tax," *Northwestern University Law Review* 108(3, 2014): 773–797, 792–795; *Richmond* (VA) *Times-Dispatch*, March 8, 1910, 1–2.

43. Einhorn, "Look Away Dixieland," 796–797.

44. There was considerable disagreement over whether the bolters had broken with a caucus injunction to vote for the rules change; a "spanking committee" composed of "eight radical and seven conservative Democrats" was appointed to decide their fate. "Minority Party Drifting," *Charlotte* (NC) *Daily Observer*, March 22, 1909, 10; Charles O. Jones, *The Minority Party in Congress* (Boston: Little, Brown, 1970), 15; Ruth Bloch Rubin, "Organizing for Insurgency: Intraparty Organization and the Development of the House Insurgency, 1908–1910," *Studies in American Political Development* 27(October 2013): 86–110, 100; Merrill and Merrill, *The Republican Command*, 295.

45. Kenneth W. Hechler, *Insurgency: Personalities and Politics of the Taft Era* (New York: Columbia University Press, 1940), 74; Sarasohn, *Party of Reform*, 75; Clark, *My Quarter Century*, vol. 2, 277.

46. Underwood (D-AL), *Congressional Record*, March 19, 1910, 3433; Clark (D-MO), *Congressional Record*, March 19, 1910, 3430.

47. Eric Schickler, *Disjointed Pluralism: Institutional Innovation and the Development of the U.S. Congress* (Princeton, NJ: Princeton University Press, 2001), 80; *Congressional Record*, March 17, 1910, 3292.

48. Fitzgerald (D-NY), *Congressional Record*, March 19, 1910, 3433.

49. *Atlanta Journal*, March 19, 1910; Scott, "A Progressive Wind from the South," 61–62; Sarasohn, *The Party of Reform*, 78–79; Harrison, *Congress, Progressive Reform, and the New American State*, 86.

50. Harrison, *Congress, Progressive Reform, and the New American State*, 85; Scott, "A Progressive Wind from the South," 62; Newlands (D-NV), *Congressional Record*, May 27, 1910, 6962–6971; Bailey (D-TX), *Congressional Record*, May 27, 1910, 6966.

51. "Only One Vote Cast Against the Campaign Publicity Bill," *Charlotte* (NC) *Daily Observer*, April 19, 1910, 3; "Senators Don't Like Campaign Publicity," *Dallas Morning News*, April 30, 1910, 1; "Fourteen Pages," *Dallas Morning News*, May 2, 1910, 6; "Unanimous Vote on Publicity Bill," *Dallas Morning News*, May 8, 1910, 2 ; "Let's People Know," *St. Albans* (VT) *Messenger*, March 12, 1910, 1; "Publicity Bill Introduced," *Morning Oregonian* (Portland), April 2, 1910, 4; "Publicity Bill Brings on Fight," *Columbus* (GA) *Enquirer-Sun*, May 11, 1910, 2; "Important Bills Disposed of by the Senate," *Idaho Daily Statesman*, June 23, 1910, 3; Sarasohn, *The Party of Reform*, 79; Harrison, *Congress, Progressive Reform, and the New American State*, 85; Bailey (D-TX), *Congressional Record*, March 3, 1910, 2689; E. W. Kemmerer, "The United States Postal Bank," *Political Science Quarterly* 26(3, 1911): 462–466, 488; Gerhard Peters and John T. Woolley, "1908 Democratic Party Platform," The American Presidency Project. http://www.presidency.ucsb.edu/ws/?pid=29589; Harrison, *Congress, Progressive Reform, and the New American State*, 239; House Committee on Interstate and Foreign Commerce, hearings on bills affecting interstate commerce, vols. 1–12 (Washington, DC: U.S. Government Printing Office, 1910); "White Slave Bill Passes," *New York Times*, January 13, 1910, 3; Bartlett (D-G), *Appendix to the Congressional Record*, January 26, 1910, 14.

52. Clark, *My Quarter Century*, vol. 2, 259–260, 269.

53. Alan Ware, *The Democratic Party Heads North, 1877–1962* (New York: Cambridge University Press, 2006), 105–111; Sarasohn, *The Party of Reform*, 88–90; H. Res. 637, 62nd Cong., 2nd sess., July 18, 1912; Nelson Polsby, Miriam Gallagher, and Barry Rundquist, "The Growth of the Seniority System in the U.S. House of Representatives," *American Political Science Review* 63(1969): 787–807; Jason Roberts, "The Development of Special Orders and Special Rules in the U.S. House, 1881–1937," *Legislative Studies Quarterly* 35(3, 2010): 307–336, 314; Changwie Chiu, *The Speaker of the House of Representatives since 1896* (New York: Columbia University Press, 1928).

54. Matthew N. Green, "Institutional Change, Party Discipline, and the House Democratic Caucus, 1911–1919," *Legislative Studies Quarterly* 27(4, 2002): 605, 622.

55. "Congress Faces Second Great Contest," *Idaho Daily Statesman* (Boise), November 11, 1910, 1; "South Seeking to Control Congress," *Cleveland Plain Dealer*, January 30, 1911, 2; "South Controls Says Iowa Man," *The State* (Columbia, SC), August 23, 1911, 9; "South Is Strong in This Congress," *The State*, March 13, 1911, 9.

56. Elizabeth Sanders, "Economic Regulation in the Progressive Era," in *The American Congress: The Building of Democracy*, edited by Julian Zelizer (Boston: Houghton Mifflin, 2004), 344; Scott, "Progressive Wind from the South," 66; "Three Parties in Congress," *Dallas Morning News*, July 31, 1911, 6.

57. Welliver, "The Triumph of the South," 731.

58. "Government Ragtime," *Fort Worth* (TX) *Star-Telegram*, June 14, 1914, 10.

59. Burton J. Hendrick, "The New Order in Washington," *The World's Work* 27(3, 1914): 314–327, 316; "Greedy for Chairmanships," *The State* (Columbia SC), January 26, 1911, 4; "Something

Is in Sight," *Charlotte* (NC) *Daily Observer*, January 29, 1911, 1; Scott, "A Progressive Wind from the South," 64.

60. Donald Ritchie, *Minutes of the Senate Democratic Conference, 1903–1964* (Washington, DC: U.S. Government Printing Office, 1998), 60,61; Burton J. Hendrick, "The New Order in Washington," *The World's Work* 27(3, 1914): 317–320; Dewey W. Grantham, *Hoke Smith and the Politics of the New South* (Baton Rouge: Louisiana State University Press, 1958), 241.

61. Welliver, "The Triumph of the South," 736; Link, "The South and the 'New Freedom,'" 314; Samuel Schaffer, "New South Nation: Woodrow Wilson's Generation and the Rise of the South, 1884–1920," PhD diss., Yale University (2010), 12.

62. The main exception to southern unity was an effort by John Thornton of Louisiana to keep cattle off the free list. Sarasohn, *The Party of Reform*, 168.

63. Arthur S. Link, *Woodrow Wilson and the Progressive Era, 1910–1917* (New York: Harper & Brothers, 1954), 39; "Insurgent Movement Nipped," *Bellingham* (WA) *Herald*, August 28, 1913, 3; "Caucus Rule Denounced," *Bellingham Herald*, August 29, 1913, 3; "Supreme Effort to Complete Tariff," *Charlotte* (NC) *Daily Observer*, September 5, 1913, 1.

64. Link, *Woodrow Wilson and the Progressive Era*, 45–46; Sarah Binder and Mark Spindel, "Monetary Politics: Origins of the Federal Reserve," *Studies in American Political Development* (2013): 1–13, 3; *Chicago Tribune*, December 23, 1913.

65. Link, *Woodrow Wilson and the Progressive Era*, 47–48; "Prolonging the Outcry," *Fort Worth* (TX) *Star-Telegram*, July 26, 1913, 6.

66. "Sauce for Goose Not for Gander," *The State* (Columbia, SC), July 3, 1913, 1; Otto Praeger, "Prospects Brighter for Currency Bill," *Dallas Morning News*, July 20, 1913, 5; "Open Sessions in Hearings," *Lexington* (KY) *Herald*, July 19, 1939, 12; Link, *Woodrow Wilson and the Progressive Era*, 49; Link, "The South and the 'New Freedom,'" 318; Abrams, "Woodrow Wilson and the Southern Congressmen," 421.

67. "Senate to Tackle Three Money Bills," *New York Times*, November 21, 1913, 13; Abrams, "Woodrow Wilson and the Southern Congressmen," 419; Binder and Spindel, "Monetary Politics," 4.

68. The definitions bill expressly prohibited certain business practices and made individual directors and officers criminally liable. The trade relations bill extended the Sherman Act's statute of limitations, outlawed additional practices such as arbitrary refusal of mine owners to sell their output and injurious price discrimination, and allowed individuals to bring suits in equity against combinations in restraint of trade. The interlocking directorates bill fulfilled Wilson's promise to outlaw the practice of individuals serving as directors for two or more financial institutions or railroads engaged in interstate commerce, with the presence of common directors in itself constituting restraint of competition. The Interstate Trade Commission bill would establish an agency empowered with extraordinary authority to gather information on any corporation operating in interstate commerce. Alexander Shanks, "Sam Rayburn in the Wilson Administration, 1913–1921," *East Texas Historical Journal* 6(1, 1968): 63–76, 67; Sanders, *Roots of Reform*, 209; James, *Presidents, Parties, and the State*, 170–172; Link, "The South and the 'New Freedom,'" 319.

69. Link, *Woodrow Wilson and the Progressive Era*, 69; Link, "The South and the 'New Freedom,'" 320; Sanders, *Roots of Reform*, 287–289.

70. Shanks, "Sam Rayburn in the Wilson Administration," 67; "The Clayton Bill and the Covington Bill," *Dallas Morning News*, March 17, 1914, 12; Arthur S. Link, *Wilson: The New Freedom* (Princeton, NJ: Princeton University Press, 1956), 436.

71. Reed (D-MO), *Congressional Record*, September 29, 1914, 15856; James, *Presidents, Parties, and the State*, 184–191; "Neither Tyrant nor Weakling," *Macon* (GA) *Daily Telegraph*, July 15, 1914, 4; John W. Davidson, "Response of the South to Woodrow Wilson's New Freedom, 1912–1914," PhD diss., Yale University (1954), 102, 212, 218.

72. "Link, "The South and the 'New Freedom,' " 319; Sanders, *Roots of Reform*, 290–297; James, *Presidents, Parties, and the State*, 176–177, 179, 162–99; *New York Times*, March 1, 1914, 12; Tindall, *The Emergence of the New South*, 13.

73. "Only Wilson Men Go to Congress," *The State* (Columbia, SC), August 24, 1914, 7.

74. "Revolt Stalks into Debate," *Louisville* (KY) *Courier-Journal*, September 18, 1913, 1.

75. Link, "The South and the 'New Freedom,' " 316, 322; Grantham, *The Life and Death of the Solid South*, 69; "Cotton Growers Threaten Party," *Charlotte* (NC) *Daily Observer*, October 6, 1914, 1; "U.S. Will Lend Cash on Cotton," *True Republican* (Sycamore, IL), August 25, 1915, 6; Sanders, *Roots of Reform*, 300; Link, *Woodrow Wilson and the Progressive Era*, 171; Henry Langford Loucks, *The Great Conspiracy of the House of Morgan and How to Defeat It* (1916), 244, 249.

76. The eighteen included Bartlett and Hardwick of Georgia, Sisson and Witherspoon of Mississippi, Rayburn, Beall, Hardy, Buchanan, Henry, and Slayden of Texas, and Murray of Oklahoma. "Senator Sheppard's Loan District Bill," *Dallas Morning News*, October 2, 1914, 5; "Shall We Force Acreage Reduction," *The State* (Columbia, SC), October 4, 1914, 4; Sanders, *Roots of Reform*, 302.

77. Link, "The South and the 'New Freedom,' " 321; "See in Rural Credit a Big National Issue," *New York Times*, January 10, 1916, 6.

78. Link, "The South and the 'New Freedom,' " 316, 322; Sanders, *Roots of Reform,* 367; "Opposition to Workmen's Compensation Law," *Macon* (GA) *Daily Telegraph*, May 29, 1912, 1; Dewey W. Grantham, "Southern Congressional Leaders and the New Freedom, 1913–1917," *Journal of Southern History* 13(4, 1947): 439–459, 457.

79. Binder and Spindel's results show a clear regional gain for the South. Binder and Spindel, "Monetary Politics"; *Chicago Tribune*, December 23, 1913, 2.

80. Johnson, "Racial Orders, Congress, and the Agricultural Welfare State."

81. Johnson, *Governing the American State*, 103; "Mayor Powell Out for Congressional Honors," *Forth Worth* (TX) *Telegram*, February 11, 1906, 6; "Pure Food: Views of the Minority," House Report 2118, Part 2, 59th Cong., 2nd sess., 20.

82. Harrison, *Congress, Progressive Reform, and the New American State*, 247; "Standing for States Rights," *Kalamazoo* (MI) *Gazette*, March 15, 1906, 1; "Pure Food and States' Rights," *Macon* (GA) *Daily Telegraph*, March 21, 1906, 4; Zach McGhee, "Senator Latimer Earning His Pay," *The State* (Columbia, SC), June 1, 1906, 1; "House Debate on Pure Food," *Idaho Daily Statesman*, June 23, 1906, 1; Richard Hooker, "President Roosevelt and Pure Food," *Good Housekeeping* 48(April 1909): 431–434, 432; William J. Cooper Jr. and Thomas E. Terrill, *The American South: A History* (New York: Alfred A. Knopf, 1990), 496; "Pure Food Fight," *Dallas Morning News*, June 26, 1906, 1; "Pure Food Bill Finally Passed House and Senate," *Kalamazoo Gazette*, June 30, 1906, 1; Williams (D-MS), *Congressional Record*, June 29, 1906, 973.

83. Sarasohn, *Party of Reform*, 23; "Government Ownership Will Not Be Tolerated," *Biloxi* (MS) *Daily Herald*, July 25, 1906, 1; "Bryan's Position," *Idaho Daily Statesman*, August 29, 1907, 4; "Editorial Opinions," *Macon* (GA) *Daily Telegraph*, September 8, 1907, 8; "Favorable to Chandler," *Dallas Morning News*, September 14, 1907, 2.

84. "Favor Railroad Across America," *San Jose* (CA) *Evening News*, February 13, 1914, 6.

85. The *Congressional Record* did not record Mann's remarks on "Jim Crow" cars, but it was widely reported in contemporary media, most of which emphasized his reticence in speaking about the issue. "Ready to Vote," *Idaho Daily Statesman*, February 8, 1906, 2; "Railroad Rate Bill," *Macon* (GA) *Daily Telegraph*, February 8, 1906, 1.

86. *Congressional Record*, February 7, 1906, 2268; Foraker (R-OH), *Congressional Record*, May 7, 1906, 6444; Money (D-MS), *Congressional Record*, May 7, 1906, 6454; "Old Parties Join Hands on the Color Line," *The Freeman* (Indianapolis, IN), May 19, 1906, 1; "The South Vindicated," *Macon* (GA) *Daily Telegraph*, May 19, 1906, 4; "A Blow at Coal Trust," *St. Albans* (VT)

Daily Messenger, May 11, 1906, 1; "Hepburn Bill in Conference," *Cleveland Plain Dealer*, May 29, 1906, 11; "Victory for the Senate on Rate Bill," *Idaho Daily Statesman*, June 3, 1906, 1.

87. Bacon (D-GA), *Congressional Record*, May 7, 1906, 6451, May 9, 1906, 6570; Tillman (D-SC), *Congressional Record*, May 7, 1906, 6452; "Conferees in Dispute," *Washington Post*, June 1, 1906, 4; "Thompson's Weekly Review," *The Freeman* (Indianapolis, IN), May 26, 1906, 4; "The Foraker-Warner Amendment," *Cleveland Gazette*, May 26, 1906, 2.

88. Harrison, *Congress, Progressive Reform, and the New American State*, 242–243, 248; "'Uncle Joe' Has Lost His Mask," *Cleveland Plain Dealer*, June 11, 1906, 1; "Congressman Beall Here," *Dallas Morning News*, March 10, 1907, 12; "Pure Food Fight," *Dallas Morning News*, June 26, 1906, 1; "Pure Food Bill Finally Passed House and Senate," *Kalamazoo* (MI) *Gazette*, June 30, 1906, 1; Williams (D-MS), *Congressional Record*, June 29, 1906, 9738.

89. See 62 H. R. 258; 64 H. R. 748; 65 H. R. 6031; 63 H. R. 1710; 62 H. R. 5948; 63 H. R. 2968; 65 H. R. 1688; 64 H. R. 7540; 64 H. R. 326; 63 H. R. 6866; 63rd Cong., 2nd sess., Report 432.

90. The Supreme Court had ruled in *James v. Bowman* (190 U.S. 127 [1903]) that a federal regulation of congressional elections was not authorized under the Fifteenth Amendment, but indicated that had the bill been more narrowly tailored, it would have been constitutional. William H. Riker, *The Art of Political Manipulation* (New Haven, CT: Yale University Press, 1986), 14; "No Popular Vote for Senators Yet," *New York Times*, May 10, 1902, 8; Gerry Mackie, *Democracy Defended* (New York: Cambridge University Press, 2003), 223; C. H. Hoebeke, *The Road to Mass Democracy: Original Intent and the Seventeenth Amendment* (Piscataway, NJ: Transaction Publishers, 1995), 163.

91. "Senators by Direct Vote Passes House," *New York Times*, May 14, 1912, 1.

92. 63rd Cong., 2nd sess., Report 432; Kathleen L. Wolgemuth, "Woodrow Wilson's Appointment Policy and the Negro," *Journal of Southern History* 24(4, 1958): 457–471, 463; "The Colored Man," *Washington Bee*, August 2, 1913, 1; Eric S. Yellin, *Racism in the Nation's Service: Government Workers and the Color Line in Woodrow Wilson's America* (Chapel Hill: University of North Carolina Press, 2013), 110–112.

93. Sosna, "The South in the Saddle," 38.

94. Schaffer, "New South Nation," 249; Yellin, *Racism in the Nation's Service*, 95; Sosna, "The South in the Saddle," 33.

95. Kathleen L. Wolgemuth, "Woodrow Wilson and Federal Segregation," *Journal of Negro History* 44(2, 1959): 158–173, 159, 161; Nancy J. Weiss, "The Negro and the New Freedom: Fighting Wilsonian Segregation," *Political Science Quarterly* 84(1, 1969): 61–79, 64; Sosna, "The South in the Saddle," 33; Gordon David, "What Woodrow Wilson Cost My Grandfather," *New York Times*, November 24, 2015, A27; Schaffer, "New South Nation," 272.

96. Anthony Gaughan, "Woodrow Wilson and the Rise of Militant Interventionism in the South," *Journal of Southern History* 65(4, 1999): 771–808, 789; Link, *Woodrow Wilson and the Progressive Era*, 183–184; Jeanette Keith, "The Politics of Southern Draft Resistance, 1917–1918: Class, Race, and Conscription in the Rural South," *Journal of American History* 87(4, 2001): 1335–1361, 1339.

97. Richard L. Watson Jr., "A Testing Time for Southern Congressional Leadership: The War Crisis of 1917–1918," *Journal of Southern History* 44(1, 1978): 3–40, 21; Keith, "The Politics of Southern Draft Resistance," 1340–1342; Janet Hudson, *Entangled by White Supremacy: Reform in World War I–Era South Carolina* (Lexington: University Press of Kentucky, 2009), 97.

98. James Mennell, "African-Americans and the Selective Service Act of 1917," *Journal of Negro History* 84(3, 1999): 275–287, 276, 277; Jeanette Keith, *Rich Man's War, Poor Man's Fight: Race, Class, and Power in the Rural South during the First World War* (Chapel Hill: University of North Carolina Press, 2004), 49–50.

99. Keith, *Rich Man's War, Poor Man's Fight*, 58–60.

100. Paul T. Murray, "Blacks and the Draft: A History of Institutional Racism," *Journal of Black Studies* 2(1, 1971): 57–76, 59, 60; Chad L. Williams, *Torchbearers of Democracy: African American Soldiers in the Civil War Era* (Chapel Hill: University of North Carolina Press, 2010), 54–55; Keith, "The Politics of Southern Draft Resistance," 1345.

101. Yellin, *Racism in the Nation's Service*; Johnson, "Racial Orders, Congress, and the Agricultural Welfare State," 151; Philip A. Grant Jr., "Senator Hoke Smith, Southern Congressmen, and Agricultural Education, 1914–1917," *Agricultural History* 60(2, 1986): 111–122, 115–116; Sosna, "The South in the Saddle," 42; *Congressional Record*, January 19, 1914, 1944, January 30, 1914, 2574–2575.

102. Sosna, "The South in the Saddle," 42; Charles Flint Kellogg, *NAACP: 1909–1920* (Baltimore: Johns Hopkins University Press, 1967), 191.

103. Jones (R-WA), *Congressional Record*, February 5, 1914, 2932; Martin (D-VA), *Congressional Record*, February 5, 1914, 2941; Smith (D-GA), *Congressional Record*, February 5, 1914, 2945.

104. McCumber (R-ND), *Congressional Record*, January 29, 1914, 2520.

105. Sosna, "The South in the Saddle," 45; Smith (D-GA), *Congressional Record*, April 29, 1914, 7422.

106. Grant, "Senator Hoke Smith, Southern Congressmen, and Agricultural Education, 120; Chas H. Thomas, "The Federal Program of Vocational Education in Negro Schools of Less than College Grade," *Journal of Negro Education* 7(3, 1938): 303–318; statement of George E. Hayne, Executive Secretary, Department of Race Relations, Federal Council of Churches, in hearings on the Economic Security Act before the Senate Committee on Finance, 74th Cong., 1st sess. (Washington, DC: U.S. Government Printing Office, 1935), 481–482; Johnson, "Racial Orders, Congress, and the Agricultural Welfare State," 153–154; Oscar B. Martin, "A Decade of Negro Extension Work, 1914–1924," Miscellaneous Circular 72 (Washington, DC: U.S. Department of Agriculture, 1926), 13; Harris, "States' Rights, Federal Bureaucrats, and Segregated 4-H Camps in the United States, 1927–1969," *Journal of African American History* 93(3, 2008): 362–388, 364.

107. Johnson, "Racial Orders, Congress, and the Agricultural Welfare State," 145; Harris, "States' Rights, Federal Bureaucrats, and Segregated 4-H Camps in the United States."

108. Lorenzo Green and Carter Woodson, *The Negro Wage Earner* (Washington, DC: Association for the Study of Negro Life and History, 1930), 222–223; "Farm Mortgage Department," *United States Investor*, December 23, 1916, 19; Green and Woodson, *The Negro Wage Earner*, 222–223.

109. Martin, "A Decade of Negro Extension Work," 13; ; Harris, "States' Rights, Federal Bureaucrats, and Segregated 4-H Camps in the United States," 364.

110. Representative Solomon Prouty (R-IA), "South Controls Says Iowa Man," *The State* (Columbia, SC), August 23, 1911, 9.

111. Schaffer, "New South Nation," 259.

Chapter 8. Minority Power

1. Donald Davidson, "First Fruits of Dayton: The Intellectual Evolution in Dixie," in *The Southern Agrarians and the New Deal: Essays after* I'll Take My Stand, edited by Emily S. Bingham and Thomas A. Underwood (Charlottesville: University of Virginia Press, 2001), 37–38.

2. "Federalization to Divide the South?" *Macon* (GA) *Daily Telegraph*, November 24, 1918, 1.

3. Tindall, *The Emergence of the New South*, 187–190; Kenneth Jackson, *The Ku Klux Klan in the City, 1915–1930* (Oxford: Oxford University Press, 1967), 15.

4. Tindall, *The Emergence of the New South*, 192–194; Alfred L. Brophy, "Norms, Law, and Reparations: The Case of the Ku Klux Klan in 1920s Oklahoma," *Harvard BlackLetter Law Journal* 20(2004): 17–48.

5. Tindall, *The Emergence of the New South*, 188, 193; David Harry Bennett, *The Party of Fear: From Nativist Movements to the New Right in American History* (Chapel Hill: University of North Carolina Press, 1988), 223–224; Rory McVeigh, *The Rise of the Ku Klux Klan: Right-Wing Movements and National Politics* (Minneapolis: University of Minnesota Press, 2009), 76–77, 80–81; George Rable, *But There Was No Peace: The Role of Violence in the Politics of Reconstruction* (Athens: University of Georgia Press, 1984), 95, 131–132; Burbank, "Agrarian Radicals and Their Opponents," 21–22; Charles C. Alexander, *The Ku Klux Klan in the Southwest* (Lexington: University Press of Kentucky, 1965), chap. 7; Clement Charlton Moseley, "The Political Influence of the Ku Klux Klan in Georgia, 1915–1925," *Georgia Historical Quarterly* 75(2, 1973): 235–255, 238–239; "Americanism Applied," *Proceedings of the Second Imperial Klonvokation, Held in Kansas City, Missouri* (Knights of the Ku Klux Klan, Incorporated, 1924), 27; Rory McVeigh, "Power Devaluation, the Ku Klux Klan, and the Democratic National Convention of 1924," *Sociological Forum* 16(1, 2001): 1–30, 5, 8; Roger K. Newman, *Hugo Black: A Biography* (New York: Fordham University Press, 1994), 101.

6. "Fight against Ku-Klux Is Slowing Down," *Raleigh* (NC) *Union Herald*, March 30, 1922, 3; House Committee on Rules, hearings on the Ku Klux Klan, 67th Cong., 1st sess. (Washington, DC: U.S. Government Printing Office, 1921); Senator from Texas, Hearings Before a Subcommittee of the Senate Committee on Privileges and Elections, subcommittee hearings, 68th Cong., 1st sess., Parts 1–5 (Washington, DC: U.S. Government Printing Office, 1924).

7. Some of the northern state parties included the pledge in their own platforms. Although the Klan initially suggested that it would support John W. Davis of West Virginia, the Democratic nominee quickly came out against them, denouncing them publicly on several occasions. His opponent, Calvin Coolidge, stayed silent. By 1924, 40 percent of the Klan's national membership came from Indiana, Ohio, and Illinois. McVeigh, 2001. "Power Devaluation, the Ku Klux Klan, and the Democratic National Convention of 1924," 5, 8; *Official Report of the Proceedings of the Democratic National Convention and Committee* (Washington, DC: National Document Publishers, 1924), 248; *The Wisconsin Blue Book* (Madison: Democrat Printing Company, 1925), 492; Arthur S. Link, "What Happened to the Progressive Movement in the 1920s?" *American Historical Review* 64(4, 1959): 833–851, 839–840; Jackson, *The Ku Klux Klan in the City*, 15; McVeigh, *The Rise of the Ku Klux Klan*, 186–187.

8. "Senator Percy Invades Vardaman's Stronghold," *Semi-Weekly Times-Democrat*, (New Orleans), August 1, 1911, 7; Albert D. Kirwan, *Revolt of the Rednecks: Mississippi Politics: 1876–1925* (Lexington: University Press of Kentucky, 1951); "Senator Percy of Mississippi," *Monroe* (LA) *News-Star*, March 16, 1922, 5; John Barry, *The Rising Tide: The Great Mississippi Flood of 1927 and How It Changed America* (New York: Touchstone, 1998), 154–155; James B. Lloyd, *Lives of Mississippi Authors, 1817–1967* (Jackson: University Press of Mississippi, 1981), 366.

9. Tindall, *The Emergence of the New South*, 238.

10. Robert S. Allen, "Texas Jack," *The New Republic*, 70(March 1932): 119–121, 119; Jordan Schwarz, "John Nance Garner and the Sales Tax Rebellion of 1932," *Journal of Southern History* 30(2, 1964): 162–180, 164–165.

11. Preston John Hubbard, *Origins of the TVA: The Muscle Shoals Controversy* (Nashville, TN: Vanderbilt University Press, 1961), 114; Tindall, *The Emergence of the New South*, 241.

12. Charles Merz, "War as Pretext," *The New Republic* 11(135, 1917): 129–131, 30

13. Ritchie, *Minutes of the Senate Democratic Conference*, 196–280.

14. *Congressional Record*, February 19, 1915, 4092; Koger, *Filibustering*, 151.

15. Thomas H. Ryley, *A Little Group of Willful Men: A Study of Congressional-Presidential Authority* (Port Washington, NY: Kennikat Press, 1975).

16. "The Cloture Movement," *Washington Post*, March 4, 1915, 6; "Senate Filibuster Is Finally Broken," *Portland Oregonian*, February 25, 1917, 6; "Wilson Wars on Senate," *Chicago Tribune*,

March 5, 1917, 1; "Some Strong Support Behind Senate Rules," *Dallas Morning News*, March 6, 1917, 1; *Congressional Record*, March 8, 1917, 39.

17. "Wilson Determined to Arm Ships," *Columbus* (GA) *Ledger*, March 6, 1917, 1; "Modification of Senate Rules Is Under Way," *Columbus* (GA) *Enquirer-Sun*, March 8, 1917, 1; "Some Strong Support behind Senate Rules," *Dallas Morning News*, March 6, 1917, 1; "Reported Legal Advisers Find President Has Power to Arm Trade Ships," *Trenton* (NJ) *Evening Times*, March 6, 1917, 11.

18. The next year, Senator Oscar Underwood would propose a majority cloture that would extend only for the duration of the war; this was rejected 34 to 41, but southerners voted 17 to 7 in favor. "Senate Cloture," *Macon* (GA) *Daily Telegraph*, March 7, 1917, 4; "Both Texas Senators Favor Cloture Rule," *Dallas Morning News*, March 7, 1917, 1.

19. "Committee Has Resolution," *Aberdeen* (SD) *Daily American*, March 7, 1917, 1; "Closing Debate in the Senate," Senate Report 447, 64th Cong., 1st sess.; S. Res. 131, 64th Cong., 1st sess., March 15, 1916; S. Res. 149, 64th Cong., 1st sess., March 24, 1916.

20. Although there were many Democrats, especially Robert Owen, who wanted a stronger cloture rule, at no point in the preceding or following years was the Democratic Senate caucus in favor of a majority rule without clear limits on duration or content, the result of vociferous southern opposition. "Modification of Senate Rules Agreed Upon," *Charlotte* (NC) *Observer*, March 7, 1917, 2; "Both Parties Agree to Limit Debates," *Macon* (GA) *Daily Telegraph*, March 8, 1917, 6; "Rules Change Will Receive Favorable Report," *Macon Daily Telegraph*, March 7, 1917, 5.

21. "West Wants Recognition," *Portland Oregonian*, March 7, 1917, 2; "House Control Causes Worry on Both Sides," *Idaho Daily Statesman*, March 26, 1917, 2; "Democrats to Organize Lower House," *Charlotte* (NC) *Observer*, March 27, 1917, 1; "New Chairmen of Committees Named," *Fort-Worth* (TX) *Star Telegram*, April 3, 1917, 15.

22. Gaughan, "Woodrow Wilson and the Rise of Militant Interventionism in the South," 789; Link, *Woodrow Wilson and the Progressive Era*, 183; Alexander DeConde, "The South and Isolationism," *Journal of Southern History* 24(3, 1958): 332–346, 335.

23. "Jeff: McLemore Is Queer Name," *Bisbee* (AZ) *Daily Review*, February 25, 1916, 1; Timothy McDonald, "The Gore-McLemore Resolution: Democratic Revolt against Wilson's Submarine Policy," *The Historian* 26(1, 1963): 50–74.

24. "Warning to Stay Off Armed Liners Will Be Defeated," *Houston Daily Post*, March 3, 1916, 3; Gaughan, "Woodrow Wilson and the Rise of Militant Interventionism in the South," 779; *Appendix to the Congressional Record*, March 9, 1916, 494; Watson, "Testing Time for Southern Congressional Leadership," 10.

25. "All Party Lines Are Wiped Out," *Charlotte* (NC) *Observer*, April 20, 1917, 1.

26. Gaughan, "Woodrow Wilson and the Rise of Militant Interventionism in the South," 789; Link, *Woodrow Wilson and the Progressive Era*, 183; Alex Arnett, "Claude Kitchin versus the Patrioteers," *North Carolina Historical Review* 14(1, 1937): 20–30, 29; Link, "The South and the 'New Freedom,'" 324; "Where Are All the Millionaires," *Current Opinion* 70(2, 1921): 251–252.

27. Robert Hormats, *The Price of Liberty: Paying for America's Wars* (New York: Times Books, 2007), 112; Link, "The South and the 'New Freedom,'" 324; W. Elliot Brownlee, "Social Investigation and Political Learning in the Financing of World War I," in *The State and Social Investigation in Britain and the United States*, edited by Michael Lacey and Mary Furner (Cambridge: Woodrow Wilson Center Press and Cambridge University Press, 1993), 329; Roy G. Blakey and Gladys C. Blakey, *The Federal Income Tax* (London: Longmans, Green & Co., 1940), 133; "All Party Lines Are Wiped Out," *Charlotte* (NC) *Observer*, April 20, 1917, 1; "Democrats and Republicans Can't Agree on Tariff Taxes," *Great Falls* (MT) *Tribune*, April 24, 1917, 1; "Revenue Boosted," *State Journal* (Lansing, MI), May 17, 1917, 1; "Start Fight to Increase Sur-Tax," *Natchez* (MS) *Democrat*, May 17, 1917, 1; *Binghamton* (NY) *Press*, May 9, 1917, 1, 9.

28. "More Hunger Rioting by Women," *Washington Post*, February 22, 1917, 1; "Government

Has Evidence," *Lincoln County News* (Lincolnton, NC), March 1, 1917; "To Press Fight for High Price Probe," *Allentown* (PA) *Democrat*, February 22, 1917, 1; William Frieburger, "War Prosperity and Hunger: The New York Food Riots of 1917," *Labor History* 25(2, 1984): 217–239; Tom Hall, "Wilson and the Food Crisis: Agricultural Price Control during World War I," *Agricultural History* 47(1, 1973): 25–46, 26, 38.

29. Watson, "A Testing Time for Southern Congressional Leadership," 23; Monroe Lee Billington, *Thomas P. Gore: The Blind Senator from Oklahoma* (Lawrence: University Press of Kansas, 1967): 68, 78; *Alexandria* (LA) *Daily Town Talk*, February 28, 1917, 4; Hall, "Wilson and the Food Crisis," 40, 43.

30. Hardwick (D-GA), *Congressional Record*, June 29, 1917, 4458; "Drop the Food Board," *Washington Post*, July 31, 1917; William Marvin, "Food and Fuel Control," *Michigan Law Review* 17(4, 1919): 310–330; "Lever Bill before Senate," *New York Times*, June 17, 1917; I. A. Newby, "States' Rights and Southern Congressmen during World War I," *Phylon* 24(1, 1963): 34–50; R. B. George, "U.S. to Move Food under Lever Control Act," *Washington Post*, October 30, 1919; see Young (D-TX) *Congressional Record*, June 18, 1917, 3803.

31. Newby, "States' Rights and Southern Congressmen during World War I," 43; "Wonderful Chance for Farmers to 'Clean Up,'" *South Alabamian* (farm and immigration supplement), March 16, 1917, 5; Young (D-TX), *Congressional Record*, June 18, 1917, 3803–3808.

32. Young (D-TX), *Congressional Record*, June 18, 1917, 3805.

33. "Why Put Cotton in the Food Bill," *The Progressive Farmer* (Raleigh, NC), July 21, 1917, 11; "South Is Still Alarmed," *Jackson* (MS) *Daily News*, July 6, 1917, 2; *Natchez* (MS) *Democrat*, July 4, 1917, 7; "Instructions to Disagree," *Greensboro* (NC) *Daily News*, July 26, 1917, 1; Watson, "A Testing Time for Southern Congressional Leadership," 24; Seward W. Livermore, "The Sectional Issue in the 1918 Congressional Elections," *Mississippi Valley Historical Review* 35(1, 1948): 29–60, 41, 44; Hall, "Wilson and the Food Crisis," 40; Newby, "States' Rights and Southern Congressmen during World War I," 43; "Drop the Food Board," *Washington Post*, July 31, 1917; Marvin, "Food and Fuel Control"; "Lever Bill before Senate," *New York Times*, June 17, 1917; Newby, "States' Rights and Southern Congressmen during World War I"; R. B. George, "U.S. to Move Food under Lever Control Act," *Washington Post*, October 30, 1919.

34. Livermore, "The Sectional Issue in the 1918 Congressional Elections," 37–38; Hall, "Wilson and the Food Crisis," 45.

35. *Wilmington* (NC) *Morning Star*, May 13, 1917, 1; Blakey and Blakey, *The Federal Income Tax*, 131–142.

36. Blakey and Blakey, *The Federal Income Tax*, 145, fn. 76; "Committee Draft Adopted," *Richmond* (VA) *Times- Dispatch*, September 6, 1917, 1.

37. For southern praise of McAdoo's control over the railroads, see "With Regret, Mr. McAdoo," *Gulfport* (MS) *Daily Herald*, November 25, 1918, 2; John K. Barnes, "Solving the Railroad Problem," *World's Work 38(5, 1919): 477–487, 477*.

38. Newby, "States' Rights and Southern Congressmen during World War I," 43–44.

39. Gaughan, "Woodrow Wilson and the Rise of Militant Interventionism in the South," 796–798; Ralph Reed, " 'Fighting the Devil with Fire': Carl Vinson's Victory over Tom Watson in the 1918 Tenth District Democratic Primary," *Georgia Historical Quarterly* 67(4, 1983): 451–479, 452.

40. Paolo Mauro, Rafael Romeu, Ariel Binder, and Asad Zaman, "A Modern History of Fiscal Prudence and Profligacy," *Journal of Monetary Economics* 76(2015): 55–70; Shanks, "Sam Rayburn in the Wilson Administration," 72.

41. Woodrow Wilson, "7th Annual Message, December 2, 1919," The American Presidency Project, http://www.presidency.ucsb.edu/ws/?pid=29560; Evans C. Johnson, *Oscar W. Underwood: A Political Biography* (Baton Rouge: Louisiana State University Press, 1980), 296–297;

Robert Justin Goldstein, *Political Repression in Modern America: From 1870 to 1976* (Urbana: University of Illinois Press, 2001), 153.

42. Ruth O'Brien, *Workers' Paradox: The Republican Origins of New Deal Labor Policy, 1886–1935* (Chapel Hill: University of North Carolina Press, 1998), 121–133.

43. "Children's Bureau Attacked in Senate," *Dallas Morning News*, January 31, 1912, 2.

44. "Filibuster on Child Labor Bill," *Dallas Morning News*, January 20, 1916, 3; "Big Fight Is On in Senate," *Kalamazoo* (MI) *Gazette*, July 19, 1916, 1; "Child Labor Is Defended before the House Labor Committee," *Columbus* (GA) *Ledger*, January 10, 1916, 1; "Spinners Fight Owen Measure on Child Labor," *Fort Worth* (TX) *Star Telegram*, January 10, 1916, 1; "Senate to Pass Child Labor Bill," *Charlotte* (NC) *Observer*, July 26, 1916, 1; Overman (D-NC), *Congressional Record*, June 3, 1916, 9234; "May Be Trouble on Child Labor Bill," *The State* (Columbia, SC), February 23, 1916, 7.

45. Tindall, *The Emergence of the New South*, 16.

46. *Congressional Record*, January 30, 1912, 1534.

47. Clarke (D-FL), *Congressional Record*, May 21, 1919, 89–90; Corrine M. McConnaughy, *The Woman Suffrage Movement in America: A Reassessment* (New York: Cambridge University Press, 2013), 245.

48. Bryan (D-FL), *Congressional Record*, March 3, 1914, 4198, 4200; James Callaway, "Casual Conversations and Observations," *Macon* (GA) *Daily Telegraph*, December 24, 1914, 4.

49. *The Tennessean* (Nashville), February 12, 1916, 3.

50. Maryland (1941), Virginia (1952), Alabama (1953), Florida (1969), South Carolina (1969), Georgia (1970), Louisiana (1970), North Carolina (1971), and Mississippi (1984) would ratify the amendment over the next several decades; Clarke (D-FL), *Congressional Record*, May 21, 1919, 89–90.

51. *Baltimore Sun*, March 3, 1903, 2; Robert DeC. Ward, "The New Immigration Act." *North American Review* 185(619, 1907): 587–593; "Senate Approves Plan," *New Orleans Times-Democrat*, February 17, 1907, 20; "Coolie Labor Barred," *Washington Post*, February 19, 1907, 5.

52. Henry P. Fairchild, "The Literacy Test and Its Making," *Quarterly Journal of Economics* 31(3, 1917): 447–460, 451; "Debate in the Senate," *Baltimore Sun*, February 18, 1897, 2.

53. "A Composite Race," *Wilmington* (NC) *Weekly Star*, May 8, 1903, 2; "Legislation of Much Interest to the South," *Charlotte* (NC) *Daily Observer*, February 12, 1914, 3; Tindall, *The Emergence of the New South*, 185; Dr. A. J. Barton, "What Dixie Will Do in 1932," address delivered January 19, 1932, *Congressional Record*, March 18, 1932, 6456.

54. "Immigrant Bill Vetoed by Taft," *Chicago Tribune*, February 15, 1913, 3.

55. This figure is likely to understate the degree to which lawmakers' preferences were moving toward restriction. See Bateman, Clinton, and Lapinski, "A House Divided?"; Link, "What Happened to the Progressive Movement," 847.

56. The article both emphasized the Jewish character of the Bolsheviks and insisted that 95 percent of Russian Jews were opposed to the Communists. "Observations and Comment," *Macon* (GA) *Daily Telegraph*, October 27, 1918, 6.

57. Daniel J. Tichenor, *Dividing Lines: The Politics of Immigration Control in America* (Princeton, NJ: Princeton University Press, 2002), 143.

58. Mennell, "African Americans and the Selective Service Act of 1917," 284–285; Williams, *Torchbearers of Democracy*, 238–239; Arthur E. Barbeau, Bernard C. Nalty, and Florette Henri, *The Unknown Soldiers: African-American Troops in World War I* (Philadelphia: Temple University Press, 1974),177; Paul Ortiz, *Emancipation Betrayed: The Hidden History of Black Organizing and White Violence in Florida from Reconstruction to the Violent Election of 1920* (Berkeley: University of California Press, 2005); see Equal Justice Initiative, "Lynching in America: Targeting Black Veterans," http://eji.org/reports/online/lynching-in-america-targeting-black-veterans.

59. There is no precise death toll for black Americans killed in East St. Louis. A congressional investigation found that at least 39 black Americans were killed, while contemporaries reported that between 40 and 150 were killed. More were undoubtedly killed in Elaine, but East St. Louis was much closer to national media centers and transportation hubs. John Hope Franklin, *From Slavery to Freedom: A History of Negro Americans*, 3rd ed. (New York: Alfred A. Knopf, 1967), 480; Guy Lancaster, *Racial Cleansing in Arkansas, 1883–1924: Politics, Land, Labor, and Criminality* (Lanham, MD: Lexington Books, 2014); Lee Williams and Lee Williams II, *Anatomy of Four Race Riots: Racial Conflict in Knoxville, Elaine (Arkansas), Tulsa, and Chicago, 1919–1921* (Jackson: University Press of Mississippi, 1972); Boren McCool, *Union, Reaction, and Riot: The Biography of a Rural Race Riot* (Memphis: Memphis State University Press, 1970); Grif Stockley, *Blood in Their Eyes: The Elaine Race Massacre of 1919* (Fayetteville: University of Arkansas Press, 2001); C. Calvin Smith, ed., "Rumors and Reactions: Reconsidering the Elaine Race Riots of 1919— A Conference," *Arkansas Review: A Journal of Delta Studies* 32(2, 2001): 91–154; Charles Lumpkins, *American Pogrom: The East St. Louis Race Riots and Black Politics* (Athens: Ohio University Press, 2008), 97, 168; Elliot Rudwick, *Race Riot in East St. Louis, July 2, 1917* (Carbondale: Southern Illinois University Press, 1964); Malcolm McLaughlin, "Reconsidering the East St. Louis Race Riot of 1917," *International Review of Social History* 47(2, 2002): 187–212; "Ku Klux Klan Being Formed on East Side," *St. Louis Times*, July 11, 1917; "Says Klan Has 4,000 Members in E. St. Louis," *East St. Louis Daily Journal*, August 20, 1922, 2.

60. Francis, *Civil Rights and the Making of the Modern American State*, chaps. 2 and 4; Kellogg, *NAACP*, 209–211; William Hixson Jr., "Moorfield Storey and the Defense of the Dyer Anti-Lynching Bill," *New England Quarterly* 42(1, 1969): 65–81.

61. "To Protect Citizens Against Lynching," hearing before House Judiciary Committee on H. R. 11279, 65th Cong., 2nd sess., Serial 66, Part 1 (Washington, DC: U.S. Government Printing Office, 1918), 4; ibid., Part 2, 16; H.J. Res. 118, 65th Cong., introduced on July 9, 1917; H. R. 11279, 65th Cong., introduced on April 8, 1918; H. R. 11554, 65th Cong., introduced on April 19, 1918; *Congressional Record*, May 7, 1918, 6177–6178.

62. Mary Jane Brown, "Advocates in the Age of Jazz: Women and the Campaign for the Dyer Anti-Lynching Bill," *Peace and Change* 28(3, 2003): 378–419, 389; Report 452. 67th Cong., 1st sess., 18; Francis, *Civil Rights and the Making of the Modern American State*, 105.

63. "Fail of Quorum," *Miami Herald*, December 21, 1921, 4; Brown, "Advocates in the Age of Jazz," 391; George Rable, "The South and the Politics of Antilynching Legislation, 1920–1940," *Journal of Southern History* 51(2, 1985): 201–220, 205.

64. Brown, "Advocates in the Age of Jazz," 392.

65. "Adjournment Gavel Is Scheduled," *Miami Herald*, September 22, 1922, 1; Francis, *Civil Rights and the Making of the Modern American State*, 122; Koger, *Filibustering*, 156.

66. Brown, "Advocates in the Age of Jazz," 393; Hixson, "Moorfield Storey and the Defense of the Dyer Anti-Lynching Bill," 73, 77; Rable, "The South and the Politics of Antilynching Legislation," 201–220, 206.

67. Rable, "The South and the Politics of Antilynching Legislation," 206; "Anti-Lynching Bill Reported in the Senate," *New York Times*, July 29, 1922, 5.

68. Charles W. Eagles, *Democracy Delayed: Congressional Reapportionment and Urban-Rural Conflict in the 1920s* (Athens: University of Georgia Press, 2010), 34, 36; H. Res. 591, 66th Cong., 3rd sess., introduced December 6, 1920; "Republicans Balk at Plan to Weaken South in Congress," *Atlanta Constitution*, December 18, 1920, 1; "Apportionment of Representatives," hearings before the House Census Committee on H. R. 14498, H. R. 15021, H. R. 15158, and H. R. 15217, 66th Cong., 3rd sess. (Washington, DC: U.S. Government Printing Office, 1921), 28, 35, 57–61; "Apportionment of Representatives," House Report 1173, 66th Cong., 3rd sess., *Congressional Record*, January 18, 1921, 1631.

69. Tinkham was subsequently allotted one minute by Siegel and given the opportunity to have remarks placed in the appendix. *Congressional Record*, January 14, 1921, 1434–1435.

70. *Congressional Record*, October 14, 1921, 6311, 6314–6315, 6340; *Congressional Record*, Appendix, October 14, 1921, 8829–8830.

71. Although it seemed initially to have been lost, after a division vote went 100 to 121 against the bill, the teller vote returned a count of 145 to 118. *Congressional Record*, June 4, 1929, 2348; "House Votes to Rob South for Robbing Blacks," *Chicago Tribune*, June 5, 1929, 16; Eagles, *Democracy Delayed*, 58; *Hartford Courant*, June 5, 1929, 11; *Baltimore Sun*, June 5, 1929, 1–2.

72. Wadsworth made these remarks during a debate over congressional investigations of election campaign spending. *Congressional Record*, June 6, 1929, 2451; Eagles, *Democracy Delayed*, 80; *New York Times*, June 6, 1929, 3; *New York Times*, June 7, 1929, 1; *Congressional Record*, March 3, 1927, 5483, 5486, 5487.

73. B. Putney, "Government Ownership of the Railroads," *Editorial Research Reports 1938*, vol. 1 (Washington, DC: CQ Press, 1938), http://library.cqpress.com/cqresearcher/cqresrre 1938042100; K. Austin Kerr, *American Railroad Politics, 1914–1920: Rates, Wages, and Efficiency* (Pittsburgh: University of Pittsburgh Press, 1968), 88–91, 139–140.

74. For a southern position in favor of public ownership, see "The Open Forum," *Charlotte* (NC) *Observer*, January 14, 1919, 6; "Federalization to Divide the South," *Macon* (GA) *Daily Telegraph*, November 24, 1918, 1; "Southern Concerns Are Being Menaced," *Macon Daily Telegraph*, February 11, 1919, 12; "Southern Shippers Want Railroads to Go Back to Owners," *Columbus* (GA) *Enquirer-Sun*, January 7, 1919, 1.

75. Tindall, *The Emergence of the New South*, 164; "Southern Concerns Are Being Menaced," *Macon* (GA) *Daily Telegraph*, February 11, 1919, 12; "Just 'Twixt Us,'" *Macon Daily Telegraph*, February 24, 1919, 6; "Costly Management," *Dallas Morning News*, April 19, 1919, 12.

76. "Southern Concerns Are Being Menaced," *Macon* (GA) *Daily Telegraph*, February 11, 1919, 12; "Southern Shippers Want Railroads to Go Back to Owners," *Columbus* (GA) *Enquirer-Sun*, January 7, 1919, 1; Kerr, *American Railroad Politics*, 88–91, 139–140; Barnes, "Solving the Railroad Problem," 477.

77. "Would Abolish Jim Crow Coach," *Macon* (GA) *Daily Telegraph*, September 6, 1919, 3; "Jim Crow Cars," *Washington Bee*, September 20, 1919, 1; "Will Not Interfere in Jim Crow Car Law," *Macon Daily Telegraph*, September 7, 1919, 1; "Favors Doing Away with Jim Crow Cars," *Savannah* (GA) *Tribune*, September 27, 1919, 1; "Jim Crow Cars Not Prohibited by Vote," *Gulfport* (MS) *Daily Herald*, November 15, 1919, 1; "Jim Crow Car Killed," *Columbus* (GA) *Ledger*, November 16, 1919, 1.

78. "Encroachments of Federal Power," *Fort Worth* (TX) *Star-Telegram*, November 17, 1919, 8.

79. Kerr, *American Railroad Politics*, 214; *Congressional Record*, December 19, 1922, 668.

80. Johnson, *Oscar W. Underwood*, 296–297; Robert H. Zieger, *Republicans and Labor, 1919–1929* (Lexington: University Press of Kentucky, 1969), 28.

81. Arthur J. Schlesinger Jr., *The Crisis of the Old Order, 1919–1933* (Boston: Houghton Mifflin, 1957), 98.

82. "Penrose in the Saddle," *Fort Worth* (TX) *Star-Telegram*, May 3, 1919, 4; "How the Shift Leaves Them," *Charlotte* (NC) *Observer*, May 28, 1919, 6; "Progressives Lose Again," *Lexington* (KY) *Herald*, May 28, 1919, 3; Brady, Brody, and Epstein, "Heterogeneous Parties and Political Organization," 221.

83. John Black, "The McNary-Haugen Movement," *American Economic Review* 18(3, 1928): 406–427, 406.

84. Tindall, *The Emergence of the New South*, 114; Link, "What Happened to the Progressive Movement?" 839; Stella Stewart, "Government Price Controls in the First World War," *Monthly*

Labor Review 52(2, 1941): 271-285, 285; Erik Newland Olssen, "Dissent from Normalcy: Progressives in Congress, 1918–1925," PhD diss., Duke University (1970), 95.

85. Tindall, *The Emergence of the New South*, 112–114; Phillips Bradley, "The Farm Bloc," *Journal of Social Forces* 3(4, 1925): 714–718, 714; James N. Gregory, *The Southern Diaspora: How the Great Migrations of Black and White Southerners Transformed America* (Chapel Hill: University of North Carolina Press, 2005), appendix table A.1.

86. Link, "What Happened to the Progressive Movement?" 845; Bradley, "The Farm Bloc," 714–715; Tindall, *The Emergence of the New South*, 133; William Atherton Du Puy, "The Farm Bloc: Just What Does It Mean to the Nation?" *Wichita Daily Times* (Wichita Falls, TX), November 20, 1921, 11.

87. Olssen, "Dissent from Normalcy," 138–139, 143; Philip A. Grant Jr., "Southern Congressmen and Agriculture, 1921–1932," *Agricultural History* 53(1, 1979): 338–351, 341.

88. "Agricultural Legislation Meets Opposition," *American Cooperative Manager* 6(14, 1921).

89. *Congressional Record*, July 27, 1921, 4341–4342, 4346.

90. "Carrier Grab Plot," *Minnesota Daily Star* (Minneapolis), July 30, 1921, 1; Olssen, "Dissent from Normalcy," 103.

91. "Purchase and Sale of Farm Products," Senate Calendar 932, Report 949, 67th Cong., 4th sess., *Congressional Record*, December 18, 1922, 621; *Congressional Record*, December 19, 1922, 666; "The Standpat Democrats Aid the Old Guard," *Capital Times* (Madison, WI), December 22, 1922, 12; Olssen, "Dissent from Normalcy," 103, 139, 147; Tindall, *The Emergence of the New South*, 134.

92. William Atherton Du Puy, "The Farm Bloc: Just What Does It Mean to the Nation?" *Wichita Daily Times* (Wichita Falls, TX), November 20, 1921, 11; Patrick O'Brien, "A Reexamination of the Senate Farm Bloc, 1921–1933," *Agricultural History* 47(3, 1973): 248–263, 255.

93. *Report of the National Agricultural Conference, January 23–27, 1922*, House Doc. 195, 67th Cong., 2nd sess. (Washington, DC: U.S. Government Printing Office, 1922), 3; Willard Cochran, *The Development of American Agriculture: A Historical Analysis*, 2nd ed. (Minneapolis: University of Minnesota Press, 1993), 118.

94. *Congressional Record*, December 3, 1924, 92–94; Grant, "Southern Congressmen and Agriculture," 342.

95. "The McNary-Haugen Bill," *Editorial Research Reports 1927*, vol. 1 (Washington, DC: CQ Press, 1927), http://library.cqpress.com/cqresearcher/cqresrre1927021000; O'Brien, "A Reexamination of the Senate Farm Bloc," 257; John Black, "The McNary-Haugen Movement," *American Economic Review* 18(3, 1928): 406–427, 407–409; Darwin Kelley, "The McNary-Haugen Bills, 1924–1928: An Attempt to Make the Tariff Effective for Farm Products," *Agricultural History* 14(4, 1940): 170–180, 176.

96. Grant, "Southern Congressmen and Agriculture," 342; Black, "The McNary-Haugen Movement," 411–412.

97. O. B. Jesness, "Changes in the Agricultural Adjustment Program in the Past 25 Years," *Journal of Farm Economics* 40(2, 1958): 255–264, 256; Kelley, "The McNary-Haugen Bills," 180.

98. Tindall, *The Emergence of the New South*, 142; Black, "The McNary-Haugen Movement," 406.

99. William Atherton Du Puy, "The Farm Bloc: Just What Does It Mean to the Nation?" *Wichita Daily Times* (Wichita Falls, TX), November 20, 1921, 11; Mauro et al., "A Modern History of Fiscal Prudence and Profligacy," 76, 55–70; Anne Alstott and Ben Novick, "War, Taxes, and Income Redistribution in the Twenties: The 1924 Veterans' Bonus and the Defeat of the Mellon Plan," *Tax Law Review* 59(4, 2006): 373–438, 376.

100. "Tar Heels Fought as a Unit," *Raleigh* (NC) *News and Observer*, August 21, 1921, 1; Roy Blakey, "The Revenue Act of 1921," *American Economic Review* 12(1, 1922): 75–108, 76.

101. Alstott and Novick, "War, Taxes, and Income Redistribution in the Twenties," 377, 425–427.

102. Norman Wengert, "Antecedents of TVA: The Legislative History of Muscle Shoals," *Agricultural History* 26(4, 1952): 141–147, 144; "Report on Nitrates and Nitrate Plants," House Report 998, 66th Cong., 2nd sess. (1920).

103. Arthur M. Schlesinger Jr., *The Coming of the New Deal: The Age of Roosevelt* (Boston: Houghton Mifflin, 1958), 322.

104. Joseph Kiernan, "The Age of Infrastructure: The Triumph and Tragedy of Progressive Civil Religion," *Penn History Review* 23(2, 2016): 10–60, 27; C. Herman Pritchett, *The Tennessee Valley Authority: A Study in Public Administration* (Chapel Hill: University of North Carolina Press, 1943), 9.

105. "Reject Ford Offer," *New York Times*, July 16, 1922, 1.

106. Wengert, "Antecedents of TVA," 145; John L. Neufeld, William J. Hausman, and Ronald B. Rapoport, "A Paradox of Voting: Cyclical Majorities and the Case of Muscle Shoals," *Political Research Quarterly* 47(2, 1994): 423–438, 429–430; Kiernan, "The Age of Infrastructure," 28.

107. Norris (R-NE), *Congressional Record*, January 13, 1925, 1737.

108. Wengert, "Antecedents of TVA," 146; Kiernan, "The Age of Infrastructure," 30; Link, "What Happened to the Progressive Movement?" 846, 847.

109. Tindall, *The Emergence of the New South*, 245–246, 248.

110. Ibid., 246; *New York Times*, October 1, 1928, 1, 3; *New York Times*, October 6, 1928, 2.

111. *Congressional Record*, April 9, 1928, 6101–6102.

112. Tindall, *The Emergence of the New South*, 250.

113. "Federalization to Divide the South?" *Macon* (GA) *Daily Telegraph*, November 24, 1918, 1; Katznelson, *Fear Itself*.

Chapter 9. At the Edge of Democracy

1. James G. Blaine, contribution to "Ought the Negro to Be Disenfranchised? Ought He to Have Been Enfranchised?" *North American Review* 128(March 1879).

2. Cited in Charles W. Calhoun, *Conceiving a New Republic: The Republican Party and the Southern Question, 1869–1900* (Lawrence: University Press of Kansas, 2006), 134, 135, 140, 142.

3. Ibid., 142.

4. Bensel, *The Political Economy of American Industrialization*; Skowronek, *Building a New American State*.

5. Cited in Katznelson, *Fear Itself*, 134–135.

6. Phillips, "The Central Theme of Southern History," 130, 131.

7. Richard White, *The Republic for Which It Stands: The United States during Reconstruction and the Gilded Age, 1865–1896* (New York: Oxford University Press, 2017), 361.

8. James G. Blaine, opening and closing contributions to "Ought the Negro to Be Disenfranchised? Ought He to Have Been Enfranchised?" *North American Review* 128(March 1879).

9. Newton, *The Ku Klux Klan in Mississippi*, 14.

10. Wade Hampton, contribution to "Ought the Negro to Be Disenfranchised? Ought He to Have Been Enfranchised?" *North American Review* 128(March 1879).

11. L. Q. C. Lamar, Wade Hampton, and Alexander H. Stephens, contributions to "Ought the Negro to Be Disenfranchised? Ought He to Have Been Enfranchised?" *North American Review* 128(March 1879).

12. Montgomery Blair, contribution to "Ought the Negro to Be Disenfranchised? Ought He to Have Been Enfranchised?" *North American Review* 128(March 1879).

13. Green Berry Raum, *The Existing Conflict between Republican Government and Southern Oligarchy* (Cleveland: N. G. Hamilton & Co., 1884), 3, 18.

14. Cited in Calhoun, *Conceiving a New Republic*, 180; *Congressional Globe*, 41st Cong., 1st sess., 383; James A. Garfield, contribution to "Ought the Negro to Be Disenfranchised? Ought He to Have Been Enfranchised?" *North American Review* 128(March 1879).

15. James G. Blaine, *Political Discussions: Legislative, Diplomatic, and Popular, 1856–1886* (Norwich, CT: Henry Hill Publishing Company, 1887), 468.

16. Sanders, *Roots of Reform*, 1.

17. The report is based on a thirteen-state definition of the South. We have updated the findings on sharecropping and tenantry, and those on education but not literacy, to include the full seventeen states, using the 1940 census. National Emergency Council, *Report on Economic Conditions of the South* (Washington, DC: US Government Printing Office, 1938), 1–2, 22, 28–36.

18. Cited in Katznelson, *Fear Itself*, 85–87.

19. Cited in ibid., 206, 144.

20. Cited in Sean Farhang and Ira Katznelson, "The Southern Imposition: Congress and Labor in the New Deal and Fair Deal," *Studies in American Political Development* 19(Spring 2005): 13.

21. Ira Katznelson, *When Affirmative Action Was White: An Untold History of Racial Inequality in Twentieth-Century America* (New York: W. W. Norton, 2005).

22. For an important discussion, see Eric Schickler, *Racial Realignment: The Transformation of American Liberalism, 1932–1965* (Princeton, NJ: Princeton University Press, 2016); cited in Katznelson, *Fear Itself*, 177.

23. Eastland (D-MS), *Congressional Record*, February 9, 1948, 1193.

24. Cited in Katznelson, *Fear Itself*, 178.

25. Hofstadter, "From Calhoun to the Dixiecrats," 150.

26. Cited in Katznelson, *Fear Itself*, 189–190.

27. Charles Wallace Collins, *Whither Solid South? A Study in Politics and Race Relations* (New Orleans: Pelican Publishing Company, 1947), 254, 264, 256.

28. Donald R. Matthews and James Prothro, *Negroes and the New Southern Politics* (New York: John Wiley, 1966), 105; Philip E. Converse, "On the Possibility of Major Political Realignment in the South," in *Elections and the Political Order*, edited by Angus Campbell, Philip E. Converse, Warren E. Miller, and Donald E. Stokes (New York: John Wiley, 1966), 240.

29. Ira Katznelson, "Reversing Southern Republicanism," in *The New Majority: Toward a Popular Progressive Politics*, edited by Stanley B. Greenberg and Thea Skocpol (New Haven, CT: Yale University Press, 1999), 241.

30. Walter Dean Burnham, "Realignment Lives: The 1994 Earthquake and Its Implications," in *The Clinton Presidency: First Appraisals*, edited by Colin Campbell and Bert A. Rockman(Chatham, NJ: Chatham House, 1996), 363.

31. Thomas Byrne Edsall and Mary D. Edsall, *Chain Reaction: The Impact of Race, Rights, and Taxes on American Politics* (New York: W. W. Norton, 1991), 251.

32. Scott Huffmon, H. Gibbs Knott, and Seth C. McKee, "History Made: The Rise of Republican Tim Scott," *PS: Political Science and Politics* 49(3, 2016): 405–413, 411; Mitch Landrieu, "Mitch Landrieu's Speech on the Removal of the Confederate Monuments in New Orleans," *New York Times*, May 23, 2017.

INDEX

Page numbers in *italics* refer to figures and tables.

manufacturing, *45*, 98, 174, 303, 307, 343; in border states, 344; in South, 44, 118, 235, 267, 343; tariffs and, 107, 118; unionization in, 184

Marie (Beaumont), 10

Martin, Oscar B., 319, 320–21

Martin, Thomas, 284, 292, 326

Maryland, 3, 21, 47, 118, 284, 426n21; black farmers in, 246; Confederate sympathizers in, 43, 81, 407n21; disfranchisement in, 227–28; Republican strength in, 210–11, 219, 343; strikes in, 164; women's suffrage backed in, 346

Massachusetts, 345

Matthews, David, 401

Maybank, Burnet, 400

Mayfield, Earle, 324, 367

McAdoo, William Gibbs, 300, 331, 337, 358, 359

McConnell, William, 204

McCormick, Anne O'Hare, 375

McCubbins, Mathew, 36

McCumber, Porter, 318

McDuffie, John, 119

McEnery, Samuel, 93, 121–22, 162, 283

McHenry, Henry, 141

McKinley, William, 56, 219, 225–26, 277, 394; anti-black violence tolerated by, 24; black rights backed by, 215; as congressman, 116, 199; lynching condemned by, 220

McLean, Angus W., 364

McLemore, Jeff, 331, 334, 339

McNary-Haugen bill, 366–69, 375

Medicaid, 402

Mellon, Andrew, 369, 371

Merriam, Charles, 263

Merrimon, Augustus, 190

Mexican War, 144–45

Meyer, Eugene, 364

migration, 41, 98, 158, 166–67, 168–70, 171, 244–46. *See also* immigration

military draft, 248, 315–17

military pensions, 23, 58, 95, 105, 144–45, 148, 155

Military Reconstruction Acts (1867), 12, 74

Miller, Thomas, 186

Mills, Roger Q., 114, 136

minimum wage, 181

mining, 90, 121, 174, 181, 342, 343

Mississippi, 41, 145, 182, 268, 284, 339–40, 343, 376, 406n25; agriculture in, 118; anti-black violence in, 130, 196, 393; black exodus from, 166; disfranchisement in,

196, 197, 212, 214; education bill and, 144, 153; Klan activity in, 325; partisanship in, 231; pro-labor sentiment in, 170; Reconstruction in, 12; secession of, 389; sharecropping in, 246

Mississippi River, 146

Missouri, 21, 81, 118, 367, 426n21; black emigration to, 158; black population in, 42, 246, 310; Confederate sympathizers in, 43; Radical Republicans in, 86; Republican strength in, 47, 79, 210–11, 222; strikes in, 184; women's suffrage backed in, 346

Missouri Pacific Railroad, 184

Missouri River, 96

monetary policy, 77, 97–98, 136, 138–39, 140, 254, *275*, *299*; bipartisan alliances over, 23, 96; federalizing of, 131–32, 134–35; Progressive movement and, 267; southern Democratic views of, 297–98; under Wilson, 291. *See also* free silver; gold standard; specie payment

Money, Hernando, 309–10

monopolies, 50, 105, 124, 230, 243, 246; in railroad industry, 360. *See also* antitrust laws; trusts

Morgan, Edmund, 3

Morgan, J. P., 189

Morgan, John, 93, 150, 173, 179–80, 203, 307

Morrill Act (1862), 104, 153, 156

Morrill Act (1890), 153–54, 156–57, 317–18, 398

Morrill Tariff (1861), 104

Morrison, William, 151

Moses, George, 370

Mound Bayou, Miss., 41

Mulroy, Quinn, 58

Murray, George H. (activist), 355

Murray, George W. (congressman), 186, 209, 215

Murray, Paul T., 316

Muscle Shoals, Ala., 372–75, 376, 378

NAACP (National Association for the Advancement of Colored People), 314, 353, 355

National Association of Colored Women, 353

National Bank Act (1863), 134

National Bank Circulation Act (1908), *256*

National Committee on Rural and Social Planning, 397

National Defense Act (1916), *256*

National Monetary Commission, 293

Princeton Studies in American Politics: Historical, International, and Comparative Perspectives

Ira Katznelson, Eric Schickler, Martin Shefter, and Theda Skocpol, Series Editors

Kindred Strangers: The Uneasy Relationship between Politics and Business in America by David Vogel

From the Outside In: World War II and the American State by Bartholomew H. Sparrow

Classifying by Race edited by Paul E. Peterson

Facing Up to the American Dream: Race, Class, and the Soul of the Nation by Jennifer L. Hochschild

Political Organizations by James Q. Wilson

Social Policy in the United States: Future Possibilities in Historical Perspective by Theda Skocpol

Experts and Politicians: Reform Challenges to Machine Politics in New York, Cleveland, and Chicago by Kenneth Finegold

Bound by Our Constitution: Women, Workers, and the Minimum Wage by Vivien Hart

Prisoners of Myth: The Leadership of the Tennessee Valley Authority, 1933–1990 by Erwin C. Hargrove

Political Parties and the State: The American Historical Experience by Martin Shefter

Politics and Industrialization: Early Railroads in the United States and Prussia by Colleen A. Dunlavy

The Lincoln Persuasion: Remaking American Liberalism by J. David Greenstone

Labor Visions and State Power: The Origins of Business Unionism in the United States by Victoria C. Hattam

A NOTE ON THE TYPE

This book has been composed in Adobe Text and Gotham.
Adobe Text, designed by Robert Slimbach for Adobe,
bridges the gap between fifteenth- and sixteenth-century
calligraphic and eighteenth-century Modern styles.
Gotham, inspired by New York street signs, was designed
by Tobias Frere-Jones for Hoefler & Co.